10/17

10-12-16

B
JACKSON

Franklin, Ruth.   M

Shirley Jackson

DUE DATE   MCN   09/16   35.00

North Bennington
Vermont
December 29 1959

Dear Mrs. Beatty,

Many many thanks. You have done us a great servic
only in the big picture book, and never dreamed th
"real" Moomin book; we have now the publisher and
ordering. Your Moomin was read with joy around ou
have really no kind of sympathy for Moomin; my hus
perhaps anti-Scandanavian) was overjoyed with Pal
every kind of sympathy for desert islands; do you
adult book?) and have also ordered that.

I have looked forward to writing you, and had prom
morning dwelling on dear books (do you know Unknow
course find myself with half an hour, a sick typew
twelve thank-you letters waiting. I have promised
a new book next Monday morning, after the children
school; that means that I must lock myself up in m
hours a day, and sneak a minute or so here and the
and making lunch ("You will eat vegetable soup aga
Mommy's beginning chapter three") so if I do not w

Yours was the only kind letter I received. I am
the unkind letters, which all come from librarians
ever going to beat the Russians to the moon if our
fantasy stuff ("There was a copy of that book abou
but of course our children could never manage to g
chapter . . ") and recommend stern measures for my
clearly never going to be able to cope with the mo
clearly fall into all kinds of psychological pitfa
Editor of the San Francisco Chronicle points out t
store in his neighborhood (he has not inspected th
proprietor wears a gold crown during business hour
for charming children? As I say, your letter was

I don't know the early science fiction, nor do any
I have asked; I spent Christmas afternoon with an
that the changes in the geography of Oz were due t
never intended to write a second book and kind of
were, with almost a new country and certainly a ne
you know the Narnia books, C.S. Lewis? If you don
last one, where the children involved discover tha
killed in a railway accident and, being dead, may

ALSO BY
RUTH FRANKLIN

A THOUSAND DARKNESSES:

LIES AND TRUTH IN HOLOCAUST FICTION

m even fright m
so vicious o
wonder about
n convince m
— but where
as me fn so
then I th
it didn't
I wish I
the whole
o its alway
Kings o the
not do any
help me
ything o one
I'm so
to me — why can't I
Florences o Henrietta
— only its so

SHIRLEY JACKSON

A RATHER HAUNTED LIFE

RUTH FRANKLIN

LIVERIGHT PUBLISHING CORPORATION

A Division of

W. W. NORTON & COMPANY

Independent Publishers Since 1923

NEW YORK LONDON

Frontispiece: Shirley Jackson by Erich Hartmann, 1947.

Since this page cannot legibly accommodate all the copyright notices, pages 585–87 constitute an extension of the copyright page.

For information about permission to reproduce selections from this book, write to Permissions, Liveright Publishing Coporation, a division of W. W. Norton & Company, Inc., 500 Fifth Avenue, New York, NY 10110

For information about special discounts for bulk purchases, please contact W. W. Norton Special Sales at specialsales@wwnorton.com or 800-233-4830

Manufacturing by RR Donnelley, North Harrisonburg
Book design by Barbara M. Bachman
Production manager: Louise Mattarelliano

Library of Congress Cataloging-in-Publication Data

Names: Franklin, Ruth, author.
Title: Shirley Jackson : a rather haunted life / Ruth Franklin.
Description: First edition. | New York : Liveright Publishing Corporation, 2016. | Includes bibliographical references and index.
Identifiers: LCCN 2016014711 | ISBN 9780871403131 (hardcover)
Subjects: LCSH: Jackson, Shirley, 1916–1965. | Authors, American—20th century—Biography. | Women authors—United States—Biography.
Classification: LCC PS3519.A392 Z64 2016 | DDC 818/.5409 [B]—dc23 LC record available at https://lccn.loc.gov/2016014711

Liveright Publishing Corporation
500 Fifth Avenue, New York, NY 10110
www.wwnorton.com

W. W. Norton & Company Ltd.
15 Carlisle Street, London W1D 3BS

1 2 3 4 5 6 7 8 9 0

For Sam and Phoebe,
as promised

"It shall be yours to penetrate, in every bosom, the deep mystery of sin, the fountain of all wicked arts, and which inexhaustibly supplies more evil impulses than human power . . . can make manifest in deeds."

—NATHANIEL HAWTHORNE, "Young Goodman Brown"

CONTENTS

NOTE ON
QUOTATIONS

IN HER LETTERS AND ROUGH DRAFTS, SHIRLEY JACKSON USUALLY typed using only lowercase letters. I have chosen to preserve her style as a way of delineating unpublished material.

North Bennington
Vermont
December 29 1959

Dear Mrs. Beatty,

Many many thanks. You have done us a great servic
only in the big picture book, and never dreamed th
"real" Moomin book; we have now the publisher and
ordering. Your Moomin was read with joy around ou
have really no kind of sympathy for Moomin; my hus
perhaps anti-Scandanavian) was overjoyed with Pal
every kind of sympathy for desert islands; do you
adult book?) and have also ordered that.

I have looked forward to writing you, and had prom
morning dwelling on dear books (do you know Unknow
course find myself with half an hour, a sick typew
twelve thank-you letters waiting. I have promised
a new book next Monday morning, after the children
school; that means that I must lock myself up in m
hours a day, and sneak a minute or so here and the
and making lunch ("You will eat vegetable soup aga
Mommy's beginning chapter three") so if I do not w

Yours was the only kind letter I received. I am w
the unkind letters, which all come from librarians
ever going to beat the Russians to the moon if our
fantasy stuff ("There was a copy of that book abou
but of course our children could never manage to g
chapter . . ") and recommend stern measures for my
clearly never going to be able to cope with the mo
clearly fall into all kinds of psychological pitfa
Editor of the San Francisco Chronicle points out t
store in his neighborhood (he has not inspected th
proprietor wears a gold crown during business hou
for charming children? As I say, your letter was

I don't know the early science fiction, nor do any
I have asked; I spent Christmas afternoon with an
that the changes in the geography of Oz were due t
never intended to write a second book and kind of
were, with almost a new country and certainly a ne
you know the Narnia books, C.S. Lewis? If you dor
last one, where the children involved discover tha
killed in a railway accident and, being dead, may

A SECRET HISTORY

SHIRLEY JACKSON OFTEN SAID THAT THE IDEA FOR "THE Lottery," the short story that shocked much of America when it appeared in *The New Yorker* on June 26, 1948, came to her while she was out doing errands one sunny June morning. She thought of the plot on her way home, and she immediately placed her toddler daughter in the playpen, put away the groceries she had just bought, and sat down to type out the story on her signature yellow copy paper. It was off to her agent the next day, with virtually no corrections: "I didn't want to fuss with it," she later said.

As origin stories go, this one—first told by Jackson and repeated countless times by others—is just about perfect. Its near mythic quality suits "The Lottery," a parable of a stoning ritual conducted annually in an otherwise ordinary village. And it sets up the reader for the surprise that follows: the angry, confused, curious letters from *New Yorker* subscribers that would soon overwhelm the post office of tiny North Bennington, Vermont, where Jackson lived. Some of the letter writers rudely announced that they were canceling their subscriptions. Others expressed puzzlement or demanded an interpretation. Still others, assuming that the story was factual, wanted to know where such lotteries could be witnessed. "I have read of some queer cults in our time," wrote a reader from Los Angeles, "but this one bothers me."

There is only one problem with Jackson's origin myth. It is not entirely true. The letters are real, all right—Jackson's archive contains a huge scrapbook filled with them. But her files show that certain details do not match up. The changes made to "The Lottery" were not as minimal as Jackson suggested they were; there is no evidence that Jackson's agent, as she would claim, disliked the story; and the period between submission and publication was a few months, not a few weeks. These details are relatively minor; they alter neither the meaning of the story nor the significance of its impact. But for the biographer, they are the equivalent of a warning siren: Caution! Poetic license ahead!

Some writers are particularly prone to mythmaking. Shirley Jackson was one of them. During her lifetime, she fascinated critics and readers by playing up her interest in magic: the biographical information on her first novel identifies her as "perhaps the only contemporary writer who is a practicing amateur witch, specializing in small-scale black magic and fortune-telling with a tarot deck." To interviewers, she expounded on her alleged abilities, even claiming that she had used magic to break the leg of publisher Alfred A. Knopf, with whom her husband was involved in a dispute. Reviewers found those stories irresistible, extrapolating freely from her interest in witchcraft to her writing, which often takes a turn into the uncanny. "Miss Jackson writes not with a pen but a broomstick" was an oft quoted line. Roger Straus, her first publisher, would call her "a rather haunted woman."

Look more closely, however, and Jackson's persona is much thornier. She was a talented, determined, ambitious writer in an era when it was still unusual for a woman to have both a family and a profession. She was a mother of four who tried to keep up the appearance of running a conventional American household, but she and her husband, the writer Stanley Edgar Hyman, were hardly typical residents of their rural Vermont town—not least because Hyman was born and raised Jewish. And she was, indeed, a serious student of the history of witchcraft and magic: not necessarily as a practical method of influencing the world around her (it's debatable whether she actually practiced magical rituals), but as a way of embracing and channeling female power at a time when women in America often had little control over their lives. "Rather haunted" she was—in more ways than Straus, or perhaps anyone else, realized.

Jackson's brand of literary suspense is part of a vibrant and distinguished tradition that can be traced back to the American Gothic work of Nathaniel Hawthorne, Edgar Allan Poe, and Henry James. Her unique contribution to this genre is her primary focus on women's lives. Two decades before the women's movement ignited, Jackson's early stories were already exploring the unmarried woman's desperate isolation in a society where a husband was essential for social acceptance. As her career progressed and her personal life became more troubled, her work began to investigate more deeply the kinds of psychic damage to which women are especially prone. It can be no accident that in many of these works, a house—the woman's domain—functions as a kind of protagonist, with traditional homemaking occupations such as cooking or gardening playing a crucial role in the narrative. In Jackson's first novel, *The Road Through the Wall* (1948), the houses on a suburban street mirror the lives of the families who inhabit them. In *The Sundial* (1958), her fourth novel, an estate functions as a fortress: an island amid chaos. In *The Haunting of Hill House* (1959) and *We Have Always Lived in the Castle* (1962), her late masterpieces, a house becomes both a prison and a site of disaster.

I've been fascinated by Jackson's work since my first reading of *Hill House*, which captivated me with the literary sophistication and emotional depth Jackson brought to what might have been a hoary ghost story. But it was only more recently that I began to appreciate the greater range of her work and its resonance with the story of her life, which embodies the dilemmas faced by so many women in the mid-twentieth century, on the cusp of the feminist movement. Jackson belonged to the generation of women whose angst Betty Friedan unforgettably chronicled in *The Feminine Mystique*: women born during or just after World War I, who were raising their families in the 1940s and 1950s. Like the housewives who felt a "strange stirring" of dissatisfaction as they went about their chores, Jackson, too, fought to carve out a creative life amid a bustling family. But—as was also the case for so many women of her time—her identity was ineradicably bound to her husband's, and their sometimes tortured intimacy reverberates seismically through her work.

Jackson began to write in earnest in college, shortly before she met Hyman, who went on to become a faculty member at Bennington College and a respected literary critic. He would always regard her as his greatest discovery, while she relied on his taste and judgment as a measure of her literary worth. The couple moved quickly into the ranks of the literary elite: at the age of twenty-three Hyman joined the staff of *The New Yorker*, which also published a dozen of Jackson's short stories, starting in the early 1940s. Her critical and commercial success mounted with each of her books, culminating in the triumph of *Castle*, her last completed novel, which was a favorite of reviewers and a best seller. At the same time, her nonfiction articles for women's magazines, which she turned into two successful memoirs about her life as a mother, won her a large popular audience and impressive fees.

Sadly, the trajectory of Jackson's creative ascent was mirrored by an arc of personal descent. Though she and Hyman shared an intellectually rich marriage and a warm family life, he could be a domineering and sometimes unfaithful partner, and he grew to resent the fact that his writing never enjoyed the public acclaim of his much celebrated wife's. As the pressures on Jackson swelled, she turned to tranquilizers to soothe her nerves and to amphetamines to help her lose weight and manage a demanding writing schedule on top of a boisterous household that included four children and a menagerie of pets. In the last years of her life, she was so tormented by anxiety and agoraphobia that she rarely left the house. Health problems related to the couple's heavy drinking and love of indulgence—both Jackson and Hyman were significantly overweight—contributed to their tragically early deaths from cardiac arrest: she in 1965 at age forty-eight, he five years later at fifty-one. Her death cut short an impressive rebound during which, recovering her physical and emotional strength, she had started two new novels.

Critics have often been puzzled by the question of how one writer could work simultaneously in two very different genres: literary suspense and domestic comedy. "One would sooner expect [Charles]

Addams to illustrate *Little Women* than Miss Jackson to write a cheerful book about family life," commented a reviewer of her first memoir. But these two aspects of Jackson's writing are profoundly interconnected. Her horror stories, which always take place primarily on a psychological level, are grounded in the domestic: in *Castle*, an entire family is poisoned at the dinner table; in *Hill House*, the nursery, referred to as "the heart of the house," is one of the sites of greatest terror. (The word poignantly repeated, mantralike, by whatever is haunting Hill House is "home.") Meanwhile, the domestic tales often need only the gentlest tap to slide into the dark, as with "Charles," in which the boy making trouble in the narrator's son's kindergarten could be either an invisible imp or (more likely) the son himself. Jackson's two authorial personas, though often in tension, were equally authentic.

In "The Third Baby's the Easiest," a magazine piece that was incorporated into her memoir *Life Among the Savages*, a clerk asks Jackson, as she arrives at the hospital to give birth to her third child, to state her occupation. "Writer," she says. "I'll just put down housewife," the clerk replies. Jackson set down these lines without rancor in a laugh-out-loud account of labor and delivery. But they vividly illustrate how great was the pressure on women of that era to assume without protest the "happy homemaker" role society urged upon them. Jackson was an important writer who happened also to be—and to embrace being—a housewife, as women of her generation were all but required to do. The tension between the two roles was both internal and external, based simultaneously in her expectations for herself and in the expectations of her husband, family, publishers, and readers.

This tension animates all of Jackson's writing. And it makes her perfectly representative of her time. Writing to a boyfriend in 1956, college student Sylvia Plath imagined a life with "babies and bed and brilliant friends and a magnificent stimulating home where geniuses drink gin in the kitchen after a delectable dinner and read their own novels." Anne Sexton opened her poem "Housewife" (1962) with the line "Some women marry houses." The themes of Jackson's work were so central to the preoccupations of American women during the postwar period that Plath biographer Linda Wagner-Martin has called the 1950s "the decade of Jackson." Her body of work constitutes nothing less than the secret history of American women of her era. And the stories she tells form a powerful counternarrative to the "feminine mystique," revealing the unhappiness and instability beneath the housewife's sleek veneer of competence.

The American midcentury was a time of both unprecedented prosperity and profound uncertainty, with the shadow of the war that had just ended—a war unlike any other—lingering uneasily in the background. The women who had entered the workforce to replace their enlisted husbands and brothers were balking at being urged back into the home—even a home stocked with gleaming new appliances, in a safe suburban neighborhood. The House Committee on Un-American Activities sought Communists lurking in the halls of U.S. government institutions and at home in those cozy suburbs. Both America and the Soviet Union tested nuclear bombs of unprecedented power and danger. And a massive social transformation, kick-started by the desegregation of public schools, was under way. All these tensions are palpable in Jackson's work, which channels a far-reaching anxiety about the tumultuous world outside the home even as it investigates the dark secrets of domestic American life. In the years that led up to the civil rights movement, she grappled with issues of racial prejudice. During a time when Jews, including her husband, were struggling to win acceptance among the WASP elite, she charted the anti-Semitic strain in American society. And the psychological suspense she generated in her novels and stories, often manifested in the fear of the self disintegrating from the inside, is inseparable from the real paranoia of a postwar America obsessed with nuclear annihilation and with the Russians who might push the fatal button.

Critics have tended to underestimate Jackson's work: both because of its central interest in women's lives and because some of it is written in genres regarded as either "faintly disreputable" (in the words of one scholar) or simply uncategorizable. *Hill House* is often dismissed as an especially well-written ghost story, *Castle* as a whodunit. The headline of Jackson's *New York Times* obituary identified her as "Author of Horror Classic"—that is, "The Lottery." But such lazy pigeonholing does an injustice to the masterly way in which Jackson used the classic tropes of suspense to plumb the depths of the human condition. No writer since Henry James has been so successful in exploring the psychological reach of terror, locating in what we fear the key to unlock the darkest corners of the psyche. "I have always loved . . . to use fear, to take it and comprehend it and make it work," Jackson once wrote in a line that could be her manifesto. In our fears and in our crimes, she believed, we discover our truest selves. And the outrage that greeted "The Lottery" shows that she was right.

IN 1960, JACKSON WROTE to her parents with an unusual request. She and Hyman had been making their wills and thinking about posterity, and she wanted her parents to promise eventually to return all the letters she had written to them. "since i hope i have a couple of years still to go the problem is not very pressing," she wrote. "but the vital thing is that you not throw them out. . . . they must be a long detailed record of many years. i am almost embarrassed when i think of the mountains of pages they must make." (Jackson tended to abandon typographical conventions in her letters and manuscript drafts, and I have preserved her style.)

Jackson's letters to her parents—most of which they did return to Hyman after her death—must be read with a certain degree of skepticism, since they often represent the efforts of a rebellious yet dutiful daughter to wrest the narrative of her life away from her parents. Still, they are indeed the best surviving account of Jackson's life, although any letters she sent before 1948 are presumed lost. She was an inconsistent keeper of diaries, but a few from her high school and college years still exist, and other scattered pages turn up at various points later on. In researching this book, I made use of numerous letters, including some to such well-known friends as Ralph and Fanny Ellison and Kenneth and Libbie Burke. Hyman's letters to mutual acquaintances, too, proved an important source of information about both of their lives, especially as he often devoted a few words to whatever his wife was currently working on. During the summers they spent apart while in college, Jackson and Hyman wrote to each other constantly, sometimes as often as twice a day; I have drawn heavily upon these letters for my story of their early life together. And Laurence Hyman, Jackson's eldest child, made available to me many years' worth of Jackson's never-before-seen correspondence with her literary agents: thanks to their careful records, I have been able to date nearly all of her work, both published and unpublished. (A select bibliography of her published writings can be found in the back of this book.) The greatest surprise and delight of this project was the discovery of nearly sixty pages of Jackson's correspondence in the early 1960s with a housewife named Jeanne Beatty, who began their intense exchange of letters with a simple fan note. These letters, hidden in a Pennsylvania barn and never before published, offer an intimate look at Jackson's family life and the state of her mind as she embarked upon the writing of *Castle*.

These and other sources have given me an unprecedented understanding of Jackson's creative process as well as her personal life—which were closely related. By all accounts, she was a powerful personality as well as a brilliant writer. "Her character was so tremendous it was always hard to believe she was just one person," Libbie Burke once said. She lived the life Plath hoped for, with her brilliant husband, her brood of children, and their legendary Vermont house, the headquarters of a social circle that included Ellison, Howard Nemerov, and Bernard Malamud, among others. On a family visit to New York when Laurence was thirteen, Jackson and Hyman decided that he ought to learn something about jazz—and took him to four nightclubs in a single evening. A devoted baseball fan, Jackson had a running joke with her editor at Farrar, Straus about using witchcraft to secure victories for the Brooklyn Dodgers.

A biography of Jackson would be incomplete without a full consideration of the life and work of Stanley Edgar Hyman—not only through the lens of their marriage and his influence on her work, but also as an important intellectual and fascinating character in his own right. Hyman was the author of several major works of literary criticism, including *The Armed Vision* (1948), a study of critical methods, and *The Tangled Bank* (1962), which explores the work of Charles Darwin, Karl

Marx, James Frazer, and Sigmund Freud from a literary perspective. He is well remembered by friends, colleagues, and former students for his generosity, his personal charisma, and his booming voice. The long-running poker game that he participated in weekly for years—along with several other Bennington professors, various college presidents, and the local garageman—was memorialized by Nemerov in a poem published shortly after Hyman's death: "hard / As it is to imagine / A fat and rowdy ghost / Pee in his empty glass / So as not to miss a hand, / That's how it happens." (The poem is called "Myth & Ritual," after a celebrated course Hyman created at Bennington, for years the most popular course in the college.) Taken together, his and Jackson's lives offer a fascinating snapshot of American intellectual life from the 1940s to the 1960s.

As a writer and mother myself, I am struck by how contemporary Jackson's dilemmas feel: her devotion to her children coexists uneasily with her fear of losing herself in domesticity. Several generations later, the intersection of life and work continues to be one of the points of most profound anxiety in our society—an anxiety that affects not only women but also their husbands and children.

Whatever his flaws as a husband, Hyman was a consistently insightful interpreter of his wife's work. He bitterly regretted the critical neglect and misreading she suffered during her lifetime. "For all her popularity, Shirley Jackson won surprisingly little recognition," he wrote in an essay published after her death. "She received no awards or prizes, grants or fellowships; her name was often omitted from lists on which it clearly belonged." He ended his lament with a prediction: "I think that the future will find her powerful visions of suffering and inhumanity increasingly significant and meaningful, and that Shirley Jackson's work is among that small body of literature produced in our time that seems apt to survive." Considering the revival that has taken place in recent years—nearly all of Jackson's books are currently in print, with a new edition of previously uncollected and unpublished materials appearing in 2015—it seems safe to say that he was correct.

I.

FOUNDATIONS

CALIFORNIA
1916–1933

> INTERVIEWER: You were encouraged to write by
> your family?
> JACKSON: They couldn't stop me.
>
> —*New York Post*, September 30, 1962

WHEN THE SS *CALIFORNIA*, AN ELEGANT STEAMER OPERATED by the Panama Pacific Line, departed San Francisco for New York City on August 12, 1933, via the Panama Canal, its passengers looked forward to a luxurious voyage. The world's largest electrically propelled commercial vessel, the *California* featured a domed dining hall with Cuban mahogany furnishings, windowed staterooms for every passenger, and a first-class gentleman's smoking room paneled in pine. The journey included passage through the Panama Canal, opened in 1914 and still a novelty. Travelers spent their days lounging by the various outdoor swimming pools and their nights in the formal ballroom, where a masquerade ball, held under "the witchery of a tropic moon," capped each voyage.

Shirley Jackson, age sixteen, was not seduced by the promise of such entertainments. It was the summer before her senior year of high school, and her parents had uprooted her from her home state of California for a

Shirley Jackson, 1915.

new life in faraway Rochester, New York. Though the sun blazed overhead, a photograph snapped on deck captured the family dressed for a
blustery day at sea, with Leslie, Shirley's father, in his customary wool
suit, and his wife, Geraldine, in a long coat with a fur collar, its lapel
sporting a lavish spray of flowers. Shirley wore a loose black dress with
short, puffy sleeves and a floppy white collar, topped with a white hat
to protect her fair skin from the sun. The dress sagged around her chest
and waist; even her white gloves fit her poorly. As she squinted into the
sun, her expression was wary. Geraldine and Leslie, too, looked som-
ber. Only Barry, her easygoing fourteen-year-old brother, appeared
pleased about the journey.

As desperate migrants from the Dust Bowl journeyed west overland in search of work and sustenance, the well-to-do Jacksons, unscathed by the Depression, were heading east. Leslie's employer, the Traung Label and Lithograph Company, had grown steadily throughout the 1920s and early 1930s. Now it was merging with the Stecher Lithograph Company in Rochester, resulting in Leslie's promotion and transfer. The Jacksons were trading a life of comfort and privilege on one coast—country clubs, social teas, garden parties—for a very similar life on the other. But though they were decorated with all the trappings of wealth, the photograph reveals them as ill at ease with one another, their stiff, formal body language radiating anxiety and mistrust.

It was wrenching to leave California, which Jackson would later remember as a lost Eden lush with avocados and other tropical delicacies then impossible to find on the East Coast. She traced her family history back to the roots of the burgeoning state: her great-great-grandfather, an architect, grew wealthy building mansions in San Francisco. She spent most of her childhood twenty miles south of the city, in tony Burlingame, "which means a suburb, and trees, and having to stop playing prisoner's base when the streetlights went on in the evening, and sitting on a fence eating pomegranates with my dearest friend," she later recalled. Before that first winter in Rochester, she would claim, she had never seen snow. Now she was embarking upon an entirely new life, a prospect that filled her with trepidation. She knew also, however, that she would have a rare chance to re-create herself, as had her ancestors, migrating westward nearly a century earlier.

HOUSES—ONE OF HER LIFETIME obsessions and the gravitational center of much of her fiction—were in Jackson's blood. "My grandfather was an architect, and his father, and *his* father," she once wrote. "One of them built houses only for millionaires in California, and that was where the family wealth came from, and one of them was certain that houses could be made to stand on the sand dunes of San Francisco, and that was where the family wealth went." Those first California houses, all built in the 1870s, were known as "millionaires' palaces." They were the most opulent residences San Francisco had yet seen: one was built of local redwood painted white to look like marble, while another featured a private art gallery. These houses were owned by the men who created San Francisco—the "robber barons" who struck gold years after the Gold Rush by investing in the railroads connecting the western United States with the East. And they were built by Samuel C. Bugbee, San Francisco's first architect and Jackson's great-great-grandfather. Nearly a century later, she would turn to them for inspiration when she needed a model for the haunted house in her most famous novel.

When gold was first discovered at Sutter's Mill, back in 1848, San Francisco, still in its infancy, was barely settled. New arrivals lived in canvas tents—poor shelter from the rainy weather. The city's first buildings were made from ships run aground in the harbor. In 1849, the population was estimated at two thousand men and almost no women. David Douty Colton was among those who arrived that year, hoping to work in mining. Charles Crocker, who came out west a year later, would make his fortune in the dry goods business. Leland Stanford joined his brothers in their Sacramento grocery in 1852. By the early 1860s, Crocker and Stanford, along with Mark Hopkins and Collis Huntington, were major investors in the new transcontinental railroad; Colton served as their lawyer. In 1863, they broke ground in Sacramento for the Central Pacific Railroad, which would run east, traversing the Sierras and the desert, to meet the Union Pacific in Promontory, Utah, making the transcontinental journey in six days instead of six months.

Samuel Bugbee came to San Francisco around the same time as the men whose houses he would eventually build. Born in New Brunswick in 1812, he married Abbie Stephenson of Maine in 1836, with whom he had three sons: Sumner, John Stephenson, and Charles. The Bugbees spent the early years of their marriage in New England, their great-great-granddaughter's later home and the setting for much of her fiction. But before long, the Gold Rush drew Samuel out west. He probably came to San Francisco in the early 1850s, his wife and sons joining him within a decade.

The flourishing city counted around 35,000 residents in 1852—a nearly twentyfold increase in just three years. By 1870, a year after the transcontinental railroad was completed, its population had exploded again, to more than 500,000. All those new residents needed houses. Samuel C. Bugbee and Son (Charles, the youngest, had joined his father in business) was the first architectural practice in San Francisco. Sumner, the eldest, also trained as an architect and worked briefly with the firm. Their office, at 402 Montgomery Street, was situated prominently in the middle of the business district. Among Bugbee and Son's creations were the California Theater (completed in 1869), Mills Hall at Oakland's Mills College (1871), Wade Opera House (1876), and the Golden Gate Park Conservatory (1879).

Middle son John Stephenson, who would be Jackson's great-grandfather, was the only male Bugbee not affiliated with the firm. A graduate of Harvard Law School, he practiced law in San Francisco and eventually spent nearly a decade in Alaska as a Superior Court judge. His wife, Annie Maxwell Greene of Massachusetts, traced her lineage to the Revolutionary War general Nathanael Greene and also counted among her relatives Julia Ward Howe, the activist and author of "The Battle Hymn of the Republic." According to family lore, Annie left her family in Boston in 1864 and traveled alone all the way around Cape Horn to San Francisco, chaperoned by a minister. John Stephenson Bugbee met the boat at the port and the minister married the couple on deck. The bride brought with her a beautiful wooden music box the size of a small table, likely of European origin, which would become one of her great-granddaughter's prize possessions. Jackson told her children that the music box, which could play a variety of melodies on zinc discs, was haunted: at times it seemed to turn itself on, but only to play its favorite selections. "It would start to play 'Carnival of Venice' at four o'clock in the morning," Laurence Hyman, Jackson's elder son, remembers. Even if Jackson claimed she hid the preferred disc, the music box would somehow manage to find it and play it. It was one of the many ways in which she delighted in putting a domestic twist on the supernatural.

AS SAN FRANCISCO SWELLED in the last decades of the nineteenth century, the wealthy looked to Nob Hill—then known as California

Street Hill—to escape the congestion downtown. Richard Tobin, an Irish immigrant and lawyer who was among the founders of the Hibernia Savings and Loan Society, was one of the first to commission a grand house there from Bugbee and Son. In 1870, the *San Francisco Chronicle* reported that construction had begun on Tobin's "large and elegant mansion" at the corner of California and Taylor Streets. The 5400-square-foot house, an elaborate Victorian, had a private chapel with stained-glass windows and a seventy-five-foot observatory tower. But it was quickly dwarfed by the monstrosities to come.

Attorney David Douty Colton's "Italian palace," an L-shaped, two-story Georgian-style building with a redwood frame, was completed in 1872. With a formal façade featuring marble steps guarded by two stone lions and Corinthian columns flanking the windows, it occupied no less than half a city block and cost around $75,000. Two years later, when construction began on a house for Leland Stanford—then president of the Central Pacific Railroad and former governor of California—a cable car line fought for by Colton ran up California Street, rendering the hill less formidable and the real estate even more valuable. Clad in granite, Stanford's "Nob Hill castle" had six chimneys, bay windows on all four sides, and front doors made out of solid rosewood and mahogany, framed by triple columns. At 41,000 square feet, with fifty rooms, its cost was estimated between $1 million and $2 million. Stanford and his wife, Jane, commissioned Eadweard Muybridge, the pioneering mid-nineteenth-century photographer, to take pictures of the exterior and the sumptuous furnishings, which included allegorical paintings depicting the continents of the world, a frescoed ceiling, marble statuary, and a salon decorated in trompe l'oeil paintings and embroidery.

Charles Crocker's home was the last of Bugbee and Son's Nob Hill creations, and the most flamboyant. The 25,000-square-foot palazzo was situated at the top of the hill on the site of twelve smaller houses, which Crocker had bought and promptly demolished. The lone holdout was a German undertaker named Nicholas Yung, who demanded $12,000 for his property. Crocker, who would eventually spend around $3.5 million on his mansion, declined to pay. Instead, he built a forty-foot-tall "spite fence" surrounding Yung's house. In retaliation, Yung threatened to erect a coffin on his roof, visible above the fence, with a skull and crossbones painted on the side—simultaneously an advertisement for his business and a menacing memento mori. Even after Yung died in 1880, Crocker refused to take down the fence.

The Sundial, Jackson's fourth novel, revolves around the Hallorans, a disagreeable family who occupy a mansion at the top of a hill, surrounded by stone wall. Crocker's Second Empire-style palace went further: it was enclosed by a wall of solid granite and crowned with a seventy-six-foot tower. A party given there in 1879 was the San Francisco social event of the decade, "an entertainment that will stand without rival possibly for years to come as regards sumptuousness, tastefulness of decorative art and nicety, elaborateness of ornamentation and illumination and prodigality of expenditure," a local newspaper reported. The menu included two kinds of oysters and nineteenth-century delicacies such as "Terrapine à la Maryland," "Mignons de Foie Grasse à la Russe," and "Galantine de Dinde au Suprême." Mrs. Crocker wore a burgundy velvet dress and an estimated $100,000 worth of diamonds.

It is hard to imagine more potent symbols of gilded age excess than the Nob Hill Bugbee mansions. That excess would soon demand a human cost. As if following the Gothic logic of a Hawthorne parable, a Poe vignette, or—indeed—a Shirley Jackson novel, each of the houses soon became a setting not only for ostentatious food and furnishings but also for a weird, melancholy family story.

Jackson never saw any of her great-great-grandfather's creations, except in pictures: all the Nob Hill mansions were destroyed in the fire that resulted from the great earthquake of April 1906. But she may have been aware of the eerie tales that surrounded them. In 1958, as she embarked upon the research for *The Haunting of Hill House*, Jackson wrote to her parents for help. Her new book, she explained, was to be about a haunted house, but she couldn't find anything suitable in Vermont: "All the old New England houses are the kind of square, classical type which wouldn't be haunted in a million years." Did her mother have any books of old California houses, perhaps with pictures of the Bugbee houses? Geraldine wrote back promptly, enclosing newspaper clippings she identified as "possible architectural orgies of my great-grandfather," including the Crocker house. "Glad [it] didn't survive the earthquake," she commented later.

Geraldine's dismissiveness was probably a reaction to the house's offenses against good taste: though the ornamentation was admired when the house was built, it would quickly have seemed outrageous, particularly during the most desperate years of the Depression. But she may also have heard about what happened to the families who lived in those houses. A local paper reported in 1891 that a "shadow of misfortune seem[ed] to rest" upon the Nob Hill mansions. Each one was virtually deserted, occupied only by a skeleton crew of servants. Colton had died suddenly in October 1878, forty-seven years old and in debt—as builders of megalomaniacal castles are apt to be. His daughter, widowed twice within a few years, eventually sold the house to railroad magnate Collis Huntington, one of Colton's former business partners. The Stanfords abandoned their home after the death of their only child, Leland Stanford Jr., in 1884 at age fifteen. They moved to Menlo Park, where they established the university bearing his name, but they kept his room in the Nob Hill mansion as a macabre shrine, complete with his boyhood possessions and his picture hanging before a window, the curtains left perpetually open so that passersby could look in. After Crocker's death in 1888, the ownership of his house was disputed by his two sons, each of whom believed it to be his rightful inheritance. Their feud with the Yung estate continued until 1904, when the lot, its spite fence still standing, was finally sold.

At the same time, the Bugbee family was struck by an epidemic dramatic enough to be remarked upon by the local media. On September 1, 1877, Samuel Bugbee died suddenly while crossing from Oakland to San Francisco on the ferry. Several years later, his son Charles dropped dead on the street. Sumner Bugbee, too, died unexpectedly during a long-distance train journey from New York, where he had been living, back to California; he was buried in Brooklyn's Green-Wood Cemetery. And John Stephenson Bugbee suffered a fatal stroke in the midst of a speech while presiding over the 1896 Alaska Republican Convention. The family propensity to meet a sudden end would resurface with his great-granddaughter.

In a lecture she often gave about writing *The Haunting of Hill House*, Jackson claimed that in searching for a model for that novel's haunted mansion, she had come upon a photograph of a California house with "an air of disease and decay." It turned out, she said, that her great-grandfather had built it. "It had stood empty and deserted for some years before it finally caught fire, and it was generally believed that that was because the people of the town got together one night and burned it down." She had her generations mixed up: John Stephenson, her great-grandfather, was the only nonarchitect in the family. But the career of another Bugbee descendant offers a possibility. After Samuel's death, a year after the Crocker house was completed, Charles Bugbee continued to run a successful practice, designing homes all over the Bay Area. Though they were built on a more modest scale than the millionaires' palaces, these houses were impressive architectural creations in the neo-Victorian style that came to be typical of the Bay Area, laden with ornamentation and studded with gables and bay windows shooting out at unlikely angles—"big old california gingerbread houses," Jackson would later call them.

Charles's nephew Maxwell Greene Bugbee, John Stephenson's son and Shirley's grandfather, joined his uncle Charles's practice in 1890. Three years later, he married Evangeline Field, one of seven children of Chauncy Field, a lawyer, and his wife, Julia. Evangeline, whom everyone called Mimi, was born in 1870 in Yolo County, west of Sacramento. At her wedding, on March 15, 1893, Mimi carried a bouquet of white lilies of the valley and a prayer book that Maxwell had given her with a ribbon marking the wedding service. She would pass the latter on to her granddaughter for good luck, telling her never to move the ribbon; Shirley didn't. The couple spent the early years of their marriage in Alameda, across the bay and south of Oakland, where they raised two children: Clifford Field Bugbee, born in 1894, and Geraldine Maxwell Bugbee, Shirley's mother, born the following year.

The house exuding "disease and decay" that Jackson mentioned in her lecture could have been one of Maxwell Bugbee's designs. The Gray House, as it is known, still stands in Ross, California, a small, elegant town fewer than twenty miles north of San Francisco. In the late

nineteenth century, the bucolic Ross Valley was a popular vacation destination for wealthy San Franciscans. Among the town's earliest settlers
were William and Elizabeth Barber, who commissioned Maxwell Bugbee to build an additional house on their property to rent to vacationers.
Completed in 1892, it featured shingled sides and a deep veranda. But
within a few years, the same shadow of misfortune came to rest upon the
Barbers. Their original home burned down. After Bugbee built them a
new house in a similar style on the same plot of land, troubles continued
to plague them. Their daughter Alice was widowed after less than three
years of marriage and never remarried. Her sister, Mary, was institu-
tionalized at Stanford Hospital and eventually committed suicide.

While the details are largely unknown, the outline of Maxwell and
Mimi's marriage hints at yet another strange and sad family story. On
the surface, the two seemed to be happy together. Maxwell was an officer
in the Masons, and his wife served as secretary of the Alameda Whist
Club. In 1902, he was admitted to the California Society of the Sons of
the American Revolution. A few years later, the Bugbees took a grand
tour that included stops in France, Switzerland, and Italy. A newspaper
profile described Maxwell as "a cultivated, refined gentleman, an artist
in his tastes, of congenial manners, entirely unassuming, and conservative in his views . . . respected professionally and esteemed socially."

His social refinement notwithstanding, Maxwell was a poor husband. Mimi, for her part, became a devotee of Christian Science, the
cultist offshoot of Christianity founded in Boston in 1879 by Mary
Baker Eddy, who promoted the idea that the material world is an illusion. Jackson's younger daughter, Sarah Hyman, describes it succinctly:
"You think things and make them real." During the first few decades of
its existence, Christian Science was the fastest growing religious movement in America, increasing from just under 9,000 members in 1890 to
more than 60,000 in 1906; the church's first San Francisco branch was
established in 1895, the year of Geraldine's birth. At its height, in the
1930s, the movement claimed more than 260,000 members—about one
in every 500 Americans.

The rise of Christian Science coincided with a general surge of interest in spiritualism and occult phenomena; Eddy herself was known to

conduct séances. The Ouija board, popularized in its modern form by Baltimore inventor William Fuld, could be found in virtually every parlor across the country by the late 1910s. Even President Woodrow Wilson was a devotee: when asked in 1914 whether he would be reelected, Wilson replied, "The Ouija board says yes." Numerous people claimed to take dictation from spirits, including one woman who said she had recorded a new novel by Mark Twain, then dead for seven years. Back in the Bay Area, Contra Costa County was the site of an outbreak of "ouijamania," in which a teenager allegedly forced her mother and sister to sit by the Ouija board day and night, believing that they were in contact with a relative who had been hit by a car several weeks earlier. Mimi, too, experimented with a Ouija board; Shirley's brother recalled her and his mother using it with him and Shirley when they were children.

Christian Scientists are famous for their belief that illness can be cured through thought alone. "Sickness is a dream from which the patient needs to be awakened," Eddy proclaimed. Perhaps Mimi suffered from a chronic illness or handicap that she believed Christian Science could cure. Or she may have been drawn by its message of personal empowerment, its exhortations that belief alone could suffice to improve one's lot in life. But it could not cure her marriage. In the early 1920s, she and her husband separated, and Mimi moved in with her daughter and son-in-law. Around the same time, Maxwell began designing a new house for his daughter's family, complete with an extra bedroom for his own wife. He died in 1927, shortly after it was finished. His granddaughter, then ten years old, would barely remember him.

"YOU COULD MAKE A story out of . . . Pop's life," Shirley's mother once told her. Leslie Hardie Jackson's family history, a classic American up-by-the-bootstraps saga, would seem more at home in a novel by Sinclair Lewis. A wealthy English family suddenly loses all its money under mysterious circumstances, perhaps in a business deal gone wrong. The father disappears, leaving a teenage son to look after his mother and two sisters. They change their name, burying all traces of their past, and travel across an ocean and a continent to San Francisco, bringing among their few possessions an heirloom wedding gown that had been Leslie's grandmother's. For a decade, the son supports his family by working a series of odd jobs, serving as a clerk, a salesman, and finally a printer's apprentice. At age twenty-four, he marries the daughter of one of the city's most established families, his bride—"one of the prettiest girls in the neighborhood, tall, brunette type, with quantities of brown hair and a clear lovely complexion"—elegant in his grandmother's dress. Their marriage took place on March 15, 1916, the date chosen to coincide with Maxwell and Mimi's anniversary.

Leslie and Geraldine must have seemed an unlikely couple. Her family, San Francisco elite, could trace its heritage to before the American Revolution; now she was marrying an immigrant with an unknowable past. But their goals were strikingly consonant, first among them a desire for material wealth. By the time of the marriage, Leslie was already working at the rapidly growing Traung Label and Lithograph Company, where he would ultimately rise to chairman of the board. Established by identical twins Louis and Charlie Traung in 1911, the company, headquartered on Battery Street, boasted the first four-color press in San Francisco, turning out posters, packaging labels for fruit crates, and seed packs featuring beautiful botanical illustrations. In the later years of Leslie's career, a perk of the job was regular trips to Honolulu to visit the Hawaiian Pineapple Company, a major client.

In an unpublished story in Jackson's archive, its title given as both "Beverley" and "Letter to Mother," the narrator, who sounds something like Geraldine (she is very proud of "my friends and my town and my clothes and my car and my country club and jewelry of all the nicest sort, and indisputably mine"), explains that she chose to marry her husband because he was the most "solid" man she knew: "i thought for a long time before i married [him], because there were plenty of other things i could have done, and men i could have married who were not so safe and solid." Throughout their lives, Leslie proved able to provide Geraldine with all the things she desired: china, jewelry, fresh flowers, furs. He also—somewhat sooner than planned—gave her a daughter. Shirley Hardie Jackson was born on December 14, 1916, almost nine months to the day after her parents' wedding.

If Shirley inherited from her maternal grandfather and his ancestors her fascination with houses, and from her mother and grandmother an interest in the spiritual world, the Jackson side also offered her something significant: a gift for visual art. In addition to his professional work in the printing industry, Leslie Jackson was a talented amateur painter with a particular fondness for ships and seascapes. The house Maxwell Bugbee designed for the family included an attic studio for him. Throughout her life, Shirley would entertain herself, her family, and her friends by drawing clever cartoons satirizing her life and her companions; at one point she even considered becoming a professional cartoonist. Economically sketched, with a few lines sufficing to suggest a person or animal (her cats were favorite subjects), Jackson's minimalistic drawings and watercolors are stylistically far removed from the bold graphics of the Traung Company's produce labels. But they serve as a reminder that she grew up in a home where art was valued—for commercial as well as aesthetic purposes.

It was not, however, a warm home. Even if Geraldine had been pleased to have motherhood thrust upon her in her first year of marriage (and by all accounts she was not), Shirley was hardly the child she had imagined. "The pregnancy was very inconvenient," Joanne Hyman, Jackson's elder daughter, says. Geraldine had been groomed to be a socialite: she and Leslie were formal in both their dress and their manners. In one of the few surviving photographs of Leslie, he sits behind his desk at work, looking every bit the proper businessman in a heavy wool three-piece suit, his tie beautifully knotted and a silk handkerchief in his pocket. His handwriting, too, was uncommonly elegant: he invariably composed letters with a fountain pen, adding generous swirls on the capital Is and Es. Geraldine appeared regularly in the society pages; in one photograph, she is captured at a theatrical premiere wearing a floor-length gown. "Seeing her . . . with her sleek little feathered pillboxes and her leopard coat[,] you'd never dream that she could be vulnerable to anyone," one of Shirley's friends once commented.

"She was a lady, Geraldine was," Laurence Hyman remembers. And she tried valiantly to shape her daughter in her image. In one of the earliest photographs of Shirley, the little girl wears an immaculate ruffled white party dress, white shoes and socks, and a giant starched bow nearly the size of her head. But it must have been clear early on that Shirley would not conform to Geraldine's ambitions for her. "I don't think Geraldine was malevolent," recalls Barry Hyman, Jackson's youngest child. "She was just a deeply conventional woman who was horrified by the idea that her daughter was not going to be deeply conventional." "Geraldine wanted a pretty little girl, and what she got was a lumpish redhead," Joanne Hyman says bluntly. When Barry Jackson—handsome, blond, athletic—arrived two years after his sister, it must have quickly become obvious which child Geraldine favored. Her criticism of her daughter—Shirley's appearance (especially her weight), her housekeeping, her child-rearing practices—never relented. Even after Geraldine and Leslie eventually moved back to California, leaving Shirley settled permanently in the East, Geraldine continued to nag and needle her daughter by mail. Though Jackson would later express her distress over the hostile letters she received from readers in the wake of "The Lottery," that sudden deluge, largely from faceless strangers, seems less damaging than the drops of poison she grew accustomed to receiving from her mother every few months—and to which, almost without fail, she dutifully and cheerfully responded.

Shirley Jackson with her brother, Barry, in San Francisco, early 1920s.

Jackson's awareness that her mother had never loved her uncondi-
tionally—if at all—would be a source of sadness well into adulthood.
Aside from a single angry letter that she did not send, she never gave
voice to her feelings of rejection. But she expressed them in other ways.
All the heroines of her novels are essentially motherless—if not lacking a mother entirely, then victims of loveless mothering. Many of her
books include acts of matricide, either unconscious or deliberate.

THE UNOFFICIAL MOTTO of Burlingame, California, which for years
adorned a mural painted on City Hall, reflected its founders' unapol-
ogetic sense of entitlement: "Living in Burlingame is a special privilege." By June 1926, when Shirley was nine, the Jacksons had installed
themselves in the modern new house Maxwell Bugbee had designed for
them (and his wife) in the growing suburb south of San Francisco—
"far enough away . . . to have palm trees in the gardens," Jackson would
later write. It was a privilege Leslie and Geraldine felt they had earned:
she owing to her wealth and family pedigree, he through his hard work
and providential marriage. Socially conservative, xenophobic, and
openly racist—reflective of the nativist prejudices common among the
American upper classes of their period—they fit comfortably in the
elite enclave.

During the early years of Shirley's life—which were also the first
few years of her parents' marriage—the Jacksons had moved often,
even itinerantly. When Shirley was born, they were likely living at 1060
Clayton Street, in the elegant Ashbury Heights neighborhood of San
Francisco. They spent a couple of years in San Anselmo, a bucolic town
in Marin County, but by the beginning of 1920, they were back in the
city, renting a house on Twenty-Eighth Avenue between Anza Street
and Balboa Street, in the Richmond district, just a few blocks north of
Golden Gate Park. Leslie had advanced to secretary at the lithography
firm, and there was a servant girl to help with the children—Shirley
had just turned three, and her brother, Barry, was one. Geraldine's parents, Maxwell and Mimi, lived next door with their adult son, Clifford, a
radio mechanic who would remain a bachelor all his life. The following

year, the family, which by that time included Mimi, moved back to Ashbury Heights, to a newly built house at 20 Ashbury Terrace, where Mimi hung out a shingle as a Christian Science practitioner—that is, a spiritual healer. Set high upon a hill, it was literally a move up. But they would stay there only a few years. Leslie and Geraldine had set their sights even higher.

The town of Burlingame was named for Anson Burlingame, an American diplomat in China, who in 1866 bought an estate there once owned by William C. Ralston, a banker. Burlingame died before he could move in, and the land wound up in the hands of Ralston's son-in-law, Francis G. Newlands, a congressman and senator who had been influential in the development of Chevy Chase, Maryland, an affluent suburb of Washington, D.C. He envisioned Burlingame according to a similar model, with large estates surrounding an exclusive club—the country headquarters for San Francisco's high society.

When the Burlingame Country Club was founded, in 1893, the town consisted mainly of horse farms and dairies. Nestled among them were a few estates owned by some of California's wealthiest families, including the Mills estate, built by Bank of California executive Darius Ogden Mills, and nearby Black Hawk, owned by Mills's sister Adeline and her husband, Ansel I. Easton, uncle of the photographer Ansel Adams. The area, according to a local historian, was "like something out of England—huge country manors surrounded by a handful of local people who helped keep the large manors running." Most of the streets were unpaved, and frequent flooding from Burlingame Creek—which ran smack through the middle of town until it was channeled underground decades later—meant that they often turned to mud. There were no shops or services aside from an itinerant vegetable farmer who passed through several times a week. Nonetheless, a tourist brochure printed in 1904 described it as "perhaps the most exclusive hometown in California."

The San Francisco earthquake of 1906 was powerful enough to rattle pantries and knock down chimneys in Burlingame. Soon the exclusive enclave was host to a flood of evacuees, many of whom were attracted by its easy commuting access to the city. By the following year, the population had quadrupled, to 1000. The new residents, accustomed to the conveniences of city living, clashed with some of the old-timers over their demands for civic improvements such as paved roads and a municipal water system. The result was that the "hill people"—including the owners of most of the largest estates—formed a separate town, called Hillsborough. (To the chagrin of longtime Burlingamers, the Burlingame Country Club fell within the new Hillsborough city limits.) In 1912, the paving of El Camino Real, which runs directly through Burlingame, set the town on the path of one of California's first state highways. That decade saw Burlingame nearly triple in size, reaching more than than 4000 residents by 1920. It also gained a library, an elementary school, two movie houses, and six churches.

A guidebook published in 1915 described Burlingame as "new, modern, spick and span—flowers, lawns, trellises, porticos, portolas, snug little individual garages. The whole place has an atmosphere of success." The town prided itself upon its friendliness: the official slogan was "You are a stranger here but once." That hospitality, not surprisingly, was extended only to white Christians. In *The Road Through the Wall* (1948), set in a town modeled on Burlingame, Jackson depicts racism and anti-Semitism among neighbors on a close-knit street virtually identical to the one where she grew up. At a time when small towns were considerably more provincial than they are today, Burlingame was one of the most insular—claustrophobically so. As the population exploded—in the years between 1920 and 1927, it nearly tripled yet again, to 12,000—houses were built so close together, with deep gardens but narrow side yards, that two people leaning out of facing windows could nearly shake hands. That proximity, in the novel, serves as a breeding ground for gossip and animosity.

The commuter town's rapid growth stemmed in part from the growing popularity of the automobile. Burlingame became a hub for automobile dealerships, and by the end of the 1920s, one in three residents would own a car, compared with one in five Americans. The names of new car buyers were printed in the local newspaper in celebration of the community's prosperity. At a time when the average American family earned $1200 per year, the typical Burlingame home cost around $7500.

Even the Depression did little to dampen Burlingame's cheer: residents were encouraged to support the economy by holding "prosperity parties," teachers donated six days' pay over six months to help the unemployed, and a portion of movie revenues was given to charity.

The Jacksons arrived in the middle of the 1920s boom. Their new home, a handsome two-story brick house with a front gable and a deep garden out back, was located at 1609 Forest View Road (now Forest View Avenue). It was only a few blocks from McKinley Elementary School, where Shirley and her brother enrolled, and a short stroll from the main commercial strip on Broadway. The Christian Science church was practically around the corner. Leslie commuted daily to his job at the rapidly expanding Traung Company. Even as the Depression hit, he continued to be promoted.

The end of Forest View Road marked the official border of Burlingame. Beyond lay the "Millionaire Colony," as Hillsborough was then nicknamed. From their backyard, the Jacksons might have been able to see into the garden of the nearest estate, built a decade earlier

Shirley and Barry, around the time of the move to Burlingame.

by George Newhall, son of an auctioneer and land speculator named Henry Newhall. Known as La Dolphine, the Newhall mansion was modeled after the Petit Trianon at Versailles, with a formal garden and a 175-foot-long driveway lined with pink and white hawthorn trees. The architect was Lewis Hobart, whose other commissions included a number of major buildings in and around San Francisco, among them—coincidentally—an estate for William Crocker, Charles's son, in Hillsborough, built after the family home in San Francisco was destroyed by the earthquake.

The action in *The Road Through the Wall*, set in 1936 in the fictional town of Cabrillo, California, takes place on Pepper Street, which happens to have been the name of one of the streets intersecting the Jacksons' block of Forest View Road (its name was later changed to Newhall). Cortez Avenue, which also figures in the novel, was a few blocks away. And the estate behind the wall, one of the novel's key symbols, was almost certainly modeled on La Dolphine, which was subdivided in 1940—around the same time as the estate in the novel is. In her notes for *The Road Through the Wall*, Jackson wrote out character sketches for each of the families and included, in parentheses, the names of their real-world models. She even mapped out the houses on her fictionalized Pepper Street, depicting them directly adjacent to one another—just as close as they were in reality.

As faithfully as Jackson followed the physical contours of the neighborhood, her novel's plot boldly clashes with the official version of Burlingame as a town of cheerful families living in tasteful homes. Only in "The Lottery" can a less appealing set of neighbors be found in Jackson's fiction. "The weather falls more gently on some places than on others, the world looks down more paternally on some people," she wrote in its richly ironic opening lines. "Some spots are proverbially warm, and keep, through falling snow, their untarnished reputations as summer resorts; some people are automatically above suspicion." Of course, in Jackson's work no one is ever above suspicion. An uncommonly close observer even as a child, she had reason to speculate that beneath the sunny surfaces of her neighbors' lives lay darker secrets: infidelity, racial and ethnic prejudice, basic cruelty. The novel's children—Jackson's peers—are treated with at least as much gravity as the adults, whom they easily equal in connivance and brutality. Harriet Merriam, an outsider who is clearly a stand-in for Shirley, commits cruelties in order to fit in with the other children on the block. One girl is mentally disabled, and several of the children manipulate her into buying them fancy presents. Marilyn, the only Jewish child, is mocked for not celebrating Christmas. The petty crimes and misdemeanors accelerate to the crisis at the novel's conclusion, in which a child is brutally murdered while the adults engage in drunken antics at a garden party.

Jackson once said that "the first book is the book you have to write to get back at your parents. . . . Once you get that out of your way, you can start writing books." The parental crime to be avenged may have simply been the Jacksons' attempt to mold their daughter into a typical upper-middle-class California girl: proper, polite, demure. In a picture of Geraldine and Shirley taken when Shirley was a teenager, Shirley sits at the piano while Geraldine hovers watchfully in the background. Music was an interest the two of them shared: Geraldine taught Shirley many of the old English and Scottish folk songs collected as the Child Ballads, handed down to her by her own mother and grandmother, which Shirley loved and sang all her life. Leslie, too, liked to sing funny music-hall songs, and later took up the ukulele and the zither.

Still, Shirley generally preferred to sit outside in the grass making up stories or to hole up in her room with the fantasies she loved: Grimm's fairy tales, the Oz books (she would eventually collect all of them), *Tarzan of the Apes*. As a teenager, she would invent a private mythology centered on the figure of Harlequin, the commedia dell'arte acrobat with a quick wit and a sly grin, scouring the local library for anything she could learn about the character. Geraldine had no use for her daughter's imagination. In a letter sent decades later, she reproached Shirley for having been "a wilful child . . . who insisted on her own way in everything—good or bad." *Come Along with Me*, Jackson's final, unfinished novel, would feature a heroine whose mother lectures her not to spend all her time lost in her imagination, "gawking at nothing."

The presence of Shirley's grandmother Mimi added a layer of oddness to the household. Even though she no longer advertised her services as a Christian Science practitioner, she continued to practice spiritual healing on members of the family. Jackson gave her children various accounts of such attempts, with her own skeptical assessment of them. Mimi once claimed that she had broken her leg and prayed over it all night, then walked down the stairs to breakfast the next morning; as it turned out, the injury was actually a sprained ankle. In another episode, which still distressed Jackson many years later, her little brother, Barry, broke his arm after Shirley mischievously told him to close his eyes and run down a hill. Her guilt over her own responsibility for the injury turned into anger as she watched Mimi and Geraldine pray over Barry for two days before they finally took him to the hospital. Later Jackson told her daughter Joanne that Mimi, who did not seek treatment for her own stomach cancer, "died of Christian Science."

Jackson channeled the anger into her fiction, in which she often portrays a grandmother figure as an aggressor. "Afternoon in Linen," one of her first *New Yorker* stories, features a grandmother who humiliates her granddaughter by demanding that she read her poetry aloud in front of guests. In the early 1940s, when she was living briefly in Greenwich Village, Jackson recalled meeting "one of my grandmother's old cronies—the one with the evil eye—down on sullivan street." Afterward, she felt she was being "followed by something supernatural and malignant." Throughout her life, she had nightmares in which her grandmother chased her. Christian Science, particularly the belief that one can influence the material world through the use of mental power, is not entirely remote from witchcraft, a subject Jackson would study and come to know well. It also—as she witnessed growing up—could be turned into a vehicle for harm.

Shirley's personal habits were another primary source of tension between her and her mother. The woman whose beauty had been remarked upon in her wedding announcement, who loved to drape herself in furs and gold jewelry, expected her daughter to have similar taste. Dorothy Ayling, Shirley's closest friend in childhood, recalled that Shirley's mother was constantly nagging her to dress neatly and behave herself. Geraldine once even ambushed her teenage daughter at the beauty salon and forced her to get a permanent. But Shirley was a redhead, which at the time was considered déclassé, more appropriate in a servant than the daughter of a socialite. And the formal outfits Geraldine loved to see her daughter wear—stiff, heavy skirts with matching jackets and gloves—tended not to flatter Shirley's large-boned figure. In a picture of the two of them riding bicycles—both dressed, as usual, in skirts and jackets, their hair in matching waves over their foreheads—Geraldine smiles encouragingly at her daughter while Shirley looks elsewhere, her entire body turned awkwardly away from her mother.

But if Jackson intended *The Road Through the Wall* as an act of revenge against her mother, she might have had in mind a crime more serious than wardrobe impositions. The relationship between Harriet and her mother is an all-too-convincing portrayal of familial dysfunction, and certain scenes in the novel appear to be drawn directly from Shirley's childhood. In the first chapter, Harriet comes home from school to discover that her mother has rummaged through her desk and read her private papers. ("Writing used to be a delicious private thing, done in my own room with the door locked, in constant terror of the maternal knock," Jackson would later write.) Mrs. Merriman forces Harriet to burn her work in the furnace while Mr. Merriam sits passively at the dinner table. Later, after the fit of rage has passed, Harriet and her mother spend afternoons writing together: Mrs. Merriam composes a poem titled "Death and Soft Music," while Harriet's is called "To My Mother."

The scene of privacy invaded was one that Jackson used repeatedly in her stories; sometimes a mother is the perpetrator, sometimes a

Shirley and Geraldine Jackson, mid-1930s.

grandmother. But certain details are always the same: the lock on the desk broken, the papers out of order. If such a violation did not actually take place, it was certainly something the young Shirley had reason to fear. She wrote voraciously as a child, including the graduation play for her fifth-grade class, and was an assistant editor of her grammar school newspaper. But she would later tell her children that she had burned all her childhood writing—in front of her mother, to make her feel guilty. Like Harriet's father in *The Road Through the Wall*, Leslie Jackson always took Geraldine's side in her arguments with Shirley. "He was not the warm and fuzzy guy we imagined him to be," Joanne Hyman recalls.

Some of Jackson's childhood writing does survive. Her early poems are written in a singsongy tone, often with a didactic religious message revealing the influence of Christian Science. Her first published work was a poem called "The Pine Tree," for which she won a contest in *Junior Home Magazine* ("The Something-to-Do Magazine for Mothers and Children") in February 1929, at age twelve. (Her excitement over the award lasted only until she found out what the prize was—a six-month subscription to the magazine.) The poem describes a pine tree who lives in a "lonely wood" and is sad because "no one ever notices me." Suddenly an angel appears and comforts the tree by telling it that God cherishes it. If the pine tree speaks for the adolescent Shirley's struggles with her mother when it says "I do no good," then it may also show that she, a lonely outsider, found more consolation in religion than she would later let on.

A poem addressed to Geraldine takes a different tone. "Written for Mother's Day on May 1926" begins with the usual cadence but soon veers off course.

A mother is the nicest thing
That ever there could be.
I have never had cause to forget,
That mine means the world to me.
How sweet to have a mother who
is always willing to help you,

always eager to sympathise,

always ready to give happiness.

How sweet is the joy given to you by that loving mother, who is
always hunting for new ways to give happiness.

If ever we feel that our mother is not quite fair to us, we must
try to overcome this unfaithful feeling, for Mothers were given to us to
love and obey, and should we not honor them as well?

Even at age nine, Shirley was capable of writing with regular rhyme and meter, as the other poems in her archive demonstrate. The problem was getting her feelings about her mother—messier and more unruly than she could accept—to fall neatly into place.

Yet another source of strain between Shirley and her mother was Shirley's friendship with Dorothy Ayling, her best friend from the time she was twelve until the Jacksons moved to Rochester, New York, in 1933. Dorothy's father was the gardener at La Dolphine—not the same class as an executive at the Traung Label and Lithograph Company. Though Geraldine never made Shirley break off the relationship, Dorothy later recalled that, in four years of friendship, she was never invited for a meal at the Jackson house. Nonetheless, the two girls were inseparable. Dorothy was a year younger and a grade behind Shirley, but they played together in the Burlingame High School orchestra, Shirley on violin and Dorothy on cello. (Dorothy went on to become a professional cellist; Shirley would abandon the violin after high school, though she sang and played the piano and guitar throughout her life.) On weekends, they went into the city or spent time together at home, playing piano duets or eating pomegranates—"two for a nickel in California at that time," Shirley remembered—on the back fence, to the dismay of Geraldine, who found fence sitting "unladylike." Dorothy would later recall some of the pranks they played together, including sneaking up to La Dolphine to peek through the windows when parties were going on. Shirley was the more flamboyant of the pair; Dorothy, "so careful," was "eager to keep me chained down to sanity," Shirley reported in her diary. Shirley also had a bossy streak, and seems to have expected the younger girl to be subservient to her. At one point, complaining that her pen had "worked overtime" and she had too much copying to do, she mused about hiring Dorothy as her secretary.

Jackson chronicled one of their excursions in "Dorothy and My Grandmother and the Sailors," written during the 1940s and first published in her 1949 collection *The Lottery*. In the story—like all of Jackson's autobiographical writings, it straddles the line between fiction and nonfiction—a girl's mother and grandmother take her and her friend Dorothy to San Francisco to buy coats, have lunch, and visit the fleet, which is making its yearly stop in the harbor. The pleasant outing is darkened by the overprotective anxieties of the narrator's mother and grandmother, which—though the girls are only around twelve in the story—have a foreboding sexual undertone: "My mother told us about the kind of girls who followed sailors, and my grandmother told us about the kind of sailors who followed girls." On the ship, the narrator realizes that she is lost. She finds "a tall man in uniform with lots of braid," whom she believes must be an officer, and he helps her find her family. After she rejoins them, her mother shakes her. "Aren't you ashamed?" she asks sternly. Apparently the girl had attached herself to one of these feared sailors. The women's anxiety infects Dorothy, who becomes hysterical a few hours later when a sailor sits down in the empty seat next to her at the movies. But the joke is on the mother and grandmother: the sailors, who clearly intend no harm to the girls, are innocent victims of the older women's paranoia.

One of Shirley and Dorothy's favorite activities was making clothespin dolls, which Jackson later described in a magazine article that was incorporated into *Raising Demons* (1957). Again, the depiction of Geraldine is revealing. In an early draft of the piece, Jackson mentions her mother's temper twice in a single sentence: "My mother used to be angry at us for doing nothing . . . [one day] she came angrily to where we were sitting on the railing of the back porch." Geraldine "must have been reading a magazine or something, because she had a bright and progressive idea, and she proposed it in precisely the voice which end-of-their-tether parents use to propose an idea which they have read in a magazine somewhere." In the published version, Geraldine's anger has faded from the picture, as has Jackson's irony, replaced by the breezy tone she customarily used for her women's magazine pieces. "I do believe that it was probably my mother's suggestion, because she was always asking us if we couldn't find something to *do*, girls, and because I can remember the bright-eyed enthusiasm with which she approached us frequently, suggesting one or another occupation for growing girls, which she had read in a magazine somewhere—that we should plan a bazaar to sell homemade cookies, for instance, or take long walks to gather sweet grass, or fern, or look for wild strawberries, or that we should learn shorthand." With her typical penchant for exaggeration, in her article Jackson claimed that the girls were so enthusiastic about the pursuit that they made more than four hundred dolls before Dorothy laid down her scissors on the dining room table and refused to continue. Shirley's childhood diary, however, records a more realistic number: thirty-nine.

AS A SICKLY, isolated child growing up in a strict New England family, Hawthorne is said to have developed an unusual quirk: he composed an inner dialogue, divided into two personalities, that substituted for conversation and companionship. One side served as storyteller, the other as audience, offering questions or criticisms. As a teenager, Jackson did something similar, but on the page. She kept multiple diaries simultaneously, each with a different purpose.

The earliest surviving diary begins in January 1932, shortly after Jackson's fifteenth birthday. It is a small datebook with a black fake-leather cover stamped with the words "Year Book," the kind that businesses often distributed for free. In these pages, she did her best to cultivate the aw-shucks tone of an all-American girl: "O Boy!" is a frequent exclamation. And the snapshot the diary gives of her life makes her look in every way like a typical suburban teenager who spends her days making fudge, playing hockey and tennis, riding bikes, gossiping with her friends, doing jigsaw puzzles, and playing card games (she favored a complicated version of double solitaire popular at the time called Russian Bank). She attended Girl Scout camp for a few weeks in the summer and regularly went to vaudeville shows and movies: the

Polish-born singer and actor Jan Kiepura was a favorite. She worried about her spending habits, her grades, and her weight: she had trouble resisting a box of chocolates. She quarreled, unsurprisingly, with her mother. There is nothing about events in the outside world: like many teenagers, she took no interest in politics or global affairs. In a year when the biggest hit song was "Brother, Can You Spare a Dime?" she preferred syrupy romantic melodies such as Fauré's "Berceuse." But she must have been watching her neighbors carefully, gathering the details of social mores that would find their way into *The Road Through the Wall.*

Only one entry reveals something more unusual. On New Year's Day 1932, Jackson made a series of resolutions, deciding confidently to "write down just what I'd like to be at the start of 1933 and . . . make myself just that." She recognized that change would be difficult, especially because of her own high standards: "I'm not easily satisfied." Most of what she aimed for was conventional: study harder, "make myself healthier (thinner)," be nicer to friends and family (she underlined "and family"), and control her spending. The last few lines are more curious. "I must lose that sense of inferiority, but not go so far as vulgarity, and, above all things, I must cultivate charm, and 'seek out the good in others, rather than explore for the evil.'"

That last phrase, significantly, is in quotation marks. Those are not Jackson's words, but someone else's. They might be her mother's: the reference to vulgarity especially sounds like something Geraldine might have said. Jackson's daughters would later complain that even as Shirley rebelled against her mother, she had nonetheless internalized that scolding voice, which she would use on them: "A lady doesn't climb trees," "A lady sits like this," and so on. After Jackson began writing fiction, Geraldine never hesitated to say that she didn't understand or simply didn't like her daughter's darker works; she preferred the magazine articles and family memoirs. "You have too many demented girls [in your books]," she once commented.

Fortunately for her writing, exploring for the evil was not something Jackson ever truly intended to give up. And even as she committed her teenage self to self-improvement, she already had a precocious ability to step outside herself, to observe herself as if she were one of the guests at her mother's teas and garden parties whom she would later caricature. "Shirley—it would be very interesting to go thru this book with a more open mind, and find out how much is sincere, and how much affectation, tho I'm afraid the result would be rather overwhelmingly in the favor of the latter," she wrote on an index card that she inserted into the front pages of the diary. Whether or not she ever did this, she was apparently aware of her own "affectation" even as she set it down on paper.

Jackson was able to step outside herself in another way as well. Even as she continued to write in the datebook, she began a second diary. This time she chose a tablet-size notepad, its cover printed with the image of an elegant young woman, her auburn hair gently waved, a yellow shawl gathered around her bare shoulders, a necklace of black beads at her throat—the proper young lady Geraldine wanted her daughter to be. The picture's title is "The Debutante." But the girl's face is scratched out with a pencil. If Shirley could not express to her mother her resentment about Geraldine's expectations, she could take it out in private.

Jackson wrote this diary entirely in the form of love letters to Harold (Bud) Young, who was a year ahead of her at Burlingame High and the concertmaster of the orchestra; he also played viola and oboe and was a member of the honor society. She described him as "my girl-shy violinist," although she seems to have been the shy one: it's not clear that they ever so much as spoke to each other. The crush existed entirely in her mind; Bud may not even have been aware of it. In the datebook, she marked as "lucky" the days on which she was able to catch a glimpse of him and enclosed a map that Dorothy, who took music lessons from Bud's father, had drawn for her of the Youngs' house, with an X marking Bud's bedroom. But the tone she created in her "Debutante" diary was unreservedly passionate—entirely different from the "O Boy!" cheer of the first diary. It also was every bit as much of a performance. Jackson was trying out different personas, figuring out what fit and what did not. For the next two years, she kept both diaries simultaneously: the black datebook to gossip about her friends and report on her activities, the "Debutante" diary for her more personal confessions. Sometimes she went for months without writing in one or the other; sometimes she wrote in both on the same day.

A significant portion of Jackson's adult writing would be epistolary: the lengthy letters she sent to Stanley Edgar Hyman, her future husband, during college vacations; her chatty reports to her parents about all the goings-on in her household, often with a side helping of news about her writing; and, late in life, the intimate letters she wrote to Jeanne Beatty, the Baltimore housewife who became her confidante. In each of these instances, Jackson's letters helped her to form her thoughts and develop her voice as a writer. The "Debutante" diary served a similar function. "Today, I shall write," she announced dramatically in November. "I feel it. I shall write of the great joys of living." She even started to abandon her crush. "Forgive me, dear, if I say it, but, these last few days, I find myself not caring so much," she wrote on November 26. "Why Bud, even you seem less important than—what? I don't know. My writing, possibly." Still, the next day, she was swooning over his performance of "Berceuse." "There has never been music more wholly yours, so softly triumphant. . . . I think, dear, that Orpheus should have had a violin, rather than a lyre." A few weeks later, she wrote of her fondness for another unabashedly romantic piece: Wagner's *Lohengrin*, with its ethereal overture for strings. "It's exquisite. Our love song—only you don't know it."

On Shirley's sixteenth birthday, she received from her mother a deep green turquoise ring (her birthstone) that she called her "Laughing Ring." The end of the year meant the departure of Bud, who graduated in December and moved on to San Mateo Junior College. Shirley would continue to run into him occasionally—she tried to figure out which streetcar he took so that she could be on the corner at the right moment—but their encounters were much less frequent. "To my friend, my love, my hero, I whisper one last goodbye," she wrote. The following day, she reflected, "I have realized that I have begun a new state of mind. I know that from now on I shall write differently in this book." Bud had served his purpose; she, too, was ready to move on.

The start of 1933 saw the United States sinking further into the

Depression, the inauguration of Franklin Delano Roosevelt on a platform of economic renewal, and the first ominous steps toward Nazism in
Europe—the last of which would prove, within a few years, of intense
concern for Jackson. For now, blissfully oblivious in her Burlingame
bubble, she began a new diary in a datebook identical to her 1932 "Year
Book." The back page contained a sheet for "Special Data," on which
she recorded the names of her crushes and best girlfriends, as well as her
ambitions: "author, actress, aviator, lawyer (almost all impossible)." She
also started a five-year diary, in which she would write intermittently.
"[Dorothy] says this diary is to tell what I think—if at all," she wrote in
the first. The second "tells what I do—if at all!" No mention was made
of the "Debutante" diary, which Shirley did not show to Dorothy or to
anyone else, and whose musings could not be so neatly categorized.

The 1933 datebook was as superficial as its predecessor: a sixteen-
year-old's worries about her grades and reports on tame adventures.
Increasingly, she wrote about movies that particularly impressed her:
not the blockbusters of the year, which included *King Kong*, *The Invisible
Man*, and *Duck Soup*, but minor dramas such as *The Match King*, about a
Swedish businessman who cons his way to success; *The Mummy*, which
she found too unreal and "horribly unhorrifying" to be frightening; and,
most interestingly, *The Kid from Spain*, featuring Sidney Franklin—a
Jew from Brooklyn turned professional bullfighter who played himself
in the film. Shirley was so impressed that she saw the movie twice in
two days; in five years, another Jewish boy from Brooklyn would prove
even more alluring. She also kept track of her writing progress. "Wrote
all evening—there was something in my pen tonight," she reported
in February. No fiction from this period survives, but the tone of her
diary entries suggests a new maturity. In one, she reported on a party
her mother had thrown—"I've been banged around, kissed, socked,
and generally man-handled"—and described the guests as if listing the
characters in a play. One of her mother's friends was a "Spanish señorita
with a Garbo complex," another was "Harlequin with a yellow streak."

These parties may well have inspired Jackson's story "The Intoxicated," written in the early 1940s and published for the first time in *The*

Lottery. A man in his thirties attending a party encounters his host's daughter in the kitchen, a "baggy and ill-formed" girl of seventeen who disconcerts him by calmly laying out a vision of apocalypse. "Somehow I think of the churches as going first, before even the Empire State building. And then all the big apartment houses by the river, slipping down slowly into the water with the people inside." The man rebukes her—"I think it's a little silly of you to fill your mind with all this morbid trash"—but she will not be dissuaded. "A really extraordinary girl," he tells her father, who shakes his head and replies, "Kids nowadays." If Jackson was anything like the girl in the story, then as a teenager she was already developing the knack for the perfectly shocking line that would come to characterize her fiction. The story also suggests that she might not have been as politically oblivious as she appeared to be: the apocalypse she imagines can be read in any number of allegorical ways. Of course, it can also be taken at face value, as a surreal vision of a world gone wrong.

That spring, Leslie and Geraldine broke the news about the Traung Company's merger. The Jacksons would arrive in Rochester in time for Shirley and Barry to begin the school year in their new home. Shirley was initially heartbroken about the move, which meant leaving her beloved California—the garden where she had spent so many hours dreaming in the grass, the back fence where she and Dorothy sat eating pomegranates—for a blustery, unfamiliar new city. "This is the last time I shall ever press the first rosebud of Spring that comes off my rosebush," she wrote sentimentally. Although she was justifiably anxious about having to finish high school in a new environment, she soon came to see the move as an opportunity for a fresh beginning. She had taken from her time in California what she needed; the question now was what she would do with it. "Get thee behind me, Cupid!" she wrote on the last day of school. "Off with the old—Come on, N.Y., I'm ready for yuh!"

The last two pages of the "Debutante" diary contain an undated story fragment that Jackson originally called "Berceuse"; later she crossed out the title and replaced it with "Melody." A girl named Karleen, attending a concert with her aunt, is deeply moved by the music. Her eyes fix on the orchestra leader—"oh, to create such music!" But Jackson has already learned that beauty and the grotesque can be effectively juxtaposed: the man's back is fat, his coat shiny. Afterward, Karleen's aunt asks if she enjoyed the concert: she wants her niece to "learn to appreciate good music, like I do." Karleen's teenage heart cringes in annoyance. She doesn't want just to appreciate music. She wants to write it.

2.

THE DEMON IN
THE MIND

ROCHESTER,
1933–1937

> All I can remember clearly about being sixteen is that it was
> a particularly agonizing age; our family was in the process
> of moving East from California, and I settled down into a
> new high school and new manners and ways, all things I
> believe produce a great uneasiness in a sixteen-year-old.
>
> —"All I Can Remember"

HANGSAMAN, SHIRLEY JACKSON'S SECOND AND MOST
autobiographical novel, begins with seventeen-year-old Natalie Waite
about to leave home for college. Natalie's home life is oppressive—her
brother, two years younger, wants nothing to do with her; her mother is
clingy and dissatisfied; her father is domineering. Quirky and sensitive,
she lives mostly in her own mind, "an odd corner of a world of sound
and sight past the daily voices of her father and mother and their incom-
prehensible actions." Her fantasy life is vivid and strange. Sometimes
she imagines that a detective is questioning her about a crime, drawing
on a deep wellspring of guilt with an unknown source. To distract herself in moments of boredom or discomfort, she imagines "the sweet

sharp sensation of being burned alive." She shares her creative writing with her father, but also keeps a secret diary, though she admits to herself that she is writing it for "ultimate publication."

Thus far, the connections between Natalie and Shirley are obvious. Even their names are similar: both contain the same number of letters and end in a "lee" sound. So what happens next is troubling. Natalie's parents give a garden party, which was a regular occurrence in the Jackson household as well. Natalie drinks a cocktail and finds herself the object of attention of one of her father's friends, an older man who offers her a cigarette and flirts with her. Like the girl in "The Intoxicated," Jackson's story about a teenager who disconcerts a party guest with talk of apocalypse, Natalie initially parries the man with clever conversation, but eventually he manages to lead her into the woods behind the house. What happens there is not described. When she awakens the next morning, she is sick and dizzy. The mirror reveals "her bruised face and her pitiful, erring body." She wishes she were dead. The remainder of the book chronicles her psychic disintegration.

If this incident is based on anything that happened to Jackson at the time, there is no trace of it. There has been speculation that she was molested as a young teenager in California by her uncle, Clifford Bugbee, a lifelong bachelor whose "sticky touch" Dorothy Ayling, Jackson's childhood friend, would recall squeamishly decades later. But Clifford is an unlikely sexual predator. For one thing, Jackson seems to have remembered him fondly, telling her children funny stories about his odd scientific inventions. When the Jacksons returned to California for a visit in 1939, the summer after Shirley's junior year at Syracuse University, her letters to Stanley—which describe the trip in minute detail, including excursions made with her uncle—reveal no discomfort at spending time with him. And her diaries from high school and early college give absolutely no hint of sexual predation.

They do, however, reveal a young woman who engaged in sexual experimentation typical for girls of her time. In 1933, shortly before the move to Rochester, Jackson got drunk for the first time at a neighborhood party—"I feel like a package of condensed giggles"—and flirted with a local actor: "I mixed him a drink, and he tried manfully."

Whatever that may mean, it does not sound like the comment of a vic-timized girl. In 1936, after starting college at Rochester, she joked in her diary about "the ruination of what we laughingly refer to as my reputation"—an incident in which her brother turned the lights on unexpectedly and exposed her canoodling with a date in the living room. Her initial embarrassment wore off quickly. "Absolved of sin," she reported a few days later.

Yet Jackson, like her fictional counterpart, would experience a mental unraveling during her first two years of college. It was serious enough that she had to withdraw from the University of Rochester and live at home for a year before making a fresh start at Syracuse University. Between 1934 and 1936, her writings indicate that she may have made at least one halfhearted attempt at suicide. No particular event appears to have sent her into this downward spiral. More likely, Jackson was overwhelmed—for the first time, but hardly the last—by the constellation of social anxiety and familial pressure that left her feeling accepted by no one.

A FLOURISHING CITY of about 320,000 on the banks of the often tur-bulent Genesee River, Rochester in 1933 was considerably more cos-mopolitan than sleepy Burlingame. In addition to theaters, dance halls, and its own philharmonic and opera company, it boasted nearly forty movie houses. With the average ticket price a quarter—well within the reach of a high school student—Jackson, who loved the movies, some-times attended as often as twice a week. Known as the Kodak City, after the Eastman Kodak Company, the city's biggest employer and great-est homegrown success story, Rochester was also home to the optical company Bausch and Lomb and the Gannett newspaper chain. The pri-vate, coeducational University of Rochester, founded in 1850, benefited from the city's prosperity: George Eastman, Kodak's founder, was a major donor. Rochester was also known for its food-packing industry: a rich harvest from local farms and orchards supplied the city's canner-ies. All those containers needed labels, which was where the Stecher-Traung Lithograph Company, Leslie Jackson's employer, came in. The company became well-known for the striking watercolor paintings that adorned its seed packets, which today are collector's items.

In spite of its economic vigor, Rochester remained bleak and industrial. And it had all the social conservatism of Burlingame—one of the city's nicknames was Smugtown, U.S.A.—with none of the mitigating factors that made California life so pleasant: the weather, the pomegranates and avocados, the eucalyptus-scented air. Jackson despised her new home from the start. "Golly, how I hate this town," she complained on September 7, 1933. In her diary, she kept track of the number of days since she had left California. The first school she enrolled in was a poor fit, and she and her brother were both miserable there. She also developed hay fever immediately upon arrival, a problem that would plague her for the rest of her life. She was literally allergic to the Northeast.

The Jackson family settled in Brighton, an upper-middle-class suburb southeast of the city center. Their new home, at 125 Monteroy Road, was a handsome five-bedroom colonial with Tudor accents, built only a few years earlier. The neighbors were professionals: doctors, lawyers, University of Rochester faculty. In general, "people were on an upward trajectory," recalls Marion Strobel, whose mother, Marian Morton, grew up near the Jacksons and knew Shirley and Barry in high school. The Jacksons were even more interested in social climbing. They hobnobbed with the city's elite at the Genesee Valley Club, a city club, and the Country Club of Rochester, where Shirley and her brother golfed. (Strobel recalled that when she was growing up in Brighton, she thought she was underprivileged because her father's club lacked a swimming pool.) Like many women of her class, Geraldine hired an African-American maid to help with housework and cooking. Shirley became close to the maid, whose name was Alta Williams, and in college wrote an unpublished story about her.

The house on Monteroy Road was walking distance from Brighton High School, where Shirley enrolled for her senior year. Two decades later, she would still recall "the sick inadequate feeling of standing in a hallway holding a notebook and wondering without hope if i would ever find the right room." The transplant from California was obviously a novelty: when the first snow of the season began to fall one afternoon,

Shirley's entire chemistry class insisted on accompanying her to the window to marvel at it. She did not bother telling her classmates that there had been a freak snowfall in Burlingame the previous winter.

Newness, however, did not translate into popularity. The school was small, with only sixty students in Jackson's graduating class. And the awkwardness of winning acceptance by long established cliques in senior year was exacerbated by Jackson's appearance. Her high school yearbook photo reveals a girl with a mass of unruly auburn hair and a stern, slightly puzzled expression. Her clothes were never quite right. "She used to wear a green sweater and a blue skirt, and in those days you didn't wear a green sweater and a blue skirt," one of her classmates would say, recalling that Jackson was also "on the heavy side." She filled her calendar with football games, parties, and plays. The California girl soon grew to love tobogganing and ice skating, and would even try skiing. But she suffered a social setback almost at once, rejected from a sorority she had hoped to join. She did not let her disappointment show, instead cultivating a pose of aloofness. Jackson "didn't give a darn about being with the in girls or the out girls," Strobel recalls her mother saying. "That just wasn't her thing."

Geraldine, focused on her own social life, paid little attention to her struggling daughter. Barry Jackson gossiped to his friends that the whole family had given up on her ever dressing or acting the way the rest

Shirley Jackson
in Rochester,
mid-1930s.

of the Jacksons did. "We just don't know what will become of Shirley," he told Marian Morton. Marian's older brother, Richard Morton, who got to know Shirley at the University of Rochester, also remembered her as an "odd duck." In a story likely written a few years later, Jackson depicts a high school girl who comes home, sobbing, because she has no date to a basketball game. "i hate that school and i won't ever go back because they're so lousy to me. . . . i hate them all and they're lousy to me and i wish i were pretty!" Her mother rather lamely tries to comfort her, suggesting that her brother take her to the game, but begins and ends the conversation by scolding her for slamming her bedroom door. After her mother leaves the room, she writes on a piece of paper, "i hate my mother . . . i wish that she would die," and sets it on fire.

By the Christmas holidays, Jackson had accumulated a small gaggle of girlfriends. Judging from the way she portrayed them later, they occupied a rung on the social ladder close to hers. In one of her unpublished stories, a high school girl tells the other unpopular girls at recess, "My father doesn't like me to go out with boys. *You* know, the things they do." In an early draft of *Hangsaman* that offers a glimpse of Natalie in high school, her only friends are Doris ("fat, and badly dressed, and stupid, and the center of a little group of girls who did things by themselves, went to movies and had parties and went swimming in the summer, in a gay chattering body whose animation never quite concealed the fact that they were ugly") and Doris's sidekick Ginny ("she played sentimental tunes very badly on the piano, and was given to much giggling flirtation with her teachers"). Sitting in the drugstore with them, Natalie "knew that she was marked, just as irretrievably as though they had all worn distinctive uniforms, as one of the little group [of] social outsiders." The humiliation of attending a school dance with these girls instead of with a date is redeemed only by her encounter there with a teacher, who compliments the poems she submitted anonymously to the school newspaper. "i knew they were yours, of course," he tells her. "even though you tried to change your handwriting, you couldn't change your own peculiar phrases and ways of looking at things." She agrees to let him publish them under her name: "i'm sort of proud of them."

The move, and the alienation that accompanied it, had a profound effect on Shirley. Back in California, Dorothy Ayling was one of the first to notice it. Shirley still considered Dorothy her closest friend; at a time when long-distance telephone calls constituted a great occasion and expense, the two wrote to each other regularly, usually with news about boys. Shirley's letters to Dorothy are lost, but the responses offer some clues about what she must have written. "When have I ever heard you say you weren't nuts over somebody?" Dorothy wrote when Shirley confided her latest crush. On the surface, Shirley sounded just about the same. But Dorothy began to pick up on signs that something was amiss. "I was just wondering . . . if your mother dropped you on your head when you were a baby. . . . Something is radically wrong in your upper story—if you have any," she wrote that winter. "Sometimes after I read your letters I wonder whether the climate's good for you," she joked a few months later.

Dorothy tried to make light of the change in her friend, but the transformation was significant. Perhaps it was the move; perhaps it would have happened anyway as Jackson matured. "I beg your pardon—may I?" she wrote in her "Debutante" diary in November, shortly before her seventeenth birthday. She now felt alienated from her own memories of a self she no longer recognized, "a girl who thought too much." Jackson marked the change in uncannily stark terms: that girl is dead, she wrote, "and her passing is, as I now see, mourned by few. She was a dreamer, and dreamers have no place in our matter-of-fact modern world. . . . A somewhat more matter-of-fact, and infinitely wiser person has taken her place." Jackson lacked the self-awareness to see that her assessment of her own infinite wisdom was somewhat premature. But, as always, she was able to step outside herself to offer self-criticism. On the same day, she wrote herself a stern note in her regular diary. The tone, and even the words, show just how deeply she had internalized Geraldine's voice. "Hereafter see that there is a distinction between your present attitude and your former one," she scolded herself. "You have always prided yourself on inherent good breeding. See that self-disgust does not destroy this rightful pride. One can be friendly without making enemies." During a year that would have crushed a girl with a weaker ego, Jackson still placed a high value on her own dignity.

She had always been moody, as nearly all teenagers are. Now, in an extension of the persona splitting of her multiple diaries, she took the unusual step of assigning names to her moods, as if they were characters in a play. The habit continued through her college years and later manifested in her fiction—most strikingly in *The Bird's Nest*, her novel of multiple-personality disorder, in which a woman's mind fractures into four distinct characters, each with her own name and defining characteristics. Jackson called her happiest persona "Irish," perhaps a reference to the features she liked best about herself: her auburn hair and green eyes. (Later, it would be one of Hyman's terms of endearment for her.) "Irish has gone—completely and utterly," she wrote during that difficult fall. "Has she left me to struggle along for myself, I wonder? Or has she merely, elusive as usual, left me when I want her most?" The trouble, as usual, seemed to be boy-related: more of the usual no-date-for-the-dance problems. On New Year's Eve, she assessed the previous year as "eventful," "rich in friends," "colorful," and "encouraging," if "not always happy." Her new year's resolution for 1934 was simpler than usual: "To be happy."

Another of Jackson's imaginary figures was Harlequin, the commedia dell'arte acrobat who became a familiar figure once again in the beginning of the twentieth century thanks to Picasso's paintings. Also known as the Italian comedy, the commedia dell'arte was a lifelong interest of Jackson's: an ornamental mask belonging to an actor who had played Pantaloon later hung in her living room in North Bennington. In the classical format, actors playing the stock characters of Harlequin, Pantaloon, Scaramouche, and others improvised variations on stock story lines, usually romantic in nature. George Sand described the commedia dell'arte as "a study of the grotesque and facetious . . . but also a portrayal of real characters traced from remote antiquity down to the present day, in an uninterrupted tradition of fantastic humor which is in essence quite serious and, one might almost say, even sad, like every satire which lays bare the spiritual poverty of mankind." This assessment applies equally to much of Jackson's fiction, which often juxtaposes supernatural or uncanny elements with realistic, even banal characters.

Traditionally dressed in a jacket of multicolored patches, a double-pointed hat, and a black mask, Harlequin—as Pierre Louis DuChartre describes him in *The Italian Comedy*, a classic treatise on the subject—is the most versatile and enigmatic of the comedy players: at once a graceful and beguiling dancer, a buffoon so absentminded that he searches everywhere for the same donkey on which he is sitting, a poet both "of acrobatics and unseemly noises." In other words, he is as unlike a shy, awkward, serious sixteen-year-old as a character could possibly be. In one famous episode, Harlequin, disguised as a doctor, advises a patient with a toothache to combine garlic and vinegar with a pinch of pepper and rub the whole concoction between his buttocks, telling him it will make him forget all about his tooth pain. Another story has Harlequin fall in love with a beautiful girl named Columbine who is guarded by her ferociously protective father. The old man is no obstacle for Harlequin, who concocts ever more elaborate ruses to trick him into handing her over.

Alienated, socially isolated, far from the sunlight of the California she missed, Jackson found in Harlequin an embodiment of lightness, charm, *sprezzatura*—qualities she valued and hoped to cultivate, but which came to her with difficulty. Sometimes she worried that to disguise her true emotions constituted "posturing"—for her, a cardinal sin. "I can't understand this desire—this requirement—to hide true things, and display to the world a suave, untroubled visage," she wrote in February 1934. "If one is bewildered and unhappy, why not show it, and why will not people explain and comfort? But instead—this pretense at calm satisfaction, where underneath there is all the seething restless desire to be off, away from all this anger at self and others, to where there are other conventions, other thoughts, other passions." Harlequin represented also the happy possibility of a life beyond her restricted world—and of a male figure who might someday come and sweep her away. When Harlequin "came" to her, as Jackson liked to put it, her confusion faded into the background and left her with the sense of peace she sought. "Knowing myself to desire so much and yet so vaguely, I catch webs of events in both hands, and pull them to me," she wrote in June, just before her graduation. "Three days more—and I step out of high school. I am going on. Towards what I want, and need, and dream of. Harlequin." A few weeks later her confusion had returned. "Life is such a casual thing at best, and such a messy thing at worst, that it's a wonder more people don't quit it than do. I'm tired and tired and tired, and if ever Harlequin was to come when I needed him—no, I don't want him to come yet. I'll always be able to stand it a little longer."

Harlequin represented to Jackson an earlier, more innocent version of the "daemon lover" figure who would later appear in the *Lottery* collection and elsewhere: a character from one of the Child Ballads, also known as James Harris, who seduces a woman only to reveal, when it is too late, that he is the devil in disguise. Like a less sinister daemon lover, Harlequin offers escape from the ordinary world into a colorful realm of pastoral landscapes and freedom. In *The Road Through the Wall*, the character Marilyn, whom Jackson endows with some of her own traits, imagines that in a past life a commedia dell'arte troupe came to rescue her from her daily life. "There's a little covered wagon that comes down the road," Marilyn recounts, as if recalling a dream, "and inside they're all talking and laughing and singing. . . . Pantaloon, and Rhodomont, and Scaramouche, and Pierrot, and . . . Harlequin. . . . He is waving and calling me, and I run down the hill as fast as anything."

A similar figure—a handsome, charming stranger who comes from another world—was the focus of the film that most affected Shirley during the spring of her senior year: *Death Takes a Holiday* (1934), a strange, Faustian fairy tale directed by Mitchell Leisen and starring Fredric March and Evelyn Venable. One night, Death appears to a duke and his friends while they are driving on a dangerous mountain road. He decides not to claim them immediately, but to spend three days as the duke's guest in his palatial villa, disguised as a prince, to learn about life among mortals. At first comedy ensues, as all the single ladies present vie for the affections of the mysterious prince, who tries to conceal his befuddlement over mortal customs such as fancy dinners, gambling, and sex. Meanwhile, newspapers report on the miraculous events taking place all over the world while Death is on vacation: a race car driver walks away unharmed from a terrible crash, schoolchildren survive a fire, all passengers are rescued from a sinking ship. Matters grow more serious when the seducer pledges his love to a beautiful young woman and she resolves to go away with him, even as her mother and the other guests try in horror to restrain her. "Remember that there is only a moment of shadow between your life and mine," Death tells the guests as he bids them farewell. "And when I call, come bravely through that shadow. You will find me only, your familiar friend."

It is easy to see why the film appealed to Jackson. First, of course, the romantic element would have been alluring to any teenager who longed to swoon in the arms of her own ardent lover, even if this brooding man had little in common with the teenage boys who were the usual objects of Shirley's affections. But more than that, Death longs to be loved by somebody who recognizes him for who—or what—he really is. He does not deceive his betrothed into committing herself to him; rather, she knows who he is and loves him anyway—exactly the fantasy of a teenager tired of "posturings," who felt that her own mother, constantly trying to mold her in another image, did not appreciate her.

And the film's premise—that Death walks among mortals, sitting beside us at the dinner table or encircling us in his arms on the dance floor—must have deeply resonated with a girl whose great theme would one day be the evil present in every human soul, hidden where we least suspect it. "What a monstrous comedy!" Death exclaims of human life. Jackson might well have thought the same.

THE 1934 UNIVERSITY OF ROCHESTER admissions application offered a space of several lines in which to answer the question "Why do you want to go to college?" Jackson wrote succinctly, "To prepare myself for a career." At a time when many women attended college simply to meet a husband, she was already certain that she would support herself after graduation. Her preferences were law, journalism, or "literary work."

The university had recently opened its River Campus: eleven handsome redbrick buildings along the Genessee, arranged around the traditional quadrangle and dominated by Rush Rhees Library, which could accommodate up to two million books. But the River Campus was restricted to men; the women's college, which had admitted its first students in 1900, was located downtown, on the corner of University Avenue and Prince Street. As was the case at most women's colleges then—newly founded Bennington College, which Jackson would later come to know intimately, was a notable and soon-to-be notorious exception—social life was rigid and traditional, dominated by sororities. Women were dissuaded from taking classes on the River Campus or using its facilities. Fellow Brighton High alumnus Richard Morton, who was in Jackson's class at Rochester, would later tell his family that the university had discouraged them both from pursuing their desired careers—for him, mechanical engineering; for her, writing. After a year at Rochester, he transferred to the University of Michigan and later became a successful engineer.

If Jackson was steered away from writing fiction into a more practical profession, the university may have been responding to the times. The college newspaper commented that the Depression, not surprisingly, had made Rochester students "more serious," with less interest in social activities. The essay questions for Jackson's English composition placement exam give a vivid picture of the era: "Contemporary American Attitudes Toward Socialism, Communism, and Fascism"; "Effects of Unemployment on Family Life" (with 25 percent of Americans still unemployed, this was the critical issue of the day); "Managing a Student's Wardrobe on a Small Budget"; "The Farmer's Desperate Situation"; "The Ethics of Motoring." Jackson opted for the only nonpolitical subject, "The Educational Value of High School Dramatics," which she broached with less than complete confidence: the paper shows her struggling to spell "playwright."

Jackson likely chose Rochester for the sake of convenience. Her grades at Brighton were mostly Bs and Cs, with a single A, in English—sufficient to gain admission, especially at a time when the vast majority of students were local, but probably not good enough for a more competitive school. The academic program, with a heavy emphasis on the sciences, was not ideal for her, and she found the social culture stifling. Her parents may have insisted that she remain in town, where they could keep watch over her. Her entrance form lists her religious preference as Christian Science, a sign either that she still felt some attachment to her family's faith or that Geraldine—who accompanied Shirley to her admissions interview—was watching as she filled out the form.

Jackson's first-year course of study included English, government, psychology, philosophy, and music appreciation. (In *Hangsaman*, Natalie's classes are virtually identical.) If Geraldine and Leslie had insisted that she stay in town, they allowed her at least to live in Stephen Foster Hall, the women's dormitory—a decision they may well have come to regret, as it allowed Jackson to take full advantage of her newfound freedom. But her initial adjustment to dorm life was difficult. Watching a sorority initiation left her deeply shaken, "sick at the things girls will do to one another." In *Hangsaman*, the freshman girls are dragged from their beds in the middle of the night and made to confess whether they are virgins. Natalie, who assesses the experience in coolly ironic terms—"the persecution of new students, once passionate, is now only perfunctory"—declines to answer, and as a result finds herself ostracized.

Natalie casts a cool eye on her fellow students, but the novel makes palpable her sense of inferiority and internal confusion in the face of the other girls. She is keenly aware of fine distinctions of social status: the "senior queens in high school," the girls "with their obvious right clothes," the girls in the "best cliques"—the same types who had rejected Shirley at Brighton. Then there were the outsiders: "the ascetic amateur writers with their poems safely locked away upstairs . . . the girls who would fail all their courses and go home ingloriously (saying goodbye bravely, but crying) . . . the girls whose hearts would break and the girls whose spirits would break." Jackson, of course, was the amateur writer with a desk full of hidden poems—she would sometimes get up in the middle of the night to write, to the astonishment of a friend sleeping over. She enjoyed parties and going out, but resented that the only girls who seemed drawn to her were the Doris and Ginny types, plain and dull—not a reflection of the way she wanted to see herself. The only person who initially befriends Natalie, a dumpy girl named Rosalind, eventually rejects her, telling her that the other girls call her "spooky" and "crazy" because she spends all her time in her room. Natalie's recourse is to create an imaginary friend, a girl she calls Tony, who

Shirley Jackson with Jeanne Marie Bedel, c. 1935.

initially seems to be the companion she longed for but who leads her nearly to her psychic breaking point.

Jackson was far luckier: she found a real friend, and an exceptional one. Jeanne Marie Bedel, whom Shirley nicknamed Jeanou, was an exchange student from Paris who also lived in Stephen Foster Hall. (It was customary in the 1930s for Rochester to host two exchange students each year, one from Germany and one from France.) Vivacious but not conventionally beautiful, several years older than Shirley and possessing a continental savoir faire, she was incalculably more sophisticated, a lover of art and literature who was the single greatest influence on Shirley to date: only Stanley Hyman would eventually have a bigger emotional and intellectual impact on her. "A true Parisian," Shirley called her. And, as the only French student on campus, Jeanou was even more of an outsider than Shirley was herself. In a picture of them taken that year, Jeanou stands a few inches shorter than Shirley, with short, tousled dark hair and deep-set eyes. (Shirley would later describe her, not especially kindly, as "a bad caricature of Beethoven.") Wearing a dark, belted coat, Shirley tilts her head back, laughing freely; her hand rests on Jeanou's shoulder. It is the happiest of all her youthful photographs, in which she normally looks guarded, even suspicious—often, of course, because she was posing before Geraldine's vigilant eye.

"Slightly mad, we were," Jackson wrote in a poem in which she called the pair of them "Gay Jeanou and Crazy Lee." With Jeanou at her side, Jackson, who was now signing her name "Shirlee," spent her freshman year exploring all that sleepy Rochester had to offer: films ("I adore gangsters," she wrote after seeing an Edward G. Robinson movie), concerts, meals in "funny little cafeteria[s]." The French bohemian and the California transplant were inseparable: they even wrote together in Jackson's diary. They walked around for hours, bonding over their mutual dislike of the city, which in comparison with Paris must have seemed unbearably stodgy—not to mention frigid. (Rochester winters were so cold that the River Campus featured a system of tunnels connecting many of the buildings, so that students did not have to go outside in the punishing weather.) Eating lunch one day, "in one hour we counted one hundred people passing and found seven interesting faces," Jackson recorded. They planned someday to spend a few weeks holed up in a hotel writing a book mocking the city, as "revenge." At a Russian restaurant they frequented, Jackson developed a crush on a "charming" pianist named Kostia, who left her with an abiding fondness for Russian classical music. As a lover of the Child Ballads and other folk music, she was especially moved by the folkloric melodies of "Procession of the Sardar," from Mikhail

Ippolitov-Ivanov's *Caucasian Sketches*, a pair of orchestral suites written in the mid-1890s. That fall she also saw a production of Bizet's opera *Carmen*, which she adored.

Jackson's old friend Dorothy Ayling, who continued doggedly to send news of Bud Young, had no interest in her new obsessions. "Don't fall too hard for the Russians. . . . They make very poor husbands," she cautioned from Burlingame. Yet Dorothy slowly realized that Shirley was pulling away from her, and she reacted with anger and jealousy. "Nobody recognized your picture at school. . . . [Jeanou] looks like she'd like to chew somebody up," she wrote sourly after Jackson sent a photograph of herself and her new friend. She called Jackson a show-off for writing to her in French. Worse, she disparaged Jackson's dreams of becoming a fiction writer, suggesting that she work as an editor at a publishing house instead. (Dorothy's own plan was to teach music in an elementary school.) Their correspondence, which until then had survived a vast geographical distance, could not withstand Jackson's changing personality, tapering to a halt within a few months.

Jeanou, with a more elevated vision, encouraged Jackson's writing, helped her with her French ("I shall *never* be able to pronounce my r's," Shirley lamented), and scolded her for not doing her homework. If she was worried about the looming cataclysm in Europe, she seems to have put it out of her mind during her stay in Rochester—at least, she did not discuss current events with Jackson. The two of them spent most of their time hanging out in cafés. Jackson cut classes whenever she had anything better to do—a concert, a play, a movie. She spent some of her rare moments apart from Jeanou joyriding around Rochester with Richard Morton, commiserating over their mutual disaffection with the university. Rather than following her syllabi, Jackson pursued her own intellectual interests: at one point she spent hours devising an invented language called Lildsune, complete with grammatical rules, and even wrote poetry in it. The assignment that occupied her most was a term paper on witchcraft, which led her to read, for the first time, a book that would greatly influence her as well as Stanley Hyman: *The Golden Bough*, anthropologist Sir James Frazer's multivolume treatment of magic and ritual among primitive cultures around the world.

That spring, Jackson published her first story. An untitled fragment of several paragraphs, it appeared in *Meliora*, the literary magazine of the women's college. The story tracks the reactions of various people in the audience as a violinist identified only as Yehudi takes the stage for his final encore, a rendition of "Ave Maria." As he plays, his mother clasps her hands in her lap, silently moved; two high school girls abandon their giggling to listen; an old man brushes a tear from his cheek. There is no applause when he finishes, only silence: "The audience filed out, not talking." Perhaps Yehudi is based on Kostia, although Jackson gives no indication that her Russian crush was Jewish, as the violinist's name suggests. Regardless, the story demonstrates her continued appreciation of the creative artist's ability to influence an audience— although it's notable that emotion, not ideas, seems to be what she values most.

All these extracurricular undertakings distracted Jackson from her coursework. She continued to do well in English, but her average plummeted to a miserable 66—low enough to earn her multiple warnings from the dean's office. ("I must really go to classes," she chided herself after one such encounter.) She also regularly missed her dormitory curfew. Geraldine tried to keep an eye on her daughter, taking her to lunch and the movies and sometimes bringing her home to spend the night on Monteroy Road. It did not help.

Jackson's abysmal grades may have been a symptom of more serious trouble. The first signs came at the start of the second term, in February 1935, which she called "a month of evil omen and disillusion." Her schedule included at least one night class, which she found burdensome. And her mood, judging from her diary, was as low as her grades. Her unrequited crush on Kostia was making her miserable: "I die a million deaths of tears," a sonnet she wrote for him began. Although she received a regular allowance from her parents, she and Jeanou were perpetually broke. She began to have dramatic mood swings: "Why does Life seem calculated to administer a deadening shock to each new jubilance?" she wondered. "Mind too confused with a million manufactured idiocies to write now," she told her diary that February. The next day she felt "sane again—at least, comparitively [sic] so." And she continued to be highly self-critical. "I have filled out yards of pages in any number of diaries, and each one grows more conceited than the last," she berated herself.

Jeanou was an emotional support for Shirley as well as a constant fount of excitement. But the intense friendship was tempestuous, marked by frequent quarrels. Once Jeanou was so angry that she threw a stack of typing paper at Shirley. She didn't hesitate to tell Shirley exactly what she thought of her, criticizing her for being "spoiled" and "selfish" and saying that her affectations could be "unbearable." At one point Jeanou wrote Shirley a note promising to stop criticizing her, but added: "I thought you would understand I do it for you, not for me. . . . You are aggravating yourself, and very often. I wonder if you don't try to be right at least as [much] as I do." Shirley was upset enough by these criticisms that she sent one of Jeanou's notes to Dorothy Ayling to ask what her old friend thought of it. Dorothy was unsympathetic. "Poor Jeanou must have a swell time arguing with you. . . . If you really want my opinion, I think it is a very exact letter, and if I could write that kind of letter, I would say the same things," she wrote back.

Despite the arguments, Jackson was bereft when her best friend returned to Paris in June 1935. France was about to undergo a dramatic political upheaval, with the socialist Léon Blum becoming prime minister the following year as head of the Popular Front coalition. Within a few years, Jeanou, like so many of her generation, would become an ardent Communist, sending reports back to Jackson about the Spanish Civil War; during World War II, she was active in the Resistance. But now, ignorant of the future, the two made a vow to meet in Paris three years later, on Bastille Day 1938. "Write to me," Jeanou begged in a good-bye letter. "Don't remember the quarrels but the nice times." She asked for reports on Jackson's schoolwork, the garden parties she went to, her life as a society "debutante," and—not least—her short stories. "Try to work and write and meet people and leave Rochester as soon as you can." As a parting gift, Jeanou gave Shirley an illustrated edition of the works of François Villon, the medieval *poète maudite* who wrote one of the most iconic lines in French literature: *Où sont les neiges d'antan*, "Where are the snows of yesteryear?"

Villon was the fifteenth century's version of a beatnik poet: his immensely popular poems were among the earliest vernacular works published in France. The poet was equally famous for the drama of his life, which included multiple robberies and the stabbing of a priest. In his "mock testaments," he willed his meager possessions, literal and metaphorical—old boots with the toes worn through, the cobwebs from his bed frame, a fist in the nose—to his friends and enemies on the Paris streets: tradesmen, friars, whores, criminals, lawyers. Nearly five hundred years after his birth, Ezra Pound wrote that Villon "has the stubborn persistency of one whose gaze cannot be deflected from the actual fact before him: what he sees, he writes."

Jackson's literary taste at the time tended more toward popular novels such as *The Forsyte Saga*, John Galsworthy's melodramatic series about an upper-class English family. The poets she admired most were plainspoken establishment writers such as Carl Sandburg and Dorothy Parker. Still, she immediately added the outsider Villon to her personal pantheon of quasi-mythological figures along with Harlequin and, later, Pan, the god of nature. "I know all things—except myself," Jackson quoted him. If Pan symbolized joy in the natural world and Harlequin represented comedy and good cheer, Villon came to stand for self-reliance and the ability to stand tall in the face of others' criticisms—a quality Jeanou also embodied. "She gave me as a parting gift the ability to face people and laugh at them, because she knew that I would need it," Jackson later remembered. "In college, there were ex-friends who stared and talked and laughed, there were records of stupidity and heights of ignorance, to be challenged and lived down. I held in my hands a dream which they tried to crush, and they failed." What others thought of her, Jackson concluded, mattered "not the smallest part of Villon's grin. I shall be happy."

"I WENT TO COLLEGE and i had a friend and she was kind to me, and together we were happy," Jackson wrote in an unpublished memoir that likely dates from her later college years. The piece describes her relationship with Kostia, the Russian pianist she and Jeanou spent time with: "she introduced me to a man who didn't laugh at me because i was ugly and i fell in love with him and tried to kill myself but i was happy just the same." Her description of the friendship merits a close look:

> my friend was so strange that everyone, even the man i loved, thought we were lesbians and they used to talk about us, and i was afraid of them and i hated them. then i wanted to write stories about lesbians and how people misunderstood them. and finally this man sent me away because i was a lesbian and my friend went away and i was all alone.

Some critics have suggested that *Hangsaman* may be read as a lesbian novel. There is a scene in which Tony, the imagined girl Natalie seems to befriend, comes to Natalie's bedside naked; later, they sleep in the same bed and bathe together; and in their final confrontation Tony appears to make a physical overture toward Natalie. "She *wants* me," Natalie realizes with horror. And Jackson's outline for the book even says that Natalie "barely escapes a Lesbian seduction," although that sounds like sensationalizing language intended for the publisher's sales sheet. On one of the drafts of that page, the line appears in the handwriting of Hyman, who often helped his wife compose publicity memos.

It is unlikely that Shirley's friendship with Jeanou had a lesbian component, or that their friendship was the reason Kostia rejected her. There is no evidence that Jeanou, who seems always to have had a man or two ready to do her bidding, was sexually interested in Shirley. And although characters who may be lesbians appear more than once in her fiction, Jackson—typically for her era and her class—evinced a personal horror of lesbianism. It's possible that the relatively extreme way in which she would later disparage lesbians reflects some repression on her part, especially considering that she and Hyman had several close male friends who were homosexual. But that is conjecture only. Jackson never spoke of experiencing sexual desire for women. When she refers to herself and Jeanou as lesbians in that piece, at a time when lesbianism was little discussed or understood, she seems to be using the idea of it as a metaphor for social nonconformity.

A novel that Jackson read during her years at Rochester offers a clue to what she might have meant. *The Well of Loneliness*, by the British author Radclyffe Hall, was published in 1928 and quickly became notorious as the subject of an obscenity trial in England. The novel's protagonist is a girl named Stephen, the daughter of parents who had longed for a son. Even as a child, she identifies strongly as a boy, wearing masculine clothes and cutting her hair short. By age seven, she begins to develop crushes on women and is continually disappointed when the objects of her affection prove more interested in men. But sexuality in the novel is expressed only obliquely. What is most palpable is Stephen's sense of herself as an outsider—a person who cannot conform to social or parental expectations and finds herself punished as a result. Jackson—a girl who often felt awkward in her own body, whose mother pressured her to dress in a way she found unappealing, who romanticized outlaw figures such as Villon—must have deeply sympathized.

And it is crucial to remember that Tony is not a real character: she is a creation of Natalie's fragmented psyche. In an unpublished document written around 1960, while she was working on *We Have Always Lived in the Castle*, Jackson noted her chagrin to discover herself mentioned in a book of literary criticism about "sex variant women in literature," which, she said, described *Hangsaman* as "an 'eerie' novel about lesbians." "i happen to know what hangsaman is about. i wrote it," Jackson retorted. She admits to having wanted to create a "sense of illicit excitement," presumably with the suggestion of a sexual charge between Tony and Natalie. But she asserts that Tony is "not a he or a she but the demon in the mind, and that demon finds guilts where it can and uses them and runs mad with laughing when it triumphs; it is the demon which is fear and we are afraid of words. we are afraid of being someone else and doing the things someone else wants us to do and of being taken and used by someone else, some other guilt-ridden conscience that lives on and on in our minds, something we build ourselves and never recognize."

The demon in the mind. This was Jackson's obsession, perhaps her fundamental obsession, throughout her life. Often it appears metaphorically as the source of the evil deeds people commit against one another, as in her story "The Lottery": what else can explain the villagers' mad adherence to a tradition that requires them to murder one of their neighbors? But it takes literal forms as well. In the early stories that would be assembled in the *Lottery* collection, innocent young women encounter an eerily seductive figure named James Harris (modeled on the character in the Child Ballad), who at first appears to be an ordinary person—a boyfriend or a colleague—but sneakily, through a sinister trick of the mind, induces in them a kind of madness. In early drafts of *Hangsaman*, too, the demon is literal: Natalie is visited by a figure she calls Asmodeus, a Hebrew name for the king of demons. "there was a devil who dwelt with natalie; she was seventeen, and the devil had been with her since she had been about twelve," one of the early drafts begins. "his was the first voice to greet her in the morning, and at night he slept under her pillow. . . . all day he rode on her shoulder, unseen by her mother, and he whispered in her ear." Asmodeus is an evil alter ego, whispering snide quips about Natalie's parents and urging her to yield her soul to him. In later drafts the literal demon disappears from the novel and the figure of the detective takes over as Natalie's inquisitor, plumbing the depths of her guilty heart.

The demon in the mind, Jackson wrote, exploits one's bad conscience, spinning ordinary worries and grievances into destructive obsession. It is striking that the sources of fear she was still writing about nearly thirty years later are reminiscent of the stresses she suffered as an adolescent: "being someone else and doing the things someone else wants us to do," "being taken and used by someone else"—in other words, yielding to Geraldine's (and later Hyman's) vision for her, which she feared would cause her to lose her own identity. Even words are to be feared: words that unfairly categorize, that criticize, that damage.

AFTER JEANOU'S DEPARTURE, SHIRLEY spent the next few months in summer school, trying to improve her grades. Her sophomore year started inauspiciously, with an English teacher she had a crush on conspicuously absent from her course schedule. But now her focus was her writing: she had a "glorious" new typewriter and was happy with what she was accomplishing with it. She had reason to suspect that her mother was going through her papers again, especially after Geraldine scolded her for writing "sexy stories." (She was living back at home—the Jacksons had moved to a larger house within walking distance of campus.) "I shall have to lock my desk," Shirley resolved. "I *would* like some privacy."

Despite Geraldine's interference, she continued to be productive. "Wrote an allegory which might mean something," she reported to her diary in September. She was most pleased with a story she called "Idiot": "The idea is driving me insane, but it's there—and the story won't end." The piece does not survive, but the title suggests that it dealt with a character who was mentally retarded or otherwise deficient— another of the outsider tropes that would later recur in different versions throughout her fiction. Jackson worked up the courage to submit "Idiot" to *Story* magazine, which rejected it. Nonetheless, her confidence in her work continued unabated. "Wrote a play tonight which delights me—it is so *myself*!" she exulted a few weeks later, chiding herself immediately afterward for conceit.

None of the girls in Shirley's small circle of friends had replaced

Shirley and Barry Jackson in Rochester, c. 1935.

Jeanou, especially in terms of intellectual excitement. But she began to date a boy named Jimmie Taylor, whom she had met one night in November at the movies: "very nice, and surprisingly fun—good dancer." For her nineteenth birthday, he took her to the Peacock Room, a rococo restaurant featuring opulent chandeliers and a live cabaret band. Jackson complained that he was dull, but she enjoyed having a boyfriend to go dancing with. After he stood her up for a date, she vowed never to speak to him again—until the next day, when he showed up at her house with a gardenia to apologize. (She still gave him "what is technically known as Hell," she told her diary proudly.) Her customary new year's musings for 1936 show that, unserious as it was, the relationship was interfering with her Harlequin equilibrium. "For people who do not care, life can hold so much of interest and so much of delight, I have discovered. There is a strange charm in feeling not able to be hurt." But she could not will herself out of emotion. "It is so desperately easy to resolve 'I will not care,' and so much easier to break that resolve!"

If the Jacksons' intention in moving Shirley home had been to keep an eye on her schoolwork, they were not successful. She failed three of her fall courses—biology, French, and psychology—and barely squeaked by in the remaining two, English and archaeology. In the spring, her grades plummeted even lower, and she was put on academic probation. By June, the university had asked her to leave. Later she would say she was thrown out "because i refused to go to any classes because i hated them."

Jackson certainly did not lack the intelligence to succeed at Rochester. Did she suffer another episode of depression that led to her failing grades? Or was it the other way around—her grades began to slip, inducing her mental disintegration? Regardless, she was deeply demoralized by her failure at college. And living at home could not have helped. Her mother pressured her constantly to find a boyfriend who would become a suitable husband—preferably someone rich who could support her in the style to which Geraldine and Leslie were accustomed, a life of country clubs and ski trips. At the same time, Geraldine continued to be highly critical of her daughter's figure, her looks, her personal style. She warned Shirley that she would never meet a man unless she lost weight and dyed her hair. All Shirley's life, Geraldine had been telling her that she was unsuitable, undesirable, unattractive. Now the University of Rochester had rejected her too. A psychiatrist who treated her in the 1960s would later say that she had her first breakdown during college.

Major depression often emerges in late adolescence. Sylvia Plath—whose novel *The Bell Jar*, which also depicts a young woman's breakdown, was likely influenced by *Hangsaman*—tried to kill herself for the first time at age nineteen, the same age as Jackson was during much of her second year at Rochester. (Plath, who also struggled with her relationship with a domineering mother, admired Jackson and hoped to meet her during a summer internship at *Mademoiselle* in 1953.) Was Jackson's depression serious enough that she tried to kill herself, as the memoir quoted earlier suggests? It is certainly possible. She had suicidal thoughts as early as sixteen. Her college diaries reveal that her mental suffering was intense. Back in February 1935, that month of "evil omen," she called her life "deadening" and wondered, "Will there ever come a break, and will there be any life to jump at the break when it comes?" She did well for several months after Jeanou left, but by November 1935 her "old fears of people" had returned. The following spring she suffered from "nerves and overwrought temperament." A poem tucked into her 1935 diary is written from the perspective of a person who might be about to jump off a bridge, looking at "the fearful cold waters below." (Several years earlier, as Jackson probably was aware, the poet Hart Crane had committed suicide by jumping off a boat bound to New York from Mexico.) The story "Janice," written during her first year at Syracuse University, depicts a girl at a party who casually tells friends that she attempted suicide because she wasn't able to return to college. In another story Jackson wrote around the same time, a girl tells a male friend about her brush with suicide—she had planned to jump off a bridge:

> "you were just going to slip off into the water?" asked victor.
> "very softly," i said.
> "with no more than that?" asked victor.

"no more than that," i said.

"tell me," said victor, "why didn't you die?"

"i forgot," i said. "i went home and wrote a poem instead."

But it is telling that the girl in Jackson's bridge story talks about committing suicide rather than attempting it. In "Janice," too, the girl does not go through with the deed. Talking, or writing, takes the place of action.

On her last day at the University of Rochester—June 8, 1936—Jackson wrote herself a letter, addressed to "Shirlee" and signed "Lee": the name of a new persona. Lee explains that she is leaving her old self behind: "You don't mind my outgrowing you, do you?" If she once was suicidal, she is no longer. "I still want to live, as you did," she writes. "And now I think I know how. . . . Through you, and all the rest in that desk, I have learned to be willing." *The rest in that desk*—the little black datebooks, the "Debutante" diary, all the pages on which she tried out new writing styles and new characters—were instruments she used to find her voice.

As her classmates returned to campus in the fall, Jackson spent what would have been her junior year at Rochester in her bedroom at her parents' house, working on her writing. Elizabeth Young, a friend from college who was close to her at the time, recalled that she set herself a strict—and ambitious—quota of a thousand words a day. None of what she wrote then appears to survive. By the spring of 1937, she had resumed her regular social schedule of dances and dinners at the country club—sometimes in the company of Michael Palmer, the son of one of her father's business acquaintances and the first boyfriend she considered marrying.

As Jackson regained her mental strength, her parents started to worry about her future. Leslie apparently told her that he would send her to any school she chose, as long as she promised that she would "stay there and behave [herself] and graduate." As a further enticement, he suggested that if she indeed "conducted [herself] like a lady" in college—probably meaning that she stop cutting classes and take her schoolwork seriously—he would let her go to Columbia University for a graduate course in writing. Geraldine did not support this plan; she wanted Shirley to stay close to home and marry Michael. But Leslie triumphed.

"I wish to further my writing career," Jackson wrote on her Syracuse application, explaining for a second time why she wanted to attend college. A hundred miles from Rochester, the university was well-known then, as it is now, for its English and journalism programs, as well as for its liberal atmosphere. (Michael Palmer disapprovingly called it "a hotbed of communism and antisocial attitudes"; he was not entirely wrong.) Her family, as usual, did not know what to make of the plan. In a posthumously published sketch, Jackson recalled her teenage decision to become a writer. "Since there were no books in the world fit to read, I would write one," she resolved. She wrote a mystery story in which any of the characters could potentially be the murderer, and decided at the end to put all their names in a hat and draw one out, "thus managing to surprise even myself with the ending." She brought the finished manuscript downstairs to read to her family. "Whaddyou call that?" her brother responded. Her father said, "Very nice." Her mother wondered if she had remembered to make her bed.

Soon their lack of interest would no longer matter. Jackson was about to meet the person who would become her most fervent admirer—and her sharpest critic.

3.

INTENTIONS CHARGED WITH POWER

BROOKLYN,
1919–1937

[Modern criticism] guides, nourishes, and lives off art and
is thus, from another point of view, a handmaiden to art,
parasitic at worst and symbiotic at best.
—Stanley Edgar Hyman, *The Armed Vision*

THE PHOTOGRAPHER PHILIPPE HALSMAN, RENOWNED FOR
his elegant portraits of royalty, politicians, actors, and other celebrities,
pioneered an unorthodox technique. In the 1950s, he began asking his
subjects to jump as he took their picture, believing that the moment of
the jump communicated something essential about a person that a more
controlled facial expression or body language might disguise. "I wanted
to see famous people reveal in a jump their ambition or their lack of it,
their self-importance or their insecurity, and many other traits," Halsman explained.

Halsman photographed Stanley Edgar Hyman in 1959 to accompany
an article on tragedy that Hyman had written for the *Saturday Evening
Post*. In the formal photograph chosen by the magazine's editors, Hyman
holds a smoked-down cigarette in his long fingers; his beard is thick,

Stanley Edgar Hyman by Philippe Halsman.

his forehead prominent, his eyes dark behind black-framed glasses. He looks the epitome of the serious literary critic. But Hyman's jump photo tells another story. On the first take, he jumped so high that the frame captured only his feet—not what Halsman had expected from a sedentary scholar. Halsman readjusted the camera and Hyman jumped again. This time Halsman caught him at the very top: eyes squeezed shut, lips twisted in a near grimace, knees drawn up beneath him. He might be an eccentric millionaire about to do a cannonball, fully clothed, into a swimming pool. Or a guest at a Jewish wedding throwing himself into an especially spirited kazatsky, a dance Hyman knew and loved. Or simply a man at a moment of intense concentration, determined to put his whole being into his act. He would not be satisfied with anything less than the best jump he could possibly achieve.

"MY ANCESTORS WERE normal people, I being the only insane person in the family," fourteen-year-old Stanley Hyman declared in a summary of his life to date. Unusually for a Jewish writer of his generation, he was a second-generation American: both his parents were born in the United States. His paternal grandfather, Louis Hyman, was part of the third major wave of Jewish migration from Europe to the United States, emigrating from Lithuania to New York in the late nineteenth century to avoid conscription in the czar's army. Stanley would say that his grandfather had been a bootlegger, which "paid, even in Russia." After Louis's arrival in the United States, he initially worked as a pack peddler in the South, where, as an observant Jew, he restricted himself to a diet of roasted peanuts to avoid food cooked with lard. After he had saved enough money, he bought a pushcart and a site for it on the Lower East Side and sent for the rest of his family.

Stanley's father, Moe (short for Moises), was born in 1891 and grew up among the tenements of Orchard Street, together with four siblings, in circumstances similar to the portrayal of immigrant Jewish life in Henry Roth's novel *Call It Sleep*—so similar, in fact, that Stanley would later tell stories he said (and probably believed) were about his parents that actually came from the novel. Eventually Louis established a small paper-manufacturing business, L. Hyman and Sons, in which Moe would join him. Decades later, L. Hyman and Sons would provide Moe's son and daughter-in-law with the yellow copy paper on which they typed nearly all their work.

In 1915, Moe married Louisa (Lulu) Marshak, the youngest of seven sisters. The couple were first cousins, but the two branches of the family were temperamentally very different. Lulu's father, Barney Marshak, also from Lithuania, was a Talmudic scholar, a "sensitive, idealistic, and deeply religious soul" who traced his lineage, according to family lore, back to the Ba'al Shem Tov, the rabbi who founded the mystical Hasidic movement. Like Geraldine Jackson, Lulu found it important to maintain certain standards: she wore a corset and stockings whenever she left the house and prided herself on the condition of her home. "She was one of those women who had to rush out and clean the ashtray every time someone flicked an ash into it," Phoebe Pettingell, Stanley's second wife, would recall. But, unlike Geraldine, Lulu also had a spontaneous, fun-loving side, especially later on, with her grandchildren. When twelve-year-old Laurence Hyman became enamored of jazz, he begged his grandparents to take him to the Copacabana, a Manhattan nightclub, to hear Louis Armstrong. Moe refused. Not only did Lulu take Laurence, they went three hours early and got the best table in the house. Laurence never forgot it.

Stanley, Moe and Lulu's first child, arrived on June 11, 1919. "It has not yet been declared a National Holiday," he would write as a teenager, tongue only partially in cheek. "Someday it will be." Before becoming pregnant with Stanley, Lulu had suffered multiple miscarriages, and Stanley arrived prematurely, perhaps as much as several months early. A tiny, weak infant, he came down with a case of pneumonia so serious that he was not expected to live. The dramatic circumstances of his birth and infancy contributed to his sense of himself, from a very early age, as exceptional: a brilliant dynamo to whom the usual rules, even those having to do with birth and death, did not apply. This self-assessment was not altogether inaccurate. Stanley would grow up to become one of the most important critics of his generation; he published *The Armed Vision*, a major work of literary scholarship, before he turned thirty.

Like Saul Bellow and Bernard Malamud, two of the other major Jewish writers of his cohort, Stanley grew up with a domineering father and a weaker, emotionally fragile mother. In their own way, Moe and Lulu Hyman were as challenging a set of parents as Leslie and Geraldine Jackson—and they had just as difficult a time appreciating their unusual child. Stanley described his father as "a willful, independent, unemotional man, bigoted in his opinions" and uninterested in discussion or debate. "A man who wanted no affection, and who possessed none to give back in return, he bred me to the same stern pattern. . . .

I became a smaller edition of my father . . . as tight-lipped and unsentimental a little boy as ever grew." Walter Bernstein, a close childhood friend of Stanley's, remembered Moe as "peremptory," with "a tough demeanor." Once, accompanying Stanley on a visit to Moe's paper business on Varick Street in SoHo, then Manhattan's industrial district, Walter absentmindedly picked up a paper clip from Moe's desk to fiddle with. Later, standing on the subway platform, he realized with horror that he was still holding the paper clip, and worried that Moe had seen him take it and would think he had intentionally stolen it. "I was scared of him," Walter admitted. Stanley, too, cultivated a tough-guy persona. Walter recalled a favorite game of his: "He would say, 'I'll let you hit me in the stomach as hard as you can if you let me hit you in the stomach as hard as I can.' I never let him."

Lulu, for her part, was asthmatic and likely depressive. Despite her shortcomings as a mother, Stanley felt protective of her. "I invariably took her side in her recurrent battles with my father, and yet it was somehow my father that I consciously aped and tried to be like," he would later reflect. An uneducated woman, she saw her brilliant, precocious son as something of a changeling, an alien. She was once called into school to hear the results of Stanley's IQ test: he had scored 180. "So?" Lulu responded. She was "frightened of his intelligence," Pettingell remembers. Lulu doted instead on her younger son, Arthur, a more conventional child with whom she was apparently able to bond more firmly. Stanley was fiercely jealous of their close relationship. But the fact that his own mother did not quite know what to do with him must have confirmed his conviction that he was a superior being.

By the time Stanley reached elementary school, Moe and Lulu had left behind gritty Manhattan for the tree-lined streets of Midwood, a newly developed middle-class Brooklyn neighborhood filled with rambling Victorian one- and two-family houses. Malamud, five years older than Stanley, grew up in the same area and attended the same high school, Erasmus Hall, but the two writers would not meet until Malamud began teaching at Bennington, in 1961. Norman Mailer, several years younger, grew up in nearby Flatbush but went to Boys High in Bedford-Stuyvesant. Then, as now, Borough Park was home to a substantial community of Orthodox Jews. Stanley attended P.S. 99, the neighborhood elementary school, "full of savage little children or grandchildren of immigrant Jews, like myself, fiercely competing to get ahead in the world through education, to become dentists or accountants or pharmacists or whatever." Many years later, teaching at Bennington, he delighted a student who had graduated from the same elementary school by singing the school song. June Mirken, who went to grade school with Stanley and later became close friends with him and Shirley at Syracuse University, recalled that he raised his hand so frequently in class that the teacher had to tell him to give the other students a chance. Stanley, more mildly, commented that he "competed with great success."

Religion was important to Moe and Lulu, as it was to most American Jewish families of their generation. The family observed rituals such as keeping kosher, and Lulu would eventually teach her daughter-in-law how to cook potato kugel and the other comfort-food staples Stanley grew up with; Shirley took particular pride in her potato pancakes, and she once tried to structure a story around the kugel recipe. Stanley and Arthur were both bar mitzvahed at Congregation Shomrei Emunah, an imposing Romanesque Revival synagogue on Fourteenth Avenue,

Stanley on vacation, age ten.

walking distance from the Hyman home. Even though Stanley detested Hebrew school and never managed to learn much of the language, he carried out his religious obligations with the zeal he brought to all his youthful passions. On Yom Kippur one year, he fasted until he fainted. At age sixteen he collected so much money for the Jewish National Fund to buy land in what was then Palestine that he received an award. In college, he formed an important friendship with Jesse Zel Lurie, one of the first Jewish journalists to report from Palestine.

But Stanley would later say that he was a "militant atheist" by the time he reached high school, which made him as much of an outcast in his family as Shirley was in hers. His atheism had its roots in the humanistic studies he began to pursue at a very early age, both independently and with a series of mentors to whom he looked for the intellectual stewardship his parents could not provide. Shirley had to wait until Jeanou's arrival, during her freshman year of college, to find an intellectual guide, but Stanley discovered the first of his as early as age eight: a girl named Berenice Rosenthal whose family lived upstairs from the Hymans. Six or seven years older, with an interest in philosophy, she instilled in him a disdain for mysticism and a love of empirical truth. Berenice loved to tell the well-known anecdote about the French mathematician Pierre-Simon Laplace, who, when asked by Napoleon why he had written a treatise on the universe without once mentioning God, answered proudly, "I had no need of that hypothesis." Stanley would later credit her with having led him away from the religion of his childhood: he would eventually come to understand the Bible as no different from any other system of mythology. Berenice, he said, "freed my mind from all the bigotry and narrowness of my home environment, made me question everything I believed or respected, taught me both to think and to evaluate. Entire new vistas opened up for me under her tutelage: microbes, hypnotism, the theater, mathematics, all of science [and] of truth-seeking." Nearly thirty years later, when Stanley discovered his daughter Sarah, then seven years old, on her knees praying to Jesus, he sent her to her room and made her read Thoreau. At the breakfast table, he sometimes made his children recite the phrase "Jesus is a myth."

The educational role Berenice played in Stanley's life was next filled by Gil, a camp counselor he met the summer before he entered high school. While the other boys were playing baseball or swimming, Stanley and Gil sat in their tent, talking about art, literature, music, and natural history. Stanley, short and heavily nearsighted, had never been athletic; now, he joked, he "became stagnant physically." But his mind was active. Gil introduced him to Lucretius's *De Rerum Natura* and to Baudelaire. "For the first time in my life I began really to read, omnivorously and far over my head," Stanley recalled several years later. Gil also demonstrated a type of masculinity far different from the model his gruff father presented. "He talked me out of thinking that poetry was only for 'pixies,' and convinced me that there were other men besides himself who used words like 'beauty,' 'rapture,' and 'sublime' without being ashamed." At camp, Stanley hunted for mushrooms alone in the woods; back in New York, he made friends with the curators of the Bronx Zoo reptile house. He would later astound a Bennington colleague with tales of putting a praying mantis and a nightcrawler together in a milk bottle so that he could "watch—with dazzling cruelty—the ensuing battle." When he and Shirley briefly lived in rural New Hampshire in the early 1940s, Stanley had an opportunity to rekindle his interest in the natural world, collecting snakes and turtles. The works of Darwin, which Stanley read in their entirety, would form one of the four pillars of *The Tangled Bank* (1962), his nearly five-hundred-page magnum opus.

While Stanley's childhood was intellectually rich, the Hymans often struggled financially, downsizing more than once to a smaller home. It was not easy to run a small paper business during the Depression, when the average income of the American family fell 40 percent. In contrast to the lush estates and bustling car dealerships of Burlingame, California, where the rich were able to avoid the worst of the Depression, Hoovervilles popped up all around New York, from a former reservoir in Central Park (now the Great Lawn) to the Brooklyn waterfront. "One got used to seeing older men and women scrounging in garbage cans for their next meal," Malcolm Cowley, an editor at *The New Republic* and soon to become an acquaintance of Stanley's, wrote in his memoir of those years. During the winter of 1931–32, New York families received

*Stanley in Brooklyn,
dressed as a pirate
for Halloween, age
twelve.*

an average of $2.39 per week in relief funds. For most of Stanley's child-
hood, at least one aunt or uncle lived with the family, and he would
later say that he grew up surrounded by affectionate female relatives.
Moe's father and uncle offered material assistance, but at one point the
Hymans resorted to selling their furniture to raise money. Moe also had
a gambling habit. "His idea of a good time was to hang around on the
street outside the barbershop with the other men and talk about baseball
and place bets," Laurence Hyman says. Eventually, the family's situation was stable enough to allow for regular summer vacations at the
Borscht Belt resorts frequented by Jews of their era. But Stanley never
forgot those years of financial anxiety.

Moe and Lulu's marriage was nearly a casualty of those difficult
years. In the spring of 1932, when Stanley was twelve, his parents temporarily separated, which put even more financial and emotional strain
on the family. In childish, awkward script, Stanley wrote pathetic letters to Moe imploring his father to come home. "Mom has periodical
attacks of asthma and crying. Chiefly crying. . . . We need you very,
very much," he pleaded. Stanley worried that his mother would commit
suicide. "She walks about all day, her eyes red with crying, muttering,
'My life is blighted, my life is blighted!' She says that she will not let you

in, but I can easily persuade her about that." He reported that they were moving into a three-room flat "to make both ends meet. . . . If you come back, we can live cheaper and everything will be all right again."

Moe did come back. He had run off with an underage girl; his brother Harry hired a private detective to track them down and persuaded Moe to come home. It was not the only occasion on which he was unfaithful. During a period when Lulu's sister Becky was living with the family, Lulu once discovered the two of them in the bathroom together in the middle of the night, Becky performing oral sex. Stanley likely did not learn about that until much later. But Moe's abandonment of the family embittered Stanley's relationship with his father. Moe's philandering also set an unfortunate example for his son.

Moe's disappearance gave Stanley a taste of what it was like to be the man of the house. During the separation, at a time of soaring unemployment, he managed to find his first job, sorting files at a local store for ten cents an hour. "At least I do part of your work," he told his father proudly. His level of independence was unequaled among his peers. As a young teenager, he was permitted to travel alone to Chicago, staying with relatives, to see the 1933 World's Fair. His earnings also allowed him to indulge on a small scale his passion for collecting, starting early on with stamps, coins (which he would collect seriously as an adult), and chewing gum, of which he would eventually accumulate more than 150 varieties. (He avowed himself to be "perhaps the greatest chewing gum collector on earth," admitting also that he was probably the only one.) Eventually his collections would include records, coins, and, most important, books: Stanley and Shirley amassed a library amounting to some 25,000 volumes, which lined virtually every wall in their house. "He knew where each one was, who wrote it, where it was in the house, what color the binding was, and pretty much everything in it," Sarah Hyman recalls. "And he could quote and quote and quote."

Stanley also kept an extensive system of files on any subject of interest, clipping articles and making comprehensive notes on anything he read. Shirley would sometimes tease him about his love of order: everything on his desk—books, pens, ashtray—had to be lined up just right

before he could work. Bernard Malamud liked to repeat a funny, if probably apocryphal, story in which a middle-aged Stanley fell asleep in his
study and awoke stark naked. After a long search, he finally located
his underwear, socks, and eyeglasses neatly stowed in his filing cabinet
under U, S, and E.

The discipline Stanley developed as a boy surely helped him cope with
his parents' chaotic marriage. It may also have been a way of subcon-
sciously siding with his mother—she of the fanatically clean ashtrays—
against his brash, dismissive father. But it would become an eventual
source of conflict with his wife, whose creative mind thrived amid the
chaos of her own desk and who had no qualms about leaving a sink full
of dishes or a floor unswept if she needed to get back to her typewriter.

IN THE FALL OF 1932, as fifteen-year-old Shirley settled into her junior
year at Burlingame High, Stanley, at the precocious age of thirteen,
enrolled as a freshman at Brooklyn's Erasmus Hall High School. Originally founded by Dutch settlers in the eighteenth century and rebuilt
in the early 1900s, the school occupied a campus on Flatbush Avenue
that was modeled after Oxford, with elegant ivy-covered buildings
decorated with gargoyles and other carvings. In addition to Malamud,
among its famous alumni were actresses Mae West and Barbara Stan-
wyck, novelist Mickey Spillane, real estate tycoon Samuel LeFrak, and
singers Neil Diamond and Barbra Streisand.

As Brooklyn's population surged in the Depression years, Erasmus
Hall expanded accordingly. By the time Stanley enrolled, the school was
so crowded that its five thousand students had to attend in three shifts,
the earliest starting at six in the morning. The school was competitive,
the best Brooklyn had to offer, but Stanley nonetheless found his education insufficient. He wrote an editorial for the school newspaper comparing Erasmus to the mythical bed of Procrustes: since standards were
set according to the average student, anyone else had to be "either cut
down or stretched out" to fit. There were strategies to help less-bright
students, Stanley complained, but "the plight of the unfortunate over-
intelligent student has been completely disregarded."

Moaning about how his own brilliance disadvantaged him was not a recipe for popularity. Stanley was initially as isolated in high school as Shirley would be in Rochester: "miserably lonely, reading prodigiously, hating everyone, and wishing I had enough courage to talk to girls." One day a boy he recognized from class sat down next to him in the locker room. Stanley, trying to make conversation as he best knew how, asked his classmate if he read Poe. "No, I read very well, thank you," came the reply. Stanley responded huffily that he didn't think puns were very clever. "I don't either," said the other boy, "but they're something I can't help, like a harelip."

That was Stanley's first encounter with Walter Bernstein, who grew up in Crown Heights and would become a celebrated screenwriter best known for *The Front* (1976). Even Stanley later acknowledged that as a child he had been "dreadfully serious," overly convinced of his own importance, and too deeply influenced by his father's Spartanism to regard fun as "anything other than the good right hand of sin." But "under Walter's tutelage," he later recalled, "slowly and carefully, I learned to laugh, the way a child learns to walk." A movie buff from early on, Walter enjoyed having the early shift at school because it meant that he could catch an afternoon film before heading home: given twenty-five cents for lunch money, he spent a dime on daytime admission to the Astor Theatre in Times Square and fifteen cents on candy. Walter even snuck out of his own bar mitzvah celebration to go to the movies; he emerged from the theater to find police cars racing up and down Eastern Parkway, his parents frantic.

Walter also brought some levity into Stanley's reading program, including the fantasy books Shirley already loved: Lewis Carroll, the Oz books, even A. A. Milne—all of which Stanley had previously derided as "childish." Walter enjoyed British humor, including the works of P. G. Wodehouse, and introduced Stanley to Gilbert and Sullivan operettas. Together with a few other friends—including Frank Orenstein, who went to college with Stanley and would become another lifelong friend—they would write a parody called *Punafore* (*Or the Class That Loved Its Jailor*) for the senior class play.

By spring of their junior year, Stanley and Walter were coauthoring theater reviews in the school newspaper, calling their column "The Prompter's Box." Walter would remember it mainly as a way of getting free tickets to Broadway plays. But Stanley took the role of critic seriously. A few months later, he wrote to the director of the Yale School of Drama to announce his intention to "enter the fold of drama critisism [sic]." The fact that college was still more than a year away did not dissuade him from asking this prominent stranger for advice regarding which college courses would be most useful in his future career.

With criticism, Stanley found the outlet for his intelligence that he had always desired. "He was born to be a critic," Walter says. Stanley's early attempts were not always successful, but he threw himself into writing with all his usual gusto. "I have read, and written, bad reviews in my time, but this certainly caps them all," Walter commented on a draft of one of Stanley's pieces. "You use ten words where three would do and you're obviously unfair for the sake of being nasty." But if his style and critical taste were not yet fully developed, Stanley's characteristic tone was already audible. A review of Thornton Wilder's Pulitzer Prize–winning novel *The Bridge of San Luis Rey* (1928), written when Stanley was fifteen, criticized the book's language as "lyric and exquisite in some places, and matter-of-fact and mechanical in others" and scoffed at the ending, in which Wilder explores a metaphysics of the meaning of life, as utterly nonsensical: "Come, come, Mr. Wilder, other people through the ages have loved, and never fell down canyons." His confidence in his own judgment, at such an early age, is nothing short of stunning.

Upon his graduation, in 1936, Stanley's yearbook quote was "Intentions charged with power." One of the stars of his class, elected for two years in a row to the honor society, he was voted "Boy most likely to be serviceable to Erasmus." At a time when private colleges and universities around the country implemented quotas limiting the enrollment of Jewish students, both he and Walter, unusually, had their choice of schools. Walter, headed to Dartmouth, urged Stanley to join him so that they could stay together. But Syracuse had just established one of the first undergraduate journalism programs, and Stanley had already decided that he was going to become a critic.

———

STANLEY'S SEXUAL AWAKENING TOOK place just after his fifteenth birthday. During the summer before his junior year of high school, he persuaded his parents to send him alone to a vacation resort in New Jersey, in a town appropriately called Mount Freedom. There Stanley encountered a man named Julie, a former burlesque comedian who was "as picturesque and checkered a person" as he had ever known. Stanley idolized Julie, largely because of his success with women, and regarded him as a role model.

Up to this point, Stanley's sexual experience amounted to "an infrequent and shamefaced masturbation." His dates thus far had been chaste. Julie, who was flamboyantly sexual, loosened his inhibitions. "He spoke of sex as though it were a perfectly normal, casual, and rather amusing form of activity, and I found myself more and more attracted to this concept," Stanley recalled. Julie was also at the center of a circle of theater people whom Stanley described as "the most real and least affected group of people I had ever known." One day, while Julie and his girlfriend were visiting Stanley in his room, they all decided to go swimming. Stanley asked the girl to leave so that he could change, but Julie told her to stay. His forehead bathed in sweat, Stanley took off his clothes without turning his back. Though he was not yet overweight, as he would later become, he had the build of a teenager who spent most of his time reading, with the thick glasses to go with it. But the incident cured him of physical embarrassment. "I have never been ashamed of my body since," he said afterward.

Despite his general strictness, Moe never insisted that Stanley adhere to a curfew: "It was my father's theory that it was no one's goddam business what I did or what time I got home, least of all his." This gave Stanley plenty of opportunity to put Julie's lessons into practice. At the start of his senior year of high school, he met Henrietta, a girl several years older who worked as a photographer's model. "She was not unintelligent," Stanley would later say, deploying the double negative intentionally, "but was as close to being illiterate as a person who has gone through high school can be." She was the first true anti-intellectual he had ever known, with an open distaste for art, literature, and music. Stanley did not mind. Walter Bernstein, who had an unrequited crush on Henrietta, remembered her as "exotic." Stanley, well aware of his friend's feelings, phoned Walter one afternoon to report that he was in bed with her—"showing off," Walter said. Stanley's competitive streak could make him cruel.

A comic sketch that Stanley wrote in high school, in the voices of a boy and a girl who give drastically different accounts of a date, offers an amusing yet telling glimpse of his attitude toward sex. The boy, wanting to preserve the girl's innocence, musters a supreme effort in his attempt not to "defile" her ("She sat there in an old red kimono, and it kept slipping open . . . the little innocent never noticed it at all"). Meanwhile, the girl bemoans her date's failure to respond to her efforts at seduction: "I wiggled, and looked at him, and opened that goddam kimono a little more, and he just sat like a wet dishrag." Even as a teenager, Stanley had no patience for the social conventions that insisted on women's purity in the face of men's aggression. If the sketch sounds more like a fantasy than like anything that might actually happen to a high school student, it nonetheless shows that he already suspected—or at least hoped—that women were just as interested in sex as men.

But in other ways Stanley was significantly less progressive. Many years later, he would reportedly say he did not believe it was possible for a woman to be raped. No matter how adamantly they might protest, he claimed, women wanted to be forced into sex, and "ultimately their excitement made them receptive." This line of thinking was not unusual for men of Stanley's era, but—influenced later by his deep reading into Freud—he may have taken it further than most.

STROLLING ACROSS THE BROOKLYN BRIDGE one night in the summer of 1936, shortly before he left for Syracuse University, Stanley had an epiphany. On his arm was Elsa Dorman, a "small, round, red-haired girl, of the type described in novels as 'pert,' " whom he had recently met and was trying desperately to impress. Several years older, Elsa was one of the first Communists he had ever encountered, and the two of

Stanley with Elsa Dorman, c. 1936.

them spent much of that summer, on the eve of the Spanish Civil War, discussing political theory. Despite his atheism, Stanley was not an easy convert: his innate individualism and skepticism of any kind of intellectual conformity made him an unlikely Communist. But that night on the Brooklyn Bridge, he suddenly was convinced. Perhaps the lights of lower Manhattan reminded him of his own family's modest beginnings in the tenements; perhaps the view onto the industrial warehouses of Brooklyn's Vinegar Hill brought home the reality that the problems of the worker were not limited to Europe; perhaps it was just the inherent romance of the bridge on a warm summer night that swayed him. The next day he signed up for the Young Communist League (YCL).

Stanley's conversion took place just as a growing number of writers and intellectuals were becoming aware of the possibilities for revolution, both politically and creatively. In the traumatic Depression years, many came to see the capitalist system as irremediably broken, its demise taking with it their hopes for progressivism. Literary journalist and social critic Edmund Wilson, who traveled around the country in the early 1930s reporting for *The New Republic* on the condition of miners and other workers (his essays were collected as *The American Jitters* in 1932), initially called for American radicals to "take communism away from the Communists," though he soon came to embrace Marxism. (Later Stanley would memorably skewer Wilson—for his critical method, not his political beliefs—in the pages of *The Armed Vision*.) But many intellectuals decided either to cooperate with the Communist Party as fellow travelers or to join. For some, this youthful moment of idealism had far-reaching consequences.

Malcolm Cowley, a colleague of Wilson's at *The New Republic* who considered himself a fellow traveler, wondered later why Communist doctrine had appealed to so many writers, especially considering how much it could cost them in terms of their literary freedom. His answer was that, in the face of the Depression, the fight against Hitler, and the Spanish Civil War, communism offered a specific plan for action. That certainly seems to have been what appealed to Stanley. If liberalism was a balm for good intentions, communism offered, in the words of his high school yearbook motto, "intentions charged with power."

Cowley later joked that "Red Decade" was a misnomer; the years between 1929 and 1939 were merely "tinged with pink." The Party's political gains were slow: in the 1928 presidential election, the Communists received around 49,000 votes, a modest increase over their showing four years earlier. But the Party's influence among writers was disproportionate. John Reed Clubs for radical young writers—founded in 1929 by contributors to *The New Masses*, the leading Marxist magazine— sprang up all over the country "to clarify the principles of revolutionary literature, to propagate them, to practice them." In Chicago, the future novelist and social critic Richard Wright got his start after wandering into a John Reed Club during an editorial meeting. In New York, Cowley found himself summoned to the club's headquarters in December 1932 to discuss an article he had written for *The New Republic* about a hunger march on Washington. Two of the men who criticized his piece, Philip Rahv and William Phillips, would soon found *Partisan Review*, which—after shedding its Communist Party connections—became the dominant highbrow cultural magazine in the United States from the 1940s through the 1960s.

More than two hundred politically engaged intellectuals descended upon New York's Mecca Temple (now New York City Center) and the New School for Social Research for the first American Writers' Congress in April 1935, a year before Stanley's political awakening. The call for delegates was written by Granville Hicks, literary editor of *The New Masses*. "He wrote in English, unlike many of his colleagues," sniped Cowley, who signed the call along with Theodore Dreiser, John Dos Passos, Langston Hughes, and numerous other writers. "Hundreds of poets, novelists, dramatists, critics, short story writers and journalists recognize the necessity of personally helping to accelerate the destruction of capitalism and the establishment of a workers' government," Hicks wrote. "A new renaissance is upon the world; for each writer there is the opportunity to proclaim both the new way of life and the revolutionary way to attain it." Delegates to the congress formed the League of American Writers, which would join the International Union of Revolutionary Writers in the struggle against fascism.

The most controversial speech of the congress was delivered by literary critic Kenneth Burke, a pioneer of language-based textual analysis who would soon become Stanley's intellectual hero and close friend. Burke's paper analyzed the semiotics of revolutionary language, arguing that if the American Left wanted to appeal to a broader swath of the public, it ought to substitute the term "the people"—more in keeping with American values—for "the masses" or "the workers." He also argued that this change would benefit the proletarian novel, of which the examples in English thus far had been uninspired. Burke was denounced as a traitor: to suggest that the Left should appropriate capitalist discourse was heretical. The fact that proletarian literature was read only by the intelligentsia rather than by workers or non-Marxists—a problem Stanley would take up a few years later—was not addressed by anyone else at the conference.

By the fall of 1936, when Stanley arrived at Syracuse, news of the Moscow show trials—Stalin's first effort to purge and execute Trotsky supporters and other dissenters—was beginning to roil the Party's American devotees. Many writers who had previously been sympathizers, including Wilson and the circle around *Partisan Review*, distanced themselves from the Soviet government. The second American Writers'

Congress, held in June 1937, abandoned the open call to revolution and instead endorsed the broad alliance against fascism known as the Popular Front. Stanley, along with Cowley and the others in the League of American Writers, initially toed the Stalinist line, denouncing Trotskyists as traitors. But in true Jewish style, Stanley admitted to having "constant doubts," scouring the works of Marx for errors and inconsistencies and remaining deeply skeptical about the Party as a monolithic institution.

Nonetheless, the YCL provided him with an instant social life in college. Florence Shapiro, an art student from Queens, recalled one of the Party's methods for helping young Communists find one another: before she got to Syracuse, she was given half of a Jell-O box and was told to find the person with the other half, who would be "on the same wavelength." That person turned out to be Stanley, and the two became friends: she found him "a typical Brooklyn intellectual . . . with a fantastic sense of humor." A senior became his political mentor and helped him discover a knack for organizing: he was soon distributing leaflets and addressing meetings of a group of steelworkers in Solvay, a suburb of Syracuse. The summer after his sophomore year of college, shortly after he and Shirley met, he took a job working at a paper mill in rural Massachusetts that supplied his father's business. His goal was to live among the workers, doing manual labor, in order to understand the conditions of their lives—and he was serious enough to go through with it.

At Syracuse, Stanley also had his first encounter with Marxist literary criticism, which was to shape his method of interpreting literature well beyond his college years. The professor who influenced him most deeply was Leonard Brown, who had begun teaching at the university in 1925, when he was only twenty-one. Brown devoted his career to teaching rather than publication; his books are few, but many of his students would remember his influence as formative. His innovation was to teach the ideas of Darwin, Marx, Freud, George Berkeley, Albert Einstein, and anthropologists such as Bronisław Malinowski, Franz Boas, and Margaret Mead alongside the touchstones of modern literature, which he believed had gravitated toward the "sociological position." During the mid-1930s, Brown was briefly fired for introducing dialectical materialism into his classes; after a popular outcry, the university quickly reinstated him, and from then on he was allowed to teach whatever he wanted. Brown also brought Burke to lecture at Syracuse several times later in the decade; Stanley would first encounter him there in 1939. While Brown favored a Marxist, scientific approach to literary study, he did not force it upon his students. "What I am attempting to teach," he told them, "is a method of criticism, not a body of personal beliefs about writers or a 'view' of literature." Stanley's copy of Brown's syllabus for the course Main Currents in Modern Literature: 1870–1939—a single-spaced, nine-page reading list in world literature and social thought—is covered with his own additions and annotations. The roots of *The Tangled Bank* extend to this course.

Stanley's infatuation with communism did not continue beyond his college years. If he suffered a specific moment of disenchantment, to parallel his epiphany on the Brooklyn Bridge, he did not mention it in his writings. More likely, as World War II progressed and Stanley began working at the thoroughly apolitical *New Yorker*, he simply grew estranged from the Party, as did so many other intellectuals. Remarkably, unlike some of his friends, he never suffered any consequences for his youthful political activities. Stanley's last known Communist affiliation was with the League of American Writers in 1941, as that group's political stance shifted to advocate American entry into World War II after Germany's invasion of Russia. From then on, literature would be his only cause.

4.

S & S

SYRACUSE,
1937–1940

> i want you more than anything in the world and you
> needn't imagine that anything you say or do is going to
> stop me from getting what i want, and you can't even stop
> me from wanting it.
>
> —letter from Shirley Jackson
> to Stanley Edgar Hyman, summer 1938

"

WAS IN THAT FIRST SWEET BOHEMIAN STAGE WHERE ALL LIV-
ing artists are Artists, and everyone who is pursuing his happy anonymous artistic way through college is a potential satellite," Jackson later
recalled of her early days at Syracuse University. When she arrived
there, in September 1937, the school was still relatively small—it
would see exponential growth after World War II. Dramatic buildings
clustered around a central quad at the top of a hill, including Crouse
College, a multistoried Romanesque Revival building, and Hendricks
Chapel, modeled after Rome's Pantheon, with a pillared façade and a
dome. Unlike at the University of Rochester, men and women attended
classes together, but their living quarters, of course, were separate. For
most of her time at Syracuse, Shirley lived in Lima Cottage, a dormitory
for about fifty women at 926 South Crouse Avenue.

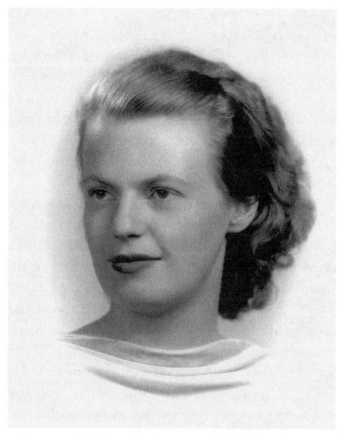

Shirley Jackson's college yearbook photograph.

Many of the male students, including Stanley, lived in the fraternity houses that lined the surrounding blocks: his was Sigma Alpha Mu, one of the few open to Jews. Campus social life centered on the Greek system and sports: the campus was anchored by Archbold Stadium, whose castlelike entryway featured turrets framing a gateway arch. But there were also numerous options for the literarily inclined, including the *Syracusan* literary and humor magazine, where Shirley would publish some of her first stories, and the *Daily Orange* newspaper, where Stanley was a writer and editor. The Cosmo, an all-night coffee shop known as "the Greeks," was a favorite student hangout.

Shirley was never a top student and would graduate without distinction, but her college notebooks demonstrate her roving intellect:

in addition to her major in English, she took courses in linguistics, geology, and criminology. She developed a fondness for Thomas Hardy and Joseph Conrad, as well as a brief affection for the Victorian poets Algernon Charles Swinburne and Ernest Dowson. Professor H. W. Herrington's course in folklore was another influence she would later acknowledge. "I am going to write my paper for this course on superstition—the need for it, the use of it, its manipulations, its use in literature, [its] effect on writers," the future author of "The Lottery" recorded in one of her college notebooks.

Switching colleges was a social challenge for Shirley not unlike her transfer to Brighton High School. She initially felt so isolated and anxious that for three days she kept her bags packed, so that she could leave at any moment. "it seemed that everyone was completely at ease and surrounded by friends but me," she later recalled. Like Natalie in *Hangsaman*, she initially left her room only for meals. Her primary pastimes were solitary: she spent hours in the record-listening room playing *Caucasian Sketches* and Prokofiev's brooding *Lieutenant Kije*. She exchanged frequent letters with Michael Palmer, the boy she had been dating in Rochester, and also with Jeanou, now a committed Communist after encountering veterans of the Spanish Civil War in Paris—she asked Shirley to send her copies of the *Daily Worker*. A story Shirley wrote around this time describes two roommates: one a transfer student named Mary who knows no one, the other a popular girl who makes little effort to help her roommate adjust. At the end of the story, Mary—who has boasted that she has "a boy back home"—fakes a love note on a photograph of a man that she puts on display. In an alternate draft, the roommate goes out with friends while Mary hides in their room, writing letters to her mother. She throws away three drafts describing her loneliness before she is able to manufacture the desired cheery tone. The first version says plainly, "Dear Mother, I want to come home."

Within a few months, however, Shirley came into her own socially, thanks to the creative writing class she was taking. The professor, A. E. Johnson, was a poet whose own work tended toward the florid;

mercifully, she did not absorb his style. But another student in the class became a close friend. Seymour Goldberg was a talented artist from Crown Heights, Brooklyn, who had already established himself in business as an interior decorator. Determined to seek out whatever adventure there was to find in the sleepy upstate town, they would head out together to explore a designated destination—a bar, a department store, the swanky Yates Hotel downtown—then return to campus to write about what they had seen. "I have . . . seldom, if ever, been as completely happy," Shirley wrote in December. "I have been relaxing into myself. I do not feel the constant strain to be someone else." Since arriving at Syracuse, she noted with satisfaction, she had succumbed to "hysterics" only once. Perhaps the dramatic highs and lows of the last few years were behind her. "I am going to catch the world in my hand," she enthused.

As always, Shirley's writing was the element of her life that brought her the greatest personal satisfaction. Now, for the first time, her peers were starting to acknowledge her talent. She carried her notebook everywhere and briefly began smoking a pipe before taking up the Pall Mall cigarettes that would be her lifelong habit. "People are beginning to grow accustomed to Jackson sprawled in a corner, scribbling away in her eternal notebook," she told her Rochester friend Elizabeth Young, whom she had nicknamed Y—pronounced "ee," to rhyme with "Lee," Shirley's new nickname for herself. "I have become a mad Bohemian who curls up in corners with a pencil." She tantalized Michael Palmer by telling him about the "epochal novel" she was working on, but refused to let him see it.

She also had a new suitor: Alfred Parsell, a senior in the creative writing class. A story he wrote demonstrates just how different she was from the typical Syracuse coed. "He knew [his roommates] didn't like her, that they thought she was crazy, and that they thought he was crazy because he went out with her," the unnamed narrator says. "He could never make them see beyond her impetuous, high-strung mannerisms and her seemingly fantastic ideas and actions." The speaker's friends are openly malicious, telling him to stand the girl up or tell her he broke his leg—anything to avoid going out with her. But the end of the piece finds the narrator and his beloved walking joyfully in the rain, "singing and shouting at the tops of their voices, splashing through puddles, dodging automobiles, and getting wetter and happier all the time." In reality, gentle, kindhearted Al was never able to make any headway with Shirley, who found him too dependable for her taste.

Jackson's successful first term at Syracuse culminated with the appearance of *The Threshold*, the class magazine produced by Johnson and his students. Published in February 1938, it quickly made the rounds of the college. "Surprisingly enough, it's good," Shirley wrote to Y. "I can write now, more fluently and better than ever before." Al Parsell had written a story called "The Good Samaritans," a turgid piece about a writer who breaks down on a book tour, unable to bear the hypocrisy of his audience. Seymour Goldberg's contribution, "Of Lydia," was a charming character sketch of an eccentric Russian woman who shares a few characteristics—notably a love of pomegranates—with Shirley, whom he liked to call by Russian nicknames. Perhaps he was a little bit in love with her, too.

"Janice," Jackson's story, opened the magazine. Barely 250 words, each one chills. There is no plot: a girl, chatting with her friends, casually mentions that she happens to have attempted suicide. Written entirely in dialogue form, with the arresting refrain "Darn near killed myself this afternoon," the story precociously displays Jackson's signature talent for combining the horrific with the mundane. Janice's conversational bomb, dropped ever so gently, shatters the placid surface of cocktail-party chitchat to reveal a hidden darkness. Jackson apparently based the main character, at least partially, on a girl she had known in Rochester; she didn't even bother changing the name. (After Y showed the real Janice a copy of the story, she refused to speak to Shirley again.) But Jackson likely chose to tell Janice's story in part because it contained elements of her own experience.

The Threshold, not surprisingly, found its way into the hands of sophomore Stanley Edgar Hyman, a dual English and journalism major. The preface alone must have gotten him sharpening his critical knife: it attacked the intellectual limitations of proletarian writers and their "specious scientific conditioning whereby the magic and the miraculous are banished and the body is gelded of its very soul." The budding literary critic scoffed at most of what he read. But "Janice" brought him up short. Stanley closed the magazine demanding to know who Shirley Jackson was. He had decided, he said, to marry her.

"YOU WERE THE ONLY live thing I had seen outside the greenhouse all winter," Stanley told Shirley after their first meeting, which took place on March 3, 1938, in the library listening room—Shirley's favorite spot on campus. The skinny, bespectacled, curly-haired Jewish intellectual from Brooklyn and the tall, redheaded, golf-playing California girl must have seemed an incongruous pair. But in many ways, their interests were perfectly aligned, as they always would be. From the first days of their relationship, Stanley took pride in Shirley as his personal discovery. He was her faithful cheerleader, encouraging her to write more and to write better; he also saw himself in the role of her educator, constantly suggesting books for her to read. Though he was entirely

Stanley Hyman outside his fraternity house in Syracuse, late 1930s.

convinced of her genius, he saw it as innate, instinctive, and perhaps even unrecognized by her. He told Walter Bernstein that she had "no idea what the things she wrote meant. Whatever came out of her head, she put on the page," Walter recalls.

Stanley had hoped to write fiction himself, but once he met Shirley, he realized that he could not compete. Stanley "wrote painfully, it was a tedious, forced thing, whereas she—the thing flowed like you turned on a faucet," said June Mirken, Stanley's old friend from elementary school, who graduated a year behind him and Shirley at Syracuse. "He talked a lot but she wrote better," another of their college acquaintances recalled. Instead, he would be the cool-headed intellectual who helped Shirley realize her full creative powers and then interpreted her work to the world: a perfect symbiosis. Between them, the criticism flowed largely in one direction. Shirley would comment on Stanley's writings, but she rarely worked them over with the same gusto he brought to hers. Throughout their marriage, he gave her detailed pages of notes on all of her novels and many of her stories. She would dedicate *The Road Through the Wall*, her first novel, to "Stanley, a critic." It became their custom to present each other with leather-bound editions of their own works, inscribed "To S with love from S."

Shirley, in contrast to her suitor, was not immediately convinced that she would marry Stanley. Age was one issue: both were sopho-mores, but she was two and a half years older, and she worried about his immaturity. (Starting with their marriage license, she took to report-ing her birth year as 1919 rather than 1916 to disguise their age differ-ence, an error that was repeated for years in the biographical and critical literature about her.) Religion was another. Shirley was untroubled by Stanley's Jewishness, but a number of her acquaintances, reflecting the disdain for mixed marriages then pervasive, expressed surprise that she would date him. Though Syracuse was less conservative than the Uni-versity of Rochester, mixing religions (and even more so races, which was illegal in most states) was nonetheless frowned upon.

Primarily on religious grounds, Shirley's parents expressed strong opposition to the relationship, which they discovered over the sum-mer, when a flurry of letters from Stanley made it impossible to conceal. Geraldine, who found out first, did not approve of her daughter's dating a Jew, but also did not forbid Shirley to continue the relationship—perhaps hoping, as parents often do, that it would quietly fade away. Geraldine did, however, suggest that Leslie, whom Stanley nicknamed "Stonewall," should not be told. The secret inevitably came out when Stanley showed up in Rochester for an impromptu visit. The couple were sitting together on the front porch when Shirley's parents drove up: she had thought they were out of town, but Leslie and Geraldine changed their plans without telling her. Unwilling to confront Leslie, Stanley leaped over the railing and ran off. Shirley had no choice but to go after him, all the while dreading the scene that would eventually ensue at home. Stanley later tried to explain that he was self-conscious because he hadn't shaved; he didn't want to meet her father for the first time "looking enough of a bum to confirm his worst suspicions." But Shirley was furious at his rudeness. Geraldine had raised her with certain standards of behavior: you don't turn tail and run at the sight of your girlfriend's parents, no matter how badly you might need to shave.

Her doubts notwithstanding, Shirley quickly recognized Stanley as the intellectual partner for whom she had been waiting all her life: attractive (if not conventionally handsome), sexual, funny, and fearfully brilliant. "Your intellect is a half-crazed centaur," she wrote in a poem addressed to him. In *Hangsaman*, Natalie muses that "no one can really love a person who is not superior in every way." For the first time, Shirley had found a man whose intellect she could truly admire.

Shirley shared with Stanley her obsessions with Villon and the commedia dell'arte, as well as new favorites Swinburne and Dowson. She adopted his all-lowercase typing style—Stanley had recently given up the shift key, likely under the influence of E. E. Cummings, whose poetry he had read so many times he knew much of it by heart—and would continue to type drafts and informal letters in lowercase for the rest of her life. They wrote each other notes in code, using Hebrew letters to spell out English words. And she started making humorous drawings to share with him, depicting herself with a cartoon character that is a cross between a penguin and an eagle: a squat figure with giant feet, a large beak, and a perpetual scowl. (They sometimes called it Boid-Schmoid.) The Shirley figure is much taller, with wavy hair sticking out from her head in every direction. In one, Shirley bends down toward the bird, who points his beak at her. The caption reads: "He wants to know why no one ever kisses him passionately."

They were a perfect pairing: writer and critic, gentile and Jew, S and S. Perhaps they completed each other too well. Natalie, in the throes of her delusion, imagines that a person could be destroyed by a "single antago-nist . . . who was calculated to be strong in exactly the right points." For Shirley, that antagonist was Stanley. Their symbiosis was always in danger of turning parasitic. "Stanley left me tonight with a powerful feeling of anticlimax, determined never to see me again," Shirley wrote in her diary on March 22, 1938, after the two of them had spent four hours together in nearby Thornden Park. She was certain he would reappear to take her out the following week. In fact, he held out for nearly two weeks before calling her again. It wasn't from lack of interest: he was alarmed by the violence of his feelings for her. "all along i had been so dazed by you that i couldn't see you more than once a week and keep my sanity," he admitted later. He went home for the Easter break determined to get a grip on himself, resume his normal routine, and cut Shirley out of his life "like a cancer." Instead, he "came back, made straight for lima cottage, and stayed there until the summer began."

At first, it was Shirley who set the terms. She bragged to Stanley that she could make him do anything she wished, and he did not deny it. "He is absolutely where I wanted," she gloated after one of those early nights together. "I am proud, and completely powerful." When things were good between them, Shirley was the happiest she had ever been. In May she began a story with the lines, "I leaned my head back against Stan's shoulders and relaxed. I was at peace." From early on, she took on the role of his caretaker: a note to herself includes reminders to "give Stan time to read," "make him go to YCL meetings," "see that he gets some sleep," and "make him laugh tonight." Yet she worried about how their balance of power could change. The idea of falling in love with Stanley frightened her: "he could break me mentally if he chose."

Love, look with favor....
Stanley

Stanley inscribed
his yearbook
photographs
to Shirley
with romantic
quotations.

For all his ardor—"Did I remember yet today to tell you that I love you?" he would ask her daily—Stanley could be cold and inattentive. "I must beg him to come, tease him and argue with him to begrudge me— and so condescendingly!—ten minutes of his time," Shirley complained to Jeanou. He was opinionated, bossy, and dismissive of Shirley's taste in literature, preferring the modernists to the nineteenth-century writers she adored. And he turned the full force of his critical acumen on her, belittling her pitilessly, just as her mother had. In one of Shirley's notebooks, he corrected her use of the abbreviation "cf." in a memo— to herself. A draft of one of her college poems displays his merciless annotations, culminating in "Marx knows [Stanley's substitute for "God knows"] you ain't no poet." When they disagreed politically, he insulted her by calling her a debutante. If he had not yet mastered the art of the literary takedown, his verbal arrows already showed expert aim: how that word must have stung.

Stanley's communism was an initial source of dispute. Politics interested Shirley "less than does sanskrit"—presumably the most boring thing she could think of. She attended a few meetings of the YCL to please him, but she never joined the Party. As a writer who was already developing a very different style, Shirley found Stanley's views on proletarian literature anathema. At Rochester, she had heard the writer Burton Holmes speak about his travels in the Soviet Union and was appalled by his reports of Stalin's repression of religion and art. "I think any nation which can do to Beauty what they have done must be a race of idiots," she wrote afterward. Where Stanley admired the gritty realism of John Steinbeck and John Dos Passos, she preferred the more esoteric high modernism of Djuna Barnes: both the early novel *Ryder* (1928), written in a bawdy mock-Elizabethan style, and the better-known *Nightwood* (1936), a dreamlike chronicle of a lesbian love affair in 1920s Paris.

During their first summer apart, Shirley briefly declared her allegiance to the Party and began reading the *Daily Worker*, probably just to annoy her conservative father. Her pose fell apart at once. Why, she wondered in a letter to Stanley, must she be branded a capitalist oppressor simply for neglecting to declare herself on the side of revolution? Couldn't she be politically neutral? His response, in a letter that ran to fifteen pages, was harsh. No one could be neutral in the class struggle, he told her. More important, as a writer, with a heightened sensitivity to injustice, misery, war, poverty, and other social problems, she had an even greater obligation to "portray life, to write true. if the major feature of life today is misery and starvation, you must show misery and starvation." Art that failed to do so would ultimately fade away: "it cannot meet the inflexible criterion of literary worth, 'is this thing true? is this the way things were?'" Hurtfully, he lumped her story "Janice"—which she had thought he admired—among the failures, calling it "a finger exercise, well done, but meaningless." He had praised it, he said, because it showed "a style graphic and economical enough to say something and say it well someday." Perhaps in an attempt to be conciliatory, he allowed that her blinkered perspective wasn't her fault; it stemmed directly from her upbringing. "when you add knowledge to [your sensitivity], and not only feel evil but understand it, you will almost certainly be a great writer." Eventually Stanley would abandon these inflexible standards and acknowledge that literature had a meaning and a purpose beyond the political. But in his youthful zeal, he was unable to look past ideology.

More problematic was Stanley's persistent interest in other women, which he saw no reason to hide. Dowson's poem about a man who confesses infidelity even as he pines for his lost love—"I have been faithful to thee, Cynara, in my fashion!"—became their personal shorthand. ("My fashion has been acting up again," Stanley would sometimes say, addressing Shirley as "Cynara," after he had been out with another woman.) As much as he loved Shirley—and he was already deeply in love with her—Stanley, embracing a self-styled polyamorous philosophy, saw no reason to limit himself to a single woman. He believed he held the moral high ground: open marriage was a Communist principle. His hero John Reed—Stanley recommended *Ten Days That Shook the World*, Reed's eyewitness account of the Russian Revolution, to anyone who would listen—was notorious for his affairs. Shirley, too, was welcome to go out with whomever she liked, he asserted rather disingenuously. She would take him up on it only once.

Stanley's dalliances with other women left Shirley profoundly unsettled. "I'll do anything you want, only don't leave me alone without you anymore," she implored him in an unsent letter that spring. One particularly upsetting incident involved Florence Shapiro, the art student from Queens whom Stanley had met through the YCL. Stanley, neglecting to mention he had a new girlfriend, invited Florence to his room one night. "He kept making remarks indicating that he liked my figure," Florence recalls. Then Shirley walked in. After that, Shirley never let Florence forget that she was in charge. "She didn't like me and she let me know it," Florence remembers more than seventy years later. The new couple had scenes in which Shirley would cry and throw Stanley out, then telephone his fraternity house over and over, worried that he had caught pneumonia outside in the cold. Later she would berate herself for her cruelty to him. "Stanley, crawling, is still powerful," she admitted soon after they met.

——

THE RELATIONSHIP BECAME more contentious over the summer of
1938. Instead of visiting Jeanou in Paris for Bastille Day, as the two
friends had once planned—a trip that, even if the Jacksons had allowed
it, the imminent outbreak of war now made virtually impossible—Shirley returned home to Rochester to resume her long-standing routine of
golf, dinner at the country club, and exploring the city's cafés and secondhand bookstores with Elizabeth Young. Stanley enjoyed his usual
freedom, first crashing with Walter Bernstein at Dartmouth and then
heading to New York for his brother's bar mitzvah before starting his
$20-a-week blue-collar job at the paper mill in Erving, Massachusetts.
This endeavor was met with skepticism: the workers at his father's paper
business, as well as the barbers at the local barbershop where Stanley
had been getting his hair cut since childhood, all predicted that he
would not last two weeks at manual labor. "they will eat those words
like radishes," he vowed. In fact, he made it through nearly two months.

While apart, Shirley and Stanley wrote to each other addictively,
sometimes twice in a day. Never published, the letters are thrilling to
read: witty, furious, and often brilliant. Shirley's warmth and humor
bubble up from her pages. As a teenager, she had developed her voice
in correspondence with an imaginary boyfriend; now, at last, her correspondent was flesh and blood—and did not hesitate to remind her of
his corporeality. "for god's sake can you think of any telepathic way
by which i can get myself into your arms and stay there?" she wrote in
early June. Stanley responded no less effusively: "i ought to stop wasting typewriter ink in letters, rush to rochester, and grab you in my arms,
which is what i want to do more than anything in the world."

Stanley filled his letters with gossip about mutual friends, humorous
anecdotes, and commentary on his reading, which proceeded at a fre-
netic pace. In a single week he mentions plays by Archibald MacLeish;
fiction by Jean Toomer, William Saroyan ("every once in awhile the
goddamned armenian writes a marvelous story, buried in all that trash"),
James Gould Cozzens, and *New Yorker* art critic Robert Coates; literary
theory by Yvor Winters; and, for a break, James Thurber's humor. He

had moments of tenderness: during a rare phone call, when he heard Shirley's voice for the first time in two weeks, he wept. But his written register tended to the brash and bawdy. He addressed Shirley by inventive, sometimes vulgar pet names ("darling slut") and was forthright about his physical longing for her. Just to look at one of her letters, he avowed, gave him an erection. He repeatedly begged her to send him a lock of her pubic hair. And he berated her for any perceived indifference, especially if she failed to write back promptly enough.

Stanley's love for Shirley, however, did not prevent him from pursuing other women, especially when he was drinking. At his brother's bar mitzvah, he drank an entire quart of scotch, sneaked out with two more bottles in his pockets, and ended up at the apartment of three female acquaintances living a life of "genuine bohemia," with people sitting all over the floor, the corners littered with empty liquor bottles, and the walls hung with bad oil paintings, generally nudes, made by friends. The girls who lived there lay around "in various stages of undress," he reported, idly swatting at the bedbugs and cockroaches. Stanley retained enough of his bourgeois upbringing to be disgusted by the filth, but he found the girls alluring. "i fondled them all indiscriminately [and] called all three of them 'baby.'" He might well have slept with one or more of them, but for the fact that he was "so drunk that i couldn't get a hard on to save my life." Also, he was afraid of the bedbugs.

Shirley refrained from commenting on this episode, but Stanley continued to detail his escapades in a manner that even a woman less sensitive and devoted might have found distressing. "i promised you a précis of the female situation here," he wrote from Erving, describing four girls in the factory who had caught his eye. One, "a polish slut of twenty-six," was "damned good-looking in a consumptive way"; another was a "buxom creature" who drove Stanley into "fearful erections" every time he worked opposite her, until he discovered that she was a "mental defective." Describing a weekend spent with his family at a Borscht Belt hotel ("typical jewish middle-class summer resort, fabulously expensive, excessively somnolent"), he related a tale about an abortive attempt at seduction that might have sparked guffaws from Walter Bernstein but understandably failed to amuse his possessive girlfriend:

i also made a play for two girls that i had seen together all that day, getting them apart and telling them practically the same thing. i was coming along pretty well with the older one when i began to feel lousy and went to bed (be it forever to my credit that when she said what, not leaving so early? why the evening is young, i said yes, too young for me). the next day the two girls drove home with us. naturally, as i could have expected, they were mother and daughter.

Stanley sometimes tried to soothe Shirley's feelings after these dalliances. "you have forever spoiled me for other girls," he told her after one episode. But he truly seems to have felt obliged to be transparent about both his beliefs and his activities: he regarded monogamy as a politically and philosophically useless enterprise, and he saw no reason to restrict himself. The obvious argument—that Shirley wanted him to—did not compel him in the least.

Stanley's insistence on his own moral rectitude was particularly hard for Shirley to handle. She tried her best to take his escapades as casually as he seemed to, but—to her shame—each one made her "all sick inside." "if it turns you queasy you are a fool," he responded unsympathetically. Rather cruelly, he made it clear that both her jealousy and her conventional insistence upon monogamy were repellent to him. "it was a copulation, simply that and nothing more," he scolded her when she ventured to complain about his sleeping around. Casual sex was one thing; his love for her was entirely separate. Indeed, he was capable of declaring his love in the most romantic terms in the very same letters that detailed his infidelities.

The cycle of infidelity, fury, and forgiveness would repeat over and over, each time resolving with Shirley's restoration of Stanley to the role in which he mattered most to her: her creative sounding board and the arbiter of her talent. "o mightiest among men," she addressed him just a few weeks after one of his betrayals (tongue only partly in cheek), lamenting that she hadn't been able to continue with the novel she had been writing, because Young had brutally damaged her self-confidence.

worst of it is, i can see damn well myself that it's good, but this constant belittling has made me feel that perhaps i may be kidding myself. . . . is she telling the truth? is there anything in the world that can prove to her (and to me, now) that i *can* write? sure, i'm a sap for trying to write a novel, but . . . it's a *good* novel.

Stanley tried to be supportive, but since Shirley refused to show him the novel-in-progress, there wasn't much he could say. "i think you are potentially the greatest writer in the world, [and] wish you had something to write about," he wrote back. In response, Shirley tried to break up with him again. With his usual equanimity—on the back of her breakup letter, he composed a to-do list—Stanley paid no attention. Jeanou told Shirley she was being rash. "Pride is nice," she wrote from Paris. "I think that love is nicer." Upon their return to Syracuse, Shirley and Stanley were once again inseparable.

"HAVE YOU PERFORMED any incantations lately?" Stanley's friend Jay Williams greeted Shirley at a party in the fall of 1938. Jay and Stanley had met the previous summer at Camp Copake, the Borscht Belt resort Walter's family frequented, where Jay, an actor, musician, and Communist, was on the social staff, teaching fencing and staging theatrical performances. Later he became involved with the Group Theatre, the influential New York drama collective, and eventually wrote a successful series of children's books. Charismatic and charming, he had a penchant for saying and doing outrageous things that appealed to both Shirley and Stanley. At their first encounter, he told Shirley nonchalantly that his backpack contained a dead baby that he planned to roast over a campfire.

By the time Stanley introduced her to Jay, Shirley had been studying the occult for several years. Her interest likely began with *The Golden Bough* and the paper she wrote about witchcraft while at the University of Rochester. During the previous summer at home, she acquired a pack of tarot cards and began to learn how to use them, a skill with which she

Jackson began seriously studying witchcraft during her college years.

would entertain friends throughout her life. (At least once, she dressed up as a gypsy and read tarot at a Bennington College fair, to the students' delight.) Together she and Elizabeth Young pored over Émile Grillot de Givry's *Witchcraft, Magic, and Alchemy*, a richly illustrated compendium of occult iconography, including demonology, folklore about witches and sorcerers, and detailed instructions for summoning spirits. And she begged Young, who was working in the English department at the University of Rochester and had privileged access to the library, to steal a rare copy of Joseph Glanvill's *Saducismus Triumphatus*, a book about witchcraft dating from the 1680s that has been credited with influencing Cotton Mather's justification of the Salem witch trials. Young declined; Shirley would have to study the book in the library.

Glanvill, a clergyman with a sideline in the occult, intended his book as a treatise to prove the existence of witches. While skeptics might declare that what appeared to be supernatural power was in fact only trickery, Glanvill attempted to give evidence that witches were real, including accounts of witches' sabbaths: meetings to which they flew naked on brooms, where they would eat and drink with the devil. He described famous hauntings and possessions such as the Drummer of Tedworth, an episode in which an Englishman reported hearing a loud drumming noise on the outside of his house. (In one of the early supernatural manifestations in *The Haunting of Hill House*, a ghostly presence pounds similarly on the characters' bedroom doors.) Shirley would later use quotations from Glanvill's book as epigraphs to each section of *The Lottery*.

Jay Williams, too, was deeply interested in magic: he had made Stanley a protective talisman, "an intricate thing with names of evil gods all over it" and other words that Shirley, despite her studies, did not recognize. Staunch atheist though he was, Stanley was superstitious enough to keep the talisman among his treasured possessions. At Jay's second meeting with Shirley, he promised to perform a black mass in which he would make the devil appear in the form of a beautiful woman riding on a tiger. Shirley was pleased by the idea. "May I ask it for anything I want?" she asked Jay. "Anything you want," he replied, "only you must be prepared to pay a price." She said that she was willing to pay any price other than giving up Stanley, and Jay frowned. "No price is too great for the devil," he said.

A few days later, she and Stanley went to Jay's apartment, "filled with books, and a typewriter, and a great many knives." Jay took down from the wall a drum that made "a soft crumbling sound," and as they drank wine and talked, he began to tap it lightly. Suddenly Shirley noticed that "the drum was talking louder." "Repeat after me," Jay instructed them, and then he spoke a word that sounded like "Mamaloi." "Mamaloi," Shirley and Stanley repeated. Drumming louder, Jay began to chant "unintelligible words in a strange language," first softly, then louder and louder. He began to point to a far corner of the room, "gesturing and calling, and the drum shouting," but Shirley did not dare turn her head to see what he was pointing at. She held on to Stanley's arm tight with both hands and began to cry. Later Stanley laughed at her for being frightened. Ever rational, he said that Jay's drumming had probably had a hypnotic effect on her and she needed to get over being afraid of ghosts, which, he told her, "are created by malignant and unknowing minds for the terrible entertainment of foolish and even less knowing minds." But Shirley sensed that Jay had access to "all the borderline evil and darkness in the world." (Stanley would eventually prove to be more afraid of the occult than he had let on.)

Shirley would later make bold, if often facetious, claims about her own occult powers, from the jacket copy on her first novel—"perhaps the only contemporary writer who is a practicing amateur witch"—to the rumor that she had caused the publisher Alfred A. Knopf to break his leg in a skiing accident. But now, only twenty-one years old, she was frightened of the possibilities the occult opened up. Owing to her Christian Science background, it was not a stretch for her to believe that another reality, beyond the material world, might exist. Glanvill, too, suggested that witchcraft was not the only aspect of the human psyche that remained mysterious to the rational mind. "We are in the Dark as to *one another's* Purposes and Intendments; and there are a thousand Intrigues in our little Matters, which will not presently confess their design, even to *sagacious Inquisitors*," he wrote in one of the passages from *Saducismus Triumphatus* that Shirley would quote in *The Lottery.*

Shirley's fear may be an indication that she believed witchcraft was possible: one cannot fear something that does not exist. Or it could be a sign of the lack of agency she felt in her own life and her corresponding longing for a way to harness power. Shirley was unable to control her mother, who now could add Stanley to her list of dissatisfactions with her daughter. And Shirley could not control Stanley—a man who was her ideal counterpart in so many ways, but who tormented her with his criticism and his unfaithfulness. What if there was a way to tap into a secret power, to exert control over things that seemed uncontrollable? Shirley would hardly be alone in desiring such magic.

Some months after the episode at the party, Jay Williams took Shirley out to dinner to give her some friendly advice. "You mustn't be so timid with Stanley," he told her. "You let him categorize you and your emotions and your reactions just like he does his own. . . . Logic is an essentially bad thing. It proves things that can't be proved." As if to emphasize the point, he gave her a little book of black magic, "full of antique formulas," so that she could conjure the devil herself. Shirley wrapped it up in silk so that it could not come into physical contact with any of her other possessions and put it away safely.

EVEN IN THE ISOLATIONIST-LEANING United States, it was clear by the fall of 1938 that Europe was on the cusp of a cataclysm. "Everybody here is talking of war," Jeanou wrote from Paris just before Germany, France, Italy, and Great Britain signed the Munich agreement giving the Sudetenland to Germany. Stanley, back in New York before the start of his junior year, felt "the next world war buzzing all around me": men his age were being conscripted in Europe, while he sat at home "scratching my abdomen lovingly and reading degenerate poetry." It would be only a matter of time, he worried, until he was drafted. In Times Square, watching Communist artists drawing political art on a street corner, he recognized Earl Browder, the general secretary of the Communist Party USA, who had run for president in 1936 on the slogan "Communism is 20th-century Americanism." "Hello, comrade," Stanley greeted him, and was pleased when Browder greeted him back.

His efforts at writing fiction unsuccessful, Stanley now turned to poetry as an outlet for his ideology. He was mainly interested in writers whose political bent suited him, especially W. H. Auden, who would soon embark on a reading tour of American colleges. On a visit to Dartmouth, the poet slept on Walter Bernstein's floor: "we stayed up most of the night talking and he is really a good guy," Walter reported. Stanley also admired Kenneth Fearing, who had become as well-known for his unorthodox writing process as for his poetry of the Depression. His method was to bring a new poem to each weekly meeting of a labor organization he belonged to, "composed mainly of semi-illiterate immigrant workers living on the East side of New York," Stanley wrote in an essay. "He reads his work to them, writes down all their criticisms, comments, and suggestions, and then takes the poem back and rewrites it until it satisfies them." Perhaps more than the poetry itself, Stanley admired Fearing's efforts to bring poetry to the masses. "No living and vital art is possible unless it is in touch with the people," he argued, echoing Kenneth Burke's remarks several years earlier at the first American Writers' Congress. At the same time, he also loved the very different work of E. E. Cummings, whose formal experimentation he found "truly liberating."

Stanley and Shirley both made a few efforts at blank verse, but they were more interested in ways they could experiment within the strictures of poetic form. Stanley wrote only a handful of poems—creative writing held his attention far less than critical thinking—but one in particular is memorable. Titled "Love Sonnet After Munich" and likely written in the fall of 1938, it is a sonnet using the acrostic "Shirley Jackson" (her name conveniently fourteen letters long). In addition to that formal constraint, Stanley wrote the sonnet in "analyzed rhyme," a complicated scheme in which vowel and consonant sounds are arranged in an alternating pattern to give the effect of rhyme without actually rhyming. Here is the first stanza:

> *Should bombers come, you would be by my side,*
> *Holding your hand in mine, your muscles numb*
> *In fear, your temples hot with frightened blood,*
> *Rivalling the warmth they knew in gayer time.*

"i don't use old eyetalian forms because they are old eyetalian forms, but because i am looking for a form strong enough to handle modern poetry, critically good and intelligible to workers," Stanley defended himself to Jay Williams. But it is clear that the form was mainly what interested him; the poem's subject matter—lovers who die together in war—is hackneyed.

Shirley's efforts were more successful. Her "Letter to a Soldier," an effort at Steinbeckian working-class realism, took the form of a traditional sonnet, with one small twist:

> *My dear,*
>   *It's lonely now that you are gone,*
> *And I grow sick of women and of rain.*
> *We all feel strange at being left alone*
> *And wonder when the Spring will come again.*
> *I have enough to eat, but I have found*

The seeds you planted will not grow this year—
The rain has gone too deep into the ground
For anything to grow. Will you be here
In time to plant again? The papers said
You would be home by summer. When you come
Bring nothing for the baby. He is dead.
The work will be less hard when you are home
But I'm afraid the season will be late
For growing things. However, I shall wait.

In contrast to Stanley's acrostic and elaborate rhyme scheme, Shirley's language and style are simple, in keeping with her subject—an ordinary farming woman writing to her husband at war. In a poem of 119 words, 100 are just one syllable. But together they tell the haunting story of a woman who seems to be writing about her farm, but is actually mourning her lost fertility. There is no Sandburg-style wordplay or linguistic absurdity of the sort she had previously been experimenting with—Stanley had pushed her in a different direction. He wrote proudly to Jay that the line about the baby "knocked the class off its feet." He was thrilled by her writing, and by her. "shoiley and i go on being happy like anything. . . . that shoiley is ten times nicer than she has ever been, so smart, so beautiful," he crowed.

Jackson wasn't certain enough of her poetry to publish it yet. In October 1938 she made her debut in the *Syracusan*, the college literary and humor magazine, which self-consciously styled itself after the still-new literary and humor magazine that was quickly becoming the place for aspiring writers to aspire to. Jackson's first piece, "Y and I," was a *New Yorker*–style "casual"—a light memoiristic essay that may or may not be fiction. It describes an apparently simple errand to buy chess pieces that turns into a madcap trip around a department store, in which Y and the narrator startle the very proper saleswomen by pretending to be Nazi spies. The ending dissolves into absurdity: the two girls are flummoxed by directions to the sporting department in the basement and slink home, defeated, to play bridge. The department-store setting is reminiscent of James Gould Cozzens's novel *Castaway* (1934), in which a man descends into madness after becoming trapped in a similar store. Stanley was fascinated by the novel and insisted that Shirley read it. But there is no darkness in her story, other than the absurdity, even in 1938, of finding Nazi spies in a small-town department store.

She satirized her experiments in the occult the following month with "Y and I and the Ouija Board," another lighthearted romp. Here the two girls find themselves in conversation with a smart-talking Ouija board, which turns out to be nursing a grudge against Y for having once dropped it. After delivering a series of wisecracks, it suggests that they all play a hand of bridge (which it wins) and then dictates a recipe for fudge. The contributors' notes at the start of the issue report that Shirley "would like us to believe that she actually owned this Ouija board, but then she also swears that the Jacksons have a family ghost named Eric the Red who lives in the checkbook." In "The Smoking Room," another story likely written around the same time, Jackson took a similarly lighthearted approach to the occult. Here the devil appears to the narrator while she is writing a school paper and asks her to sign a contract selling him her soul, but she outsmarts him into selling her his soul instead. He is finally cowed by the appearance of the dorm mother, who tells him he is a fire hazard and threatens to report him to the dean of women. Nothing in either of these stories suggests that the author had spent much of her summer poring over arcane handbooks of the supernatural, or that she took any of it at all seriously.

IN THE SPRING OF 1939, as the Spanish Civil War ended with victory for Franco's reign of murderous oppression and Germany peremptorily invaded Czechoslovakia, Shirley was preoccupied with troubles of a more mundane sort: a series of pregnancy scares. Jay Williams gave her various charms to bring on her period, which achieved the desired results. Unwilling to continue relying on magic alone, she acquired a pessary: a type of diaphragm similar to the one immortalized in Mary McCarthy's *The Group*, in which a character famously leaves her newly acquired birth control device under a park bench. As McCarthy's novel—which was published in 1963 but takes place in the mid- to late

1930s—makes clear, a woman was technically supposed to either be married or have a health reason for requiring the device, but the rules were not always strictly enforced. "All you need is a straight face, a quick story, and a consciousness that . . . dammit, you can do it," Shirley counseled a friend. Walter Bernstein and Frank Orenstein, with whom Stanley shared all the details of his sex life, were suitably impressed. "What do you do to get the pessary out, stand Shirley on her head and shake her?" joked the less experienced Walter. When they separated again for the summer break, Stanley held on to the pessary. Shirley, who was headed back to Rochester, probably did not want to risk the possibility that Geraldine, with her propensity for snooping, would discover it. (In *The Group*, the diaphragm's owner likewise struggles to figure out where to store it safely—surely not in her room at a proper hotel for unmarried women.) Even so, the symbolism of Stanley keeping the token of her sexual liberation could not have been lost on Shirley.

Stanley's plans for the summer were typically ambitious. That year he and Shirley had studied modern literature with Leonard Brown, the star of the Syracuse English department, whom they both came to idolize. At first Brown offended Shirley by chauvinistically suggesting that Stanley had written one of her term papers for her, which led Stanley to worry that Brown and others saw their intellectual relationship as "one-sided." "One-sided—when it takes both of us to keep him on his feet," Shirley snorted. But she came to be as fond of Brown as Stanley was; two decades later, she would dedicate *The Haunting of Hill House* to him. Brown, they would later write, had taught them that the goal of reading and criticizing was "to know and understand, not to like or dislike, and the aim of writing was to get down what you wanted to say, not to gesticulate or impress." Stanley may not always have followed that precept, but at least he believed in it.

Now Brown encouraged his star student to put his talent for literary criticism to use by writing a handbook of poetic form. As a measure of his extraordinary esteem for Stanley, he promised to lecture from the book-in-progress in the poetry course he was teaching that summer, using the pages as soon as they rolled out of Stanley's typewriter—but only if Stanley could complete them in time.

The pressure did not dissuade Stanley from making his customary visit to Walter at Dartmouth, where he proudly displayed Shirley's pessary to anyone who would pay attention. He then spent several weeks in New York, where Shirley managed to join him, staying with Stanley's YCL friend Jesse Zel Lurie and his wife, Irene, in their apartment on West Tenth Street. The highlight of their New York City sojourn was a visit to the remarkable 1939 World's Fair, with the slogan "Dawn of a New Day." There Shirley and Stanley had their first look at the new-fangled invention called television, as well as the electric typewriter, the fluorescent lightbulb, and nylon fabric—famously said to be made from coal, air, and water. As the Nazi threat loomed, the fair promoted cultural awareness and diplomacy, with more than sixty countries participating. Many years later, Stanley would write an article for *The New Yorker* about the time capsule that was buried at the fair, which contained writings by Albert Einstein and Thomas Mann, a pack of Camels, a Mickey Mouse watch, and other tokens of the era. (The time capsule is scheduled to be unearthed in 6939, five thousand years after it was buried.) By the beginning of July Stanley was back in Syracuse, working at a furious pace on his book, with the goal of completing two chapters each week.

Shirley returned to Rochester to prepare for an adventure to rival her cruise through the Panama Canal six years earlier: a cross-country family road trip culminating in an extended visit to San Francisco, to which she hadn't returned since the move to Rochester. She was excited about the trip, but anxious about leaving Stanley to his own devices for most of the summer—so much so that she even sent him a sketch she had written during one of their breakups, in which she spilled out into her notebook all her desperation at the thought of losing him. "People don't just part like that," it concludes. "They don't have so much together and then so much apart—He can't have anything apart from me because he has taken so much from me." Ever editing herself, she crossed out the word "part" in the first sentence and wrote in "separate": even at her lowest, her style still mattered. The original title of the piece was "Prayer," which Shirley removed before sending it to her atheist boyfriend. "i decided i wanted to say something and did," she told him.

Stanley's only reaction was aesthetic: he called the sketch "marvelous" and encouraged her to write "more in the same style, a great deal more." But he was apparently unwilling to hear what she was trying to say. He loved her as much as ever, and told her so in each letter, but he remained unconvinced of monogamy's merits. Though he was working a punishing schedule on the book, he reserved the hours after ten p.m. to "read or fuck." What he needed more than anything else, he told her matter-of-factly, was to "look at someone's face beside my own in the mirror when i get up in the morning." As usual, he had a few prospects in mind, including a cute redhead in his apartment building and an older woman named Tony, who shared his interest in literary criticism and pressed books upon him.

Stanley's drudgery was interrupted by a visit to Syracuse by Kenneth Burke, the iconoclastic critic who had already made a name for himself as the author of several major works of literary theory. Though nominally a Marxist sympathizer, he was equally famous for his idiosyncratic approach to literary study: fearing the "assembly line" of academia, he had dropped out of Columbia just before graduating and fled to Greenwich Village to begin his writing career. When Burke arrived at Syracuse that summer, he was fresh from the third and final American Writers' Congress, where he had delivered "The Rhetoric of Hitler's 'Battle,'" a magisterial lecture analyzing the language of *Mein Kampf.* The congress, like many of its attendees, had essentially abandoned its original Communist leaning: Malcolm Cowley reported in *The New Republic* that aside from an address by Edvard Beneš, the former president of Czechoslovakia, "there was not much talk of the political situation; it was an ominous background that was taken for granted."

Stanley was instantly captivated by Burke's brilliant conversation. To listen to him, he wrote to Shirley, was "an intellectual thrill of the highest order. . . . the man is really the finest brain and the loosest tongue i have ever seen." Burke's absorption in his thoughts was so complete that if he and Stanley were conversing while walking down a hall and Stanley turned to go down the stairway, Burke would keep walking and talking until he ran into the wall: "they used to tell those stories about einstein, and i never believed them." He was ecstatic when Brown invited him and Burke to spend an afternoon at Brown's cottage in Borodino, by Lake Skaneateles. Stanley was relaxing on the dock with a typescript of Burke's latest opus when a page blew into the water. He was aghast, but Burke only laughed. "Aha, your subconscious is trying to destroy my manuscript!" he said. It was the beginning of a friendship that lasted for the rest of Stanley's life and had an immense impact on both his intellectual development and his career. Cowley, a friend of Burke's, also gave a talk at Syracuse that summer, but Stanley found him less impressive. "i didn't realize what a thrill (actual physical thrill) it was to hear burke until i heard cowley, who after all is just an ordinary mortal," he reported to Shirley. The two men remained friendly—Cowley, along with other *New Republic* colleagues, attended Stanley and Shirley's wedding the following year—but would never be close.

Shirley must have been glad to hear Stanley more enthusiastic about Burke than about the fetching redhead upstairs. She set off on her cross-country journey—in the days before interstate highways, a weeks-long drive—anxious about the extended period of time before they would see each other again. Her parents' disapproval notwithstanding, she faithfully wrote to Stanley at each stop, in letters that were so long and rapturous that she sometimes ran out of ink in the middle and had to switch to pencil. By now, the terrible years of drought were over and the atmosphere of the Midwest and the Plains states was more cheerful. "Minnesota comes close to my idea of heaven—it's all farming country, and very green," she wrote. "I never knew what hay really smelled like—so sweet." In South Dakota, she was awed by the grasshoppers— "a foot and a half long . . . with incredibly nasty dispositions"—and by the friendliness of the locals: "I'd forgotten what it was like to sit in a gas station for an hour and talk to other people driving through." In the Black Hills, she rediscovered her love of mountains, for which, she suddenly realized, she had been "acutely homesick" in the East. The peace she found in nature was a consoling antidote to the din of her anxiety:

> Someday . . . I shall have a little house with no sides on top of a mountain. It must be a mountain with pine trees, and little streams and deer and even bees. . . . We stopped on top of one today, and I

went far off by myself and sat and looked, and I didn't even think about you, my darling. I just remembered all the times at home—even with you—that I've wanted something and couldn't tell what it was. . . . Way deep inside me all the restlessness has gone away, and I could stay here from now on, even without you. I wouldn't *want* to, but it wouldn't drive me crazy, or into that desolate, no-insides feeling I'd have anywhere else. I think that my restlessness and nervousness at home is an insane seeking for some over-whelming stability which I find here in this vast quiet.

In early August 1939, nearly six years to the day after they set sail for New York, the Jacksons arrived in San Francisco. Two years after the Nanking massacre, in which Japanese troops committed murder and mass rape in the Chinese capital, the city, fearful that Japanese aggression would soon reach the West Coast, was gripped by anti-Japanese hysteria. Chinese merchants displayed signs reading "We Are Chinese," and Shirley's uncle Clifford, who took her and Barry sightseeing, wouldn't allow either of them to enter a Japanese-owned business. When Barry offered a piece of Japanese candy to a Chinese beggar child, the boy, insulted, slapped it out of his hand. More interested in curios than politics, Shirley, who had recently taken to wearing a charm bracelet with skull ornaments, was thrilled to find a hand-carved miniature skull, "the most delicate and intricate little thing," for only a quarter.

She was overjoyed to be back in her native city. "i'd forgotten, hadn't i? i mean, about fog and about hills and about oceans and things? because it's wonderful." The only drawback was having to deal with her grandmother, who had found an apartment for the Jacksons to stay in, perched on a hill beside the Presidio, "very practical . . . with a garage and a radio and a piano and lots of ashtrays," but only two beds for the four of them. "she has been concentrating for two weeks on making mary baker eddy and god think of a place for barry to sleep," Shirley wrote with her customary irony about Christian Science.

Stanley, who had never been farther west than Chicago, complained sourly that Shirley's letters sounded like a "movie-travelogue." He must have been deeply envious of both her adventures and her freedom. His writing was proceeding at a remarkable clip—by the end of July, he had written nearly six chapters of his book—but he was burning out. Until then, he had been "solidly chaste and completely faithful" for the entire summer, but it was "not from lack of trying," as he told her. Now he renewed his efforts.

At the same time, tensions between Shirley and her parents, likely exacerbated by the enforced proximity of the transcontinental car ride, were on the verge of exploding. That summer Geraldine and Shirley had enjoyed a rapprochement of sorts: they had even begun sitting on Shirley's bed together in the evenings, talking and smoking cigarettes. Before leaving Rochester, they attended a luncheon at which the menu was composed entirely of Shirley's least favorite foods: cold tomato soup, cottage cheese salad, cauliflower. Geraldine couldn't help but get a kick out of Shirley's discomfort: when lobster was served as the main course ("a form of fish, i believe . . . [it] makes me sick"), she took one look at her seafood-averse daughter's face and "indulged in a fit of coughing which left her with a very red face and nearly crying." But afterward Geraldine took Shirley out for a sandwich and the two of them laughed together about the incident.

Now their truce disintegrated. *The Grapes of Wrath*, Steinbeck's masterpiece about the plight of migrants to California in the wake of the Depression, had appeared a few months earlier. Stanley stayed up all night reading it and judged it "one of the finest modern novels," despite its commercial appeal. Shirley's antiproletarian father forbade her to read the novel, but she did so anyway. He found out and they argued, with Leslie, a corporation executive and staunch conservative, fulminating against the "dirty Reds" who were overrunning California. Shirley meekly ventured that Communists might not be as bad as he thought they were, which resulted only in his refusing to speak to her for the rest of the day.

That night, over dinner with some old family friends, Leslie took advantage of a lull in conversation to announce, "My daughter's one of those Reds." Everyone turned to stare at Shirley, who sat silently, "a little drunk and . . . mad and sort of ashamed." The rest of the table got into the fun, asking her to sing the Internationale. Looking around for a supportive face, Shirley saw her mother and brother both laughing at her; her father sat silently. In desperation, she knocked over her glass of champagne, creating a distraction. Later, she worried that her father might be angry enough to forbid her to return to Syracuse. "stanley, please help me," she implored.

Stanley did not do well when confronted with emotional scenes. Not only was he unable to reassure her—the best he could do was to call Leslie "a first-class bigot and a thoroughly stupid old fathead"—but he had something devastating to tell her. In a previous letter he had admitted to sleeping with an ex-flame named Martha, who had already stoked Shirley's jealousy the previous summer. Now he had gone to bed with the cute redhead upstairs—and had somehow neglected to use a condom. He was terrified that the girl might become pregnant. Still, always mindful of his work, he enclosed in the same letter a few more chapters of the book for Shirley to comment on and asked for her advice regarding whether to publish it now or add another section. "see that you love me despite my ridiculous transcendental groin (oh the flesh is so weak, and the spirit generally willing into the bargain) and that you tell me so regularly," he concluded.

Shirley initially responded with fury. "i've read your letter four times and still all i can get out of it is that you're probably a father by now," she wrote.

> instead of slapping your wrist i ought to kick you in the face you bastard. sometimes you get a little beyond your abilities and when that happens . . . you generally try to solve things your own way and someone gets hurt. it's usually me. by which i mean that when you fuck a lady you don't know very well you do it with [a] condom and if you don't you damn well don't fuck her.

But she didn't send this letter. How could she have? Stanley had already made it clear that her recriminations were useless. The more she expressed her jealousy, the less he paid attention. Instead, she waited a few days and wrote another letter. This one was solely about the book: she did not allow herself a single word about the incident with the redhead. It was neither the first time nor the last that she would swallow her rage at his infidelity.

The following week Shirley became so sick she was admitted to the hospital. At first the doctors thought it was mumps, then diphtheria; the final diagnosis was a virulent throat infection. Unable to eat or drink, she lost fifteen pounds over the next few weeks. The mental stress of Stanley's repeated infidelity was compounded by her betrayal by her parents. After publicly mocking her, Leslie had left for Rochester, leaving Geraldine and Barry—who had laughed right along—to wait in San Francisco until Shirley recovered, a process that involved daily visits to the doctor for painful injections. So inept was Geraldine as a nurse that, trying to irrigate Shirley's throat, she inadvertently made her swallow a large quantity of hydrogen peroxide, making her even sicker. More poisonous than the peroxide, though, was the belittling and the criticism to which Geraldine had subjected Shirley all her life—priming her to accept a relationship with a man who treated her disrespectfully and shamed her for legitimate and rational desires.

"guess what started it. you and your goddamned ideas," Shirley wrote to Stanley. She was joking—the night she became sick she had gone on a roller coaster, something he had always dared her to do. Still, the metaphorical connection is too rich to ignore. Only days after choking back the words she so dearly wished to say to him, she fell ill with a swollen throat! In a moment of feverish delirium, she thought she saw him enter her hospital room, only to walk out. "you wouldn't stay . . . just closed the door and went away and i could hear your footsteps going down the hall."

Shirley's illness showed Stanley that he was more dependent on her than either of them had thought. He was taken aback by the depth of his concern. "i was half certain that you were dead," he scolded after she failed to send an update on her condition promptly enough. He consoled himself by buying a turntable and records, so that they would "have some music for when we set up housekeeping." On his list were symphonies by Beethoven, Tchaikovsky, Brahms, and Schubert; Bach concerti; Sibelius's *Finlandia*, and miscellaneous Debussy and Wagner, as well as one concession to the pop music of the day: jazz trumpeter

Ziggy Elman's "And the Angels Sing," featuring a klezmer-style solo. Stanley, who admitted that he "never knew, liked, or understood music" before meeting Shirley, was proud to have become a music lover "on the professional scale." But he still couldn't tell the difference between two notes on the piano "unless they are half a kilometer or more apart."

Shirley returned from California bearing a hand-carved wooden chess set as a gift for Stanley. In return he had bought her a complete book of Hogarth's drawings, bound in leather and weighing ten pounds, "the most beautiful book ever printed. . . . the only way i can get it back is to marry her." The two would maintain the custom of buying each other extravagant gifts into their marriage. But if Shirley's illness had initially shocked Stanley into fidelity, he quickly succumbed to yet another "stupidity," as he put it in a letter to Jay: going to bed with a close friend of Shirley's while she was in the next room, "quite drunk, shouting obscene remarks of an uncomplimentary tenor."

Shirley's reaction frightened Stanley so badly that he wrote to Walter for advice. He was worried, he confessed, that she was mentally unstable. Walter approached the situation calmly and sensibly: Stanley should write down Shirley's symptoms, he suggested, and try to figure out what, if anything, triggered her "attacks." "If it's all you say it is," he warned, "it isn't anything to play around with." But Walter also refused to downplay Stanley's responsibility for Shirley's behavior. "A whole lot depends, I think, on your attitude towards her," he wrote. "If you will sacrifice some of your 'integrity' and think of the possible effect on her before you do or even say anything, it might help and will undoubtedly calm her down a lot and make her feel happier and more secure." It was good advice. But Stanley did not heed it—not then, and not in the years to come.

SHIRLEY HAD CAPPED OFF her successful run in the *Syracusan* the previous spring by being elected fiction editor. But shortly after she assumed the post, the other editors decided the magazine should stop publishing stories. "Print them yourself," a friend suggested when she complained.

Thus was born *Spectre*, the "official magazine of the Syracuse University English Club," which Shirley and Stanley launched together that fall. The masthead listed Shirley as editor, Stanley as managing editor, June Mirken on the editorial staff, and Florence Shapiro as an illustrator. Florence joined at Stanley's insistence, but Shirley, who had not forgotten their old enmity, managed to kick her off the publication after the first issue. Stanley also did the magazine's p.r., proudly collecting all the press clippings that mentioned it. Later he would maintain files of both his and Shirley's reviews.

"We called the magazine *Spectre* for obvious reasons," Shirley and Stanley wrote coyly in their first editorial. The name might have been an homage to William Blake—the front page bore his lines "My Spectre before me night and day / Like a wild beast guards my way"—but it was more likely a veiled reference to Marx's warning in *The Communist Manifesto* of the "spectre haunting Europe." (In case anyone missed the reference, an essay in the second issue cited the Marx quote—in a literary context, of course.) They presented it as primarily a literary magazine, but it was not exactly apolitical. Under the heading "We the Editor," Shirley and Stanley opened each issue with an editorial dedicated to a pressing political or social issue. Though the advent of war in Europe would have seemed to be the foremost topic of concern, they used their first editorial to explain the magazine's philosophy. "We haven't any editorial policy except printing what's good," they insisted. "We like experimental forms and we like traditional forms." With "so much that was more important going on outside," some might think it was a bad time to start a literary magazine. But even college literature should reflect reality, they argued, and "it is a good time to start a magazine when people are thinking."

The first issue was written almost entirely by Shirley, Stanley, and their friends. June Mirken contributed a story, "Sorority Girl," about the subtle but pervasive anti-Semitism on campus. Ben Zimmerman, one of Stanley's fraternity brothers, wrote a story about a lynching. Walter Bernstein, under the pseudonym "Myron R. Pleschet," sent in an essay comparing Goya and Daumier. Stanley wrote an essay called "The Need for a New Poetic Form," about the question that had been preoccupying him for several years now: how poetry could better reach the masses, with Auden and Fearing as the primary exemplars. And

Shirley contributed a short story, "Call Me Ishmael" (the title was Stanley's), in which a girl and her mother have vastly different responses to a vagrant woman they encounter on a street corner. Printed, unusually for her, entirely in lowercase, the story revolves rather abstractly around the question of what is real versus what derives meaning solely from other people. The mother, a Geraldine figure, primarily understands the world based on the reactions of others; only the girl is capable of authentic human response. The story is cerebral and a little pedantic, but it still has the quality of strangeness that so often characterizes Shirley's writing—the sense that reality, though still recognizable, appears as if distorted in a mirror.

By the time the second issue appeared that winter, Shirley and Stanley had succeeded in making *Spectre* something of a cause. The first issue had featured a drawing of a nude man, done in a stocky socialist realist style. To generate controversy, Shirley and Stanley goaded the magazine's faculty adviser into objecting to the nudity, which gave them an opening for a cri de coeur about censorship. "If you want to have nude bodies in a campus publication, without corrupting public morals, they have to be female bodies," Shirley and Stanley wrote, deploying the irony that was already a trademark of both their styles. The "censorship" of the art gave them an excuse to broaden their argument to the current political climate. Earl Browder had been banned from speaking at various colleges, including Harvard, Yale, and Dartmouth (where Walter got into trouble for protesting Browder's disinvitation). Regardless of one's political beliefs, the editors insisted, this constituted an insult to intellectual freedom. And the censorship of *Spectre*, they argued somewhat grandiosely, stemmed from a similar impulse. "Censorship, or Repression, or Dictatorship, or Reaction, or whatever you want to call it . . . is the stuff Fascism fattens on."

But *Spectre*'s primary political cause was discrimination against blacks, which was then just beginning to become a major social issue, especially among Jews. (Apart from June Mirken's story in the first issue, the magazine was silent on the subject of anti-Semitism at Syracuse.) Black students could be admitted to Syracuse but were forbidden to live on campus. At the same time, Marian Anderson, the African-American singer whose operatic voice electrified audiences in the late 1930s, had become a cause célèbre when the Daughters of the American Revolution refused to allow her to perform before an integrated audience in Washington, D.C.'s Constitution Hall. Anderson "sells out every time she comes here, but they won't allow negro girls in the college dormitories," the editors protested in the third issue. "Maybe it's all right if you're no closer than the sixth row." After interviewing various Syracuse administrators, they wrote, they had been unable to determine why so few black students were admitted to the university. The primary argument—that there was no place on campus for blacks to live—was prima facie ridiculous: "The overwhelming majority of white students on campus have no slightest objection to living with negro students, and would be pretty stupid and bigoted if they did." But the editorial ended on a note of optimism about the future: the NAACP had recently started a branch on campus. "We wish them all the luck in the world."

Most of what *Spectre* published was typical college literary magazine fare, but a few items stand out. "Big Brown Woman," an appreciation of Bessie Smith by Stanley, reveals his growing range as a critic. Stanley had recently developed a serious interest in jazz and blues, and whenever he was in New York, he visited the nightclubs as often as he could afford to. One of his favorite hangouts was Nick's in Greenwich Village, which held Sunday jam sessions featuring musicians such as Sidney Bechet, Muggsy Spanier, and Jelly Roll Morton, with famous bandleaders Duke Ellington, Louis Armstrong, Count Basie, and others making occasional appearances. Stanley especially favored Nick's because the club declined to enforce the usual two-drink minimum; you could listen all night for the relatively low cover of seventy-five cents. Watching these musicians play, Stanley had an epiphany: popular culture was just as appropriate a subject for criticism as highbrow art. In his writing about blues music, which would remain a lifelong area of fascination, he took on a new tone: warm, enthusiastic, sincere.

At the time, recordings by African-American artists, primarily blues and gospel, were known as "race records." Under a segregated system, the recordings were produced by white-owned record companies and marketed to African-American consumers; white collectors of black music were highly unusual. Alta Williams, the Jackson family's black maid, helped Stanley acquire many of his Bessie Smith records. His observations about them were acute. On the recording of "Trombone Cholly," with Charlie Green, "Bessie talks to that trombone and it stands up and talks back to her." When Louis Armstrong "picked up a phrase or a bar and . . . turned it back on her and sent it up and up and up, clear and round, it was like Bessie singing a duet with herself." And when she sang, he wrote,

> She would rest her bare bronze arms easily at her side, open her well-rouged lips until you could see all of the big white teeth, half close her eyes, and start to sway. . . . Then she would lean forward and let her big full voice roll out over the house. . . . There was nothing you could do about it except sit back and listen and let the sound pour over you like a heavy surf.

Spectre also marked the only time Shirley published poetry under her own name. Three of her poems appeared in the second issue: "Letter to a Soldier" as well as "Black Woman's Story," spoken in the voice of a woman whose husband is lynched, and "Man Talks," about a worker on the skids. Each was a sonnet in traditional form, but the magazine printed them as prose poems, in paragraphs, so that the reader must do the work of discerning the hidden sonnet. The effect is a little obscurantist: Why go to such effort to disguise a poem? Just as she couldn't break prose into short lines and call it free verse (as Stanley had once lectured her), Shirley also couldn't put a poem into paragraph form and call it prose.

The fourth issue was *Spectre*'s last. The cause of its demise was said to be Shirley and Stanley's joint review of three new poetry books: two by Syracuse students and one by her former professor A. E. Johnson. They signed the piece with their initials—hardly a disguise, especially considering that they published many pieces under pseudonyms, including poems and stories by Shirley writing as St. Agatha Ives and Meade Lux (the latter pseudonym an homage to the boogie-woogie pianist Meade Lux Lewis). They went easy on the younger poets, but singled out Johnson as "advocat[ing] retreat and weakness. . . . Professor Johnson is hidden away from the world, and happy in his illusion." Considering what Stanley, who had been practicing the art of the takedown since high school, was capable of, the criticism was not that harsh; but it was apparently the last straw for the Syracuse administration. Commencement 1940 would be the end of *Spectre*, although that fall June Mirken was able to resurrect its spirit in a new, longer-lived magazine called *Tabard*. The relative mildness of the review raises the suspicion that the administration's displeasure might have had more to do with *Spectre*'s polemics about racial discrimination at Syracuse than with the editors' opinion of an English professor's poetry. "The college was glad to be rid of both us and the magazine," Stanley wrote later with pride.

Meanwhile, Shirley and Stanley were trying to settle on their plans for after college. Stanley's hopes of publishing the poetry textbook he had written the previous summer had come to nothing. Despite Brown's encouragement, the educational publisher Scott Foresman had rejected the book, and Stanley shelved the project. Walter Bernstein had already published two stories in *The New Yorker*—"most of which I wrote," Stanley reported glumly of one of them—and spent two weeks working there as a reporter in the summer before their senior year, of which Stanley was hardly able to conceal his jealousy. And if Shirley's father had ever been serious about sending her to Columbia's graduate writing program, that offer was no longer on the table. A story by Shirley in the third issue of *Spectre*, "Had We but World Enough" (another of Stanley's allusive titles), hints at their frame of mind in the spring of 1940. A boy and a girl, walking in the park, want to get married but are waiting for him to get a job. They entertain themselves by fantasizing about how they will set up housekeeping together:

> "If we had fifty dollars every week we could have a swell place. I'd buy furniture and dishes and things."
>
> "We'd have to have a place with a telephone," he said.
>
> "To handle your business calls, no doubt? I don't want a telephone; I want a brown and yellow living room with venetian blinds and comfortable chairs . . ."

"We'd have children, too."

"The hell with you," she said. "You think I'm going to have children and ruin my whole life?"

They laughed. "Twenty children," he said. "All boys."

The answer came in early May, when Stanley received a letter from Bruce Bliven, editor of *The New Republic*, informing him that he had won the magazine's college writing contest. The prize was a summer job in the magazine's New York office. The pay was low and the job was temporary, but it was a start. Stanley accepted at once. If there had ever been any doubt that the two of them would move to New York immediately after graduation, there was no longer. A cartoon Shirley drew around that time depicts her with her arms out wide and her head thrown back in exultation. The caption reads: "She says that from now on with her[,] art is everything."

5.

THE MAD BOHEMIANS

NEW YORK,
NEW HAMPSHIRE,
SYRACUSE, 1940–1942

"well, i like the title," said stanley. "what's the plot?"

"what plot?" i asked.

"the plot of the novel," said stanley, wide-eyed.

"don't be silly," i said. "i let the characters make the plot
as they go along."

"you mean you don't have any idea what's going to
happen?"

"not the slightest," i said proudly.

"but," said stanley rather breathlessly, "people don't write
novels like that."

"*i* do," i told him very smugly indeed.

—*Anthony* (unfinished novel)

N AN INFORMAL CEREMONY—"A BRIEF THREE-MINUTE THING,"
as Stanley described it—Shirley and Stanley were married on Tuesday,
August 13, 1940, at a friend's Manhattan apartment. On the marriage
license, Shirley listed her birth year as 1919. It was as if the three miserable years she had spent in Rochester had been erased and her adult life
had officially begun when she entered Syracuse and met Stanley—

*Shirley's drawing of herself and Stanley in New Hampshire, fall
1941. The figure with the beak is the bird she called her "familiar."*

which, in truth, it had. In a gruffly worded invitation, Stanley advised
friends to "miss the ceremony and come for the liquor." Formal dress was
not expected, he emphasized, and neither were presents: "it is not that
sort of wedding."

If Stanley's tone sounds grim for a man about to be married, it was
likely because the months leading up to the wedding had been filled
with tension. The couple faced determined parental opposition from
both sides. Moe had first confronted Stanley about the relationship
in the summer of 1938, when he discovered long-distance charges on
the phone bill and realized Stanley had been calling "that Mick," as
he referred to his son's *shiksa* girlfriend. In the spring of 1940, back

at their home in Brooklyn, the two of them had their first serious talk about what would happen when Stanley and Shirley were married— *when* and not *if*, he reported to her afterward. The dire news out of Europe must have increased Moe and Lulu's opposition to the marriage. Moe had distant relatives still in Lithuania; two years earlier, his synagogue had been one of the few in New York to hold a service commemorating Kristallnacht. Moe told Stanley he wouldn't say Kaddish for him—the signally harsh measure of essentially declaring his son dead, or at least dead to the family—but "he would be awfully sore and awfully hurt and he wouldn't talk to me for years." Moe also enlisted his friends in the campaign. Stanley got a call one day from his former boss at the paper plant in Erving, who said that he understood perfectly well the desire to sleep with non-Jewish women—in fact, he had a number of such mistresses himself—but, out of respect for his mother, he didn't marry them. Stanley insisted that his relationship with Shirley was, as he put it, "the real business," and by the end of the conversation the man was offering to help them both find jobs in New York. Lulu, for her part, seems to have kept quiet about the matter; she could not have been pleased, but she also would not ostracize her elder son.

Leslie and Geraldine Jackson were no happier about the marriage than Moe was. In the two years since a scruffy Stanley literally jumped off the porch rather than meet his future in-laws face-to-face, the Jacksons' attitude toward him had deteriorated even further. "they will do anything in the world, says my father, to prevent my marrying you, even unto bribery and threats," Shirley reported. The cross-country road trip the previous summer had likely been motivated at least in part by their desire to put distance between their daughter and her unsuitable boyfriend. In the spring of 1940, Shirley's parents announced that for a graduation present they were buying her a plane ticket to spend the summer in California—a major extravagance in the early days of air travel and another obvious effort to separate the couple. They were crestfallen when she told them she would not go: her plan was to move to New York immediately and look for a job. But Geraldine did not give up. "i have come to the conclusion that my family is not so dumb,"

Shirley wrote to Stanley while she was at home in Rochester over the Easter holiday.

> last night they dressed me all up with a red skirt like carmen and my hair done high and red red nails and expensive perfume and red carnations in my hair and silver sandals and a couple of drinks, and they took me to the opera. . . . my mother wore white satin and silver fox and diamonds, and we sat in the mezzanine among a lot of other women all looking perfectly beautiful, and we went out during intermission and met everyone my family knows and they all said to me shirley how wonderful that you're back for a while you're looking lovely will we see you in june? and then mother would say oh we're thinking of taking shirley to california with us in june she loves the coast so you know. and then of course the friends would say how perfectly wonderful shirley how lucky you are dear don't i wish i could go in your place.

A so-called genteel anti-Semitism was the norm in upper-middle-class social milieus such as the one Geraldine and Leslie inhabited, as the best-selling novel (and later hit film) *Gentleman's Agreement* (1947), the story of a magazine reporter who poses as a Jew, would soon demonstrate. After visiting Shirley and Stanley at home in Greenwich Village early in their marriage, the writer and lifelong anti-Semite Patricia Highsmith commented in her diary: "[T]he Jews disgusting!" Leslie, a staunch conservative who also despised Communists and every other left-wing group, was a longtime member of San Francisco's Bohemian Club, an elite, primarily Republican social club that since the late 1800s has hosted a high-powered political retreat every summer at the Bohemian Grove, a 2700-acre campsite in Sonoma County. Geraldine's prejudice seems to have been social rather than ideological—like Mrs. Merriam, the mother in *The Road Through the Wall* who makes her daughter break off a friendship with a Jewish girl, she simply valued conformity more than anything else. Now, Leslie offered to use his connections in the printing business to help Shirley get some kind of publishing job—on the condition that she wait six months after graduation to marry Stanley. Alta Williams was the only member of the household who supported Shirley's decision.

Intermarriage was still unusual in the United States in 1940. Only a year earlier, *The Atlantic Monthly* ran a first-person article by an anonymous Christian woman titled "I Married a Jew." The author cautioned that intermarriage meant "being barred from certain circles. They can say what they like about Germany, but democratic America is far from wholeheartedly accepting the Jews." The same week as Shirley and Stanley's wedding, *The New Yorker* published "Select Clientele," a story by the Brooklyn-born Jewish writer Irwin Shaw, in which three young people are enjoying themselves on a bike ride in the country when locals call them Jews and throw rocks at them. Shaw's stories had dealt with anti-Semitism before, but now he brought it home. "The disease was growing stronger in the veins and organs of America," realizes Sam, the story's Jewish narrator. "All the time there were more hotels you couldn't go to, apartment houses right in New York City you couldn't live in. Sam sold stories to magazines that published advertisements for vacation places that said 'Distinguished clientele' or 'Exclusive clientele' or 'Select clientele.' A hotel advertises that its hotel is exclusive, Sam thought, if it allows in everybody but six million Jews and fifteen million Negroes." One of those magazines was none other than *The New Yorker*, which continued to carry ads for restricted hotels well into the war years—ads that no doubt appealed to people like the Jacksons. Some of the resorts they visited on their cross-country trip in 1939 may have been restricted.

Florence Shapiro remembers anti-Semitism at Syracuse as being obvious but mostly benign: "Whispering. Silence when I entered a room." Jewish students were segregated in certain fraternities and sororities, and Shirley was occasionally confronted by classmates who were shocked by her nonchalant attitude toward Stanley's religion. Despite her traditional upbringing, however, Shirley seemed to be immune to anti-Semitism, as she seemed also immune to racial prejudice. In one of her unpublished college essays, Shirley laughs at another girl's assumption that Stanley's Jewishness is the reason she won't bring him to a school dance. (In fact, it was simply his antipathy to organized social events.) She became enraged when a boy she knew from Rochester asked her if she was "still messing around with Hyman, mixing races." Stanley, inured to such remarks, laughed it off.

Shirley identified strongly with Stanley's sense of himself as an outsider, an identification that would only deepen after they moved to the insular communities in New Hampshire and Vermont where they would later live. Though her family was part of the mainstream social culture, she had always felt like an outsider herself: unappreciated by her mother, not fitting in with the sorority-girl cliques at Brighton High or the University of Rochester, at home only among the bohemians and other misfits. She may also have seen marrying Stanley as the ultimate rebellion against her parents. Her sketch "I Cannot Sing the Old Songs" reads like the scene that ensued when Shirley tried to break the news of their engagement to the Jacksons—or her fantasy of it. The mother in the story cries. The father says that he's ashamed of his daughter. "What are we going to tell our friends?" he asks the mother. Meanwhile, the daughter struggles to keep from laughing. "Jesus, you poor old man," she thinks. In fact, Shirley did not invite her parents to her wedding; she told them about it long after the fact, when she was pregnant with her first child, making up a more recent date. For many years, Leslie and Geraldine did not know the date of their daughter and son-in-law's actual anniversary.

Shirley and Stanley's friends had assumed for some time that they would get married after graduation—at one point he even gave her, perhaps half in jest, a cheap engagement ring, which she did not wear for long: during a fight one night, she "bounced it off Stan's skull," he threw it at her, and the ring disappeared, never to be found again. But she went through her own period of uncertainty. A novel she started in college, provisionally called *Anthony*, takes up the question of what marriage means. Anthony and Paul are roommates and best friends; after Mary becomes Paul's girlfriend, he wrestles with the question of whether he wants to marry her and lead a traditional life or remain with the far less conventional Anthony (who wears red nail polish as a concession to his "unfailing sense of the dramatic"). The novel is episodic: scenes told from the perspective of various characters are interspersed with dialogues in which the unnamed author defends her technique to an interlocutor named Stanley, who doesn't quite understand what she is trying to achieve.

"i'm not made to be free, and have different people always trying to tie me down," Paul tells Anthony in one version of the scene in which he announces he will marry Mary, which Jackson rewrote half a dozen times. "i'm going to make myself an average, normal, married man, with children, and a home, and mary, and then i'll hide my head in the haystack of the usual—" Anthony cuts in: "and try to pretend you're happy." In each version, Paul leaves the home he has made with Anthony to be with Mary: he cannot imagine not having a wife. Anthony, for his part, is presented as not quite human: wondering at one point whether he is jealous of Mary, he concludes that "jealousy had no part in his life; he was free of human emotions, although chained by needs." The dilemma is an intriguing one. But the disjointed perspectives of *Anthony* never quite come together, and it's not entirely clear whether Shirley was deliberately trying to write in the mode of Djuna Barnes or truly couldn't decide how to tell her story.

In her late novels, Jackson's female characters are often split versions of herself—most clearly in *We Have Always Lived in the Castle*, in which Merricat and Constance represent both wanderer and homebody, one a bundle of barely controlled animosity, the other a calming domestic presence. Here, Paul and Anthony seem to stand for two ways of living—part Stanley and part Shirley. Shirley knew that the conventional kind of marriage offered by men like Al Parsell and Michael Palmer was not what she wanted. Michael knew it, too: he warned her that college would be the happiest time of her life, because only then would she be free from responsibility. "When you get out of college and go to work, you'll be . . . in some grimy office . . . slaving your damn fool head—yes, that same red head—off for three meals a day. . . . And there, when you're good and bored, and know that I'm right—which will be after about six weeks—you'll drop me a line, and I'll come to you, on my white charge, and sweep you off your feet, and then together we'll work our damn fool heads off for three meals a day," he told her.

Shirley did not want a husband who worked in the usual "grimy office"; she already believed that she could only love a man whom she found superior to her in every way. The life she and Stanley could build together, as she imagined it, would be fundamentally different from Michael Palmer's grim vision of marriage as two people slaving away for three meals a day. They would not have to hide their heads in "the haystack of the usual"; they would be mad bohemians together, fulfilling each other creatively and intellectually. No other man she knew could offer anything like it.

Shirley and Stanley's wedding was attended only by a small, motley group of friends. Bruce Bliven and Malcolm Cowley, whom Stanley had gotten to know during his summer working on *The New Republic*, were there; so was Tom Glazer, the Jewish-American folksinger who later became famous for the novelty song "On Top of Spaghetti." Walter Bernstein was not: he had gone to Los Angeles for the summer and would soon be drafted. Stanley's parents knew about the wedding but did not come. For the next few years, Lulu would write and send gifts to Stanley, but his father made no attempt to contact him. Reconciliation would not take place until several years later, after the birth of Laurence, Stanley and Shirley's first child. For now, they were on their own.

THE REPUTATION OF GREENWICH VILLAGE as a mecca for writers, artists, and bohemians of all types was already in decline by the early 1940s. Many of the writers who had made it famous—Djuna Barnes, Mabel Dodge Luhan—had already moved away: to Paris, Taos, or other more romantic destinations. A real estate market analysis done by the major newspapers in 1943 noted that the neighborhood appealed particularly to "business couples." Bohemianism had even been co-opted as a marketing strategy: ads for the department store Wanamaker's targeted consumers with a taste for Sibelius and E. E. Cummings. After "Professor Sea Gull," Joseph Mitchell's 1942 *New Yorker* profile of homeless scribe Joe Gould, mythologized Gould as the supposed creator of an "oral history" of the Village that comprised thousands of overheard conversations and ran to some nine million words, the Minetta Tavern on Macdougal Street hired Gould to be a "bohemian-in-residence"—in exchange for one free meal a day, he would sit at a table by the window and scribble in his notebooks. In a follow-up piece written more than twenty years later, Mitchell, who by then had become a close friend of both Shirley and Stanley's, determined that the oral history most likely did not exist.

Still, for a writer there was probably no better place to be. E. E. Cummings was still living in his studio on Patchin Place; Dawn Powell, who wrote a series of novels set in the Village, was another longtime resident. Mary McCarthy lived there briefly in 1936 and 1937, after her divorce from her first husband, enthusiastically embracing the life of a single girl in the city (complete with tiny studio apartment) before settling down temporarily with Philip Rahv and then Edmund Wilson. (Of a dinner party at which she met Lillian Hellman for the first time, she recalled that "[t]he guests at those dinners were mostly Stalinists, which was what smart, successful people in that New York world were.") Delmore Schwartz would return in 1945, declaring that it was "1919 all over again." *Partisan Review* made its headquarters on Astor Place; Meyer Schapiro lectured on art at the New School for Social Research on West Twelfth Street; and the headquarters of the Boni Brothers, who published Upton Sinclair, D. H. Lawrence, and Thornton Wilder, were on Fifth Avenue near Thirteenth Street. "The city had never looked so bright and frisky before," commented Alfred Kazin. Jackson's story "The Villager," written in 1944, sums up the mood: "When she was twenty-three she had come to New York from a small town upstate because she wanted to be a dancer, and because everyone who wanted to study dancing or sculpture or book-binding had come to Greenwich Village then."

The neighborhood was largely white but socioeconomically diverse. The wealthiest residents clustered in the handsome brick and brownstone town houses north of Washington Square Park and in the stately apartment buildings along Fifth Avenue. But there was plenty of space for writers and artists in the cheaper outskirts of the neighborhood, where a substantial population of Italian immigrants lived in crowded tenements. Jackson and Hyman took a tiny apartment in a walk-up building at 215 West Thirteenth Street, between Seventh and Eighth Avenues.

In a series of casuals detailing her adventures as a single girl in the city, which she later turned into the popular book *My Sister Eileen*, *New Yorker* writer Ruth McKenney had some fun with the condition of the real estate in the Village's seedier corners. "Every time a train roared by, some three feet under our wooden floor, all our dishes rattled, vases swayed gently, and startled guests dropped drinks," she wrote in an essay called "Mr. Spitzer and the Fungus," subtitled "The housing situation in Greenwich Village and how dismal it is." A "pleasure-loving robber" steals her radio, a bottle of gin, and four milk bottles she is planning to redeem for a nickel apiece. With the subway crashing by every three minutes, "village urchins" playing on the street, and the sounds of the man upstairs beating his wife or perhaps his mother, the apartment is "a symphony of noise." When she complains to the landlord about the mold growing in the bathroom, he tells her she should enjoy observing nature.

Jackson and Hyman, too, felt the pinch of poverty. As an editorial assistant at *The New Republic* for the summer, Hyman earned $25 per week—only a few dollars more than he had made at the paper mill in Erving. (For comparison, Cowley was paid $100 a week when he became literary editor a decade earlier.) Hyman quickly earned himself a reputation as a hard worker and was well liked in the office, not least for his sense of humor. After his first piece was published, he bombarded Bruce Bliven, the magazine's editor, with a series of prank postcards, all signed by people with the last name Hyman, attesting that it was the best thing ever to appear in the magazine. Bliven even kept him on for a few extra weeks as a favor.

When the position had to end that fall, Bliven wrote Hyman letters of introduction to editors all over town: "he is highly intelligent, writes rapidly and well, has the gift of humor and I think has the makings of a crack newspaper man." Hyman wrote his own letter to Gustave Lobrano, then a young staffer at *The New Yorker*, who within a few years would be Jackson's editor there. "i choose you because i have no idea who is in charge of reading applications for employment from bright young men with convictions of innate superiority who have just been graduated from coeducational universities in the east," the first draft inauspiciously began. This missive—presumably in edited form—somehow made its way to the desk of William Shawn, then the assistant editor in charge of the "Talk of the Town" section. It probably helped that Hyman dropped Walter Bernstein's name.

In those days, "Talk of the Town" opened with a page or two of brief, unsigned items—sometimes humorous, sometimes pointed—known as "Comment." In January 1941, Shawn invited Hyman to contribute Comments; he would do so for the next decade. He also began writing freelance book reviews for *The New Republic*, the Marxist magazines *The New Masses* and *The Jewish Survey*, and other publications. The work was demanding: one of Jackson's early drawings of the two of them shows Hyman staggering under a giant pile of books. Still, it wasn't enough to live on. Hyman was desperate enough to take a job in a sweatshop, sewing brassiere straps, but he was so bad at it that he was fired. For several months in 1941, he collected unemployment. They economized by using the same coffee grounds for several days in a row, but "we have to have oranges, don't we, hell, you get scurvy or something," Jackson grumbled.

Jackson held a series of odd jobs, including staving off creditors at an advertising agency and writing scripts for a radio station—mostly commercial pander aimed at housewives ("How can I make my dinner table look attractive without spending much money?"). In a satirical piece, she parodied the indignities of the job interview: "i am twenty-three [actually twenty-five], just out of college, authority on all books and a great writer, can type, cook, play a rather emotional game of chess, and have a republican father which is no fault of mine." A stint selling books at Macy's during the Christmas season served as fodder for "My Life with R. H. Macy," in which Jackson poked fun at the store's practice of referring to employees by number rather than name and the cryptic abbreviations she was expected to decipher (her receipt for a pair of free stockings reads "Comp. keep for ref. cuts. d.a. no. or c.t. no. salesbook no. salescheck no. clerk no. dept. date M.... 13-3138"). The piece would appear in *The New Republic* the following year.

With the exception of a few short poems printed under pseudonyms in *Tabard*, the Syracuse literary magazine that June Mirken was running in place of *Spectre*, Jackson published nothing for a year and a half after graduation. She tried her hand at *New Yorker*–style casuals and "Talk of the Town" pieces, but nothing other than the Macy's piece seems to have made it past a first draft. Her poem "Portrait of the Artist, with Freudian Imagery" captures her discouragement:

> *She might have disguised herself as a pencil*
> *Moving, unseeing, between a world of men*
> *And another world of words; but there, again,*
> *She would have found no paper long enough, and no ink plenty. . . .*

Hyman submitted it to the poetry editor at *The New Yorker*, who returned it with the terse comment "Not for us, it seems." Jackson expressed her frustration with magazine work, politics, the impending war, and all other annoyances of their life in New York in a single immortal couplet, verbosely titled "song for all editors, writers, theorists, political economists, idealists, communists, liberals, reactionaries, bruce bliven, marxist critics, reasoners, and postulators, any and all splinter groups, my father, religious fanatics, political fanatics, men on the street, fascists, ernest hemingway, all army members and advocates of military training, not excepting those too old to fight, the r.o.t.c. and the boy scouts, walter winchell, the terror organizations, vigiliantes, all senate committees, and my husband":

> *i would not drop dead from the lack of you—*
> *my cat has more brains than the pack of you.*

BY THE TIME HYMAN began working at *The New Yorker*, the war had managed to invade that magazine's mild-mannered pages. For most of the 1930s, *The New Yorker* had clung stubbornly to its original identity as a humorous publication, declining to take political positions and treating even the most ominous news with the evenhandedness that consistently characterized its tone. In April 1933, E. B. White opined in a Comment that recent developments in Germany had sent the nation "a thousand years into the dark," but the remark was buried low in the column, after an item on trout fishing. In 1936, White noted the irony that some American Christians who opposed the Nuremberg laws continued to patronize "restricted" establishments, but his editorializing struck a false note: "Americans' philosophy seems to be that it is barbarous to persecute Jews, but silly to suppose that they have table manners. Of the two types of persecution, Germany's sometimes seems a shade less grim." This takes the ironic pose one step too far.

Irwin Shaw, one of the most prolific *New Yorker* fiction writers in those days, may have done more than any of the magazine's other writers to raise awareness of the coming disaster. "In almost everything I wrote . . . this thing was hanging like a backdrop," he said later. The magazine was known for its reluctance to engage with overtly Jewish topics, but Shaw managed to work them in. His story "Sailor off the Bremen" describes an anti-Nazi demonstration encroaching upon a bohemian New York City scene that would prefer to ignore politics. (This story, incidentally, seems to mark the first appearance of the term "concentration camps" in the magazine.) In Shaw's "Weep in Years to Come," published in July 1939, a newsboy continually shouts "Hitler!" in the background as a couple leave a movie theater. Initially they carry on with their conversation, but eventually the subject of the war takes over—a metaphor for what was taking place in the city at large.

Walter Bernstein, who had drawn an unlucky number, was the first of Hyman's friends to be drafted; he left for Fort Benning in February 1941. In March, Hyman received his first notification from the Selective Service. As a married man, he was classified 3-A: deferred, for the time being. But the war found its way into his Comments, which had initially tended toward the innocuous. Now, in an item about advice that Eleanor Roosevelt had recently offered young women on how to avoid being the victims of crime, he included a reference to a speech given by a Navy admiral to families in Honolulu, warning about anonymous phone calls used to track ship movements. (Appearing less than six months before

Pearl Harbor, it now feels eerily prescient.) At Gimbel's one morning shortly after the Office of Production Management seized the nation's supply of raw silk, he watched as women responding to an advertisement allowing unlimited purchases of silk stockings stampeded the hosiery department. Hyman wrote about the scene in the language of a military exercise: "The terrain unquestionably favored the invaders, many of whom were clad in light cotton dresses. . . . The defenders, back of the counters taking orders, were hard pressed to maintain their lines in the face of opponents who deployed with skill and single-mindedness. . . . Such is our bulletin from the front during what may be the last days, for all we know, when a woman can walk into a department store and buy as many pairs of silk stockings as she has a mind to." The magazine still sought the humor in virtually any situation.

A summer heat wave brought "tense and humid days," making New Yorkers so testy that—as Hyman reported in another of his Comments—a man in Coney Island bit a police officer. Five people died; the warm front stretched as far west as the Dakotas, setting records in Indiana. Shirley, always affected by seasonal allergies, suffered from an excruciatingly painful headache that would not go away. Her parents convinced her to make a trip to Rochester to visit the family doctor, who diagnosed her with a sinus infection and said she needed sleep, exercise, and green vegetables.

There was then, as there is now, no shortage of doctors in New York. Shirley's parents were using her illness as an excuse to induce her to come home. Geraldine and Leslie, as a matter of pride, would not come to New York, but they longed to see their daughter, even if they disapproved of her life choices. "This is a week I have owed them for so long," Shirley wrote to Stanley plaintively from Rochester. Still unaware of the marriage, they greeted her with a box of her favorite peanut brittle and did not mention Stanley at all: when he called on the phone, Geraldine and Leslie shut themselves in their bedroom until the couple finished talking. Stanley, who spent the week in Syracuse with friends, wanted to visit, but Shirley discouraged him, worried about her parents' reaction. "Like always I don't know how to see you [in Rochester] and it is so funny and different if you come here and I am always scared." Stanley was dismissive. "there is some incredible psychological hold that house has on you that puts us back three years as soon as you go through the door," he harrumphed. But he obediently stayed away, arriving to collect Shirley for the trip back to the city at a time when no one else was home.

Back in Manhattan, Shirley and Stanley came upon an advertisement for a remote cabin on the evocatively named Toad Hollow Road, outside the town of Winchester, in southern New Hampshire. A dozen miles from Keene, the nearest major town, it was fully furnished and came with a wood-burning kitchen stove. "The house looks fresh and clean and cool," their prospective landlady, Gwynne Ross, assured them. Across the dirt road was a brook that had been dammed up to make a swimming hole, "marvellous if you like cold water." It wasn't the "house with no sides on top of a mountain" Shirley had once dreamed of, but it was close. Perhaps there, in the quiet, she would finally be able to calm the "insane seeking for some overwhelming stability" she had once lamented.

The conditions, Ross cautioned, were rustic. There was a telephone, but no gas or electricity. The kitchen had running water, but the bathhouse was a shed outside. More important, the plumbing was not designed to be used during the winter, and the pipes would have to be buried so as not to freeze. "Have you ever lived through a winter in the country before? There is quite a technique to it," Ross warned them. Sandbags had to be stacked around the outside of the house and an adequate supply of wood stockpiled. "With reasonable care, damage can be prevented, but you have to be on the qui vive all through the winter." The rent was only one hundred dollars for the entire year. Her warnings notwithstanding, they took it.

Although Shirley's driving skills were rudimentary at best (Stanley could not drive and never would learn), they bought an old car from her former nemesis Florence Shapiro for twenty-five dollars—it was "a real tin lizzie," Florence recalls—and headed for New Hampshire. "It has been wonderfully warm and incredibly lovely, with the leaves turned red and me not yet turned blue," Stanley wrote in October to

Louis Harap, a friend of Jesse Zel Lurie's and the editor of *The Jewish Survey*, for which he wrote occasional reviews. He was happily nursing blisters and calluses from chopping wood and shoveling dirt, they had found and adopted two kittens, and *The New Yorker* continued to run his Comment items every other week or so. "The farm seems to agree with you," Shawn told him. In cartoons depicting their rural life, Shirley gently poked fun at Stanley's ineptness at surviving in the country. "He's either drowning or fishing," she comments to the eagle-penguin character as Stanley flails in the creek, only his arms visible above the water. Her drawings were changing. The bird now functioned as the straight man or sounding board to whom Shirley's comments—funny, wry, or bitter—were directed: her audience. In one drawing, Shirley labels him a "familiar."

Stanley's main adaptation was growing a beard, which gave him the professorial look he would always cultivate. He invited Harap to visit— and to help out: "there is still wood to be cut, a cesspool to be dug, and many other features of a pleasant weekend." Shirley, he reported, had "gone completely rustic . . . baking bread and putting up cinnamon jelly with a passionate, unquestioning fury." She would send Harap a story to publish "as soon as she can get away from the oven to the typewriter."

In fact, both Shirley and Stanley found country life suited to productivity. Shirley managed to place her Macy's piece in *The New Republic*—the magazine paid her only twenty-five dollars, but it was her first
commercial publication. "Shirley Jackson, the wife of Stanley Hyman,
is living in New Hampshire and writing a novel," her author's note read.
From this point on, her identity was double. Her byline was "Shirley
Jackson," and always would be. But in her personal life, like almost all
women of her era, she used her husband's name. This doubling could
play out in amusing ways: her agent's office would sometimes send royalty statements or other formal correspondence addressed to "Shirley
Jackson" but with the salutation "Dear Mrs. Hyman." She never commented on why she chose not to use the name Hyman professionally,
though in later years she was grateful for the relative anonymity it gave
her. When the family moved to Westport, Connecticut, after the publication of "The Lottery," many of their neighbors did not realize that
the woman they knew as Mrs. Stanley Hyman was the writer Shirley
Jackson.

Hyman, in addition to his *New Yorker* work, speculated that he might
spend the long winter evenings writing a biography, perhaps of the abolitionist Wendell Phillips. Walter Bernstein had signed a contract that
fall with Viking on the strength of his *New Yorker* pieces, one of which
had been selected for the magazine's first anthology, *Short Stories from the
New Yorker* (1940), an effort to establish its bona fides in serious fiction.
Bernstein assuaged Hyman's jealousy somewhat by introducing him to
his agent, whom he considered both "mentor and friend": Frances Pindyck of the Leland Hayward Agency, a motion-picture talent agency
with a sideline in writers. A petite, bubbly, intelligent Jewish woman
from New York who graduated from Syracuse a decade before Jackson and Hyman, Pindyck counted among her clients Dashiell Hammett
(*The Thin Man*) and Betty Smith (*A Tree Grows in Brooklyn*). Within a
few months she would be shopping around Jackson's work, too.

Jackson started and abandoned several novels over the next few
years, so it's hard to say exactly what she was writing in New Hampshire. It might have been *I Know Who I Love*, an unfinished novel about

a young woman named Catharine, "thin and frightened, born with a scream and blue eyes," the daughter of a stern minister who would have preferred a son—Geraldine, in disguise. (The first section of the novel would eventually be published posthumously under the same title.) The bulk of the story has to do with Catharine's painful memories of high school ("worse for Catharine than any other time in her life"): the girls who tease her by singing "Ratty Catty, sure is batty," her mother's disapproval of a girl she befriends, the boy at a party who refuses to kiss her in a kissing game. She envies the girls with high heels and curly hair who go to school dances while she and "her three or four friends gave little hen parties where they served one another cocoa and cake, and said, 'You'd be cute, honestly, Catty, if you had a permanent and wore some makeup.'" She fantasizes about returning someday, "a famous artist with a secretary and gardenias," and scorning the people who once mocked her.

The minister dies young, and Catharine, a secretary at age twenty-three, brings her mother to live with her, who despite this gesture calls her "an ungrateful, spoiled child. . . . I don't know what I did to deserve a daughter like you." Her only happy memories are of a man whom she met in business school, who calls her "Cara" and jokes with her about her parents' disapproval. She keeps a letter from him in a cedar box with her other treasures: a charm bracelet, a matchbook from a nightclub, and a rejection slip for a watercolor she once submitted: "She kept it . . . because it had been addressed to her name and address by someone there at the magazine, some bright golden creature who called writers by their first names and sat at chromium bars and walked different streets than Catharine did." The autobiographical elements are obvious—the hen parties, the boyfriend who is the target of parental disapproval, the magazine rejection. But Jackson was starting to show a greater ability to distance herself from them, translating elements of her own experience into an alien environment.

In contrast to the isolationist indifference shown by many Americans to the catastrophe that was threatening Europe, American Jews were visibly more anxious—as was Jackson, now married to a Jew. Her growing concern about the war is evident in a story she wrote for Harap for a contest run by *The Jewish Survey*. "The Fable of Philip" depicts an anti-Semitic art student who tries to rally his classmates against the Jewish students, who he complains are advancing unfairly by paying others to do their work for them ("they've got money to burn") and taking opportunities from others. Eventually he is suspended for an act of vandalism against a Jewish professor, and his family, which includes a Jewish grandfather, disowns him. Even the German-American Bund proves unhelpful, and in the end he settles for a job in the wholesale paint business. As the title suggests, this "fable" is a simple piece of writing with an obvious political message, more a piece of propaganda than a true short story. Harap, failing to understand Jackson's intentions, was dismissive. "I cannot, as a friend of yours, allow this story to be published," his rejection letter began. The plot lacked "movement," and Philip was "a stereotype right out of *The Jewish Survey*'s rogue's gallery." Jackson took the criticism hard—she remembered it in an angry letter to Harap several years later. Throughout her life, she had trouble handling rejections; later Hyman and her agents would shield her from them as much as possible.

Her consolation was her first magazine story. "My Life with R. H. Macy" appeared in *The New Republic* on December 22, 1941. The magazine's second issue after Pearl Harbor, it was devoted almost entirely to analysis of the war. The lead editorial blamed officials in Washington for following a policy of appeasement, which had made it impossible to prepare adequately for the possibility of war, but urged the public not to indulge in "either excessive pessimism or optimism." Other articles examined Japan's possible strategy and encouraged support for Russia as "our strong and admired ally." Earlier in the year, the magazine had surveyed its contributors about whether they supported an immediate declaration of war against Germany. Along with about half the respondents, Hyman came out in favor: "We should prosecute the war on Hitler with all possible fervor, including the immediate creation of a second front in Europe and the rapid crushing in that gigantic pincers of the old pincers-master himself," he had written. Now the question was moot.

THE LANDLADY'S PREDICTIONS about winter in the country proved accurate. Temperatures averaged as low as single digits. Shirley and Stanley brought in an extra stove, but it wasn't enough. Shirley's cartoons depict them both wrapped in blankets; the bird, too, wears a scarf. Even in top form, Shirley probably did not have the constitution to endure a New Hampshire winter in an insufficiently insulated house. But now her health was a little more delicate than usual. Around the start of the new year, she began to suspect she was pregnant.

In January 1942, Shirley and Stanley decamped to Syracuse for the rest of the winter. There they could get by nearly as cheaply as in New Hampshire, and they still had an assortment of acquaintances at the university, including their mentor Leonard Brown and their old friend Seymour Goldberg, who became a near constant companion. One night after dinner, reminiscing about *Spectre* and people they had known, they realized their college stories were fertile material for fiction. Troubled by how much he had already forgotten, Stanley resolved to keep a journal and persuaded Shirley to join him: they would write every day and periodically share their journals with each other.

Shirley, of course, was no stranger to journal keeping, and lately her cartoons had become a kind of personal chronicle. But she hadn't tried to write a daily diary since high school. It was in her letters—from the

scribbled notes to Elizabeth Young and Jeanou in random pages of her college notebooks to the lengthy missives to Stanley she typed during the summers—that she gathered her thoughts and assessed her life. Now, the return to journal writing reopened her confessional vein. Her "official" typewritten journal, the one she shared with Stanley, was cool and analytical. But now and for the rest of her life, there would be other spasms of diary writing: just a page or two at a time, hidden among a pile of drafts for a novel or notes for a lecture, often written at a moment of crisis.

Stanley, on the other hand, kept his journal every single day for a month and a half (often signing off with the Pepysian flourish "And so to bed"), then abandoned it entirely. When he set his mind to something, he did it—but only as long as it held his interest. His love of routine is evident in his daily habits. He typically stayed in bed until late morning or early afternoon; Shirley would get up earlier to prepare coffee for him. (Arthur, his brother, would later remark that Stanley had preserved one aspect of their traditional Jewish upbringing: like a Talmudic scholar, he managed to have his wife take care of all the day-to-day matters so that he could concentrate on his studies.) Their room didn't include a full kitchen, so they took most meals at the Greeks, their old college hangout, which stayed open until two in the morning and conveniently allowed them a generous line of credit. After a late breakfast or early lunch, Stanley would return home to work through the afternoon. He continued to write Comments for *The New Yorker* as well as reviews for *The New Republic*, and read both magazines from cover to cover the day they came out. He also scoured the newspaper daily, filing away articles he thought might later be useful for Comment ideas or reviews. Throughout his life, Stanley maintained a system of taking rigorous, organized notes on all his reading. As he read, he would make tiny notations on a bookmark; later he would type them up and file them.

Shirley's habits were less regular, as they always would be: she often spent the afternoon drawing cartoons or having coffee with a friend. They were sharing a single typewriter, and Stanley generally commandeered it. After her resounding rejection from Louis Harap, she felt uncertain about how to proceed. "Shirley is still working on funny pieces, but hasn't turned out anything yet that is really good," Stanley wrote to Harap. She followed through with attempts at a few stories drawn from the lives of their college friends: one centered on June Mirken's painful breakup with a boyfriend. Shirley wanted to write about the episode because it troubled her, but she was unsure how to make it into a story. To do so, she mused, she'd "have to put it down first the way it happened and then go back and cut out all the drama until it stopped being what had happened and turned into a story. it's a good story . . . the only thing wrong with it is that it happened." Later she would often use the technique of basing a story on an anecdote someone told her, "thinking about it, turning it around, thinking of ways to use a situation like that in order to get a haunting note." Eventually she would realize that, as she put it in a lecture, an "accurate account of an incident is not [a] story." But she hadn't yet figured out how to transform a life event into fiction.

In Stanley's opinion, her stories needed to have a "wow ending, like Mr. Hemingway," whose collected stories he had given Shirley for their first Christmas together. This advice was largely in sync with the literary taste of the time, particularly as it was influenced by *The New Yorker*, which in the years since its inception in 1925 had expanded beyond its initial purview as a humor magazine into a destination for at least moderately serious fiction. By the early 1940s, the "*New Yorker* short story" was already an identifiable type. Exemplified by writers such as Shaw, James Thurber, and John O'Hara, this style of fiction was brief (no more than a few pages), genteelly oblique, and virtually plotless. Instead, the writer used precise observations and keen aperçus to illuminate some cold truth about contemporary life, often revealed in a bitter twist at the end. The "wow ending" was far from universal: Thurber's stories in particular often meandered to a close. But when it was done well—O'Hara and Shaw were particularly skilled in this regard—the final stab could reverberate through the entire story to alter the reader's perception of what had taken place.

The *New Yorker* style was not universally admired—even the magazine's editors sometimes felt uneasy about it. Katharine Angell (later

Katharine White), who joined the magazine's staff in August 1925, six months after its founding by Harold Ross, and was in charge of the fiction department for many years, wrote to an early contributor that "we want fiction and we want short stories, and yet when it comes right down to it Mr. Ross feels the stories we use have to be quite special in type—*New Yorker*-ish, if that word means anything to you." Lionel Trilling, the soon-to-be eminent literary critic who had recently been hired as the first Jewish full-time professor in Columbia University's English department, objected to the magazine's already notorious slick and glossy style in a critique of *The New Yorker*'s fiction in *The Nation* in the spring of 1942. All the authors, Trilling argued, were "the same anonymous person, and you feel about them that, just as any scientist might take over another's research or any priest take over another's ritual duty, almost any one of these writers might write another's story in the same cool, remote prose. . . . Somehow, despite their admirable technical skill and despite their high earnestness, these stories have a mortuary quality; they are bright, beautiful, but dead." Part of the problem, Trilling believed, was the magazine's strict limits on length: the stories have "just room enough to make the sharp perception but not room enough for a play of emotion around it." And their themes were as indistinguishable as their style. Trilling found the stories "grimly moral," invariably devoted to a social lesson about "the horrors of snobbery, ignorance, and insensitivity and . . . the sufferings of children, servants, the superannuated, and the subordinate."

Trilling had a point, but his judgment suffered from a certain snobbery about *The New Yorker*'s populist appeal, and his focus on the socially conscious stories is a little strange: with the exception of Shaw's recurring theme of anti-Semitism and the occasional comment on racial prejudice, the stories were largely amoral, more about the decadence of the upper middle classes than anything else. Hyman, writing in *The New Republic*, rose to his employer's defense. "It is worth noting that *The New Yorker*, allegedly a 'humor' magazine, prints a higher percentage of good serious stories than any of the heavy literature magazines," he fired back at Trilling. He acknowledged the limitations of the short form and the magazine's lack of interest in experimental writing, but declared most of the fiction to be "excellent," if of a clearly identifiable type: "tight, objective sketches with a strong undercurrent of emotion, aimed at capturing a mood, a feeling or a situation." And some pieces transcended the form. He singled out E. B. White's "The Door," a small masterpiece of paranoia; Thurber's haunting depiction of loneliness in "One Is a Wanderer"; and a very different story by the unknown writer Alex Gaby called "An Action Photo Has Been Taken," which Hyman aptly described as "one of the punchiest and most horrible stories about chauvinism against the Negro ever written." Unlike Trilling, he saw the magazine's social consciousness—admittedly limited—as a point in its favor.

The stories Hyman praised, however, were not the ones he advised Jackson to imitate. His fondness for the "wow ending" was more in sync with the magazine's typical contributors—commercial writers such as Shaw, O'Hara, or Sally Benson, whose semiautobiographical stories were made into the movie *Meet Me in St. Louis*—than with the "quiet, impressionistic" Thurber/White style he admired so much. Perhaps he didn't think Jackson was capable of the more sophisticated style of writing. More likely, he simply believed it was more practical to swim with the mainstream rather than against the tide, considering that they were both still struggling to get published.

The war ultimately proved a more fertile source of inspiration than the gossip of their Syracuse days. One night Jackson tried another story drawn closely from life, about their friend Seymour Goldberg's experience in a bar with a Nazi sympathizer, but Hyman thought it "just didn't click." Undeterred, Jackson started over. By midnight she had produced an entirely new story: "a very good slick funny piece," in Hyman's opinion, "that looked as though rewriting would make it commercial." It described a young woman having lunch with her batty Aunt Agatha, who announces that she is planning to take in a Viennese war refugee, the son of her hairdresser. The plan falls apart when the young cousin who lives with the aunt acts out bizarrely: he builds a machine to imitate the sounds of bombs and takes to chanting, in German, "We will kill you."

Hyman's involvement with Jackson's stories had previously been minimal—he suggested titles or made small changes. Now he set to work, toying with the piece for the next few days until they both were satisfied. The writer and the critic again worked in symbiosis. Aunt Agatha became Aunt Cassandra. He realized that bombs had never been dropped on Vienna, so they changed the boy's country of origin to Holland. He even typed up the revised copy. Together they sent it off to Frances Pindyck, the agent Walter Bernstein had recommended, who agreed to shop it around.

SHIRLEY AND STANLEY always kept their door open to anyone who wanted to drop by in the afternoon, and usually someone did. Evenings were spent with a rotating group of friends and neighbors who came over to drink cheap wine and listen to music. Once unable to appreciate music, Stanley had turned to record collecting with all the fervor he had once devoted to curating his arsenal of chewing gum. In addition to jazz and the blues, he was starting to branch out into folk music: Appalachian ballads, as well as the work of leftist singer-songwriter Woody Guthrie and Burl Ives, a former peace demonstrator newly drafted into the Army. Stanley was ahead of his time: the visitors with whom he shared these records often had no idea what to make of them.

The constant parade of visitors may have meant only that after a long autumn virtually on their own in the woods, Shirley and Stanley were eager for company. But it could also have been a sign that they did not care to spend much time alone together. There were moments of lightheartedness: one night at the Greeks, they challenged each other, along with Goldberg, to identify the brands of four random cigarettes by smoking them blindfolded. (Only Shirley got a perfect score.) They joked about the future baby, nicknaming it "Simon Hyman." A doctor in Syracuse said Shirley was "probably but not certainly pregnant"; he advised her to eat sensibly and drink milk, but not to bother quitting smoking, which was common advice at the time. But Shirley's journal mentions often how unhappy they were together. Most of their conversations she found "too dull to record." A comic piece Stanley was trying to write about growing a beard owed all its merit to jokes he had stolen from her. One afternoon Goldberg gave Shirley a drawing lesson. Stanley praised her work, but later he criticized her ability to appreciate fine art, an argument that ended with her in tears. "he was more interested in telling me what was good than in knowing why i didn't realize it was good, and got me finally after a few hours into a state of helplessness where i felt the whole world was standing around pointing at me and calling me names." They went to bed "furiously angry" and stayed that way into the next day, "until time worked its wonders and we made friends again. thought that sort of stuff was passing," she wrote sadly.

The return to Syracuse also triggered a relapse of Stanley's old habits. In mid-February, Shirley went to Rochester for a few days to keep Geraldine company while Leslie was away. It was one of her last trips there: Leslie would soon be transferred back to California, where the Jacksons spent the rest of their lives. Stanley was invited but refused to go along: he claimed he was too busy, but he still felt justifiably little fondness for Geraldine. Shirley left Syracuse with all her usual anxiety about what Stanley might do while she was out of town. Almost as soon as she left, Stanley ran into her old nemesis Florence Shapiro. A few days later he invited Florence over for an evening, buying a half gallon of Sauternes in preparation. But after a few hours of talking and playing records, all through which Florence claimed the wine was "mild as water," she became violently ill. Stanley put her in the shower and stood her in front of an open window to sober her up, then gave her coffee and took her home. That seems to have been the extent of their encounter.

In a repeat of their previous pattern, Stanley showed Shirley his account of the episode in his diary as soon as she returned. She was not amused, though she feigned nonchalance. "if i had to marry a guy who fancies himself as a gay dog, i can hardly expect him to be housebroken so quick," she scolded herself lightly in the diary she shared with him. But it stung her that he had chosen Florence, of all people, for his attentions. Shirley deemed her "coarse and vulgar," but couldn't hide her jealousy. "whatever i say i can't deny that she has a beautiful body and after all i am too fat."

Her more private writings show just how much distress the incident caused her. At home in Rochester, she kept a toy stuffed cat that Stanley had given her while they were in college. They named it Meadelux, in homage to the boogie-woogie pianist Meade Lux Lewis, and Shirley's letters to Stanley from Rochester often included an amusing reference to how Meadelux was doing. Now, in a sketch that remains unpublished, she depicted a woman in despair, trying to resist calling her husband (who happens to be named Stanley) on the telephone, and pouring out her heart instead to a stuffed cat named Meadelux. As her anxiety mounts into a full-blown panic attack, she fears that she will lose her mind:

> it got quieter and quieter and things in the room got bigger and bigger. she grabbed the pillow beside her and held onto it with both arms. it got bigger and bigger as she held on to it.
> o boy, she said. here i go, meadelux.

What happens next—a "madness of crying and tenseness and fear and hatred and remembering and seeing again"—must have been something like the "attacks" several years earlier that had frightened Stanley so badly that he had asked Walter Bernstein what to do. Once again, he had failed to follow Bernstein's advice—to think about the effect on Shirley before he acted out with another woman—and once again his behavior had sent Shirley into a state of psychological crisis, "the only thought in her one of fear of him and knowing nothing to hold on to but a pillow and a sawdust cat. . . . and then the worst of all, the realization that it was only beginning, that what was past was not past but a foundation for what was coming." The horror was not only Stanley's behavior; it was that she could not hope it would ever improve.

> he said he'd take care of me, meadelux, she said. he told me he'd take care of me and he didn't. . . .
> he would do it again, as it had been again and again and again, as it had been and would be and her hating it and loathing him and herself and everything of their life together and everything they had and wanted and loved together and everything nice that had been would go and turn into cheapness and horror while stanley sat at a dinner and talked with another girl and left her

alone and silent and afraid and only hearing stanley's voice saying cruel words. . . .

i am a psychopathic case, she said, and i am going to go insane.

The woman in the story tries to talk herself away from the edge. "i
am very hysterical, she said severely to meadelux. when i am logical,
she went on, and i can certainly be logical if i want to, i know just how
foolish this all is, and i think that i will leave stanley, and yet i know
that i won't leave stanley." In the end, the fear of being on her own was
greater than her rage at Stanley's infidelity. "it isn't jealousy . . . it's
[being] hurt and being left alone."

Aside from the occasional date with Michael Palmer when she was
at home during college vacations, Shirley had never taken advantage
of her open relationship with Stanley. As she put it rather bitterly in
another story written around this time, "why should i be [unfaithful]?
he wouldn't care if i were." Worse, she feared that her own infidelity
might condemn her to another round of the same torturous cycle: if she
was unfaithful to Stanley, then he would have no compunction about
being unfaithful to her again. But now she decided to try it: out of anger,
or impatience, or desperation. Stanley had an acquaintance named Jerry
who was constantly complaining about his own romantic troubles. Shirley's journal is oblique, but it's fairly clear what happened:

poor little boy. heard something about his ethel, was astonished
to find out how unenthusiastic i was, kept calling him armand.
afterwards he talked about many people we used to know. . . .
stanley finally threw jerry out, which was good, because he was
getting back to ethel.

"no more," she wrote after this account. "journal finished."

The typewritten journal ends there. But Shirley wasn't finished.
There was the not insignificant matter of her pregnancy. What on earth
would happen, she wondered, when a baby came into this relationship?
Stanley had bought her a spiral notebook to use for drawing cartoons;
on one of its pages, she scribbled a diary entry that reveals how deep the

fissures in the marriage were. "If it's sex I can't do anything about it," the entry reads in part. "He forced me God help me and for so long I didn't dare say anything and only get out of it when I could and now I'm so afraid to have him touch me."

Sex clearly wasn't the only problem in their relationship, but it was an important one. Is Shirley saying that Stanley raped her? It would go some way toward explaining, among other things, the episode at the garden party in *Hangsaman* when Natalie is a victim of sexual violence. The scene may function as a stand-in for an encounter early in their relationship in which Stanley somehow forced or simply pressured Shirley into sex. A letter she sent to him during their first summer apart refers, seemingly half in jest, to "my rape." Natalie's violation at the garden party takes place in a gap in the text—just as Shirley's journal entry about Jerry omits a description of their sexual encounter, indicated only by the evocative word "afterwards." Janna Malamud Smith, who grew up with the Hyman children during the years her father, Bernard Malamud, taught at Bennington College, writes chillingly in her memoir that the teenaged Sarah Hyman once told her—"explaining to me a view she attributed to her father"—that there was no such thing as rape: "However adamant, female protest was simply foreplay. Women wanted to be forced, and ultimately their excitement made them receptive, no matter what their claim."

There are other indications that Shirley did not relish sex in the same way that Stanley did. She never answered any of his sexually explicit letters in kind. While visiting her parents the previous summer, she wrote to him wishing he could come for just a few minutes—not to "get fucked," she made a point of saying, "but just [to] hold onto you." Now she worried it had all been a mistake.

> We should never have gotten married and I keep thinking that now we are we have to make the best of it—but doesn't a man ever get ashamed to think that the only way he can look like a man before his wife is to say cruel things to her until she cries. . . .
> Tantrums and hatred and disgust—what a married life—

The possibility of divorce had not yet entered Shirley's mind. Her best hope—for companionship, for fulfillment, for love—was the child she was carrying. "Maybe when I have my baby," the journal entry concludes, "I can talk to it and it will love me and it won't grow up mean." In motherhood, perhaps she would find the stability she longed for.

6.

GARLIC IN FICTION

NEW YORK,
1942–1945

> In some respects, having a baby is roughly like being in
> the path of a major hurricane. Or like having all your rela-
> tives come at once for a two-week visit. . . . Or like dis-
> covering suddenly that you have only one hand when you
> thought you had two. Or like discovering suddenly, as a
> matter of fact, that you have only two hands when you
> hoped you had four.
>
> —*Special Delivery*

"MY MENAGERIE NOW INCLUDES TWO SNAKES, ONE SMALL
snapping turtle, twenty-three salamanders, eight frogs, and several million polliwogs," Hyman reported happily to Louis Harap in May 1942.
Now that the weather was warmer, he and Jackson had returned to New
Hampshire, and he was again indulging his childhood fascination with
natural science—by summer, the snake count reached nine. He gathered food for them himself, catching chipmunks, frogs, or a handful
of grasshoppers for his pets. The weather, at last, was beautiful, and
Jackson's pregnancy was proceeding easily. Harap was drafted in July,
but he did make it up to visit beforehand, and so did Jesse and Irene
Lurie. Jackson and Hyman spent their days swimming, picnicking, and

Self-portrait, c. 1942.

picking wild berries. Hyman's *New Yorker* Comments were still running at least once a month, and he was publishing occasional book reviews in *The New Republic* and elsewhere. He had also been in contact with a young man named Ralph Ellison.

"Sometimes we have such good luck in acquiring our friends that it's impossible not to suspect that fate had a hand in their appearance," Ellison later recalled. Born in Oklahoma City, he attended Tuskegee Institute in Alabama before coming to New York in 1936, just as the initial glow of the Harlem Renaissance was starting to fade. Hyman may have noticed his writing as early as 1938, when Ellison, mentored by Langston Hughes and later Richard Wright, made his debut in *The New Masses*, reviewing a biography of Sojourner Truth. In 1942, he was named managing editor of *Negro Quarterly: A Review of Negro Life and Culture*, a new journal of African-American writing backed by left-leaning intellectuals, including the novelist Theodore Dreiser and the Harlem Renaissance philosopher Alain Locke. Ellison's plans for the magazine were ambitious: to stimulate "discussions concerning the relationship between Negro American culture and history and that of the nation as a whole" while covering sociology, literary and cultural issues, and politics from a socially radical perspective, with writing from "the best critical minds, whether black or white." But the initial response from white critics was disappointing. Ellison discovered that while many of the critics he admired "knew the spirituals well enough to sing a few verses and had been touched by jazz and Negro American dancing styles, few were prepared to give these cultural products the finest edge of their sharply honed minds."

Hyman—young, eager for exposure, and passionately antiracist—was an exception. After reading the magazine's first issue, he immediately sent Ellison a postcard offering his services as a reviewer. Ellison was already aware of Hyman's work, complimenting him on an article he had recently published about Steinbeck in the *Antioch Review*. "Between the sophisticated *New Yorker* and the deadly earnest *Quarterly* there ought to have been a chasm," writes Ellison's biographer Arnold Rampersad. But the two men's interests were already aligned. Like Hyman, Ellison was attracted to folklore and mythology as an influence on fiction (including his own)—an interest that had begun at Tuskegee, when he followed T. S. Eliot's footnotes on *The Waste Land* to Jessie Weston's book *From Ritual to Romance*, a key text in myth and ritual criticism, which interprets the Grail legend as rooted in primitive myths of the death and rebirth of a fertility god. In 1940, Ellison published an essay in *The New Masses* that began with an extended reference to *The Grapes of Wrath* as a novel that had recently "explod[ed] upon the American consciousness"—including, of course, Hyman's.

Their affinities were personal as well as intellectual. Both men were active and respected in the New York intellectual scene, yet in important

ways outsiders to it. "A Jew married to a gentile, Hyman saw himself as a cosmopolitan intellectual—just as Ralph, labeled a Negro, saw himself as a citizen of the world," Rampersad writes. The two men met for the first time that summer and started seeing each other regularly in the fall, when Jackson and Hyman returned to New York. Hyman's first piece in *Negro Quarterly*, a review of the novel *Tap Roots* by the white Southern writer James Street, appeared in the fall 1942 issue.

After a burst of writing that spring, Jackson had been less productive. Fran Pindyck had shopped around a few of her stories without success. Jackson amused herself by drawing cartoons and putting together an illustrated ABC book called *The Child's Garden of New Hampshire, or, How to Get Along in the Country*, written in a parody of the gruff New England style. "D is for Deer—which is a season"; "I is for Idle, which is the kind of hands we find work for" (illustrated by an axe and a pile of chopped wood); "S is for Stanley, easily recognizable by the *New York Times* he carries in his hand"; "U is for Uppity, which is what summer folks are"; "Y is for Yesterday, which is when the mailman started out." For a time, she may have seriously considered becoming a cartoonist.

Jackson's humor could not mask the very real alienation she felt from her neighbors in Winchester. Part of the reason she and Hyman urged their friends from New York to visit was that they felt isolated:

their only local friends were a pair of Communists who ran a dog kennel. The fancy-newspaper-reading, Sauternes-drinking renters hardly fit in, and their neighbors let them know it. A cartoon depicts their house surrounded by figures listening at the windows as Jackson complains, "I can't understand how the neighbors find out that we have company from New York." They also clashed with their landlady, who lectured them about the "mutual assistance" country people expected after they neglected to help repair the bathhouse, which they had managed to burn down. (Jackson's cartoon about the incident shows Hyman calmly regarding a kerosene lamp as it bursts into flame.) Jackson would later say that "The Lottery" grew out of this period in their lives—not, as is commonly thought, from the insular community of North Bennington, Vermont, where they were living when she wrote the story. She would give many explanations—or partial explanations—for that story's genesis; still, the influence of New Hampshire seems meaningful.

Perhaps to her relief, their second stay in New Hampshire was even shorter than the first. In July 1942, William Shawn, then *The New Yorker*'s managing editor for "fact" pieces, offered Hyman a full-time job at a salary of thirty-five dollars a week, plus bonuses for extra productivity, doing much the same work as he was already: writing Comments, casuals, and perhaps some "Talk of the Town" items. The war had hit the magazine hard: some of the staff had already been drafted, while others, including A. J. Liebling and Janet Flanner, were sent abroad to cover the news from Europe. Walter Bernstein, for whom Harold Ross had found a job with *Yank*, the Army's new weekly magazine, also sent occasional dispatches back to *The New Yorker* from Europe and the Middle East, including the first interview with the new Yugoslav leader Marshal Tito conducted by an American journalist. *The New Yorker* was "a worse madhouse than ever now, on account of the departure of everybody for the wars, leaving only the senile, the psychoneurotic, the maimed, the halt, and the goofy to get out the magazine," E. B. White complained in a letter to his brother.

Hyman would be among them. Called before the draft board again in March 1943, he failed his physical. He later liked to joke that the Army doctor told him he had the organs of a middle-aged man. He probably did, thanks to his sedentary lifestyle, but in fact it was his poor eyesight that disqualified him. He and Jackson would have to watch the war from afar. His friend and colleague Joseph Mitchell was also disqualified from war service, because of a history of ulcers. Mitchell's inability to participate in the war effort was a source of guilt and resentment for the rest of his life: he complained of sitting at home in New York while friends like Liebling and Flanner wrote "reputation-making" articles. Hyman may well have felt the same.

When he offered Hyman the job, Shawn warned that "living in New York has its disadvantages, the newest of which is the prospect of air raids." The city had been transformed by the war. Workers mobilized to help with war production efforts—everything from building ships in the Brooklyn Navy Yard to making uniforms at Brooks Brothers. Ration books were issued for sugar, gasoline, and soon coffee; anyone wishing to buy a new tube of toothpaste, made from metal, had to turn in the old one. Typewriters, too, were rationed—a special hardship for writers. At the war's height, a ship laden with supplies or men left New York harbor every fifteen minutes. In the quiet of the New Hampshire woods, the war could be ignored; in the city, it could not.

Wartime chaos notwithstanding, it was Hyman's dream to work at *The New Yorker*. Now, at age twenty-three, he had achieved it. Although he wrote little for the magazine in his later years, he kept the title of staff writer until his death. Even after he began teaching at Bennington, he wrote nearly all his correspondence on *New Yorker* letterhead—a symbol of his attachment to the magazine and his pride in the status it conferred. Whenever he visited the office, he replenished his supply. His colleague Brendan Gill would later write of Hyman's "magic briefcase": he would leave Bennington with a briefcase full of whiskey and would return with it weighing exactly the same amount, now full of *New Yorker* stationery.

On September 1, as German troops were beginning their ill-fated advance on Stalingrad, Jackson and Hyman traded their cabin in the woods for a brick row house at the top of a hill in Woodside, Queens, then known as "the borough of homes." The extension of the subway in 1918 had generated a housing boom, and the quiet streets were lined with new semidetached English-style houses with gardens in the front and the rear. Their new house was just around the corner from Jesse and Irene Lurie, who were soon to have a baby of their own, and a short subway commute to Manhattan. Their experiment in country living was over—for now.

FOR MANY YEARS, Shirley maintained a running joke that she was conducting a contest between the number of children she produced and the number of books she wrote. Eventually the books pulled ahead, but at first the children kept pace, with a new arrival every three years, almost to the day. Laurence Jackson Hyman (Laurie) was born on October 3, 1942, followed by Joanne Leslie (Jannie) in November 1945, Sarah Geraldine (Sally) in October 1948, and Barry Edgar in November 1951. Like nearly all men of his era, Stanley was a hands-off parent, preferring to sequester himself with his typewriter behind a closed door. "Bring 'em to me when they can read and write," he liked to say. Shirley once commented that at age two, Laurence's definition of "Daddy" was "man who sits in chair reading."

But Shirley, all her children remember, was an imaginative and unconventional mother. Several years before Dr. Benjamin Spock's best-selling *Baby and Child Care* would advocate a more relaxed style of child rearing than the strictly routinized methods that had become standard in America, she embodied his intuitive, casual approach. Though she couldn't help channeling some of Geraldine's admonishments—"A lady doesn't climb trees," she would tell her daughters, whom she made wear garters and high heels as teenagers—she was determined to give her children an upbringing altogether different from her own: down to earth, creative, loving. Early in *Hill House*, Eleanor, the protagonist, encounters a little girl having a tantrum because she cannot drink her lunchtime milk out of her usual cup painted with stars. "Insist on your cup of stars," Eleanor silently bids the girl. "Once they have trapped you into being like everyone else you will never see your cup of stars again." Shirley, who would one day decorate the kitchen ceiling with stars, wanted to be the kind of mother who offered a cup of stars.

It was far from inevitable that Shirley would become a mother. In the literary circles she and Stanley were part of, having children was considered unusual. Visibly pregnant at a *Partisan Review* party, Diana Trilling, Lionel Trilling's wife, was approached by the wife of another writer who asked her incredulously if her husband was letting her have the baby. Midge Decter—who, with her husband Norman Podhoretz, the future editor of *Commentary*, was friendly with Jackson and Hyman in the 1950s—remembers that "it was the men who needed looking after. . . . They had many demands." It was an area in which she—who also had children—felt a connection with Shirley. "It was very tough for women to admit, even to themselves, that what they wanted was children or a household. It was not part of the bohemian life," Decter recalls.

But it was a life for which Shirley was instantly, innately suited. Stanley was physically distant—a kiss on the forehead was enough for him—but she, unlike her own mother, was intimate and warm, inviting the children to cuddle in bed with her. Every night, even if a party was in progress, Shirley came upstairs at bedtime and went from room to room, bidding each child good night. She sang them all kinds of songs, from the Child Ballads her father loved to a gruesome ditty called "The Grattan Murders" that would eventually appear in *The Haunting of Hill House*: "The first was young Miss Grattan—she tried not to let him in, / He stabbed her with a corn knife, that's how his crimes begin. . . ." When Laurence had trouble sleeping as a baby, she played boogie-woogie records by her old favorite Meade Lux Lewis—the only way he would be consoled. She was indulgent enough to send the children to bed at night with a piece of candy or a glass of orange soda, and she could be permissive—or absentminded—to the point of laxness. Laurence was allowed to roam more or less wherever he wanted, but the younger children had to stay within a certain distance of the house. She would sit on a stool in the kitchen, looking out the window, to make sure they were still where they were supposed to be. "She was afraid she would lose us," Sarah remembers.

At times Shirley could be a tough disciplinarian—one of Sarah's friends would later recall, with lingering terror, a slumber party at which Shirley sternly quieted a room full of giggling girls. But she also had a sense of humor about the children's misdeeds. One day Laurence, twelve or thirteen years old, balked when she told him to take a bath. Shirley went into the kitchen, came back with an egg, and smashed it on his head. "Now you need a bath," she told him. When others accused the children of misbehaving, she could be fiercely protective, whether they deserved it or not. Once she jumped out of her car to confront Laura Nowak, a neighbor in North Bennington, over a minor altercation involving their daughters and a lollipop. Her fits of temper, however, were brief. In *Life Among the Savages*, she tells of screaming over the phone at a neighbor whose son Laurence had accused of bullying him (falsely, as it turns out). The two mothers are so furious that each hangs up on the other, but all is forgotten when they meet in the grocery store the next day.

Shirley had always had an imaginative, even magical mind, filled with witchcraft lore, myths, and fantasies of her own devising. Stanley, ever the rationalist, had limited patience with that aspect of her character. He tolerated no suggestion of religious belief and scolded her for believing in ghosts, though he later refused to read *The Haunting of Hill House* because he found it too frightening. Now she lavished her imagination upon her children, who became happy participants in her fantasy life. When Sarah had a series of dreams about an imaginary country, Shirley encouraged her to draw maps of it and (perhaps recalling the language she once invented) make up languages spoken there. When eight-year-old Laurence asked his mother how he ought to spend a dime, she suggested that he give it to the birch tree in front of their house. He promptly went outside and asked the tree for a dime's worth of wind. To Shirley's amusement, a massive hurricane struck that night. "All we could figure was that wind must be very cheap indeed for him to get that much for a dime," she wrote to her parents. Her moods could be volatile. "She could go from happy to upset in the blink of an eye," Joanne remembers. "You never knew what you were going to get." Later, when Shirley was suffering from the agoraphobia and anxiety that troubled her final years, Joanne, arriving home from school, would "listen to the house" as she entered, trying to gauge her mother's mood.

Birthdays and Christmas—a holiday Stanley also embraced, in contradiction of both his background and his atheism—were celebrated lavishly. Shirley spent months poring over catalogs from New York department stores, antiquarian booksellers, and other far-flung merchants. She took pride in coming up with uncommon gifts that would surprise and delight every member of the family—even her brother Barry's son, whom she hardly knew. Since all four children were born in the fall, the period from the beginning of October through Christmas kept her "reeling from one birthday cake to another." If the Brooklyn Dodgers made it to the World Series, as they often did in the glory days of the early 1950s, Laurence's birthday celebration usually involved at least one game at Ebbets Field. The celebrations could send the family into debt: Shirley's files include an irate letter to Gimbel's department store in response to a series of increasingly stern notices of overdue bills, explaining that because of her "irregular income," she would have to wait to pay her bill until she received her next check.

Shirley's collection of Christmas ornaments included some that her father's family had brought over from England as well as cardboard cutouts from her first Christmas tree as a baby; she also hung up the same Christmas lights that the Jacksons had used during her childhood, the wires becoming more frayed every year, until the entire strand had to be wrapped with tire tape. But she also created her own family traditions. On Christmas Eve, the family trimmed the tree together, but when the children went to bed, the living room was bare of presents. By the time they came down in the morning, it would be filled, with a separate area for each child. "They would put sheets over the doors so we couldn't see, and then it would be our heart's desire," Sarah remembers. At one Christmas alone, gifts for the children included a trumpet for Laurence; for Joanne, a puppet theater; for Sarah, a desk stuffed with all kinds of drawing and writing supplies; and for Barry, an eight-foot wooden train. Shirley and Stanley celebrated each other no less extravagantly: his Christmas presents to her over the years included a set of four-thousand-year-old Egyptian scarabs and an antique magic ring from England; among hers to him were an antique flintlock musket and, in 1953, a tape recorder, then costly, cutting-edge technology. Friends and acquaintances in New York and elsewhere received shipments of Vermont apples or cheese. Geraldine and Leslie rarely joined their daughter's family at Christmas, but they sent gifts—usually impersonal ones—for Shirley, Stanley, and the children. (One year Shirley and Geraldine both sent each other ice buckets, which, Shirley joked, reflected their lifestyles.) Instead, the Hymans usually celebrated with Frank Orenstein and June Mirken, their old friends from Syracuse, who were Laurence's godparents, and later with June's husband, anthropologist Sidney Mintz, and their son, Eric. When the Ellisons joined them, Shirley always remembered a box of "dog candy" for their beloved pet.

In the Hyman household, intellectual curiosity and creativity were cultivated and nurtured. There was singing around the piano and dancing in the living room and art projects at the kitchen table: Shirley's old clothespin dolls even made a reappearance. One year, dismayed to discover the children's lack of familiarity with the Bible, Shirley and Stanley read from it every night at the dinner table. Shirley also read her favorite books aloud to the children at bedtime: the Oz series, *The Hobbit* by J. R. R. Tolkien (which she preferred to *The Lord of the Rings*), fairy tales. At age nine, Laurence was given a set of oil paints; at twelve, he took up jazz trumpet. By the time he was fourteen, he was performing in nightclubs with professional musicians, a pursuit Shirley and Stanley supported and encouraged. For years, the family played poker together on Sunday afternoons, whether the children wanted to or not. "Shut up and deal," Stanley would growl.

The children, too, nurtured their mother's imagination. Fascinated by the evolution of a child's consciousness, Shirley delighted in their developing minds. She would write of her astonishment at overhearing Laurence and Joanne talking about the colors in a sunset, or Sarah sitting down at the piano and announcing that she was going to compose a piece that would sound exactly like the cats running down the stairs. Such episodes provided Shirley with a deep well of material that she would draw on many times for the comic essays she published in women's magazines throughout the late forties and fifties and collected in *Life Among the Savages* and *Raising Demons*. The children were not always happy about the way she gobbled up their accidents and

Shirley with Laurence in Greenwich Village, c. 1944.

adventures to regurgitate for public consumption. Sarah, often the family troublemaker, was especially annoyed when Shirley punished her for misdeeds, only to translate them later into cute stories. She smarted when kids at school teased her about her mother's revelations: "Every month, our family was exposed again in *Ladies' Home Journal*." Shirley, whose memory of her own mother's very different invasion of her privacy as a child remained acute, did not seem to be aware that she was committing a similar violation.

What is most evident in the stories Shirley told about her children, however, is her deep pleasure in them. That pleasure is evident in a beautiful fragment written sometime in the midfifties, inspired when Joanne, thrilled to find a new litter of kittens, remarked, "The nicest thing about these kittens is we got them for nothing." Children, of course, do not come "for nothing"; and Shirley's children, especially Laurence and Sarah, would eventually exact a high emotional toll. But in her happiest moments she felt as she depicts herself in this unfinished essay, marveling at "the kind of gratuitous abundance which is lavished upon us everywhere," as in moments when the whole family is suddenly overcome by laughter while sitting at the dinner table. To live with four children, to watch them grow and develop skills and talents, to be allowed to share their most intimate thoughts and ideas, was an "indefinable luxury. . . . Our investment is clothes and food and education and a few well-worn aphorisms, and our return is deep pleasure and delight." After her own difficult childhood, in which her mother never seemed to take "pleasure and delight" in her idiosyncrasies, she was determined to do just the opposite.

SHIRLEY'S JOY IN LAURENCE is palpable in a letter written in early 1943 to Louis Harap, who was then serving in the Army. Shirley filled in her friend on every quotidian detail—Laurence's height, his weight, the progress of his teeth—and covered the pages with hand-drawn pictures of the baby. She was quiet, though, on the subject of her work. "i do very little writing these days," she confessed, with an accompanying cartoon of Laurence sitting on top of her head. She was learning to squeeze her writing into the in-between moments: when the baby was napping or after his last nighttime feeding. In the afternoon, she would take him out for a walk and perhaps a chocolate milk shake. Stanley was more sardonic about the experience of new parenthood: Laurence "looks just like every other baby but slightly uglier," he told Harap. But even he, Shirley reported, was succumbing to the charms of fatherhood: Stanley pushing a baby carriage around the block was something to behold.

Her drawings, however, suggest a different story. In the cartoons Shirley drew after Laurence's birth, the eagle-penguin "familiar" is largely absent: now the focus is on Shirley and Stanley, and the humor is more sarcastic. In one cartoon, captioned "6 o'clock feeding," Stanley, freshly shorn of his New Hampshire beard, sits next to baby Laurence, dressed in an identical shirt and posed in an identical posture, as Shirley approaches—her hair, as usual, sticking out in all directions—with a tray holding a wine bottle and a baby bottle. (The wine is labeled Sauternes.) "Dear, you know the doctor said you weren't to carry anything heavy," he admonishes from behind *The New York Times* as Shirley struggles in, laden with groceries. (Stanley's *Times* reading is a frequent motif in the cartoons; Shirley preferred the *New York Herald Tribune*.) In another, Shirley, holding the baby by his ankle, discovers Stanley taking a nap: "I did three paragraphs all at once and it tired me out," he says. The typewriter sits conspicuously in the background.

As the reference to Sauternes suggests, with its unfortunate reminder of the recent Florence Shapiro episode, Laurence's arrival had not diminished Stanley's interest in other women or Shirley's anxiety about it. In another cartoon, Shirley depicts their living room filled with voluptuous beauties, Stanley leering amid them, as she opens the door to friends. "Oh, no, we haven't got company—just a few friends of Stanley's dropped in," she says. Others seem to be revenge fantasies. "Honest to God, Stanley, the butcher *swore* it was roast beef," she says as her husband tucks into a plate of something that looks suspiciously like entrails, two of the cats looking on with interest. In another, she steals up behind him, brandishing a hatchet, as he relaxes with the newspaper.

The cartoons, however, are dominated by concerns about work, rather than infidelity. Sometimes Shirley is sympathetic to the demands made on her husband. In one drawing, Stanley, reading standing up, leans on a pile of books as high as his chest. "[The editor] says to send them back immediately if I can't have a review ready by tomorrow noon," the caption reads. Others bring into relief the dilemma that Shirley was just starting to confront—a dilemma that would persist for the rest of her life. An early drawing depicts a muscular woman, looking disgruntled, dragging her husband off by his hair as another couple look on worriedly. "I understand she's trying to have both a marriage and a career," one says to the other.

AT THE TIME of Laurence's birth, Jackson was suffering through one of the longest dry spells of her professional life. Her husband's new staff position at *The New Yorker* made it no easier for her to break into that prestigious publication. Despite Pindyck's efforts, she did not publish a single story in 1942. But on Christmas Eve, she received the news that fiction editor Gus Lobrano had finally taken two of her stories: "After You, My Dear Alphonse" and "Afternoon in Linen." The accompanying check, minus the agency fee, was for $252—the equivalent of nearly two months of Hyman's salary. Jackson and Pindyck celebrated modestly with a meal at Hamburger Hearth, a diner on Madison Avenue, at which Jackson formally agreed to let Pindyck represent her. "We're going to be hitched!" Pindyck wrote to her happily afterward, enclosing the contract. In fact, Pindyck was the first of a string of agents with whom Jackson sometimes had contentious relations before she settled down with the venerable firm of Brandt & Brandt in the early fifties. She and Pindyck wouldn't make it to their third anniversary.

Jackson's *New Yorker* success inaugurated a year of fecundity. By the end of 1943, she had sold a total of eight stories, including two more to *The New Yorker*—the same number as John Cheever, one of the most prolific contributors, sold in his first year of writing fiction for the magazine. Jackson also published in *Charm*, a new magazine for young working women, and *House and Garden*, earning around $800 for the year. Hyman's salary, before bonuses, was $1820. Their days of worrying about scurvy were over. "now that we are making a lot of money we are living fine. we even saw a movie not long ago," she told Harap.

Jackson's new productivity had partly to do with the change in her household routine: with Hyman working all day at the *New Yorker* office, she no longer had to fight for her turn at the typewriter. Of course, she also had a baby to take care of! But while Jackson sometimes complained about the mental calisthenics required to be at once a housewife and a writer—the "nagging thoughts" about finishing the laundry or preparing lunch that often interrupted her creative work—she also seems to have derived imaginative energy from the constraints. Writing in the interstices—the hours between morning kindergarten and lunch, while a baby napped, or after the children had gone to bed—demanded a discipline that suited her. She was constantly thinking of stories while cooking, cleaning, or doing just about anything else. "All the time that I am making beds and doing dishes and driving to town for dancing shoes, I am telling myself stories," she said in one of her lectures. Even later, when the children were older and she had more time, Jackson would never be the kind of writer who sat at the typewriter all day. Her writing did not begin when she sat down at her desk, any more than it ended when she got up: "a writer is always writing, seeing everything through a thin mist of words, fitting swift little descriptions to everything he sees, always noticing."

Practical demands notwithstanding, giving birth to Laurence seems to have unlocked Jackson creatively. Her new burst of productivity began only a few months after he was born—a period when many mothers (and fathers) are still woozy with sleep deprivation. It can be no accident that both of her first two *New Yorker* stories center on a child.

Jackson's new confidence was marked by a visible shift in her writing habits: she began typing all her drafts on yellow paper, which became her signature. This was more than a superficial change. Just as some writers find it crucial to use a certain type of notebook or a favorite pen, Jackson's yellow paper became integral to her self-image as a writer. "A book is a comfortable stack of pages of yellow copy paper, with typed words on them, a familiar and fitted country in which I am perfectly at home," she once wrote. Bound between hard covers, her books felt foreign; on her beloved yellow paper, they belonged to her alone. Just as she had once adopted his habit of typing in all lowercase letters, Hyman began sharing her yellow paper.

"In the country of the story the writer is king," Jackson would say in a lecture she gave in later years on the techniques of fiction writing. "He makes all the rules, with only the reservation that he must not ask more than a reader can reasonably grant." This confidence came to her slowly, as she used these early stories—many made it into magazines, while others went into the drawer—to perfect her strategies. One of the most dangerous pitfalls for beginning writers, she would eventually conclude, is that "their stories are, far too often, just simply not very interesting." The writer's challenge is to reach out and grab the attention of even the most distracted or lazy reader: no story will be interesting "unless the writer, using all his skill and craft, sets himself out deliberately to make it so." She called this technique "garlic in fiction": the use of adjectives, images, or symbols, "sparingly and with great care . . . to accent and emphasize."

Already Jackson was honing the efficiency of style that would be one of her defining characteristics as a writer. She was learning, as she later advised others, to let a story "move as naturally and easily as possible, without side trips into unnecessary spots of beauty." Uninteresting details must be made interesting: rather than describing a chair as hard and straight, the writer might show the protagonist holding on to it for balance in a moment of weakness. She perfected dialogue, one of the most difficult things to get right. "It is not enough to let your characters talk as people usually talk because the way people usually talk is extremely dull. . . . Your characters will start all their conversations in the middle unless you have a very good reason for their telling each other good morning and how are you." Repetition and consistency would be key in her work: "a character who says habitually, with one of those silly little laughs, 'Well, that's the story of my life,' is not ever going to turn around and say, with a silly little laugh, 'Well, that's my life story.' "

All these techniques are visible in Jackson's first *New Yorker* story. "Alphonse," like some of the socially conscious stories that Stanley admired, gently but pointedly pokes fun at the racism typical of the American middle class—a theme that would recur regularly in Jackson's early fiction. Mrs. Wilson (Jackson often gave especially ordinary names to her most treacherous characters) is taken aback when her son Johnny brings home his friend Boyd, who is black. She never says anything outwardly racist, but her attitude toward the child is evident in her condescending assumptions about the boy's appetite ("There's plenty of food here for you to have all you want") and his family ("I guess all of you want to make just as much of yourselves as you can"). Boyd innocently parries her at every turn, but eventually declines to accept the Wilson family's old clothing, provoking an outburst from Mrs. Wilson about his ingratitude. Still, the story ends cheerfully: the boys continue happily with their game, unaware of the true intent behind Mrs. Wilson's remarks. The dialogue is tuned with marvelous subtlety—Jackson had finally gotten the *New Yorker* tone just right. But what is truly new in this story is her empathy with Boyd. Ralph Ellison noted it admiringly in a letter to Hyman: "Unlike most *New Yorker* stories in which Negroes appear, 'Alphonse' succeeds in being 'about' the Negro child almost as much as it is about the cheap liberalism of the white kid's mother," he wrote.

In "Afternoon in Linen," a girl named Harriet, embarrassed when her grandmother demands that she read her poetry aloud in front of a guest and her young son, humiliates her grandmother in revenge. (Another poetry-writing child named Harriet, a partial surrogate for Jackson, would appear a few years later in *The Road Through the Wall*.) Its docile-sounding title notwithstanding, the story is a savage snapshot of children's gleeful cruelty to others. Jackson was presenting the world from the true perspective of a child: not through the gauzy veil of the usual women's-magazine fare, but unvarnished, its brutality on full display. The technique suited her wonderfully.

At the time, the *New Yorker* fiction department was experiencing a transition. Lobrano, a college friend of E. B. White's who had previously been an editor at *Town and Country*, took over the department from Katharine White in 1938, when the Whites left Manhattan for Maine. A tall, well-mannered Southern gentleman, Lobrano seems to have been a little too outdoorsy for the *New Yorker* offices, preferring to play badminton at his home in Westchester or to fish at his family's lodge in the Adirondacks, which was decorated, in the classic style, with a moose head over the fireplace. Favored contributors were invited to join him there to enjoy the rustic atmosphere. Jackson was already familiar with country living from her stay in New Hampshire. But Lobrano doesn't ever seem to have invited her to visit the lodge. It was a male-bonding activity from which she was excluded.

Badminton and fishing could do only so much to soothe the nerves of *New Yorker* writers who had begun to chafe at the magazine's notoriously stringent editing. In an obvious reference to Lionel Trilling's critique the previous year, Shaw complained to Lobrano in 1943 about "the patronizing sniffing of critics when they call my stories 'New Yorker' stories, meaning thereby something pallid and cold that is inexplicably used to pad out the space between cartoons and the Talk of the Town. . . . You're overworking your famous urbanity and objectivity to a point where too much of your stuff has a high, even gloss, whether it's on the subject of death, disaster, love, anything." Lobrano sweetened the deal by offering the magazine's top writers a "first-reading agreement," which entitled regular contributors to an annual bonus if they agreed to show him anything they wrote before offering it elsewhere, as well as a bonus if they managed to sell more than a certain number of stories to the magazine each year. And gradually he and Katharine White, who continued to edit fiction part-time after moving to Maine and is generally credited with shaping the magazine's literary vision, grew more open to fiction that did not fit the *New Yorker* mold: by the end of the decade, they would publish stories by J. D. Salinger and Vladimir Nabokov in addition to, of course, "The Lottery."

The department's evolution, however, was slow. And the fact that Jackson had gotten two stories into *The New Yorker* was no guarantee that Lobrano would take others. Her next seven were rejected—not always politely. "Pretty formula[ic] and unconvincing . . . my suspicion is that Miss Jackson is a good deal better when she stays close to reality," Lobrano wrote in response to "Company for Dinner," about a man who accidentally comes home to the wrong house; neither he nor his wife initially notices the difference. "[She] seems to have not much flair for whimsy or fantasy." Jackson must have found this critique frustrating, since the majority of the stories she had submitted were realistic. In "Little Old Lady in Great Need," the most accomplished of this group (it would find its way to *Mademoiselle*), an elderly lady manages to swindle a butcher out of his own dinner, lecturing her great-granddaughter all the while on how to act like a lady. (Some of her lines—"A lady does not permit herself to show anger in public," for instance—sound like particularly choice tidbits from Geraldine.) But it was a little more one-dimensional than the magazine's usual work.

Jackson finally made it back into *The New Yorker* with "Come Dance with Me in Ireland," which appeared in May 1943. Again the subject is the essential hypocrisy of human beings and their mindless cruelty to one another. An elderly man selling shoelaces shows up at Mrs. Archer's apartment building one day; he looks faint, so she invites him in to sit down. She and her friends are as superficially courteous as Mrs. Wilson in "Alphonse"; they are also just as thoughtless, wondering openly whether the man is drunk and speaking of him rudely in the third person. The old man gets the last word: he announces proudly that he once knew Yeats, quoting, "Come out of charity, come dance with me in Ireland." The women's so-called charity is nothing of the kind. But the man's reproach likely goes over their heads: they are only dimly aware of who Yeats is.

Even in these early years, cruelty and alienation were the dominant themes of Jackson's fiction. A cashier in a liquor store behaves generously toward a blind man and his wife, only to discover himself the victim of a scam ("On the House"). A sad old man, strolling through the park on a sunny day, tries to impress others by lying about his connections to celebrities ("It Isn't the Money I Mind"). In "Colloquy," one of the most evocative pieces, a woman visits a psychiatrist who, unnervingly, is unable to empathize with her distress. He speaks of "international crisis" and "cultural patterns" when all she wants to know is whether she is going crazy. By the end of the story, she is reduced to parroting his words back to him, giving them a new meaning:

"What is going to help?" Mrs. Arnold said. "Is everyone really crazy but me?"

"Mrs. Arnold," the doctor said severely, "I want you to get hold of yourself. In a disoriented world like ours today, alienation from reality frequently—"

"Disoriented," Mrs. Arnold said. She stood up. "Alienation," she said. "Reality." Before the doctor could stop her she walked to the door and opened it. "Reality," she said, and walked out.

SHIRLEY AND STANLEY lasted only a year in "the borough of homes." In October 1943, they moved back to the more congenial Village, taking a second-floor apartment at 36 Grove Street for $900 a year, around the corner from Edna St. Vincent Millay's famous former residence at 75½ Bedford Street. Other than increased rationing—coffee, meat, cheese, and canned goods were now added to the list—the war had changed Greenwich Village very little. The Grove Street apartment, in a redbrick town house, was "a nice big old place" with three fireplaces, Stanley

Washington Square Park by Berenice Abbott, 1935, not long
before Jackson and Hyman moved to Grove Street.

told Kenneth Burke, with whom he had begun to correspond regularly. They were just around the corner from Isaac Rosenfeld, Saul Bellow's close friend, whose apartment was a social center for the *Partisan Review* crowd, including the critics Harold Rosenberg and Alfred Kazin.

Laurence's birth did not put a damper on Shirley and Stanley's social style; their parties sometimes went on all night. Philip Hamburger, one of Stanley's *New Yorker* colleagues, recalled seeing Laurence's crib piled so high with guests' coats that he had trouble locating the baby. Jesse Zel Lurie was astonished when Shirley served "hideously green mashed potatoes" for dinner, tinted with food coloring. The regular kind bored her, she explained. *New Yorker* reporter Andy Logan would remember a Thanksgiving meal at the Hymans' attended by half a dozen of the magazine's young staff, to which she contributed a bottle of cheap white wine. Shirley was holding Laurence in one arm and "rustling up dinner with the other, audibly daring the gravy to lump." (It didn't.) The very genteel Shawn was "pleased but alarmed" to hear about the dinner. "I don't believe this sort of thing ever happened at *The New Yorker* before," he said to Logan.

Some of the guests who visited the Hymans over the years, including Walter Bernstein, remember Shirley as notoriously lax about standards of hygiene. "The baby's diaper was always full," Bernstein recalls. If Shirley had ever tried to conform to Geraldine's expectations for her as a housekeeper, she now abandoned any such pretense. Later, in Vermont, her neighbors would gossip about her sloppy habits. But her casual style was the norm in the Village. Bellow would joke that if there were a magazine called *Bad Housekeeping*, Isaac Rosenfeld's wife could have been the editor.

One frequent visitor to the Grove Street apartment was Ralph Ellison, who had quickly become close to both Jackson and Hyman after their initial contact in New Hampshire. Despite the similar intellectual interests of the two men, their personalities were a study in contrasts. Always known for his fastidious clothing and manners, Ellison was surprised, at their first meeting, when Hyman appeared "hatless and wearing a short-sleeved sport shirt, lugging his ever-present briefcase." Their writing styles, too, were sharply different. Hyman's first *Negro Quarterly* piece began with a typically bold salvo: "The thing to do with a book like *Tap Roots* is to get the worst things said first. In many respects it is a bad book and a cheap book." Ellison agonized over every word, so cautious and at times indecisive that, despite his enormous talent, he would famously struggle with bringing his works to completion. "Where Ralph tended to be self-conscious, solemn, ideological, and ponderous, Hyman was direct, engaging, and smart," writes Ellison's biographer Arnold Rampersad.

The pair quickly became partners in an intellectual endeavor that would be crucial to both of them. Around this time, Hyman and Ellison both began to read deeply in the myth-ritual criticism written by the classicists and folklorists of the previous generation known as the Cambridge School: Jane Ellen Harrison, Gilbert Murray, Lord Raglan, and of course Frazer. According to these theorists, myth should be understood not as a corrupted version of history (a theory known as "euhemerism"), but as a narrative that derives from ritual and purports to explain it. As Hyman would later write, "Myth is neither a record of historical fact nor an explanation of nature. It is the spoken correlative

of a ritual, the story which the rite enacts or once enacted." The implications of this theory were far-reaching, with potential consequences
for the study of not only religion but also literature. More than a decade
later, Hyman would create Myth, Ritual, and Literature, a brilliant and
original course tracing the ritual origins of the Old and New Testaments as well as folk songs, ballads, and the blues. It was an intellectual
endeavor for which he—with his traditional Jewish education, his atheism, his rigorous literary training, and his love of music—was uniquely
suited, and which resonated deeply with the themes of Jackson's work.

Hyman also introduced Ellison to his mentor Kenneth Burke, who
would play an important role in Ellison's intellectual life as well. After
hearing Burke deliver his lecture "The Rhetoric of Hitler's 'Battle' " at
the third American Writers' Congress in 1939, Ellison had immersed
himself in the critic's work. When Burke visited New York (he and
his wife, Libbie, lived on a farm in rural Andover, New Jersey, with
no plumbing or central heating), the three men, along with Jackson,
sometimes met for dinner at one of Burke's favorite spots, the Farm-
food vegetarian restaurant on West Fortieth Street. (Burke, who was
partial to cheese blintzes and loved to come up with idiosyncratic forms
of language, called their dinners there "going a-blintzing.") Ellison

*Hyman reading
the manuscript of*
Invisible Man,
c. 1950.

acknowledged Burke's influence in a letter written in 1945 while he was working on *Invisible Man*, his seminal 1952 novel examining the black experience in America: "I am writing a novel now and perhaps if it is worthwhile it will be my most effective means of saying thanks. Anything else seems to me inadequate and unimaginative."

Reflecting on their friendship many years later, Ellison would credit Hyman as a crucial influence on his fiction. If Ellison was struggling with a project, Hyman often stepped in to encourage him. In 1943, when Ellison was about to ship out to the merchant marine, Hyman urged him first to finish "Flying Home," the story that would be his breakthrough work. Ellison was "reluctant," but at Hyman's insistence, he sat down at the typewriter in the living room on Grove Street and "brought the yarn as close to completion as time permitted, then headed for the North Atlantic." By the time he returned, it was already in print: Hyman had submitted it to *Cross Section*, an anthology of new writing that also published one of Jackson's stories, "Behold the Child Among His Newborn Blisses." For both, it was their first "appearance between hard covers," Ellison proudly remembered. The influence flowed both ways: Ellison also read Jackson's and Hyman's drafts and offered comments. Two years later, when the opening to *Invisible Man* came to Ellison at a friend's farm in Vermont, he wrote to Hyman immediately to share both his excitement and his anxiety. "This section of the novel is going very well—though God only knows what the hell it's all about. Of one thing I'm sure, any close symbolic analysis of it [a joking reference to Burke] will reveal how completely crazy I am." Over the course of his long and often painful effort to write the novel, Ellison would regularly call upon Hyman for guidance, at one point saying that he was "invaluable" during the process. Rampersad and others have suggested that absent Hyman's influence and encouragement, Ellison might not have written *Invisible Man*.

AS SHIRLEY ENJOYED her string of successes in 1943, Jeanou was struggling with the new realities of life in Nazi-occupied Paris. In March, she was arrested for Resistance work and spent nearly a year and a half in prison. Scheduled to be shot or deported—she did not know which—in August 1944, she would be spared by the liberation of Paris. By then, much of her family had been deported to Germany, along with her lover, a Russian national. Shirley learned of Jeanou's predicament a few months after her release and asked a friend who was still serving in Europe to visit her. He would bring her with him to the Army mess hall so that she could enjoy a meal that included meat. Also scarce were tea, canned milk, chocolate, soap, or stockings, all of which Shirley mailed to Paris at Jeanou's request.

Meanwhile, Shirley and Stanley were bystanders to the war that roiled the world. "we live quietly, writing books and being in a constant state of chilled horror at our son," she wrote to Louis Harap in February 1944. "he leers, and talks back (his two words: good, light, but he can make them sound very ugly), and eats with his fingers and looks at his father and snorts contemptuously. he is already so strong that it is wiser to appeal to his good judgment than force. . . . he likes to wrestle, and to walk along the street yelling, and to lift ladies' skirts on the street, but he is already healthier than any of us ever were." A few months later, she reported proudly that Laurence was strong enough to lift the kitchen chairs, with "muscles in his back like Joe Louis." Her father, in a letter, referred to him as "young Samson." Unfortunately, he also was strong enough to climb out of his crib at night, interrupting her evening writing time.

Although Jackson criticized herself as unproductive, in 1944 she sold a dozen stories, including another four to *The New Yorker*. It was an unusual feat for an up-and-coming writer, especially a woman: only more commercial female writers, such as Sylvia Townsend Warner and Sally Benson, appeared more frequently. Many of Jackson's *New Yorker* stories would eventually find their way into the somber-toned *Lottery* collection: small domestic incidents, realistically depicted, that take on a darker meaning with the revelation—if only partial—of something sinister in the background. What is unsaid is often more important than what is said. In "A Fine Old Firm," Mrs. Friedman drops in on her neighbor Mrs. Concord to tell her that their boys are serving together in the Army. It soon becomes clear that Mrs. Friedman's friendly interest in the Concords is not reciprocated. The conversation ends when Mrs. Friedman offers Mrs. Concord's son an interview with her husband's law firm after he returns, only to be told that the boy will be joining the firm in which his grandfather was once a partner, "a fine old firm." The tension between the Jewish newcomers and the WASP old-timers is so subtly drawn, the anti-Semitism so lightly suggested, that on first reading it may pass over the reader's head.

"A Fine Old Firm" appeared in *The New Yorker* in March 1944, laid out opposite a full-page ad for a brand of hardware used by the military. D-day came just two months later. By then, most of Stanley's friends had been drafted: Harap, Ellison, Bernstein, Frank Orenstein, Ben Zimmerman. Shirley and Stanley learned the news of the invasion when *The New York Times* arrived that morning; they ate breakfast with the radio on. When Shirley went out to do her errands, people stopped her on the street to read the newspaper she was holding. In the bakery, the owner, who had four sons overseas, was weeping openly. It was "the most terrible day" of her life to date, Shirley felt at the time.

As a gentile married to a Jew, Shirley was well aware that if she and Stanley had been living in Europe, their whole family would have been deported and murdered. The fight against the Germans felt personal for both of them, as Shirley made clear in an unfinished novel she was working on around this time, tentatively titled *Soldier Leaving*. The main character is Harriet, a young housewife in New York City whose husband, Paul, is preparing to leave for the war. Harriet is Christian, Paul is Jewish, and Billy, their son, is about a year old. Harriet is racked by nightmares in which an unknown menace threatens her and her child. "they were chasing her and she was running down the two flights of stairs and she was carrying billy and the fire was ahead of her and they were chasing her and then the fire had burned away the stairs and she fell still holding billy and when she went up to billy afterwards he was a picture from a magazine, cut and burned and with a caption saying 'innocent children slaughtered.'" Friends warn her that "smart jews are going to get the hell out of this country."

The war appears in Jackson's stories primarily as a backdrop to the human dramas: the wives (loyal and less so) left behind, the children

taken aback by the sudden reappearance of a father who has been serving in the Army. In "Henrietta," an unpublished early story, a teacher
mistakes the ravings of a refugee student as paranoid delusions, but to
the reader it's obvious that she's having flashbacks to a concentration
camp. In "The Gift," a soldier home on leave asks a department store
clerk to help her pick out a present for his girlfriend, who turns out to
be a figment of his imagination. Jackson was especially interested in the
consequences for women left on their own when their husbands went
to war. In "Trial by Combat," a young woman staying in a rooming
house while her husband is overseas discovers that an elderly neighbor
is stealing from her, but decides not to confront the thief: not speaking up becomes as deliberate an act as provoking a confrontation. In
"As High as the Sky," a mother inspects her two young daughters as
they sit together on the couch, anxious that their father, seeing them for
the first time in years, will be presented with a model tableau of family
life. "Homecoming" emphasizes a wife's anticipation of her husband's
return and the pleasure she takes in the necessary housekeeping duties.
"This is the part of the house he never saw, that no one knows about,"
she muses before her open linen closet. "The laundry when it comes
back, the wash on the line fresh from the tubs. . . . Women with homes
live so closely with substances, bread, soap, and buttons."

Only one of these early stories gives a sense of what Jackson's writing meant to her. In "When Things Get Dark," a young woman named
Mrs. Garden receives a letter from Mrs. Hope (the names even more
symbolic than usual), an elderly lady she met on a bus a few days earlier. The cryptic letter offers vague support: "When things get dark,
remember there are always friends thinking of you and wishing you
well." As it happens, Mrs. Garden is in need of friendly advice: she
recently discovered that she is unexpectedly pregnant—her husband,
too, is overseas—and is debating what to do about it. But when she
seeks out Mrs. Hope for counsel, the older woman doesn't even remember meeting her. Writing letters, it turns out, is just the way she passes
the time; she has no special interest in Mrs. Garden. She has even written to Hitler: "when he first started killing and rampaging . . . I said for
him to look into his heart and find love." Mrs. Garden is the first of Mrs.

Hope's addressees to contact her, and she is pleased to learn that she is "doing some good." But Mrs. Garden is so distressed by Mrs. Hope's indifference to her that she flees the room. "Wait a minute," Mrs. Hope calls, handing her the letter. "You don't want to forget this. . . . Keep it near you, to read when things get dark."

Fourteen years later, Jackson would write a story that was almost an exact counterpoint to "When Things Get Dark." Never published during her lifetime—it appeared posthumously as "The Possibility of Evil"—it also features an old woman who writes letters, this time maliciously, spilling secrets and sowing dissent among neighbors. The letters in "When Things Get Dark," on the other hand, are well intended—little beacons of hope sent into the night—yet useless. If Jackson saw her own stories as idle letters cast into the dark and wondered whether they could do any good, she was relieved at last to be publishing her writing and earning a living from it. "after a while you get to feeling like there's something you got to do and say before you float away just floating like on air," she wrote in an unpublished essay. "and you try to tell them and all that comes out is god god life life."

AS A RESULT OF HYMAN's *New Yorker* gig and his prolific freelance book reviewing, he quickly became known in New York publishing circles as something of a wunderkind. But the novelty of writing Comments every week soon faded. To his enduring frustration, the magazine's editors were uninterested in his attempts to write anything longer. At the age of twenty-four, he determined the time was right to undertake a full-length work of literary criticism.

Instead of focusing on a certain writer or movement, Hyman decided, he would criticize the critics themselves. As he eventually formulated it, the idea was to examine "the acts of criticism to which men from Plato and Aristotle through Coleridge to [contemporary critics] . . . have been led by their varying reactions to the subject matter, successes, and failures of the most important writings—the Bible, Shakespeare, the finest English poetry, etc." There would be chapters on Edmund Wilson, Yvor Winters, T. S. Eliot, Van Wyck Brooks, and Kenneth Burke, among others, each representing a particular mode of literary criticism: evaluative, biographical, psychological, Marxist, and so on. The book was a direct outgrowth of the ideas Hyman had been developing as early as college, when he first realized that a work of art could be interpreted in a virtually limitless number of ways, on a spectrum ranging from political to personal. He floated his idea for the book to Burke, who was enthusiastic, if sardonic. "The general outline suggests richly ironic possibilities. I.e., you can squeeze each critic successively into a bin that is too narrow for him—and then in your wind-up you can give them all hell for being so restricted," Burke told him.

In the fall of 1941, Scott Mabon, an editor at the distinguished publishing firm Alfred A. Knopf, had contacted Hyman after hearing he might be at work on a book. Mabon wasn't interested in the biography of abolitionist Wendell Phillips that Hyman proposed, but he praised Hyman's review of *Mildred Pierce*, a recent Knopf novel by James M. Cain. This was quite a compliment, considering that Hyman had panned it. A year later, after requesting a review copy of another Knopf book, Hyman was floored to receive a letter from Alfred A. Knopf himself, inviting him and Jackson to lunch at the Knopfs' Tudor country house in Purchase, New York. Jackson, too, received a personal note in which the publisher congratulated her on "Alphonse," calling it "a swell little piece" and expressing the hope that she would someday become a Knopf author.

Knopf, who had founded his publishing firm in 1915 at the age of twenty-three, was as well-known for his brusque demeanor and flamboyant taste in clothing (a *New Yorker* profile described him as "bold and piratical") as for his roster of Nobel Prize winners: Knut Hamsun, Sigrid Undset, Thomas Mann. In early 1943, Jackson and Hyman spent a pleasant afternoon at his estate, "eating squab and drinking godknows-what"—Knopf's cork-lined wine cellar was the stuff of legend. But they left mystified, as Knopf had said nothing about publishing either of them.

Their mystification did not last long. That August, a few months after his rejection by the draft board, Hyman signed a contract with Knopf that gave him an advance of $500 and a laughably optimistic deadline of

December 30, 1944, less than a year and a half away. The book's working title was *The Critical Method*. In January 1944, he resigned from *The New Yorker* to work on it full-time, although he continued to write Notes and Comments. His ambitious plan was to spend the first six months of the year reading and taking notes on several hundred books of criticism and the last six months writing. "he seems to be writing hard, all day long," Jackson reported.

Jackson supported Hyman's efforts: the morning he began work on the book, she placed a rose on his desk and cooked him a special breakfast of chicken livers. But she felt pressure to complete a book of her own. "did stanley tell you i am writing a novel? i decided that i might as well, just to keep stanley from sounding too superior about his old book," she wrote to a friend in May 1944. Pascal (Pat) Covici, who joined Viking in 1938 after founding his own publishing firm with partner Donald Friede, had been impressed enough by her *New Yorker* stories to offer her a contract for an as yet unwritten work of fiction. Covici's list already included John Steinbeck, Nathanael West, and Lionel Trilling, among many others. Years earlier, he had been responsible for bringing to press *The Well of Loneliness*, the lesbian novel Jackson had admired in college, in defiance of the libel suit brought against the book.

Eventually Jackson would grow fond of Covici, to whom she dedicated her last completed novel, *We Have Always Lived in the Castle*. But she quickly regretted signing that contract. Her novel about the Jewish soldier leaving for the Army would not progress; she managed only around thirty-five pages. She tried something entirely different: a refashioning of a witchcraft story from Glanvill's *Saducismus Triumphatus*, the seventeenth-century account of witchcraft trials that she had once hoped her friend Elizabeth Young would steal from the University of Rochester library. One of the cases Glanvill documents involves Elizabeth Style, an alleged witch who is accused of bewitching and torturing a young girl named Elizabeth Hill. When brought to trial, Style confessed that the devil had appeared to her ten years earlier in the shape of a handsome man and as a black dog. "He promised her Money, and that she should Live gallantly, and have the Pleasure of the World for 12 Years, if she would with her Blood sign his Paper, which was to give her soul to him. . . . When she hath a desire to do harm, she calls the Spirit by the name of Robin, to whom when he appeareth, she useth these words, O Satan give me my purpose!" One of Style's accomplices would come to repent of her choice: "He promised her, when she made her Contract with him, that she should want nothing, but ever since she hath wanted all things."

In Jackson's version, called simply "Elizabeth," Elizabeth Style, in a sly joke, is a literary agent who works for a man named Robert Shax. (Shax, a name Shirley would later use for a number of her favorite cats, is the name of a king of demons.) When the story takes place, he and Elizabeth have worked together for nearly eleven years. Their agency is unsuccessful, and Elizabeth spends her days shaking money out of potential clients and stealing their ideas for her own manuscript-in-progress. Shax is married, and he and Elizabeth have been conducting a long-term affair that she hopes, fruitlessly, will end with him leaving his wife. Instead, one day he brings her an unwelcome surprise: without consulting her, he has hired a new secretary, a buxom young blonde named Daphne Hill. Elizabeth insults and torments the girl, then fires her while Shax is out of the office for the afternoon. The story sputters to a halt soon afterward: Jackson was unable to bring the plot to a satisfying conclusion. Novel writing would almost always come with difficulty for her. Her stories, especially as she became more and more practiced, often required little revision, other than normalizing the capitalization and, sometimes, changing names—especially if she had used real-life models. But her novels were painful processes, full of false starts and dead ends.

Instead, Jackson decided to put together a book of stories. It would be called *The Intoxicated*, after her story about the man at a party who encounters a teenage girl prophesying the apocalypse, and would feature just about all her published and unpublished material to date. Harap was critical: the scope of her stories was "limited," he wrote, urging her to work on a novel instead. Shirley found his comments patronizing. "if you think a 'full career as a writer' comes with the length of a novel you are more ambitious for me than i am for myself," she shot back. But Covici, already an esteemed and (to Jackson) intimidating editor, insisted that she abide by their agreement. In early 1945, she submitted what she had of "Elizabeth." Unimpressed, he offered to release her from her contract. Fran Pindyck, Shirley's agent, offered the novel to an editor at Knopf, since the firm had previously asked to see her work, but he, too, thought it was unready for publication. Jackson put it aside. She would eventually publish part of it as a short story in the *Lottery* collection.

A distraction from her failed novels arrived from an unexpected source. Burke had recently mentioned to Hyman that Bennington College, a progressive new women's school in Vermont, was looking for young instructors, having lost several to war service. "can't you just see stanley teaching a seminar in a girl's college?" Jackson laughed, perhaps not altogether enthusiastically. Over dinner in New York, Burke formally introduced Hyman to Bennington's president, Lewis Webster Jones, a former economist and professed "illiterate in the arts" who now found himself in an unlikely new role. Founded only a dozen years earlier, the college offered a famously experimental curriculum with an emphasis on faculty who— like Burke—made up for in brilliance what they lacked in advanced degrees. Now Jones was looking for a critic who could teach introductory courses in literary theory, joining a department that included Burke as well as drama critic Francis Fergusson and poet Theodore Roethke.

After visiting the college, situated on 140 hilltop acres just outside the rural town of North Bennington, in southern Vermont, Jackson and Hyman came away delighted. Even though her city shoes were inadequate to the ice, Jackson was amazed by the surrounding mountains covered with clean white snow—a dramatic contrast to the sooty sludge of Greenwich Village in the winter. The idea of raising children in Vermont, where they could see "real cows," also appealed to her. Perhaps here, in the country again, she would find her long sought stability, the balm for her restlessness. In the spring of 1945, Hyman joined the Bennington College faculty.

7.

SIDESTREET, U.S.A.

BENNINGTON,
THE ROAD THROUGH
THE WALL,
1945–1948

"It's such an old house," Mrs. MacLane said, looking up at
the dark ceiling. "I love old houses; they feel so secure and
warm, as though lots of people had been perfectly satisfied
with them and they *knew* how useful they were. You don't
get that feeling with a new house."

—"Flower Garden"

BENNINGTON COLLEGE, FOR DECADES CONSIDERED THE
most radical campus in America, was dreamed up by a preacher. Vincent Ravi Booth, appointed pastor of the First Congregational Church
in Old Bennington, Vermont, in the summer of 1919, was dismayed to
find that his pews were empty come fall—the town's summer residents
had all left for the season. How could he fill the seats? What the area
needed, locals told him, was a women's college. Both Smith and Mount
Holyoke, in nearby western Massachusetts, were overcrowded, turning
away qualified applicants for lack of dorm space. A similar college in
Bennington stood a good chance of success.

Within thirteen years, a coalition of progressive educators and

Students on the Bennington College Commons in the 1940s.

wealthy Vermonters had realized Booth's vision. Their ambitious project was to reimagine the education of American women. The first women's colleges, driven by the need to prove that women and men were intellectual equals, had modeled themselves on men's colleges. But the traditional curriculum, oriented heavily toward the classics, had begun to feel out-of-date. Bennington, the early planners decided, would be a new kind of college designed especially to meet the needs of modern women, organized around science, history, sociology, languages, fine arts, and philosophy. The emphasis would be on "the actual," said Robert Devore Leigh, Bennington's first president: "the changing world which our students are living in." As John Dewey, the founding father of progressive education, famously opined, education was not "preparation for life," but life itself. "It was a wild and wonderful place," recalls the critic Barbara Fisher, who studied with Hyman at Bennington in the early 1960s. The writer Susan Cheever, also an alumna, has written that the college was "as much a state of mind as it was a place."

The purpose of college, according to Bennington's first course catalog, was to provide a grounding for education that the student could continue throughout her life. The emphasis was on the independent pursuit of knowledge. There would be no grades, exams, or prizes to serve as motivators; students were evaluated in lengthy written comments. (For those who wanted to continue on to graduate school, the comments would be translated into grades solely for use on a transcript.) The women would spend their first two years exploring a possible major, then move on to self-directed advanced work, supervised personally by a member of the faculty. Each division would offer an introductory course—not a traditional survey, but a sampling of what was "significant, vital and representative in the field," focusing on modern Western civilization and contemporary American culture. Faculty, too, would learn by doing: initially, they determined their course offerings after meeting each year's students and discussing their interests. And the winter "non-resident term"—first two months long, later three—gave students the opportunity to pursue internships in their chosen fields; it also got them off campus during the most brutal months of the year.

Most important, intellectual development and character development were considered inseparable. To that end, each student was assigned a faculty counselor who would meet with her weekly to offer advice on her coursework and anything else she might need help with. "Bennington regards education as a sensual and ethical, no less than an intellectual, process," reads the college's commencement statement, which has been read aloud at every graduation since 1936. "It seeks to liberate and nurture the individuality, the creative intelligence, and the ethical and aesthetic sensibility of its students, to the end that their richly varied natural endowments will be directed toward self-fulfillment and toward constructive social purposes." This was extraordinary at a time when some leading educators deliberately discouraged their female students from developing a critical intelligence they would be unlikely to use in their postcollege lives. Many colleges included a "marriage education" course designed to prepare students to be housewives. As Mills College put it in an infamous slogan adopted in the early 1950s, "We are not educating women to be scholars; we are educating them to be wives and mothers."

Isolated on a bucolic campus surrounded by mountains, Bennington students enjoyed a level of personal freedom to equal their intellectual freedom. The college's philosophy with regard to student social life was summed up by Mabel Barbee Lee, the first dean of admissions, in a polemic for *The Atlantic* in April 1930 against "social paternalism" in women's colleges. At a time when "house mothers" monitored students' movements in their dorms and strict curfews, known as parietals, were the norm, Lee argued that female students should be "granted browsing privileges in the field of experience." At Bennington, there were initially only three rules: silence had to be maintained in the library at all times and elsewhere on campus after ten p.m.; no cars could be driven on the road by the student houses after ten p.m.; and a student who planned to be off campus after eleven p.m. had to fill out a slip saying where she could be reached. (Miriam Marx, Groucho Marx's daughter, was

*Bennington
student houses,
c. early 1940s.*

one of the few students to be expelled in the early years for disciplinary reasons: in addition to other offenses, she loudly drove her car on campus late at night.) Eventually another rule was added prohibiting pets at college, after complaints were made about students bringing puppies, kittens, mice, and even lambs into the dorms. "It was the kind of place where a notice went out to everybody before Parents Weekend saying, 'Please take your liquor bottles off the windowsill while the parents are here,' " remembers Marilyn Seide, Walter Bernstein's sister, who graduated in 1952. When the writer Kathleen Norris arrived at Bennington in the early 1960s, she was shocked to see one of her classmates openly taking speed during class. Her father, contacting the college out of concern for his daughter after a breakup, was told blithely by a counselor, "We do count [the students], now and then."

The "Bennington girls" attracted by this culture of independence— not exactly the churchgoers Reverend Booth had sought—were known for being "arty, avant-garde, a little unconventional," as Seide puts it. They also were rich, or at least their parents were: for years Bennington was the most expensive college in America. When Suzanne Stern graduated in 1956, her parents showed up for commencement with a case each of champagne and beluga caviar. Bernard Malamud, who began teaching at Bennington in 1961, noted that the students were "very bright, very perspicacious about literature; it's something to hear them analyze a story." But he was initially so dismayed by their casual clothing that he insisted they wear dresses to his creative writing class. In response, Betty Aberlin, who went on to become an actress, showed up in a full-length evening gown, accessorized with cowboy boots. Nonchalance regarding personal appearance was something of a Bennington tradition: the town's community council scolded the first class of students for wearing "scandalizing attire" off campus, but quickly gave up the fight. Long before it became a political statement to burn one's bra, Bennington girls were known for going braless; at a time when upper-class young women were brought up according to standards like Geraldine Jackson's—carefully coiffed, with skirts to the midcalf—they grew their hair long and wore blue jeans. Shirley, writing to Jeanou soon after her arrival, commented approvingly that the students wore no makeup and dressed in dirty shirts and pants. Their teachers, too, could be casual. The first time Stern encountered Burke, at a poetry reading— "this wild man . . . with his hair flying around like Einstein"—she mistook him for a janitor.

Hyman would have been an unlikely candidate for a job at a traditional college, not least because he did not have an advanced degree. But the Bennington faculty—the term "professor" was not used—were young and dynamic, mainly practitioners in their fields rather than academics; only a few had doctorates. "The idea was to be an actual creator in your field rather than a teacher," says Fisher. The years Hyman taught at Bennington—from 1945 until 1946, then again from 1953 until 1969—were a golden age for the college, which boasted an astounding collection of thinkers and artists. In addition to Burke and Roethke, the literature faculty included W. H. Auden, Stanley Kunitz (hired in haste in 1946 when Roethke, in the grip of a manic episode, said he would emerge from his campus house only if Kunitz was brought in to replace him), Howard Nemerov, and later Malamud. Erich Fromm taught psychology; Martha Graham taught dance. In the fifties and sixties, the fine arts division included critic Clement Greenberg, painters Jules Olitski and Paul Feeley, sculptor Anthony Caro, composers Lionel Nowak and Marc Blitzstein, and cellist George Finckel.

These names are virtually all male—unusual for a women's college. The combination of the predominantly male faculty, the small student body (the college maintained an enrollment of fewer than four hundred students until the mid-1960s), the remote location, and the culture of permissiveness and informality fostered particularly intimate connections between faculty and students. Classes were often conducted in the living rooms of student houses, with the instructor sitting in an armchair and students lounging on couches or the floor. And the weekly counseling sessions encouraged students and their advisers to form close relationships. A faculty member with ten "counselees," as the students were called, could easily spend more time advising than teaching. Stern remembers Burke, her counselor, knocking on her window in the middle of the night to invite her to go for a walk and "kick around a few notions." Professors and students often socialized together. "When we had parties, sometimes I would find a professor on the floor of my closet the next morning," says Victoria Kirby, a 1962 graduate.

Many women found these relationships deeply nurturing, both personally and intellectually. Others felt they were exploitative. "It was a model for sexist behavior," says the writer Joan Schenkar, who graduated in 1963. Liaisons between students and faculty—sometimes discreet, sometimes open—were tolerated on campus until the late 1960s, when Edward Bloustein, then the president, cracked down. A guest at a New York cocktail party Kathleen Norris attended referred to Bennington as "the little red whorehouse on the hill." One faculty member was known for prowling the all-night study room for conquests. Many of the students interviewed for this book had a story to tell about a sexual encounter, often unwanted, with a professor. Sometimes the students were the aggressors. "More than once," Norris writes in her memoir, "I received an engraved invitation to an on-campus orgy; a more perfect expression of debutante wantonness could not be conceived." When Phoebe Pettingell, who would become Hyman's second wife after Jackson's death, arrived at Bennington in 1965, the art students who lived in one cottage kept a chart on the wall of their stairway ranking the art faculty, with critical ratings and "caricatures of certain body parts." Those girls, Pettingell says, "collected faculty scalps."

Hyman would eventually become a dazzling and charismatic teacher. His signature course, Myth, Ritual, and Literature, which he inaugurated in 1956, was for years the most popular class in the college. "He was as brilliant as Shakespeare," recalls the poet and novelist Sandra Hochman, who studied with Hyman in the late 1950s. But he initially found his responsibilities overwhelming. His course load during his first year included Methods of Literary Criticism, in which he lectured on the critical approaches he was writing about in *The Armed Vision*, and Forms of Literature, for which he assigned two dozen novels by Stendhal, Flaubert, Hawthorne, Melville, Tolstoy, Dostoyevsky, Faulkner, and others. He described his foray into teaching as "learning something of a Monday to teach it of a Tuesday": he had to spend "three days a week on campus and the other four from morning to night reading the stuff." The students found him standoffish, partly because he insisted on addressing them by their last names, as his college professors had addressed him, but also because he delivered the kind of formal lectures he had enjoyed at Syracuse, which was not the Bennington style. One said his method of argument resembled "the mating combat of male elks."

The schedule left Hyman very little time to work on the criticism book he was supposed to be writing. His deadline, originally December 1944, had already been extended to January 1, 1946. On January 6, he wrote to his editor at Knopf asking for another extension. His plan was to resign his post at the end of the spring term and devote the rest of the year to finishing the book.

Although the permissive milieu appealed to her in many ways, for Jackson, too, adjustment to life at Bennington was somewhat difficult. The "faculty wife" of the 1940s and 1950s was expected to concentrate her energy on organizing social activities and supporting her husband's work. Jackson eventually channeled her feelings about this role into a satirical essay for the Bennington alumnae magazine. The faculty wife, Jackson wrote, anticipating *The Feminine Mystique* close to a decade before its publication,

> has frequently read at least one good book lately, she has one 'nice' dress to wear to student parties, and she is always just the teensiest bit in the way. . . . It is considered probable that ten years or so ago she had a face and a personality of her own, but if she has it still, she is expected to keep it decently to herself. . . . Her little pastimes, conducted in a respectably anonymous and furtive manner, are presumed to include such activities as knitting, hemming dish towels, and perhaps sketching wild flowers or doing water colors of her children.

The illustrations for the piece—done by fellow faculty wife Helen Feeley, married to the painter Paul Feeley and a good friend of Jackson's—depicted women without faces.

In addition to her professional career, Jackson's housedresses and casual demeanor set her apart from the neatly-put-together faculty wives. In an early photograph taken on the Bennington lawn, she relaxes in a sundress and sunglasses, a cigarette between her fingers, her hair pulled back in a ponytail; many of the other women dressed more formally, their hair carefully styled.

Jackson mingled in the Bennington community: she and Hyman often attended movies, concerts, or lectures at the college, and she occasionally read tarot cards for students. When Hyman invited students over to the house, Jackson was sometimes happy to play the role of hostess, especially for her favorites. She nicknamed Suzanne Stern "Mimosa" and complimented her beauty. Miriam Marx, who became close to the family and babysat for some of the children, remembers Jackson's excellent potato pancakes. But Jackson could also withdraw or act hostile. "He would invite us over . . . and Shirley would be there looking glum and grim and say nothing," remembers Joan Constantikes, a 1956 graduate. "She was kind of overshadowed by Stanley," Marx says. "My mother used to enjoy feeling superior to the students he'd bring over," recalls Sarah Hyman. "She'd say condescendingly, 'Really, you've never cooked?' . . . She would make sure that everyone in the house knew that they were her inferior." When she drove to campus to pick Hyman up, as she often did in later years, she "always seemed a little annoyed or anxious to get him the hell out of there," says Marjorie Roemer, who graduated in 1959.

In a very funny scene in *Hangsaman*, a novel largely set at an unnamed women's college that is obviously Bennington, the wife of an English professor dresses down a student who is flirting with her husband. "I sometimes think that housework must be really the *most* satisfying work of all. . . . It must be *wonderful* to see—well, *order* out of *chaos*, and know that you've done it yourself," the student coos in an transparent attempt to be ingratiating. "I suppose you've never scrubbed a floor?" the professor's wife responds acidly. (The student's comment to the faculty wife anticipates almost verbatim a line by Betty Friedan: "What kind of woman was [the housewife] if she did not feel this mysterious fulfillment waxing the kitchen floor?") In her article about the faculty wife, Jackson was more direct: "By the end of the first semester, what I wanted to do most in the world was invite a few of my husband's students over for tea and drop them down the well."

———

MANY OF THE BENNINGTON COLLEGE faculty lived on campus, in a grouping of red-painted wood houses called the Orchard. But the Orchard houses were small, and Shirley and Stanley were expecting a second child in November. They decided to rent a house in the village of North Bennington, about a mile up the hill from the college's north gate. (The larger town of Bennington, several miles away, offered more shops, restaurants, and other businesses, but most faculty preferred to be closer to the college.) Their first home there, a Greek Revival house at 12 Prospect Street, was three stories and sixteen rooms, including a conservatory and two pantries—quite a departure from the single-floor Grove Street apartment. More than a hundred years old, it had four Doric columns across the front that led Howard Nemerov, who soon became a close friend to both Shirley and Stanley, to nickname it "The Church of Christ Hyman." In *Life Among the Savages*, her best-selling memoir of family life, Jackson writes of her horror at seeing it for the first time: nothing had been touched since the previous resident died several years earlier, including two petrified doughnuts still sitting on the breakfast table. But the doughnuts were mercifully cleared away, the house was duly fixed up, and the Hymans moved in. There were four bedrooms on the second floor, a long narrow hall that would be lined with bookcases, front and back staircases, and multiple attics. Jackson called it their "little nest"—"lovely and sunny and dirty and agreeable and bigger than anything we've ever seen."

"Our house is old, and noisy, and full," *Savages* begins. A picture of the Prospect Street house, or a tidier approximation of it, appears on the book's cover. "When we moved into it," Jackson writes, "we had two children and about five thousand books; I expect that when we finally overflow and move out again we will have perhaps twenty children and easily half a million books. . . . This is the way of life my husband and I have fallen into, inadvertently, as though we had fallen into a well." In fact, Shirley and Stanley had only Laurence, then age three, when they moved to Vermont; his sister Joanne was born there. But the way Jackson describes "falling into" her life as a mother rings true. Jeanou,

The Hyman house on Prospect Street in North Bennington.

for one, found it hard to imagine the indolent teenager she had once known as a capable housewife, washing diapers and baking brownies. And Jackson, as she writes at the start of *Savages*, still entertained fantasies of a different kind of life, without children or books, in a quiet apartment "where they do the cleaning for you and send up your meals and all you have to do is lie on a couch." But she had always loved a home filled with friends and conversation. And this busy, boisterous, stuffed-to-the-seams household suited her surprisingly well.

The house was less than half a mile from the village's central square, which opened out from the corner of Prospect and Main Street. There was a public library, a post office, and a smattering of businesses: Percy's newsstand, which also served as a taxicab company and a pool hall; Jimmy Powers's boot and shoe store, also selling men's work clothes; Peter Panos's ice cream parlor and restaurant; a drugstore and a barbershop. Up the road was the North Bennington Village School, which served students from elementary through high school in a single red-brick building. A little farther out, supplying employment for many of the villagers, lay a sawmill, a woodworking plant, and several furniture companies. At the top of the hill sat the railway station, from which a direct train at one point ran daily to New York. The village was—and still is—anchored by Powers Market, a grocery store then run by

Michael Powers and his son Larry, who joined his father in the business in the spring of 1945 after he came back from the war, right around the same time as the Hymans arrived. Although many of the locals preferred to do the bulk of their shopping at the less expensive A&P on the outskirts of town, the market was the main gathering spot for the village. Anyone who dropped by for a loaf of bread or can of vegetables got a healthy serving of gossip along with their groceries. In *Life Among the Savages*, Jackson writes of her surprise at discovering, on her first visit to North Bennington in search of a house to rent, that Michael Powers "not only knew our housing problems, but the ages and names of our children, the meat we had been served for dinner the night before, and my husband's income." She may not have been exaggerating.

Some of the villagers were welcoming. Within days of the Hymans' arrival, a neighbor brought over a mother cat and four kittens, to Shirley's delight. But North Bennington, like so many tucked-away New England towns, was not an easy place to be a newcomer. Many residents had lived in the village for generations. Brooklyn-born Malamud, another uneasy Vermont transplant, told of an acquaintance who was corrected by the local mechanic after describing as a Vermonter an octogenarian who had lived in town since he was seven; the man had been born elsewhere. "Vermonters generally wanted nothing to do with you unless your family had arrived before the American Revolution," Malamud's daughter, Janna Malamud Smith, writes wryly. "Natives were polite but deeply reserved and wary." They weren't always polite, especially the children. Three-year-old Laurence was beaten up by two boys who lived next door. Barry, the youngest of the family, remembers kids throwing stones at him as he walked down the street.

The adults' surface politeness often masked deeply held biases. For starters, the locals were highly suspicious of the college. It was a source of employment—Larry Powers's mother worked there for a time as a maid—and sometimes of fascination: when the Bennington dance students, lacking space on campus, started using the North Bennington school gym for rehearsals, Larry and other local boys would peer curiously through the windows at the scantily clad women. "Those young ladies were like models," Powers remembers. But the ultraliberal

Bennington College community could not have been more culturally removed from its socially conservative, bedrock Republican neighbors up the road. "The students were seen as sort of weird, kooky, by the townspeople," recalls Anna Fels, whose father, William Fels, was president of Bennington from 1957 to 1964. They were thought of—not entirely without reason—as "Commies" or "pinkos," Barry Hyman remembers.

Shirley socialized in the village: she shopped at Powers Market, greeted her neighbors at the post office, joined the PTA. But she and Stanley could never truly integrate themselves into the community. The Hymans "added color to the village," Larry Powers says—a polite way of saying they stood out. Shirley "wasn't your ordinary housewife," remembers Laura Nowak, whose husband, Lionel, a composer, taught at the college. Stanley was even more conspicuous, with his professorial beard and horn-rimmed glasses, strolling down the street carrying one of the canes he had begun collecting: one, made of python vertebrae, once belonged to James Joyce; another, which was hollow, he filled with brandy. In later years, there was a French restaurant at the bottom of Main Street called the Rainbarrel that he and Shirley patronized; some evenings the whole family would parade down for dinner, all in a line. "I would walk in the back, trying to be invisible, because I knew I would get beat up the next day," Barry remembers.

Sometimes the village talk was friendly: extra tomato plants were offered, or a puppy from a new litter. But often it was not. The atmosphere of North Bennington in the late 1940s had much in common with the town in Grace Metalious's 1956 novel *Peyton Place*, which depicts in vivid detail the poison that can lurk beneath New Englanders' politeness. The garbageman gossiped to Larry Powers about the number of liquor bottles he collected at the Hyman house. In addition to the parties they regularly threw, Stanley also participated in a rotating weekly poker game that included Howard Nemerov, Lionel Nowak, the artist Paul Feeley, various presidents of Bennington College, and the man who ran the local garage. The game often went on all night: Laurence remembers heading off to school in the morning with the "remnants" still going. People criticized the way Shirley kept her home: her

Greenwich Village ways were not up to the standard of country women, who had little to do but scrub their floors. At a time when women were urged to embrace the role of housewife, Jackson's ambivalence and self-consciousness about housework is evident throughout her work, both fiction and nonfiction. In "Men with Their Big Shoes," a story written soon after the move to North Bennington, Mrs. Hart (her very name suggests her vulnerability), pregnant and recently transplanted to the country, hires Mrs. Anderson, an older local woman, to help her around the house. Mrs. Anderson turns out to be bitter and passive-aggressive; she despises her own husband and implies that Mr. Hart is cheating on Mrs. Hart. She gossips about Mrs. Hart in the grocery store and reports back what others say:

> Mrs. Hart thought of Mrs. Martin, keen-eyed and shrill, watching other people's groceries ("Two loaves of whole wheat today, Mrs. Hart? Company tonight, maybe?"). "I think she's such a nice person," Mrs. Hart said, wanting to add, You tell her I said so.
> "I'm not saying she isn't," Mrs. Anderson said grimly....
> "I wish," Mrs. Hart began again, a quick fear touching her; her kind neighbors watching her beneath their friendliness, looking out quietly from behind curtains. . . . "I don't think people ought to talk about other people," she said desperately.

By the story's end, Mrs. Hart cannot maintain her sense of self against the onslaught of Mrs. Anderson, who threatens to move into her house and take over her very life. She realizes "with a sudden unalterable conviction that she was lost."

THE ASSORTMENT OF VISITORS who often came up to spend the weekend—friends who were likely to be Jewish, homosexual, or African-American—also set Shirley and Stanley apart from the homogeneous community of North Bennington. Barry Hyman speculates that Ralph Ellison, whom Stanley invited to lecture at the college in November 1945

and who visited frequently from then on, might have been the first
black person some villagers had ever seen. "As a black man he stuck
out in North Bennington but acted as if he didn't," Arnold Rampersad,
Ellison's biographer, writes. "Strolling with his camera [Ellison was an
avid and talented photographer] about North Bennington, or on the
campus grounds, he was a figure few could miss. To many of the towns-
folk, clannish and wary of the liberal college ever since it opened in
1931, the fact that he stayed with the Hymans made him almost as sinister as the fact that he was black."

The important story "Flower Garden," which Jackson began writing within months of the move and reworked over the next few years,
addresses both the ugliness of small-town racism and the deep-seated
pressure to conform to local standards. Mrs. Winning (her name, again,
no accident) is a no-longer-young woman who married into "the oldest
family in town"; she, her husband, and their two small children live with
his parents in a big old house that his family has owned for generations,
where her mother-in-law sets the rules. Mrs. Winning once hoped to
live in the little cottage down the hill, but she has given up this dream,
and one day she learns the cottage has been sold. The newcomers, from
the city, are Mrs. MacLane, a widow about Mrs. Winning's age, and
her five-year-old son. Curious to get a look at the cottage, Mrs. Winning pays them a visit, and soon the women and their children become
friends. Mrs. Winning finds much to admire about the urbane and
sophisticated Mrs. MacLane—the colorful sandals she wears, the beautiful blue bowl on her coffee table, and most of all the glorious flower
garden she plants on all four sides of her house. The Winning house is
dark and austere, and flowers will not grow in the shade of the ancient
maple trees around it.

One day while they are out for a walk, Mrs. Winning's son taunts
a biracial child on the street, calling him "nigger," and Mrs. MacLane's
son joins in. Mrs. Winning is shocked when Mrs. MacLane makes her
son apologize, and even more shocked when her new friend suggests
that the boy's father work for her as a gardener. The garden grows
beautifully under the man's care. But Mrs. MacLane's status in the town
begins to wither. The villagers gossip about her relationship with the

"colored man." Her son is excluded from the other children's activities. Mrs. Winning finds herself implicated in the gossip and realizes that she must turn against her friend or lose her own standing. She affects innocence when Mrs. MacLane asks if the gardener is the reason for her ostracism. "The nerve of her," Mrs. Winning thinks defensively, "trying to blame the colored folks." After a neighbor's tree limb crashes down into her garden during a storm, Mrs. MacLane and her son move back to the city.

Jackson had explored prejudice before—racism in "After You, My Dear Alphonse," anti-Semitism in "A Fine Old Firm." But "Flower Garden," with symbolism reminiscent of Hawthorne's parables, is significantly more complex than either of those stories. In an early draft, Jackson told the story from the perspective of the newcomer, a New Yorker named Mrs. Hanson. That version captures well the city woman's desire to befriend her rather chilly neighbors, to behave in a way that wins their approval. She suffers acutely from their little barbs, no matter how subtle: early in the story, the character who would become Mrs. Winning, here named Mrs. Worthing, gently chides Mrs. Hanson for letting her son dig in the front yard. Her own children have gardens in the back of the house, "where it doesn't show." One episode in particular—Mrs. Hanson's son strays a few blocks away and is returned by a kindly neighbor—sounds suspiciously like Jackson's experience: more than one of her children tells of being brought back home after wandering into the village on his or her own.

The early draft is dominated by Mrs. Hanson's emotions: her profound longing to connect with her neighbors and her hurt and anger at being driven back to the city. In her revision, Jackson might have considered that Hanson sounded a little too much like Hyman; she also made the situation more general by not specifying which city the newcomer has arrived from. But the major change is the shift in perspective to Mrs. Winning's, which allows Jackson to speak for the village, giving an internal glimpse at attitudes normally expressed obliquely, through a glance or a snide remark. She depicts Mrs. Winning's racism with great subtlety: it is apparent, but not explicit, in her rudeness to the biracial boy, her condescending notice of his good looks ("they're all beautiful children"), and her shock at Mrs. MacLane's offer of work to his father. She comes reluctantly to the realization that she must ostracize Mrs. MacLane. Despite her treachery, by the end of the story the reader feels a kind of pity for the contortions she has suffered through a lifetime of conforming to the Winnings' expectations. She consoles herself with the thought of her family, "a solid respectable thing," but it is a false consolation: the cost of this form of respectability is too high. Though she does not realize it, she is every bit as lost as Mrs. Hart.

IN ONE OF SHIRLEY'S CARTOONS, likely drawn shortly after Laurence was born, she depicts herself bending over the stove to heat a bottle as the baby lies on the floor, screaming. Toys are strewn all around him, a sagging clothesline stretches the length of the room, and one of the cats is reaching into the fishbowl. Stanley peers over the clothesline, commenting, "What he needs is a baby sister."

Joanne Leslie, the Hymans' second child, arrived on November 8, 1945, six months after her parents' move to Bennington. Stanley wanted to name her Jean, after his mother's sister Jenny, who had recently died; Shirley preferred Anne. They compromised, although not very successfully. The resulting Joanne "seems as arbitrary to the child as it does to everyone else," Shirley lamented in an undated fragment about her elder daughter—perhaps because Shirley sometimes called her Anne and Stanley called her Jean. "as soon as she could talk she renamed herself toby, which is the name of our dog. now her name changes daily, depending upon her mood and the weather." In her family writings, Jackson usually referred to her elder daughter as Jannie, another compromise. As a college student, Joanne nicknamed herself Jai, which she kept from then on.

Laurence had always been a rough-and-tumble child, big and strong for his age, fond of pranks, plots, baseball, and cowboys. In "Charles," her first family story and one of her funniest, Jackson describes him returning home from kindergarten every day with a tale of some outrageous sin that his classmate Charles committed: hitting the teacher, saying dirty words, talking back. She cannot wait to meet Charles's mother in person at the next PTA meeting, but when she asks the kindergarten teacher to introduce her, she gets a surprise. "Charles?" the teacher asks. "We don't have any Charles in the kindergarten." Laurence had "a thousand bright questions and sly, funny comments to make about everything that was going on," wrote Catherine Osgood (Kit) Foster, who taught English at Bennington and, with her husband Tom, was a friend of the Hymans. One night after dinner, Stanley tried to teach Laurence to count, using his fingers. Laurence grew tired, but Stanley urged him on, asking how many toes he had. "Only these few," Laurence answered, looking wearily at his feet. As he grew older, Jackson depicted him as often irritable and impatient with her, eager to be off doing his own thing. Laurence acknowledges the portrait is accurate.

Blue-eyed, curly-haired Joanne was all girl: gentle, a little shy, obedient. In *Savages*, she tends to pipe up with "I'm good, aren't I?" just as her older brother is being accused of some monstrous misdeed. From an early age, she loved dolls, clothes, and shoes: Jackson describes discovering her one morning dressed for play in an organdy party dress over pink pajama pants. At the age of four, she asked for high heels; at five, she had a knack for tying a scarf smartly around her neck. She occasionally went through phases of whimsy: in an amusing episode in *Savages*, she insists on calling herself "the second Mrs. Ellenoy" and reports on the antics of her seven stepdaughters, all named Martha. But as a teenager, she was the most conventional of the Hyman children, interested in clothes and boys—not terribly different from the kind of daughter of whom Geraldine might have approved. In 1959, when Geraldine and Leslie suggested that one of the children join them in California for a summer, it was Joanne who was chosen to go. (The visit was not a success: Joanne felt that she, too, disappointed Geraldine.) "Jannie is our beauty . . . sweet and popular," Jackson described her on the cusp of adolescence. She loved her daughter, but her writing shows that she didn't always know what to do with her. When Sarah arrived—fearfully intelligent, deeply uncanny Sarah—it was soon clear that she was the child with whom Jackson would identify most.

Laurence had begun attending nursery school, which freed up Jackson's mornings for writing. But the arrival of a new baby meant she once again had to adjust her schedule. She managed, in part, by giving the children a remarkable amount of autonomy. Laura Nowak once came to the house to pick up Joanne, then around two years old, to play with her daughter. Jackson was writing and didn't come to the door. Instead, five-year-old Laurence had gotten his sister ready for her outing. "He had a little jacket for her . . . just as efficient as can be," Nowak says.

Jackson, too, was becoming more efficient as a writer. "She was always working," says Joanne. "While dinner was cooking, she was sitting there working on plots and stories, making little notes sitting on this tiny stool in the kitchen." By the time she managed to sit down at the typewriter, the stories were often already half finished. Many of Jackson's stories—"Flower Garden" was a notable exception—underwent very little revision. Kit Foster told of playing Monopoly one evening with Jackson and Hyman when Jackson abruptly withdrew from the game and went into her study, where she could be heard banging away at her typewriter. Less than an hour later, she emerged with a story that was sent off to her agent the next morning and published with only a change in punctuation.

But Jackson also sought advice from both Foster and Hyman. Although she would be "tense and even impatient" while listening to their comments, "her fine discriminating mind guided her to choose only the best suggestions," Foster recalled. She was "least tense and most attentive" to Hyman's remarks, and almost always followed his suggestions, at least in the early days. Once Jackson read them both half a story about two women sharing a house in the suburbs: "The dialogue was excellent, acerbic and even gritty, polite on top but on the edge of storm underneath." Hyman found the story plotless and insignificant. "What truth about human nature does this story show?" he asked. Jackson could not answer. There was no point in writing a story, he told her, unless it has a general truth in it: "A slice of life, no matter how convincing or moving it is, is not a story." Jackson abandoned the draft.

WHEN JOANNE WAS BORN, Jackson and Hyman were in a difficult place financially. Hyman was no longer on *The New Yorker*'s payroll: instead, the magazine gave him a "drawing account" of $50 weekly, the usual arrangement for nonsalaried staff writers. It was essentially an advance that the writer had to earn back by selling a certain number of articles (or, in Hyman's case, Comment items and book reviews) to the magazine. Any deficit remaining at the end of the year had to be paid back or—more commonly—was carried over to the next year. This system generated considerable anxiety among the magazine's writers, who had to do complicated calculations to figure out where they stood. "Half the people here were always in debt," Joseph Mitchell later recalled, even prominent, well-established figures such as James Thurber and Wolcott Gibbs. At the end of 1944, Hyman's debit balance was more than $2,646—nearly the equivalent of his starting salary at Bennington. The Hymans' money problems were serious enough that Hyman managed to beg some of the remainder of his advance from Knopf, despite having turned in only one chapter of the promised book.

Jackson took out her stress on her agent, Fran Pindyck, whom she accused of not working hard enough. Pindyck had sold a dozen of Jackson's stories in 1944 and only two in 1945—one of which, "Seven Types of Ambiguity," was held by *Story* magazine for nine months before publication (and payment). At the beginning of 1945, *The New Yorker* offered Jackson a first-reading agreement, complete with a $100 bonus, and then failed to take a single one of her stories. (She was in good company—the magazine also rejected all of J. D. Salinger's submissions that year.) Even when Jackson did get stories into the magazine— "Whistler's Grandmother" and "It Isn't the Money I Mind," two minor pieces sold the previous year, were her only stories to appear there in 1945—her rates were significantly lower than many other writers'. In 1942, for "The Man Who Was Very Homesick for New York," a story of around 1500 words, Cheever, one of the magazine's regular contributors, earned $365, or 24 cents per word. For "Whistler's Grandmother," a slightly shorter story published three years later, Jackson got $185— only 13 cents per word. The magazine tended to offer lower rates to women writers; in 1948, when Jean Stafford's first story was accepted, she also received a $100 signing bonus and an initial rate of 18 cents per word, despite having already published two novels, one of them a best seller. (Cheever's signing bonus was several hundred dollars.) After the agency extracted its commission, Jackson made less than $500 in 1945— one-third her previous year's earnings.

Pindyck fired back that the low rate of sales wasn't her fault. Despite how little there was to show for it, she had been aggressively shopping Jackson's stories all year. Early on, when Jackson tended to become despondent whenever she received a rejection letter, Hyman asked Pindyck to tell her only of her acceptances. If it was unavoidable, he broke the news to her himself: "Be a darling and [tell] Shirl as gently as you can," Pindyck wrote to Hyman once when *The New Yorker* had passed on yet another of her submissions. This arrangement caused some complications in the office—rejection letters were passed on to authors as a matter of routine—but Pindyck, out of fondness for Jackson, was willing to go to extra trouble for her sake. Now, infuriated by the accusation, she sent Jackson a scathing three-page letter enumerating precisely how many rejections each of her active stories had racked up—one was on its twenty-fourth submission. "Our authors always get such [rejections] and it has been a special effort to keep yours out of the routine for fear that by letting such a letter get through, you might have a moment of unhappiness," Pindyck wrote acidly. Now, she felt, Jackson had abused her kindness.

Jackson apologized, but their relationship did not recover. A few months later, Pindyck's assistant informed Jackson that Pindyck, without saying good-bye, had gone to California for "a well-earned rest." In California, she met and married screenwriter and author Morton Thompson, and a few years later they moved to a farm in Connecticut. She never returned to the agency. After Thompson died suddenly of a heart attack in July 1953, Pindyck shot herself in their bedroom.

In the meantime, Leland Hayward had been purchased by the Music Corporation of America (MCA), and by spring 1946 it was fully incorporated into the larger agency. With Pindyck's departure, Jackson and Hyman were both handed on to an agent named Jim Bishop, formerly a war correspondent for *Collier's*. Bishop immediately set to work trying to sell a collection of Jackson's short stories. Pat Covici at Viking, who had previously been interested in her work, offered an advance of only

$150, with the stipulation—still—that she publish a novel first. Bishop refused and asked for the stories back. His strategy was to insist on a two-book deal, with the short stories to be published first and the novel second. (Then, as now, publishers were reluctant to publish short-story collections, which typically sell far fewer copies than novels.) "In a crisis I can always retreat to the point where I permit the publisher to bring the novel out first, followed by the stories," he explained to Jackson. He also tried to find out why it had been so long since *The New Yorker* had taken any of her stories. Gus Lobrano, spouting a standard euphemism, reassured him that Jackson was "still very dear to their hearts"; but, as it turned out, another year and a half would go by before she appeared in the magazine again.

Jackson found Bishop's attitude energizing. "You can bait [publishers] with the news that I am now working on a cheerful novel about a college girl, suitable for serialization in anything printed on slick paper, which I will have in your lap, done up in red and green ribbon, by Christmas Day," she told him in August 1946. This suggests that she was already thinking about *Hangsaman*—some early attempts at it seem to date from around this time—although "cheerful" is hardly an accurate characterization of the finished book. She may also have returned to *I Know Who I Love*, her novel about a "thin and frightened" young woman named Catharine, writing character descriptions and multiple outlines. "This is to be the story of a strangely haunted woman, whose life becomes a cheap tragedy," one synopsis begins. Now the focus of the story shifted from Catharine's early romance with the art student to her marriage to a New Hampshire man. (Jackson modeled the house they live in on the Winchester cabin.)

Catharine feels conflicted between her desire to be an artist and her fear that her talent is insufficient; she also chafes against the conventionality of her husband and the farming community around them. "much grim humor, in country people," Jackson noted to herself. Catharine begins to dream of the devil, who appears first as a romantic young man and becomes increasingly terrifying. Jackson, too, suffered throughout her life from dreams in which the devil appeared to her in various guises and tried to lure her into his trap; these became more frequent during periods of psychological stress. (The novel's title came from a folk song: "I know where I'm going / And I know who's going with me / I know who I love / And the devil knows who I'll marry.") Finally, Catharine has a nervous breakdown. But this subject, too, proved fruitless: Jackson was unable to get past the first section.

Jackson sent Bishop a few more stories, none of which sold. Sometime in the fall of 1946, she finally hit on her subject. As always when the conditions were right, it came quickly. "Shirley has finished five-sixths of her first novel ever to get past the halfway point, and will finish this one, for sure. It is red hot," Hyman told Jay Williams. *The Road Through the Wall* was ready to go out to publishers in the first week of 1947. "Seventy thousand words, count 'em, seventy thousand," Hyman crowed. On a visit to New York, he proudly delivered it to Bishop.

Bishop went first to Hiram Haydn at Crown, who rejected the novel. He was not discouraged. "I have never known of so many requests from so many diverse publishers as have asked for a look at your book," he reported to Jackson. The winning match was made by Tom Foster, Kit Foster's husband, a local poultry farmer and book reviewer with a sideline as a scout for the new literary house of Farrar, Straus. In early March, Bishop sent Jackson a telegram—Farrar, Straus was interested. The firm offered her a two-book deal: a $1500 advance for both the story collection and the novel, with the novel to appear in early 1948. (For the sake of comparison, in 1946 Cheever received from Random House a generous $4800 for his first novel; in 1949, Farrar, Straus would also offer Flannery O'Connor, a decade younger than Jackson, $1500 for hers.) Bishop's strategy had failed—the novel would have to come out first after all. Jackson did not seem to mind.

"MY GOODNESS, HOW YOU WRITE," John Farrar, Jackson's new editor, wrote to her after reading *The Road Through the Wall*. The novel is set, almost in its entirety, on a single block—Pepper Street, clearly modeled on Forest View Avenue, the street in Burlingame where Jackson grew up—and focuses primarily on one girl, Harriet Merriam, and her efforts to fit in. But the interactions among the neighbors on the block could take place anywhere, including North Bennington, Vermont. The novel's true setting, as one reviewer would call it, is "Sidestreet, U.S.A.": anyplace where everyone knows everyone else's business and passes judgment on anyone who does not conform. In fact, the plot has obvious similarities to "Flower Garden," which Jackson rewrote just after she finished the first draft of the novel. Harriet, a moody, unattractive girl of fourteen who likes to write poetry, befriends the outsider Marilyn, ostracized because her family is Jewish. The prejudice of the other neighbors—always expressed in the most polite terms, as in "A Fine Old Firm"—is unmistakable. When one family organizes all the children on the block for a reading of Shakespeare's plays, Marilyn is excluded on the pretense that she will be offended by *The Merchant of Venice*, with its depiction of the usurious Shylock. Finally Harriet's mother orders her daughter to break off their friendship. "We must expect to set a standard," she says. "However much we may want to find new friends whom we may value, people who are exciting to us because of new ideas, or because they are *different*, we have to do what is expected of us."

We have to do what is expected of us: this is the very definition of conformity. Those words could have been spoken by Geraldine—and perhaps they were. (Mrs. Merriam's first name is Josephine, with its obvious similarity to Geraldine; this character is one of the cruelest in the novel, her gossip by far the most poisonous.) They could also have been spoken by Mrs. Winning in "Flower Garden," or Mrs. Winning's mother-in-law, or the other villagers who condemn the outsider Mrs. MacLane for her kindness to a black man. Another subplot in the novel deals with racism: Harriet exhibits the knee-jerk hostility to the Chinese typical of that place and time, and is shocked when a friend does not. *The Road Through the Wall* had its roots in Burlingame, California, but it could not fully bloom until Jackson experienced the impact of that stifling mind-set as an adult.

One of the ironies of Jackson's fiction is the essential role that women play in enforcing the standards of the community—standards that hurt them most. The psychological intrigues that dominate their lives have the power to bring down the neighborhood. *The Road Through the*

Wall, like "Flower Garden" and the majority of Jackson's stories, exists almost entirely in the world of women and children: nearly all the action on the street takes place after the men have gone off to work. The fact that these works are dominated by women does not necessarily make them feminist, a term with which Jackson did not identify. Still, the way she portrays certain of her characters' attitudes strikingly anticipates the movement to come: one neighbor, who regards herself as "something more than a housewife," is scorned by the others for putting on airs. But no escape is possible from the hothouse of hostility in which these women live. Things start to fall apart not long after Harriet's rejection of Marilyn, and the pace of disintegration continues until the novel's calamitous conclusion.

Friendships between girls or women are central to much of Jackson's work, and here she is a particularly close observer of the small secrets and rituals by which these intimacies are created: in one scene Harriet and Marilyn write their hopes for the future on slips of paper and bury them by the town creek. Elements of this friendship are reminiscent of Shirley's friendship with Jeanou, including their not-to-be-kept vow to meet in Paris on Bastille Day 1938. A best friend can function as a kind of double, particularly for a girl, and when the writing on the slips is revealed, later in the novel, it is hard to know which was written by Marilyn and which by Harriet. One reads, "In ten years I will be a beautiful charming lovely lady writer without any husband or children but lots of lovers and everyone will read the books I write and want to marry me but I will never marry any of them. I will have lots of money and jewels too." The other: "I will be a famous actress or maybe a painter and everyone will be afraid of me and do what I say." Both girls, also, contain elements of teenage Shirley—Marilyn loves the commedia dell'arte, Harriet agonizes over her weight. And their hopes for the future are in some ways expressive of her own hopes. What is witchcraft, after all, but the desire to generate fear in others and instill their obedience?

The note Jackson sent with the revised book read, simply, "Herewith the baby." Farrar was delighted; Roger Straus, his partner, congratulated her on "a magnificent job." The novel includes more than a dozen characters, but Jackson's control over the material is superb. She parcels out scenes rhythmically, careful to maintain the book's taut atmosphere. (Notes in her drafts show that Jackson, likely at Farrar's suggestion, counted the number of pages in each chapter and took care to balance them.) Every description is calculated for what it reveals, both about the character to whom it refers and the person whose attitude it represents. When Helen Williams, the girl who is Marilyn's chief tormentor, moves away, Marilyn notices the poor quality of the family's furniture and regrets how easily she had been intimidated: "Helen dressed every morning for school in front of that grimy dresser, ate breakfast at that slatternly table . . . no one whose life was bounded by things like that was invulnerable." Jackson was beginning to explore the technique of using houses and their furnishings as expressions of psychological states. One unfortunate family lives in "a recent regrettable pink stucco with the abortive front porch [that was] unhappily popular in late suburban developments." As always in these descriptions, she has a knack for the unexpected word: tropical fish in a mural swim "insanely," and the apple trees on Pepper Street produce "wry unpalatable fruit." In "Notes for a Young Writer," a lecture on writing fiction composed as advice to her daughter Sarah, Jackson would relish the "grotesque effect" of the "absolutely wrong word": " 'I will always love you,' he giggled."

Compared with Jackson's masterly late novels, *The Road Through the Wall*, unsurprisingly, is a slighter work. But it is marvelously written, with the careful attention to structure, the precision of detail, and the bite of brilliant irony that would always define her style. There are wonderful moments of humor, as when one of the neighborhood girls, hoping to decorate her living room with high-class art, accidentally orders a set of pornographic photographs. And there is this astonishing aperçu from the novel's prologue: "No man owns a house because he really wants a house, any more than he marries because he favors monogamy." Both house and marriage are valued for the status they confer upon their possessor rather than for their intrinsic worth. In a novel that encompasses adultery, murder, and suicide, this may be the darkest line.

———

WHEN FARRAR, STRAUS BOUGHT *The Road Through the Wall*, the firm was still in its first year of business. Roger Straus, a would-be publisher in search of a partner, had teamed up with John Farrar—recently ousted from Farrar & Rinehart, his first endeavor—to create Farrar, Straus and Company. The two men had entirely different temperaments. Straus, who hailed from the New York German-Jewish elite (his grandfather had been a cabinet secretary; his grandmother was a Guggenheim), was known for both his business savvy and his skill at handling difficult authors. "He seemed to possess countless sensitive social tentacles," writes Boris Kachka in *Hothouse*, his history of the company. Straus also had what Kachka delicately terms "a keenly developed sense of quid pro quo—or, as [Straus] took to calling it, 'You blow me, I'll blow you.' "

The more reserved Farrar, who would be Jackson's primary editor, came from a High Episcopalian Vermont family that was rich in pedigree but poor in cash: he attended Yale on a scholarship. In 1920, at age twenty-four, he became editor of *The Bookman*, a book review journal. Six years later, he cofounded the Bread Loaf Writers' Conference, where Jackson would eventually serve on the faculty. His wife, Margaret Petherbridge Farrar, who joined him as an editor at Farrar, Straus, created the *New York Times* crossword puzzle in 1942. Straus was the commercial man, but Farrar was the firm's literary backbone. In those early years, Kachka writes, "everything of quality was brought in by Farrar."

From the outset, Farrar, Straus intended to be a literary house. "A new imprint on a book gathers character through the years," announced the firm's first catalog, in the fall of 1946. "Our list will be a general one. . . . We shall shun neither the realistic nor the romantic." Farrar, Straus's first literary success was Carlo Levi's *Christ Stopped at Eboli* (1947). But the company was best known in its early years for a blatantly commercial diet manual by the bodybuilder Gayelord Hauser called *Look Younger, Live Longer* (1950), which sold about half a million copies and guaranteed the firm's stability, at least for the time being.

When Jackson first met him, Farrar had "an owlish aspect," with wire-rimmed glasses and red hair. He once described himself as having "no sense of humor and a vile temper," but from the start Jackson's relationship with both him and Margaret was warm and intimate. "I hope you will let me know whenever you feel like talking about the book, about any book, about anything," Farrar wrote to her shortly after they first met. She and Margaret bonded over puzzles, which Jackson also enjoyed; for her part, Margaret found the book "so beautiful and so devastating, I can't get it out of my mind." John proposed changing the title to *The Innocents of Pepper Street*, but when Jackson balked, arguing that the wall was the book's central symbol, he backed down. The copyediting was almost nonexistent; in return, she made not a single mark on the proofs. The book's cover was dominated by the brick wall, with parallel rows of surreal lime-yellow trees extending eerily on either side.

The publisher's standard request for biographical information flummoxed Jackson. Hyman ended up filling out the sheet for her. It paints an idiosyncratic picture:

> She plays the guitar and sings five hundred folk songs . . . as well as playing the piano and the zither. She also paints, draws, embroiders, makes things out of seashells, plays chess, and takes care of the house and children, cooking, cleaning, laundry, etc. She believes no artist was ever ruined by housework (or helped by it either). She is an authority on witchcraft and magic, has a remarkable private library of works in English on the subject, and is perhaps the only contemporary writer who is a practicing amateur witch, specializing in small-scale black magic and fortune-telling with a Tarot deck. . . . She is passionately addicted to cats, and at the moment has six, all coal black. . . . She reads prodigiously, almost entirely fiction, and has just about exhausted the English novel. . . . Her favorite period is the eighteenth century, her favorite novelists are Fanny Burney, Samuel Richardson, and Jane Austen. She does not much like the sort of neurotic modern fiction she herself writes, the Joyce and Kafka schools, and in fact except for a few sports like Forster and [Sylvia

Townsend] Warner, does not really like any fiction since Thackeray. She wishes she could write things as leisurely and placid as
Richardson's, but doesn't think she ever will. She likes to believe
that this is the world's fault, not her own.

Out of all this, only the detail about witchcraft remained in the
final version—an obvious attempt at generating publicity. It looks out
of place on *The Road Through the Wall*, the least spooky of all Jackson's books. When the line appeared again on the *Lottery* collection the
following year, reviewers took notice—not always in a way Jackson
appreciated. But for now, it attracted little attention.

On November 13, 1947, Jackson and Hyman sat separately for
the photographer Erich Hartmann. Hyman's picture has a debonair
quality—an image befitting the brash young author of *The Armed
Vision*, which was scheduled at last for the following spring. His hair is
closely cropped, and his expression is not exactly a smile, but something
close. (In the version that was sent out with Hyman's publicity materials, he wears a forbidding scowl.) Dressed in a dark wool jacket and pat-
terned tie, he holds a smoldering cigarette that casts a plume of smoke
toward his face. Jackson looks very young and very serious; she tilts
her head slightly to the right, just as Hyman does, and her enigmatic
half-smile is almost the mirror of his. Her hair is pulled back with a clip,
and a string of chunky beads hangs around her neck. Behind her round
glasses, her gaze is penetrating.

Jackson thought Hyman looked like "a man of distinction," but she
was disappointed in her own photos, one of which she thought resembled "Alexander Woollcott [a distinctively jowly *New Yorker* writer] imi-
tating an owl." She was being overly critical—the picture that became
her standard publicity shot is an attractive one. Margaret Farrar found
it "perfectly delightful and fetching." But Jackson was always sensitive
about her appearance. Throughout her life, she would consent to be
photographed only with great reluctance, and eventually she refused
entirely. Fifteen years after it was taken, that same photograph would
appear on *We Have Always Lived in the Castle*.

The Road Through the Wall was published on February 17, 1948:

Stanley Hyman's author photograph for The Armed Vision, *taken by Erich Hartmann in November 1947.*

"we hope [it] is a day you like," Farrar's assistant wrote to Jackson, with a nod to her superstitious tendencies. She dedicated it "To Stanley, a critic." They both came to New York for the "ritual week," which included a cocktail party in Jackson's honor on publication day. At the time they were especially broke, and so anxious about the book's potential sales that Hyman took it upon himself to complain to Straus about the firm's publicity efforts. Straus, using all his sensitive social tentacles, sent back a soothing response in which he cautioned against too much optimism in the current "mediocre market" but assured Jackson and Hyman that the firm was making an "all-out effort." "We believe in Shirley as a writer," he promised. "We are all interested in the same thing—selling books—and we are all interested in the stature of Shirley as a writer now, tomorrow, ten years from tomorrow or twenty years from tomorrow." Still, he allowed that reviews would be a crucial factor, and to reviewers a first-time novelist was "an unknown quantity."

Alas, Straus's cautions were validated. A few critics loved the novel: one recognized Jackson's gift for diagnosing the "little secret nastinesses" of the human condition, and another praised the "direct, unsentimental way" she wrote about children. But most were put off by the book's negative depiction of humanity. "If you sometimes have bad days when you seem to remember all of the stupid, inane, embarrassing things that you ever did, then you will find a bit of yourself on every page, for Miss Jackson has selected only such incidents to carry her story, if indeed there is a story," sniped one critic. Others found the ending contrived and melodramatic. Even *The New Yorker* could manage only a backhanded compliment: Jackson's "supple and resourceful" style managed to make her "shopworn material appear much fresher than it is." Some friends were also less than enthusiastic: Jeanou, to whom Jackson proudly sent a copy of the novel, loved the descriptions of suburban life but was disappointed in the ending, which she found melodramatic. The reaction of Geraldine and Leslie, who had recently moved back to the Burlingame area, has not survived, but it could not have been positive. Early sales were disappointing—only around 2000 copies. Straus had projected 3500, the minimum necessary for Jackson to earn back her advance. In response, Farrar, Straus decided to delay her book of stories until the following year.

Jackson, it seems, was not overly disheartened by the reaction. At any rate, it hardly discouraged her from using fiction to tell her readers—or her neighbors—unpleasant truths about themselves. And with this first investigation of a small town in which neighbors gradually undo one another, she laid the groundwork for the thunderbolt that would come next.

8.

A CLASSIC IN
SOME CATEGORY

"THE LOTTERY,"
1948

The morning of June 27th was clear and sunny, with the
fresh warmth of a full-summer day; the flowers were blossoming profusely and the grass was richly green.

—"The Lottery"

"THE LOTTERY" IS A KIND OF MYTH; AND OVER THE YEARS,
various myths have been told about its writing. Jackson's neighbors in
North Bennington would say that she had been inspired to write it after
village children had thrown stones at her while she was out for a walk
with her baby. In one version of the lecture she often gave about "The
Lottery" and its aftermath, Jackson said a book she had been reading
about "choosing a victim for a sacrifice" had led her to the idea. At the
time she wrote the story, Hyman and Jay Williams were collaborating
on a proposal for an anthology of myth and ritual criticism, for which
Hyman had begun to collect numerous books, one of which might well
be the one she refers to. Jackson's interest in myth and ritual dates back
to her collegiate reading of *The Golden Bough*, anthropologist Sir James

Shirley Jackson in her study, late 1940s.

Frazer's compendium of ancient rites and customs. Frazer's main area of interest is the rituals surrounding the death and rebirth of a vegetation god, a fertility rite that is relevant to "The Lottery"; he also describes the use of scapegoats, another of the story's themes.

The most enduring myth, however, was created by Jackson herself, in the version of her "Lottery" lecture that was published after her death as "Biography of a Story." As she told it, she was out doing errands one bright June morning "when summer seemed to have come at last, with blue skies and warm sun and no heavenly signs to warn me that my morning's work was anything but just another story." She was pushing Joanne, around two and a half, in a stroller; Laurence was

at kindergarten. The idea came to her, she said, on the way home—
"perhaps the effort of that last fifty yards up the hill put an edge to the
story"—and as soon as they arrived, she put Joanne in her playpen,
put away the groceries, and sat down to write. She was finished by the
time Laurence arrived home for lunch. "I found that it went quickly and
easily, moving from beginning to end without pause," she would recall.
"As a matter of fact, when I read it over later I decided that except for
one or two minor corrections, it needed no changes, and the story I
finally typed up and sent off to my agent the next day was almost word
for word the original draft."

As with some of the other stories Jackson told about her life, this one
takes some liberties with the factual record. For one thing, she puts the
story's date of composition as sometime during the first week of June,
three weeks before its publication in the *New Yorker* of June 26, 1948,
which would have meant an unusually quick turnaround from manuscript to print. A note in Jackson's handwriting on the draft of "The
Lottery" in her archive indicates that she submitted it to MCA on March
16, 1948. Jim Bishop had recently left the agency, and another agent,
Eleanor Kennedy, was now handling Jackson's submissions. Kennedy
wrote to Jackson on April 6 that Gus Lobrano liked the story but had
"some reservations about it" and would send on a detailed critique: "He

Sir James Frazer,
mid-1930s. His book
The Golden Bough
deeply influenced
Jackson.

assured me that if you can put it in proper shape for them, they will take it," she wrote. Jackson submitted the revised story on April 12. On April 26, she received a telegram from Kennedy. Lobrano had bought "The Lottery" for $675—about three times what he had paid for any of Jackson's previous stories.

Details aside, it is stunning to think that this story composed in only a few hours—on this all the accounts agree—has proved to be one of the most read and discussed works of twentieth-century American fiction. Hyman told his friend Ben Belitt, a poet and fellow Bennington professor, that he recognized it as a masterpiece from the moment he read it. "It was the pure thing . . . the mythic thing you find in Greek literature," Belitt commented. Other perceptive readers were also impressed from the start: "It is not likely the story will be forgotten, even though others of yours come along to assault," John Farrar wrote to Jackson. But the reaction of Joseph Henry Jackson, the literary editor of the *San Francisco Chronicle*, was more typical—admiring, yet puzzled. "No one writes a story in a vacuum," he wrote to Jackson. "Something pulled the trigger that set 'The Lottery' off in your mind. What was it?"

"The Lottery," of course, did not come out of a vacuum. It was an obvious continuation of the preoccupations that had haunted Jackson for years. In a publicity memo written for Farrar, Straus around the time *The Road Through the Wall* appeared—only a month before "The Lottery" was written, if the March date on the draft is accurate—Jackson mentioned her enduring fondness for eighteenth-century English novels because of their "preservation of and insistence on a pattern superimposed precariously on the chaos of human development." She continued: "I think it is the combination of these two that forms the background of everything I write—the sense which I feel, of a human and not very rational order struggling inadequately to keep in check forces of great destruction, which may be the devil and may be intellectual enlightenment." In all her writing, the recurrent theme was "an insistence on the uncontrolled, unobserved wickedness of human behavior."

Nowhere is this more obvious than in "The Lottery." The story, with shades of *The Scarlet Letter*, unfolds in Jackson's signature plain style, which is perhaps what fooled some of its initial readers into believing it was fact. Much of it is devoted to a deceptively simple account of exactly how the ritual is conducted. Jackson sets the scene with her usual economy, depicting how the children, out of school for the summer, gather first, the boys horsing around and choosing "the smoothest and roundest stones" to fill their pockets. The men assemble next, "surveying their own children, speaking of planting and rain, tractors and taxes," followed by the women, "wearing faded house dresses and sweaters. . . . They greeted one another and exchanged bits of gossip as they went to join their husbands." Tessie Hutchinson arrives late; distracted by her housework, she forgot what day it was. "Wouldn't have me leave m'dishes in the sink, now, would you?" she jokes. The details and the dialogue are virtually timeless: were it not for the reference to tractors, these villagers could be residents of Puritan Boston, gathered to witness the punishment of Hester Prynne.

The story proceeds calmly through every detail: the jovial manner of Mr. Summers, the retired man who conducts the ceremony, because he has "time and energy to devote to civic activities," and who also runs the village square dances and the youth group; the black wooden box, shabby and splintered, from which the slips of paper will be drawn. Those who are missing must be accounted for—Clyde Dunbar is at home with a broken leg, so his wife will draw for him; Jack Watson draws for his mother, who seems to be a widow. (Looking back, the reader may wonder if the elder Watson was the victim of an earlier lottery.) Then the lottery proceeds, with the men coming up first to draw for their families.

Once it is discovered that Bill Hutchinson has drawn the slip of paper marked with a black dot, the story's emotional climate alters drastically. Tessie, Bill's wife, protests that he was rushed through the drawing. "It wasn't fair!" she exclaims repeatedly. The others quiet her. The Hutchinsons—Bill, Tessie, their three children—draw again to determine who it will be. This time Tessie gets the black dot. "All right, folks," says Mr. Summers, "let's finish quickly." The purpose of the stones becomes apparent as the story builds to its disturbing conclusion:

The children had stones already, and someone gave little Davy Hutchinson a few pebbles.

Tessie Hutchinson was in the center of a cleared space by now, and she held her hands out desperately as the villagers moved in on her. "It isn't fair," she said. A stone hit her on the side of the head.

Old Man Warner was saying, "Come on, come on, everyone." Steve Adams was in the front of the crowd of villagers, with Mrs. Graves beside him.

"It isn't fair, it isn't right," Mrs. Hutchinson screamed, and then they were upon her.

Jackson would claim that the only editorial change requested by *The New Yorker* was to change the date on which the lottery took place to June 27, so that it would match the cover date of the magazine (which was actually June 26). This is impossible to confirm, because the first few pages of the first draft have been lost. But it is the kind of change that editor Harold Ross, who insisted that the magazine's fiction had to correspond with the season in which it was published, was known to make. In April, Kennedy tried to persuade the magazine to rush publication but was unsuccessful: had she succeeded, the date of the lottery might have been April 27 instead. The revised copy in Jackson's archive reveals additional small changes—one or two by Hyman; others in response to marginal queries in Lobrano's handwriting, asking her to make certain details of the process more clear. (In the first version of the story, she neglected to describe the actual drawing of lots.) Lobrano also was concerned that the story's meaning was too opaque. "The most important thing is somehow to clarify your intention—that is, the underlying theme of the piece—just a bit more," he told Jackson, suggesting that she amplify "one or two snatches of talk"—perhaps Old Man Warner's complaint that nothing is good enough for young people. Could she give him a few more sentences about the dangers of breaking away from established tradition? "Not at all necessarily in such bald terms," Lobrano cautioned. "He might even complain about the deviations from the original ritual."

Jackson agreed to his request, adding one of the story's key passages: Old Man Warner's speech warning the villagers not to abandon the tradition.

"They do say," Mr. Adams said to Old Man Warner, who stood next to him, "that over in the north village they're talking of giving up the lottery."

Old Man Warner snorted. "Pack of crazy fools," he said. "Listening to the young folks, nothing's good enough for *them*. Next thing you know, they'll be wanting to go back to living in caves, nobody work any more, live *that* way for a while. Used to be a saying about 'Lottery in June, corn be heavy soon.' First thing you know, we'd all be eating stewed chickweed and acorns. There's *always* been a lottery," he added petulantly.

The townspeople take it for granted that the lottery serves a civic function, though that function is never articulated. "Some places have already quit lotteries," one woman remarks. "Nothing but trouble in *that*," Old Man Warner replies. Part of the reason is superstition: the lottery, which takes place near the summer solstice, fulfills the function of the ancient fertility rites detailed in *The Golden Bough*. (Hyman, with his ear for folklore, is said to have contributed the "corn be heavy soon" line, but if so, it must have been in conversation: that line is written on the manuscript in Jackson's handwriting.) But more than that, the lottery is an event in which the entire town joins together. The participation of each member is so crucial that even little Davy Hutchinson must join in throwing pebbles at his mother. Tessie's friend Mrs. Delacroix, one of the kindlier characters, will choose a stone "so large she had to pick it up with both hands."

Even with Jackson's clarifications, the meaning of "The Lottery" was not at all obvious to *The New Yorker*'s editors. She would later tell Thurber that when Lobrano called to say the magazine had accepted the story, he asked if she wanted to comment on its meaning. "I could not—having concentrated only on the important fact he had mentioned, which was that they were buying the story," she said. (It was her first piece to appear in *The New Yorker* since "It Isn't the Money I Mind," in August 1945, nearly three years earlier.) Lobrano continued to push, asking if the story was about the ignorance of superstition, or if it could be considered an allegory that made its point by ironically juxtaposing ancient customs with a modern setting. Sure, she said, that sounded fine. "Good," Lobrano answered, "that's what Mr. Ross thought it meant."

By the late 1940s, the magazine's fiction was starting to break free of the "bright, beautiful, but dead" style that Lionel Trilling had savaged in his 1942 essay for *The Nation*. Fiction writers who had their first stories in the magazine during those years included Nabokov, Salinger (whose *New Yorker* debut, "Slight Rebellion off Madison," came in 1946 after two solid years of rejection), Stafford, Roald Dahl, and V. S. Pritchett. Cheever's "The Enormous Radio" (1947) showed the magazine's tastes evolving to embrace work that might previously have been thought too weird or difficult. A young couple, middle-class New Yorkers who live in a typical high-rise, mysteriously receive a new radio. Trying to tune it to her favorite station, the wife discovers that the radio picks up her neighbors' conversations. She listens obsessively to the vicious fights that go on behind their sedately closed doors and eventually grows despondent. "We've never been like that, have we, darling?" she begs her husband to reassure her. Of course, the reader knows that these two are just as secretly wretched as all the rest.

Ross, who frequently complained about the grim stories the magazine was running and was famously resistant to anything that smacked of obscurity, initially balked at "The Enormous Radio." "He'd say, 'Goddammit, Cheever, why do you write these fucking gloomy goddamm stories!' And then he'd say, 'But I have to buy them. I don't know why,'" Cheever recalled. Nevertheless, Ross supported the publication of "The Lottery" when Jackson resubmitted it in April. The only dissenter among the editors was William Maxwell, who found it "contrived" and "heavy-handed." Among the writers, opinions were more divided, as Brendan Gill, then a young staffer at the magazine, cheekily informed Jackson. "I think, and have thought from the second I finished it, that it is one of the best stories (two or three or four best) that the magazine ever printed," Gill wrote to her. "Lobrano thinks it's overwhelming, which—tell it not in Gath—surprises and delights me. On the other hand, Mitchell, Liebling, and others are as opposed to it as I am in favor of it."

Despite the portentous way in which she would describe the story's composition, Jackson presented herself as having been utterly unaware that anything unusual would happen upon its publication. And indeed, nothing about *The New Yorker* of June 26, 1948, suggested that it was something other than an ordinary issue of the magazine. The cover depicted a row of people fishing on a darkened beach, illuminated by the glow of campfires. There were ads for Dewar's, Pontiac, United Airlines, Elizabeth Arden, Tiffany, DuMont televisions, and the new Pitney-Bowes postage meter. The "Talk of the Town" section included humorous pieces about knickers coming back in style and the process of adapting subway turnstiles for the imminent fare increase from a nickel to a dime. "The Lottery" was the second piece in the issue, between a short story by Sylvia Townsend Warner and an article from Argentina by Philip Hamburger about the corruption of the Peróns. The magazine also included a review of women cabaret singers, among them Ella Fitzgerald; a humor column devoted largely to the upcoming Republican presidential convention; a "Letter from Paris" by Janet Flanner; and a long review of Evelyn Waugh's novel *The Loved One* by Wolcott Gibbs. Aside from the bombshell on page 25, there was nothing unusual about it at all.

THE FIRST LETTERS were dated June 24, just after the issue hit newsstands. "Shirley Jackson's 'The Lottery' . . . despite a certain skill of expression, impresses me as utterly pointless," wrote Mrs. Victor Wouk of Park Avenue, who wondered whether Jackson was "not overly preoccupied with the gruesome." "If the sole purpose . . . was to give the reader a nasty impact it was quite satisfactory, I suppose," wrote Walter Snowdon of East Thirty-fifth Street. "I frankly confess to being completely baffled by Shirley Jackson's 'The Lottery,'" wrote Miriam Friend, a young mother living in Roselle, New Jersey, asking the editors to send an explanation before she and her husband "scratch right

*Jackson kept many of the letters she received about
"The Lottery" in a large leather-bound scrapbook.*

through our scalps" trying to figure it out. Interviewed sixty-five years later, Friend still remembered how upsetting she had found the story.

These were the start of a torrent of letters that *The New Yorker* would receive about "The Lottery." By now the story is so familiar as a cultural touchstone that it is hard to remember how uncanny it originally seemed: "outrageous," "gruesome," "shocking," or just "utterly pointless," in the words of some of the readers who were moved to write to the magazine or to Jackson personally. Within a month there were nearly a hundred letters, "not counting two newspaper columns and ten notes canceling subscriptions," Hyman reported cheerfully to Ben Zimmerman. By the beginning of August, the total was up to 150, and more were starting to come in from abroad. The magazine issued a press release to say it had never before received so much mail in response to a work of fiction.

In "Biography of a Story," Jackson gave the final total as more than 300 letters. Only 13 were kind, she claimed, "and they were mostly from friends." (One had overheard people on the Fifth Avenue bus saying to each other, "Did you read that story in *The New Yorker?*") The rest, she reported with mordant humor, were dominated by three main themes: "bewilderment, speculation, and plain old-fashioned abuse." Readers wanted to know where such lotteries were held, and whether they could go and watch; they threatened to cancel their subscriptions; they declared the story a piece of trash. If the letter writers "could be considered to give any accurate cross section of the reading public . . . I would stop writing now," she concluded.

Jackson probably did not exaggerate the sheer number of letters. A giant scrapbook in her archive contains nearly 150 of them from the summer of 1948 alone, and she would receive letters about "The Lottery" for the rest of her life. But though there were some canceled subscriptions and a fair share of name-calling, the vast majority of the letter writers were not hostile, simply confused. More than anything else, they wanted to understand what the story meant. The response of one Connecticut woman was typical. "Gentlemen," she wrote, "I have read 'The Lottery' three times with increasing shock and horror. . . . Cannot decide whether [Shirley Jackson] is a genius or a female and more subtle version of Orson Welles."

Although a decade had already passed since Welles's famous broadcast of *War of the Worlds*, some did take the story for a factual report. "I think your story is based on fact," wrote a professor at the University of Cincinnati College of Medicine. "Am I right? As a psychiatrist, I am fascinated by the psychodynamic possibilities suggested by this anachronistic ritual." Stirling Silliphant, a producer at Twentieth Century-Fox, was also fooled: "All of us here have been grimly moved by Shirley Jackson's story. . . . Was it purely an imaginative flight, or do such tribunal rituals still exist and, if so, where?" Andree L. Eilert, a fiction writer who had once (and only once) had her own byline in *The New Yorker*, wondered if "mass sadism" was still a part of ordinary life in New England, "or in equally enlightened regions." Nahum Medalia, a professor of sociology at Harvard, also thought the story might be factual, though he was more admiring: "It is a wonderful story, and it kept me very cold on the hot morning when I read it." But the fact that so many of the readers accepted "The Lottery" as truthful is less astonishing than it now seems, since *The New Yorker* at the time did not designate stories as fact or fiction as it does today, and the "casuals," or humorous essays, were generally understood as falling somewhere in between.

Arthur L. Kroeber, an anthropologist at the University of California, Berkeley, wondered about Jackson's motivations: "If Shirley Jackson's intent was to symbolize into complete mystification, and at the same time be gratuitously disagreeable, she certainly succeeded." Kroeber's daughter, the novelist Ursula K. Le Guin, was nineteen when "The Lottery" came out, and remembers that her father was indignant about the story "because as a social anthropologist he felt that she didn't, and couldn't, tell us how the lottery could come to be an accepted social institution." Since the fantasy was presented "with all the trappings of contemporary realism," Le Guin says, her father felt that Jackson was "pulling a fast one" on the reader. Jackson's literary friends were no less bewildered. Arthur Wang, then at Viking Press and soon to found Hill and Wang, wrote to Hyman that he had discussed the story with friends for nearly an hour: "It's damned good but I haven't met anyone who is sure that they . . . know what it's about."

Only a few of the letter writers dared to hazard an interpretation. "In this story you show the perversion of democracy," a reader from Missouri wrote confidently. "A symbol of how village gossip destroys a victim?" wondered a reader in Illinois. A producer at NBC believed it meant that "humanity is normally opposed to progress; instead, it clutches with tenacity to the customs and fetishes of its ancestors." Some ventured wilder guesses. Marion Trout, of Lakewood, Ohio, suspected that the editorial staff had become "tools of Stalin." "Is it a publicity stunt?" wrote a reader from New York, while others wondered if the printer had accidentally cut off a concluding paragraph. Other readers were simply confused by the plot—not everyone understood that Tessie was stoned to death. "The number of people who expected Mrs.

Hutchinson to win a Bendix washer at the end would amaze you," Jackson commented wryly to Joseph Henry Jackson. Still others complained that the story had traumatized them so greatly that they had been unable to open the magazine since. "I read it while soaking in the tub . . . and was tempted to put my head underwater and end it all," wrote a reader in St. Paul.

But the largest proportion of the respondents did admire the story, even if they did not understand it. "Only a true genius could have written 'The Lottery'—a story that persists in staying in the thought of the reader, whatever interpretation may be reached, and compelling him to keep on wondering about it," wrote a friend of Jackson's parents. H. W. Herrington, who had been Jackson's folklore professor at Syracuse, wrote that the story had disturbed his sleep as well as his waking thoughts, but that he had been "singing over it too as one must over a fine piece of art." Jackson wrote back that the idea for the story had originated in his course, which may have been at least partially true, although she had read *The Golden Bough* before transferring to Syracuse.

Jackson and Hyman's friends were mostly generous with their compliments. Herbert Weinstock, Hyman's editor at Knopf, said it was "one of the most impressive stories *The New Yorker* has ever published." Kenneth Burke judged it "a very profound conceit. . . . [T]he story starts the bells of possibility ringing." Ralph Ellison, who spent Christmas with Jackson and Hyman that year, was more critical: he thought Jackson had "presented the rite in too archaic a form" and with too much understatement, though he was willing to admit that "it is a rich story and perhaps it succeeds precisely because of the incongruity to which I am objecting." He also noted, approvingly, that he and Jackson were "beginning to work the same vein."

Harold Ross, for his part, never went on the record with his opinion. But he wrote to Hyman in July that "The Lottery" was "certainly a great success from our standpoint. . . . Gluyas Williams [a *New Yorker* cartoonist] said it is the best American horror story. I don't know whether it's that or not, or quite what it is, but it was a terrifically effective thing, and will become a classic in some category."

Jackson, though she was asked repeatedly, never would offer a consistent explanation of "The Lottery." Her friend Helen Feeley said Jackson told her that the story had to do with anti-Semitism. In fact, its theme is strikingly consonant with the French Holocaust survivor David Rousset's book *L'Univers concentrationnaire* (1946), which argues that the concentration camps were organized according to a carefully planned system that relied on the willingness of prisoners to harm each other. The book was translated into English as *The Other Kingdom* in 1947 and was reviewed in *The New Yorker*, possibly by Hyman, who was a frequent contributor to the magazine's section of brief, anonymous reviews.

Others have said that all the characters were based on actual people in North Bennington, and an early version of "Biography of a Story," in which Jackson considers specific people in the village and how they would behave in such a situation, backs up this interpretation. She said something similar to Bennington professor Wallace Fowlie when he told her that critics had been explaining it in terms of ritual: "Shirley's beautiful piercing eyes sparkled with an expression that was half surprise and half amusement. 'The scene of that story is simply North Bennington. Just listen to the people here in town and the way they slaughter one another with words and stories and slander.'" Joanne Hyman, the toddler who was in the playpen while her mother wrote the story, says Jackson told her it drew from her first experience living in New England—the brief period she and Hyman spent in Winchester, New Hampshire—rather than their life in North Bennington. Sometimes she refused entirely to say what it meant: when Jennifer Feeley, Helen's daughter, read the story in high school and asked Jackson about it, Jackson responded huffily, "If you can't figure it out, I'm not going to tell you."

Others have commented that "The Lottery" reflects a culture of casual violence common in Vermont at the time. Janna Malamud Smith writes that she was unprepared for the "rural harshness" that others took for granted; as a child, she was shocked to hear a friend of her parents' talk casually about local factory employees torturing a mentally disabled coworker. Jackson depicts some of this harshness in "The Renegade," written around the same time as "The Lottery," in which Mrs. Walpole—another city woman who feels out of place in the country—is informed by a neighbor one morning that her dog has been killing chickens. As she makes her way around the village doing her errands, everyone she meets has heard the rumor, and all kinds of gruesome solutions are offered: tying a dead chicken around the dog's neck, letting a mother hen scratch out the dog's eyes, or—most horribly—forcing the dog to run while wearing a spiked collar, so that it cuts off her head.

Still, Jackson almost certainly did not intend "The Lottery" as an insult to rural Vermonters, even if some of them read it that way. The best interpretation is likely the most general, something like what she wrote in response to Joseph Henry Jackson's query: "I suppose I hoped, by setting a particularly brutal ancient rite in the present and in my own village, to shock the story's readers with a graphic dramatization of the pointless violence and general inhumanity in their own lives." *The New Yorker*'s Kip Orr, who was charged with the task of responding to all the letters on Jackson's behalf, echoed this position in what became the magazine's standard formulation. "It seems to us that Miss Jackson's story can be interpreted in half a dozen different ways," he wrote to reader after reader. "It's just a fable . . . she has chosen a nameless little village to show, in microcosm, how the forces of belligerence, persecution, and vindictiveness are, in mankind, endless and traditional and that their targets are chosen without reason."

In the summer of 1948, only three years after the end of World War II, the American public was still reeling from the horrifying scenes from the death camps of Europe, not to mention the aftermath of Hiroshima and Nagasaki. The term "Cold War" had been coined a year earlier in a speech by financier and elder statesman Bernard M. Baruch before the South Carolina House of Representatives, gaining currency after it was repeated by Walter Lippmann in the *New York Herald Tribune*. In the United States, Kip Orr's "forces of belligerence, persecution, and vindictiveness" had recently assumed a new form in McCarthyism. The House Committee on Un-American Activities had already begun its infamous hearings regarding alleged Communist influence in the movie industry, and Hyman's old friend Walter Bernstein was one of the screenwriters targeted. Soon Whittaker Chambers would expose Alger Hiss as a Communist operative within the U.S. government. When Arthur Miller's play *The Crucible*—an allegory of the witch hunt

for Communists set against the background of the Salem witch trials—
came to Broadway a few years later, a friend of Jackson's commented to
her on its similarity in theme. It is no wonder that the story's first readers reacted so vehemently to this ugly glimpse of their own faces in the
mirror, even if they did not understand exactly what they were seeing.

In Jackson's story, the target of the lottery is indeed chosen at random, as Orr pointed out. But it seems hardly "without reason," at least
on the part of the author, that she happens to be both a wife and a mother.
On the morning she wrote the story, Jackson was pregnant with her
third child—a fact she omitted from "Biography of a Story"—and was
occupied with taking care of her second; she had a break from the first
for only a few hours. Published nearly a decade before Betty Friedan
conducted the survey of Smith College graduates that would lead to *The
Feminine Mystique*, the story depicts a world in which women, clad in
"faded house dresses," are defined entirely by their families. Though
"The Lottery" has an anachronistic quality, with an atmosphere at once
timeless and archaic, in fact it describes the world in which Jackson lived,
the world of American women in the late 1940s, who were controlled by
men in myriad ways large and small: financial, professional, sexual.

Tessie Hutchinson, the lottery's victim, in many ways resembles
Jackson: her distraction, her self-consciousness about her housekeeping, her disheveled appearance. (Just as Tessie insists on finishing her
dishes before she arrives at the lottery, Jackson carefully notes that she
put away her groceries before sitting down to write the story.) Female
sacrifice is a motif in "The Renegade" as well: the dog is named Lady,
and the story ends with Mrs. Walpole metaphorically switching places
with her, imagining the sharp points of the collar closing in on her own
throat. If "The Lottery" can be read as a general comment on man's
inhumanity to man, on another level it works as a parable of the ways
in which women are forced to sacrifice themselves: if not their lives,
then their energy and their ambitions. The story is at once generic and
utterly personal.

Jackson was less thrilled by the sudden recognition than she had
expected to be. "One of the most terrifying aspects of publishing stories
and books is the realization that they are going to be read, and read

by strangers," she wrote later. "I had never fully realized this before, although I had of course in my imagination dwelt lovingly upon the thought of the millions and millions of people who were going to be uplifted and enriched and delighted by the stories I wrote. It had simply never occurred to me that these millions and millions of people might be so far from being uplifted that they would sit down and write me letters I was downright scared to open." (In reality, the mail Jackson may have been most "scared to open" was more likely to be the invariably critical letters she received regularly from her mother.) Her tone is at least semi-jocular; she goes on to quote some of the more outrageous letters she received, including one from a convicted murderer and another from a group of "Exalted Rollers" who acclaim her as a prophet and ask when she will publish her next revelations. But her lecture broadcasts a level of anxiety about her fame that foreshadows the crippling agoraphobia of her later years—in which she feared going to the post office, among other things. "I am out of the lottery business for good," she concludes.

At the end of "The Lottery," as the villagers close in on Tessie, the slips of paper blow out of the black box and mingle with the stones on the ground. Like the letter used for blackmail in Poe's "The Purloined Letter," the platitudes Mrs. Hope sends out indiscriminately in "When Things Get Dark," or the wicked little notes Mrs. Strangeworth leaves for her neighbors in "The Possibility of Evil," they serve as reminders of all the ways in which the written word can wreak havoc.

IN A STROKE OF particularly evil luck, the appearance of "The Lottery" coincided almost exactly with the publication of *The Armed Vision*, Hyman's long gestating work of criticism. The title, which came from Coleridge's *Biographia Literaria*, refers to the level of discernment attainable by the ideal critic: "The razor's edge becomes a saw to the armed vision; and the delicious melodies of Purcell or Cimarosa might be disjointed stammerings to a hearer, whose partition of time should be a thousand times subtler than ours." At more than 400 pages of tiny print, this impressive book was the apotheosis of the "scientific" approach to literary criticism that Hyman, guided by his dual

*Hyman in 1947,
while he was
writing* The
Armed Vision.

mentors—his Syracuse professor Leonard Brown and his critical idol
Kenneth Burke—had been perfecting since college. In twelve densely
argued chapters that began with a vicious takedown of Edmund Wilson, the *New Yorker* critic who was one of the dominant literary voices of
the 1940s, and climaxed in an encomium to Burke (the book progressed
from "villains to heroes," as one reader noted), Hyman analyzed major
contemporary critics as exemplars of different approaches: evaluative,
Marxist, psychological, and so on. He argued the merits and faults of
each in exhaustive detail, building to a conclusion in which he attempted
to integrate the approaches in "the ideal critic."

The Armed Vision's journey to publication was full of stumbles.
Hyman found his dealings with Knopf so aggravating that he tried
more than once to break his contract. His editors must have been no
less annoyed by his conduct, which was, in truth, sometimes childishly
obstinate. To begin with, he did not deliver the manuscript until April
1947—nearly two and a half years after the deadline. By that time,
his original editor had left the firm, turning the book over to Herbert
Weinstock, a scholar of classical music who would become an important writer on opera. On a personal level, Hyman and Weinstock got
along well: Weinstock and his partner, Ben Meiselman, were among the
Hymans' houseguests in North Bennington. (Weinstock was among
the very few relatively uncloseted gay men in New York publishing in
the 1940s.) But professionally their relationship was rancorous.

Hyman's desperate financial situation may have driven him to be more aggressive than usual with Knopf. Although he admitted it to almost no one, Bennington—which offered no tenure—had declined to renew his contract in the spring of 1946, after his first full year of teaching. His firing, for that was what it amounted to, was apparently more a referendum on his personality than on his teaching skills: the college president, Lewis Jones, found him abrasive. (Some of his colleagues believed him to be a victim of academic politics.) Upon his return, in September 1953, he would establish himself triumphantly as one of the superstars of the literature department. But for now he was out. "Stanley himself felt he had failed as a teacher," says Phoebe Pettingell. After the book was finished, he planned to return full-time to *The New Yorker*—to write profiles, he hoped—and perhaps to New York City. But for the time being, he and Jackson decided to stay in North Bennington.

In some ways, Hyman's firing was a boon: it meant more time to work on his already overdue book. On a practical level, however, he and Jackson were broke. Hyman's weekly "allowance" (as he called it) from *The New Yorker*, cut from $50 to $35 that year, was nowhere near enough to support a family of four, not to mention his book-buying habit. Jackson's story income was essential to their household, and after "The Lottery," her greater earning power would be obvious. But in 1946, the year Hyman stopped teaching, she sold only one story: "Men with Their Big Shoes," for which *The Yale Review* paid just $75. In 1947, *The New Yorker* declined to renew her first-reading option. Hyman was forced to ask both Jay Williams and Ben Zimmerman for loans. At least one trip to New York that year had to be canceled for lack of funds. Their situation began to improve in the spring of 1947, when Jackson signed her contract for *The Road Through the Wall*. Six months later she sold "The Daemon Lover" to *Woman's Home Companion* for $850, and her fees would rise from then on. But for now, they needed money.

Since Hyman had taken most of his advance early, he was due only $150 when he finally delivered the full manuscript, in April 1947. At once he began agitating for more cash. When Weinstock enthused over the book, Hyman suggested that if he liked it so much, he might consider increasing the advance. That was not possible, so Hyman started pressuring Weinstock to give him a contract for the next book, based on only an outline and a brief description. His idea was to study Darwin, Marx, Frazer, and Freud ("the greatest and most influential minds of the past century") as literary writers, "on the theory that their great influence has been due, as much as anything, to their creative and imaginative powers." *The Tangled Bank*, the book that eventually grew from this germ, would be a remarkable compendium of virtually everything Hyman had ever read or thought about. But Weinstock can hardly be blamed for not immediately seeing its potential.

Weinstock did not hold back in expressing his admiration for *The Armed Vision*: the book, he wrote to Hyman, was the most exciting manuscript to cross his desk in his three and a half years at Knopf, and he predicted it would become "what is loosely called a classic in its field." The scholar William York Tindall, to whom Weinstock sent it for evaluation, largely agreed, beginning his report with the line "This is an important book." But Weinstock worried—not unreasonably—about Hyman's ability to complete the next project on time. He offered $1000 as an advance for the new book, then called *Four Poets*, to be paid whenever Hyman began work on it and thought he could complete it within a year.

Hyman wanted the money at once—a request that Weinstock found more appropriate for a banker than a publisher. It did not help that Hyman had yet to turn in his revisions on *The Armed Vision*. In a final desperate stab, Hyman prevailed upon *The New Yorker*'s treasurer to loan him $1000 with his future Knopf contract as a guarantee, provoking a stern rebuke from Alfred Knopf himself. "The basic point, it seems to me, is that you simply cannot, the book world being what it is—and who are we to set it right—count on getting . . . 'money for rent and groceries' from the kind of book you write," the man who had once served squab to Hyman now scolded him. "It is a pleasure and a privilege to publish such books, but we cannot finance them as if they had sales possibilities which we are all but certain they have not." A profile of Knopf that appeared in *The New Yorker* a little over a year later quoted him lamenting "the crassness of present-day literary men. 'My God!' he said last year, speaking of a writer who was asking for what he considered a premature and excessive advance. 'This man tells me he needs money to pay his grocery bills. What the devil do I care about his grocery bills?'" The writer, of course, was Hyman. The same profile notes that Knopf contracts were considered "a good deal longer, and a good deal more tiresome, than the contract of any other American publisher," whch must have been slight consolation. The line about the groceries would be repeated in Knopf's *New York Times* obituary, nearly forty years after Hyman's request.

Insulted and furious, Hyman asked to be released from his contract, but Knopf wouldn't even do that. "We will rest on our contract and hope that as time goes on you will think less badly of us than you no doubt do now," he replied. (In the scrapbook in which he kept correspondence and reviews for *The Armed Vision*, Hyman taped below this letter the news report of Knopf's skiing accident.) Jim Bishop, Hyman's agent, told him there was nothing he could do—the Knopf editors liked the book and viewed it as "one of the prestige items of the year." But "they don't think it will sell worth a damn," Bishop said, "and neither do I."

In the end, Hyman backed down. But he was incensed a few months later to learn that the book's price, owing to its long page count, had been set at $6.95—nearly $70 in today's money—which he considered "criminal and farcical": "It will make me a general laughing-stock and reviewers' butt . . . [and] will kill absolutely any chance for a sale the book might have had." (*The Road Through the Wall*, by comparison, sold for $2.75.) Since Hyman was depending on the book's royalties to bring in some much needed income, this was not a trivial matter. He had hoped to earn more by selling off individual chapters to literary magazines, but their fees were as low as $25. The disparity between his income and Jackson's rankled him. "You see our difference in scale," he complained to Ellison.

This time Hyman had the contract on his side: it stipulated that the book's price could be no higher than $5. "If Alfred A. Knopf Inc. . . . cannot fulfill in 1947 a contract that was made in 1943, Mr. Knopf should have accepted the chance I gave him in a letter some months ago to break the contract peaceably and let me go elsewhere," he wrote gleefully, threatening to take up the matter with the Authors Guild. After a hasty consultation with the firm's lawyer, Knopf conceded that round to Hyman. But various altercations still lay ahead over the fees Hyman was charged for alterations, the index, and so on. By the time *The Armed Vision* was published, Hyman had racked up nearly $500 in additional charges on top of his $500 advance, all of which would have to be recouped against sales before he could start earning royalties.

Materially and emotionally, Jackson supported Hyman through these travails. The book was dedicated to her, "a critic of critics of critics," and in the acknowledgments Hyman thanked her for doing "everything for me that one writer can conceivably do for another." That may be a sly inside joke: Jackson and Hyman had publicly spread the rumor that Knopf owed his skiing accident to Jackson's witchcraft. She had to wait for him to go skiing in Vermont, she said; federal laws prevented her from doing magic across state lines. (The joke would come back to embarrass her the following year, when, in the wake of her *Lottery* publicity, an interviewer asked her, quite in earnest, how she had broken Knopf's leg.) Hyman's files reveal that she read the manuscript carefully and made numerous notes. In a jocular "review" of the book that Hyman pasted into his scrapbook, she wrote that she had read it "perhaps more often, and with greater loving and painstaking care, than almost anyone else, excepting possibly mr hyman himself." (The two writers made a game of coming up with fake blurbs and reviews of each other's books, purportedly authored by Shakepeare, Samuel Richardson, and other idols.) Still, Hyman, always competitive, chafed at having lost out to Jackson in the race to publish their first books. "I am delighted that I have finally gone into type, since Shirley, who has already had page proofs on her opus, has practically stopped twitting me," he wrote to Weinstock in the fall of 1947. And Jackson also used her joke review as an opportunity to slide in the dagger, noting that her qualifications for writing it were her "relations with mr hyman, which are of course about what you might expect, he having done everything for me that one writer could possibly do to another." That slip at the end from "for" to "to" was surely intentional.

The Armed Vision was finally published on May 24, 1948. The jacket copy, written by Weinstock, hailed it as "an important publishing and literary event . . . a critical book of major importance, a book over which rivers of ink will eventually be spilled." But Hyman's experience with Knopf had left him demoralized. Even the minor details rankled, especially the fact that his book jacket didn't include an author photograph or biographical information (which "makes the author feel like an author," he wrote pathetically to Weinstock). Instead, the space was used to advertise other Knopf books that he happened to dislike. "The literary future I see under this contract is three more books, say the next ten years, in peonage, with the advance for each book whistled past my nose and applied to styling charges, index fees, reset costs, etc., to the accompaniment of nasty notes and bills," he lamented. "Better to languish unpublished, say I." He didn't feel like an author. He felt betrayed.

The critical reaction did little to soothe his bruised ego. Weinstock had gotten mixed results in his quest for blurbs: Wallace Stevens had commended the book as "exciting from beginning to end," but the critic Mark Schorer, whom Hyman had elsewhere called a "narcissus," wrote back that he was "unable to lift my gaze from the pool." In his reader's report, Tindall had predicted the difficulty of generating positive publicity for *The Armed Vision*, since just about every critic who might write about it was savaged in its pages. "Kenneth Burke cannot review the book for every journal," he wrote snidely. (Weinstock prefaced his requests for blurbs with the apologetic note, "I feel certain that whether you like this book or not you will find it vastly interesting.") Alas, Tindall was right. The book's obstreperousness would have been hard to take from anyone, but it must have seemed especially threatening coming from Hyman, a Brooklyn Jew pitting himself against a generation of WASP literary scholars. When Saul Bellow, a decade earlier, announced his intention to do graduate study in English literature, the chair of his department at Northwestern University discouraged him with a blatantly anti-Semitic remark: "You weren't born to it."

A few of the early notices were positive: W. G. Rogers, whose syndicated column "Literary Guidepost" ran in newspapers all over the country, praised Hyman's "brilliant display of scholarship . . . cogent thinking . . . [and] vigorous writing." Another reviewer called it "distinguished" and "explosive." But Joseph Wood Krutch, a drama professor at Columbia whose biography of Poe had earned a negative mention in *The Armed Vision*, set the tone for much of what would follow in a lengthy piece in the *New York Herald Tribune* on June 20. Krutch's review betrays a bizarre hostility to criticism in general: "One lays down [the book] with the bemused conviction that . . . the function of the poet is merely to provide some raw material upon which the critics can fling themselves," he wrote. In his view, Hyman was a parasite eating away at a far more worthy set of hosts.

Hyman's own publications were no kinder to him. In *The New Republic*, John Farrelly called the book's goal of developing a scientific approach to criticism "questionable" and its evaluations "arbitrary." *The New Yorker*, in a brief, unsigned review, judged Hyman's writing "uncomplicated and often witty" but his conclusions "marked by an almost breathless irresponsibility and lack of judgment." (The next review praised a new critical anthology, edited by Hyman's nemesis Schorer, as "thoughtfully planned and instructive.") Brendan Gill sent a nice note, but admitted that he had read only to chapter 4. Hyman's old friend Louis Harap lectured him that his understanding of Marxist criticism was inadequate.

Despite his obvious disappointment, Hyman managed to have a sense of humor about the reaction. A cartoon he preserved in the scrapbook shows a man surrounded by a mountain of books and magazines as his wife holds up a tiny clipping: "Look, George, a favorable review!" He repeated with amusement a report that the Yale Co-op, misconstruing the title, had shelved the book under Military Affairs. And he treasured the complimentary notes he received from friends and colleagues. But the criticism stung him—he complained to Ellison of Krutch's "nasty petulance"—and so did the low sales. During the first six months after publication, *The Armed Vision* sold only 1500 copies, grossing just over $700, which left Hyman nearly $250 still to recoup. "Aside from being up against a financial wall, I have no complaints," he wrote wryly to Jay Williams, who responded with another loan. He did not receive his first royalty check until September 1950. For the next two years, the book sold only a few hundred copies a year, earning Hyman less than $300 in royalties. In February 1952, Knopf announced its intention to melt the plates, taking the book officially out of print. Hyman would not publish another work of literary criticism until 1961.

AS *THE ARMED VISION* limped along, "The Lottery" sprinted ahead. It was anthologized immediately in the *Prize Stories of 1949* as well as *55 Short Stories from the New Yorker* (1949), a volume celebrating the magazine's twenty-fifth anniversary. Vladimir Nabokov marked the table of contents in his copy with a grade for every story: "The Lottery" was one of only two that he deemed worthy of an A. (He gave an A+ to "Colette," his own story in the volume, as well as to Salinger's "A Perfect Day for Bananafish.") The composer Nicolas Nabokov, Vladimir's cousin, expressed interest in making "The Lottery" into an opera, with Jackson writing the libretto: "We may be the Gilbert and Sullivan of this generation," she joked. In March 1951, a version of "The Lottery" was broadcast on the NBC radio program *NBC Presents: Short Story.* "An ugly story, 'The Lottery,'" wrote Harriet van Horner in the *Washington Times.* "But how brave of radio to do it!" The story was also adapted for Albert McCleery's television program *Cameo Theater.* Rod Serling, creator of *The Twilight Zone*, later recalled that the TV show made the "anti-prejudice message much more pointed."

The story was anthologized for students as early as 1950, and it is still included in textbooks for high school and college English courses. It has been used to teach medical students how to evaluate the ethics of scarce resources (whether to allow an elderly patient to occupy a valuable intensive-care bed, for instance) and to dramatize questions of self-interest for high-school students (one teacher randomly awarded one student a grade of 0 on an assignment and gave all the others a grade of 100 to see how they would react). After coming to power in 1948—coincidentally, the same year "The Lottery" was published—the government of South Africa included the story on a list of banned books along with Lillian Smith's *Strange Fruit* and Richard Wright's *Native Son*, among others. Hyman would later say that Jackson was proud of this distinction: "she felt that *they* at least understood the story." There are Marxist, feminist, symbolic, and religious interpretations. One scholar

*Jackson reading
"The Lottery"
during a lecture in
Michigan,
July 1962.*

analyzed the method of selecting the victim and determined that some villagers actually have a greater chance of being selected than others: since the first drawing selects the family and the second selects the particular victim, villagers from small families are at a disadvantage.

Even though her earnings from permissions fees were substantial, Jackson eventually grew annoyed that "The Lottery" was reprinted much more often than anything else she wrote. She worried, not without justification, that she might become known for that story and nothing else— which for many years after her death was indeed the case. At one point, she asked her agent to raise the permissions fee to encourage editors to "let the poor old chestnut rest for a while." The only difference the price hike made was to bring in more money.

Grudgingly, Jackson agreed to record "The Lottery" for Folkways Records in 1959. Along with her recording of "The Daemon Lover," on the B side, it is the only recording of her voice that still exists. The agoraphobia of her late years had not yet begun, but she preferred to avoid New York City if possible, and refused to make a special trip to do the recording. Laurence, then a technically adept senior in high school, did it for her on a reel-to-reel recorder at Bennington. Jackson, nervous, brought along a glass of bourbon; the clink of ice cubes in her glass is occasionally audible. Her voice is low, with the slightest hint of an English affectation. She reads the story calmly, almost without expression. A sharpness enters her tone only when Tessie Hutchinson begins to speak. Jackson's voice ascends shrilly as she reads the lines: "It isn't fair, it isn't right." She gives the final line of the story a curious inflection: "And *then* they were upon her." Like the pointed collar around the throat of the dog Lady in "The Renegade," the recording cuts off abruptly before her voice has a chance to die out, making the last line sound like a question: And *then* they were upon her? The irony is audible. They have been upon her all along.

9.

NOTES ON A MODERN
BOOK OF WITCHCRAFT

THE LOTTERY: OR,
THE ADVENTURES OF
JAMES HARRIS, 1948–1949

[S]he was running as fast as she could down a long horribly clear hallway with doors on both sides and at the end of
the hallway was Jim, holding out his hands and laughing,
and calling something she could never hear because of the
loud music, and she was running and then she said, "I'm
not afraid," and someone from the door next to her took
her arm and pulled her through and the world widened
alarmingly until it would never stop and then it stopped
with the head of the dentist looking down at her. . . .

She was back in the cubicle, and she lay down on the
couch and cried, and the nurse brought her whisky in a
paper cup and set it on the edge of the wash-basin.

"God has given me blood to drink," she said to the
nurse.

—"The Tooth"

FOUR MONTHS AFTER "THE LOTTERY" WAS PUBLISHED, JACKSON arrived at the hospital to give birth to her third child. As she would tell it, the clerk who admitted her asked her to state her occupation. "Writer," she answered. "Housewife," the clerk suggested. "Writer," Jackson repeated. "I'll just put down housewife," the clerk told her.

This story appears in a magazine piece Jackson called "The Third Baby's the Easiest," a hilarious account of labor and delivery that would later be included in *Life Among the Savages*. Comedy aside, it perfectly illustrates the dilemma of her Janus-like dual identity—a dilemma that would become even more pronounced as her books achieved greater success and her fame grew. She was Mrs. Stanley Hyman: housewife, PTA member, faculty wife, mother to Laurence, Joanne, and now Sarah. And she was Shirley Jackson: the author, when she wrote that piece, of one finished novel, numerous short stories, and a forthcoming

Jackson in North Bennington, late 1940s.

Jackson with baby Sarah. Photograph by Ralph Ellison.

collection that included the literary sensation of 1948. That tension would never be resolved; if anything, it would grow more pronounced over the coming years. But Jackson also would grow skilled at manipulating it—and at using it in her fiction to illuminate the problems that defined women's lives of her era.

THAT THIRD BABY WAS Sarah Geraldine Hyman, who arrived October 30, 1948, just after Jackson sent off the proofs of her short story collection. Shirley wanted to name the baby Sue, but this time Stanley won: she was named for his grandmother. The family immediately began calling her Sally, which stuck throughout her childhood. (In this book, she is referred to as Sarah, the name she now uses formally.)

Shirley and Stanley had expected another boy, but they were delighted by their second daughter. Though she was a placid, easy baby—"fat and happy," Shirley wrote to her parents—it was soon clear that she would be the most creative, most intelligent, and ultimately most challenging of the children. ("Three children are enough for you to take care of," replied Geraldine, who never refrained from offering her opinion about her daughter's life. "Don't ever think of any more.") As a child, Sarah would read Freud and Emerson, along with all of Shirley's Oz books. She could stay alone in her room all day, reading or drawing; she was a tomboy who wore Laurence's old pants and came home with holes in the knees; she refused to comb her hair. ("Her general appearance is of a child barely kept in a state of cleanliness by stubborn determination," her mother once ruefully described her.) In *Life Among the Savages*, Jackson writes that she rejected "any notion of being a co-operative member of a family, named herself 'Tiger' and settled down to an unceasing, and seemingly endless, war against clothes, toothbrushes, all green vegetables, and bed. Her main weapon was chewing gum . . . with which she could perform miracles of construction on her own hair, books, and, once, her father's typewriter." As if suspecting even at birth her daughter's unconventionality, Shirley named as Sarah's godmother Jeanou—the vivacious intellectual who had done so much to break her out of her parents' mold—though the two would never meet.

Laura Nowak, whose daughter Alison was one of Sarah's close friends, remembers her as "mischievous"—at age four, she got up from a nap and wandered down to the village square on her own, where she went into the market and asked Larry Powers for a popsicle before Shirley noticed she was gone. As she grew older, she became captious, and the mischief turned into a desire to provoke. "She always presented herself as different and strange," Barry, the youngest of the siblings, says. "Anything controversial or offensive or weird or bizarre, she would adopt it and talk loudly about it—in school, in the town, anywhere." Sarah agrees, though she puts it differently: "I tried to be the most interesting kid." For years she picked an argument at the dinner table virtually every night: meals ended with either her or Shirley storming upstairs. Once when Sarah was about seven, she asked a question about sex while the whole family was eating out at a restaurant. "If you say that again, I'll butter your nose," Stanley warned her. Naturally she repeated it, just to see if he was serious. He was.

In some ways, she was Shirley's favorite; she was certainly more like Shirley than any of the other children. "sally has always been our sweet baby, the wickedest and funniest of our children, the little odd delightful silly one . . . our family fairy goblin," Shirley wrote when her daughter was eight. She shared Shirley's love of cats and her interest in magic and the macabre. Elizabeth Greene, who was Sarah's camp counselor one summer and became her close friend, recalls the two of them making a magical charm for a friend who was going through a difficult time. "She had a lot of light, a lot of openness to what lies beyond . . . one foot in the other world," Greene says. Sarah also was a talented writer who published her first story at age sixteen. When Jackson gathered her thoughts on fiction writing in "Notes for a Young Writer," Sarah was her intended reader. But she was just as much of an outsider as Shirley had been as a child, and she had more than her share of troubles. At age fifteen, she was kicked out of boarding school; the summer she was sixteen, a few weeks before Shirley died, she attempted suicide. "She had a self-destructive side," Greene says. That, too, she got from her mother.

"THERE IS A RIGHTNESS and a kind of burnished quality about every-thing you do," John Farrar wrote to Jackson after he read the manu-script of her short story collection. The success of "The Lottery" had spurred Farrar, Straus to ramp up its efforts on behalf of the new book, which was now to be titled *The Lottery* so as to capitalize on the author's new notoriety. Pyke Johnson, the publicity director, planned a cam-paign in which envelopes containing slips of paper would be inserted inside the books, with prizes—stone paperweights, witches' brooms, cauldrons—awarded to readers whose slips bore a black dot. "I never heard anything so ghoulish in all my life, but if the post office can stand it, I can," Jackson told him. To her parents, she was more blunt: the publicity campaign was "so excruciating that i will never show my face out of Vermont again." Fortunately, the postmaster overruled the plan.

The book's subtitle was not as easily settled. Farrar suggested *Notes from a Modern Book of Witchcraft*. Jackson did not want to abandon the witchcraft theme entirely: she decided to use passages from Glanvill's *Saducismus Triumphatus*, the seventeenth-century witchcraft chronicle that had first fascinated her in college, as epigraphs to each of the book's five sections. But she also had another unifying concept in mind. The collection would include several extremely accomplished stories that she had written the previous year but had not yet published (*The New*

Yorker turned them all down), which would serve as cornerstones of the book. They all worked along a similar model: an apparently mundane situation—a dinner guest, a visit to the dentist—that takes a Hawthorne-like detour, sharp yet subtle, into the uncanny.

The first, "Like Mother Used to Make," was probably written around January 1947, and was inspired by an anecdote from her friend Ben Zimmerman's life. A man named David arrives home from work to prepare for the arrival of his next-door neighbor, Marcia, for dinner. His apartment is a scene of perfect order, with the furniture invitingly arranged, a bowl of flowers, a beautifully set table; he has even baked a pie. Marcia's apartment, which he enters briefly to leave a note, is the antithesis: so cluttered that it reduces him to despair. Their dinner is interrupted by the unexpected arrival of a male coworker of Marcia's. He thinks David's apartment is actually hers, and she plays along, sneakily stealing credit for the comfortable atmosphere and even the pie. At the story's end, David has no choice but to surrender his apartment to Marcia and her friend and retreat to her unpleasant quarters, which he begins, helplessly, to tidy. Like Mrs. Hart in "Men with Their Big Shoes," the innocent David finds his home invaded by an unsettling, alien presence that he is somehow powerless to ward off.

In an early draft of the story, Marcia's intrusive coworker is named, innocuously, Mr. Lang. For the *Lottery* collection—now to be subtitled *The Adventures of James Harris*—Jackson changed his name to Mr. Harris. This figure wends his destructive way through the book, disrupting the lives of various characters, nearly all of them women. (David, whose feminine gifts for homemaking and cooking Jackson emphasizes, is a rare male victim.) In the Child Ballad that bears his name, which may have been one of the old English songs Jackson learned from her mother, James Harris is the "Daemon Lover" who seduces a woman by promising to show her "how the lilies grow / On the banks of Italy." It is not until she is aboard his ship that she discovers he is the devil in disguise, when he reveals that their true destination is the snowy mountain of Hell.

What would happen if James Harris walked the streets of New York? Just as she had with "Elizabeth" and "The Lottery," Jackson updated the legend. A tall man in a blue suit, he slips in and out of the stories in the *Lottery* collection, taking on different personas. Sometimes, as in "Like Mother Used to Make," his presence is sinister but tangential. Elsewhere, he brings women to the point of disintegration—the true theme of the collection.

Just before she began work on these stories, Jackson became preoccupied with a real-life case of a woman's disappearance. On the afternoon of December 1, 1946, Bennington student Paula Welden headed out for a walk on Vermont's Long Trail near Glastenbury Mountain, on the outskirts of Bennington proper, and never returned. The case dominated the local paper for weeks. The most likely theory was that she had suffered a hiking accident, but rumors spread that she had been seen in a car with a man. A waitress in western Massachusetts claimed she had served a man accompanied by a girl fitting Welden's description; when he went up to pay the bill, the girl asked the waitress where she was and how far it was to Bennington. A psychic said that Welden had walked through a covered bridge and along the banks of a river, where she would be found alive inside an old shack. Others suggested that she might have "run away to start a new life." Search parties combed the area for days, but Paula Welden was never found.

Jackson wrote one story explicitly based on Welden's disappearance, called "The Missing Girl" (the title came from one of the news articles about the case she carefully saved). But the motif of women who lose their way dominates *The Lottery*—the phrase "she was lost," or variants of it, is repeated again and again. These women are secretaries a bit past their prime and still unmarried, or mothers stuck at home with their children, longing for companionship yet terrified of their gossiping neighbors. Women and men are depicted as occupying different realities, with men literally driving women insane. "Sometimes," the narrator of "Got a Letter from Jimmy" reflects as she does the dishes one evening, "sometimes I wonder if men are quite sane, any of them. Maybe they're all crazy and every other woman knows it but me, and my mother never told me and my roommate just didn't mention it and all the other wives think I know. . . ." (The original draft, one of her earliest stories, was based closely on an episode in which Hyman, feuding with Walter Bernstein, refused to open a letter from his friend; Jackson changed the name to Jimmy to match the James Harris theme.) The story ends with the narrator's fantasy of murdering her husband.

Written within a few months of each other, three of the longer stories function as a kind of trilogy: Hyman jokingly compared it to *The Divine Comedy*. In "Pillar of Salt," Margaret and Brad, former New Yorkers who now live in New England, return to the city for a brief visit. Slowly, ominously, things start to go wrong. There is a fire in an apartment building near a party they attend; later, walking on a Long Island beach, Margaret discovers a human leg. Gradually it becomes clear that these outward signs of disintegration and alienation mirror her inner state. The story ends with her standing on a street corner, paralyzed, overwhelmed by the prospect of crossing: "she wondered, How do people ever manage to get there, and knew that by wondering, by admitting a doubt, she was lost."

Margaret's husband is a stolid presence throughout the story, unable to understand quite what her problem is. But elsewhere in the collection, the woman's disintegration is linked to romance. James Harris, the daemon lover, comes along to sweep her out of the tawdry tedium of her life—the trips to the dentist, the diapers and dishes—and promises her something better; but the consequences are dire. If she goes with him, she will give up not only her life but her soul. In "The Daemon Lover," the midpoint of the trilogy, a no-longer-young woman (her marriage license gives her age as thirty, but in truth she is four years older) waits in her apartment for a fiancé—Jamie Harris—who never arrives. Desperate, she goes out in search of him, but as she gradually descends deeper and deeper into hysteria, the reader finally wonders whether he ever existed at all. James Harris is a similarly elusive figure in "The Tooth," the final story in the trilogy, in which country housewife Clara Spencer travels to New York to visit the dentist and encounters, or believes that she encounters, a mysterious man named Jim. Her mind befogged by drugs and by pain (and possibly by his menacing presence), she has visions of him holding out his arms and calling to her; by the end of the story, she imagines she is running away with him.

Another story makes the dangers of escape even more explicit. In "The Beautiful Stranger," which Jackson also likely wrote around this time but did not try to publish, another woman named Margaret (a name Jackson used repeatedly for characters with whom she seemed particularly to identify) greets a man who she thinks is her husband on his return from a business trip and realizes that, Martin Guerre–like, he is literally a different person. Her husband, we learn through gradual hints, was abusive and cruel. The stranger is warm and companionable: he mixes her a martini the way she likes it and laughs with her over dinner. "This is not the man who enjoyed seeing me cry; I need not be afraid," Margaret tells herself. But one afternoon she goes out on her own to run errands: "I must see something today beyond the faces of my children. . . . No one should be so much alone." (In *The Feminine Mystique*, Friedan writes, "Sometimes a woman would tell me that the feeling [of loneliness at home] gets so strong she runs out of the house and walks through the streets.") Strangely, she is unable to find her way home. "The evening was very dark, and she could see only the houses going in rows, with more rows beyond them and more rows beyond that, and somewhere a house which was hers, with the beautiful stranger inside, and she lost out here."

In "Company for Dinner," an early precursor to this story, a man accidentally walks into the wrong house and believes it to be his. "The Beautiful Stranger" takes that simple irony—people are interchangeable; all marriages are equally dull—and complicates it. The stranger and the husband look identical; only the wife can tell the difference between them. On some level, she knows she is making a deal with the devil, but even the devil—a kind, handsome daemon lover—is preferable to her contemptible husband. (The story was originally titled "Document of Loneliness.") Yet escaping an unhappy marriage turns out not to be that easy. What appears to be a solution is only a trick: she will lose her way.

Most clearly, the figure of the daemon lover represents Jackson's fears about the world outside the relative safety of her marriage—the simultaneous lure and danger of the unknown. But when Jackson married Hyman, she saw him, too, as a kind of daemon lover, sweeping her out of her parents' upper-class, bourgeois lifestyle into a world as alluring, and as foreign, as the land of wonder offered by James Harris. If some elements of their marriage had lived up to her expectations—the intellectual stimulation he offered, their shared jokes, their symbiosis of writer and critic—others clearly had not. "you once wrote me a letter . . . telling me that i would never be lonely again. i think that was the first, the most dreadful, lie you ever told me," Jackson would later write to Hyman in an undated letter enumerating possible reasons for divorcing him. The line uncannily echoes the confession by one of Glanvill's witches of her relationship with the devil: "He promised her, when she made her Contract with him, that she should want nothing, but ever since she hath wanted all things."

"ONCE IN A LONG while a book publisher, because of definite signs and general intuition, feels the touch of magic that makes for an important book. . . . We believe we have such a book," John Farrar and Roger Straus wrote to reviewers and booksellers in March 1949, a month before publishing *The Lottery: or, The Adventures of James Harris*. The book was featured in early reviews in both the daily and Sunday *New York Times*, the Associated Press called it "a work of genius and the publishing event of the year," and the U.S. government bought fifteen hundred copies for Army and Navy libraries. Two days before the official publication date of April 13, *The Lottery* had already gone into a second printing. Within two months it sold five thousand copies, almost unheard of for a collection of short fiction.

Jackson was thrilled by the sales—the previous Christmas, with no advance yet for Hyman and a number of her stories circulating but not yet accepted, she had been reduced to asking her parents for a loan. (After the book appeared, Geraldine wrote that she and Leslie were "very pleased and proud that the new book is dedicated to us—our little girl getting so well known" but characteristically refrained from saying anything about its contents.) But Jackson found Farrar, Straus's promotional efforts distasteful, if effective. They were playing up the book as "the most terrifying piece of literature ever printed, which is bad enough, and . . . [saying it] will give ulcers to anyone who reads it," she complained, rightly believing that such insinuations trivialized her work. Publicist Pyke Johnson was telling any reporter who would listen that Jackson had used witchcraft to break Knopf's leg. "Boy, that story is sure going to sell copies," he told her, slapping her on the back.

His instincts were correct. "With attractive features and a pair of quite un-evil eyes behind glasses, she does not resemble a witch," wrote W. G. Rogers in a profile of Jackson for the Associated Press (head-lined "Shirley Jackson Is 'Sure 'Nuff' Witch"). He brought up the story about Knopf and asked Jackson to tell him all about black magic. "for-tunately he had just bought me two drinks, so i was able to tell him, very fluently indeed, about black magic and incantations and the practical application of witchcraft to everyday life, most of which i remembered out of various mystery stories," she wrote to her parents. The part about the mystery stories, Jackson's indulgence throughout her life, wasn't true. Her library of witchcraft books, as Rogers noted in his piece, now numbered in the hundreds of volumes. Rogers's remark in his review of *The Lottery*—"Miss Jackson writes not with a pen but a broomstick"—would be repeated by countless wags in the years to come. Reviewers also compared her to Saki and Truman Capote, neither of them "writers i admire particularly," she grumbled.

Jackson claimed to be embarrassed by the witchcraft talk. She told her parents it made her feel "as though i had a very bad hangover and everyone was telling me the screamingly funny things i had done the night before." If she really had a broomstick, she said, she would fly to California and hide in their cellar. In fact, Rogers's article made it clear that he did not take the story about Knopf seriously. He concluded that Jackson was like a witch in only one way: "She is hard to pin down."

Despite her distaste for self-promotion, Jackson proved adept with reporters, slipping in and out of her personas with the agility of James Harris. Bowing to stereotypes of the period, she preferred to present herself to reporters and critics—virtually all of whom were men—as a women's-magazine-certified happy homemaker who tossed off her sto-ries during breaks from dusting. "I can't persuade myself . . . that writ-ing is honest work," she said cheerily in an interview with Harvey Breit of *The New York Times Book Review*, validating on one level the com-ment from the hospital clerk who switched her occupation from writer to housewife. "Fifty percent of my life is spent washing and dressing the children, cooking, washing dishes and clothes and mending. After I get it all to bed, I turn around to my typewriter and try to—well, to create concrete things again. It's great fun, and I love it. But it doesn't tie any shoes." Writing was "relaxing," she said later in the interview: "I do it because it's fun, because I like it." Breit, too, fell into her trap, emphasizing Jackson's domesticity: "She looks not only wholesome but very much on the dayside. . . . She subtly radiates an atmosphere of coziness and comfort."

The tug-of-war between these three dimensions of Jackson's character—writer, housewife, and witch—is evident in various drafts of a biographical note that her publisher asked her to write for publicity purposes. In one version, she is sanguine—perhaps excessively so— about the children's influence on her writing:

> i don't like housework, but i do it because no one else will. my older daughter and i are practically learning to cook together. i write in the evenings mostly, i guess, although sometimes i let the children help me write in the mornings. they are all very sympathetic about my writing, and my son no longer tries to justify me to his friends.

The draft concludes: "i like cats and dogs and children and books. i wish i didn't have to write this."

But another version in a strikingly different tone suggests that magic may have meant more to Jackson than she was willing to admit to her parents. "I am tired of writing dainty little biographical things that pretend that I am a trim little housewife in a Mother Hubbard stirring up appetizing messes over a wood stove," it begins:

> I live in a dank old place with a ghost that stomps around in the attic room we've never gone into (I *think* it's walled up) and the first thing I did when we moved in was to make charms in black crayon on all the door sills and window ledges to keep out demons, and was successful in the main. There are mushrooms

growing in the cellar, and a number of marble mantels which have an unexplained habit of falling down onto the heads of the neighbors' children.

At the full of the moon I can be seen out in the backyard digging for mandrakes, of which we have a little patch, along with rhubarb and blackberries. I do not usually care for these herbal or bat wing recipes, because you can never be sure how they will turn out. I rely almost entirely on image and number magic.

Whether understood as a parlor trick or something more, Jackson's magic was of a piece with her housewife persona: it had a thoroughly domestic cast. "i'm a kind-hearted mama who studies evil all the time," one of her late characters says. (The line is a reference to Robert Johnson's "Kind Hearted Woman Blues.") One of her favorite "tricks," friends would recall, was to slam a kitchen drawer jumbled with utensils and name the one she wanted; when she opened the drawer again, it would invariably be on top. She and her editors had a running joke regarding her ability to engineer victories for the Brooklyn Dodgers. "I suggest you write to Shirley and have her order from her usual source of supply a series of light sun-showers for Saturday, to end with your

Witches assembling for the Sabbath, from Johannes Geiler von Keisersperg, Die Emeis *[The Ant-Colony], Strasbourg, 1517. Reprinted from Émile Grillot de Givry's* Witchcraft, Magic, and Alchemy.

arrival at the stadium," a mutual friend wrote to John Farrar in a letter that accompanied tickets to a Dodgers-versus-Yankees World Series game in 1949. "I'll be glad to reimburse her for all materials used in the order: Eye of newt, and toe of frog . . . the usual stuff." She was said to have turned up at Ebbets Field "with a string of rattles and other gadgets" to hex the Yankees. Alas, Jackson's magic was insufficient: the Dodgers lost.

All that was fine, as long as no one else took it seriously, or suspected that she took it seriously. But in some ways she did. Witchcraft, whether she practiced it or simply studied it, was important to Jackson for what it symbolized: female strength and potency. The witchcraft chronicles she treasured—written by male historians, often men of the church, who sought to demonstrate that witches presented a serious threat to Christian morality—are stories of powerful women: women who defy social norms, women who get what they desire, women who can channel the power of the devil himself. In classic accounts of the witches' sabbath, a gathering of sorcerers and witches presided over by Satan, the sexual and domestic connotations are obvious: witches attend naked, flying to the sabbath via their chimneys. In the earliest chronicles, they flew on pitchforks; later the pitchforks turned into brooms, another symbol of home and hearth. To call oneself a witch, then, is to claim some of that power. *Everyone will be afraid of me and do what I say*, reads one of the notes left by the creek in *The Road Through the Wall*, a note written by a victimized girl.

And magic, for Jackson, was inextricably connected to her writing. "i like writing fiction better than anything, because just being a writer of fiction gives you an absolutely unassailable protection against reality; nothing is ever seen clearly or starkly, but always through a thin veil of words," she wrote in a brief talk she often gave, in different versions, to introduce her readings; a version of it appears in *Come Along with Me*, a posthumously published collection of her writings edited by Hyman, as "Experience and Fiction."

a story can derive from anything. my daughter sally pointed this out to me most vividly one irritating morning, when i was wrestling with the refrigerator door, which would never open easily; sally came into the kitchen and told me that fighting the refrigerator was useless; what i needed was magic. when i thought about it, it seemed like a better idea, so i abandoned the refrigerator and went in to the typewriter and wrote a story about trying to unstick the refrigerator door and when the story sold i bought a new refrigerator. thus experience plus magic equals fiction.

This is jocular, of course. But on some level writing was a form of witchcraft to Jackson—a way to transform everyday life into something rich and strange, something more than what it appeared to be. In "The Third Baby's the Easiest," Jackson quotes Othello's lines about how he wooed Desdemona by telling her stories of his adventures: "She loved me for the dangers I had pass'd, / And I loved her that she did pity them." The line that follows, which she does not quote, resonates silently: "This only is the witchcraft I have used."

JACKSON EARNED BACK her advance and began to accumulate royalties even before *The Lottery* was published. In the second half of 1949 she also sold three stories to *Good Housekeeping*, at $1000 apiece. (After giving birth to Sarah, she told Ralph Ellison, she came out of the hospital "full of ultra-violet rays and story plots.") After she and Hyman paid all their bills and their income tax, there was enough money left over for them to acquire a television set—"one of the first ones, with a tiny screen," a childhood friend of Joanne's recalls—on which they loved to watch baseball games and boxing matches.

Jackson was also finally able to fix her teeth, which had been a longtime source of discomfort: "The Tooth" offers an all-too-vivid description of the "crash of pain" that accompanies a toothache. Her teeth had deteriorated to the point that many would no longer hold fillings, and her dentist recommended she replace her top teeth with an artificial plate. She was surprised by how pleased she was with her appearance afterward. "now that i am not constantly uncomfortable because my teeth looked so terrible, i have no trouble with things like speaking in public . . . or being interviewed. also i grin in all the photographs," she wrote to her parents. This was not quite true—Jackson would always be a nervous interview subject. In a rare moment of praise, Geraldine told her daughter that she was "very brave to go to New York all alone and have all those teeth out" but reprimanded her for not notifying her parents in advance: "You must always tell us about yourself. You must not forget that you are still our little girl."

Jackson's new teeth were a necessity rather than a luxury, because she was suddenly in demand as a lecturer. Bennington suffered a minor crisis in June 1949, when several faculty members resigned to protest the expulsion of Miriam Marx after a series of rules violations. Apparently she had been warned that another offense would lead to expulsion, but since her graduation was only six weeks away, some of the faculty saw the punishment as unnecessarily cruel. The poet Stanley Kunitz, Marx's counselor, was one of the professors to resign; another was James T. Jackson, who taught a course in the short story. A series of guest lecturers took over the course, including Jackson. She was initially nervous, asking Wallace Fowlie how it was done: "What do you say first? And then *what* do you teach?" But she turned out to be a gifted teacher. "the girls and i talk very seriously about the Art of Writing and then they ask me very timidly where they can sell their stories and i tell them there's nothing to it," she told her parents. One of the students recalled that she gave her first public reading of "The Lottery" in the class.

The experience inaugurated in Jackson a love of lecturing that would continue throughout her life. Her shyness and anxiety vanished when she took the stage, and she talked fluidly and engagingly about writing, often from just a few pages of notes, using many examples from her fiction. That summer, Jackson was invited to read at the Cummington School of the Arts, in the Berkshires; Hyman, annoyed by the attention being paid to her, grumbled that she went on "interminably." John and Margaret Farrar also invited her to a new conference they had started at Marlboro College, a tiny school on the site of a former farm in nearby Marlboro, Vermont, outside Brattleboro. The First Annual Marlboro College Fiction Writers' Conference included *New Yorker* writer Peter DeVries and novelists Charles Jackson and Dorothy Canfield Fisher.

(Hyman was invited, too, but only after he sent the Farrars a peeved letter asking why he had been excluded.) After her one brief stint at Bennington, Jackson would never teach formally again, but she found she loved the intimate atmosphere of writers' conferences: she participated in the Marlboro conference for several years before moving on to the Suffield Writer-Reader Conference in Suffield, Connecticut, and the prestigious Bread Loaf Writers' Conference. Eventually these conferences would also serve as havens where she was able to be celebrated for her writing, far from Hyman's critical gaze. But for now they went together: Hyman lectured on "Fiction and Folk Material," and Jackson conducted a master class in fiction writing. Afterward, Margaret Farrar complimented her on her "modesty" and the "supreme skill of her stories." She and Hyman both "had a fine time being writers for two days," Jackson reported.

Wasn't she always a writer? That remark illustrates how acutely Jackson felt the push and pull of her writer and housewife personas after *The Lottery* was published. She was, at last, an established fiction writer with a real income, an income that even allowed her to hire a housekeeper to do light cleaning and prepare breakfast and lunch for the children, so that she could work uninterrupted in the mornings. But there was still plenty of housekeeping: all the little chores, as she put it, that "no one but me ever remembers to do—things like keeping the toys together, and filling the cigarette box, and about five hundred small things like that." Considering that many of Jackson's friends and neighbors would later comment on the messiness of her house, it may seem odd that the housewife aspect of her persona took up so much of her mental energy. But even if she wasn't naturally gifted at housekeeping, she was keenly aware that it was expected of her. As Friedan would make abundantly clear in *The Feminine Mystique*, women in the postwar period were told to be "perfect wives and mothers; their highest ambition to have five children and a beautiful house; their only fight to get and keep their husbands." The ideal woman of the era was one who could proudly put "Housewife" in the spot for "Occupation" on her census form. "Our readers are housewives, full time," the editor of a women's magazine—likely one of the ones Jackson wrote for—told Friedan. "They are not interested in national or international affairs. They are only interested in the family and the home."

Housekeeping was also a source of tension in her marriage. Jackson never made any pretense of being a flawless housekeeper, "trim and competent." She inevitably found herself as she does in the essay "Here I Am, Washing Dishes Again"—with the dishpan heaped high, inventing stories to distract herself through the task. The orderly house was a fantasy, not a standard she strived to uphold. But unlike her, Hyman was compulsively tidy—everything on his desk had to be perfectly lined up before he could begin work. She would later move to a separate room to write (and eventually to sleep as well) because she liked to tape photographs or drawings that inspired her on the wall at random, while he could not tolerate even a picture hanging crookedly. Jackson jokes in an unpublished fragment that "any kind of problem can be solved by putting it in a box and putting the box away." Surely some of the obsession with housekeeping in Jackson's writing stems from the desire metaphorically to put things away—anxieties, fears, all the messes of life—and her corresponding inability to do so.

In fact, though Jackson strived for some order in the home, she feared too much of it. She loved rooms that were filled with books and cats and color and sunlight, even if there were papers strewn on the floor or clothing draped over the chairs. More often than not, housekeeping done too perfectly in one of her stories is a sign that something is amiss. In "Pillar of Salt," the distraught protagonist deliberately unmakes her bed (which she made "before going out to breakfast, like any good housewife") and then remakes it, "taking a long time over the corners and smoothing out every wrinkle," in an effort to calm her unsettled mind. In a piece published in *Vogue* in 1949, Jackson lamented modern innovations such as plastic for bringing an artificial sterility into the home and eliminating "anything natural or real—the honest touch of dirt, the use of wood or stone for practical endurance, the unclean standard of air we have been breathing for so long." Artificiality in the environment, she argued, would bring about artificial emotions as well. "A woman's house no longer loves her, as a good family house should love its housewife. . . . No one cares any more about the deeper personality that comes with solid, unshakable affection, with the sympathy of personalities that grow together through attention and loving care and laborious painstaking work." She ended the piece with a Stepford-like vision of the future: "Soon, in our charmingly fabricated living rooms, our glittering kitchens, where no food ever either perishes or is eaten, we women will find ourselves completely useless, an anachronism like the horse and buggy, or a failed invention like the zeppelin. And we deserve it, too." A little chaos was good for the soul.

But the *idea* of the house—what is required to make and keep a home, and what it means when a home is destroyed—is important in just about all of Jackson's novels. Already as a child, she had responded to the moods of houses: "even the bookends have personalities," she once wrote of her bedroom in Rochester. The relationship between a person's surroundings and his or her mental state was one she understood well. "The crack in the kitchen linoleum is a danger to the structure: the well spaced coolness of the sheets on the line is a sensual presentation of security," she writes in the early story "Homecoming." Later, in *The Haunting of Hill House*, the mood of the house will have a devastating effect on some who set foot in it.

At times, Jackson chafed at the dual role. In a piece called "Fame," she satirically reports on a phone call she received from a woman writing a gossip column for the North Bennington newspaper. The call comes just a few days before *The Road Through the Wall* is to be published, but every time Jackson tries to get in a word about her book, the caller steers her back to domestic details. When the story appears, it doesn't mention the book—only that "Mrs. Stanley Hyman" was "visiting Mr. and Mrs. Farrarstraus of New York City this weekend." Jackson was exaggerating for comic effect, as she so often did in these pieces. The actual column, which she saved in her *Road Through the Wall* scrapbook, did include the title of the novel, though it identified the author by her married name. Still, her news looks out of place among the other items in the gossip column, such as "William Barber of Main street is quite ill with the grip [sic]" and "The Baptist church choir will rehearse Thursday evening at 7:30."

On the one hand, as she showed in "Fame," Jackson wanted her neighbors to know that she was different—that her life was bigger than the confines of North Bennington. At the same time, she feared their scrutiny and their gossip. In the story "Mrs. Spencer and the Oberons," the snobbish Mrs. Spencer—another Geraldine figure—maintains a bizarre vendetta against the Oberons, a new family in town whose casual, friendly way of life offends her buttoned-up sensibilities. Mrs. Spencer's behavior is never anything other than correct; her "kitchen [is] immaculate, dinner preparing invisibly, her table set and lovely in a quiet stillness of shining glass and white damask." The Oberons (their name alludes to *A Midsummer Night's Dream*) are more like the Hymans: "Children being fed all kinds of things. . . . Grown-ups laughing and drinking and probably never getting anything to eat until all hours. People trampling through the house, wrinkling rugs, upsetting ashtrays, pressing into the kitchen to help make a salad, dropping cigarettes, putting glasses down on polished furniture, making noise." To Mrs. Spencer, this behavior is "vulgar and untidy and nasty." But everyone else in town is charmed by the Oberons. By the end of the story, Mrs. Spencer is the one who finds herself ostracized, wandering lost on a dark night, trying to follow the dreamlike sounds of laughter and singing that reach her from the Oberons' distant house.

If Jackson's story makes it clear that her sympathies are with the Oberons, she worried nonetheless about the disapproval of neighbors like Mrs. Spencer. After four years in North Bennington, she was still a newcomer in a village where most of the locals had grown up together, attending the same school and settling down to the same kind of lifestyle—a working-class job for the husband, a life at home for the wife. The woman in *The Road Through the Wall* who is scorned by the others for imagining herself to be "something more than a housewife" will be brutally punished for her pretensions. Jackson may have feared a similar kind of cosmic retribution. Who was she, after all, to call herself a writer?

And news of "The Lottery" was making its way back to North Bennington, whether or not the locals read the story. (If the postmaster may not actually have had to give Jackson the largest box in the post office, as she would later claim, he could hardly have failed to notice the piles of extra mail pouring in.) Before "The Lottery" came out, Jackson joked to a friend that her "literary reputation here in North Bennington" was well established: "I am now constantly being approached to Write Things for People, like the Girl Scouts, and the Home Talent Show, and the Fireman's Benefit. . . . I am now town writer. Fame is a great thing." But now she really was town writer, in a way the locals appreciated far less. "The general consensus was that this outsider came in, lived in the town for a few years, and then wrote some nasty story making them all look bad and uncivilized," Barry Hyman says.

In the wake of her second book's publication—the reviews, the interviews, the fuss about witchcraft—Shirley's anxiety flared up. "you can imagine how i feel, in the middle of all this. sort of small, and scared. . . . naturally, i'm having a wonderful time being fussed over, and i love it, but i feel like an awful fool most of the time," she confessed to her parents. During the summer of 1949, she may have experienced her first brush with agoraphobia. She declined to commit to another Bennington course: "no more teaching . . . i'd rather stay home." Even staying at home wasn't safe enough anymore—not in this town where she had never felt at home, where she had always sensed her neighbors' resentment beneath the small talk. In "The Summer People," written a few months after "The Lottery," a couple who have been vacationing peacefully for years at their small-town summer home discover that the locals turn on them when they decide for the first time to stay past Labor Day. The grocer declines to deliver their food; the kerosene man says he doesn't have enough to replenish their supply; their car is tampered with and their telephone lines are cut. The message is clear: strangers will be tolerated only as long as they respect their boundaries.

The inconveniences of life in North Bennington were beginning to outweigh the benefits. The increase in publicity meant that Jackson had to make more frequent trips into New York, a five-hour train ride away. The local school was inadequate to their needs: Laurence, now seven years old, was at the top of his class, and Jackson worried that he was being insufficiently challenged. Even the big old house was starting to feel crowded, especially with their latest addition, a three-year-old shepherd mix named Toby, "the biggest dog in town" at close to a hundred pounds.

With Hyman no longer teaching at Bennington, there was no reason to stay. Jackson and Hyman considered moving to a few different towns in Connecticut, as well as Cambridge, Massachusetts. But their plans shifted from hypothetical to urgent when their landlord, as if enacting a scene from "The Summer People," announced that he wanted them out by December 1. One of Hyman's *New Yorker* colleagues, who lived in the posh suburb of Westport, Connecticut, stepped in to help them find a house to their liking. It was just outside Westport in a town called Saugatuck: a Victorian on Indian Hill Road with five bedrooms, two bathrooms, and an acre of land, with woods facing the back. Hyman would be able to commute easily by train to the *New Yorker* offices.

The only problem was the cost—$200 a month, four times as much as they were paying in North Bennington. Hyman's income from *The New Yorker*, now around $300 a month, was not sufficient. In spring 1949, Eleanor Kennedy, the MCA agent then representing both him and Jackson, had managed to liberate him from his obligations to Knopf, and he was finally, as he wrote to Jay Williams, "in a position to sign up with someone else and get a whopping advance in four figures, two of them dollars and two of them cents." He and Williams had been unable to interest a publisher in their anthology of myth and ritual criticism. He wound up signing a contract with Harper & Brothers for his book on Darwin, Marx, Frazer, and Freud, with an advance of only $500 and another wildly optimistic deadline of December 31, 1950. This time Hyman worked an extension clause into the contract—he knew he would need it.

It would be Jackson, in fact, who paid for the house. On the basis of the stories she had already sold to *Good Housekeeping*, the magazine offered her a contract in the fall of 1949 for eight stories a year, with an advance of $1500 each quarter. (While the fee seemed high to her, the magazine paid its male writers more: Charles Jackson received $2500 apiece for similar stories in 1948.) She wasn't happy with the kind of pieces the magazine required her to write—sentimental fiction about children and homemaking. In "The Wishing Dime," editor Herbert Mayes's favorite of her stories, two children are given a dime that they believe to be magical, but it's obvious to the reader that their wishes come true through a succession of happy accidents. Geraldine, suddenly a literary critic, told her daughter this work was beneath her. Jackson responded bluntly that it was worth doing for the guaranteed income, which would give her freedom to work on a new novel without having to scramble to place individual stories: "at a thousand bucks a story, i can't afford to try to change the state of popular fiction today, and since they will buy as much of it as i write, i do one story a month, and spent the rest of the time" on serious work, she explained blithely. By December 1, the Hyman household—Shirley, Stanley, Laurence, Joanne, Sarah, Toby the dog, and half a dozen cats, along with eleven tons of furniture and books (mostly books)—was installed on Indian Hill Road.

10.

THE LOVELY HOUSE

WESTPORT,
HANGSAMAN, 1950–1951

> Upstairs Margaret said abruptly, "I suppose it starts to
> happen first in the suburbs," and when Brad said, "What
> starts to happen?" she said hysterically, "People starting
> to come apart."
>
> —"Pillar of Salt"

"SMART NEW YORKERS ARE FLOCKING" TO CONNECTICUT'S
Gold Coast, *Life* magazine reported just a few months before the Hymans
joined the migration. Less than an hour and a half from the city via
the electrified New Haven Railroad or the newly completed high-speed
Merritt Parkway, the "quietly luxurious" area was quickly becoming
home to an increasing number of high-powered business executives
and their Bugbee-style mansions: H. S. Richardson, chairman of Vick
Chemical, founded by his grandfather; Chester LaRoche, president of
the C.J. LaRoche advertising agency and also of the Fairfield County
Hunt Club; printing executive Nelson Macy, of Corlies, Macy & Company; and many others. (In a move only slightly less outrageous than
Charles Crocker's "spite fence," Richardson, unsatisfied with the rocky
shoreline by his house, had sand brought in so that his children and
grandchildren could play in comfort.) The businessmen tended to

cluster in and around the most exclusive towns, including Greenwich, Darien, and Fairfield, commuting each day via "club cars" that offered the wealthiest patrons amenities not found in coach class, such as air-conditioning. Though *Life* declined to mention the less savory details, some of these towns were "exclusive" in more ways than wealth. Darien was restricted to WASPs; Jews and African Americans were not permitted to buy real estate there or even visit the beach. In *Gentleman's Agreement* (1947), the relationship between the main character (who is pretending to be Jewish in order to investigate anti-Semitism) and his girlfriend takes an ugly turn when the couple is invited to a party in Darien and many guests mysteriously decline to attend.

Westport, a former colonial shipping center just west of Fairfield and east of Darien, was the least conservative of the Gold Coast towns, a center for "idea people"—writers, artists, and actors. J. D. Salinger rented a house in Westport at right around the same time as the Hymans—it had formerly belonged to F. Scott Fitzgerald—to use as a writing retreat while he finished *The Catcher in the Rye*. Formed in 1945, the Westport Artists Club already counted 148 members by the time the Hymans arrived, including cartoonists Helen Hokinson and Wood Cowan and sculptor James Fraser, who had designed the buffalo nickel. The Westport Country Playhouse, housed in an old cow barn and tannery, was founded in 1931 by former Broadway producers Lawrence Langner and Armina Marshall (also husband and wife) and attracted such actors as Bert Lahr, Ethel Barrymore, and Paul Robeson. Thornton Wilder played the stage manager in his play *Our Town* there in 1946 and returned for the lead role in *The Skin of Our Teeth* two years later.

Despite its wealth and sophistication, Westport was a close-knit community that could be nearly as insular, in its own way, as North Bennington. The Hymans would be criticized by their neighbors for their perceived unfriendliness and lack of interest in participating in town affairs. After another resident accidentally hit Laurence with her car while he was riding his bike, causing serious injuries that necessitated a lawsuit against her insurance company, Jackson and Hyman felt that the neighborhood turned against them. As it turned out, their fears that their neighbors were gossiping about them were not unfounded. Their stay in Westport would prove to be short-lived.

WHEN THE HYMANS decamped from North Bennington, their books took up an entire moving truck. Their collection at that point amounted to about seven or eight thousand volumes—only a fraction of what it would ultimately total. Bookcases would soon occupy nearly every available inch of wall space in the Indian Hill Road house, overflowing into stacks and piles. Over the years, their library grew steadily. At one point Stanley attempted to catalog all the books, but even he, with his love of order and his meticulous filing system, could not keep up. After the Hymans returned to North Bennington, eventually they opened up their house's attic to store their books, which by the early 1960s numbered around twenty thousand. By the end of Shirley's life, the collection totaled somewhere between twenty-five and thirty thousand volumes, possibly more.

Shirley and Stanley's main source of books, aside from the review copies that poured in from *The New Yorker* and elsewhere, was the Seven Bookhunters. This group of men traveled around the country buying books from secondhand bookstores and reselling them, often at a high markup. (There were actually only four bookhunters; the firm's founder, Louis Scher, chose the number seven because he liked the way it sounded.) Whenever Stanley and Shirley needed an obscure, out-of-print, or otherwise hard-to-obtain title—such as one of the works of myth and ritual criticism Stanley was assiduously collecting—they put in a special request to Scher, a "plump, disarmingly affable, and almost incredibly energetic Frenchman with a large head and a sharp nose." As Stanley described him in a *New Yorker* profile, Scher was "as familiar with secondhand bookstores from [New York] to San Francisco as a policeman is with his beat." He dressed for his trade in "a nondescript felt hat, a rumpled shirt and tie, a gray jacket lumpy with possessions, and a pair of morning trousers . . . because they wear like iron and don't show book dirt." So absentminded that he was said to have once wrapped up his own hand in a package of books, he nonetheless had a remarkable memory and was capable of sorting through thousands of books and picking out a few titles that customers had requested.

Scher was apt to be prickly—clients who complained about prices would get "CB," for "cheap bastard," stamped in red on their file cards. For his favorites, however, he would do "almost anything," including finding whatever books they might want "as quickly and as cheaply as possible," alerting them of new books they might be interested in, allowing "virtually unlimited" credit (which Stanley naturally took advantage of), and performing assorted non-book-related favors, such as bringing them along to baseball games and boxing matches. (He liked to root for the visiting team, "because that keeps things lively.") Stanley was accorded the ultimate privilege: every year he accompanied Scher on a book-buying trip, sleeping in cheap hotels or on the benches of railway stations, eating and drinking with Scher's friends along the way, and buying as many as a thousand books.

Though Scher's interest in books extended only to buying and selling them, he and Stanley would play poker whenever Stanley was in the city, as well as bridge and *belote*, a "vicious French game" that was Scher's favorite. He also was a fine cook who taught Shirley to make French onion soup and vichyssoise. By the time Sarah was born, in 1948, they were so close that Shirley and Stanley asked Louis to be her godfather; throughout her childhood, he regularly sent her expensive and rare children's books. When the Hymans moved to Connecticut, Scher and one of his associates came up from New York to help organize their library.

"Life at Castle Jackson is certainly looking up," Stanley chortled to a friend soon after the move to Westport. The town was "a vast improvement" over North Bennington, Shirley told her mother, and compared with their drafty old place on Prospect Street, the house on Indian Hill Road was "so pleasant, and so comfortable." But she was already worried that it might be too small: she and Stanley had no choice but to put their desks in the living room, where they also kept the television, and if a baseball game was on in the afternoon, both were tempted to knock off work early. A memo Shirley wrote to Farrar, Straus regarding her progress on her new novel promised that she would turn in the manuscript "before the World Series."

The house was especially suitable for the children. Shirley made the entire basement into a playroom, where she installed the heirloom family music box, to which Joanne loved to dance. Though she bemoaned all the unanticipated expenses of a suburban house—it cost $7.50 a week to hire a man to mow the lawn, a job that sedentary Stanley would never bother with himself—she loved the garden, which had forsythia, honeysuckle, rhododendrons, irises, rosebushes, and an apple tree complete with a tree house. When the trees were in bloom, the yard was entirely hidden from the road, "sheltered and private." Once summer came, they fenced off an area where baby Sarah could safely play and furnished the rest of the yard with a wading pool "big enough for all the neighborhood children," a log-cabin playhouse, a sandbox, a croquet set, horseshoes, a sprinkler, and a barbecue. They even moved the kitchen table onto the back porch so that the children could eat outside.

They also acquired, for $500, a green two-tone 1940 Buick— "about the same style middle-aged family car that everyone else around here drives." The car was Shirley's idea: she wanted to be able to drive Stanley to the train station and take the children to the beach and bring her own groceries home, "just like everyone else." In a neighborhood where driving was the norm, having a car was a way of fitting in; and after their experience in North Bennington, Shirley feared standing out. But it was also a way to assert her independence from Stanley, who had no interest in driving, never would learn to do it well, and—though he would come to rely on her as his chauffeur— was initially skeptical of Shirley's efforts. She passed her driving test after two weeks of lessons and was frankly proud of her new skill. "one of the things the driving school taught me was not to listen to people blowing horns and yelling at me; these are of course all inferior drivers who are careless and must be forced to go slowly," she joked to her parents. Surprisingly, Geraldine was supportive. "There is no reason in the world why you won't make a good driver," she wrote, although she added that she hoped Shirley had good insurance. Over

the years Shirley would grow increasingly attached to her cars, especially a series of tiny Morris Minors that she began to acquire in the
late 1950s. "She always had one red arm and one white arm, because
the car was so small that she had to have her arm out, winter or summer," Sarah remembers. Driving would later be an important symbol
of independence in Jackson's work: in *Hangsaman* and *The Bird's Nest*,
her second and third novels, her protagonists run away (unsuccessfully) on the bus, but Eleanor will drive herself to Hill House, feeling competent and free—at least until she arrives. In *Come Along with
Me*, Jackson's final unfinished novel, the protagonist—who sets off
for a new life after the death of her husband—renames herself Angela
Motorman.

In Shirley's letters from the spring of 1950, she sounds happier and
more confident than ever before. Her social life, as always, was full.
New Westport friends included *New Yorker* writers Peter DeVries and
James Geraghty, along with their families, as well as Salinger, who
would come over to play catch with Laurence on the front lawn. Jay
Williams and his wife, Bobbie, lived in nearby Redding; Malcolm and
Muriel Cowley, who had assisted in the house hunt, were in Sherman.
Walter Lehrman, who met Shirley and Stanley in 1945 through a girl-
friend at Bennington and who shared Stanley's interest in folklore and
the blues, came up often from New York, as did June Mirken, Ralph
Ellison, and Walter Bernstein. One night when Lehrman was visiting,
a neighbor stopped by with an old friend of hers from college—Bette
Davis. Shirley got out her guitar, and the writers and the actress all
sang folk songs together.

As Ellison's work on *Invisible Man* progressed, he continued to lean
on both Hyman and Jackson for guidance. On a visit to Vermont a few
years earlier, he and Hyman had jointly written an outline of the novel,
then called *The Invisible Man*. That outline helped Ellison, under contract with the small firm Reynal and Hitchcock, get a more lucrative deal
with Random House. In April 1951, Ellison wrote to his friend Albert
Murray, a younger student at Tuskegee who would become a well-
known literary and music critic, that he had "finished most of [*Invisible
Man*] at Hyman's place in Westport." That time it was Jackson, who was

looking over her page proofs for *Hangsaman*, who proved most helpful. "I had been worrying my ass off over transitions; really giving them more importance than was necessary, working out complicated schemes for giving them extension and so on," Ellison wrote. "Then I read [Shirley's] page proofs and saw how simply she was managing *her* transitions and how they really didn't bother me despite their 'and-so-and-then-and-therefore'—and then, man, I was on."

Professionally, it was useful for Jackson as well as Hyman to be closer to New York. She joined the Pen and Brush, a Greenwich Village club for women in the arts, where she enjoyed meeting her agent for cocktails and hoped, one day, to bring her mother, no doubt out of the desire to demonstrate her success. She was especially pleased that Hyman, who didn't "belong to anything yet except the folklore society, which doesn't have a bar," wasn't allowed in unless she accompanied him. (He, as usual, was working on everything other than the book he was supposed to be writing: book reviews, conference papers, and, at last, two longer pieces for *The New Yorker*: the profile of Scher and a history of the Brooklyn Bridge.) Jackson was mentioned often in articles about promising young authors, including a piece by Cowley in *The New Republic* in which he included her in a group of emerging writers along with Bellow, Stafford, Capote, and Eudora Welty. Invited to a dinner where everyone was "a rich writer and had written a best-seller," she was pleased and surprised to discover that all the guests had heard about her sensational short story collection. Still, she and Hyman found the other guests "very dull and too shrimp newburg-y for us . . . no chips on the china, napkins for everybody, eighteen matched cocktail glasses, and so on. . . . there's money in writing, if you work it right." ("Don't you like matched china and napkins for everybody?" Geraldine wrote back cluelessly.)

Jackson's letters to her parents from this period are filled with references to how challenging it was to make a living as a writer—"if i don't get these three stories out today we will never be able to pay the grocery bill"—as well as a subtle pride that she was able to pull it off. Eleanor Kennedy, her third agent at MCA, had retired in 1949, so she had been passed on to yet another agent, Rae Everitt, the head of

MCA's literary department. *Lottery*'s success meant that Everitt could ask Farrar, Straus for a larger advance for Jackson's next novel. At a cocktail party where a tipsy Jackson encountered Roger Straus, she called him "the biggest crook in town" and announced that she wanted $25,000 for the new book. Fortunately for her, he laughed off both the insult and the demand. "as long as he is amused when i call him a crook in front of half a dozen of his other authors i can't leave [the firm]," she wrote to her parents. More realistically, Everitt hoped for $5,000: "we'll take four, we figure, and can be talked into three, but it will take a lot of talking." In fact, $3,000 was the advance they settled on in June 1950, when Jackson submitted the first third of the novel that would become *Hangsaman,* now titled *Natalie.* (Another early title was *Rites of Passage.*) Everitt found it "intriguing" and "wonderful as hell," and Straus congratulated Jackson on "a brilliant job." The book was scheduled for April 1951.

Since money was coming in from multiple sources, the amount of the advance was not as crucial to Jackson as it had once been. "The Lottery" had been made into a television play, bringing in nearly $1000, and June Mirken was now fiction editor at *Charm* and buying all the stories by Jackson she could. One of these was "The Summer People," the eerie tale Jackson had written in the wake of "The Lottery" about what happens to an elderly couple who unexpectedly decide to stay another month in the house they rent every summer. *The New Yorker* had passed on the story two years earlier, with Lobrano arguing that it was a "subsidiary theme" to "The Lottery" and felt "anti-climactic" in comparison. After "The Summer People" ran in *Charm* in 1950, it was selected for *Best American Short Stories 1951.* By the summer of 1950, in addition to her retainer from *Good Housekeeping,* Jackson had sold two more stories to women's magazines. "With six thousand bucks in a lump, we are finally ahead, and hope to stay that way for a while," Hyman wrote triumphantly to Zimmerman.

The money, as always, would go quickly. In addition to the playhouse and all the other outdoor amusements for the children, Jackson bought a spinet, which she had been longing for, and a washing machine, her first. Hyman bought her a fur coat; he also loaned $1000 to his father,

joking that the surprise "should take ten years off his life." A bigger luxury, if more practical, was a live-in maid named Emma, whom Jackson
called, with only slight hyperbole, "the greatest blessing" ever to happen to the family. ("You'd better work hard at your writing to be able
to keep her," Geraldine warned.) Emma made the children's breakfast,
allowing Jackson to sleep in and wake up to a pot of hot coffee; she also
prepared lunch and dinner, so that Jackson could write uninterrupted in
the afternoon. Best of all, with Emma to look after the children, Jackson was free to go into the city as she pleased. Life at Castle Jackson
was looking up indeed. Yet 1950 would soon bring a series of unhappy
events, some minor and others much more significant, that combined to
shatter Jackson's equilibrium and erode her confidence.

AT THE END OF February, Dylan Thomas, on his first reading tour
in America, visited Westport. Poet John Malcolm Brinnin, director of
the Poetry Center at the YM-YWHA (now the 92nd Street Y), was
his escort in the New York area. Brinnin, who had idolized Thomas
ever since reading his first published poems sixteen years earlier, was
taken aback by the poet's obvious ill health, unpredictable behavior, and
prodigious alcohol consumption. As soon as his morning flight landed,
Thomas headed to the airport bar for a double scotch and soda. His eyes
were bloodshot, his teeth broken and brown with tobacco stains, and
his body racked with a cough so violent that he sometimes vomited on
the street. He would pass out with a lit cigarette in his hand, coming to
only when it burned his fingers. At the literary parties to which Brinnin
brought him, he made passes at women aggressively and indiscriminately; once he grabbed the writer Katherine Anne Porter, then nearly
sixty, and hoisted her up in the air. Yet at his public events, where he
read his own works as well as poems by Yeats, Hardy, Auden, and others, Thomas enthralled audiences with his hypnotic voice.

Thomas spent a few days at Brinnin's home in Westport, and one
afternoon the two men were invited to the Hymans' for cocktails. After
dinner at a local Italian restaurant, the group returned to Indian Hill Road
to watch boxing on television. Jackson and Thomas began a game of

imagining plots for murder mysteries, of which they were both devotees, and tried to outdo each other in gruesomeness. Then Thomas read some of his poetry. Brinnin is oblique about what happened next: "As usual, we stayed too late and drank too much and the evening ended gracelessly, with some of us out in the snow, and some of us silent before a dead television set." When they got back to Brinnin's house, around three o'clock in the morning, Thomas was so drunk that Brinnin literally had to push him up the steps to the front door, where he refused to enter. "Now you know exactly what you've brought to America," he told Brinnin.

Jackson and Thomas had some kind of intimate encounter that evening, the details of which are unclear. Brendan Gill gives an account of the scene in his gossipy memoir *Here at the New Yorker*, which serves mainly as an example of the rumors that spread about that night. (The book includes other unkind and possibly apocryphal stories about Jackson; Gill's section on her opens, bizarrely, "Shirley Jackson Hyman wrote under her maiden name.") According to Gill, Jackson and Thomas (whom he describes as "a tubby little man, with thinning hair and brown teeth with holes in them") were both drunk when he made a pass at her. Jackson jumped up and ran through the living room, past Hyman watching television, with Thomas following her. They did several circuits around the house, up the front stairs and down the back, until Hyman—"irritated at having his view of the ball game repeatedly interrupted by the great beasts jogging past him"—grabbed Thomas by his belt, bringing him down.

Brinnin told Paul Ferris, Thomas's biographer, that Gill's account was untrue. In his version, he went outside, drunk, to vomit and saw Thomas and Jackson "fooling about" in the snow: he heard "squeals of girlish laughter, his or hers," and went back into the house. As they drove home, Brinnin says, Thomas confessed that the cold night air had made him impotent. Brinnin clearly thought alcohol was also a factor.

Jackson's version is different still. In an untitled fragment, a woman named Margaret—the name Jackson also used in "The Beautiful Stranger" and "Pillar of Salt"—is tipsy and bored by her guests, a pretentious writer and his prissy wife (perhaps stand-ins for the Gills). As the writer drones on about Kafka, she slips out, tired of putting on a

Dylan Thomas in New York City, c. 1950.

"bright alert face." On the porch she finds another man, smoking a pipe. Though they have hardly spoken previously, she feels an uncanny affinity with him.

"are you afraid sometimes?" margaret asked him.

"not very often."

"i'm afraid of staying," margaret said. she saw him nod, against the light from the door. encouraged, she went on, "i'm afraid of being with myself so much. i forget to look outside." . . .

they were quiet for a minute and then margaret turned and put her arms around his neck; oh, god, i'm drunk, she thought for a minute and then it was gone. . . .

he had put one arm around her in return; the other hand was holding his pipe; when he laughed and tightened his arm around her she was appalled and thought, oh god, oh god. . . .

"what am i doing?"

"you are sitting here," he said carefully, as though choosing his words to convey an exact meaning, "in a position of great comfort, me with my arms around you and you with your arms around me. although as a gesture it was completely meaningful, as an attitude it is still noncommittal." . . .

margaret laughed, thinking oh god, oh god. "i'm not even afraid," she said.

"no."

"i won't ever *be* afraid."

"no."

"can you cross a border line as easily as that?" margaret asked, wondering.

"easily."

"and never go back?"

"never." . . .

she began to laugh again helplessly, shaking his arm and the porch rail. she put her head against his shoulder and was lost, slipping slowly into the darkness of not knowing, and not caring, and not wondering, and not believing.

On her way inside, she encounters the pretentious writer's wife, who tells her that she saw what Margaret was up to and assures her that she will not mention it to Margaret's husband. "there ought to be a name . . . for a woman who has to find someone to mind her children when she wants to be unfaithful to her husband," Margaret volunteers, self-deprecatingly. She returns to the cocktail party. "i have a secret, she was thinking, sitting in her chair looking unafraid at the people around; i have a brave, brave secret locked in, locked in, with me."

The depiction of the encounter in Jackson's story is far less tawdry than Gill's story of the "great beasts jogging" around the house or Brinnin's report of Jackson and Thomas in the snow. It also seems more plausible, especially considering Brinnin's assessment of Thomas's physical condition. "I'm afraid of staying," Margaret tells the man in the story. Despite her love for her house, her children, even her husband, there was a part of Jackson that longed for escape. Escape might come in the magical form of James Harris, who speaks to Clara in "The Tooth" of a place "[e]ven farther than Samarkand . . . the waves ringing on the shore like bells." Escape could come, more prosaically, through mental release, with or without alcohol: elsewhere in the fragment, Margaret cherishes "the little moments of unconsciousness that came so easily and went with a breath; they were precious to her in a way that moments of acute awareness never were; drunk, perhaps, or lost running, the beautiful departure of self, slipping away to tend to things of its own, and then the abandonment of heart and mind without its monitor." And here it comes in the form of a beautiful stranger, a mysterious man on the porch who is content to sit with his arm around her, speaking quietly. But it is never without danger—of people gossiping, of random cruelty, or of one's own dissolution.

The story Jackson would dedicate to Thomas illustrated that danger more starkly. "A Visit: For Dylan Thomas" was written in September 1950 and published by a magazine called *New World Writing* in 1952; later it would be reprinted as "The Lovely House." The story, which Jackson more than once referred to as one of her favorites, is so mysterious and uncanny that to paraphrase it ruins the effect, but here an outline will do. A girl named Margaret (again) goes to visit a friend who lives in a beautiful house in the countryside, a storybook mansion surrounded by a river and hills, with stone sculptures and walls bedecked with tapestries and a room with a stone mosaic on the floor depicting a girl's face, with lettering underneath: "Here lies Margaret, who died for love." Soon the friend's brother arrives, with Paul, a friend of his own, who charms and seduces Margaret, taking her on picnics and telling her the history of the house. Driven by curiosity, Margaret goes to visit the castle's resident madwoman, a great-aunt hidden away in a stone tower: her name, too, is Margaret, and she is distressed to hear that Paul has returned. "He should have come and gone sooner," she says, "then we'd have it all behind us." Jackson's dialogue is so subtle, the story unspooled so carefully, that on first reading one may well not realize that Paul is an imaginary figure, visible only to Margaret. He cannot reciprocate her love; he can only return to haunt his manor, preying upon lonely girls with a propensity to die for love.

ONE MORNING IN EARLY JUNE, Shirley awoke at around four o'clock to find Emma, the new maid, standing by her bed. "Come downstairs, I want to show you something," she whispered to Shirley, who got out of bed and went to get her bathrobe. "That's all right, come like you are," Emma urged, and Shirley followed her downstairs barefoot, wearing only her nightgown. A little girl was in her bed, playing with a bluebird, Emma told Shirley; other people were outside. Shirley awakened Stanley, who listened to Emma babble for a few minutes and then retreated to his study. Shirley convinced Emma that she needed to go back to her parents' house to rest and called a taxi; by the time the children awoke, Emma was gone. Shirley told them she had taken ill during the night—"which heaven knows was true," she wrote to her mother. Apparently, as she found out later, Emma's husband had just told her that he was leaving her for "someone younger and prettier," prompting her to drink most of a bottle of whiskey. "it was a combination of mental distress and drink and, aside from the scare it gave *me*, not very serious," Shirley explained. Geraldine was not fooled. "You sound as if the episode made you nervous," she wrote back. "Don't you know that things like that should not be taken seriously. . . . Anyway, it will be a story for you to write."

The scare it gave her was considerable. Sweet, reliable Emma, whom the children and Shirley had so quickly come to love and depend upon, had turned, literally overnight, into someone unrecognizable. And all it took was a combination of infidelity and drink—two things with which Shirley, too, was well acquainted. "Can you cross a border line as easily as that . . . and never go back?" Margaret asks the man on the porch. For weeks Shirley refused to leave the children with a babysitter; she was loath to let a stranger into the house, even to clean it. She was so distracted by the incident that, uncharacteristically, she forgot about

Father's Day—for which her mother promptly reprimanded her. Shirley apologized: "that was [the week of] our little difficulty with emma and i didn't remember anything." Geraldine, perhaps suspecting that her daughter could not manage long without a maid, took it upon herself— from three thousand miles away—to find Emma's replacement. One day Elmira, "a nice girl from the South," appeared on the doorstep. Elmira quickly won Shirley's trust, perhaps because she reminded Shirley of the maid her family had employed during her childhood. Before long, Elmira's mother, too, would join the household.

But the aftereffects of Emma's crack-up lingered, first in the form of Shirley's chronic headache, which started up again. Five years earlier she had discovered that codeine helped to ease the pain, and now she needed a new prescription. The "real fancy doctor" she went to, who treated all the Westport society ladies, examined her and decreed that nothing was physically wrong; the cause of her headache was psychological, "nervous tension." He happened to be a psychoanalyst on the side—would Shirley be interested in a consultation? Certainly not, she told him; "i wasn't fool enough for that sort of thing." The doctor tried another tactic. Had she ever wanted to lose weight? She told him she "didn't care one way or the other," an obvious untruth—her letters to her mother often mention whether her weight has recently gone down. The doctor told her that "losing weight was psychological just as the headaches were, so that it would be very easy for me to go on a diet, and then through some psychic about-face i would then lose my headaches." Whether Shirley believed this or not, she decided to give it a try— perhaps because the doctor assured her she did not have to alter her eating and drinking habits. She certainly didn't have to give up alcohol, he said, "because in this hot weather everyone wants cold drinks." All she had to do was report back to him once a week for an injection—at twenty-five dollars a pop—and take the "magic pills" he provided her.

Thus Shirley became one of the many 1950s housewives to diet with Dexamyl, a combination pill that included both amphetamines and barbiturates and was also used to treat depression and anxiety. Stanley, whose waist size by now was up to 40, took it as well. Over the years other prescriptions would be added to the cocktail: Miltown, the spectacularly popular "mother's little helper" introduced to the market in 1955; later Valium and Seconal; and eventually the antipsychotic Thorazine, which may have exacerbated Shirley's anxiety rather than alleviating it. The drugs were believed to be safe; Sarah remembers her parents offering her Dexamyl to help her lose weight as a teenager. And Shirley was initially successful: by September, she would lose twenty pounds. But using prescription drugs can be another of those borders that is all too easy to cross, with consequences impossible to foresee.

EVERY SUMMER, THE NEW YORK CITY papers ran appeals for the Fresh Air Fund, a program established in the late nineteenth century to bring underprivileged city children to the country for a brief summer respite from the heat and the crowds. "Think how much . . . a two-week escape will mean to boys and girls who call the tenements their home," readers were urged. Some children went to camps paid for by the fund; others were hosted by families in "Friendly Towns" who offered "board and lodging—and love—to their young guests." A little girl reported that she "went swimming and on picnics. . . . They taught me how to play tennis and Bad Mitten and [the family] loved me very much and I got to love them too."

Eager to share the family's new riches, Shirley volunteered as a host. She asked for a boy of eight and a girl of five, as playmates for Laurence and Joanne, specifying only that they not insist on going to church. Her rationale shows that she had swallowed the program's rhetoric wholesale. "Perhaps these days, when we are all growing up most horribly, a certain basic humanity is essential in even the tiniest things . . . it seemed to me important that before my children knew how bad the world could be, they might learn once, for two weeks one summer, that human love and affection is deeper than anything else, even charity," she wrote in "Fresh Air Diary," her chronicle of the experience. Anxious the night before the children's arrival, she imagined herself in the position of their mother, worried about sending her child off to a stranger's home. "Is she wondering if, in a world gone all dirty and black, there is any hope of some small clean place for a child to live a little longer? Because,

God help me, I am wondering so too." The looming Korean War, which broke out that summer, may have contributed to her fears. But she wondered also if she herself—"and this is the ultimate question, of course"—was adequate. She knew the house was up to the task, with the wading pool and the playhouse and the sandbox. But what about her? Would she be able to comfort a stranger's homesick child? Would she be cross and unjust, as she feared she too often was with her own children, or kind and tolerant? Could she genuinely love a child not her own, or was what she offered merely charity?

Things did not go as planned. To the dismay of the society ladies who assembled at the train station, the Fresh Air children were "unattractive and undernourished." She was appalled to hear the other Westport mothers making loud comments like "Imagine having that one over *there*" and "I'm so glad I got a pretty one." Instead of the boy and girl she had requested, Shirley wound up with two boys; the girl, it turned out, had missed the train. Bobbie was stout, unhappy looking, and anxious; Larry, stupid, sly, and greedy. Both were devout Catholics. Joanne cried all afternoon because "her girl" had not shown up. Laurence decided that he hated both boys; he was selfish with his toys and jealous of Shirley's attention.

In virtually all the stories she wrote about her family, Shirley used humor to disguise any serious problems. Now she could not—likely the reason "Fresh Air Diary," despite multiple submissions, was never published. It is simply too honest. She was unable to hide her contempt for Larry: he was kind to Joanne only when he knew Shirley was watching; he called Bobbie "Fatty"; he was "alternately ingratiating and insulting." "My granny makes hamburg like that, only hers is better," he told Shirley. Bobbie was relatively more agreeable, but cringing and apologetic, and Shirley resented his obvious efforts to curry her favor. Their Brooklyn accents were so strong—"aks ifn they should go inna watah"—that Stanley had to translate. Finally, a girl named Kathy arrived and Larry was transferred to another family, but Kathy spent the first evening running away. The whole situation made Shirley so tense that on her weekly visit to the doctor, she burst into tears and could not stop crying. He offered her a sedative and told her to send the children home. Her mother agreed, advising Shirley—rather belatedly—not to "overtax" herself.

Matters came to a head when a weekend guest arrived with his new wife, who volunteered that she had once been a Fresh Air child and now bitterly opposed the program. "How would *you* like . . . to have someone show you a kind of life you couldn't ever have, and then take it away just as you found out how wonderful it was?" she asked Shirley. When another guest asked Shirley if she could conceive of sending her own children off to a stranger, she was forced to admit that she could not. "Were we, then, actually benefiting anybody, by doing something for others we would not have done to ourselves?" she asked. Did the program actually inscribe class distinctions rather than erase them? Was it hopeless for her to expect her son to understand that "these people are his brothers and that these kids are kids like himself," despite the difference in their circumstances? When the two weeks were up and the children prepared for their departure, Shirley decided that she had failed. "Somehow, while trying very hard, I had not been able to stretch my initial sympathy for [Bobbie] over two weeks . . . I had not been patient enough, I thought, I had not been tolerant."

Shirley did not question the program's underlying paternalistic assumptions—only her own ability to live up to them. She held herself to an impossible standard: in fact, her "Fresh Air Diary" reveals the multitude of small kindnesses she bestowed upon these children. Though she was relieved to see Larry go, she kissed him good-bye and told him that if he didn't like his new hosts, she would come and get him. When Kathy, homesick, cried inconsolably, Shirley sang to her until she fell asleep. But in her mind it was not enough, because she did not come to truly love the children: proof that she was "inadequate," just as she had feared.

ON A BRIGHT FALL morning two days before his eighth birthday, Laurence rode his bicycle down the driveway and onto Indian Hill Road without looking and was hit by an elderly lady who could not stop in time. Thrown off the bike, he suffered a severe concussion, a bad gash to his shoulder, and a broken thumb—miraculous, considering what could have happened. "Laurie just got killed by a car," the friend who had been with him ran up to the back door to announce. The impact was so severe that Laurence's bike had to be pried off the car's bumper. A neighbor who happened to be a policeman took charge of the scene; he put temporary bandages on Laurence's wounds and offered Shirley a lit cigarette, saying, "Don't *you* lose your head." She and Stanley both rode in the ambulance to Norwalk Hospital in Bridgeport. There they waited for hours, Laurence crying alone in a room they were forbidden to enter, until a doctor was summoned. Finally they were told that their son's skull was fractured and he had been put into a dark, silent room to be observed for brain damage: they would not be allowed to see him again for several days. After they came home, late that night, Stanley poured a water glass full of whiskey for both of them. For days, Shirley needed a combination of whiskey, Ovaltine, and sleeping pills to fall asleep.

Within a few days, Laurence was out of danger. His skull was not fractured, after all, though he had to stay in the hospital for several more weeks. He also was acting like himself, "hopping mad" at the nurse for giving him baby food and begging for extra helpings of ice cream. "Except for a splitting headache he seems to be in perfect possession of himself," Shirley wrote to her parents. He did not remember the accident and wanted to know all the gory details, which she found painful to recount. Family and friends rallied around the Hymans, especially Stanley's father, who doted particularly on Laurence and was still traumatized by the memory of a similar accident that had taken place when Stanley was twelve, leaving him in bed with a concussion for nearly two months. But Shirley remained in a state of high anxiety. She wrote to Geraldine and Leslie nearly every day with updates on Laurence's condition, then regretted the letters. "there is nothing at all to worry about now, and the main thing is to take it easy and try to forget it," she reassured them. But for her that was impossible. One evening Stanley persuaded her to go to a *New Yorker* dinner party. His editor, William Shawn, whom Shirley described as "a highly neurotic and frightened little man," was so anxious about the disasters that might befall his own children that it took him much of the evening to work up the courage to ask about Laurence. "it is the last time stanley will ever persuade me to go somewhere against my better judgement—i told him so perhaps fifty times last night and today," Shirley vowed.

The aftermath of the accident was nearly as difficult for Shirley as the initial trauma had been. The morning afterward, while she and Stanley were waiting at home for word from the hospital, an insurance agent representing the car's driver (a "sweet-faced old lady," as Shirley remembered her) visited them: "he remarked that of course everything would be all right, and that of course the important thing was saving the boy's life, and that right now of course no one wanted to talk about insurance or such. . . . in our haste to reassure the sweet-faced old lady we practically acquitted her of blame." Later she learned that the true purpose of the visit had been to elicit "incriminating statements" from her and Stanley in their distracted state, to ensure that they would not be able to prove that the "sweet-faced old lady" had been at fault. The experience left her demoralized and disillusioned. "if it is your child she injures next, please profit by our experience," she wrote in an unpublished polemic about the experience. "leave your child lying on the street, go as quickly as you can to gather witnesses who will if necessary extend the truth a little, make sure that the police and the bystanders realize clearly that none of this was your child's fault, and announce clearly and distinctly before the child is moved that you intend to sue; if your child dies, you will very likely win."

The next month brought a hurricane to the celebrated Gold Coast. "half our town is gone. . . . all of the beach and the beach houses are either submerged or on their way out to sea," Shirley reported. She would joke about Laurence—finally out of bed—having brought it on by asking the birch tree out front for a dime's worth of wind. But it was a disaster: three hundred books they had been storing in the garage were ruined, along with the sandbox, the playhouse, and various of the other small pleasures that she had been so pleased to accumulate.

Laurence's thumb was not healing properly; it would have to be broken again and reset. The cough that had been plaguing Joanne was finally diagnosed as asthma, which the doctor thought was partly psychological, a result of her distress over Laurence's condition. "we are thinking of hiring a resident doctor to take care of all of us, since it seems to be a full-time job," Shirley wrote to her parents. And the sweet-faced old lady's insurance company declined to pay Laurence's hospital bills; Shirley and Stanley had to sue her in order to recover any money. Shirley's only consolation was that somehow, in the midst of all this, she had managed to finish her second novel.

HANGSAMAN IS A WEIRD, rich brew of autobiography and fantasy, combining elements of Jackson's unhappy years at the University of Rochester, the social culture of Bennington College, her marriage to Hyman, and literary allusions ranging from *Alice in Wonderland* to Victorian pornography; even Emma's crack-up went into the mix. The title comes from another Child Ballad, "The Maid Freed from the Gallows," popularized as a blues song known as "Gallows Pole" or "Hangman Tree": "Slack your rope, Hangsaman, / O slack it for a while, / I think I see my true love coming, / Coming many a mile." In the song, a young man or woman about to be hanged is visited by various family members: "Father, have you brought me hope, have you paid my fee? / Or have you come to see me hanging on the gallows tree?" All refuse: they have come to watch the hanging. Only true love offers salvation.

On the surface, *Hangsaman* is the story of Natalie Waite, one of the many precocious children in Jackson's fiction, whose similarities to her creator have already been discussed. Her name references the occultist Arthur E. Waite, who wrote a guide to the tarot that was popular in the early twentieth century and also collaborated with the artist Pamela Smith on a widely used tarot deck. (When Jackson read tarot cards, she usually used an older version, known as the Tarot of Marseilles, but she was familiar with the Waite-Smith deck.) The Hanged Man is one of the most important cards in the deck, with a complex iconography. The card depicts a man hanging by one leg from a T-shaped tree, the other leg crossed behind him to form an upside-down figure 4; as Waite observes, the compulsion to turn the card so that the man is right-side up is virtually irresistible. Its appearance in a tarot reading is said to indicate not a death sentence, but the possibility of spiritual transformation. Waite notes that the figure's face "suggests deep entrancement, not suffering," and that the image as a whole evokes "life in suspension." It is the most mystical of all the cards, he writes: "He who can understand that the story of his higher nature is imbedded in this symbolism will receive intimations concerning a great awakening that is possible, and will know that after the sacred Mystery of Death there is a glorious Mystery of Resurrection." T. S. Eliot, who mentions the Hanged Man in *The Waste Land*, seems to have understood the card along metaphorically similar but pre-Christian lines, associating it with the symbol of the Hanged God in Frazer's *Golden Bough*. As Frazer tells it, the people of ancient Phrygia, who worshipped a god of vegetation named Attis, believed that they maintained the fertility of the land with an annual ceremony reenacting the god's death and resurrection.

The reference to the card in the novel's title suggests that a spiritual transformation will take place therein. The book's earlier title, *Rites of Passage*, may also refer to the ancient initiation rituals Frazer describes, which Jackson would have known both from her own reading of *The Golden Bough* and from Hyman's recent intense immersion in myth and

The Hanged Man tarot card, from The Pictorial Key to the Tarot, *by Arthur Waite.*

ritual criticism. Applying unsuccessfully for a 1948 Guggenheim Fellowship to support the book, Jackson described it as "a novel with contemporary setting centering around the ritual pattern of the sacrificial king." (The fellows in fiction that year included Saul Bellow, Elizabeth Hardwick, and J. F. Powers.)

When the novel begins, Natalie is about to go away to college, leaving behind an unhappy home: her father is controlling and insensitive, her mother smothering. In the first chapter, Mr. Waite, a book critic who writes for "The Passionate Review," critiques a writing assignment he has given his daughter. The exercise, it turns out, was to write a description of him, which Natalie has done with astonishing candor: "He seems perpetually surprised at the world's never being quite so intelligent as he is, although he would be even more surprised if he found out that perhaps he is himself not so intelligent as he thinks." Rather than being offended, her father applauds her precise language, then offers a few self-serving criticisms. "You overlook one of my outstanding characteristics, which is a brutal honesty which frequently leads me into trouble. . . . My honest picture of myself has led me to aim less high than many of my contemporaries, because I know my own failings, and as a result I am in many respects less successful in a worldly sense." Coming on the heels of *The Armed Vision*, this description reads so clearly as a caricature of Hyman that some of his friends commented on the resemblance.

As the chapter progresses through a garden party hosted by the Waites, Jackson's attack grows more pointed. Books set out for the guests' enjoyment include *Ulysses*, *The Function of the Orgasm* (a then fashionable volume by the psychoanalyst Wilhelm Reich, whose theories about channeling sexual energy via an "orgone box" attracted Bellow and other intellectuals of the period), *Hot Discography* (a catalog of jazz recordings), the abridged edition of *The Golden Bough*, and an unabridged dictionary—a brief and ludicrous snapshot of Hyman's interests. Mr. Waite dresses for the party in a "fuzzy tweed jacket" that makes him look "very literary indeed. . . . It was almost equivalent to a brace of pistols and a pair of jackboots; Mr. Waite was arrayed for his own interpretation of a street brawl."

The novel's portrayal of the relationship between Mr. Waite and his wife—in her attitude toward her daughter she is all Geraldine, but she sometimes speaks in Jackson's voice—is even more damning. The kitchen, which her husband never enters, is the only room in the house that Mrs. Waite feels is truly her own. In a bleak moment, she confides her frustration to her daughter in a speech reminiscent of the bewildered housewife in "Got a Letter from Jimmy":

> I always used to wonder how people made happy marriages and made them last all day long every day. . . . Don't ever let your husband know what you're thinking or doing, that's the way. . . . When I met your father he had a lot of books that he said he read, and he gave me a Mexican silver bracelet instead of an engagement ring . . . and I thought being married was everything I wanted. . . . Don't ever go near a man like your father.

Natalie escapes from this poisonous environment the only way she can—mentally. In an early draft of the novel, she hears the devil Asmodeus speaking to her; in revisions, Jackson changed this literal possession to fantasies in which Natalie's personality begins to divide. She imagines a detective repeatedly questioning her about the murder of her father, or a team of future archaeologists excavating the Waite house and coming upon her skull ("Male, I should say, from the frontal development"); later, she will write of herself in the third person. At the garden party she tries drinking as another form of escape—it is her first experience with alcohol—and the result is her disastrous, obliquely suggested sexual encounter in the woods with one of the guests.

After Natalie arrives at college, her disintegration continues. Her experiences there reflect Jackson's early difficulties at Rochester, but the college is unmistakably Bennington, as Jackson acknowledged in an outline for the novel:

> It was decided to construct the college buildings entirely of shingle and "the original beams"; it was supposed that modern dance and the free use of slang in the classrooms might constitute an aura of rich general culture. It was decided that anyone who wanted to

study anything should be accommodated, although gym was not
encouraged. . . . It was unanimously voted that students should
be allowed to drink, stay out all night, gamble, and paint from
nude female models, without any kind of restraint; this, it was
clear, would prepare them for the adult world. . . . The faculty
members were to be drawn almost entirely from a group which
would find the inadequate salary larger than anything they had
ever earned. . . . A great deal was said about old English ballads.

Here Natalie meets Arthur Langdon, a well-regarded English professor, and his much younger wife, Elizabeth, one of his former students, who complains about her loneliness as a faculty wife and drinks
heavily as consolation for his flirtations with others. Elizabeth is particularly tormented by a pair of students named Anne and Vicki, who
flatter her husband's ego and condescend to her. (Another distinctively
Bennington detail: when Anne and Vicki throw a cocktail party, they
serve gin in toothbrush glasses "confiscated from the common bathrooms, rinsed inadequately, and dried on other people's bath towels"—
no matching crystal here.) Only Natalie sympathizes with Elizabeth,
leading her home when she is too drunk to walk by herself and trying to
console her when she confesses, "Natalie, I want to die."

The first sign that all is not well with Natalie comes when other girls
in her dorm complain that things have gone missing—a dress, money,
jewelry—and Natalie reflects on her own possessions: "if she had lost
any clothes or jewelry she would hardly have known it, since she had
worn the same sweater and skirt for a week." Soon after, she becomes
aware of the presence of "the girl Tony," who is another of her mind's
projections, although that may not be immediately clear to the reader.
Clues throughout that Tony is unreal, including a scene in which Natalie goes to sleep in Tony's bed but wakes up in her own, are subtle.
One night she is awakened: Tony appears naked at her bedside, takes
her hand, and leads her to a room filled with all the things that have
been stolen, chattering about the little girl who has come to sleep in
her bed—a scene reminiscent of Jackson's experience of being woken
by the babbling Emma. Natalie runs away in fear, but she cannot resist

Tony's pull. Together they play solitaire with tarot cards, "old and large and lovely and richly gilt and red"; they sleep in the same bed, "side by side, like two big cats"; and eventually they run away, taking a bus to a town that loosely resembles Rochester.

Now the atmosphere grows still more unreal. Natalie has passed through the looking glass; she quotes a line from Lewis Carroll, "Still she haunts me phantomwise." She sees tarot symbols encoded in the signs and shop windows; at a cafeteria, she and Tony meet a man with one arm. This section explicitly draws upon Jackson's wanderings around Rochester with Jeanou, with whom she was still corresponding sporadically; her diary from her first year of college even mentions a "strange, one-armed man" she saw in a café. Finally, in the woods by an abandoned fairground, Natalie believes, to her horror, that Tony is trying to seduce her. Of course, if Tony is not real, this is impossible. But it provides the push Natalie needs to shock herself back into sanity. She returns to college feeling she has survived a trauma. "As she had never been before, she was now alone, and grown-up, and powerful, and not at all afraid."

Many of *Hangsaman*'s readers, then as now, are bewildered by the ending and its abrupt shift from a mood of danger to one of serenity. But when understood in the myth and ritual context, it becomes clear. Classicist Jane Ellen Harrison, author of *Themis* (1912), a book of myth and ritual criticism that was one of Hyman's touchstones, argues that in ancient cultures, the ritual enacting the death and rebirth of a vegetation deity—Frazer's Hanged God—should be understood also as a ritual of initiation into society: like the god or his representation, youths die symbolically and are reborn as adults. In an article called "Myth, Ritual, and Nonsense," published in summer 1949, around the time Jackson began working on *Hangsaman*, Hyman mentions the scholar Joseph Campbell's theory that all myth can be traced back to a "monomyth," which he describes as "an elaboration of the three stages of [ethnographer and folklorist Arnold] Van Gennep's *rites de passage*, thus: 'a separation from the world, a penetration to some source of power, and a life-enhancing return.' " That, in brief, is precisely the plot of the strange final section of *Hangsaman*. Unfortunately, to the average reader not steeped in Harrison, Campbell, and Frazer, the book's underlying structure was opaque.

———

"MARY HAWORTH'S MAIL," A popular advice column, was syndicated in newspapers nationwide from the early 1940s until the mid-1960s. In June 1951, just after *Hangsaman* was published, a letter appeared under the headline "Should She Leave Husband?" The writer identified herself as a mother of three, married for eleven years to a college professor named Stan, who has been unfaithful to her. "Do I owe it to the children," she wonders, "to keep my marriage together for practical reasons?" The letter is signed "S. J." Jackson saved the clipping among her papers.

Hangsaman can be interpreted in many ways, but on one level it is unmistakably a document of Jackson's rage at her husband. The novel's subtext—never far beneath the surface—is sexual danger, always invoked in code. Perhaps that is why what happens to Natalie at the garden party is not made explicit: the scene may represent the encounter in which Stanley "forced" Shirley into sex, about which Shirley felt she had to remain silent. His presence is otherwise inscribed all over the novel. In addition to the book critic Mr. Waite, the professor Arthur Langdon embodies elements of Stanley: his teaching style, his attention to his students, his infidelity. In a story called "Still Life with Teapot and Students," written around the same time as *Hangsaman*, Jackson puts herself explicitly in the faculty-wife role, entertaining two students—in the original draft, their names are Vicki and Anne—who come over for tea. She knows them well because they studied writing with her, which allows her a candor that she usually represses. "You still making passes at my husband?" the wife in the story asks Anne. Both girls affect surprise at the discovery that such a thing might bother her. Why doesn't she just overlook his affairs? Vicki asks. "I mean, it's not anything serious, ever, is it?" The wife realizes she cannot defend herself further, because "any more talking would destroy the handsome invulnerability she had set up for herself." After the students leave, she pours herself a drink. "So I did it, she told herself defiantly. He can't say a word without admitting everything. No more respect for his wife than that, she thought, every fat-faced little tomato who walks into his class." When one of Hyman's Bennington colleagues brought a girlfriend to a party at her house, Jackson used the same striking term: the professor had arrived, she announced, "with his latest tomato."

In fact, her jealousy may have been misplaced. There is no question that Hyman enjoyed the dynamic of being a male faculty member at an all-girls college—particularly one as permissive as Bennington, with a student population both so intelligent and so free-spirited. Walter Lehrman remembers him saying, "You know what Bennington's really about? Sex." But Hyman's former students insist that he—unlike many of their other instructors—did not have affairs with students. "Stanley didn't do that. He exuded admiration and delight, but he did not make a pass," says Suzanne Stern, a student of Hyman's in the mid-1950s. Many commented on his lack of physical appeal, especially in comparison to his colleague Howard Nemerov, whose seductive qualities are well remembered. "There was nothing inherently attractive or romantic about Hyman as a figure. But he was dazzling," says Marjorie Roemer, an English major and 1959 graduate. Another student, who graduated in 1965 and was close enough to the Hymans to spend a few weeks at their house babysitting while Shirley and Stanley were on vacation, recalls Stanley's telling her that he had a "hundred-mile rule"—no cheating within one hundred miles of Bennington.

Hyman may not have always stuck to this rule. Regardless, it created a loophole by allowing him to look up former students on his regular visits to New York. And the move to Westport—which allowed him more convenient access than ever before to the city, now less than sixty miles away—facilitated this. He normally spent two days a week there, working in the *New Yorker* offices; in the evenings, he often played poker with Walter Lehrman, Louis Scher, and others. But he also had the opportunity to meet women for dinner, drinks, and whatever might follow. "This was the world of the double standard," says Phoebe Pettingell. "Part of the ethos was that you didn't get involved with people you might get too emotionally attached to." And he may not always have been able to control his behavior. Lehrman and his wife, Jinny, were regular overnight guests at the Hymans'. One night Jinny went to bed early while the rest of the household stayed up playing poker. While she was in bed, Stanley, thinking she was asleep, came into the room, uncovered her, then covered her back up and left. Lehrman considered the incident "just ordinary drunken curiosity," but others might have taken such things more seriously—especially Jackson.

The years in Westport—where her initial happiness was so quickly eroded by one debacle after another, all of which she had to face largely alone, far from the friends she had made in North Bennington—seem to have been when Shirley first began thinking about divorce. In a letter to Stanley that runs to nearly six typewritten pages, she would later lay out the reasons she believed their marriage would inevitably end— that is, why she would someday gather the courage to leave him. Not only did he belittle and neglect her, but he lavished attention on other women—especially former students whom he visited in New York. "i used to think . . . with considerable bitter amusement about the elaborate painstaking buildup you would have to endure before getting [one] of your new york dates into bed," she wrote. "they had been sought out, even telephoned, invited, spoken to and listened to, treated as real people, and they had the unutterable blessing of being able to go home afterward. . . . i would have changed places with any of them."

Up to this point, the women in Jackson's stories required a magical escape from their unhappy marriages, in the form of James Harris or another beautiful stranger. But in "A Day in the Jungle," written in the spring of 1951, a woman simply walks out on her husband, packing a suitcase and leaving a note. It was "so shockingly, so abominably, easy, that her only vivid feeling about it was surprise that the institution of marriage might pretend to be stable upon such elusive foundations," the story opens. The woman goes to a hotel, where she naps and relaxes with a mystery novel; she lunches in a restaurant and flirts with a stranger. Her reverie is interrupted by a call from her husband, who has tracked her down, and she agrees to meet him for dinner. On the way to the restaurant, she grows bizarrely, irrationally frightened of some unknown menace: the neon signs swinging dangerously above her, the "devouring earth" lurking beneath the sidewalk, ready to open up and swallow her. "What am I doing?" she wonders. "This is madness, this is idiotic; I am not supposed to be *afraid* of anything; I am a free person, and the path I have chosen for myself does not include fear." But when she sees her husband waving to her at the restaurant, he seems "wonderfully safe and familiar," and as she greets him she thinks, "I have been alone for so long."

Jackson—as Margaret tells the Dylan Thomas figure on the porch—was afraid of staying. But not as afraid as she was of leaving. Not yet.

IF HYMAN WAS bothered by his wife's portrayal of him, he didn't show it. "Shirley finished the novel last night, and sends it off tomorrow. I think it is a beaut," he wrote to Ben Zimmerman at the end of November 1950. His own book, yet again, was stalled. He complained to his editor that he had been "in peonage" to *The New Yorker*, writing long pieces, including his profile of Louis Scher, which he submitted that fall but was not published for more than two years. After the next one—a gargantuan history of the Brooklyn Bridge—was in, he promised, he would have a year off from the magazine to work full-time on the book. He requested an extension to December 31, 1951.

"my novel is coming out in april and no one likes it[,] even me," Jackson wrote to her parents just before Christmas. It wasn't true that no one liked it: Jackson's friends had been typically effusive with their praise. Nemerov—whose first book of poetry, *The Image and the Law*, had appeared a few years earlier—complimented her "delicate and certain" tone, and Jay Williams wrote that it was "a splendid, mature, beautiful book." But Jackson smarted at rejections from the women's magazines where she had hoped to place excerpts; the editors admired the book but thought it was unsuitable—in other words, too unconventional—for their readers. Elliot Schryver at *Woman's Home Companion* compared Jackson to Djuna Barnes and remarked, perceptively, "It's a story that terrifies you because the madness is kept on the near side of the fence where you yourself dwell." Margaret Cousins, Jackson's editor at *Good Housekeeping* and a friend, said she felt "wrung dry" upon finishing the novel. But her admission that she did not understand "half of what is going on" foreshadowed the most common criticism of the book—that it was simply too obscure.

Farrar, Straus was optimistic about *Hangsaman*'s prospects: the first printing was 7500 copies, and advertising was aggressive. A new publicity picture was arranged, in which Jackson looks severe, her hair pulled tightly back from her face. She wears a business suit and pearl earrings; the only sign of unconventionality is the large scarab pin on her lapel. Alas, reviews were mixed. *Time* magazine would mention *Hangsaman* along with *The Catcher in the Rye*, another novel about an adolescent with a precarious grip on sanity, as "one of the most successful U.S. novels of the year, a perfectly controlled, remarkably well-written account of a college girl's descent into schizophrenia." Jackson's friend Kit Foster, writing in the *Bennington Weekly*, found *Hangsaman* "a considerable advance" over *The Road Through the Wall*: "realistic, sharp descriptions and dialogue combine with a spine-tingling, hallucinatory inner monologue to produce the sensation of life in two worlds." In *The New York Times*, daily reviewer Orville Prescott called it "a beautifully written and thoroughly exasperating novel," observing that the parts of the book dealing with Natalie and her parents were "almost unfairly brilliant" but that the story of her breakdown was too opaque. The reviewer for *The New York Times Book Review* loved the book—"One cannot doubt a word Miss Jackson writes"—but missed its point entirely, treating Tony as a real character. Those who understood it tended to find the ending problematic. W. T. Scott, writing in the *Saturday Review*, complained that "the structure of the novel falls apart; it cannot contain both the satirical reporting of the first half and the nightmare fantasy of the second," and W. G. Rogers, the Associated Press book critic who had earlier quizzed Jackson about witchcraft, found the climactic scene "part magic and part gobble-de-gook."

In June 1952, a year after *Hangsaman* appeared, Diana Trilling published a column in *The New York Times Book Review* that inadvertently revealed the extent of the disconnect between Jackson's work and the broader reading public. Trilling blamed the general decline in fiction sales in America (which Roger Straus tended to invoke whenever Jackson complained about her own sales) on the generally poor quality of contemporary novels, for which the usual explanation, she said, was that the modern world had become "so complex and awful that the novelist is unable to deal with it," just as painters had turned away from rep-resentative art to abstraction. Trilling disagreed: she simply found the novels superficial, "fashion-drawings of what the sophisticated modern mind wears in its misery—and it is no accident that their authors are so welcome in the pages of our expensive fashion magazines." The central question, she continued, was whether writers would use their talent to "assert the human possibility" or continue to "give rein to the perverse and destructive will which is somewhere in all of us." On both counts—the fashion magazines and the negative view of humanity—she might have been speaking of Jackson.

Critic John Aldridge published a response to Trilling's essay the fol-lowing week. In his mind, the problem wasn't that writers were strik-ing "fashionable poses of doom," but that the novel itself had run out of subjects. The taboos that had energized eighteenth- and nineteenth-century fiction were now all but broken down: the drama surrounding love had faded into "the lesser drama of sex," while money and social ambition had disappeared as sources of tension with the blurring of class lines. The tendencies in the novel that Diana Trilling had criticized, he concluded, were simply "necessary adjustments to a changed cultural situation." As a result, he believed, novelists such as Salinger, Stafford, Capote, and Carson McCullers were immaturely resorting to childhood as a source of inspiration.

Neither Trilling nor Aldridge mentioned a novel that had just appeared a few months earlier, one that refuted both their arguments: Ralph Ellison's *Invisible Man*, which Hyman had had such an impor-tant role in shaping. Steeped in mythology as well as the history of the African-American experience in the United States, Ellison's novel—the darkly surreal coming-of-age story of a young black man struggling against the perversities of racism—was no fashion drawing for the sophisticated modern mind, but a profound investigation of a human being as marginal to society as Natalie in *Hangsaman* or the lost women of Jackson's earlier stories. It's notable that Aldridge failed to mention race as a social taboo, since—as Ellison demonstrated—it was in fact still a potent source of tension. (Homosexuality, also not on Aldridge's list, was obviously another.) But the critics who embraced *Invisible*

Man nearly unanimously—it won the National Book Award in 1953—tended to see it less as a novel about black identity than as a depiction of an American Everyman. "What language is it that we can all speak, and what is it that we can all recognize, burn at, weep over, what is the stature we can without exaggeration claim for ourselves; what is the main address of consciousness?" asked Saul Bellow in *Commentary*, praising Ellison for not adopting a "minority tone" in his writing. *The Adventures of Augie March* (1953), Bellow's breakthrough novel, represented his own attempt to write a coming-of-age story that was at once identifiably Jewish and generically American.

It was easier for critics of the early 1950s to regard as universal a story about a black man or a Jewish man than a story about a woman. But telling women's stories was—and would always be—Jackson's major fictional project. As she had in *The Road Through the Wall* and the stories of *The Lottery*, with *Hangsaman* Jackson continued to chronicle the lives of women whose behavior does not conform to society's expectations. Neither an obedient daughter nor a docile wife-in-training, Natalie represents every girl who does not quite fit in, who refuses to play the role that has been predetermined for her—and the tragic psychic consequences she suffers as a result. During the postwar years, Betty Friedan would later write, the image of the American woman "suffered a schizophrenic split" between the feminine housewife and the career woman: "The new feminine morality story is . . . the heroine's victory over Mephistopheles . . . the devil inside the heroine herself." That is precisely what happens in *Hangsaman*. Unfortunately, it was a story that the American public, in the process of adjusting to the changing roles of women and the family in the wake of World War II, was not yet ready to countenance.

The first printing of *Hangsaman* did not sell out. Fortunately, Jackson already had another book in the works. This one would be a best seller.

II.

CABBAGES
AND SAVAGES

BENNINGTON,
*LIFE AMONG
THE SAVAGES,*
1951–1953

I have never liked the theory that poltergeists only come
into houses where there are children, because I think it is
simply too much for any one house to have poltergeists *and*
children.

—"The Ghosts of Loiret"

T IS THE ENDURING QUESTION OF SHIRLEY JACKSON'S CAREER.
How could she simultaneously write the dark, suspenseful fiction that
would define her legacy—"The Lottery," "The Daemon Lover," *The
Haunting of Hill House, We Have Always Lived in the Castle*—and the
warm, funny household memoirs that brought her fame and acclaim in
the 1950s but have largely been forgotten since? With the publication of
Life Among the Savages and its sequel, *Raising Demons*, a wide audience
of enthusiastic readers gobbled up the adorable (and often embellished)
antics of Laurie, Jannie, Sally, and Barry, recorded by their flustered,
bemused mother. Even reviewers who had not found *Hangsaman*

The jacket for
Life Among the
Savages *(1953).*
The house is
modeled on the
Hyman house on
Prospect Street in
North Bennington.

willfully obscure marveled that a writer whose last novel had featured sexual assault and schizophrenia was now spinning madcap *I Love Lucy*–style yarns about a visit to the department store, the night all the family members (even the dog) wound up in the wrong beds, or the time the furnace and the car both died while her husband was away on a business trip. This was a novelist who had once referred to herself as "this compound of creatures I call Me"; still, it was a generous range. "The Lottery" was as different from *Savages*, one reviewer remarked, as "a thunderstorm from a zephyr."

But *Savages* is recognizably a book by Jackson, owing not least to its gentle touch of the macabre. The book concludes with a document purporting to show evidence of a poltergeist in the house—written in a parody of Glanvill—and one of the family cats is called Shax, after the demon. An early draft went further, with an episode in which Jackson is visited by a ghostly former resident of the house they have just moved into. But in the final version she toned this down, choosing instead to suggest a homier mode of the uncanny by claiming that the furniture left behind by the previous owners had its own opinions about its arrangement: "No matter how much we wanted to set our overstuffed chairs on either side of the living room fireplace, an old wooden rocker . . . insisted upon pre-empting the center of the hearth rug and could not in human kindness be shifted." Although Jackson states matter-of-factly in the book that she has "always believed in ghosts," the house in *Savages* is haunted only in the way that all houses are haunted: with the memories created by the family who call it home, along with the faint impressions left by those who have gone before.

Like virtually all humor writing, *Savages* straddles the line between fiction and fact; it is autobiographical but not necessarily true. Shirley listened closely to her children's talk—she and Stanley loved to repeat their latest hilarities, and notes in her files show that she jotted down the children's best lines as inspiration. The Hyman children affirm that many of the stories are based on real-life incidents, some of which appear in very similar form in Shirley's letters to her parents. Apologizing for a long delay between letters, she once wrote that "the reason i always think i have written you is because i write the same material in stories; if i sent you the first drafts of all my stories you would have twice as many letters." Geraldine, not surprisingly, loved the household stories so much that she would thumb through all the women's magazines at the newsstand to be sure she hadn't missed one. "It is just like a visit with you and Stanley and the children to read one of your stories," she wrote with pleasure from California, though she would also carp at her daughter for her too honest depiction of her "helter skelter way of living."

In her literary fiction Jackson zeroed in on the moments of greatest confusion, discomfort, or depravity in her characters' lives, but in *Savages* she omitted the painful bits to focus on the cheer. In her own way, she was finally following through on that long ago admonishment to "seek out the good . . . rather than explore for the evil." Many of the drafts reveal rawer versions of episodes that would eventually be buffed and polished for public consumption. Telling the story of Laurence's

accident, for instance, Jackson conveys only a hint of her own anguish
and certainly nothing of her cynicism about the sweet-faced old lady.
Instead, that episode in *Savages* begins with him coming home from the
hospital safely healed, full of pride over his ordeal, and eager to hear all
the gruesome details ("Was there a lot of blood?"). As she had been telling herself—with Hyman's encouragement—since the earliest stages of
her career, "an accurate account of an incident is not a story." Creative
transformation was always required.

It took time for Jackson to make her way into this genre: a few
early attempts at *New Yorker*–style humor fell flat. As with her fiction,
she found true inspiration after the children's arrival. Starting with
"Charles," the story about Laurence blaming his own kindergarten misdeeds on an imaginary classmate, Jackson discovered a lucrative market
for her household stories in women's magazines such as *Good Housekeeping* and *Woman's Home Companion*, as well as in general-interest publications such as *Harper's* and *Collier's*. In these pieces—many of which
were incorporated into *Savages*—Jackson essentially invented the form
that has become the modern-day "mommy blog": a humorous, chatty,
intelligently observed household chronicle. Before Jean Kerr's *Please
Don't Eat the Daisies* (1957) or Erma Bombeck's *At Wit's End* (1967), she
brought something of an anthropologist's eye to her tribe of "savages,"
treating "the awesome vagaries of the child mind," as one reviewer put
it, with a combination of "clinical curiosity, incredulity, adoration and
outrage." (In a line reminiscent of "The Lottery," the same reviewer
noted that "[t]his tribe lives among us; its jungle is everywhere.") No
one had written about life with children in quite this way before.

Jackson made it look easy. Her files brim with fan mail from admiring readers, many of them mothers who were aspiring writers in
search of advice. Some wondered at Jackson's ability to get anything
done while caring for four children—which also mystified some of her
friends. "She not only had a working life and a life with children, but a
very demanding husband and an enormous household," recalls Midge
Decter. (In "Fresh Air Diary," Jackson confesses her impatience with
such comments: "This is a remark I have never been able to answer,"
she muses after a weekend guest wonders how she can take care of her

children and still find time to write.) Others were more critical of their own deficiencies. "Why, I asked my blundering self, can't I produce something *that* good?" asked one reader, recognizing the wealth of material provided by just about any brood of kids. Jackson occasionally wrote back, suggesting practical strategies such as planning out a piece before sitting down at the typewriter and, not surprisingly, ignoring the housework to carve out more writing time. "Despite interference from the children, I manage to get stories written about them," she joked to her agent after Laurence suffered yet another minor calamity that required stitches.

Its deceptive simplicity notwithstanding, this form required every bit as much control as any of Jackson's writing. Her household stories take advantage of the same techniques she developed as a novelist: the gradual buildup of carefully chosen detail, the ironic understatement, the repetition of key phrases, the instinct for just where to begin and end a story. Her style, too, is as painstakingly refined as in her serious fiction. In an episode describing the last day of summer vacation, Jackson tries to generate enthusiasm in Laurence and his friends by telling them she always loved school. In an early draft, she reports their reaction as follows: "there was nothing for any of them to say in the face of that bald lie. they sat and stared at me, deadpan." In the final version, these lines, now a single sentence, acquire a new pungency: "This was a falsehood so patent that none of them felt it necessary to answer me, even in courtesy."

Even more than her style, Jackson's voice makes these stories compulsively readable: many of the fan-mail writers looked upon her as their new best friend. The persona she created was both charming and approachable, a mother at once loving and perennially distracted—perhaps by the stories she was planning as she chauffeured her children to school or heated a can of soup for lunch. She clearly would rather be on the floor reading to her children instead of dusting around them, but she might like best of all to check into a hotel by herself, with housekeeping and room service. Not only has she no talent for housework ("Not for me the turned sheet, the dated preserve, the fitted homemade slipcover or the well-ironed shirt"), but even the maids she hires turn out to be alarmingly incompetent: one disappears shortly before her parole officer shows up, while another turns out to be a born-again Christian who ices cookies with the lettering "Sinner, Repent." She admits to a "pang of honest envy" as her husband departs for a business trip; when the children misbehave in public, she disguises her frustration by smiling "sweetly and falsely."

Just as motherhood is not sentimentalized nor idealized, neither are the children. Sometimes, Jackson admits, she finds herself "open-mouthed and terrified" before them, "little individual creatures moving solidly along in their own paths." Laurence (always called Laurie in the stories, as he was in real life as a child), restless and cheeky, despises school and relishes any kind of practical joke; if a phone call comes for Jackson during breakfast, he is apt to embarrass her by telling the caller she is still asleep. (In an author's note, Jackson says he explicitly requested that she include "Charles" in the book.) Joanne, called Jannie, is adorable and a little bit wacky, refusing to go anywhere without a troop of imaginary friends and insisting that they be addressed by name, offered cookies, and read to. Sarah (Sally), at around age three, enters "with complete abandon into a form-fitting fairyland," subjecting her mother to "tuneful and unceasing conversation . . . part song, part story, part uncomplimentary editorial comment." Standing on her head in the backseat of the car—the only position in which she consents to ride (this was the pre-seat-belt early 1950s)—she sings, "I'm a sweetie, I'm a honey, I'm a poppacorn, I'm a potato chip." "When I ask you 'What's your name?' you must say 'Puddentane,'" she commands her unobliging older brother. After an afternoon excursion to a farm, she regales her siblings with a tale of watching giants roast marshmallows over a campfire. Jannie turns out to be more skeptical than her mother, who finds Sally's stories more disconcerting than she cares to admit:

> "I don't believe it when Sally tells about giants. Do you?"
>
> "Certainly not," I said. "She's just making it up." And recognized clearly that there was no ring of conviction whatever in my voice. "My goodness," I said heartily, "who's afraid of *giants*?"

Stanley is noticeably absent from these stories. When he appears, it is usually only to demonstrate his incompetence in any and all practical matters, though he does get some of the book's best lines: when Laurence asks, "Who was Aristides the Just?" Stanley replies distractedly, "Friend of your mother's." His blunders are harmless. At one point, his attempt to kill a bat is foiled by a cat, who runs off with the intruder in her mouth, nodding "contemptuously" at Stanley. Later, he orders a package containing 150 coins from around the world and 100 counterfeit coins; they arrive jumbled together, forcing him to spend hours sorting out the real from the fake. (Shirley had come up with the idea of Laurence starting a coin collection as a way of keeping him busy while he was recuperating from his accident—"if anything were to be collected, for heaven's sake it might as well be *money*"—but Stanley, always the collector, joined in with equal enthusiasm, and would continue to accumulate rare coins long after Laurence lost interest.) In *Raising Demons*, he would be treated less tolerantly. But for now, Jackson chose to depict him as hapless, clueless, and largely peripheral to the workings of the household.

If Stanley was annoyed by this, he displayed it only briefly, when a reporter from the *Albany Times-Union* came to profile Jackson after *Savages* was published. "She has her career, I have mine. We don't intrude upon each other's," he insisted. He also "firmly refused" to pose for any pictures with her. Instead, the photograph with the article depicted Jackson in an overstuffed armchair, all four children tumbling around her, a black cat in her lap, and the dog, Toby, at her feet. Unusually for a publicity photograph, she is smiling broadly. She and the children are the stars of this show.

IRONICALLY, THIS UTTERLY innocent portrayal of the Hymans as an all-American family—one reviewer of its sequel wrote that the books would be "good red, white and blue publicity" if translated into Russian—was written while they were under investigation by the FBI for alleged Communist activity. Suspicions were first raised when Shirley and Stanley arrived in Westport. As movers were

Jackson, all four children, and Toby photographed for the Albany Times-Union *in 1953, just after* Life Among the Savages *was published.*

unloading the truckload of books, one of the cartons broke open. Inside were numerous books and pamphlets by Stalin, Earl Browder, Howard Fast (then the editor of *The New Masses*), and others. One of the movers informed the FBI, kicking off an investigation that would continue for the next two years.

Fortunately, the agents in charge of the case did not discover that Stanley had actually been involved with the Communist Party during his years at Syracuse University. But they did determine quickly from his phone records that among his associates were several known Communists. Walter Bernstein had already been blacklisted and was working

under a pseudonym, when he could. Jay Williams, too, had been a literature director of the Party as recently as 1947 and was still on Party mailing
lists. The agents identified Shirley as a writer but declined to make her a
target of the investigation.

Their focus was on Stanley. Agents interviewed the Hymans' landlord
as well their neighbors in Westport and several people affiliated with Bennington College. The landlord confirmed that the Hymans had "a tremendous number of books in their home," with "bookcases all around the
house"—so many that the agents wondered whether Stanley might be "a
custodian of Communist Party property." Stanley, the landlord testified,
was "not friendly" and did not "mix in any activities" in the Westport
area. The Hymans did receive frequent visitors from New York, but as far
as he knew, there was nothing to indicate that they were "un-American
or connected with subversive activities." The other people interviewed
were either unaware of who Stanley was or echoed the landlord's judgment. A neighbor said that Stanley and Shirley largely kept to themselves,
but the lights were on in their home "practically every night" and various
cars could be seen coming and going. An administrator at Bennington
said that "although she did not like either [Stanley] or his wife personally, she never observed any indication of disloyal activities or disloyal
associations" on their part. A Bennington faculty member, too, said that
he "intensely disliked" Stanley but had no reason to question his loyalty
to the United States.

If Stanley was aware that he was under investigation, he does not seem
ever to have mentioned it to anyone. Shirley's writings contain only one
veiled hint. In a draft of *Savages*, she identified the family's decision, in
spring 1952, to move back to Vermont as motivated by "a growing tension, a sort of irritable pressure which none of us could define." The finished version of the book omits this line. Did she remove it out of caution
that it might be read as a reference, however oblique, to the investigation?
Or did the author of "The Lottery," exquisitely sensitive to disturbances
in the local atmosphere, simply pick up on the climate of suspicion that the
FBI investigation must have created? Either way, after a year and a half of
life in Westport, she and Stanley were already contemplating a return to
North Bennington.

———

REGARDLESS OF WHETHER Jackson was aware of the FBI investigation, one event in particular catalyzed her desire to leave Westport. In June 1951, the relative anonymity that she had been enjoying came abruptly to an end. The family had chosen to leave North Bennington for a variety of reasons, including the village's distance from New York and Hyman's loss of his teaching job, but foremost among them was the response of their neighbors to "The Lottery": in the village, Jackson would be forever recognized as the author of that story. For a year and a half in Westport, nearly everyone knew her only as Mrs. Stanley Hyman—until a publicist from *Ladies' Home Journal*, which was running one of her stories for the first time, drove up to Connecticut in search of her. Just as he stopped in the drugstore to inquire about the elusive Shirley Jackson, Laurence happened in to buy some chewing gum and volunteered that the mysterious writer was his mother. The local paper promptly trumpeted the news: the author of "the famed short story 'The Lottery'" was living in the neighborhood! Jackson was plainly nonplussed. "I wish this was timed better," she complained to the reporter. "I am not exactly interested in the public eye right now."

Jackson was never interested in the public eye. In addition to her hatred of publicity photos, she would eventually refuse to engage in any promotional activities for her books at all. But at that moment in her life, she was especially hostile to scrutiny. The "irritable pressure" she was suffering from began with the string of bad luck in 1950—Emma's crack-up, the Fresh Air Fund fiasco, Laurence's bike accident and the ensuing complications—and continued through the following year, spreading like an ugly stench from the household into her professional life. The critical reaction to *Hangsaman* was lukewarm. Several stories she wrote remained unsold, including "The Missing Girl," inspired by the Paula Welden case, and "The Lie," about a woman who returns to her hometown to expunge a guilty secret from her conscience. Jackson began but did not finish a new novel, alternately called *Abigail* or *Another Country*, about a pastoral dream world not unlike the commedia

*Jackson with
Laurence
and reporter
Jane Connors
of WLIZ
(Bridgeport,
Connecticut),
1951.*

dell'arte: "it was a novel i liked but no one else did so i put it away," she commented later. And she wasted several months working on a treatment for a movie about the dancer Isadora Duncan. The actor-turned-producer Franchot Tone, best known for his starring role in *Mutiny on the Bounty* (1935), had sent Jackson a telegram out of the blue in the spring of 1951 asking her to collaborate on the project. She was initially thrilled, especially after the director Robert Siodmak, "a flowery character," offered to fly the whole family to Capri while she wrote the movie. But in the end nothing came of it except months of protracted and frustrating negotiations.

Meanwhile, Herbert Mayes, her editor at *Good Housekeeping*, was pressing Jackson to fulfill her obligation to the magazine, which was still advancing her $1500 quarterly with the expectation that she submit at least eight publishable pieces a year. But he rejected almost everything she sent him as "too depressing" ("Still Life with Teapot and Students"), too long ("Fresh Air Diary"), or otherwise unsuitable. The magazine published a couple of the pieces that would make their way into *Savages*, but strangely, Mayes wasn't as interested in Jackson's nonfiction. Instead, his taste ran to exactly the sort of stories she least liked to write: wholesome fables about lovers overcoming minor obstacles or children misbehaving adorably. In a tart letter, he suggested she reread her own story "The Wishing Dime" for "a quite definite idea of the short fiction we like." Until she managed to hit the mark, not only would there be no more money from *Good Housekeeping*: in March 1951 Mayes demanded that she repay $4000.

This disastrous outcome of a contract that had seemed so promising brought an end to Jackson's relationship with the MCA agency, which she blamed for the debacle. She had her eye on Bernice Baumgarten of Brandt & Brandt, known as "the toughest agent in the business." In November, Jackson sent her a brief, no-nonsense letter requesting representation. Within a month, Baumgarten was shopping her stories. The wife of author James Gould Cozzens, whose novel *Castaway* had fascinated Jackson and Hyman in college, Baumgarten had smooth, elegant dark hair and blue eyes. The author and film critic Stanley Kauffmann, another of her clients, remembered her as "small, quiet, and neat." But her manner was deceptive: Baumgarten was an aggressive negotiator. Jackson would later say that "there is nothing she likes better than getting someone . . . by the throat."

Baumgarten had started at Brandt & Brandt as a secretary in 1924; she became the head of the book division two years later, at the age of twenty-three. By the time she retired, in 1957, her client list included Thomas Mann, E. E. Cummings, Edna St. Vincent Millay, John Dos Passos, Ford Madox Ford, Mary McCarthy, and Raymond Chandler. Like Jackson, she used her maiden name professionally, though Carl Brandt senior, the agency's founder, suggested that she change it because Baumgarten sounded too Jewish. (Cozzens, notorious for his anti-Semitism, once remarked that part of the reason he and Baumgarten chose not to have children was that he didn't want a son of his to be kept out of Harvard's exclusive—and restricted—Porcellian Club.) Also like Jackson, Baumgarten was the primary breadwinner for much of her marriage, supporting her husband through a dozen less-than-lucrative novels. And she was a blunt talker with a wry sense of humor that Jackson appreciated. "Personally I think all children are born immoral," Baumgarten wrote after Mayes rejected a story because he didn't approve of the way a child's behavior was depicted. She told her client Jerome Weidman, after reading a scene in his novel *The Third Angel* (1953) in which the hero rapes a prospective girlfriend on their first date, that bringing a dozen long-stemmed roses would be more appropriate. Weidman said the man couldn't afford roses. "He can certainly afford a philodendron plant," Baumgarten replied. When Hortense Calisher, whose short stories had begun appearing in *The New Yorker* shortly after Jackson's, asked Baumgarten whether she should take a job teaching writing at a correspondence school, Baumgarten told her, "When we come to sell your soul, we'll get a damn fine price for it."

Baumgarten delighted Jackson at once by demanding $5000 from Farrar, Straus for her next novel. Eventually she was also able to work out a compromise between Jackson and Mayes regarding her debt to *Good Housekeeping*: Mayes wanted her to promise to repay $100 a month, but Baumgarten got him to agree to accept 10 percent of Jackson's earnings on each magazine sale, up to a total of $2900. Despite this considerable sacrifice on Jackson's part, Mayes maintained a grudge against her for years: she was effectively barred from the pages of *Good Housekeeping* as long as he remained editor.

After the stream of *Good Housekeeping* income went dry, the Hymans could no longer afford the Westport house. But for the time being they were stuck there: Shirley was pregnant again. (The headline of the newspaper story about her was " 'Shirley Jackson' Is Westport Mother-to-Be.") In August, Shirley's doctor abruptly informed her that he had miscalculated her late-fall due date; he now believed the baby would arrive in September. After that month came and went with no signs of labor, he suggested that she be prepared to wait another month. By mid-November, there was still no baby. Shirley made light of the situation in *Savages*, depicting the children's surprise when she came down to the kitchen each morning: "You're *still* here?" they would ask. But the uncertainty was frustrating for everyone. Stanley asked Ralph Ellison, who had time on his hands while waiting for the galleys of *Invisible Man*, to stay in Westport so that he could be on hand to drive Shirley to the hospital. Ellison came up in early November and wound up spending the better part of the month with the Hymans. "The damn baby wouldn't show up," he later recalled. Shirley took castor oil, to no avail; finally she went to the hospital anyway. Barry Edgar Hyman, Shirley's fourth and final child, arrived on November 21, 1951, putting the children temporarily ahead in the book–child sweepstakes. Ellison, appropriately, was his godfather.

When Shirley came home from the hospital, she handed the baby to six-year-old Joanne and said, "This one's for you." Nearly from birth, Barry showed a "quiet determination" that marked him as the most serious and self-directed of the Hyman children. Sarah believes that Stanley preferred Laurence and Joanne, but she and Barry were Shirley's favorites: "Barry was always good." While he was still a baby, the family began calling him "Mr. Beekman," because his perpetually earnest expression was reminiscent of "a small worried businessman, very sober and thoughtful." By age five, he could sing twelve-bar blues; at six, he began taking percussion lessons at the college and writing his own compositions; at twelve he picked up the guitar, which he has played ever since. (He is now a professional musician.) Starting in elementary school, he became the only one of the four to receive all As on his report cards. Sarah remembers that at seven, Barry was regularly winning the family poker game and could carry on "a rational conversation" with Stanley: "He could sit there and talk about Louis Pasteur." "barry is unbearable; he now thinks he knows everything," Shirley wrote to her parents when he turned nine, an age at which his pastimes included doing algebra problems for fun. When John Glenn, amid great fanfare, became the first American astronaut to orbit the Earth, in February 1962, ten-year-old Barry, caught up in the general hoopla, insisted on getting up at dawn to watch the rocket launch on television. He also had a strong moral compass: when the family ate in a restaurant, Barry always instructed the waiter not to bring any side dishes that he did not like, even if they came with the meal, because the sight of wasted food disturbed him so deeply.

As a toddler, Barry was extremely attached to his mother: he dashed after the car, screaming, if Shirley tried to so much as run an errand without him. (In *Demons*, Jackson gave this trait a positive spin: he cried, she wrote, because he loved riding in the car so much that he could not bear to see anyone drive away without him.) But he quickly became the most self-sufficient of the siblings, showing something of the early independence Stanley manifested as a child. Laurence, nine years older, built a tree house for Barry and Sarah to play in and would sometimes appear to give him and his friends a baseball lesson, but he was often away at camp or playing gigs with his band. Like the rest of the siblings, Barry found his own group of friends in North Bennington and wandered freely around the village. At age seven, he went off on his own to visit his uncle and aunt in New Jersey—Stanley's brother, Arthur, and his wife, Bunny—for two weeks. When he was twelve, he befriended the son of the English sculptor Anthony Caro, who was teaching at Bennington, and went with the Caros to England for a summer vacation.

As a joke, Laurence liked to call gentle-natured Barry "Killer"— "the least accurate nickname possible." Barry was a frail child who suffered from repeated bouts of pneumonia and asthma; he spent the week before *Savages* was published in the hospital, inside an oxygen tent. The other siblings always believed that Shirley favored Barry: perhaps because he was ill so often, or because his separation anxiety had been so pronounced, or simply because he was the easiest to get along with. Laurence and Sarah would both get into serious trouble; Joanne, as soon as she hit adolescence, exasperated her mother by being precisely the kind of typical teenager, obsessed with boys and clothes and cosmetics, that Shirley had never been. But Barry was "quiet and unobtrusive," one of his babysitters remembers; he stayed out of the way. Shirley "loved Barry because he was a teddy bear. . . . He understood everything he was told and he wasn't always saying, 'What does that mean?' " Sarah remembers. "Which [Joanne] did because she really didn't know, and I did because I wanted to get at it deeper. Laurence was too proud to ask questions. He'd just listen and nod."

Savages ends with Shirley bringing Barry home from the hospital. In a draft, her joy at having a new baby is inscribed in every detail of the scene. She toned down her emotion in the final version, which focuses on the reactions of the older children as they crowd curiously around the bundle. "I guess it will be nice for you, though," nine-year-old Laurie concludes. "Something to keep you busy now *we're* all grown up." It's a laugh line, and a funny one. But Barry was indeed the last child at home after Laurence headed off to college and Joanne and Sarah went to boarding school. When his mother died, he was only thirteen.

———

BECAUSE JACKSON DELIBERATELY obscured the setting, *Savages* feels as though it could take place anywhere in Sidestreet, U.S.A. In fact, this celebration of the household was written during a period when the Hymans had no permanent home. Jackson started it in North Bennington, wrote much of it in Westport, and finished it in a series of rented houses back in North Bennington before finally settling into 66 Main Street, where she would spend the rest of her life.

In early 1952, finally ready to give up on what Stanley called "the sordid Westport experiment," the Hymans decided to return to North Bennington. After a few years away, the problems with the village—the school, the locals—no longer seemed as bad; certainly the episode with the "sweet-faced old lady" had made Westport no better. And Lewis Jones, the president with whom Stanley had clashed, had since left the college, reopening the possibility of a teaching job. But the question of where to live was not easily answered. Very few houses were available in the area, to buy or to rent. There was not much time to decide—the Westport house had been sold, and the Hymans were to be evicted as of May 1. (The FBI investigation may well have played a role in encouraging the Hymans' landlord to drive them out.) By early April, they were so desperate that Stanley asked Kenneth Burke if they could rent a barn on his property in rural Andover, New Jersey: "Shirley, no friend of the outhouse or the water pump, has made her peace with the idea."

Sparing Shirley and Stanley a reprise of New Hampshire, their Bennington friends Paul and Helen Feeley found them a cottage to rent temporarily in the Orchard, the campus faculty-housing enclave. "I feel ten years younger with a roof over my head," Shirley sighed. The house, which belonged to music professor Paul Boepple and his family, came with an electric mixer, a newfangled Bendix washing machine, and a dishwasher (Shirley's first). "You had to wash the dishes before you put them in," remembers Joanne. "She quickly trained us to do it." On the piano sat a gigantic bronze bust of Beethoven, which was so heavy it could not be moved. "beethoven sits there . . . and glares over my shoulder while i work," Shirley complained. The house was also small: they had to put almost all their belongings into storage. Shirley and Stanley would not see their own books for another year and a half.

Still, the Feeleys were nearby, as were the Nemerovs and the Durands, a husband and wife who were the local family doctors. Shirley loved the apple blossoms that were just beginning to come out on the trees, and the fact that the children were right near their friends: "there is a constant pack of kids all ages wandering around. . . . even sally can just run wild." Laurence fell right back in with his old group of boys—the Cub Scouts organized a picnic in his honor to welcome him back—and joined a baseball team. Joanne discovered horseback riding, which she loved. Shirley and Stanley gave a big housewarming party for all their old friends as soon as they got back. "Been away a spell, you folks, I guess," the grocer greeted her.

Alas, the Orchard was not as idyllic as it appeared. The house had only a single desk that Stanley often covered with his coin collection, so Shirley sometimes had to take her typewriter outside to find room to work. Over the summer a pack of teenagers from town burglarized a number of the cottages, stealing television sets and typewriters. A suitable house elsewhere came on the market, but the Hymans did not have enough money for the down payment. Shirley had long since spent the $2000 advance she had received for *Savages*; she was due nothing else until publication, still nearly a year away. She finally managed to sell another story to *The New Yorker*, her first since "The Lottery"—a comic account of a visit to the house by a group of foreign exchange students. And she gave a lecture and reading at the Bread Loaf School for English, along with Robert Frost, Katherine Anne Porter, and Allen Tate. The following year, Stanley would be reinstated at Bennington, where he would remain on the faculty until his death. But for the time being, they were living on his *New Yorker* drawing account and her magazine sales, with no hope of seeing a substantial sum of money until she could get a contract for a new novel.

By the time the Boepples returned, in August 1952, the Hymans still had not found anywhere to live. In desperation, Shirley packed up and moved the family to a local inn: "picturesque, ancient, expensive, catering largely to parents of college students and old ladies who want to spend two weeks sketching the covered bridges." Ten days later, they were finally visited by a stroke of good fortune. The psychologist Erich Fromm, the well-known author who taught at Bennington, had taken his ailing wife to Mexico; their house was available for a year's lease. It was a brand-new ranch—not exactly Shirley's taste—in a fairly remote location several miles from campus, on the other side of the Walloomsac River, accessible, in true old Vermont style, via a covered bridge. It was a good thing Shirley had learned to drive—otherwise, the children would have had no way to get to school. But the house was modern, with four bedrooms and a picture window in the study, where Shirley liked to sit and listen to the owls calling outside.

The fact that the house belonged to Fromm also intrigued her. To her amazement, he had left all his files and notebooks out in plain view in the wing of the house he had used as his office. Even though she was sorely tempted to peek, she packed them up and put them discreetly in the attic. She and Stanley were both amused that the couch Fromm used for analysis was "inexplicably" double. In typically contrarian fashion, Stanley would use Fromm's library to write a polemic against his theories for *Partisan Review*.

They could hardly have chosen a more auspicious place for Jackson to begin the book that would become *The Bird's Nest* (1954). A psychology professor at Bennington had pointed her toward Morton Prince's *The Dissociation of a Personality* (1906), a lengthy case history of a young woman whom Prince diagnoses as suffering from what was once commonly known as multiple-personality disorder. He prefers to call it dissociated or "*disintegrated* personality, for each secondary personality is a part only of a normal whole self." Each personality, however, has "a distinctly different character . . . manifested by different trains of thought, by different views, beliefs, ideals, and temperament, and by different acquisitions, tastes, habits, experiences, and memories." Other personalities might have no awareness or memory of what their "host" did while another personality was in control. Prince's patient is astonished, for instance, to discover letters, to herself and to others, that she has no memory of writing. The fictional possibilities of the story were obvious. Many details from the life of Prince's patient would ultimately find their way into *The Bird's Nest*, although Jackson invested them with an emotional charge that was lacking in Prince's dry, academic text.

She initially tried to write the book in the style of a case study: its working title was *The Elizabeth Case*. Jackson named the Dr. Prince character Dr. Wright; she called the patient Elizabeth, the same name she had used in her story about a literary agent who is in league with the devil. The choice was apt: Prince's patient, unable to think of another explanation for her odd behavior, worries that she is possessed, and Dr. Wright also resorts to demonic possession as a figure of speech to describe Elizabeth's most intractable personality. As she had done in *Hangsaman*, in which the voice inside Natalie's head evolves from being a literal demon to the manifestation of her psychic breakdown, Jackson once again looked to psychology to explain phenomena that appeared to be supernatural. Eventually, in *Hill House*, she would employ this technique to perfection.

But Jackson had to put her new novel aside to to finish *Savages*, which she managed to do just after the new year. She sent the manuscript off on January 5, 1953, after an anxious Christmas spent in Fromm's "dismal little house," uncertain about what lay in store.

MARGARET FARRAR RECOGNIZED the potential of *Savages* as soon as she saw the rough draft. The book was "completely delightful and entertaining reading—not Shirley on a broomstick at all," she reported to her colleagues. To Jackson she was even more enthusiastic: "Every time I think of the 'savages' I feel better about life. It's a gem of a book." The only editor with reservations was new partner Stuart Young, who found the stories "warm and affectionate and reasonably pleasurable reading" but didn't think they would sell. Fortunately, both John Farrar and Roger Straus disagreed. "With the proper enthusiasm and promotion," Farrar predicted, the book would "far outsell anything Shirley has done." To Jackson's chagrin, they decided to delay publication until June 22, 1953, to take advantage of the summer market for lighter books. "It seems too bad in a way that it takes longer to have a book than a baby, but that should be excellent timing for it," Margaret Farrar—who, if not

an equal partner with her husband, had significant editorial responsibilities—reassured Jackson. The subtitle would be *An Uneasy Chronicle*.

Jackson always had a litany of complaints about the way Farrar,
Straus handled her books, and *Life Among the Savages* was no different: she found the jacket copy inane, the page proofs didn't reach her on
time, the advertising budget was too small. Despite these problems, it
was clear well before publication that the book would be an enormous
success. In March, the Family Book Club bought rights to *Savages* for
$7500, split between Jackson and the publisher; another excerpt was
sold to *Reader's Digest* for $5000. Even the children got excited about
the book, especially when they learned that their photograph would be
on it instead of Jackson's—a creative compromise. She hung the jacket
on the kitchen wall, "so they can admire themselves while they dine."
Their own name for it was "Life Among the Cabbages."

By publication day, advance orders had already driven the book into
a third printing. Orville Prescott kicked things off with a rave in *The
New York Times*, calling *Savages* "the funniest, the most engaging, and
the most irresistibly delightful book I have read in years and years."
Jackson was so delighted that she wrote him a thank-you note. The
book debuted on the July 12 *New York Times* best-seller list at number
16, selling around five hundred copies a day. (Also on the list that summer was Norman Vincent Peale's *The Power of Positive Thinking*, one of
the first blockbuster self-help books.) "Staggered" by the news, Jackson
gloated that Hyman now had no basis for complaining, as he did whenever he discovered her writing a long letter, that she ought to be spending her time on stories: "when i am making three hundred dollars a day
just sitting around he can't open his mouth whatever i do." Geraldine,
thrilled that her daughter had finally made the best-seller list, felt that
her own taste was vindicated: "Funny how people like the amusing ones
and will read them when a serious novel seems to leave them cold." By
the end of August, *Savages* had risen to number 8—one notch above
the Revised Standard Version of the Bible. Jackson was so buoyed by
her success that even a nasty letter from a reader did not trouble her. "If
you don't like my peaches, don't shake my tree," she wrote back saucily.

For once, most of the reviewers at least understood what Jackson was

Barry, Sarah, Joanne, and Laurence, photographed for the
jacket of Life Among the Savages.

trying to accomplish, even if they didn't all approve of her turn toward
the quotidian. But there was a notable gender divide. Male reviewers—
still the majority, even for a book about child rearing—tended to find
the children rambunctious and the household unpleasant. "Cute Kids,
but Mommy's Better When She's Sinister" was the headline in the *New
York Post*, whose reviewer called Jackson's humor strained and the children "very cute, very bright and very bad." In his column in the *New
York World Telegram*, Sterling North, who would achieve renown for
his young-adult best seller *Rascal* (1963), adopted a condescending tone.
"There is no reason, I suppose, why a mother should not write at some
length about her four children (ages one to ten), about the cat named
Shax and the dog named Toby and the continuous bedlam in what must
be one of America's most chaotic households. But when that mother is a
prose stylist of the caliber of Shirley Jackson it is something of a shock
to read such ephemeral fluff," he sniffed.

Women, on the other hand, responded to the familiarity of the setting: for the first time, they saw their own travails depicted in literature. "Never, in this reviewer's opinion, has the state of domestic chaos
been so perfectly illuminated," wrote Jane Cobb in *The New York Times*

Book Review, where she was identified as "a free-lance critic with her own share of domestic responsibilities." Margaret Parton, in the *New York Herald Tribune*, wrote that "it is the very familiarity of the material which makes it such pleasant reading—emotional catharsis, no doubt." For these readers, Jackson wasn't introducing the unfamiliar customs of a foreign tribe. She was describing their own daily routine, though with the ironic distance that is virtually impossible to achieve regarding one's own household.

Not all the critics agreed that *Savages* was a departure for Jackson. Joseph Henry Jackson of the *San Francisco Chronicle*, who had been following her career closely since *The Road Through the Wall*, found *Savages*, in its own way, as uncanny as Jackson's other work, in part because of the "chilling objectivity" with which she depicted the children's fantasy life: "any parent will recognize the other world into which children can withdraw at an instant's notice, and the helplessness of the adult faced with it." In the most perceptive review of the book, Edmund Fuller, a biographer, critic, and novelist whose fictionalization of the life of Frederick Douglass was remarkable for its time, also recognized the continuity among Jackson's works. "Shirley Jackson has built her reputation on a combination of the fantastic and the macabre added to what is actually as clear-eyed and minutely observant a scrutiny of contemporary life as any fiction writer is offering," Fuller wrote. He judged *Savages* her best work yet, establishing Jackson as "a humorous writer second to none, in a vein not unlike James Thurber or E. B. White, at their best." (A few years later, a reviewer of *Raising Demons* would call Jackson a "female Thurber.") She had "pinned down the contemporary middle class intellectual couple with young children definitively—the happenings, the sayings, the crisis. . . . It sounds like home."

As always, the publicity was Jackson's least favorite part. She had a disastrous interview with Mary Margaret McBride, the host of a popular women's advice radio show. Jackson was insulted when McBride announced at the start of the interview—live on the air—that she was unfamiliar with *Savages*: "i thought she might at least have read my book, so i said something to that effect." After the interview, McBride offered an attempt at apology, confessing that it was the first failure she had ever had. "You're such a nice woman and I just hope I didn't scare you to death," she wrote to Jackson. Later Jackson would say that McBride had called her "the most uncooperative person she ever had on her program." Geraldine wasn't amused by her description of the debacle. "You *must* learn to hold your temper," she scolded.

The book's sales more than compensated for such ordeals. The success of *Savages* finally allowed Shirley and Stanley to buy a house of their own.

MORE THAN HALF A CENTURY after she last lived there, 66 Main Street in North Bennington is still known as the Shirley Jackson house. Fifty years old when the Hymans bought it, in September 1953, it is a handsome, solid two-story wood-framed house a few blocks from the center of North Bennington, with seventeen rooms—"big, in that fine old high-ceilinged fashion," Shirley described it—a barn full of pigeons, a driveway marked by two stone pillars (one perpetually crooked), and more than two acres of land. Shirley and Stanley were able to buy it for $15,000—"an extremely reasonable price"—because it had been divided into four apartments; two tenants were still in place. Within a few months, one had sneaked out in the middle of the night, owing a month's rent; the other was in the midst of a divorce. For a while, Shirley and Stanley kept one of the apartments vacant to rent to friends—Ben Zimmerman and his wife, Marjory, were among those who lived there—but eventually they would take over the entire house.

Many say that 66 Main Street was the model for the ramshackle but dignified mansion in *We Have Always Lived in the Castle*. "It seemed to go on and on," remembers Anne Zimmerman, who was born while her parents were living in the back apartment. There were two sets of stairs, front and back, and many of the rooms connected. To the right of the entrance was the front room, for watching TV and playing music, with Stanley's study next to it. (Although he stopped drinking for a while around the time of the move, he nonetheless created a bar in the adjacent kitchenette.) To the left was the living room, where a tall Christmas tree would be erected every December, and the dining room, with a big

The house at 66 Main Street, where the Hymans
settled permanently in North Bennington.

oblong table and bookcases. After Laurence, as an adolescent, developed a talent for carpentry, he built furniture for many of the rooms, including a gigantic cabinet that his parents used to display their collections: for Stanley, coins, antique weapons, and canes; for Shirley, china cats and an assortment of esoterica—"totems . . . and masks, and *objets* from a thousand anthropological capitals," remembered Claude Fredericks, a poet, playwright, and translator who joined the Bennington faculty in 1961. On the wall, an Indian miniature was juxtaposed with an Azande *shongo*, or throwing knife; on the shelves, jostling for space, were a group of Australian *churingas* (elliptical totems); a terra-cotta statue of Silenos from ancient Thebes, its penis erect; an Iroquois rattle made from a turtle shell; a collection of Japanese netsukes; a ship harp from West Africa; and a Corsican vendetta knife. At the bottom of the staircase stood a statue of a Greek or Roman goddess holding a lamp. The town rumor mill transformed it into a statue of the Virgin Mary holding a beer can.

The kitchen, Shirley's domain, ran the width of the house at the rear. On the ceiling she pasted silver stars of all shapes and sizes. Later, when she was dieting, she would cover the walls with calorie counters. As her success mounted and the money began to pour in, she invested in improvements: new linoleum, a new Frigidaire "with a big freezing compartment and all sorts of silly little boxes for keeping butter and cheese and a slide for eggs to roll down and the inside all colored blue and gold," a new pink dishwasher, yellow paint for the walls, turquoise cabinets. Eventually the exterior of the house would be painted gray with white trim; there would be new couches and curtains for the living room, brown leather chairs for the study, a new washing machine and dryer. Shirley's beloved cats, too numerous to count, would wander in and out at will. Friends recalled hearing her talk to them as if having a conversation.

After the first tenant moved out, Laurence took over the upstairs back apartment. Joanne and Sarah had a suite of their own, two bedrooms with a shared library in between (Laurence built bookcases for them, too). Barry was next door, across from the master bedroom. Shirley had a study of her own next to the bedroom; at some point, probably in the late fifties, it became her bedroom as well. As the Hymans' book collection expanded, Laurence built a library in the attic. (Stanley always removed the book jackets, which he thought were vulgar.)

Guests were always welcome—with or without children. Naomi Decter, Midge Decter's daughter, remembers Stanley telling her and her sister in mock seriousness, "Whatever you do, don't jump on the bed"—if they did, a magical creature who lived in the woods behind the house would come and take them away to his fantasy land. Naturally, as soon as Stanley closed the door, they began jumping on the bed as hard as they could. A rotating series of friends settled in the back apartment for short- or long-term stays. "It was full of life, full of kids, full of bustle," says Midge Decter. It was also full of animals—at least three dogs over the years and countless cats. Some guests would complain about the mess and the cat smell, but others did not seem to notice. Decter remembers the house as homey and untidy, but not dirty. "It was writing clutter . . . not filth, not at all."

"The doors were always open," remembers Marilyn Seide, Walter Bernstein's sister and a Bennington alumna. In the late years, when Shirley was suffering from agoraphobia, students were no longer as welcome, and Bennington alumni from the early and mid-1960s remember her as taciturn and withdrawn. But throughout the fifties, the Hymans were famous for their parties. Shirley served exotic delicacies she brought back from New York: pickled cantaloupe and cinnamon jelly from Altman's, stuffed grape leaves and feta from Sahadi's. She loved to seek out the latest in gourmet foods, the more extravagant the better: one year for Father's Day she and the children presented Stanley with a four-foot-long smoked cheese. And there was a bottomless well of alcohol. "Everything was somehow provided for everybody," remembers Catherine Morrison, a student at Bennington in the midfifties. (After Morrison told Shirley that she had never witnessed a birth, Shirley once came to her dorm room to fetch her when one of the cats was having a litter of kittens.) Shirley had a way of taking care of the social niceties without appearing to pay much attention to them. One year Midge Decter and her husband, Norman Podhoretz, visited while Shirley and Stanley were celebrating their anniversary. "There was this great spread—where it came from, how it had been produced, or when, you wouldn't know," Decter says. "She did everything as though it was not the least bit of trouble."

Students and faculty would gather in the front rooms, forming one circle around Shirley and another around Stanley as each held forth, "rarely letting anybody else interrupt." As the years went on and she put on more weight, Shirley "took up literally half the sofa," her friend Harriet Fels, wife of Bennington president William Fels, recalled. "But when she opened her mouth, everything changed. . . . She was witty, brilliant, and she knew it and used it." The atmosphere was homey and welcoming. "Stanley and Shirley were particularly protective of the [Bennington] girls," Morrison says. "They were a surrogate family." At one gathering, Suzanne Stern entertained a group of faculty members by doing imitations. She was delivering a lecture on *Moby-Dick* in the style of Howard Nemerov when Nemerov walked in. The group was delighted. "Don't stop!" everyone yelled. Stanley once deftly defused an argument that had broken out between Podhoretz and another guest.

During another party, late in the evening, Shirley startled Claude

Fredericks by showing him a human skull, which she said had belonged to a doctor. The top of the cranium had been sawed off and reattached with hinges; Shirley opened and closed it as if it were a cigarette box. She tried to hang her commedia dell'arte mask on the skull, but the mask wouldn't stay put. "She began to speak to it as if it were a child, as if the skull were the ghost," Fredericks later remembered. " 'What, you don't want it on, it hurts your eyes, you're tired of it on?' she asked the creature. . . . There was something unpleasant and ghostly there in the dark, something obscene as she gently, tenderly, almost reverently put the skull back in its place on the shelf." He was relieved when the arrival of other guests "cleared the air."

Even during her most social years, Shirley would sometimes withdraw from parties to write, just as Kit Foster remembered her doing in the house on Prospect Street. "We'd all be sitting at dinner and Shirley would excuse herself . . . and retire to her room. Whenever she needed to write, she wrote," Morrison says. "Hours later she would come out with a draft of something and rejoin if anybody was still there." Morrison understood Shirley's behavior as almost involuntary. "The ideas were churning, churning all the time. I had the sense she felt that if she didn't write them, she was going to lose them." Another guest remembered her "sitting on the edge of the group" at house parties, "absorbing lemur-like every shade and texture of the person she was talking to. I always had the feeling that she knew just what it was like to be another person, that she grasped and understood to an almost frightening degree."

As the sale on the house was finalized, Shirley, riding high on her new best-seller status, was jubilant about the future. After years of living from one check to the next, she and Stanley now had a house, a car, and money in the bank, thanks to *Savages*. "it may be bad luck to say it, but right now there doesn't seem to be anything more we need in the world . . . we are about as lucky as we can be," she wrote to her parents. "keep your fingers crossed, and knock on wood; there doesn't seem to be anything that can go wrong."

12.

DR. WRITE

THE BIRD'S NEST,
1953–1954

> Everything was going to be very very good, so long as she remembered carefully about putting on both shoes every time, and not running into the street, and never telling them, of course, about where she was going: she recalled the ability to whistle, and thought: I must never be afraid.
>
> —*The Bird's Nest*

"THIS IS YOUR WIFE," THE CAPTION OF THE BELL TELEPHONE ad reads. Above it, five identical women's heads are lined up in a row. One head wears a chef's toque; the next, a nurse's bonnet; another, a chauffeur's cap; and so on. Thanks to the telephone, readers are told, "the pretty girl you married" can order groceries, call for a sick child's medicine, find out what time to meet her husband's train, and more. Behold the modern American housewife: five women neatly bundled into one.

The ad makes literal an argument common in the women's magazines of the late 1940s and 1950s: that a housewife need not consider herself "just a housewife." Rather, she is a specialist in multiple fields at once: "business manager, cook, nurse, chauffeur, dressmaker, interior decorator, accountant, caterer, teacher, [and] private secretary," as one article put it. The fact that many housewives apparently needed to be reassured of their own significance demonstrates that they found the media's glorification of their role far from convincing. But those who hoped for more might have been scared off by the many cautionary magazine stories of the era about women who struggled—and failed— to integrate career and home. One feature described a woman who had tried to pursue a promising career as a concert performer until "the tension of trying to fulfill multiple roles" caused her to have a nervous breakdown. How much safer it was to domesticate those multiple identities into a single category—and better for the family, too. "Few men ever amount to much when their wives work," the woman concluded. The success of Herman Wouk's best-selling novel *Marjorie Morningstar*, about a woman who dreams of becoming an actress but is sidelined by an unhappy love relationship, demonstrates how powerfully the theme resonated.

Just as pressure mounted for women to give up careers and embrace domestic life, there was a sudden uptick of popular interest in multiple-personality disorder, a psychiatric diagnosis that had fallen out of fashion fifty years earlier. "Split personality seems to be the literary vogue this season," one of the reviewers of *The Bird's Nest*, Jackson's third novel, commented in 1954, pointing to two other books with a similar theme. (One, *The Three Faces of Eve*, would be made into a popular movie.) Postwar Americans generally showed an increased awareness of mental health issues—a result of veterans returning traumatized from the war as well as of the growing popularity of individual psychotherapy and pop psychology. In Hollywood, psychoanalysis was openly discussed: Marilyn Monroe saw five different analysts, including Anna Freud, starting in 1955. But the particular focus on multiple-personality disorder may well have had more to do with the cultural anxiety surrounding the reorientation of women's lives around the domestic sphere. The idea that a woman's identity might comfortably encompass more than one persona—wife, mother, and professional, for instance—threatened a male-dominated culture invested in glorifying the stability of family

This Is Your Wife

How the telephone helps her to be five busy people

This is the pretty girl you married.

She's the family chef. And the nurse. And the chauffeur and maid.

And when she's all dressed up for an evening out—doesn't she look just wonderful!

How does she do it?

Of course she's smart and it keeps her busy, but she never could manage it without the telephone.

When the "chef" needs groceries, she telephones. Supplies from the drugstore? The "nurse" phones her order.

A train to be met? The telephone tells the "chauffeur" which one. A beauty shop appointment? A call from the "glamour girl" makes it easily and quickly.

Handy telephones—in living room, bedroom, kitchen and hobby room—mean more convenience and security for everybody.

Working together to bring people together... BELL TELEPHONE SYSTEM

695
September, 1957

life based on traditional gender relations and keeping women out of the workforce. This anxiety is at the heart of *The Bird's Nest*, in which a dramatic battle of wills takes place between a male doctor struggling to cure a patient on his terms and her multiple personalities, which will not be easily subdued.

When Elizabeth Richmond, a clerical worker at the town museum, arrives at her desk one Monday morning, she discovers that the wall of her office has been removed. As she sits at her typewriter, she can extend her arm into a gaping hole that reveals the building's "innermost skeleton." The museum, it seems, has begun to list dangerously, its foundations sagging; the efforts to repair it have only made things worse. The relationship between the building's disrepair and Elizabeth's own mental state is strongly implied. "It is not proven that Elizabeth's personal equilibrium was set off balance by the slant of the office floor, nor could it be proven that it was Elizabeth who pushed the building off its foundations," the novel tells us, "but it is undeniable that they began to slip at about the same time."

Elizabeth is a shy woman, only twenty-three years old, whose personality is so "blank and unrecognizing" that her coworkers barely register her presence. She has "no friends, no parents, no associates, and no plans beyond that of enduring the necessary interval before her departure with as little pain as possible." Since her mother's death, four years earlier, she has lived with her loud, abrasive Aunt Morgen, who harbors an unexplained grudge against her late sister. Lately the placid surface of their life together has been marred by disruptions. Elizabeth has begun to receive threatening letters addressed to her at work: "ha ha ha i know all about you dirty dirty lizzie." Aunt Morgen accuses her of sneaking off to meet a man in the middle of the night, but she has no memory of leaving the house. Visiting friends one evening, she repeatedly insults them—also without being aware of it. And her head aches nearly all the time.

"I'm frightened," Elizabeth tells Victor Wright, her psychiatrist, at their first meeting. Pompous but well-meaning, given to quoting Thackeray ("A man's vanity is stronger than any other passion in him") and fulminating against modern trends in psychoanalysis, he believes at first that she has a mental blockage similar to a clog in a water main; if he can find the source of the trauma and clear it away, she will be cured. When he puts her under hypnosis, a standard treatment in the 1950s, something unexpected happens. Elizabeth's stuttering speech and confusion disappear and a second persona emerges, calm, helpful, and agreeable; Dr. Wright even finds her attractive. But as he gazes upon her features, they are replaced by "the dreadful grinning face of a fiend." Here is a third, Gorgon-like Elizabeth: "the smile upon her soft lips coarsened, and became sensual and gross, her eyelids fluttered in an attempt to open, her hands twisted together violently, and she laughed, evilly and roughly, throwing her head back and shouting." This personality calls him "Dr. Wrong," threatens him ("Someday I am going to get my eyes open all the time and then I will eat you and Lizzie both"), and is locked in a continual struggle for dominance over the other two.

Demonic possession is the first thought to cross the doctor's mind: "Hence, Asmodeus," he mentally commands after the third personality appears. But, acknowledging that "one who has raised demons . . . must deal with them," he remembers his psychology, quoting Morton Prince, author of *The Dissociation of a Personality* (the psychology text Jackson consulted while researching the novel), on the "disintegrated" personality. According to Prince, in a case of multiple personality, each "secondary" personality constitutes part of the "normal whole self." Prince theorizes that such fragmentation occurs as a result of trauma: Dr. Wright speculates that in Elizabeth's case it was the death of her mother, in which she is implicated in a way that is not yet clear. He initially hopes to vanquish the demon, freeing the second personality to exercise her charms—perhaps in his company. But he soon realizes that his real task is to reassemble the personalities as one, as the nursery rhyme that gives the book its title prefigures: "Elizabeth, Beth, Betsy and Bess / All went together to find a bird's nest." After a fourth personality emerges, Dr. Wright comes to think of them by those names. Elizabeth is the original dull character; Beth, utterly charming, with whom he falls a little bit in love; Betsy, her evil twin, childish, vulgar, and cruel; and Bess, vain and materialistic. He sees himself "much like a Frankenstein with all the materials for a monster ready at hand, and when I slept, it was with dreams of myself patching and tacking together, trying most hideously to chip away the evil from Betsy and leave what little was good, while all the other three stood by mockingly, waiting their turns." But how will he put them back together? And what will be the result?

Next to *The Sundial*, published four years later, *The Bird's Nest* is Jackson's most overtly comic novel: at one point Aunt Morgen sets out four coffee cups, "one for each of you," and there is a tour-de-force set piece in which she watches dumbly as each of the personalities, in turn, takes a bath. The inadvertently amusing Dr. Wright, who narrates two of the sections, is one of Jackson's most skilled creations. Calm and avuncular, Dr. Wright is a less sympathetic predecessor of Dr. Montague, the psychic investigator in *Hill House*: a man of science, somewhat deficient of imagination, who believes that he is trying to do the best for his patient but unconsciously acts in his own interest rather than in hers. Imagining himself as Prince Charming coming to the aid of Beth, a maiden in distress, he sees Elizabeth ultimately as "a vessel emptied" that his job is to fill. The multiple puns embedded in his name are no accident: Dr. Wright explicitly, though misguidedly, connects his role with that of the author; and on a page of notes for the novel Jackson scrawled DR WRITE. "I daresay a good writer is much the same as a good doctor," he pronounces early on, "honest, decent, self-respecting men, with no use for fads or foibles, going on trying to make our sensible best of the material we get, and all of it no better and no worse than human nature, and who can quarrel with that for durable cloth?" (An early version of this character was even more pompous and verbose; Jackson may have realized that such a powerful voice in the book could not be entirely unsympathetic.) Jackson's aim in her writing, of course, was hardly to make the "sensible best" of her material, a moralistic cliché that sounds like a positive version of her teenage resolution to "seek out the good in others."

Jackson's publishers recognized *The Bird's Nest* as a tremendous leap forward from *Hangsaman*. "You have written a simply beautiful and wonderful novel. I might even say a perfect novel," Roger Straus wrote. But they promoted the book as "a psychological horror story," which annoyed her. "it's really more like *moby dick*, penetrating to the depths of the human heart, and whatnot," she told her parents. That verbal shrug shows that Jackson wasn't entirely serious about the comparison—or that she couldn't allow herself to make it without an accompanying self-deprecation. But, like Melville's novel, *The Bird's Nest* offers an intimate study of a character under extreme psychic stress. In its exploration of the original trauma that provoked Elizabeth's disintegration, the book foreshadows the themes that Jackson would explore with profound pathos in her late novels: the longing for home, particularly for the care—maternal or sisterly—to be found there; and the tragedy of losing a mother, or of being rejected by her.

Elizabeth's splintering, as we are meant to understand it, is an exaggerated form of a universal condition: Who, Aunt Morgen wonders late in the novel, does not have "a chameleon personality," starting the day wise and calm and ending it in a more cynical mood? This was the condition of the American housewife in the 1950s, pressured by the media and the commercial culture to deny her personal and intellectual interests and subsume her identity into her husband's—to fill in "Occupation: Housewife" on the census form and be glad to be doing so. This pressure, Betty Friedan wrote less than a decade after *The Bird's Nest* appeared, forced American women to "deny reality, as a woman in a mental hospital must deny reality to believe she is a queen." Women of the 1950s, as Friedan put it, were "virtual schizophrenics."

AS JACKSON TURNED HER focus to *The Bird's Nest* in the fall of 1953, Hyman resumed teaching at Bennington. After a successful visit to Smith and Amherst the previous spring, he was "hungry to go back to teaching," as he told his old friend Kenneth Burke, still an important figure in the Bennington literature department. Frederick Burkhardt, a professor of philosophy, was now the president of the college, a post he would keep until 1957, when he became president of the American Council of Learned Societies. By the time Jackson and Hyman moved back to Bennington, Hyman had already gotten to know Burkhardt through the regular poker game, which he continued to join whenever he and Jackson visited their Vermont friends. He and Burkhardt shared an interest in Charles Darwin—Burkhardt would later edit Darwin's correspondence—and in horse racing; Burkhardt would sometimes drive out to Saratoga Springs with Jackson and Hyman for a day at the races.

Hyman was now in a much stronger professional position than he had been during his first, unsuccessful teaching stint: he had published one book (with Knopf, no less) and was under contract for another, and he had finally managed to get two long pieces into *The New Yorker*. In the spring of 1953, the literature faculty unanimously voted for his reappointment, with a starting salary of $4,700. "I assume that all this is due to your devious efforts on my behalf," he wrote to Burke in thanks.

For the first time, Hyman was able to teach what he truly wanted to teach. His syllabi stand out for their rigor and their creativity. For the first semester of the department's introductory course in literature— which he taught nearly every year—he assigned *A Portrait of the Artist as a Young Man*, *Stephen Hero*, *Dubliners*, and part of *Ulysses*, as well as Kafka's *Metamorphosis*, the first half of *Invisible Man*, Thoreau's *Walden* and *Life Without Principle*, and more. (He required the students to read *Portrait of the Artist* in its entirety before the first class; they would then reread it together during the term.) For an advanced course called Form in the Novel, he had the students alternate readings from two major works: on Mondays they studied *Moby-Dick*, on Thursdays, Shakespeare. The same pattern was repeated the following semester with the *Odyssey* and *Ulysses*.

The course for which Hyman was best known was Myth, Ritual, and Literature, which he began teaching (as "Folk Literature and Folklore") in 1953 and established in its enduring form in 1956. The course originated with his discovery, in his twenties, of the work of Jane Ellen Harrison, the classics scholar who was one of the first to explore the implications of the myth-ritual theory for literary study. Harrison's book *Themis* "changed my life," Hyman once wrote, recalling chauvinistically that it made him acknowledge for the first time "the existence, and thus the possibility, of an absolutely first-rate analytic mind in a woman." The theory is based on the assumption that myth originated as the "spoken correlative" of ritual—"the story which the rite enacts or once enacted"—and not as a record of historical fact or as an explanation of natural phenomena: myth "arises out of the ritual, and not vice versa." Harrison argued that the Greek gods themselves evolved from ritual and social custom: a god is "the projection of collective emotion, the reaction of man on his fellow man." Beneath the legends of Olympus lay an older, nearly forgotten Greek religion, organized around a version of the primal death-and-rebirth rituals that James Frazer would later explore in great detail in *The Golden Bough*. Harrison found evidence for her theory throughout Greek poetry and drama: the hymn of the Kouretes (ritual male dancers who venerated the goddess Rhea) discovered on Crete; the Dionysiac theater; the works of Hesiod, Ovid, and Virgil; and much more. As Hyman would write, she "found Greece marble and left it living flesh."

By the time Hyman began teaching the course, he had been reading deeply in the field for at least five years, probably more. The roots of his interest extended all the way back to his childhood in Brooklyn, to his Orthodox Jewish upbringing and his early skepticism about religion. As a child and young adult, he had sought a rational understanding of the world through natural science, which led to his later interest in Darwin. His immersion in Marxism further ingrained his skepticism; when he first read *The Golden Bough*, likely at Syracuse after meeting Jackson, he became convinced that modern religion was not divinely inspired, but based in ancient harvest rituals. When he read *Themis*, it all fell into place. Harrison's contribution, as she herself saw it, was nothing less than to shake the foundations of Western religion: with

Jane Ellen Harrison, author of Themis. *Portrait by Augustus John.*

her book, "a hand was laid upon their ark," she proudly wrote. If every foundational Western myth—the Creation story in Genesis, Jonah and the whale, the Gospels, the Dead Sea Scrolls, and more—could be traced back to primal ritual, then the worshippers who lined the pews of churches and synagogues were fundamentally no different from the primitives in Frazer who burned their gods in effigy and conducted magical ceremonies to ensure a plentiful harvest. At the same time, if the greatest works of Western literature, from Greek tragedy to Shakespeare, were also founded upon such rituals, to read them is to be powerfully connected with a lost world. The theory was so all-encompassing as to constitute an almost religious epiphany. "That's what Stanley found so appealing about it—that it was true in a higher, transcendental sense," says Phoebe Pettingell, who took Myth, Ritual, and Literature with Hyman before they were married and edited his posthumously published articles on the subject. One of Hyman's colleagues said he described his conversion to the views of Harrison and the other Cambridge School ritualists as "a kind of Pauline rapture . . . all the nonsense turned luminous."

Hyman never would publish a book about the subject, although the Frazer section of *The Tangled Bank* touches upon it. Instead, he poured his years of study into the course, which in itself could be said to constitute his greatest intellectual achievement. The idea was to examine the relationships among various "expressive aspects of culture"—the Old and New Testaments, early English and Scottish ballads, Greek tragedy, the blues—by tracing the ritual origins of each. "Its formal beauty as an arrangement of readings was considerable," remembers Jean McMahon Humez, who took Myth, Rit, and Lit (as it was nicknamed) in the early sixties. In keeping with Hyman's love of order, everything was divided neatly in half—the week, the semester, the year. Mondays were for studying primary materials, while Thursdays were dedicated to criticism: part of Hyman's aim was to teach the students how to read literary theory. He required them to have read the Bible through by the first class; if they hadn't finished it, he told them sternly to drop the course. For the rest of the semester, they would study it book by book. In addition to the usual analytical papers, students were required to complete a creative work: artists could submit paintings; creative writers, stories.

The course was much more than a brilliant syllabus. "The life of that course was in Stanley's performance of it," says Humez. Although he was a talented teacher, it never came effortlessly: he once confessed to Nicholas Delbanco, a younger colleague, that "before each class, invariably, I have my routine: I take a piss, check my fly, wish I were dead, and begin." Eventually, after the course became the most popular in the college, sessions were held in the Barn, the biggest lecture hall on campus, with stadium-style seating. Hyman, dressed in a shabby tweed jacket, Birkenstock sandals, and socks, would pace up and down the aisles, his eyes twinkling. (In his later years, his student Barbara Fisher says, he looked a little like Toulouse-Lautrec: short and stout, with a heavy beard.) After Hyman's death in 1970, Walter Lehrman, a professor at the University of Akron and his close friend, was asked to teach it for a year, but he felt inadequate to Hyman's breadth of knowledge. The course would not outlive its creator.

Myth, Rit, and Lit established Hyman as a major figure in a literary powerhouse that included the writers Howard Nemerov and later Bernard Malamud as well as scholars Wallace Fowlie, Francis Golffing, and Harold Kaplan. (Burke was a more sporadic presence: he taught one course every other year.) "He was a very large figure on a very little campus," remembers Anna Fels, whose father, William Fels, succeeded Burkhardt as president in 1957. Colleagues spoke of Hyman's intellect with awe. Fowlie called him "an almost legendary figure, [like] one of his own mythic heroes surrounded by mystery, revealing only what he wished to reveal." Claude Fredericks, who joined the faculty in 1960, was initially terrified of "big black-bearded Stanley, flushed and fat," but was soon won over by his congeniality. "A man who is capable of inspiring a myth has verified his life in a way that transcends what is said about him," wrote Kaplan, who taught at Bennington from 1949 until 1972. Hyman was also a well-liked administrator, known for his collegiality. Golffing called him "one of the most patient and courteous listeners I have ever known." At meetings or lectures on campus, "he dominated the scene with the forcefulness and whimsicality of his speech," said Fowlie; when he was absent, "we found ourselves wondering what he would say or think, what he would approve or denounce."

Even at Bennington, where close faculty-student relationships were the norm, Hyman surprised his colleagues with the depth of his devotion to his students. Greta Einstein, who graduated in 1956, remembered him as "infinitely giving and enormously responsive, not only to the intellectual needs of his students but to the totality of their persons." Many others echoed her assessment. Some of the faculty thought he was given to overpraise, but "when we saw what he often drew from them, we felt that it was not error that operated in his judgments but . . . a kind of limitless hope for intelligence and talent," said Kaplan. When his counselees had difficulties that involved other instructors, Hyman often intervened, helping them to obtain extensions or other special considerations.

As before, Jackson—with ample reason—was intensely jealous of Hyman's relationships with his students. Often, it seems, she mistook his expressions of fondness for a more intimate connection. Unlike many of his colleagues, Hyman appears to have stuck to his hundred-mile rule; in the few instances in which he became romantically involved with a former student, it seems that nothing sexual took place until after she graduated. But the details of the relationships may have mattered less to Jackson than the attention Hyman bestowed upon these young women—attention she felt she and the children deserved more. Their own family could not compete with "your three hundred beloved babies," she complained to him in the letter outlining her reasons for wanting a divorce. "time grudged to your wife or your children or your friends is lavishly spent on a student who drops in to borrow a book. perhaps you are right in saying that this is what makes you a good teacher, and you can only do your work well if you love your students, but you must then admit that your children are justified in thinking you are indifferent to whether or not they say goodnight, and your wife is justified in thinking you are indifferent to whether or not she intrudes on your bed." And she smarted at the "unbridled delight" he was unable to hide every morning when she drove him to the college: "i see how you change from your usual glum preoccupied personality at home, change during the short space of the ride up to college, into someone eager and happy and excited, almost unable to wait until you can get into the world you love."

In college, Walter Bernstein and others had sometimes been amazed by Hyman's obtuse disregard for the connection between his own behavior and Jackson's mental health. By this point in their marriage, he had long since dropped any claim to an ideological explanation for his infidelity, but the behavior continued nonetheless. It's not clear whether Hyman failed to understand how hurtful his actions were to Jackson or whether he simply did not care. What is clear is that the flourishing of his teaching corresponded with a steep decline in her mental equilibrium. The problems began almost immediately.

Shirley and two friends were rowing a boat to a tiny island made of rock. Atop it was a house, also made of rock. The landlady let them in. "You came at a bad time," she told them. "The devil has gotten into the house." Inside, too, the house was all rock, even the tables and chairs. In front of the fire was a tall man with strange light eyes. He stood up and left the room, smiling.

"We can drive the devil away," she told the landlady. They went upstairs to sleep. When she came down for breakfast in the morning, the man with light eyes was there. "I didn't know you looked like that," she said to him. He transformed into a big black dog, then into a giant rock, then into a cat, and then back into a man. "Do you want to talk to me?" he asked her. "No," she said. "Everything you say is a lie." And she ran upstairs.

He came again that night. "I will show you where we are going and what I will give you," he told her. She closed her eyes and saw herself walking down wide black steps toward a big red room with candles burning on the walls and a golden throne at one end. "No matter what I say," she told him, "I am only dreaming and when I wake up I will not have made any promises to you." "Come along," he said, and held out his hand; she took it. "Do we go over the water?" she asked. She

was trying to wake up, but she couldn't. "You'll see when we start,"
he told her. "I didn't promise anything," she said as she awoke. "Even
*dreaming I didn't promise. I'm sure of it."**

Usually, when working on a new novel, Jackson was entirely absorbed in her manuscript, writing quickly and for hours at a time. These bursts of productivity alternated with periods of ennui during which she indulged in escapist activities: mystery novels, television, movies. The stretches of absorption were always accompanied by tension and anxiety, especially when the writing was difficult—and in the beginning the novels were always difficult. But never before like this.

Soon after she began writing *The Bird's Nest*, in late 1952 or early 1953, Jackson began to feel "a sudden and unusual general fear . . . applied to all things: security, work, general health." She started drinking heavily, more than ever before. Like the fictional Elizabeth, she began to suffer from headaches that often came on very suddenly. She felt extreme hunger and exhaustion, but also a total loss of interest in either eating or sleeping. More than anything else, she felt irresistibly tempted to give up writing the book, convinced she could find no other relief from her "symptoms," as she called them. After finishing a very rough draft of the first two sections, she took a break from the novel over the summer, writing some lighter stories and enjoying the success of *Savages*. But once she went back to it, after the move to 66 Main Street, the trouble started up again, worse than before.

Jackson called it "nervous hysteria": she had crying jags, fits of temper, nightmares, "extravagant worries." Some of it, she thought, could be explained by her anxiety over whether she and Hyman could afford the new house, as well as the stress of moving. There was also the news, that fall, of the sudden death of Dylan Thomas. After an

---

*A document describing this dream and the two others that follow is tucked between the pages of a file containing Jackson's notes and drafts for *The Bird's Nest*. This, as well as a reference made to the dreams in a memo describing her psychological breakdown, strongly suggests that it dates from the same time. Jackson describes the dreams at length; I have paraphrased, staying as close as possible to the original phrasing. All dialogue is verbatim.

alcoholic binge in New York, where he had come for another reading tour arranged by John Malcolm Brinnin, the poet died at St. Vincent's Hospital in Greenwhich Village. After their encounter more than three years earlier, Shirley had not seen him again, but he continued to figure powerfully in her imagination. "A Visit," dedicated to him, had recently appeared in print.

She was also under enormous pressure from John Farrar and Roger Straus, who were urging her to turn in the book by January 1954 so that it could be ready for publication in June. To meet the deadline, she had to work constantly: no evenings off except an occasional Saturday night bridge game or movie with the kids. Bernice Baumgarten, her dutiful and protective agent, tried to keep her publishers at bay, periodically reassuring them that Jackson was "steaming away" on the book. Indeed she was, sometimes writing up to twenty pages in an evening and ten more the next morning. But she was plagued by false starts. One early draft began with Elizabeth narrating her problems in first person to a therapist—perhaps Jackson found it a little too reminiscent of her friend and former neighbor Salinger's novel *The Catcher in the Rye*. Another draft, also discarded, was narrated entirely by Dr. Wright, in the manner of a case study. In addition to finding the right voices, Jackson had trouble controlling the appearances of the different personalities in the text—it wasn't always clear when one shifted to another, and their distinct characters weren't yet apparent.

In late fall of 1953, Jackson submitted a revised version of the first two sections to Farrar and Straus. She teased her editors by refusing to tell them how the book would end, and challenged them to guess which personality would come out on top. "I've always wanted to write a mystery story," she wrote. "Now I've got a beauty." The new version begins by describing Elizabeth's troubles in the third person, then shifts to Dr. Wright's narration. Each personality is defined by its own characteristics: Betsy slams doors and grins like a fiend, Beth smiles gently, Elizabeth is vacant and confused. (Bess does not appear until later in the novel.) Satisfied, Jackson read parts of it at the college, something she had never before done with a work in progress. "it scared them to death," she reported happily.

Shirley and Stanley received a telegram from a friend in the country offering them a place to stay for the summer. It was a large white farmhouse set alone in the middle of a field, with a few trees behind it and a brook. The teenage son of the owner was on hand to show them around. On the third floor was a locked door. "We don't go in this room unless we have to," he told her, but she insisted she wanted to see it. The room was furnished with a single bed, a wooden rocking chair, and a dresser; otherwise it was empty.

Later, she left Stanley eating dinner and went upstairs to open the locked room. Inside was the same tall man with strange light eyes. He looked at her in a friendly way, and she felt glad to see him, but she knew she should not have anything to do with him. Answering that telegram was a mistake, she realized. It was a ruse, leading her into a trap. But in some way she wanted to be trapped.

By the time of Jackson's Bennington reading, she had been walking in her sleep for a month. "I am myself in a state of such extreme tension that I have no patience with anything," she confessed. As she worked on the third section, in which Betsy seizes control and runs away to New York to search for her mother, her nightmares became so severe that she was afraid to go to bed or to sleep with the lights off. Sometimes she awoke in the middle of the night to find herself bending over to check on one of her sleeping children; she wondered whether this had to do with a private joke that the four personalities corresponded to her four children. She began to lose her memory: first just a slight absentmindedness, then forgetting entire conversations; she put objects back in the wrong places and repeatedly addressed Mr. Powers, the grocer, as "Mr. Hyman." Her speech wandered; her typing became almost impossible to read, littered with misspellings. She worried whether it was safe for her to drive, but continued to do so anyway.

Her writing, too, went poorly. She found the Betsy section "very weak, very tentative, very bad." She could not focus at all during the day; she would sit at the typewriter for hours but write as little as half a page. Only Dexamyl—in "unhealthy quantities"—allowed her to concentrate at night. In despair, she reread her previous work and wondered if she would ever write well again; somehow all her talent seemed to have evaporated.

Then suddenly things turned around: she had a new insight. In a single evening, she revamped the Betsy section: "changes vital and exciting, no chance of stopping." Hyman, too, read it and was pleased. But the symptoms only got worse.

Up to this point in the novel, the reader has not heard Betsy's internal voice; we have seen her only from the perspective of Dr. Wright—or Dr. Wrong, as she calls him. Jackson's revision, which was as inspired as she judged it to be, was to transform Betsy from a demon into a frightened child, showing that the doctor truly is wrong about her. In the early draft, she was calm and self-possessed. Now she is a little girl lost, terrified of being discovered, unsure how to act, and bereft without her mother. She mimics the words and expressions of those around her so that she will blend in and not give herself away: "she must on no account be thought strange or different." When she is anxious, she consoles herself by thinking of her mother. "My mother loves me best," she repeats like a mantra. But an unpleasant thought intrudes; she tries to push it back, but it will not go away. There is someone else: the callow and disinterested Robin, her mother's boyfriend, a strange bird who fouls the nest. She doesn't like him. "Why did Robin run away?" she asks herself, and then remembers: "Because I said I'd tell my mother what we did."

That is not the only violation, or even the worst one. The worst was when her mother denied her. They were at the beach, the three of them, and Betsy went off to gather seashells. When she came back, she overhead Robin saying to her mother, "I *hate* that child." And what did her mother say in response? "Had her mother said 'But she's my Betsy; I love her';—had her mother said that? Had she?" Or did she say she preferred Robin? "My mother loves me best, Betsy told herself forlornly, my mother was only teasing about not loving me best . . . my mother loves me better than anyone."

Now the reader knows what Dr. Wright does not: this is Betsy's essential moment of trauma, the moment at which her personality was arrested and ceased to develop. We do not know how old she was that day at the beach, but clearly she was quite small—young enough to play games and gather shells. The trauma is her desertion by her mother. And the bird's nest, then, represents the childhood home, which Betsy desperately seeks but which holds unspoken terror. On the bus to New York, the woman sitting next to her turns toward her maternally, "as though promising a home, and safety," but turns out to be deceptive and malevolent. Betsy wanders the streets of New York in search of her mother, going from one apartment building to the next, turned away at each by people who laugh at her. In *The Haunting of Hill House*, motherless Eleanor, too, will seek a home, with consequences even more dire.

What Betsy wants is what every child wants: to be loved more than anyone else. It is something that Shirley herself never had. Not from her own mother, certainly, whose replies to her own cheery letters frequently contained a note of reproach, whose occasional visits to North Bennington were always fraught. Shirley was tense and nervous in her mother's presence, and the asthma that Geraldine invariably suffered from exposure to the family cats was yet another problem for which her mother blamed her.

Nor did her husband act as though he loved her more than anyone else. Apparently oblivious to Shirley's distress, Stanley pressured her to finish the novel as quickly as she could: even though he was teaching again, they needed the money for their house payments. He may not have realized how seriously disturbed she was. He was distracted by his own problems—"going crazy," as she put it, trying to keep up with his students, who seemed to read even faster than he did. When her writing went poorly, the symptoms disappeared. When it went well, she could type for hours as if in a trance, the words "smooth and inevitable and inexorable, with no conscious planning." Then she would stop suddenly—in the middle of a word, even—in complete exhaustion. She normally wrote in fits and bursts, but this was "a painful exaggeration."

As she finished the Betsy section, believing the book was close to complete, her headache returned. While cooking, she cut her fingers repeatedly and was unable to type. On New Year's Eve 1953, she was plagued by the smell of chlorine in the tap water, which was so unbearable that she could not wash, brush her teeth, or do dishes; only she could detect it. One day she was convinced she had appendicitis; the next, heart failure. She suffered from internal pains, coughing spells, dizziness to the point of blacking out. After a long session of work, she was as exhausted as if she had given birth. The more deeply she immersed herself in the book, the worse her symptoms got. On her worst days, she wondered if she was dying. All the illness vanished entirely every time she decided that she would give up the book.

She went to the grocery store to buy coffee and the grocer said to her, obscurely, "It is time that this was ended." She followed him back to her house, leaving notes on trees and telephone poles for her friends to come and find her. She was surprised to see that the house was made entirely of straw, with walls, furniture, ceiling woven in intricate patterns. "My home is not straw," she said to the grocer. "You have forgotten our relationship," he responded pleasantly. Just then her friends arrived to take her away, but the grocer told them not to interfere: she was his wife. "I am not," she said, shocked, but he took their marriage certificate out of his pocket and showed it to her. "This is not true," she said, over and over, but her friends did not believe her. "The written word is so important," the grocer—her husband—told her, amused. "Do you see how true it actually is?"

He went to the fireplace, selected a log, and gave it to her. It fit perfectly in her hand, and she enjoyed the feel of it for a moment before swinging it against the side of his head. When he fell to the floor, she reached into his pocket for the marriage certificate and found only a blank sheet of yellow manuscript paper, signed with her name. "A blank story," she thought, "like a blank check." She ran from the house, but there he was again, waiting for her on the corner. She turned and ran in another direction, two small boys chasing her. As she ran, she tore up the piece of paper, strewing the scraps behind her, a trail for the boys to follow.

"i am tangling with things in [The Bird's Nest] which are potentially explosive (and thus things in myself potentially explosive)," Jackson wrote in a lengthy note composed midnovel, in late 1953 or early 1954, apparently in an effort to record and analyze her symptoms. She knew that she would not have chosen the subject of multiple personality had she not found it, even unconsciously, "a vehicle for existing emotions."

On one level, the "explosive" material clearly touched on her own feelings about her mother. All of Jackson's heroines are essentially motherless, or at least victims of mothers who are not good enough. Harriet Merriam in *The Road Through the Wall* is bullied and manipulated by her superficial, gossiping mother; in *Hangsaman*, Natalie Waite's mother cannot intercede in her daughter's destructive relationship with her father or protect her from harm at their garden party; in *The Sundial*, Maryjane Halloran is a victim of her domineering mother-in-law, and her own daughter Fancy suffers as a result. Eleanor Vance in *Hill House* is an orphan, as are Merricat and Constance in *We Have Always Lived in the Castle*. Elizabeth would be the first of Jackson's characters to commit matricide; the act also takes place in her last two completed novels.

This does not mean that Jackson actually wished to kill her mother, any more than the frequent appearance of sexual molestation in her fiction means that she was literally molested. But it is clear that, even from California, Geraldine managed to insert herself into her daughter's life in a way that Jackson resented, criticizing her appearance and offering unsolicited advice on household help, clothing, furniture, and other domestic matters. Her letters to Jackson are masterpieces of passive-aggression, disguising harsh critiques beneath a veneer of sweetness. She needled Jackson constantly about her weight: "How about you and your extra pounds? . . . You will look and feel so much better without them," she wrote to her daughter shortly after *Lottery* was published, less than six months after Sarah's birth. "We're so proud of your achievements—we want to be proud of the way you look too. And really dear—you don't do a thing to make yourself attractive," she wrote the following year. Even in the household stories, which Geraldine preferred to Jackson's serious fiction, she found plenty to criticize. "Dear, you are getting in a rut," she wrote after reading one of her stories in *Woman's Home Companion*. "Your stories are getting a little repetitious and why oh why do you dwell on the complete lack of system and order in your household. . . . Please don't spoil your wonderful gift

for writing by writing any more about your helter skelter way of living."
And it rankled Jackson that she and Hyman still occasionally had to ask
her parents for loans during their dry spells—as they did in the spring
of 1953, before her payments for *Savages* came in. But she suffered the
sniping without complaint. Killing off Geraldine's fictional counterparts
was the only way she could silence that disapproving voice.

The nightmares she suffered, however, were not about Geraldine.
They were about Stanley, and about marriage in general. "all my ailments seem to come from him," she wrote in an anguished diary entry,
her words riddled with typos. The first dream—which she transformed,
with surprisingly few alterations, into the posthumously published story
"The Rock"—was a variation on the daemon lover theme: the tall mysterious man, the journey over the water, the knowledge that he will
deceive her. What was new was the element of resistance: even asleep,
knowing that she was dreaming, she attempted to fend him off, whereas
the women in her earlier stories—Clara in "The Tooth," the unnamed
bride in "The Daemon Lover," and others—welcome James Harris's
advances. But on some level, as Jackson realized in the second dream,
she wanted to be trapped. Because to be married, to bind one's life to
another person, is to be entrapped; and she wanted to be married. Or
did she? Was her marriage just a house of straw, her husband a stranger?
And if so, how could she get out of it, and what would be left of her if
she did?

Then there was the question of multiple personality: what it meant in
the culture, and what it meant to Jackson in particular—Jackson, who
embraced "that compound of creatures I call Me"; who teased interviewers by playing up either her housewife persona or her witchy tendencies, but always kept the writer under wraps, hidden from view. In
The Bird's Nest, when Elizabeth is "cured," after the trauma is exhumed
and the personalities are subdued, nothing is left of the person she once
was. She is reborn as a new creation, an "empty vessel" to be filled by
Dr. Wright and Aunt Morgen, who act in the role of parents. Toward
the end of the novel, the doctor quotes another nursery rhyme: "There
once were two cats of Kilkenny / Each thought there was one cat too
many / So they fought and they fit / And they scratched and they bit /

Till . . . instead of two cats there weren't any." Is that what must always happen when two—or more—personalities are at war? Would one of Jackson's personalities—the writer, the housewife, or the witch—eventually have to subdue the others, or would they destroy one another, annihilated by their own conflict? And what would be the consequences for her marriage? *"The written word is so important. . . . Do you see how true it actually is?"*

EVEN THOUGH *THE BIRD'S NEST* got better reviews than either of Jackson's two previous novels, critics—again predominantly male—largely failed to understand her intentions. Reviewers admired her skill in creating a suspenseful story and adroitly managing all four personalities, as well as her measured, often humorous tone. But they tended to play up the book's macabre aspects rather than its understanding of the human psyche, many comparing it to Robert Louis Stevenson's *Dr. Jekyll and Mr. Hyde*. "I can think of no other living writer who can match Shirley Jackson's gift for velvet-padded shock," wrote a reviewer in the *Roanoke Times*, comparing her to Roald Dahl for her adeptness in "thrusting civilized horror on the reader." Another wrote, rather alarmingly, that "anybody who gives away much of the plot of Miss Jackson's stories should be burned in oil." Dan Wickenden, in the *New York Herald Tribune*, noted the author's own dual personalities: "Shirley Jackson the housewife and mother has once more yielded to Shirley Jackson the literary necromancer, who writes novels not much like any others since the form was invented." The "two Miss Jacksons," he continued, had little in common other than their writing talent and their sense of humor. In England, the *Spectator*'s critic called the book "more gripping than a detective story," which must have pleased Jackson, with her love of mystery novels.

Only a few critics recognized that Elizabeth's troubles might not be as unusual as they appeared. "Most men are at least two people. . . . So it is quite appropriate that women, who are twice as complicated as men, should be allowed a four-part disharmony," wrote Sterling North, one of the few critics who had disparaged *Savages*, in his column, now calling Jackson "one of the wisest, wittiest, and most compassionate writers of her time." North concluded his review with "a brief aside to lovers and husbands: If you do not realize that your girl, too, is many women, in fact a miniature harem, you are probably unworthy of your plural monogamy." Florence Zetlin, a freelancer for a small Virginia paper who was one of the few women to review the novel, noted that "the most horrifying of all experiences are those that lie deep within the human psyche and cause man to fear himself." But a number of critics were confused by the shifting between the personalities; others found all the psychology talk too clinical. *New York Times* critic Orville Prescott judged the novel's plot "too bizarre for the necessary suspension of disbelief" and wondered if psychiatry was a fruitful subject for fiction at all.

Jackson was distressed at the reviewers' emphasis on Elizabeth's insanity, which many of them mistook for schizophrenia. The misunderstanding was heightened with the movie version, titled *Lizzie* (1957), which starred Eleanor Parker (now best known for playing the Baroness Schraeder in *The Sound of Music*) as Elizabeth and the comic actress Joan Blondell as Aunt Morgen. (Blondell described her character as "an old souse, a diz-whiz girl who nips the booze but underneath has the traditional heart of gold.") Jackson was thrilled to have sold a book to the movies for the first time, but she willingly gave up the right to have a say on the film: it was "arty and pretentious," she said, "to go all oversensitive at the prospect of changing a plot or a word," and "if I faint dead away when I see [the film] I will keep it to myself." Nonetheless, she found it more unnerving than she expected to have her characters come to life on the screen in a way utterly different from how she had imagined them. "Abbott and Costello meet a multiple personality" was her assessment of the film. Elizabeth, transformed into "Lizzie" (a character that does not exist in the novel), becomes a drunken slut; Aunt Morgen is bawdy and flirtatious; and the doctor cures his patient with an incoherent combination of Rorschach inkblots, Freudian analysis, and Jungian therapy. The film was rushed to open ahead of *The Three Faces of Eve*. But while *Eve* went on to win an Academy Award, critics were lukewarm on *Lizzie*. The *Newsweek* reviewer offered an apt summary: "Major mental muddle melodramatized."

Jackson would always insist—as she did to a reporter who profiled her for *The Knickerbocker News*—that Elizabeth was not clinically insane; the diagnosis was actually "hysteria," the all-purpose female malady of the nineteenth and early twentieth centuries. "they made [Elizabeth] into a lunatic, which she can't be, by definition," she complained of the film. If Elizabeth was a lunatic, so was Jackson. So were virtually all the other women of her generation.

13.

DOMESTIC DISTURBANCES

RAISING DEMONS,
1954–1957

"One who raises demons . . . must deal with them."
—*The Bird's Nest*

JACKSON HAD PREDICTED THAT ONCE SHE FINISHED *THE Bird's Nest*—"fiendish book"—she would "sleep for a year." In fact, she was forced to embark immediately upon a new project: a short chapter book for the Random House Landmark young-adult history and biography series, a recent initiative spearheaded by Bennett Cerf. The other authors in the series were of a high caliber—former *New Republic* editor Bruce Bliven contributed a book about the American Revolution; Sterling North wrote a biography of Lincoln—and the gig was cushy: the books tended to earn significant royalties, and Jackson's would be no exception. In March 1953, Cerf proposed that Jackson contribute a history of the Salem witch trials, and she eagerly accepted: she already had "enough of a library on the subject to get the material easily." Even though she was likely unaware of the extent to which she was personally implicated—the FBI closed its file on her husband the previous year, shortly after the Hymans returned to Bennington—she was further

Shirley Jackson and her children in the dining room at 66 Main Street. Photograph by Erich Hartmann, 1956.

energized by the persecution of American Communists undertaken by Joseph McCarthy, the senator who lent his name to an entire era. Now, because of her problems writing *The Bird's Nest*, the children's book was overdue. Amazingly, despite her condition. she managed to write it in about a month "by a kind of dogged grinding out."

The Witchcraft of Salem Village has a somewhat stilted tone—writing for older children doesn't seem to have come naturally to Jackson. (She would eventually write two charming and engaging picture books, *Nine Magic Wishes* and *Famous Sally*.) But what's striking about *Witchcraft*, its lackluster style notwithstanding, is Jackson's attention not only to the phenomenon of witch hunting, but also to the social context in which it flourished. The witch trials, as she demonstrates, did not come out of nowhere: they were the product of the specific circumstances of the Massachusetts Bay Colony in general and Salem Village in particular. Likewise, the women who were targeted were not accidental victims, but social outcasts or others outside the mainstream. Her emphasis on these themes, novel at the time, anticipates a number of more recent treatments of the witch trials. As for the McCarthyism connection, which no contemporaneous reader could have failed to see, Jackson herself thought it was too obvious even to mention. "The main trouble will lie in making the book *not* a comment on the present day; the parallels are uncomfortably close," she observed.

In 1692, when the witchcraft frenzy began, the entire Massachusetts colony was "disturbed and uneasy," Jackson writes. The new English governor had revoked the colony's charter, rumors of war with France were in the air, taxes were punitive, and the colonists were even under attack by pirates. Daily life in the village was difficult, requiring hard labor and adherence to strict rules: no dancing, no toys for the children (seen as possible tools for witches), and two lengthy church services every Sunday. This community under stress was fertile ground for the preachings of Cotton Mather and other clergy who warned about the devil's personal impact on people's lives. Even the villagers' weekly routine facilitated the spread of rumors, because residents who lived on the outskirts did not have time to go home between morning and afternoon church services and normally spent that period visiting their neighbors, spreading news and gossip.

As Jackson tells it—her account, though novelistic, sticks closely to the historical facts—the trouble began when a group of village girls, including the daughter of minister Samuel Parris, began spending time with Tituba, the Parris household's West Indian slave, who read their palms and told them about witchcraft. Soon they began to behave strangely: falling suddenly into fits, seeing nightmarish figures, screaming that they were being poked by invisible hands. In addition to Tituba, they pointed fingers at several other village women, among them Sarah Goode and Sarah Osburn. "They could not have chosen better," Jackson remarks mordantly. Sarah Goode's reputation was "already doubtful"; she was poor and wandered begging from door to door, acting "half crazy." Sarah Osburn "spent a large part of her time sick in bed, and everyone knew her for a cross, disagreeable old woman whose house was always in disorder." It was no accident that the girls had singled out this pair: "Their mothers had surely talked among themselves of the shiftlessness of Sarah Goode, and the slovenliness of Sarah Osburn, and had perhaps even told one another that such behavior was the devil's handiwork." Although the tone of this book is entirely objective and political rather than personal, Jackson must have been thinking also of a certain contemporary New England woman who, Hester Prynne–like, was sometimes the target of village gossip, who was said to keep a disorderly home, and who felt herself to be on the margins of a closed society. Later the targets would be even more defenseless: a mostly deaf elderly woman and a five-year-old girl sent to prison along with her mother.

The combination of political tension and fear of the devil—uncannily similar to the fear of communism that infected 1950s America like an evil spell—formed an explosive mix that generated "uncontrollable hysteria." The afflicted girls wandered around the village "like a kind of sideshow, giving performances wherever they had an audience." The girls may have truly believed that they were being tormented by witches; or they may have simply realized that to say so was "a wonderful way of attracting attention." On an emotional level, Jackson also emphasizes how exciting the spectacle must have been, both for the girls who were allegedly afflicted and for the other children watching, who had been taught that witches were "as concretely dangerous as sickness or broken bones or storms which might bring trees crashing down upon the houses." (Joseph McCarthy, too, clearly relished the fame and national attention that the Senate hearings brought him.) Within five months, more than two hundred people would be imprisoned.

The problem, of course, was that there was no way to argue against the evidence presented. Anyone who defended or even sympathized with the accused witches was automatically suspected of being a witch herself. (Men made up only a small proportion of the accused.) Clergymen incited the villagers against one another, urging them to expose anyone who had slighted them in any way. One woman was arrested because her friends remembered a quarrel she had had years ago with her husband. "As in all such epidemics where there is no actual disease germ to be communicated, the sickness was not controllable," Jackson writes. "Everyone was in danger, because no one . . . has ever spent a lifetime cautiously enough to escape all criticism." When one of the afflicted girls admitted she had been lying, her friends accused her of being a witch herself; her only defense was to recant. By September 22, 1692, twenty people had been executed—insisting all the while upon their innocence. An unknown number died in jail. Paradoxically, those who confessed to witchcraft were spared, as long as they denounced their accomplices—in contrast to McCarthy's victims, who were generally blacklisted whether they confessed or not.

As quickly as it began, the epidemic ended: "People simply stopped believing that their friends and neighbors were witches." But the harm to the colony could not be repaired, just as the shadow of McCarthyism created an enduring fear of "Reds" that would loom over the American political theater for decades. So many people had fled Salem to avoid unjust accusation that the population of the village declined precipitously. The residents had been so focused on witch hunting that they neglected planting, cultivating, taking care of the roads, and all the other chores necessary to maintain a society. Food became scarce and taxes rose even higher. Salem Village slowly decayed; it no longer exists on the map. (The town that now stands in its place, five miles from Salem proper, is called Danvers.) Though twelve of the jurors in the trials publicly asked for forgiveness, the names of the accused witches were not formally cleared until 1957—the year after *The Witchcraft of Salem Village* was published.

Apart from an afterword describing the history of the church's persecution of witches, Jackson restricts her book to the historical context of Salem Village. But the similarity between the wild accusations of the Salem Village girls and the persecution of American Communists—a germ that had infected her own household—was clear. The term "witch hunt" was used in connection with McCarthyism as early as 1950. *The*

Crucible, in which Arthur Miller used the witch trials as an allegory for Red-baiting, was first produced in 1953. Like his predecessors among the Salem witch hunters, McCarthy claimed that the community was being infiltrated from within by a potentially fatal menace; he was aided by a credulous popular press that spread and amplified his rumors; and he inflicted damage upon countless innocents who were convicted in the court of popular opinion based on the most circumstantial evidence. In *The Witchcraft of Salem Village,* Jackson lamented that the automatic assumption of guilt by association made it difficult for "intelligent and thoughtful people to stop a great popular hatred like the hatred toward the witches." She might easily have substituted "Communists."

Even if she was happily oblivious to the fact that her neighbors in Westport and North Bennington had been asked to inform on her household, Jackson nonetheless knew about McCarthyism at first hand. Walter Bernstein, as she was well aware, was among the screenwriters targeted in the late 1940s by the House Committee on Un-American Activities; for years after that, he had to work under a pseudonym, if at all. (Stanley's telephone calls to Bernstein were one element that stoked the FBI's interest in the Hyman household.) Shirley and Stanley's acquaintance Marc Blitzstein, the composer and Broadway librettist who was among the early supporters of the *Negro Quarterly,* was also called before the committee to testify. A decade later, Blitzstein, who was homosexual, would be murdered by a sailor he had propositioned in a bar in Martinique—the victim of another form of persecution that was no less repugnant to Jackson and Hyman, who bitterly mourned his death.

In a letter she sent to children who wrote to her after reading *The Witchcraft of Salem Village,* which was included in a later edition of the book, Jackson alluded to Salem's message for the present day. Witchcraft, she wrote, has lost its power to terrify: "If the bewitched children of Salem Village came screaming and writhing into a modern courtroom, it would probably be assumed . . . that they were the willing victims of a new teenage dance craze." But if "fashions in fear change," people do not. The intelligent are in the minority, their measured voices in constant danger of being drowned out by the din of the mob. "We are not more tolerant or more valiant than the people of Salem, and we are just as willing to do battle with an imaginary enemy," she wrote resignedly. "The people of Salem hanged and tortured their neighbors from a deep conviction that they were right to do so. Some of our own deepest convictions may be as false. We might say that we have far more to be afraid of today than the people of Salem ever dreamed of, but that would not really be true. We have exactly the same thing to be afraid of—the demon in men's minds which prompts hatred and anger and fear, an irrational demon which shows a different face to every generation, but never gives up in his fight to win over the world."

AFTER COMPLETING *The Witchcraft of Salem Village*, Jackson succumbed to a state of extreme exhaustion. "i've been feeling very tired and depressed for most of the summer," she confessed to her parents in the fall of 1954. Dutiful as she was, she generally sent updates on the household at regular intervals, in spite of her mother's constant carping; now, she hadn't written to Geraldine and Leslie in months. It wasn't personal, she explained; she had been "working off my wild writing schedule last winter" and hadn't been able to muster "energy or spirit to write" anything at all, not even letters. She finally went to see Dr. Oliver Durand, the local general practitioner, who told her that she simply needed rest and prescribed her sleeping pills—likely Seconal, a powerful barbiturate used widely in the early 1950s. "so i've been sleeping ten hours a night and a good part of the day, and spending the rest of my time doing just as little as possible."

She could afford to do so, because money was still coming in: the movie rights for *The Bird's Nest*, a substantial royalty check for *Savages*, plus a lucrative assignment from *Life* magazine for—inevitably—a family story, with a deadline months away. And *Savages'* popularity meant that Bernice Baumgarten could sell just about anything Jackson gave her, even old stories dusted off from the drawer: one went to *McCall's* for $2000, Jackson's first sale to that high-paying publication. By the end of 1954, she was beginning to feel calmer, "eating and sleeping again like other people," but she was still not ready to write. The article for *Life*, normally a week's work, took her two months to finish. Her pace would not be back to normal for another year.

Stanley was sometimes supportive—he took Shirley out to dinner to celebrate the sale to *McCall's*. Knowing how financially necessary her writing was, however, he quickly grew impatient with her lack of productivity. His own cure for Shirley's problems was to fill up her schedule, giving her lists of books to read and even signing her up for singing lessons at the college, something she had talked about doing but never undertaken. With her customary light tone, Shirley told her parents that "stanley says he is going to kill oliver [Durand] for deciding that my jitters were due to overwork, because now i am all calm and collected again i still don't work, and he wants oliver to find something that he can diagnose as underwork." Geraldine was initially sympathetic. "You were trying to do too much—writing all night and taking care of kids all day," she wrote back. "You are the hub of your whole family . . . so keep yourself as well as you can. Without their mother around your whole family will fall flat on their little faces." But she, too, worried about the Hymans' finances—perhaps suspecting that she and Leslie might be asked for another loan. "When do you start the next novel?" she was soon asking. "Better hurry up and get started. Christmas will be here before you know it."

Despite the pressure, Shirley was not yet able to begin a new novel. Instead, she spent the fallow period absorbed in family life—which was good for a few stories, as always—and planning the sequel to *Savages*, which "obviously . . . must be called 'On the Raising of Demons.'" She and the children started a garden, with raspberry bushes and radishes and carrots and lilacs. Barry, age three, had largely recovered from the asthma and pneumonia that had plagued him as a baby and was revealing his personality as a gentle, easygoing child: "our small clown," Shirley called him. Sarah, now six, had begun to read in earnest and was placing her own rare-book orders with Louis Scher of the Seven Bookhunters. While Joanne was away at camp, Sarah spent the summer of 1955 working her way through Shirley's entire collection of Oz books, staying up all night to read and sleeping during the day. Joanne, a precocious nine-year-old, discovered dancing and, along with the rest of America, Elvis Presley. Shirley was surprised to find that she enjoyed his music too, though

Joanne, Laurence, Barry, and Sarah, c. 1956.

she would come to prefer the hit "Blueberry Hill," by Fats Domino, the rhythm-and-blues singer-songwriter and pianist. "i actually like rock and roll," she wrote to her parents—perhaps hoping to shock them—"and every evening while i am making dinner . . . laurie puts on my fats domino records, and everyone else goes away and shuts all doors and tries to listen to armstrong or presley, but fats domino can drown out any of them."

At age twelve, Laurence continued to disappoint Shirley with his lack of interest in academics, but he had discovered two new skills: carpentry and baseball. "since we have been in despair all these years because he could hardly read and write, it's nice to discover that he does have some kind of a talent," Shirley wrote wryly. North Bennington established its first Little League, which attracted both faculty and local families, making some progress toward resolving the long-standing cold war between the college and the village. (It helped that the faculty contributed generously to the creation of a baseball field.) "Our whole family life is completely tied up with the Little League," she wrote proudly to Baumgarten, sending the scores from Laurence's games in lieu of stories.

Laurence also took up the trumpet, and it was quickly apparent that he had considerable talent for that as well. Shirley and Stanley decided that he ought to hear "some real jazz," so in the spring of 1956 they took him on a tour of New York City nightclubs. The first stop was the Metropole, "loud and noisy," with two different bands. Then Jimmy Ryan's, "small and very fancy," where Laurence was initially denied entry: Stanley persuaded the management that he and Shirley were the boy's parents and would not let him drink "anything stronger than coke." Next was Nick's, where the manager recognized Shirley and Stanley from their days in Greenwich Village and seated them at the front table, practically underneath the band. "stanley kept having to duck his head because he was right under the trombone and laurie was delighted, because he was about two feet away from the trumpet player." When they finished playing, she and Stanley were "limp," but Laurence was "applauding wildly." They ended the night at Eddie Condon's. "at one in the morning we looked at laurie and he was sound asleep sitting up at the table, but we nearly had to drag him out to get him home," Shirley wrote. "he kept asking to stay for just one more number."

Much of this material found its way into magazine stories: Farrar, Straus was encouraging Shirley to put together a sequel to the wildly successful *Savages*. The company was preparing to celebrate its tenth anniversary in the fall of 1956, and Roger Straus hoped to have a new Shirley Jackson book as "an additional plume" in his hat. With the provisional title *On Raising Demons* (later the "On" was dropped, against Shirley's wishes), the book again included a nod to her studies in witchcraft, with an epigraph describing the conjuration of demons taken from the Grimoire of Honorius, a compendium of magical knowledge from around 1800. Otherwise, the book's demons were entirely of the household variety: Laurie and Jannie, moving steadily into adolescence; Sally, absorbed more and more deeply by her own imaginary world (one of the book's reviewers called her "a little chip off the old broomstick"); and Barry, her sidekick and ready accomplice.

Jackson stuck closely to the winning formula she had developed in *Savages*: breezy tales of mostly harmless misadventures, relayed by a mother who is reassuringly self-deprecating with regard to her own imperfections.

As the children grew older, they could no longer be relied upon for ador-able material, so Jackson increasingly sought out the humor in her own predicaments. *Demons* opens with a hilarious account of the stress of mov-ing, from the cryptic abbreviations the moving company uses on its list of the family's furniture and other possessions (with some difficulty, Shir-ley and the children figure out that "S. & M." stands for "scratched and marred," "M.E." for "moth-eaten," and so on) to the furious phone calls required in order to get the items delivered to the new house. A scene in which she repeatedly telephones the man in charge of the company, only to be told by his secretary (a moment after she hears his voice on the line) that he is away for the day or otherwise indisposed, seems too funny to be true, but in fact it comes almost verbatim from a letter Jackson wrote to a former neighbor in Westport asking for advice on how to handle her prob-lems with the local moving company. All she changed was the man's name.

More often, though, Jackson transformed the stories with a fictional twist. In an episode in which she takes a rare weekend away, she leaves behind a seemingly random stream-of-consciousness memo of instruc-tions ("Barry Sunday breakfast cereal, bottle, lunch applesauce, cats milk Sunday morning, milk in refrigerator, did you leave casserole in oven Sat-urday night?"), which Stanley ignores, taking the children out to the ham-burger stand instead. A note she actually once left before a solo trip, which included detailed descriptions of how to light the stove and prepare coffee, demonstrates just how unfamiliar Stanley was with the workings of the kitchen, like so many men of his era. (When in doubt, Shirley told him, ask Laurence where the food is.) Blatantly disregarding her mother's advice, Jackson played up her own distraction in an episode in which she wakes up at ten thirty one morning to discover that the three older children have wandered off on their own, Sally telling the milkman that their mother has "gone to Fornicalia to live" and Jannie informing a friend's mother that she had gotten no breakfast because Shirley "had not come home until way, way late last night." In another of the book's funnier moments, Shirley receives a birthday card in the mail at the wrong time of year and puzzles over who the sender could be (a person with "almost illiterate" handwrit-ing who is so cheap as to use two-cent stamps) until she realizes that she accidentally sent to herself a card she intended for Stanley's great-aunt.

All the comedy notwithstanding, *Demons* is pervaded by an under-current of anxiety that was absent in *Savages*. Much of the anxiety has to do with money: despite the Hymans' improved financial situation, there is still never quite enough of it. Stanley keeps tabs on the cash, and Shirley resorts to subterfuge (sometimes with the children's collusion) to win his consent for the purchase of any big-ticket item. Grocery money can be wrung out of him only "by a series of agile arguments and a tear-ful description of his children lying at his feet faint from malnutrition." In order to get the electric razor she wants to give him for Father's Day, she has to buy it from the electric company and charge it to their bill, in installments. After her car is totaled in an accident, he grumbles about replacing it but finally gives in: "since we were in debt for the rest of our lives anyway with the house payments we might as well buy a car too and go bankrupt in style."

No casual reader of this book would dream that Jackson had actually outearned Hyman for years. With the success of *Savages*, the disparity in their incomes dramatically increased. In addition to his Bennington sal-ary, which went up to $5200 in 1955, Hyman still got a weekly "drawing account" from *The New Yorker* of around $75 a week for his work on Com-ments and "Talk of the Town," as well as for the short book reviews he was still regularly writing. But the real money to be made at the magazine was in profiles and other journalistic articles, which, despite his efforts, were not his métier. Though Hyman's contract was renewed every year, he was only ever able to get a few long pieces into *The New Yorker*, to his great chagrin. An article he submitted in 1953, about the time capsule buried during the construction of the 1939 New York World's Fair, was deemed to be in such bad shape that another staffer was tasked with rewriting it; he and Hyman shared the byline. Hyman's last published reported piece, a humorous account of a visit to the Seminars on American Culture at Cooperstown, appeared in 1954. By 1958, he was once again in arrears to the magazine. In 1959–1960, he spent more than a year working on a pro-file of Jackie Robinson, the second baseman who made baseball history as the first African American to play in the major leagues. William Shawn accepted the piece, but it never ran in *The New Yorker*. The profile finally appeared in *The New Leader* in 1997, long after Hyman's death.

Meanwhile, Jackson seemed able to turn just about anything into a moneymaking opportunity. In 1956, the Hymans were audited; while Stanley went over the figures with the man from the IRS, Shirley listened from the kitchen, making notes. "if i can sell the story we break even," she told her parents. (The piece didn't sell, but she made use of it in *Demons*.) "Nothing is ever wasted; all experience is good for something," she would later advise in her lecture "Experience and Fiction." In addition to her advances, royalties, and magazine sales, foreign rights were proving a significant source of revenue: *Savages* appeared in German, Italian, Norwegian, and Swedish, among other languages. Hyman's income for 1956 totaled around $9900; Jackson's was greater than $14,000.

In public, Hyman admitted only pride in Jackson's earnings; he sometimes even bragged that his wife made more money than he did. Jackson, too, was openly proud of her earning power, especially in front of her parents, who had so often seen her in debt (and helped to bail her out). But she resented the amount of control he kept over their finances—as well as his criticism whenever he found her devoting time to a non-moneymaking activity, such as writing letters to relatives or friends. At one point he justified the purchase of a new dishwasher by rationalizing that every minute Jackson saved on doing housework was "potential writing time." When *Savages* was on the best-seller list in the summer of 1953, Jackson bragged that "stanley cannot say a word about my writing such a long letter; he usually protests that all these pages would make a story." Many of these remarks may have been made in jest, but there was a serious undertone. Later, at a crisis in their relationship, Shirley would accuse Stanley of sabotaging her literary work by forcing her to write magazine stories for money.

The financial pressure added to the stress on Shirley and Stanley's delicately balanced marriage. In *Savages*, Stanley appeared as a kind of accidental bumbler, but in *Demons*, the tensions between him and Shirley are readily apparent. In addition to depicting him as cheap, Jackson alludes more than once to his infidelities. In one story, after a longtime female friend of Stanley's announces her intention to come for an overnight visit, he unsubtly suggests that Shirley clean the house from top to bottom and prepare a special dinner—which she does, grumbling, as he sings the other woman's praises. (In a stroke of luck for Shirley, the woman's trip is canceled at the last minute.) In another of the stories, based on an actual incident, Stanley is invited to judge the Miss Vermont contest, which involves traveling to Burlington to spend several days in the presence of a group of nubile young beauties. Shirley claims she finds the whole idea hilarious, but she finds a way to twist the knife. In one scene, the whole family is discussing the beauty pageant at the lunch table:

> "Daddy is going to see a lot of girls," Sally told Barry. She turned to me. "Daddy likes to look at girls, doesn't he?"
>
> There was a deep, enduring silence, until at last my husband's eye fell on Jannie.
>
> "And what did you learn in school today?" he asked with wild enthusiasm.

Some of the critics who reviewed *Demons*—both men and women—found this depiction overly exaggerated, as it likely was. Writing in the *Houston Post*, Derland Frost complained that Jackson portrayed her husband as "the classically dogmatic but essentially simpleminded buffoon whose main purpose in life seems to be to allow himself to be outwitted by wife and children." Another reviewer wished that "the author's husband had won more of a role than that of somehow hanging ominously over the dazzling prospect of every new purchase." And a few noted the uncommon acidity of the segment about being a faculty wife, an angry piece originally published in the Bennington alumnae magazine, in which Jackson suggests that only Bluebeard, the fairy-tale aristocrat who murders his wives and hides their bodies in a room in his castle, would make a worse husband than a professor. The admissions director, concerned that the article portrayed Bennington too negatively, had all the copies of the magazine removed from display during commencement; Jackson informed her sweetly that she had already sold the piece to *Mademoiselle*.

As she had in *Savages*, in *Demons* Jackson again conceals her identity as a writer. In the story about moving, she notes that the family's possessions include "typewriters," plural, but Stanley is the only person ever depicted using one. She often presents herself as at a loss for what to do with herself when the children are out of the house. Preparing Barry's winter clothing for school—he entered kindergarten in the fall of 1956—Shirley realizes sadly "how strange it was going to be now during the long empty mornings." When she drops him off, he is immediately so engrossed in the classroom toys that he doesn't even hear her say good-bye. "I drove home very slowly because I had plenty of time before I had to pick him up at eleven-thirty and when I got home at last I went and sat in the study and listened to the furnace grumbling down cellar and the distant ticking of the alarm clock up on my dresser." That "sat in the study" is the only hint that she will use the extra time for work.

In *The Feminine Mystique*, Friedan myopically criticized Jackson as part of "a new breed of women writers" who wrote about themselves as if they were "'just housewives,' reveling in a comic world of children's pranks and eccentric washing machines and Parents' Night at the PTA." By depicting her days as if they were restricted to housework and child care, Friedan wrote, Jackson played a role analogous to that of Amos and Andy, dressing up an ugly truth in the costume of comedy. "Do real housewives then dissipate in laughter their dreams and their sense of desperation?" Friedan asked. "Do they think their frustrated abilities and their limited lives are a joke?" Jean Campbell Jones, in *Saturday Review*, sounded a similar note, lamenting that "somehow one expects more of Miss Jackson, who has after all, in her pre–Little League days, done some memorable short stories" (though Jones also called the book a "shrewd and witty social document" as well as a "fresh and beguiling family chronicle)." And another female critic noted aptly that "if Miss Jackson's role as wife and mother . . . had actually been quite as continuously hectic as the book implies, the book never would have got itself written."

In Jackson's defense, one could argue that she didn't have to tell her readers that she was a writer—the evidence was right there on the page. Failing to read between the lines, Friedan and Jones also overlook the genuinely subversive element of Jackson's family chronicles. Part of the joke is that Jackson herself is an inept housewife—and thus she implicitly deflates the expectation that every woman must fulfill that role. She pokes fun, also, at the idea that her children ought to be at the center of her universe, unashamed of her delight at taking a weekend away or her need for two martinis to get through the dinner hour. For Edmund Fuller, again an admiring critic who enjoyed *Demons* as much as he had *Savages*, Jackson's gift for mining "the humor of frustration" distinguished the book. "Some such humorous family chronicles are essentially on the saccharine side—but not this one, for the author's merriment has a distinctly tart and tangy flavor," he wrote.

For the most part, critics were won over by Jackson's unsentimental realism, many agreeing with Farrar that the book was even better than its predecessor. By now most reviewers were no longer surprised that she should be the author of books in two wholly distinct genres, although one called her a "writer with two heads." While some found the children too charming to be true, most were utterly convinced that Jackson was depicting her own household. "310 pages from life," wrote Paul Molloy breezily in the *Chicago Sun-Times*. Another critic noted that Jackson's "charm in writing lies in her ability to bring her reader into her home." Many emphasized how typically American the family was—somewhat surprising, in a country still rife with tacit anti-Semitism, considering that Shirley's identity as "Mrs. Stanley Hyman" was often mentioned: "an unusual but not really so different American family"; "as normal as hot dogs . . . the stuff that Americana is made of." The political reporter Mary McGrory, in an example of a truly poor match between reviewer and subject, may have been the only critic who had no sympathy for *Demons* whatsoever. McGrory, who had covered the Army-McCarthy hearings for the *Washington Star*, found *Demons* all too realistic: the book made her feel, she wrote, like "someone trapped on a sofa immobilized by a doorstep [sic]-sized family album and a relentless, acid commentator." McGrory concluded that Jackson "ought to go back to frightening people frankly"—otherwise, "impressionable girls reading her unvarnished recital of domestic life might take a vow of spinsterhood."

What makes *Demons* feel so genuine—and to some degree counteracts Jackson's apparent bitterness toward Hyman—is her fascination with the children: their conversation, their ideas, their particular talents and desires. "The savages are older and more sophisticated now," wrote Lewis Gannett in the *New York Herald Tribune*, but "the mood is the same: mingled awe, fatigue, exasperation and affection." Others commented on the tone of nostalgia that characterizes some of the stories, though Jackson usually tempers it with just enough bite to keep them feeling realistic. The children are indeed growing up, and with their newfound independence comes a palpable longing—their own and their mother's—to hold on to things the way they are. The book's conclusion is an unapologetically sweet Christmas story that lovingly recounts the Hyman family traditions: the electric lights held together by a generation's worth of tire tape, the ornaments that belonged to Shirley's grandmother, the children's sheer joy in it all. The story ends with what Straus called, with his characteristic hyperbole, "the two best lines any book ever ended with": as Sally says "Last Christmas—," Barry interrupts her with "Next Christmas—." A mother must always be dizzyingly Janus-faced, simultaneously looking ahead at what is to come and backward at what has gone before. Her constancy, even in the face of change, keeps everything in place.

SHIRLEY'S INCREASING HEALTH problems were another aspect of her life that she omitted from *Demons*. Rarely thin even as an adolescent, in her late twenties and thirties she had increasingly put on weight. Although she loved fresh vegetables, which reminded her of her childhood in California, and would splurge on avocados and artichokes if they were available at the grocery store, the food she typically cooked tended to be high in calories: meatballs, cube steak, the potato pancakes and potato kugel (pudding) that Stanley's mother had taught her to make. "it's not a real potato pudding unless [you grate] a couple of knuckles into it," she once wrote, sounding like a typical Jewish mother. "It was the standard American diet," Barry remembers. "There was always enough to eat and it was good. And whatever we wanted to eat, we weren't denied. . . . She loved to serve food, she loved to eat, and she loved to see people eat." Shirley took pride in her cooking and tried to find the best ingredients available in North Bennington: other children had sandwiches on mass-produced Wonder Bread, but the Hymans' sandwiches were made with Pepperidge Farm. She paid attention to the smallest details: when she put butter on toast, she spread it all the way to the corners. The days of food coloring in the mashed potatoes were long past, yet Shirley did invent some creative dishes. Her recipe for "spiced meatballs" included mustard, chili sauce, and pickle juice. Sarah's favorite dinner was something Shirley called "turkey Sallies," a cream cheese pastry dough stuffed with a meat and sour cream filling. She enjoyed baking as well—her grandmother's recipe for nut cake was a staple. "She liked being in the kitchen and having smells like that in the house," remembers Laurence.

The family ate together most nights, and the large oval dining table was the setting for some of the children's most enduring memories, such as the year Shirley and Stanley read the Bible aloud after dinner, a chapter each night. Sometimes all the Hymans would head down to the Rainbarrel, North Bennington's only real restaurant, run by a French-Algerian couple whom they befriended. Once Laurence was old enough to be responsible for the younger children, Shirley and Stanley regularly went out to dinner on their own, and they would happily drive twenty miles or more to try a new restaurant or patronize an old favorite. When they visited New York, they went out for food that was exotic at the time: fried rice, tacos, shish kebab, schnitzel, stuffed grape leaves. Brendan Gill, who unkindly described Shirley as "a classic fat girl, with the fat girl's air of clowning frivolity to mask no telling what depths of unexamined self-loathing," remembered eating breakfast with her and Stanley at the Royalton Hotel, down the street from *The New Yorker*'s offices on West Forty-Fourth Street, where Stanley always stayed while visiting the magazine. As Gill recalled, "Each of them ordered and ate a substantial breakfast of orange juice, buckwheat cakes with maple syrup, buttered toast, and coffee; then they ordered and ate the same breakfast again. They got up hungry."

Gill's story sounds exaggerated. (How could he know they "got up hungry"?) Others, however, have also testified to both Shirley's and Stanley's large appetites. Stanley, who enjoyed food no less than his wife, was seriously overweight for much of his life. Kenneth Burke recalled that when they ate together in the cafeteria at Bennington, Stanley would choose meat and potatoes while Burke, who prided himself on a healthy diet, ate only vegetables—a habit to which he later credited his long life. (He died in 1993, at ninety-six.) Carol Brandt, who would become Shirley's agent and friend after Bernice Baumgarten retired at the end of 1957, believed that Stanley deliberately encouraged Shirley to eat fattening foods as a form of aggression, perhaps "for reasons of professional jealousy." When the three of them lunched together in New York, Brandt said, "he would . . . urge food on her. Thick cream pies. . . . I had to watch him stuffing her like a goose." Shirley, for her part, did not try to rein him in until much later. "our doctor (who never gains a pound) shakes his finger warningly under our noses and we glance gleefully at one another and call to make a reservation at l'auberge [a favorite restaurant]." Stanley would not attempt to lose weight until 1964, after a serious health scare.

Despite the pressure her mother put on her to lose weight, Shirley's early attempts at dieting were desultory. In her high school diaries, she would confess to eating an entire box of chocolates and then resolve to lose weight. She tried again in 1950, when the "fancy doctor" she saw in Westport started her on Dexamyl, but that effort was derailed when she became pregnant with Barry the following year. In an unpublished essay likely written around the time of that pregnancy, she declared that she was done with worrying about her weight. "i have suddenly realized that i am fat, plump, stout, heavy, matronly, oversized, better-than-average, obese, and rotund," she wrote cheerfully. "far from being the sleek trim character in the ads, i am the one they deal with in 'matronly dresses, fifth floor.' " (Shirley's taste in clothes, which tended to long, flowing dresses in bright colors, emphasized her bulk.) So what if Laurence's friends made fun of him because his mother was fat, as he confessed over the dinner table one night? Their mothers thought about little other than their weight, and it made them miserable. Every once in a while their obsession—"calories are small demons which lurk constantly on the outskirts of the unguarded life"— infected her: when Laurence made such a remark, for instance, or when she tried to buy a new dress from an eighteen-year-old salesgirl, or "when any one of the thousand small humiliations . . . in stock for us portlies slaps me in the face." (Her story "Mrs. Melville Makes a Purchase," in which a plus-size woman suffers various indignities while shopping for clothing, is a masterpiece in detailing such humiliations.) Then she resolves to have salad for lunch and avoid the usual "small odds and ends at bedtime"—and promptly gives in. The trouble is that she simply loves "the beautiful and lovely and fascinating foods mankind has devoted himself to inventing since he first learned to heat up meat . . . the wonderful imported candies, the elaborate desserts, the rich sauces, the cheese and potatoes and creams and sweets." Stanley's *New Yorker* colleague Gardner Botsford would tell of a night spent at an inn with the Hymans in a suite of rooms that shared a connecting bathroom. Late at night, Botsford was awakened by the sound of their raucous laughter from the bathroom. Initially puzzled, he realized at last that they were weighing themselves—and finding the results hilarious.

Even though Shirley inveighed against "the claptrap . . . that the overweight are more mortal than others," she had to acknowledge that her weight made her susceptible to heart disease, high blood pressure, or "any one of half a dozen frightful prospects." The time finally came, in September 1956, a few months before her fortieth birthday, when Dr. Durand warned her that her weight and her blood pressure were much too high: at around five feet seven inches, she was well over 200 pounds. (By various estimates, she would eventually weigh as much as 250.) He sketched out a strict weight-loss plan amounting to about a thousand calories a day. Breakfast was to include toast, coffee, grapefruit juice, and maybe a scrambled egg; for lunch and dinner, she was allowed a small serving of lean meat, fish, or poultry with raw vegetables or juice.

Shirley threw herself into the diet with enthusiasm. She taped calorie counters to the kitchen walls and logged her meals in notebooks, keeping track even when she cheated: "SINFUL," in capital letters, appears next to a lunch of two cheeseburgers. She also doggedly recorded everything she drank—normally at least two or three cocktails or glasses of bourbon a night. "i figure i will just have to get the food down to fewer calories to make room for the cocktails," she wrote blithely. To her parents she described it as "a very lenient diet" that she would have no problem sticking with: "i gave up eating candy a long time ago, and have no trouble doing without desserts and sweets in general, but i do mind potatoes and bread." Fortunately, the pills Durand prescribed for her included "one of those relaxing dopes"—Miltown—which "does take the edge off that jumpy feeling you get when everyone else is eating potatoes." Geraldine offered encouragement: this was an area in which she had experience. "I know excess weight is hard on your heart and your blood pressure and I hated to see you using yourself so badly," she wrote. "Try nonfat milk. It isn't bad if you want to like it. And it is fun if you make it so to count calories." Baumgarten wrote that Shirley's plan for apportioning calories between food and alcohol seemed so sensible that it almost—almost—gave her the courage to try it herself. (Margaret Cousins, at *Good Housekeeping*, was another professional contact with whom Shirley bonded over their mutual weight-loss struggles.)

After three weeks, Shirley had lost four pounds; her blood pressure was also lower. She vowed to keep at it for a year. Stanley was not yet ready to join her, but he promised her a new fur coat if she got down to a size twelve (roughly the equivalent of a present-day six), a sign either that he believed such an achievement worthy of a rare extravagance or that he never thought she would manage it. In fact, she did not. In November 1956, with the family birthday season in full swing, she started to slip: "sinful" appears more and more frequently in her diet log. However, by the following February, she had lost about twenty pounds, putting her below 200. She was still dieting the following summer, although losing "slowly." There were many slips, especially during the summer break. But Shirley more than kept her word, mostly sticking with the diet through the spring of 1958, though she eventually gave up. "stanley and i are a pair of stout, good-eating burghers," and she dieted only when she felt "conscience-stricken," she told a friend in 1960. "richness is all. . . . so it's hard to buy clothes. who needs clothes? my mother is a size eighteen but she never had any fun."

Dieting did not prevent Shirley from writing: she recorded the date she finished her first draft of *The Sundial* in her diet log (July 8, 1957), and notes for *The Haunting of Hill House* appear in another diet notebook. But it is sad to look at all the notebooks she neatly filled with meal plans and calorie calculations and imagine what else she might have written there had she not expended so much mental effort on losing weight. It is sad also because her effort was in vain: she would not succeed in keeping the weight off, and the image of her that persists is the overweight, homely, unkempt Shirley of her late years. Based on what is now believed about yo-yo dieting, the repeated efforts at weight loss may even have damaged her health; certainly whatever weight she managed to lose did not forestall her early death.

But more than that, food was important to Shirley, both in her personal life and in her writing. She felt at home in the kitchen and took pride in having all the latest appliances. "If you wanted to spend time with my mother, you would go to the kitchen. . . . It was always very comfortable and emotional, a warm and safe kind of place," Barry recalls. "There was comfort eating and comfort drinking and comfort coffee and comfort cigarettes. They were always consuming something. And enjoying it." In her early story "Like Mother Used to Make," the homemade pie baked by David and then appropriated by Marcia is a symbol of all the care he puts into his home. In "Dinner for a Gentleman," Mallie, a fairy godmother figure who appears in a number of Jackson's lighter stories, whips up a meal for a young woman to serve to a male dinner guest and leaves behind a magical cookbook filled with menus to be served during their future married life together. Meals prepared by Mrs. Dudley, the surprisingly good cook at Hill House, offer an oasis of consolation amid the psychological torments of the house. And *We Have Always Lived in the Castle* revolves around Constance's kitchen and the food she lovingly prepares there after the fateful meal involving arsenic in the sugar bowl.

It would be hard for almost anyone to stick to a diet of a thousand calories a day. It was especially hard for Shirley—who sent Vermont cheese and apples to acquaintances every fall, who loved to try new recipes and trade them with friends, who sought out delicacies in New York to show off at her parties—to deny herself this basic comfort. Yet she managed it for substantial periods of time, even under significant external stress.

———

THE HYMANS CELEBRATED Christmas 1956 with all the usual fanfare. Shirley had lost eighteen pounds since fall; as a concession to her diet, she drank bourbon while the others sipped eggnog. Laurence, showing off his carpentry skills, presented Stanley with a gigantic breakfront for the dining room in which he could store his collections; for Shirley, he made a special table for jigsaw puzzles with a cover to protect loose pieces. She and Stanley gave him a newfangled clock radio; there was a sewing machine for Joanne, a typewriter for Sarah, "who wants to be a writer," and a punching bag for Barry. "altogether, an elaborate and wild christmas," she recorded with satisfaction.

Soon afterward, though, Shirley noticed that something was troubling Sarah, always the strangest and most sensitive of the children. At first she wondered whether her younger daughter—"brilliantly intelligent," with moods that ranged from "wild and defiant" to "tender and perceptive"—was just going through a difficult developmental adjustment. Every day she came home from school, went straight to her room, and shut the door; when Shirley tried to coax her out, she would say she wasn't feeling well. When she did leave her room, she was "unbelievably cross," snapping at everyone, even Barry, to whom she was closest among the siblings. Always thin, she lost her appetite entirely, and often left the dinner table in tears after being told to eat. At night, she woke screaming from nightmares. Begging to stay home from school, she complained constantly of stomachaches, headaches, a sore throat, colds; at school, she made excuses to see the nurse. As a result, she missed a significant amount of schoolwork, and her grades began to drop. But when Shirley took her to Durand, she refused to cooperate, screaming "like a wild animal" when the doctor tried to draw her blood. With shades of *The Bird's Nest*, Shirley privately wondered "if she could possibly be demented, out of her mind." Durand tried to reassure her that there was nothing physically wrong with Sarah, nor, he suspected, mentally; but something was frightening her terribly. At bedtime, Shirley implored her to explain what was going on. "What can you do when you're so scared of something and you don't dare say what it is?" was all that her daughter would say. Shirley tried to console her, came downstairs, and "cried all over the story i was writing."

In early April 1957, Shirley got a call from the mother of one of Sarah's classmates. Had Sarah ever mentioned anything unusual about Florence Holden, the third-grade teacher? the woman wanted to know. Her son—whom she, too, had taken to the doctor because he was "generally not well"—had told her that Miss Holden was systematically abusing him and several other children in the class, including Sarah, who had been whipped with a yardstick and had a clothespin fastened to her ear. The teacher called her a liar and a thief, and made her stand in front of the class to be humiliated. Sarah still remembers the incident more than half a century later: "She was a bitter woman and she did not like me." Other children were tied to a metal beam in the room as punishment for "being naughty"; the teacher had allegedly even banged one boy's head into the radiator. They all were told that if they said anything to their parents or anyone else, their punishment would be even more severe.

The teacher's behavior was unjustifiable under any circumstances. But it is not surprising that Sarah was among the children singled out for punishment. When she felt like it, she could be captivating: after Shirley brought her to visit the literary agency Brandt & Brandt, Baumgarten wrote that Sarah had "the whole office in the palm of her hand." But she also had a rebellious streak. Laura Nowak, whose daughter Alison was in the same class, remembers Sarah as "the most mischievous" of the Hyman children. (Alison recalls her as "very intense . . . very intellectual.") Early in the term, she had come home wondering whether it was all right to correct the teacher's grammar. Shirley and Stanley told her not to, but that is no guarantee she obeyed.

Shirley and a group of other parents showed up unannounced at the next school board meeting, on April 17, demanding that Miss Holden be immediately dismissed. Shirley believed, naïvely, that no other response to the children's testimony was possible. "These poor little kids have been going along for months absolutely defenseless . . . at least now we may have given them some confidence that they will be protected and do not need to be afraid to tell about such things." Instead, the town split into factions. Miss Holden, generally well-liked, was a thirty-nine-year veteran who had taught the parents of some of Sarah's classmates. She was known to be a strict disciplinarian—in fact, the previous year she had been placed on probation for similar actions—but what child didn't deserve a little physical punishment from time to time? Many of the townspeople had come through her classroom; they had all survived, and so would their children. "When a teacher hit a kid, that was just expected back then," says Joanne.

The controversy, covered almost daily by the *Bennington Banner*, galvanized the insular village. By the following week, it was clear that Miss Holden's supporters outnumbered those who wanted her fired. The school board held another meeting at which the pro-Holden group submitted "letters of appreciation" for the teacher signed by more than fifty parents, testifying to her "integrity, diligence, and understanding." Meanwhile, the *Banner* portrayed the anti-Holden group, which numbered around twenty, as a small band of upstarts who had flouted the chain of command by disrupting a school board meeting rather than making their complaints privately to the principal. Miss Holden claimed that the boy who had hit his head on the radiator did so accidentally after she startled him when approaching to admonish him for not paying attention. Tensions were so high that the reporter who covered the tempest for the *Banner* found himself under fire for not giving sufficient space to the pro-Holden faction, despite the fact that his reporting was distinctly biased in their favor. In no article did he quote any of the parents who had made complaints.

In the end, Miss Holden suffered no consequences. She was allowed to finish the school term, and the following year she was eligible for retirement. Shirley felt just as she had when confronted with the "sweet-faced old lady" who had hit Laurence with her car in Westport. She was certain that her side was in the right: she knew Sarah and the other children were telling the truth, and she never dreamed that Miss Holden would be allowed to keep her job in the face of such obvious abuse. She and the other anti-Holden parents had been outnumbered, but they had also been outmaneuvered. She had underestimated the strength of the North Bennington village community, which closed ranks when challenged by a relative newcomer—all the goodwill generated by the Little League notwithstanding.

The author of "The Lottery" and *The Witchcraft of Salem Village* ought not to have been taken off guard by the way the locals banded together. Previously, the harassment Shirley and Stanley had endured was fairly minor: gossip about her housekeeping, the boozy parties they threw, their African-American friends. But it was one thing for the villagers to make her suffer and yet another for them to defend her daughter's abuser: like Hester Prynne in *The Scarlet Letter*, Shirley took punishment willingly on herself but fought fiercely to protect her children. After the school board incident, the harassment of the family became more vicious. The Hyman children remember finding garbage dumped in their yard and even swastikas soaped on the windows. It took Sarah several years to recover from the trauma of her abuse: by 1960, Shirley could finally report that she went off to school each day "without terror." Though her health and her interest in academics returned, she continued to struggle with authority through high school.

Shirley could not admit her defeat. She told her parents that "the old sadist had been bounced"; a few years later, recounting the episode to a friend, she said that the teacher had ended up "in an institution, of course." She did confess the truth to Baumgarten, who took her side completely and reassured her that one day it would make "a tremendous story." Shirley never would try to turn the episode into a story—she left unfinished the notes she made about it. But it infected the tone of much of her future writing, especially *We Have Always Lived in the Castle*, in which the villagers who torment Constance and Merricat are portrayed with particular venom. "The people of the village have always hated us," Merricat confides. As usual, the novel's setting is not identified, but in every way it suggests New England.

Jackson began her fourth novel, *The Sundial*, in the late fall of 1956 and finished writing it about nine months later, shortly after the school fracas. It seems especially influenced both by the threat she felt to her family's security and the generalized unease about the developing atomic age that was in full throttle by the mid-1950s. It is a novel about apocalypse—the characters all come to believe that the world is about to end—but also about control: like fish in an aquarium, they end up sealed inside the estate that serves as their fortress against what they imagine will happen. They are Jackson's most absurd group of characters, and she mercilessly milks the comedy from their grandiosity and pretension. But on another level she must have envied them. Eventually she, too, would shut herself within her house, barricaded against the chaos outside.

14.

WHAT IS THIS WORLD?

THE SUNDIAL,
1957–1958

"I keep figuring how it will be." She spoke very softly, very clearly, to a point just past him on the wall. . . . "Everything that makes the world like it is now will be gone. We'll have new rules and new ways of living."
— "The Intoxicated"

THE FIRST COMPLETED HYDROGEN BOMB WAS TESTED OFF Bikini Island in March 1954. A thousand times more powerful than the atomic bomb dropped on Hiroshima, the bomb generated a blast so strong that scientific instruments were unable fully to quantify its force. Its detonation rattled an island 176 miles away and shot a nuclear cloud more than forty thousand feet in the air—"thirty-two times the height of the Empire State Building," *The New York Times* reported. Americans got to see the bomb's force with their own eyes in *Operation Ivy*, a short documentary film made by the government to chronicle an earlier experimental test. In an apparent effort both to reassure the public about American superiority and to demonstrate the enormous power of nuclear weapons, President Eisenhower declassified the film and it was broadcast repeatedly on national television on April 1. As sailors watch from afar, a gigantic fireball engulfs the horizon, then fades into a slowly

Shirley Jackson, mid-1950s.

unfurling mushroom cloud. The sequence of the explosion is played twice for maximum effect. "The fireball alone," the film's narrator intones, "would engulf about one-quarter of the island of Manhattan."

While Americans worried about a hypothetical disaster at home, the bomb's repercussions could already be felt abroad. Meteorologists had miscalculated both the power of the explosion and the direction of the wind carrying radioactive fallout, which threatened two dozen American sailors on the Pacific island of Rongerik, more than two hundred people on the Marshall Islands, and the Japanese crew of a small fishing boat that happened, unluckily, to be in the area. One of the Japanese fishermen witnessed the explosion. "The sun's rising in the west!" he called to his shipmates. Two hours later, ashes began to rain down on them. By the time the boat pulled into port, several weeks later, many of the crew were suffering from radiation sickness; one eventually died.

Apocalypse was in the air, quite literally. A decade later, cultural critic Susan Sontag would argue that the citizens of the world suffered a collective trauma in the mid-twentieth century "when it became clear that, from now on to the end of human history, every person would spend his individual life under the threat not only of individual death, which is certain, but of something almost insupportable psychologically—collective incineration and extinction which could come at any time, virtually without warning." One expression of that trauma, Sontag wrote, was the sudden increase in science fiction films during the 1950s and 1960s, which often take nuclear war as a theme or a subtext. In *The War of the Worlds* (1953), based loosely on the H. G. Wells novel, creatures from Mars invade Earth because their planet has become too cold. In *The Incredible Shrinking Man* (1957), the main character is shrunk by a blast of radiation. *The Mysterians* (1959) features extraterrestrials who have destroyed their own planet with nuclear warfare. *The World, the Flesh and the Devil* (1959) is devoted to the Robinson Crusoe–style fantasy of occupying a deserted city and starting a new civilization. And the Soviet launch of Sputnik I in October 1957, kicking off the "space race," not only demonstrated the Soviet Union's superiority in the arms race, but also triggered enormous anxiety about new disasters that might rain down from the sky.

Despite the popularity of this genre in the 1950s, Jackson wrote only one published story that truly qualifies as science fiction: "Bulletin," a whimsical vignette from 1953 about a professor who travels ahead to the year 2123. His time machine returns empty but for a few fragmentary documents that show both how drastically the world has changed and how it hasn't, such as an American history exam that refers to "Roosevelt-san" and "Churchill III" and contains a list of true-or-false statements that includes "The cat was at one time tame, and used in domestic service." But in *The Sundial*, a social satire, she took the mood of impending apocalypse and turned it on its head.

The Sundial, Jackson said, was written from the inside out.

"Prominent in every book I had ever written was a little symbolic set that I think of as a heaven-wall-gate arrangement," she told an audience at Syracuse in the summer of 1957, shortly after finishing the manuscript. In each of her novels, she said, "I find a wall surrounding some forbidden, lovely secret, and in this wall a gate that cannot be passed." Somehow, she had never been able to get through the wall, and it occurred to her that the thing to do was to start from the inside and work her way out. "What happened, of course, was the end of the world. I had set myself up nicely within the wall inside a big strange house I found there, locked the gates behind me, and discovered that the only way to stay there with any degree of security was to destroy, utterly, everything outside."

Starting with *The Sundial*, each of Jackson's final three completed novels begins and ends with a house. Here it is the Halloran estate, built several generations earlier by the first Mr. Halloran and now occupied by dysfunctional descendants: Richard, a senile old man, and his wife, Orianna; Richard's sister, known to all as Aunt Fanny; Maryjane, widow of Lionel, who was Richard and Orianna's son (when the novel begins, he has just died under suspicious circumstances, and Maryjane believes that her mother-in-law pushed him down the stairs to ensure her ownership of the house); Fancy, Maryjane's daughter; and a small crew of servants and hangers-on. Like the estate in *The Road Through the Wall*, the house is separated from the rest of the world by a stone wall that completely encircles it, "so that all inside the wall was Halloran, all outside was not." The first Mr. Halloran, who made his fortune in some unspecified business, built the house because he "could think of nothing better to do with his money than set up his own world." Everything was constructed according to a strict order: the tiles on the terrace and the marble pillars holding up the balustrade all perfectly symmetrical, a precisely square blue pool, a "summer house built like a temple to some minor mathematical god." Only the sundial, in the midst of it all, is off center, a reminder "that the human eye is unable to look unblinded upon mathematical perfection." Jackson planned the design meticulously, illustrating her notes for the novel with sketches showing the layout of the house and gardens.

One morning before sunrise, Aunt Fanny wanders into the garden

Jackson's sketch of the Halloran estate's garden for The Sundial.

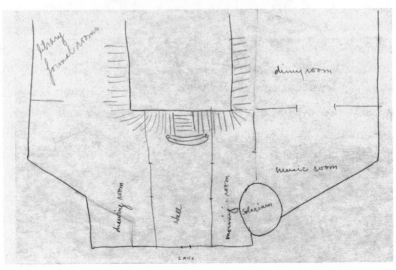

Jackson's sketch of the Halloran estate (interior).

and has a vision in which her father speaks to her of an impending apocalypse. "Humanity, as an experiment, has failed," Aunt Fanny declares grandly to the others. ("Splendid. I was getting very tired of all of them," her sister-in-law responds.) In "one night of utter disaster," the entire world will be destroyed, with only the house left standing. Its inhabitants, emerging "safe and pure," will be "charged with the future of humanity; when they came forth from the house it would be into a world clean and silent, their inheritance." The date of the apocalypse is set for August 30, about three months hence; Jackson later joked that she chose it because it was also her deadline. In the novel, as per her usual practice, no year is specified and there are few markers of temporality. The story could be set in the past or in the future—it does not matter.

The critic R. W. B. Lewis, an acquaintance of Jackson and Hyman's, wrote that apocalyptic fiction has "a pervasive sense of the preposterous: of the end of the world not only as imminent and titanic, but also as absurd." Perhaps Jackson's funniest novel, *The Sundial*, like Stanley Kubrick's classic film *Dr. Strangelove* (1964), derives much of its very black comedy from the spectacle of how singularly unfit its characters are to contend with an event of such cosmic significance. If they are the "chosen people," as one character puts it, the future of humanity looks very bleak indeed: these inheritors of the earth are petty and self-indulgent, preoccupied with their social class (which they lord over the villagers who live literally below their house high on a hill) and their interfamilial squabbles. Aunt Fanny is insufferably passive-aggressive ("No one needs to worry over me, thank you"); Orianna, her detested sister-in-law, enlists members of the household to spy on one another and stands behind her husband's wheelchair so that he cannot see the boredom on her face. Shortly after their honeymoon, her husband asked if she married him for his money. "Well, that, and the house," she told him matter-of-factly. All the house's residents are utterly certain of their own superiority. At one point they are visited by representatives of the True Believers, a doomsday cult preparing for the imminent arrival of spacemen from Saturn to take them away. In a very funny scene, the True Believers, who might be characters out of one of those campy

1950s science fiction films, attempt to assess the Hallorans' prepared-
ness for the apocalypse—do they eat meat or drink alcohol? do they
use metal fastenings on their clothes?—and are roundly ejected from
the mansion.

Jackson said more than once that *The Sundial* was her favorite of her
novels: "Nothing I have ever written has given me so much pleasure,"
she claimed in her lecture about the book. After her two-year block, it
poured out of her quickly and easily, untroubled by the usual false starts
and self-doubt: she began it in fall 1956, around the time of President
Eisenhower's reelection, and was finished the following summer, just
before the Sputnik launch. Her enjoyment is evident in the novel's comedy, especially her lengthy detailing of the housekeeping necessary to
prepare for the end of the world. Aunt Fanny startles the proprietress of
the village bookshop by asking for a Boy Scout handbook on surviving in the wild, as well as elementary textbooks on engineering and
chemistry and a guide to herbs, announcing that she has "an immediate need for a good deal of practical information on primitive living."
(The villagers, incidentally, have little to redeem them: they get their
lifeblood from tourists who make pilgrimages to the site of a grisly murder some years ago in which a local teenager killed her father, mother,
and younger brothers with a hammer, Lizzie Borden–style.) Eventually the Hallorans will remove all the books from the library and burn
them in the barbecue pit, filling the shelves with antihistamines, first-aid
kits, instant coffee, suntan lotion, toilet paper, citronella, cigarettes, and
other indispensables—perhaps a reflection of the midcentury mania for
building bomb shelters. (A booklet issued by the U.S. government in
the early 1950s, titled "You Can Survive," gave helpful tips on what to
store inside a bomb shelter.) But Jackson plays it coy when it comes to
the actual moment of apocalypse. The book ends with the Hallorans—
most of them, anyway—barricaded in the house, waiting.

The motto on a sundial normally contains a reference, often morbid,
to the passing of time and the approach of death, such as *"Tempus fugit"*
or *"Carpe diem."* In an early draft, Jackson chose "It is later than you
think"; after considering numerous options, most of them biblical—
"Watch, for ye know not when the time is"; "The time is at hand"—she

settled on "What is this world?" The line comes from Dryden's retelling of Chaucer's "Knight's Tale": "What is this world? what asken men to have? / Now with his love, now in his colde grave / Allone withouten eny companye." Particularly appropriate for the atomic age, it emphasizes our lack of control over our fate, and the speed at which our circumstances can change. It reminds us also that the Halloran estate, a world in itself, is a microcosm of our own world, intended to "contain everything": a lake with swans, a pagoda, a maze and rose garden, items of silver and gold, a library stocked with marble busts and leather-bound books, and inspirational quotes—"When shall we live if not now?"—inscribed on the walls.

Like Elizabeth Richmond in *The Bird's Nest*, the Hallorans are an extreme case, an exaggeration of a common human condition. But every family does create its own world, and every house is an expression of the world in which that family lives: its experiences, its history, its inside jokes and preoccupations. This is poignantly illustrated by Aunt Fanny, who preserves in the attic of the mansion a perfect replica of the apartment in which her parents lived before they moved to the estate: the knickknacks and photographs and books and Victrola in the living room ("this furniture had been built to endure, and endure it would"); the kitchen with oilcloth on the table and the high chair used by Aunt Fanny and her brother; beds made up in the bedrooms. A family, as Mrs. Halloran says at the end of the novel, is "a tiny island in a raging sea . . . a point of safety in a world of ruin."

And a writer, like a homemaker, also creates his or her own world and stocks it with objects of beauty and fascination. In one of her lectures on writing, Jackson spoke of the way objects in her house became characters in stories in which she might imagine, for instance, that "the waffle iron, unless watched, is going to strangle the toaster." In the next breath, she gave this whimsical notion a serious cast. "The very nicest thing about being a writer is that you can afford to indulge yourself endlessly with oddness, and nobody can really do anything about it, so long as you keep writing and kind of using it up, as it were. All you have to do—and watch this carefully, please—is keep writing. So long as you write it away regularly nothing can really hurt you."

———

BY THE TIME SHE began writing *The Sundial,* Jackson had been dissatisfied with Farrar, Straus for many years. Each book seemed to bring new problems. She blamed the disappointing sales of *The Road Through the Wall* and *Hangsaman* on the firm's failure to put sufficient promotional muscle behind them: not only was she dissatisfied with the advertising, but Farrar, Straus consistently neglected to supply books to the Bennington Bookshop, a sure source of sales for her. (Tom Foster, Jackson's friend and the local scout for the firm, agreed that they were "always a little behind" with regard to marketing her books.) With *Life Among the Savages,* the production department forgot to send her page proofs; on *The Bird's Nest,* a production editor annoyed her by suggesting that the book should carry a disclaimer averring that it was fiction. The original jacket art for *Raising Demons* depicted five children, not four. And years after she had moved back to North Bennington, the secretarial staff continued to forward letters to her in Westport. Most of these "millions of petty irritations" were indeed petty, but they added up to give Jackson the impression that her publishers didn't care enough about her books, or about her, to treat her as a truly important author.

It may simply not have been an ideal match between author and publisher. For some time the aging John Farrar had been relegated to the background; from *The Bird's Nest* on, his main role seemed to be sending "fond little notes" and books to her children. Jackson saw him more as an "indulgent old uncle who pats me on the head" than as a professional who treated her as a colleague. Straus, whom Jackson rarely saw or heard from, was the firm's dominating force, directing his energies primarily toward prizewinning European literary heavyweights, such as François Mauriac, Alberto Moravia, and Marguerite Yourcenar. Since the house was now publishing sixty-five books a year, it's not surprising that Jackson felt her work was getting less attention. But she was essentially stuck with Farrar, Straus, because each of her contracts granted the firm the right of refusal on her next work.

That changed after *Demons,* which fulfilled the option clause on *The Bird's Nest*; Baumgarten had deliberately neglected to include a new one in the *Demons* contract. Jackson was now free to look elsewhere, and she let it be known that she was ready to do so. Straus knew that he could not persuade her to stay himself. Instead, he dispatched Robert Giroux, the firm's newest editor, formerly of Harcourt Brace. As reticent and modest as Straus was outspoken, Giroux was already known, as Baumgarten told Jackson, as "probably the best editor in publishing today." At Harcourt, Brace, he had worked with Thomas Merton, T. S. Eliot, Flannery O'Connor, Jean Stafford, George Orwell, and E. M. Forster. He would later say that he left the firm over its refusal to publish *The Catcher in the Rye*. In his office at Farrar, Straus, where his authors would eventually include Susan Sontag, Isaac Bashevis Singer, and Elizabeth Bishop, he kept a framed Thurber cartoon depicting a dog in a meadow, baying soulfully and obliviously at the moon, while another dog bounds toward it, ready to pounce. Giroux called the drawing "Author and Publisher."

Giroux prepared to pounce. On March 21, 1956, he took the train up to Bennington for the express purpose of meeting Jackson. He spent time with the whole family that afternoon; the next day, Jackson and Hyman attended a cocktail party that Tom and Kit Foster hosted in Giroux's honor, with the writer Dorothy Canfield Fisher, a local celebrity, among the guests. Giroux reported to Baumgarten that everything had gone splendidly: he found Jackson and Hyman "completely delightful," and the children were "the best behaved kids" he had met. Jackson's account was a little more acid: Mrs. Fisher had patted her on the arm and asked her what she was studying at Bennington, and Tom Foster put too much ice in his martinis. She also suggested to Giroux that her next contract ought to include a clause requiring Straus to ensure Laurence's admission to Exeter, where, despite his undistinguished academic record, she still hoped to send him. "What is the biggest advance that yacht-owning pirate ever gave to any writer in his life? Because I want to top it by fifty cents," she told Baumgarten. But Giroux's gambit worked. Jackson signed on for another book with Farrar, Straus, now with Giroux as her editor, with an advance of $5000.

With regard to the content of Jackson's books, Farrar, Straus had taken a hands-off approach. Straus negotiated her fees and Farrar handled the personal side of the relationship, but other than to offer vague praise, they mainly refrained from commenting on her prose. That was not the case for Giroux, who wrote Jackson long and thoughtful letters upon reading each installment of *The Sundial*. After seeing the first seventy pages or so, he was already prepared to declare the novel her best yet. "How you managed to make a houseful of characters so clearly identifiable right off is something of a miracle," he wrote to her in March 1957. By the end of July, she had submitted the full manuscript, and his quibbles were minor. If she meant to convey that the big house was "the chosen Ark," he was concerned that the logistics of how it would weather the storm required more explanation. He also worried that the other characters reacted too casually to a dramatic plot twist in the last chapter. "All this is a tribute to the enormous suspense and credibility which you have created in the earlier part of the book," he assured her.

Jackson took both suggestions into account in her revision, which she finished much more quickly than usual. For the first time in more than a decade, she had only one child to take care of. Joanne was away at camp, and after hearing how much she enjoyed it, Sarah spontaneously decided to join her there. Laurence, trumpet-obsessed at fourteen, had gotten a summer job at the Music Inn, a hotel and concert venue fifty miles away in Stockbridge, Massachusetts. Located on the former estate of a countess, the Music Inn specialized in jazz, blues, and folk, with concerts held outdoors under a tent. Shirley and Stanley had first taken him to visit the previous summer, when Stanley gave a lecture there about jazz. When Laurence got out of the car, he "decided on the spot that this was where he planned to spend the rest of his life," Shirley told her parents. The staff normally consisted of college boys, but the owner made an exception for Laurence, allowing him to work part-time taking care of the sports equipment and generally helping out around the place. Like Stanley's summer at Mount Freedom, it was an enormous amount of independence to offer a young teenager, with consequences that Laurence's parents did not entirely foresee. For now, they were pleased with the arrangement. "He says bop musicians only tip a quarter and every time someone comes in and insists on carrying one small suitcase and letting the bellhop take the others, you can figure the small suitcase has a bottle of whiskey in it," Shirley reported. Visiting him there, she and Stanley got to meet Dizzy Gillespie, the bebop trumpeter who had recently toured the Middle East as "the ambassador of jazz." That left at home only Barry, who had reached an age "when a set of soldiers and box of blocks are sufficient occupation for hours."

Jackson and Hyman made a small vacation of her appearance at the Syracuse Summer Writing Workshop, organized by their former professor Leonard Brown; Malcolm Cowley, Randall Jarrell, and Delmore Schwartz also lectured. Jackson's talk, to her chagrin, took place in the same room where she had failed her final exam in Spanish nearly twenty years earlier. Brown, with whom Jackson and Hyman had sporadically stayed in touch, teasingly asked her whether she had "ever learned to keep a neat notebook of story ideas, or . . . still took notes on old scraps of paper." (Of course, a "neat notebook" never would be Jackson's way.) She spoke to around sixty students about writing *The Sundial*—"I would not like to have any of you believe that I cook up this kind of thing in a cauldron"—and read a frightening scene in which one of the characters tries to escape from the Halloran house and, after a nightmarish ride with a sinister taxi driver, finds herself lost in a disorienting fog, "an impenetrable, almost intangible, weight of darkness pressing down." The students asked "millions of idiotic questions and some embarrassing ones . . . and they thought of all sorts of things I couldn't answer." They also wanted to know the book's ending, but she told them they would have to wait until it came out.

The truth was that she wasn't entirely certain about the ending. Could she really leave the question of apocalypse unresolved? Hyman read the manuscript and told her to change the ending; she refused, and they argued. "stanley was so annoyed that he couldn't sleep . . . and sat up reading and snarling until about four-thirty and then tried to come to bed quietly and of course woke me . . . so it is now seven-thirty and stanley is sound asleep and i have been up since four-thirty and i refuse to change the ending of the book because why should he sleep when i can't?" she grumbled. It seems she considered going through with the Day of Judgment and allowing her characters to emerge into the new "world of loveliness and peace" they were anticipating. But she was right finally to leave them on the cusp, waiting for an apocalypse that may or may not arrive—a last note of ambiguity that suits the novel's perfectly tuned satire.

In the end, the only changes Jackson made between the drafts were to alter some of the characters' names and flesh out a few scenes. By late August, she had sent the final version to the typist. Now that the book was done, she actually had time on her hands. "I am most anxious to start a new book," she wrote to Giroux, "so if you have any old plots lying around send them to me fast."

As always, however, something went wrong. This time it was the jacket copy. Jackson loved the design: an all-text cover that repeated the title and her name in alternating rows and with alternating blocks of color—orange and fluorescent yellow. The effect was kaleidoscopic and dizzying, almost an optical illusion. But she was insulted by the mistakes in the book's description: names of characters were misspelled and elementary details of the plot were wrong. She also objected "violently" to the plot summary and the character descriptions, offering instead a brief and oblique outline of the book. Ideally, she wanted the back flap to be left entirely blank. "I realize that this must sound like a childish temper tantrum, but it seems to me that *Sundial* is so precariously balanced on the edge of the ridiculous that any slip might send it in the wrong direction," she concluded. "I tried to keep it on that uneasy edge . . . but I wouldn't like to see anyone breathe on it too hard." Giroux yielded. The copy was edited to her specifications and the back flap contained only a list of her previous works—no photograph.

At the same time, a big change was taking place at Brandt & Brandt: Baumgarten had decided to retire. James Gould Cozzens, her husband, had seen enormous success with his thirteenth book, *By Love Possessed*, which was the top-selling novel of 1957. (When it hit the best-seller list, Jackson and Hyman sent Baumgarten a congratulatory telegram warning her not to "let your old man steal the spotlight.") After years of commuting from their farm in remote Lambertville, New Jersey, to her Park Avenue office, Baumgarten was ready to leave the business.

Baumgarten's departure was a "development of great importance in the publishing scene," Giroux told a colleague. It was also a great loss to

*Bernice Baumgarten
(1903–1978) was Jackson's
agent from 1951 until her
retirement in 1957.*

Jackson: the two of them, if not exactly intimates, had developed a close and trusting working relationship. In contrast to a previous agent who "spent more time taking people out to lunch and asking me for news about the children than she ever did making money," Jackson was reassured by Baumgarten's straightforwardness and tough-mindedness: "i don't think bernice has ever taken anyone out to lunch in her life and she has certainly never said two words to me about anything but business. . . . i wouldn't like to have her for a sister, but i do love doing business with her." (Baumgarten generally revealed so little of her personal life to her clients that many of them did not realize she was married to Cozzens.) The critic and novelist Mary McCarthy, another of Baumgarten's authors, would remember her "tremendous, never-failing control" and "straight, reflecting, considering look, as if she always wanted to measure the truth of what she was saying."

In the six years they worked together, Baumgarten had sold four of Jackson's nine books for adults, engineered an acceptable resolution to the *Good Housekeeping* debacle, generated lucrative new relationships for her with *Woman's Home Companion* and *McCall's*, and gotten her into the Random House Landmark series with *The Witchcraft of Salem Village*—a book that cost Jackson little effort and paid enormous dividends. Baumgarten squeezed as much money as humanly possible out of the notoriously parsimonious Straus, hitting him up for advances every time Jackson needed cash—often before a contract had been signed. And she was an excellent manager, constantly suggesting new magazines to which Jackson might contribute and placing her work skillfully and strategically. Together with Giroux, she nominated Jackson for a grant from the National Institute of Arts and Letters in 1956 (alas, without success). Jackson acknowledged Baumgarten's impact on her career by dedicating *The Sundial* to her. "I know that you are bound for great success," Baumgarten wrote in her valedictory letter.

Baumgarten left Jackson with a parting gift that would shape the rest of her career. In December 1957, before Giroux had a chance to pounce again, she negotiated a three-book contract for Jackson with Viking Press. "i keep getting sad little letters from people around farrar and straus saying how they are so sorry i am leaving them . . . and i write sad little letters back which read like lee's farewell to his troops although actually i am delighted to be leaving them and i bet they are just as happy to see me go, since we have been fighting for fifteen years," Jackson wrote. The person who was probably the most sorry to see the relationship end was Jackson's neighbor Tom Foster, who—as a reward for his role in bringing Jackson to the firm—received significant royalties on her sales. Had she stayed at Farrar, Straus for her next two novels, her highest selling ever, he would have stood to benefit considerably. As it was, he continued to receive royalty checks from Farrar, Straus into the 1990s.

Pascal Covici, a legend in the publishing world, was to be Jackson's editor at Viking. Born in 1885, the grandfatherly Covici, known to everyone as Pat, was the son of Romanian-Jewish immigrants. Though he never finished college, he started his own publishing firm early in his career with partner Donald Friede, publishing writers such as John Steinbeck, Clifford Odets, and Nathanael West. When he moved to Viking, in 1938, Steinbeck came with him; Viking published *The Grapes of Wrath*, a Pulitzer Prize winner, the following year. Covici cultivated a list of writers with serious literary clout who were also commercially viable: in addition to Steinbeck, they included Graham Greene, Joseph Campbell, Marianne Moore, and Saul Bellow—who, like Jackson, made the best-seller list under Covici's guidance. Jackson described him as "an old old man who is tremendously respected in publishing and has the fanciest office i ever saw." Bellow, who dedicated *Herzog* to Covici, later recalled him as "one of those men in broad-brimmed fedoras who took drawing rooms on the Twentieth Century Limited in the John Barrymore days, people who knew headwaiters and appreciated well turned-out women. . . . Pat knew how to order a fine dinner, how long to let wine breathe, how to cherish a pretty woman, how to dart into the street and stop a cab by whistling on his fingers, [and] how to negotiate a tough contract."

Jackson's contract was actually quite advantageous to her. For the first time ever, she had a guaranteed stream of income. She would receive a total advance of $15,000 for three works of fiction, one of which was to be a short-story collection, with payments spaced out as she wished. There would be no more wrangling over money—Jackson could simply request installments as she needed them. "What it does is to give you money on call at intervals and, I hope, keep you easy in your mind," Baumgarten wrote.

Ease of mind was perhaps too much to hope for, given Jackson's fragile nerves. And eventually the money would prove not to be enough; it was never enough. But with Jackson looking ahead to significant expenses—boarding school for the older children and college rapidly approaching—she indeed found it a relief, at least initially, to have a dependable source of income from Viking.

LIKE JACKSON'S THREE previous novels, *The Sundial* did not earn back its advance. The book's ambiguity was too much for many reviewers, who split just about evenly between admiring and mystified. Almost unanimously, they praised Jackson's writing, especially the novel's bitingly funny opening scene, in which ten-year-old Fancy asks if she ought to push her grandmother down the stairs, "like she killed my daddy." One reviewer said the book had "the deadly mannered charm of an Oscar Wilde drama," and others compared Jackson to Hawthorne, Kafka, Poe, and Ivy Compton-Burnett, the English domestic novelist whom Jackson thought her tone often resembled. ("i always start like ivy and have to write it off," she confided to a friend.) "As a

satire of much common behavior, its darts strike home," wrote Edmund
Fuller, a consistent (and consistently perceptive) fan of Jackson's work.
But others had a hard time keeping the many characters straight ("an
assemblage of weirdies," one called them); many also got key points of
the plot wrong. And the dénouement, or lack thereof, was a particular
sticking point. "A bizarre tale with an enigmatic ending," wrote critic
John Barkham.

The book had "all the big brains puzzled." Reviewers judged it to be
blatantly symbolic, but what it was meant to represent they weren't sure.
The theories ranged as widely as the interpretations of "The Lottery" had
ten years earlier. Could it be an allegory of the atomic age: "hell bombs
and space platforms bristling with atomic artillery and . . . [other] stylish
nightmares of our day?" asked Charles Poore in *The New York Times*.
Numerous critics mentioned the recent Sputnik launching. "As H-Hour
of an apocalyptic D-Day approaches," wrote William Peden in the *Saturday Review*, the book presented "a shocking picture of a society paralyzed by conceit." Another wondered if the sundial was "the hub of a new
universe" or "the symbol of life eternal." A review that Jackson found
particularly amusing argued that the entire book was an allegory of the
Catholic church, with Mrs. Halloran standing for the "Mother Church,"
the statues in the garden for remnants of paganism, Aunt Fanny for the
Old Testament prophets, and so on. "A novel such as this is a kind of
literary Rorschach test," Robert Kirsch wrote sensibly in the *Los Angeles
Times*. "The right answer is the one you provide for yourself."

And again, some reviewers simply could not reconcile themselves
to the idea that Jackson might legitimately write two different types of
books: humorous memoirs and serious fiction. "Some kind of dissociation of personality is certainly going on in Miss Jackson, one half of her
flying off toward the women's magazines, the other half out-Kafkaing
K," wrote one. In a long piece in the *New York Post* that compared *The Sundial* unfavorably to a new book by the lesser-known novelist Frederick
Buechner, critic William Bittner, who taught Jackson's work in a course
on postwar fiction at the New School for Social Research, lamented
that she—who "ahead of all the rest" had understood "the nature of the
human predicament in our time and made art out of it"—had "fiddled

her time away with *Life Among the Savages*," to the detriment of her fiction. "Why parturition (an activity my cat goes through without losing a bit of the enthusiasm she has for the better things of life) should be able to make temporary dopes out of intelligent human beings I do not know; but when one of the finest literary talents of our time wastes her ability on books about brats, to the complete stagnation of her own development, I feel like throwing bricks," Bittner wrote insultingly. Others took issue with the book's misanthropy, with one reviewer calling Jackson "a very bright lady with a savage vision of our world." (Jackson herself acknowledged that it was "a nasty little novel full of mean people who hate each other.") Reviewing *The Sundial* in *The Nation* together with John Dos Passos's *The Great Days*—both "novels striven for but not quite attained"—another critic wondered whether the problem was less Jackson's writing than the general literary climate: "One is tempted to think that we have now had a surfeit of elegant sensibility and formal artistry in fiction." It was the old Diana Trilling/John Aldridge debate revived, with the same lack of awareness that the woman-centric fiction Jackson was writing was fundamentally different from the mainstream. Only Eleanor M. Bloom, one of the few women to review the book, seemed to recognize Jackson's interest in women's issues as a crucial element separating her from Mailer, Salinger, Bellow, and the Beats. (Jack Kerouac's *On the Road* had recently inaugurated that iconoclastic, but still male-dominated, movement.) "Miss Jackson is, for my money, the most exciting writing talent in America today, and that includes all of the angry young men," she wrote.

With her future at Viking already sealed, the reviews had no power to damage Jackson's contractual situation—or her self-confidence. By the time *The Sundial* was published, she had already written a new story called "Louisa, Please Come Home." As long and complex as "Flower Garden," it would also go through two dramatically different drafts. The first version was a kind of sequel to "The Missing Girl": what might happen if, several years after a Paula Welden–like disappearance, an impostor showed up, claiming to be the absent daughter and knowing all the details about her life? Would she be able to infiltrate the family, fooling even the parents of the missing girl? In Jackson's telling, the parents are all too easy to convince, but the girl's sister and aunt are skeptical from the start. Their suspicions are vindicated when the girl and her husband (a family friend who has abetted in the deception) are exposed as con artists—but not before they make off with money, expensive clothing, and jewelry.

That draft was clever and pointed, but Jackson was dissatisfied with it. In the next version, the tale of the impostor was relegated to a sidebar. Instead, Jackson focused on the missing girl herself, here named Louisa Tether. For no obvious reason, nineteen-year-old Louisa decides to run away from her family, carefully strategizing so as not to be discovered— she buys a round-trip train ticket, to avoid suspicion—and eventually settles in a nearby city, where she finds a room in a boardinghouse and a job in a stationery store. Three years later, she has just about eradicated all traces of her former life when she encounters an old friend on the street, who insists on bringing her back to her parents: each year, on the anniversary of her disappearance, her mother has delivered a plea on the radio for her to come home. But when she arrives, her family refuses to believe that she is the real Louisa—it turns out that the friend has already brought two impostors. Rather than argue, Louisa goes along with them. "I hope your daughter comes back someday," she tells her own parents.

Carol Brandt, now Shirley's agent, judged this version a "powerful and brilliant horror story," but she wondered why Jackson had left Louisa's motives unexplained. What made her run away from home? Jackson declined to answer, but it seems clear that Louisa does not in fact need a reason. Like the wife in "A Day in the Jungle," or the later character of Angela Motorman in *Come Along with Me*, she wants simply to disappear, to begin a new life, untethered from the old, even if that means giving up everything. Jackson's next novel—its working title was now *The Haunted House*—would be centered on another woman who does precisely that. The consequences for her, as for Louisa, are dire.

IN EARLY JANUARY 1958, as Sputnik I crashed to Earth and the United States prepared to launch its own satellite, Jackson and Hyman went down to New York together so that she could meet Carol Brandt and

Pat Covici. As their train pulled into the stop at 125th Street, where trains coming from the north then paused before continuing to Grand Central Station, Jackson was startled by the sight of "the most hideous building" she had ever seen. It was an ordinary tenement-style apartment house, but something about it felt "unspeakable . . . horrifying," she remembered later. As the train pulled away, something strange happened: it disappeared. Her initial thought was to turn around immediately and head back to Vermont: "I didn't want to spend another minute in a city with that building in it." In the confusion of arriving and checking into their hotel, she put the building out of her mind. But that night it appeared to her again in "one of those bad nightmares which get you out of bed to turn on the lights and make sure it was only a dream." For the rest of her stay in New York, she dreaded the moment when she would pass the building again on the way home. Finally her anxiety was so paralyzing that she and Hyman switched to a night train so that it would be dark when they passed 125th Street and she would not have to see it.

After returning to Vermont, Jackson was still obsessed with the hideous-looking tenement. She wrote to a friend at Columbia to ask if he knew of any explanation for its ghastly appearance. "When we got his answer I had one important item for my book," Jackson remembered later. "He wrote that he had had trouble finding the building, since it only existed from that one particular point of the 125th Street station; from any other angle it was not recognizable as a building at all. Some seven months before it had been almost entirely burned in a disastrous fire which killed nine people. What was left of the building . . . was a shell. The children in the neighborhood knew that it was haunted."

Like so many writers' best stories, this one seems only to be partially true. There was a fatal fire in Harlem in April 1957, in which three people (not nine) were killed and five injured; but the apartment building where it took place was at 229 West 140th Street, too far to be seen from the 125th Street train station. If Jackson received the letter she describes from a professor at Columbia, no record of it exists in her files. But she may well have glimpsed an uncanny-looking apartment house from the train that got her thinking about how houses become haunted. The feeling Jackson had when she saw the building, she would say later, was the closest she had ever come to a supernatural experience. "I have always been interested in witchcraft and superstition, but have never had much traffic with ghosts, so I began asking people everywhere what they thought about such things, and I began to find out that there was one common factor," she wrote. "Most people have never seen a ghost, and never want or expect to, but almost everyone will admit that sometimes they have a sneaking feeling that they just possibly *could* meet a ghost if they weren't careful—if they were to turn a corner too suddenly, perhaps, or open their eyes too soon when they wake up at night, or go into a dark room without hesitating first."

Regardless of what exactly she saw, Jackson came back from New York eager to begin a new novel about a haunted house: "the kind of novel you really can't read alone in a dark house at night." But she needed a good house for inspiration. For some time she had been collecting postcards and newspaper clippings of old houses: Wallace Fowlie gave her some from France, and Hyman bought her a box of hundreds of postcards depicting houses from around the world. She and Laurence would sometimes drive around the back roads near North Bennington and look for houses that might be haunted. There were a lot of abandoned farmhouses, but nothing suitable: the New England houses were too square and neoclassical, a "type which wouldn't be haunted in a million years." She wanted something ornate, like the Château de Monte-Cristo, a turreted Renaissance castle built by Alexandre Dumas père; Neuschwanstein Castle, a fairy-tale-like Romanesque Revival palace in Bavaria; or Grim's Dyke, a combination Gothic Revival/late Elizabethan mansion in London that had belonged to W. S. Gilbert. Closer to home, many have speculated that Jennings Hall, an ivy-covered gray stone mansion perched on a hill on the Bennington campus, was the model for Hill House, but there is no evidence for this: Jackson's files contain no picture of it, and the house is much plainer than the others in her collection. A better local candidate is the Edward H. Everett mansion near Old Bennington, which at the time was being used as the noviciate of the Holy Cross Congregation and is now part of the campus of Southern Vermont College. The former home of a wealthy glass bottle manufacturer, the mansion was the site of a contentious legal dispute

The Everett Mansion in Bennington, Vermont, shortly after its completion in 1912.

between Everett's daughters and his second wife. It is said—still—to be haunted by the ghost of Everett's first wife, a woman dressed in white who roams the house and grounds. A picture of the mansion, suitably foreboding, is in Jackson's files.

Unsatisfied with New England, Jackson turned to the West Coast, asking her parents to send pictures of the Winchester House in San Jose, California, or "pictures and information (particularly pictures) of any other big old california gingerbread houses." Whether she remembered that some of those old "gingerbread houses" had been designed by her ancestors was unclear. But Geraldine responded at once with a handful of clippings, including images of the Crocker House, which she identified correctly as one of her great-grandfather's creations. She also sent a tourist brochure for the Winchester House, now known as the Winchester Mystery House. Only forty miles from Burlingame, it had been built by Sarah Winchester, the widow of gun magnate William Wirt Winchester, after the death of her husband and daughter. A medium reportedly told her that spirits were taking revenge on her for all the people who had been killed by Winchester firearms. The only solution was to build a house that was in flux: as long as rooms, corridors, and stairs were constantly added, the medium said, the confused spirits would not attack. Sarah Winchester followed her instructions, employing carpenters to work continually on the house for thirty-eight years, until her death in 1922. Its idiosyncratic design includes gables and turrets bursting out at all angles, corridors that lead nowhere, stairs with uneven risers, trapdoors, and ornamentation featuring spiderwebs and the number thirteen (Winchester believed both had spiritual significance). Hallways are as narrow as two feet; doors open both inward and outward in unexpected places, with some on the upper floors leading directly to a sudden drop. "An unguided person would be completely lost within fifty feet of the entrance," warns the brochure. Hill House would incorporate some very similar features, including the disorienting layout, and the novel mentions the Winchester House.

Jackson's architectural creation includes elements of many of her models, but she invested it with an emotional valence that was distinctly her invention. "No human eye can isolate the unhappy coincidence of line and place which suggests evil in the face of the house, and yet somehow a manic juxtaposition, a badly turned angle, some chance meeting of roof and sky, turned Hill House into a place of despair," she writes. The house's "face"—she does not call it a façade—seemed "awake, with a watchfulness from the blank windows and a touch of glee in the eyebrow of a cornice"; it "reared its great head back against the sky without concession to humanity." Shown to her bedroom by Mrs. Dudley, the sinister housekeeper who seems to try deliberately to unnerve her ("We live over in the town, six miles away. . . . So there won't be anyone around if you need help. . . . We couldn't even hear you, in the night"), the protagonist, Eleanor Vance, finds even the geometry of the room unsettling: "It had an unbelievably faulty design which left it chillingly wrong in all its dimensions, so that the walls seemed always in one direction a fraction longer than the eye could endure, and in another direction a fraction less than the barest possible tolerable length." Downstairs is a labyrinth of rooms, many windowless; the doors, hung off center, swing shut of their own accord. "A masterpiece of architectural misdirection," one character calls it.

Now that Jackson had found her house, she needed ghosts. She consulted a number of well-known historical accounts of haunted houses: the report of John Crichton-Stuart, who led a team of psychical researchers to investigate Ballechin House in Scotland in the late 1890s, as well as the book *An Adventure*, in which Charlotte Anne Moberly and Eleanor Jourdain, two British women on a European vacation, describe their uncanny experience of stumbling on a scene from the past while visiting the Petit Trianon, Madame du Barry's house at Versailles. An episode late in *Hill House*, in which Eleanor and Theodora unexpectedly come upon a group of people—perhaps ghosts—picnicking in the grounds behind the house, shows the influence of their chronicle, as does Jackson's use of the name Eleanor, found nowhere else in her work, for her main character. In her notes for the novel, Jackson refers to *An Adventure* as "one of the greatest ghost stories of all time."

As Jackson began to write, further inspiration came from an unlikely source of the supernatural: the newspaper. In early 1958, the New York media reported on the curious case of a Long Island family apparently plagued by a poltergeist. One afternoon in early February, Mrs. Herrmann called her husband at the office to tell him that bottles in the family's ranch house—"a symbol of orderly suburban family life," wrote one reporter—were "blowing their tops": their screw tops had spontaneously opened, spilling the contents everywhere. Next, while twelve-year-old Jimmy Herrmann was brushing his teeth, two bottles slid off the bathroom ledge and landed at his feet. The episodes continued almost daily for several weeks: a sugar bowl sitting on the dining table exploded while a detective was questioning the family; a ten-inch globe flew off a bookcase and hurtled across a hall to land at the feet of a visiting reporter; a statue of the Virgin Mary fell off a dresser. The story made the front page of *The New York Times*. Police, scientists, and parapsychologists all examined the case, but no single theory dominated. The disturbances eventually ceased as abruptly as they had begun.

The investigators focused on Jimmy Herrmann, who was around the same age as the girls who claimed to be plagued with witchcraft manifestations in Salem, and who was often in the room or nearby when the actions took place. It seemed impossible for him to be moving the objects physically, but a parapsychologist from Duke University who visited the house suggested that Jimmy could be unconsciously exercising psychokinesis (also called parakinesis): using mental power to produce physical effects. An article about the case cited *Haunted People*, a book by Hereward Carrington and Nandor Fodor, psychical researchers who sought psychological explanations for phenomena that appeared to be supernatural. Carrington and Fodor point out that poltergeist-type episodes tend to take place in the vicinity of children around the age of puberty. "It is a legitimate inference that the life force which blossoming sexual powers represent is finding an abnormal outlet," writes Fodor, whose theories were deeply influenced by Freudian psychology.

Jackson, curious, got a copy of Carrington and Fodor's book. Even had she not acknowledged it to Fodor, its influence would be obvious. The vast majority of poltergeist incidents cited in *Haunted People* have one element in common—an element that appears over and over in the long list of cases the book references, and that will be immediately obvious to any reader of *Hill House*. The most frequent characteristic of a poltergeist manifestation, one that happened to have special resonance for Jackson, is precisely the same as the incident in the novel that originally brings Eleanor to the attention of Dr. Montague, the psychical investigator who organizes the visit to Hill House—an incident that took place when Eleanor was twelve. It is a shower of—of all things—stones. Like the missiles cast at Tessie Hutchinson by her neighbors, the ashes that rained down upon the unsuspecting crew of the Japanese fishing boat, or the satellites hurled into orbit only to come crashing back down, they are a small apocalypse in the air, a harbinger of disaster.

15.

THE HEART OF
THE HOUSE

THE HAUNTING OF
HILL HOUSE, 1958–1959

> we are afraid of being someone else and doing the things
> someone else wants us to do and of being taken and used
> by someone else, some other guilt-ridden conscience that
> lives on and on in our minds, something we build our-
> selves and never recognize, but this is fear, not a named
> sin. then it is fear itself, fear of self that I am writing about
> . . . fear and guilt and their destruction of identity. . . . why
> am i so afraid?
>
> —unpublished document (1960)

"THERE ARE GOING TO BE, EVENTUALLY, THE REASONS WHY
our marriage ends, and you ought to know that it will not be a vague
sudden emotion, or quarrel, which drives—has driven—me away,"
Shirley wrote in the long letter to Stanley in which she made clear how
serious her grievances against him were. It is one of the most painful
documents in her archive. She wrote of her loneliness in the face of
his indifference to her and the children, his inveterate interest in other
women, his belittling her, his obsessive devotion to teaching and to his

Shirley Jackson, late 1950s.

students, female all, "which leaves no room for other emotional involvement, not even a legitimate one at home." She wondered if "this is the
lot of wives and i have no cause to complain," but she could not believe
that. She concluded the letter with a final accusation. "you once wrote
me a letter (i know you hate my remembering these things) telling me
that i would never be lonely again. i think that was the first, the most
dreadful, lie you ever told me."

The letter is dated September 9, with no year. But a reference to the
Suffield Writer-Reader Conference—Shirley told Stanley that she did
not want him to accompany her there the following year—means that
it was likely written in 1958, after the couple returned from a joint trip
to the conference. Shirley was deep into writing *The Haunting of Hill
House* that fall and completed the manuscript the following spring. Hill
House—a house that contains nightmares and makes them manifest,
in which fantasies of homecoming end in eternal solitude—is the ultimate metaphor for the Hymans' symbiotic, tormented, yet intensely

committed marriage. Early drafts demonstrate that marriage was crucial to Shirley's vision of the novel from the start. In one version, the sister of Erica, the protagonist (later to be named Eleanor), wants to set her up with a man. "Carrie wanted me to get married, for some inscrutable reason," Erica says. "Perhaps she found the married state so excruciatingly disagreeable herself that it was the only thing bad enough she could think of to do to me." To be married, Shirley always feared, was to lose her sense of self, to disintegrate—precisely what happens to Eleanor in the grip of the house.

Each of the houses that anchor Jackson's final three completed novels—*The Sundial, Hill House,* and *We Have Always Lived in the Castle*—has its own distinct personality and indeed functions as a kind of character in the book. Her interest in houses and their atmosphere extends back to the beginning of her career: to her early fiction, which so often describes the efforts of women to create and furnish a home, and to the first family chronicles she wrote for women's magazines. Her preoccupation with the roles that women play at home and the forces that conspire to keep them there was entirely of a piece with her cultural moment, the decade of the 1950s, when the simmering brew of women's dissatisfaction finally came close to boiling over, triggering the second wave of the feminist movement. In *Hill House*, which appeared in 1959, Jackson gathered powerfully all the objects of her longtime obsession: an unhappy, unmarried woman with a secret trauma; the simultaneous longing for a mother's love and fear of its control; the uncertain legacies handed down by previous generations; and finally the supernatural as a representation of the deepest psychic fears and desires. The result, a masterpiece of literary horror on a par with Henry James's *The Turn of the Screw*, is arguably her best novel, and certainly her most influential.

As with all great ghost stories, readers have been divided over how to understand *Hill House*. Are the ghosts intended to be real, or are they the psychological manifestations of Eleanor, the book's most disturbed character? On this fundamental question the novel remains deliberately enigmatic. But what cannot be questioned about *Hill House* is Jackson's technical mastery. From the book's first lines, her absolute control over the rhythm and timbre of her sentences is obvious:

No live organism can continue for long to exist sanely under conditions of absolute reality; even larks and katydids are supposed, by some, to dream. Hill House, not sane, stood by itself against its hills, holding darkness within; it had stood so for eighty years and might stand for eighty more. Within, walls continued upright, bricks met neatly, floors were firm, and doors were sensibly shut; silence lay steadily against the wood and stone of Hill House, and whatever walked there, walked alone.

No mere ghost story has ever been so beautifully written. Stephen King, one of Jackson's most devoted fans, has written that "there are few if any descriptive passages in the English language that are finer" than the opening to *Hill House*. "It is the sort of quiet epiphany every writer hopes for: words that somehow transcend the sum of the parts."

No live organism can continue for long to exist sanely under conditions of absolute reality. The line reads at first like the start of a different book: what does it have to do with the description of the house that follows? But what it reveals is of crucial importance for the story to come. Hill House is itself a living force that adapts to its inhabitants and responds to their personalities and their histories. The fact that it is "not sane" shows that the circumstances that exist there, supernatural though they may appear, in fact constitute "absolute reality," or at least one form of it. "An atmosphere like this can find out the flaws and faults and weaknesses in all of us, and break us apart in a matter of days," Dr. Montague says. What Eleanor Vance will face inside is not a haunting from another world, but a confrontation with the reality of her psyche—the world of her own secrets and fears.

THE NOVEL BEGINS with Eleanor's journey to Hill House. Thirty-two years old, she has spent all her adult life dutifully caring for her mother, "lifting a cross old lady from her chair to her bed, setting out endless little trays of soup and oatmeal, steeling herself to the filthy laundry." Since her mother's recent death, she has been living with her sister, whom she hates. Eleanor cannot remember a time when she was happy: "Her years

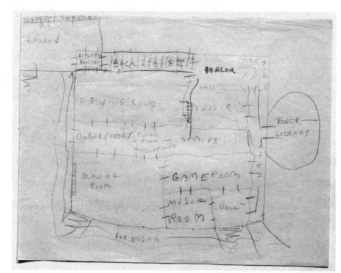

*Jackson's sketch
of Hill House
(downstairs).*

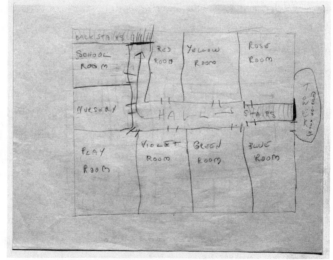

*Jackson's sketch
of Hill House
(upstairs).*

with her mother had been built up devotedly around small guilts and small
reproaches, constant weariness, and unending despair." Having spent so
much time in isolation, she suffers from painful self-consciousness, which
makes her anxious at even the thought of a simple conversation. When a
letter comes inviting her to join the group of researchers at Hill House,
she does not hesitate: all her life, she has been clinging to the belief that
"someday something would happen."

Like Dr. Wright in *The Bird's Nest*, Dr. Montague is a character

Jackson might have borrowed from a Trollope or Thackeray novel. He is "round and rosy and bearded and looked as though he might be more suitably established before a fire in a pleasant little sitting room, with a cat on his knee and a rosy little wife to bring him jellied scones," and his cure for insomnia is an hour of Samuel Richardson before bed. He has sent invitations to a dozen people he selected based on evidence of their prior psychic ability; in the end, only two turn up. For Eleanor, the relevant incident was the shower of stones that fell on her childhood home for three days after the death of her father, "during which time Eleanor and her sister were less unnerved by the stones than by the neighbors and sightseers who gathered daily outside the front door, and by their mother's blind, hysterical insistence that all of this was due to malicious, backbiting people on the block who had had it in for her." Theodora, who arrives next, is clairvoyant, with disconcerting powers of empathy. She is Eleanor's opposite, an artist, bright and cheerful and flirty, with a bohemian lifestyle and a partner whose sex is pointedly never specified. (In early drafts of the novel, she is openly lesbian.) After spending only a few hours with her, Eleanor already realizes that it is "oppressive to be for long around one so immediately in tune, so perceptive," as to be able to read minds. Finally they are joined by Dr. Montague and Luke Sanderson, the heir to the estate, whose aunt—the owner of Hill House—has insisted that a member of the family be present during the investigation.

It took several tries—as was typical—for Jackson to settle on the exact source of Hill House's horror. In an early draft, the main character, arriving at the house, knocks on a heavy wooden door. In the next, she finds a knocker with a lion's head. In the final version, the knocker Eleanor uses has become a child's face. She is entering a family home, but it is a home that has gone badly wrong. The house was built by a man named Hugh Crain, who, like the first Mr. Halloran in *The Sundial*, had a vast and unexplained fortune. The disasters began at once. Crain's first wife died when her carriage overturned in the driveway, leaving him to raise their two little girls. The second Mrs. Crain died in a mysterious fall. Later he was married again, this time to a woman who was consumptive, and left the girls behind at Hill House, traveling with his new wife from one European spa to another. After she died, Crain closed Hill House and sent his daughters away; they would later quarrel bitterly over which of them would inherit the house. The elder sister wound up living there with a female companion, a girl from the village, who claimed after the sister's death that she was the legal inheritor of the house. The younger sister lost a fight against her in court, but hounded her until she committed suicide. "Gossip says she hanged herself from the turret on the tower, but when you have a house like Hill House with a tower and a turret, gossip would hardly allow you to hang yourself anywhere else," Dr. Montague remarks. As if to symbolize the children's unhappiness, a distinctive cold spot, a classic sign of haunting, lies just before the doorstep of the nursery: "the heart of the house," one character calls it.

The supernatural manifestations begin on the second night. Eleanor awakens to a sound she believes is her mother knocking on the wall to summon her; it turns out to be an unknown presence banging on the bedroom doors, seemingly in search of someone inside. Soon it becomes clear that whatever is in the house has its eye on Eleanor. Mysterious messages appear on the walls written in chalk and in blood: "Help Eleanor Come Home." At one point Dr. Montague's wife, a blowzy medium who arrives in the midst of the weeklong investigation to provide some much needed comic relief, insists that the group contact the house's spirits using a planchette, a device similar to a Ouija board. The message that arrives is addressed to Eleanor. "What do you want?" Mrs. Montague asks. "Home," comes the response. Over the next night of manifestations, the pressure inside Eleanor's head mounts unbearably. "It is too much, she thought, I will relinquish my possession of this self of mine, abdicate, give over willingly what I never wanted at all; whatever it wants of me it can have. 'I'll come,' she said aloud."

At one point the characters try to define fear, and their answers are notably similar. "I think we are only afraid of ourselves," Dr. Montague suggests. "Of seeing ourselves clearly and without disguise," Luke elaborates. Theodora simply phrases it a different way: "Of knowing what we really want." Eleanor confesses her own personal fear: "I am always afraid of being alone." In the crucial scene that immediately follows, Eleanor awakens in the night to hear a voice babbling in the next room and clutches at the hand of Theodora, sleeping beside her. The voice turns into the cry of a child, sobbing, "Please don't hurt me. Please let me go home." She screams; the lights go on, and she sees that Theodora is not next to her after all, but in bed across the room. "God God," Eleanor says, "whose hand was I holding?"

If this, as Jackson wrote in her notes on one of the drafts, is the "key line" of the novel, what does it mean? The critic Daryl Hattenhauer has argued that Eleanor is holding her own hand, but the novel indicates that this is not the answer: at one point during the scene Eleanor clutches the other hand with both of hers. Another scholar writes, similarly, that Eleanor's fear comes from her disillusionment: she thought that she had company in the dark, but finds herself alone yet again. An alternate interpretation also seems possible. The people we hold by the hand are our intimates—parents, children, spouses. To discover oneself clinging to an unidentifiable hand and to ask "Whose hand was I holding?" is to recognize that we can never truly know those with whom we believe ourselves most familiar. One can sleep beside another person for twenty years, as Shirley had with Stanley by this point, and still feel that person to be at times a stranger—and not the "beautiful stranger" of her early story. The hand on the other side of the bed may well seem to belong to a demon.

But it is, once again, a poisonous mother-daughter relationship that is central to *Hill House*—just as Shirley's poisonous relationship with her own mother, whose relentless criticism had conditioned her to accept Stanley's belittling and betrayal, underpinned the damaging dynamic of her marriage. "Fear and guilt are sisters," says Dr. Montague, and Eleanor's anxiety is rooted in her guilt over her mother's death, which, she finally confesses, happened because she failed one night to respond to her mother's knocking on the wall. (When Shirley failed to respond on time to Geraldine's missives, regardless of their content, her mother took it poorly.) Eleanor reversed roles with her invalid mother, she the caretaker and her mother the dependent; in Hill House the roles reverse again, the hallways filled with ghostly children who pound on the doors and laugh at the keyhole but will never be allowed inside. In the end, the house itself takes on a kind of maternal role—"housemother," Luke puns—its furniture "padded" and "motherly," yet "hard and unwelcoming"; like the burned-out tenement Shirley glimpsed from the train, it is "vile," "diseased," "unclean," just as Eleanor's mother was in her illness. Eleanor's final crescendo of insanity transforms her into a child of the house, dancing and playing in its rooms. In her "Experience and Fiction" lecture, in which she discusses the writing of *Hill House*, Jackson writes that she sleepwalked one night and found on her desk the next morning a piece of her yellow writing paper on which she had scrawled, "DEAD DEAD." No such paper can be found among the drafts of the novel in her archive; instead, there is a page on which she scribbled, "FAMILY FAMILY." In the world of the novel, the two are essentially the same.

"The house *is* the haunting (can never be un-haunted)," Jackson wrote in her notes for the novel; on another page she wrote, "The house is Eleanor." Jackson clearly intended the external signs of haunting to be interpreted as manifestations of Eleanor's troubled psyche; over and over, in her notes and lectures about the book, she states that she does not believe in ghosts. But the novel makes it clear that something in the house brings out the disturbance in Eleanor. En route to Hill House, Eleanor indulges in fantasies of creating a home, picturing herself in various houses she passes along the way—a mansion guarded by stone lions, a cottage with a blue door and a white cat on the step—in each of which she imagines living a different kind of life. Later, she lies to the group about where she truly lives, conjuring a make-believe apartment based on these fantasies. Her final breakdown occurs after a conversation with Theodora in which Eleanor asks if they can live together after leaving Hill House and Theodora rejects her. When Eleanor submits to the house, she experiences a feeling of oneness with it, a heightened sense of its sounds and structure: "Somewhere upstairs a door swung quietly shut; a bird touched the tower briefly and flew off. In the kitchen the stove was settling and cooling, with little soft creakings. . . . She could even hear, with her new awareness of the house, the dust drifting gently in the attics, the wood aging." Eleanor is unmarried and alone, with no place to go, no home to return to; her first desire is a longing for home. And in the end she achieves it by surrendering to the pull of Hill House. "I am home, I am home," she thinks in her last moments of delusion, racing madly through the house before driving her car into a tree.

In an early version of the novel, the spirit voice that the protagonist

hears whispers to her to go away. But at some point in the writing process, Jackson realized that staying in Hill House was more frightening
than leaving it. Like an abusive relationship—or an ineluctably entangled
marriage of nearly twenty years—the house is both impossible to remain
in and impossible to escape. In the end, of course, Eleanor's delusion that
she is coming home to join whatever has been calling her turns out to
have been painfully wrong. The novel concludes with the same lines it
opened with, which show that her fantasies of unity go unfulfilled. Just as
Shirley's hope that marriage would bring an end to her loneliness turned
out to be in vain, Eleanor will not take her place in Hill House among the
ghosts with whom she imagined herself in communion. Whatever walks
there still walks alone.

IN THE MIDST of her work on *Hill House,* Jackson found a new intellectual home: the Suffield Writer-Reader Conference. Founded by the
poet William Jay Smith in 1956, the conference, held on the grounds of
a private school in Suffield, Connecticut, gave amateur writers a chance
to interact with professionals in a casual, intimate atmosphere. Jackson
was first invited in 1958 by Louis Untermeyer, a poet and author of children's books, who became a friend; she would return nearly every year
until her death. During her first summer, the other faculty, a group of
distinguished poets, critics, and fiction writers, included Untermeyer,
Malcolm Cowley, Padraic Colum, Shirley Barker, George Abbe, and
Jackson's old friend Jay Williams; Hyman attended as a guest lecturer.
Their obligations were light: each faculty member was required to give
a single public lecture and to read and critique student manuscripts.
The others regarded Jackson as "outrageous," she proudly told a friend,
because she insisted on having a pitcher of water and a bowl of ice delivered to her room an hour before lunch and dinner, so that she could set
out a bottle of bourbon and host guests for a drink before meals. She
was given a room in a private guest house, "so i can conduct my orgies
away from the students," but she had to share the house with Marjorie
Mueller Freer, a writer of saccharine juvenile fiction whose presence she
found grating. "she kept coming into my room at night and sitting on

my bed while she put up her hair and we had what she called—i swear to this—girl-talk. . . . i honestly found myself solemnly discussing things like My First Dance and Should I Cut My Hair? (really i don't think so marjorie dear, it looks so nice the way it is.)"

In the lectures Jackson gave in the late 1950s and early 1960s, at Suffield and elsewhere—"one [new] lecture a year usually manages to get you through"—she analyzed her own writing techniques and shared succinct, specific advice about exactly how she achieved her effects. In "Memory and Delusion," delivered her first summer at Suffield, she emphasized that the writer's intelligence must constantly be working, "always noticing": "I cannot find any patience for those people who believe that you start writing when you sit down at your desk and pick up your pen and finish writing when you put down your pen again." Everything the writer observes is possible fodder for a story. When a green porcelain bowl on the piano suddenly shatters during a bridge game, she keeps the image of the scattered pieces in her memory storeroom, waiting for the right moment to deploy it: as an image of destruction ("what I can remember is the way the little pieces of the bowl lay there so quietly after they had been for so long parts of one unbroken whole"), or as an illustration of a sudden shock, or to represent the loss of a treasured possession. "All things are potential paragraphs," she writes; the writer must decide upon their emotional valence.

The following summer, just after completing the *Hill House* manuscript, Jackson gave a lecture called "Garlic in Fiction," a masterpiece of clarity that reveals how thoroughly in command of her talent she was. The greatest danger to the writer, she said, is a reader who decides to stop reading, and so the writer must use every weapon in the arsenal to snare his or her attention. But images and symbols, if used too frequently, will overpower the story, just as garlic will overpower a dish; they must be employed only as accents. For each character in a story or novel, she explains, she uses one basic image or set of images that the reader will associate with the character. For Eleanor, there are five: a little old lady she meets on her way to get her car, who tells her she will pray for her; two stone lions outside one of the houses she passes; the oleander bushes surrounding another house; a white cat on the step of a cottage; and the little girl she encounters in the diner who refuses to drink her milk because it is not in the cup painted on the inside with stars that she prefers at home. ("Insist on your cup of stars," Eleanor silently bids the girl, poignantly, since her childhood—like Jackson's—clearly did not include such a cup, or a mother who would have indulged her whims.) The five symbols will recur throughout the novel, and each time they do, Jackson explains, they remind the reader of Eleanor's essential loneliness and homelessness. They become "artificially loaded words" that, deployed correctly, have a powerful impact.

Holding forth at Suffield, in her lectures and the lengthy question-and-answer sessions that followed, Jackson relaxed happily into her authority as a writer. Unlike Bennington, where despite her growing fame she was always identified as "Mrs. Stanley Hyman," Suffield was an oasis where she was recognized and celebrated as an individual. Refusing to allow Hyman to accompany her there, she explained that "it is now one of the only places where i feel i have a personality and a pride of my own, and i cannot see that go, too, under your mockery."

Jackson also took her first plane trip in July 1958: she went with Stanley and Barry to lecture at a book festival at Eastern Michigan College in Ypsilanti. Neither of them was distressed, but she was "frightened enough for three." After the plane ride, the lecture did not faze her, though the auditorium was "roughly the size of radio city," with an audience of more than six hundred people. The president of the University of Michigan invited her to lecture there the following year, but Jackson declined to commit. In fact, she would never set foot on a plane again.

Her car, however, was a source of pleasure and freedom—and another place where she could escape Hyman's eye. That summer, Jackson acquired, for $1850 (less than *Woman's Home Companion* paid for a story), the first of a series of tiny Morris Minor convertibles, black with red leather seats, which she called "the pride and joy of my life." Later, after the money for the movie rights to *Hill House* came in, she considered buying an Austin-Healey convertible, but when she sat down in it she realized she wasn't "the sports car type"; she couldn't even reach the brake. Many of Stanley's former students remember seeing her tooling around North Bennington in the "Morris," as she called it, one arm stuck out the window. She liked to drive fast, taking the turns at full speed. Barry, sitting in class in the North Bennington Village School, could tell it was his mother driving by from the way she revved the motor. In September 1958, she drove by herself to New York and back to attend the wedding of her friend Barbara Karmiller, a former Bennington student; afterward they had champagne and caviar and she headed home, "sailing along in my little car." The following summer, when all the children were out of the house and Stanley spent a month teaching in New York, she went on long spontaneous drives, stopping to spend the night at inns she happened to find along the way. She and Stanley also traveled together, taking a road trip to Massachusetts and Maine because Shirley had never seen the coast; she loved Maine's little fishing towns.

That was before her agoraphobia set in. During Jackson's worst periods, in the last years of her life, she found it impossible even to walk from the house to her beloved car. The ability to drive—since Westport an important element of her identity, allowing her both convenience and independence—had been taken away from her. (Eleanor notably begins her own journey to Hill House by stealing the car she shares with her sister; that she drives herself to her new home, with various encounters on the way both real and imaginary, is crucial to the novel.) As Jackson began the process of recovery, her first challenge was to get behind the wheel once more. When she was finally able to gather her strength to begin the novel she would not finish, Jackson endowed its heroine with a name potently symbolic of her own longing for freedom and autonomy: Angela Motorman.

"HILL HOUSE IS REALLY swinging," Jackson wrote to Carol Brandt after her return from Suffield. But the main character would go through at least three different versions—one, incongruously, a spinster with a swagger not unlike Aunt Morgen in *The Bird's Nest*—before Jackson settled on the final, significantly more subdued version of Eleanor. By September 1958, she had made little progress: every week she threw out half of the manuscript and started over. Most of her work was done in a private study upstairs: Hyman had kicked her out of the downstairs study, she claimed, because her desk was always too messy. But she finished the book at a second typewriter she kept in the dining room, adjacent to his work space. Perhaps she was trying deliberately to discomfit him: Jackson tended to talk out loud when she was writing, and "yell and swear and laugh and sometimes cry," which made him nervous. For the first time, he refused to read her manuscript: he found the concept of ghosts too frightening.

Fortunately, Pat Covici at Viking proved to be the most patient of editors. Rather than give Jackson a firm deadline, he liked to ask her to submit her novels "when the dogwood blooms in Central Park," which they both took to calling "Dogwood Day." Brandt, whose instinct for soothing Jackson's nerves would prove very strong over the coming years, encouraged her to put the book aside and write some short stories. She quickly submitted a whimsical piece called "The Very Strange House Next Door," which Brandt sold to the *Saturday Evening Post* for $2250—Jackson's first story to be published there and her highest fee to date. Nearly ten years earlier, Jackson had written a series of stories about a housekeeper named Mallie who acts as a kind of fairy godmother, creating home-cooked meals and handmade curtains seemingly out of thin air. Now she resurrected the character, perhaps as an antidote to *Hill House*—a cheerful domestic version of the evil powers at play there. The story, however, has a darker subtext: the family who employ Mallie are newcomers in town, and eventually the locals hound them out because of their odd ways. Like "Flower Garden," which has a similar theme, the story is told from the perspective of one of the villagers, who is blissfully unaware that she may have done anything wrong. ("I don't gossip," she announces in the first line of a story that consists of virtually nothing but gossip.)

With her own touch of the fairy godmother, Brandt also managed to finesse several professional difficulties that dogged Jackson. Back in the fall of 1957, after Roger Straus refused to advance her any more money, Bernice Baumgarten had signed her up to contribute a few sections to a guide for new parents to be published by Little, Brown. Titled *Special*

Delivery: *A Useful Book for Brand-New Mothers*, the book would inter-
sperse words of advice from Jackson with humor pieces by Mark Twain,
Ogden Nash, and others, as well as professional advice from a doctor
and a nurse. Jackson found the whole project embarrassing, explaining
bluntly when it came out that she did it for money. In fact, her contributions are charming and down-to-earth, particularly next to the articles
written by the "professionals," which give a taste of the conventional
wisdom of the era. (The nurse advises bringing a loose-fitting dress or
girdle to wear home from the hospital, "as it usually takes a few weeks to
regain your pre-baby figure.") Jackson, by contrast, is candid, uncon-
descending, and thoroughly realistic. On the difficulty of getting babies
to sleep through the night, she writes, with her customary understated
humor, "No one has ever solved this problem adequately." She urges
new mothers not to adhere strictly to a schedule, as many pediatric
experts of the time advised: "No baby ever developed an excruciating
disease because he got a swift sponging instead of a bath." "We Just
Came to See the Baby" is an all-too-realistic depiction of a gaggle of
judgmental elderly aunts descending upon a helpless young mother at
the very moment the baby decides to nap. A piece urging new mothers to go ahead and hire a babysitter—"in ninety-nine cases out of a
hundred the baby will wake up, take his bottle calmly, submit to being
burped and changed, and go back to his bed and to sleep without any
sign of shocked disbelief at seeing a stranger"—ends with a very funny
story about a mother who left her two children with their usual sitter
and went out for the evening without mentioning that she had recently
given birth to a new baby, whom she had left sleeping on the porch.
Jackson presents this anecdote as having happened to a friend, but it
sounds like something she could conceivably have done herself.

The editor at Little, Brown who signed Jackson up for *Special Delivery* had promised that her name would "only appear in some small note
somewhere," with no indication that the book had been written or
edited primarily by her. But when the book came out, in April 1960,
the publisher could not resist capitalizing on her fame, trumpeting her
authority in providing "a sane and sage approach to the hilarious and
homey situations which accompany the advent of motherhood." Covici

was displeased, but Brandt soothed him with the promise that Jackson would do nothing to support the book promotionally.

Brandt also worked the miracle of mending Jackson's relationship with Herbert Mayes, the *Good Housekeeping* editor who had demanded that she repay her advances from the magazine but refused to buy her stories. After Mayes moved in the fall of 1958 from *Good Housekeeping* to *McCall's*, Brandt took him out to lunch and asked him to do her a personal favor by "burying the hatchet." He astonished both her and Jackson by agreeing. Betty Pope, the editor who replaced Mayes at *Good Housekeeping*, promptly offered Jackson another contract with the magazine, which she accepted, again to her later regret. At the time she needed the money, but after the movie rights to *Hill House* were sold— for the sum of $67,500—that was no longer a concern. And Pope edited her work heavily, often without running the changes by her before publication: "[she] thinks she is making them cleverer when she takes out my exquisitely formed phrases and substitutes madison avenue slang." Perhaps because Jackson had little financial motivation, the pieces she wrote—"In Praise of Dinner Table Silence," "The Fork"—were beneath her usual standard. The arrangement ended amicably in 1961.

Jackson was intimidated by Brandt's personal style: "eight feet tall with lots of gold bracelets studded with rubies and enormous hairdos and the right shade of lipstick and a kind of little tolerant laugh," the kind of woman who made Jackson nervous that she would overturn a martini onto her "perfect gray suit." She was always anxious about her own clothes on visits to New York, where her relaxed style of dress stood out among the business suits and formal dresses worn by most professional women in the gray-flannel-suit era of late 1950s New York. Myron Kolatch, Hyman's editor at *The New Leader* in the early 1960s, was astonished when she showed up for lunch one day in a loose-fitting housedress and bobby socks, then the rage among teenage girls. She often mentions rushing to buy new clothes before lunch with her agent or editor.

But Brandt, whose son Carl would follow her into the business, had a gentle, maternal manner that Jackson came to find reassuring. A dozen years older and the mother of two grown children, Brandt offered advice about problems with the Hyman children—starting in the fall of 1958, when Laurence, a high school junior, was promptly kicked out of boarding school less than a month after he started. Her supportive words were a sharp contrast to Geraldine, who all but blamed Laurence's problems on Shirley's permissiveness: if she hadn't let him spend so much time running around playing jazz with older boys and men, she reprimanded her daughter, he might have had an easier time settling down at school. When Jackson complained of arthritis in her fingers, Brandt sent her the name of a doctor she knew in New York and offered to make an appointment for her. And she seemed to understand when to give Jackson a little push and when to let her breathe. "Shirley, from my experience, is the kind of person who will come up with three ideas out of the blue just at the moment that you despair of having a letter from her. . . . Let her simmer on the back of the stove for a few weeks," she told Betty Pope. "Don't press the book and force the ending against the handicaps and difficulties you're having," she wrote to Jackson in spring 1959, when she was struggling to complete *Hill House*. "Take it easily and gently." Jackson managed to finish a week later.

From the start, it was clear that Jackson's experience with Viking would be different from her treatment at Farrar, Straus. In their letters to her, Covici and the rest of the staff took a deferent tone. "You are the most reasonable of authors," Marshall Best, one of the firm's top editors, assured her after she had complained about punctuation changes on the manuscript, promising that the house rules would be bent to accommodate her style. Covici himself was fairly hands-off, giving Jackson a list of changes recommended by the editors but emphasizing that they were suggestions, not directives. He had faith that given enough time, Jackson could perfect the manuscript on her own—and he was right. She would not become as close to him as she had once been to John and Margaret Farrar, but she appreciated his light touch and his supportive manner, dedicating to him *We Have Always Lived in the Castle*, their second book together. *Hill House* was dedicated to Leonard Brown, the Syracuse English professor who had been a formative influence on both her and Hyman.

Hill House was a financial and critical triumph. A month before the publication date of October 16, 1959—appropriately close to Halloween—Viking ran an unusual announcement in *The New York Times*, generating advance sales of about eight thousand copies and considerable buzz. Though there was the usual wonderment at Jackson's dual writing personas, reviewers responded far more enthusiastically than they had to any of her previous novels. Some treated it as little more than a particularly well-written horror tale. In *The New York Times*, Orville Prescott—often one of Jackson's more skeptical critics—called it "the most spine-chilling ghost story I have read since I was a child," although he was unsure whether she intended it to be "taken seriously" or had simply designed it "to give delicious tremors to readers who delight in one of the oldest varieties of folk tale." Some thought the book was too obviously Freudian: *Time* opened its piece with the snide line "When busy Housewife Shirley Jackson finds time for a new novel, she instinctively begins to id-lib." Jackson professed to think this was hilarious, claiming she had "never read more than ten pages of Freud," though she later invoked him regarding *Castle*. But most critics recognized that *Hill House* was, as the *Providence Journal*'s reviewer put it, "a strong and scary parable of the haunted mind" in the vein of Hawthorne, Poe, or James. Along with Bellow's *Henderson the Rain King*, John Updike's *The Poorhouse Fair*, Louis Auchincloss's *Pursuit of the Prodigal*, and others, the book was a finalist for the National Book Award—Jackson's first and only nomination. The winner was *Goodbye, Columbus*, Philip Roth's impressive debut.

Though *Hill House* did not make the best-seller lists, it sold far better than any of Jackson's previous novels—around 12,000 copies for the hardcover edition in the first six months. For a condensed version, *Reader's Digest* offered $35,000, split between Jackson and Viking, which guaranteed another 25,000 copies in print. Jackson was thrilled about the deal. "when i left farrar and straus two years ago [Covici] had enough faith in me to persuade viking to take me on with a big advance and not bother me until i had finished the book," she wrote to her parents. "now, of course, they will be more than paid back." For the first time, a novel of hers had finally earned back its advance and was even making a profit. She and Hyman paid off their mortgage and all the smaller debts they had accumulated, including $1,800 to Geraldine and Leslie. "you come after the mortgage and before the dentist," she told them. The money also meant that she could take her time before embarking on a new novel, which for Jackson was a mixed blessing: she consistently wrote best under a deadline. It would take her well over a year to get *Castle* off the ground.

The sale of movie rights was a huge financial boon. "i just deposited twenty-four thousand bucks in the bank and am feeling a bit lightheaded," she reported after receiving an installment of the $67,500, an astronomical fee for the time. She used the money to remodel the house, buying a new washing machine and dryer, drapes for the living room, brightly colored sheets for all the beds, and a player piano; even after Stanley bought *New Yorker* stock for the children, they had enough left over to open their first savings account. In staid North Bennington, the idea of colored sheets was so shocking that Jackson's fellow faculty wife Helen Feeley still remembered them decades later.

Robert Wise, whose film *West Side Story* (1961) was about to win numerous Academy Awards, would direct the movie, to be called *The Haunting*. (His next project was *The Sound of Music*, another blockbuster.) Julie Harris, then best known as a stage actor, starred as Eleanor Lance—not Vance—and Claire Bloom, who had appeared opposite Charlie Chaplin in *Limelight*, played Theodora, now unambiguously portrayed as a lesbian. Production began in October 1962, with interiors filmed at the MGM Studios in London. For exterior shots of the house, Wise chose Ettington Hall (now the Ettington Park Hotel), a gigantic Gothic mansion near Stratford-upon-Avon, which was said to be haunted by the ghost of a girl who threw herself from the balcony one Friday because she could not marry her lover. Bloom and Harris were reportedly terrified when they got their first look at the house. Wise decided, superstitiously, not to film on Fridays.

In keeping with the novel, Wise chose not to explicitly depict anything supernatural. "Shirley Jackson writes along that very fine line . . . just on the edge of reality and unreality," he told a reporter. "There's no ectoplasm in this picture, no ghosts, no manifestations, no monsters, no hairy claws coming out from behind the draperies." Instead, Wise generated suspense through the clever use of camera angles, including a special wide-angle lens that produced a distortion effect. For the soundtrack, he amplified recordings of the moanings and creakings typical of an old house, and he photographed the house through filters that blocked out the natural green of its surrounding gardens. Nandor Fodor, the parapsychologist whose book about poltergeists Shirley had consulted, served as a technical adviser. Jackson did not participate in the filming—as with *Lizzie*, she said that once she had been paid for the rights, the director could do whatever he wanted with her book—but she did meet with Wise and screenwriter Nelson Gidding to discuss their vision for the film. Gidding told her he saw Hill House as something like an insane asylum, with the manifestations coming from the demented perspective of the patients—was that what she had intended? "No," she replied, "but I think it's a very good idea."

For once, Jackson was delighted by a promotional campaign: the advertisements for the movie were marvelously creative. A few months before it opened, ads ran in the New York papers requesting contact with anyone who had had a supernatural experience: "Wanted: Accounts of Persons Who Have Seen a Ghost." Those who had were directed to write to The Haunting, in care of MGM, "All replies confidential." Reviewers were almost unanimously won over. Wise had given the novel its due by filming it as "a top-notch ghost story, old-fashioned and therefore filled with the horrors of the unseen and unexplained," wrote critic Judith Crist in the *New York Herald Tribune*. Others expressed relief that he hadn't made it into a typical grade-B horror movie. Only Brendan Gill of *The New Yorker* managed to be snide. "Most of the devices it employed in trying to make my flesh creep go back to the days of *The Bat*," he wrote. Jackson said publicly that she was pleased with the adaptation. "When I saw it, I was terrified. I couldn't believe that I had written this," she told a reporter. In private, she bemoaned the changes made to the plot, but said the house—the real star of the movie, anyway—was wonderful.

By the time *The Haunting* opened, on September 18, 1963, Jackson could barely make it to New York for the premiere. She had been housebound for more than a year, suffering from a debilitating combination of agoraphobia and colitis, her own form of imprisonment. Hyman accompanied her: she could not travel alone. Eleanor, rather than return to her family, had driven herself into a tree; Shirley, mercifully, chose a less violent, if no less drastic, effort at self-preservation. "I have written myself into the house," she chillingly told a friend. She would have to write herself out of it.

16.

STEADY AGAINST THE WORLD

WE HAVE ALWAYS LIVED IN THE CASTLE, 1 9 6 0 – 1 9 6 2

i will so write ten pages if i like. . . . i was feeling very silly because i thought you were not going to answer my child-ish letter, which i so much enjoyed writing. . . . do you find it crazy, kind of, sending a letter out into the blue and then just wondering where it got to finally and how it was received and whether someone said goodlordlook at the length ofthis and then used it to light cigars with?

—Shirley Jackson, letter to Jeanne Beatty

THE LETTER, UNPROMPTED AND UNEXPECTED, ARRIVED TWO weeks before Christmas 1959, an early gift. Jackson had just published a piece in *The Reporter* lamenting contemporary trends in children's books, which tended to favor inspirational tales about historical figures or sensible, practical stories—"how Violet, Girl Horticulturalist, found love and a career in a greenhouse"—rather than the magical kingdoms and adventure sagas that had absorbed her as a child. Children these days, she complained, knew their way around Mars better than the Land of Oz. "Every now and then," she wrote, "even these days, I meet some-one else who knows the names of the four countries of Oz. . . . There are fewer of us every year, I suspect."

The letter opened with a list of the four countries of Oz (Gillikin, Munchkin, Quadling, Winkie). It also contained books: one from the *Moomin* series by the Finnish writer Tove Jansson, a cheerful fantasy about a family of oddly shaped creatures who have various adven-tures, as well as another book called *Palm Tree Island*: "better than *Treasure Island*, a hundred times better than *Swiss Family Robinson*." And it showed that the letter writer, a housewife in Baltimore named Jeanne Beatty, was a kindred spirit: in addition to knowing the Oz books, even the more obscure ones, every bit as well as Shirley did, she was searching, somewhat desperately, for someone to talk to about the books she loved—fantasy and science fiction, but also contempo-rary literature.

Shirley did not always answer her fan mail, but she found this letter irresistible. "I have looked forward to writing you, and had promised myself a pleasant morning dwelling on dear books . . . and of course find myself with half an hour, a sick typewriter ribbon, and twelve thank-you letters waiting," she wrote back, kicking off an intense correspon-dence that lasted for well over a year. On both sides, the letters became personal and intimate almost immediately, moving quickly from books to children, husbands, and writing: Shirley was about to start *We Have Always Lived in the Castle*. "I have promised myself absolutely to begin a new book next Monday morning, after the children have gone back to school," she told Jeanne in her first letter. "That means that I must lock myself up in my cave for four dogged hours a day, and sneak a minute or so here and there for writing letters and making lunch ('You will eat vegetable soup again today and like it; Mommy's beginning chapter three') so if I do not write [to you] now I never can."

The writing did not proceed exactly according to plan. Though Shirley had the title of her new book from the start—Pat Covici found it "lovely," but a Viking sales representative worried that it was "too long for anyone to remember"—she would not complete it until April 1962, more than two years later. She spent 1960 embroiled in the most difficult struggle she would ever experience writing a novel, unable to find her way in. That fall, she decided to discard the entire draft and begin anew; she kept the title and the basic theme but drastically altered the main characters. The following spring, when she was nearly immobilized by colitis, in pain and largely unable to leave home, the book began to take shape. By January 1962, she had four chapters. Two more came quickly in February; she was finished by the end of April.

But in 1960, she did virtually no writing, other than a few pieces for *Good Housekeeping*—and her letters to Jeanne Beatty. Those letters total more than sixty pages, often single-spaced, of Shirley's signature yellow copy paper. Their subject matter ranges widely: from the Oz books to C. S. Lewis, J. R. R. Tolkien, and Frank Baker's comic mystery novel *Miss Hargreaves*, about a young man who invents a fictional character and discovers, to his astonishment and eventual chagrin, that his invention has come to life; Sarah's troubles with the third-grade teacher (three years earlier, but still on Shirley's mind); the arthritis plaguing her fingers; the literary tour of Europe she and Stanley had been invited to lead the following summer; the pleasure she took in the Suffield writing conference, to which she encouraged Jeanne to apply; recipes for beef stew, brisket, potato pudding, and, from Jeanne, a classic of the era: canned grapefruit slices frozen in gin and served on toothpicks. Discussing children, Shirley treated Jeanne—twelve years her junior, with four children eight and under—as a kind of younger sister, writing with the confident authority she displayed in *Special Delivery*, which came out that spring: "i cannot really remember what it is like to have a child under two, and glad i am for it." ("Dear Master Parent," Jeanne teased her after reading the baby-raising manual.) Shirley sent a photograph of some of the household pets: Bix, a newly acquired Great Dane, curled up with a black cat named Piney Brown, with another black cat, Harlequin, visible in the background. And she showed off, relishing Jeanne's admiration of her work and playing the role of "Important Writer." In an aside about her newly acquired stereo, she couldn't resist adding that Ralph Ellison helped put it together. "do you know his great book *invisible man?* because it was written in our house with sally sitting on his typewriter tormenting [him] and he would really rather set up electronic equipment than write." She also alluded to her romantic encounter with Dylan Thomas, now dead for six years: "he taught me to say 'not bluidy loikely,' and i can do it fine. . . . someday i will know clearly how i felt about dylan."

As the friendship progressed—only through the mail; the two women would never meet face-to-face—Shirley did not shy away from the more difficult aspects of her life. She joked about her moods, calling herself "sharly (snarly shirley)" and "shurley (surly shirley)." She complained about the isolation of North Bennington, "with no trains and only an occasional nasty bus and roads not fit to travel on most of the time, so we are forced to find all our social life in one small college community." She described her nightmares about the daemon lover, which by the end of the year had begun to recur. And she wrote at length about Stanley, whom she described to Jeanne, in her second letter, as "my husband, professor of literature at bennington college, vindictive winner of bets, poker player, writer of profiles for the new yorker, stern bearded disciplinarian, who will not read hill house because he is mortally afraid of ghosts."

In the beginning, Shirley presented their family life as quirky but happy, full of inside jokes and private games. When Stanley went to Detroit for a month to give a series of lectures, she told Jeanne it was a tradition for her and the children, at the precise time of his lecture, to stop whatever they were doing and send him mental wishes of good luck. But soon a note of melancholy crept into her tone. Stanley refused to

A photo of Jackson's pets, sent to Jeanne Beatty in 1960.

enter her office because her books were not alphabetized and her shades and pictures were always crooked. He begrudged "every minute" she did not spend writing fiction or articles, and once "in a fury figured out that considered in terms of pure writing time my letters are worth forty dollars a page." And her haphazard working habits irritated him.

> he sits down at the typewriter and says today i will write ten pages with half an hour for a cigar after lunch and today he writes ten pages and on tuesday he writes letters . . . and answers all the letters he has gotten since last tuesday and on sunday he files everything. . . . so when he sees me spending a Working Day making a doll house out of an old carton he gets very nervous. or sometimes i look at pictures of old houses or sing to myself or sit on the back steps telling myself stories and stanley frets.

Some of Stanley's impatience surely had to do with his frustration that his orderly routine did not translate into efficiency at the typewriter: he still had not finished *The Tangled Bank* after more than a decade, largely because of his demanding teaching schedule. He made no real headway on the writing until early 1959, when a fellowship from the American Council of Learned Societies finally allowed him to take a semester off, but he had to stop after finishing the Frazer section so that he could write the never published profile of Jackie Robinson for *The New Yorker*. He would finally complete the book in the summer of 1961.

Jeanne empathized with Shirley. She had attended Oberlin College and Johns Hopkins University, taking courses in English, mathematics, and botany, and was evidently brilliant, but had given up her studies to marry and raise children. Her husband, an engineer, worked long hours, and she often broke off her letters in order to tidy the house before he got home: "Of course I will meet him smiling." He, too, believed that time she spent writing or reading was time wasted. "What am I doing reading the Sunday papers? (It's Sunday.) Why am I not washing fingerprints off the woodwork and vacuuming spiderwebs off the ceiling? . . . What are women for, anyway?" He had made her give away her piano—"House wouldn't hold both it and play pen and we're *not* giving the baby away"; she couldn't even have a record player. She wouldn't leave him, at least partly because she suffered from depression and depended upon his stability ("he solidifies the atmosphere"). But when Shirley described how she had spent part of the previous summer driving around by herself in her Morris Minor, Jeanne felt "purest saturated envy for your aloneness, your morris, and your wandering. . . . I want loneness, no kids, no responsibilities but me, or nothing [no writing] comes. Except a couplet now and then put down on kitchen paper, and one of those got put out by mistake for the milkman." In a poem she sent to Shirley, her longing is palpable:

> *make me a poem   make me a psalm*
> *make me a song when the lights lie down*
> *make me a charm so the dark won't find me*
> *and the frightful things rise up behind me*

It's easy to understand why Jeanne was thrilled to receive Shirley's letters, which she carefully numbered and preserved. She was an anonymous housewife—albeit an extraordinary one—flattered by the attention of a famous writer. As for Shirley, she had not had a female friend whose mind was so well calibrated to hers since Jeanou, back in her days at the University of Rochester, with whom she had long since fallen out of touch. Her closest friend at Syracuse had been June Mirken, charming and witty and sympathetic, but June was Stanley's friend first, and an element of rivalry always existed between them. At Bennington, Shirley had friends among the faculty wives, including Helen Feeley, Laura Nowak, and Harriet Fels, but these were social acquaintances: she went out to lunch with them and chatted with them at cocktail parties, but she did not unburden her heart to them. (Some also were prone to making catty remarks about her behind her back.) And all her male friends were Stanley's friends as well: Ralph Ellison, Joseph Mitchell, Howard Nemerov.

In Jeanne, Shirley had finally found an ear attentive to her and her alone, a person who not only was truly interested in what she had to say about the things that mattered to her most, but also posed no threat of exposing her to anyone else she knew. "it is a wonderful pleasure to write to you," Shirley confided. "i go from month to month and year to year never writing letters because i cannot write little letters which are polite and unnecessary mostly because i can't stop, as you see. . . . it's like sitting down to talk for an hour, and far more agreeable than most conversations." Shirley had always loved to write for an audience, whether imagined or real: the letters to Bud Young she scribbled in her high school diary, the voluminous correspondence she and Stanley carried on during the summers they spent apart in college, her regular reports on family life to her parents back in California. Now she had Jeanne, who—like the character in *Miss Hargreaves* who astonishes her creator by coming to life—seemed to magically combine the best attributes of all Shirley's correspondents: she was a real person who wrote back, but the fact that she was far away and knowable only through her letters meant that she served as a screen onto which Shirley could project her vision of the ideal friend, without any risk of disillusionment. The novel Shirley was writing, or trying to write, would ultimately center around two women who are perfect complements: one light, the other dark; one older, the other younger; one domestic, the other untamed; one sane, the other unhinged. Together they form an inseparable, self-contained unit; apart, they are vulnerable to destruction.

As *Castle* stalled, writing to Jeanne became Shirley's only solace. "my book is so completely bogged down that i am almost frightened. quite seriously, writing these long letters to you (and, oddly, i do not write so to anyone else, perhaps because *your* letters are so delightful) does more good for me (selfish) than anything i can think of; it somehow relaxes and directs." She waited impatiently for Jeanne's responses—out of eagerness to hear from her friend, but also because she couldn't wait to write back. One letter ended "my turn my turn," urging Jeanne quickly to pass the baton. Jeanne couldn't help but be a little insulted. "I resent being called a vacuum between letters. No, I resent being one," she wrote. At the same time, she was glad to help. "If it soothes and pleases you to write, here I am, an everlovin' raccoon blanket. . . . You write letters to keep down the underbrush so the ground's clear for more

ambitious building; any letters I write are a triumph over the underbrush of daily days."

If Shirley was trying to "keep down the underbrush" so that her
mind would be clear to focus on *Castle*, she was unsuccessful. Did she
have trouble making progress on the novel because she spent too much
time writing to Jeanne (as Stanley surely would have scolded, had he
caught her at it)? Or did she write so often to Jeanne because she could
not write the novel and needed another outlet? The latter seems more
likely—once the novel picked up steam, their correspondence dwindled.
A major theme of the letters is the novel's failure to thrive. "damned
book is nagging me so i wince," Shirley wrote in February 1960. "it is
a perfectly splendid book, nicely planned, and if done carefully should
work out true and complete; it has only one disadvantage—everything
in it has been done before, by me or someone else. it is as unoriginal
as an old sponge." She reminded herself that her novels almost always
began this way; the false starts and dead ends were simply part of her
process. But that didn't make the difficult period easier to get through.

While much of Shirley's original draft has been lost or destroyed,
it's possible to piece together some of *Castle*'s initial plot from her letters
to Jeanne. She was inspired by a famous case that took place in Victorian England, in which a man named Charles Bravo died mysteriously of
antimony poisoning. His wife, Florence, was significantly wealthier and
insisted on keeping her money in her name; he may, in fact, have accidentally swallowed poison that he intended for her. The couple's maid
might also have been involved. (The case was never solved.)

In Shirley's novel, the two main characters were originally named
Constance and Jenny; as in the final version, they are sisters who live
together in "a big old brown house saturated with family memories."
Jenny is married, and the two sisters have jointly decided to murder
her husband. (In a humorously vicious touch, Shirley named him after
Louis Harap, the editor and friend of Stanley's with whom she had
a falling-out some fifteen years earlier, after he criticized her writing.) "they are going to kill him because he is a boor i think," Shirley
wrote. But she wasn't sure how. "i want something highly suspicious

but possibly natural, like mushrooms but i don't really know one end of a mushroom from another." She borrowed handbooks on plants and mushrooms from her friend Libbie Burke, Kenneth Burke's wife, and made careful notes on the poisonous ones: *Amanita pantherina,* false blusher ("highly poisonous"); *Amanita muscaria,* fly agaric ("highly poisonous"); *Amanita phalloides,* death cap ("deadly poisonous"). Her characters were constantly on her mind. "cooking now is putting something into a casserole and sitting on my red stool making notes," she wrote in March. "about one-third of this will get into the book and the rest is just saturating myself with the two of them and trying to get ivy compton-burnett out of my system."

The summer, though, was bad for her morale. Her evening lecture at Suffield drew a record-breaking audience, but she felt like a hypocrite giving writing advice—"do not impose your own prejudices upon your story; let your story tell itself"—when she couldn't make progress on her own novel. With all three younger children in camp and Laurence touring Europe with his band, she and Stanley took a road trip to the Maine seashore and to Salem, which she had longed to see but found disappointingly filled with tourist traps: "there weren't any witches. . . . but there was the Witch City Auto Body Wrecking Company and the Witch City Dry Cleaners and the Witch Grill. . . . after much searching i got to see a manuscript written in court of the trial of Rebecca Nurse and she really did say all those heartbreaking things." They hoped to wander farther, but Stanley tripped and hit his jaw, doing major damage to his teeth. Together they took an emergency detour to New York, where he visited a dental surgeon and she met with Brandt and Covici, who asked her if the book would be ready by the following spring. "dogwood day, and i was eating eggs benedict and drinking martinis and pretending i was a lady being taken out to lunch. the book will not be ready a year from dogwood day." She hadn't heard from Jeanne since April, and the silence saddened her: "i would have sent you a postcard but you hadn't written for so long." Driving home by herself, she was caught in a heavy rainstorm and spontaneously decided to spend a night at a hotel in Albany, a luxury she could now afford. She told the desk clerk she wanted a room with air-conditioning and television, plus a bottle of bourbon and a bowl of ice, and spent "a lovely evening all by myself watching television and drinking bourbon"—closed off, safe, secure.

In early September, Shirley returned Libbie Burke's plant guides with a note apologizing for keeping them for so long: though the book was progressing slowly, she reported, two chapters were now done. But by the time Jeanne finally wrote again later that month, explaining that she had been overwhelmed at home, Shirley had decided to give up on the whole draft. "i am really seared by all this, although the clouds are lifting slightly," she wrote. "i have spent eight months trying to make a novel out of that thing and almost convincing myself i could, and it is an absolute relief to be able to look at it and say there isn't any novel there." As a sign of the psychic cost of her failure, the nightmares that had plagued her periodically over the last twenty years—her "pact-with-the-devil series of dreams," she called them—had returned.

Brandt was "heartily falsely cheerful" about the delay: she put on her most encouraging voice and said she would break the bad news to Covici, and in the meantime Shirley should "take a nice long rest." Stanley's reaction was rather different: "he said you have a nice long rest over my dead body you rested all summer you don't have to write this novel if you don't want to but you get the hell up to that typewriter and write *something* or your fingers will fall off." Shirley found his tough-love approach reassuring, especially after he took her out to dinner at the Rainbarrel. "maybe i will write another book," she told Jeanne. All the while, Covici kept up his gentle pressure, sending her a copy of his favorite cookbook, *Simple Cooking for the Epicure*, with a sweet but pointed note: "Good food helps my disposition. Does it help your inspiration?" To her parents, Shirley was philosophical: "these times come, and there is not much to do except wait them out."

This time the waiting took longer than usual. A major setback came in early 1961, when Shirley came down with what she thought was a lingering intestinal flu. It was soon clear that she was actually suffering from colitis, a painful and debilitating inflammation of the colon that can be correlated with high blood pressure, high cholesterol, and smoking. The symptoms, which include intense abdominal pain and sudden attacks of diarrhea and nausea, would be distressing for anyone, but for Shirley they were particularly upsetting. Always self-conscious about bodily functions, she initially tried to conceal her problems from Stanley. "She lived on Alka-Seltzer," Sarah remembers. Dr. Durand prescribed paregoric acid, an over-the-counter diarrhea remedy, which she was to take six times a day, as well as "sulfa pills the size of eggs." Her diet was severely restricted: no coffee, orange juice, salad greens, or various other raw vegetables, among other foods. Her meals consisted largely of cottage cheese and perhaps "a nice bracing cup of cocoa" in the morning. After several months of this, all she longed for was "a cold green salad with tomatoes and avocados and french dressing with lots of garlic," but after she indulged, she regretted it.

Shirley's illness posed serious challenges for her lecturing schedule. In April, she and Stanley were both scheduled to speak at Fairleigh Dickinson University in New Jersey. The five-hour car ride caused her tremendous anxiety ("every time i saw a sign reading 'next gas station forty-four miles' i would get worried"); then she had to sit through Stanley's event, a three-hour panel discussion. "then a coffee hour with the students (no coffee for me, thanks) and then a cocktail party (*that* they didn't take away from me, thank heaven)." Her hosts took her and Stanley out to dinner at a fancy restaurant, where she suffered paroxysms of guilt when she was unable to eat the expensive steak that was ordered for her. Somehow she made it through her own lecture, before an audience of five hundred, with Stanley in the front row, ready to escort her out if necessary. With the exception of Suffield, it would be several years before she would travel again without him or someone else to accompany her.

In addition to Shirley's illness, the summer of 1961 was rocked by a Hyman family tragedy: the sudden death of Moe Hyman, Stanley's seventy-year-old father, from a heart attack. He and Lulu had come up to Bennington the previous New Year's Eve, laden with all the customary kosher delicacies from New York: delicatessen meats, brandied cherries, chicken livers. It had been apparent to all that Moe's health was declining, but his death still came as a shock. To Stanley he left his signet ring; Laurence, his favorite grandchild, inherited his collection of expensive

clothing: "a lot of silk shirts and fine sweaters, if he can bring himself
to wear them." Shirley, Laurence, and Joanne accompanied Stanley to
New York for the funeral, leaving the younger children in Bennington in
the care of Laura Nowak: Sarah's behavior could be unpredictable, and
Laura sensed that they "didn't want to take a chance." Shirley refused
to attend the ceremony itself, citing her "terror of such things." But she
was fascinated by the rituals, especially the tradition that Jews identified
as Cohens, or descendants of ancient priests, are forbidden to enter a
cemetery or go near a dead body, "even the present-day members of the
family named cohen—who are very far from being priests, considering
that one of them is a small-time gangster." She and her Jewish sister-
in-law, tasked with taking charge of the food served after the burial,
were bewildered by Lulu's kosher kitchen: "we used the wrong dishes
(put cheese and stuff in the dishes which are to be reserved entirely for
meat) and put everything back where it didn't belong."

Shirley's colitis may have contributed to her decision not to attend
the funeral. The illness plagued her, on and off, for the rest of 1961.
Paradoxically, it proved good for her novel, since it kept her close to her
desk: "there's nothing like being scared to go outside to keep you writing," she wrote to her parents. During that anxious fall, as Soviet and
U.S. tanks came to a standoff in Berlin and the first rumblings toward
war in Vietnam were audible, both Covici and Brandt nudged her again
to ask whether her novel might appear on Viking's 1962 list. "No one
has the desire to needle you or push you or hasten you, and if it makes
you nervous to commit yourself, don't," Brandt assured her. But this
time Shirley was finally able to give an affirmative answer. Covici would
have the manuscript by next Dogwood Day.

AS JACKSON STRUGGLED with *Castle*, a shipment of books from England arrived for Stanley. Among them was one that he had ordered for
her "half-seriously": *Sex Variant Women in Literature*, by Jeannette H.
Foster. (The book, which first appeared in 1956, is now considered a
minor classic of lesbian critical theory.) Jackson read one chapter and

decided the book was "clearly trash," but before putting it aside, she checked the index. There was her own name, with a reference to *Hangsaman* as "an eerie novel about lesbians."

Jackson tells this anecdote at the start of a five-page document in which she lays out, in considerable detail, the crisis she came to while working on *Castle*. These pages have previously been identified as an unsent letter to Howard Nemerov, but this seems unlikely: Nemerov was in residence at Bennington in 1960, the year the document must have been written, and Jackson would have been unlikely to write him a letter when he was living nearby. Moreover, none of her surviving letters to him—his archive includes only a few—is written in this style. It's possible, of course, that Jackson may have written other, more personal letters (of which this was one) to Nemerov, to whom she was close during the last years of her life. But what the document most resembles is a letter to Jeanne Beatty—perhaps composed during the lull in their exchange in the summer of 1960, when Jackson might have hesitated to intrude on her friend but missed having her usual outlet. Like many of the other letters to Jeanne, it is typed on Jackson's yellow copy paper and begins with no salutation, just the opening phrase, "now, can you help me?" And it is written in the intimate stream-of-consciousness style, sprinkled with jokes and puns, that characterizes Jackson's letters to Jeanne, with references to some of the other subjects their correspondence touched on.

It also deals with something Jackson may well have wanted to discuss with Jeanne: the question of lesbianism in her work. As mentioned earlier, Jackson was vehemently opposed to the idea that her fiction might have a lesbian subtext—perhaps *too* vehemently opposed, considering how often figures who may be understood as lesbian appear in her fiction. Now, she writes, the idea that she belonged in a book about "sex variance" had "completely disintegrated *castle*," because misreading Jenny and Constance as lesbians would distort the novel's meaning. Stanley told her to "write about what you want to write about and the hell with what dirty old ladies say," but she couldn't dismiss the concern (although she admitted that she would rather be "called names" by Foster than write books that were "cleaned up so she would not have any excuse for calling me names"). No one would believe that she had actually set out to write about the Charles Bravo murder; all readers would see were two women nefariously colluding against a husband. "my most basic beliefs in writing are that the identity is all-important and the word is all-powerful," Jackson wrote.

> i want my jenny in *castle* to be absolutely secure in her home and her place in the world, so much so that she can dispose of her husband without concern . . . but when jenny's identity depends entirely upon her thoroughly romantic association with constance, then i am tagged again. jenny wants to see the world, with always one foot on base at home, constance never wants to leave home. they are again two halves of the same person, and must i then suspect that? together they are one identity, safe and eventually hidden. do they hide because they are somehow unnatural? am i never to be sure of any of my characters? if the alliance between jenny and constance is unholy then my book is unholy and i am writing something terrible, in my own terms, because my own identity is gone and the word is only something that means something else.

Jackson's judgment of lesbianism as "unholy," though extreme, was not unusual for her time. But what disturbed her more than the idea of being "tagged" as a lesbian writer was that she might not have control over her own fiction—that her work might mean something entirely different from what she intended. On one level, to be sure, she wrote for herself; but she wrote also to be read and to be understood. The letter continues:

> i am writing about ambivalence but it is an ambivalence of the spirit, or the mind, not the sex. . . . it is fear itself, fear of self, that i am writing about, fear and guilt and their destruction of identity, and any means at hand will do to express them; why am *i* so afraid?... i am frightened by a word. . . . but i have always loved (and there is the opposition: love) to use fear, to take it

and comprehend it and make it work and consolidate a situation where i was afraid and take it whole and work from there. so there goes *castle*. i can not and will not work from within the situation; i must take it as given. . . . i delight in what i fear. then *castle* is not about two women murdering a man. it is about my being afraid and afraid to say so, so much afraid that a name in a book can turn me inside out.

The fear Jackson refers to is not fear of lesbianism—or, at least, not only fear of lesbianism. It is the fear of what lesbianism represented to her, something that on one level she fervently desired even as she feared it: a life undefined by marriage, on her own terms. Constance and Merricat are indeed "two halves of the same person," together forming one identity, just as a man and a woman are traditionally supposed to do in marriage. Not finding that wholeness in marriage, Jackson sought it elsewhere: first with Jeanne Beatty, and later with her friend Barbara Karmiller, also younger, who came back into her life shortly after she finished *Castle*. Indeed, the novel, in its final version, is not about "two women murdering a man." It is about two women who metaphorically murder male society and its expectations for them by insisting on living separate from it, governed only by themselves.

"FOUR PEOPLE HAVE READ the first two chapters . . . and all independently announce that it is the best work i have ever done. . . . i finally got it into a kind of sustained taut style full of images and all kinds [of] double meanings and i can manage about three pages a day before my eyes cross and my teeth start to chatter," Jackson wrote to Jeanne Beatty as the novel began to take shape. "Sustained taut style" is an apt description of this allusive, hypnotic book, which, at only 214 pages, is the briefest of her novels. In draft after draft, she mercilessly stripped out extraneous backstory, dialogue, and exposition. The final version is as economical and evocative as "The Lottery": on one level absolutely straightforward, but with a network of hidden meanings stretching like roots beneath the surface.

my name is mary katherine blackwood. i live with my sister constance.
i have often thought that with any luck at all i might have been a
werewolf, because the middle fingers on both my hands are the same
length, but i have had to be content with what i had. i dislike
washing myself, and dogs, and noise. i like my sister constance, and
richard plantagenet, and amanita philloides, the death-cap mushroom
everyone else in my family is dead.
the last time i glanced at the library books on the kitchen table they
were more than five months overdue, and i wondered wther i would have
chosen differently if i had known that these were the books that were
going to lie, forever, on the kitchen table. few things were ever
moved around in our house, anyway; we dealt with the small surface
transient objects, the books and the knitting and the dishes we used,
but below these lay a solid foundation of stable possessions. tables
and chairs and beds and pictures and rugs and dressers were dusted and
swept under, but set back always in their proper places, and the
tortoise-shell toilet set on our mother's dressing table was never off-
place by so much as a fraction of an inch. it was comforting to know
that nothing would be moved, it was safe. perhaps constance and i both
thought that an accidental jostling of our mother's tortoise-shell comb
would bring the house tumbling onto our heads; certainly we were very
careful.
it was on a friday in april, five months and two weeks ago as time is
correctly counted, that i chose the books in the library.

The first page of a draft of Jackson's manuscript for
We Have Always Lived in the Castle.

Castle is told entirely from the perspective of Mary Katherine Blackwood (Merricat, as her sister calls her), Jackson's most ambiguous heroine. Eighteen years old, she lives with her sister, Constance, and their
uncle, Julian, an invalid, in their longtime family mansion. The rest of
the Blackwoods are dead, poisoned six years earlier at the dinner table
by someone who put arsenic in the sugar that the family members used
to sweeten the blackberries served for dessert on the fateful night. The
novel teasingly withholds confirmation that Merricat was the murderer,
but there can be no real question in the reader's mind. She chose the
poison deliberately to spare Constance (who does not use sugar on her
berries), ten years older, whom she adores: "She was the most precious

person in my world, always." Protective of her little sister, Constance took the blame, washing out the sugar bowl immediately to hide the evidence, and stood trial. Even though—or perhaps because—she was acquitted (for reasons that are never made clear), the residents of the village ostracize the family.

Like the house in *The Sundial*, the Blackwood mansion sits physically at a remove from the village beneath it, surrounded by a barrier—in this case a fence put up by Merricat and Constance's father. When Merricat goes into town to do errands a few days each week—Constance never goes past the garden—the townspeople stare at her and children chant rude rhymes. "Merricat, said Connie, would you like a cup of tea? Oh no, said Merricat, you'll poison me." Other than those brief excursions, the two women are entirely self-sufficient. Constance does all the cooking and gardening because Merricat, according to their personal system of household rules, is not allowed to handle food, but together they take satisfaction in "neatening the house," preserving its order exactly as their parents left it. "We always put things back where they belong," Merricat explains. "We dusted and swept under tables and chairs and beds and pictures and rugs and lamps, but we left them where they were; the tortoiseshell toilet set on our mother's dressing table was never off place by so much as a fraction of an inch. Blackwoods had always lived in our house, and kept their things in order; as soon as a new Blackwood wife moved in, a place was found for her belongings, and so our house was built up with layers of Blackwood property weighting it, and keeping it steady against the world."

The women's domestic security is disrupted by the arrival of their cousin Charles, who appears to take a romantic interest in Constance but is more interested in assuming control of the estate and, thus, the family money hidden within it. Merricat, jealous and fearful at losing Constance and their way of life, plays pranks on Charles and finally, though perhaps accidentally, sets the house on fire. (She puts Charles's still burning pipe in a wastebasket full of newspapers, but it's not entirely clear that she grasps the almost certain consequences of this act.) The fire department, led by a village man who takes particular pleasure in tormenting Merricat, puts it out in time to spare the first floor. But then the fire chief, deliberately removing the hat that marks him as an official, leads the villagers in a violent rampage. While the sisters hide in the garden, their neighbors (with shades of "The Lottery") throw stones through the windows, smash heirloom china and furniture, and destroy Constance's harp, which falls to the floor "with a musical cry." Charles, whose voice is heard several times urging the firemen to rescue the safe in which the sisters keep their money, does not defend his cousins or otherwise intervene. After the disaster, it becomes clear that the fire served as a kind of purification ritual by which the villagers were at last able to make peace with the Blackwoods. The sisters set up house with their surviving furniture and cookware in the shell that remains, and now their neighbors, instead of pointing and jeering, stop by periodically to leave offerings of food on the doorstep. "We are going to be very happy," Merricat repeats to Constance.

As always while she was writing, Jackson paid careful attention to the physical space in which the novel takes place, drawing a map of the village depicting the shops, the main roads, and the path leading to the Blackwood house. The village, as described in the novel, sounds very much like North Bennington, with wealthier homes on the outskirts and a main street where all the villagers mix; in Jackson's sketch, the similarities are even more obvious. Some of Jackson's friends would later say she told them that Merricat's experiences in the village were based on her own. "We knew we were different," says Joanne Hyman. "Our parents were Democrats, we were atheists. We didn't fit in. We were . . . not paranoid, but a little bit self-conscious." Jackson also made diagrams of the dining room table, showing where each family member sat on that fateful last night, and her children remember her asking them to reenact the scene at the Hymans' oval dining table, with each of them representing a member of the Blackwood family.

While the novel's geography is carefully defined, motives are left uncertain, although the careful reader will notice hints. Why do the villagers despise the Blackwoods? What happened to Constance in town that made her decide never to venture beyond the garden? Why is Uncle Julian fixated on the night of the murder, obsessively recording every detail that he can remember? And, most crucially, what drove Merricat to murder most of her family? Early drafts give explicit answers to all these questions: regarding the murder, their mother treated Constance like Cinderella, forcing her to cook and clean in drudgery. In the final version, a single crack in Constance's docility is seen when, on the night of the murders, she tells the police that "those people deserved to die"—but she could be covering for Merricat. In another ambiguity, she also is the only of the sisters who expresses regret over the loss of the family, remarking once that she would "give anything to have them back again."

In *Hill House*, Jackson left the novel's most frightening elements unspoken, beneath the surface. She uses the same technique in *Castle*, but takes it to an extreme: *everything* is left mysterious. In contrast to the maximalist prose that characterizes the work of Kerouac or Bellow—Kerouac's *Big Sur* appeared in 1962, the same year as *Castle*; Bellow's *Herzog* came two years later—Jackson reduces episodes that could have been entire scenes to a single sentence. Isaac Bashevis Singer—the "Yiddish Hawthorne," Hyman called him in a review—complimented Jackson on *Castle*'s mysteriousness, which he found "European in spirit." "Where is it written that a writer must explain everything?" he wrote to her. "I am, like you, against too much motivation. The less[,] the better." In early versions, Constance and Charles engage in fantasies about their future together; in the final, their plans are only alluded to. Merricat's thinking as she starts the fire also was elaborated in the draft version: "there were newspapers in the wastebasket and his pipe, burning, on the table. it was a good omen, although i already knew that he put his pipe down all the time and forgot it. all i had to do was brush the pipe and ashtray off the table and into the wastebasket. sometimes things like that turn out all right and sometimes they turn out all wrong." In the final version, she simply sweeps the pipe into the wastebasket, with no further comment.

The most crucial revision Jackson made between the drafts was her shaping of Merricat's character, which is so crucial to the book in its final form that Jackson's own shorthand for the novel was "Merricat." The "Jenny" figure, as Jackson described in her unsent letter, is "absolutely secure in her home and her place in the world"; Constance is the one who is uncertain, who needs protecting. At an intermediate stage of the manuscript, an older version of Merricat, who returns home from an unspecified job in the city to take care of Constance, is still presented as the adult in the family. By the final draft, their positions are entirely reversed. Constance, as her name suggests, is the embodiment of peace and stability, angelic with her blond hair and rosy skin, even her harp. Merricat is untame, uncontrollable, her world governed by superstition rather than reason. Like a witch or a devil, she is accompanied everywhere by her black cat, and believes that she keeps herself and Constance safe through her magic rituals. Her peculiarities are evident from the book's iconic first paragraph, as astonishing as the opening to *Hill House*:

My name is Mary Katherine Blackwood. I am eighteen years old, and I live with my sister Constance. I have often thought that with any luck at all I could have been born a werewolf, because the two middle fingers on both my hands are the same length, but I have had to be content with what I had. I dislike washing myself, and dogs, and noise. I like my sister Constance, and Richard Plantagenet, and *Amanita phalloides*, the death-cup mushroom. Everyone else in my family is dead.

In her "Garlic in Fiction" lecture, Jackson described her technique of zeroing in on a few specific words that take on a special significance in the context of each novel. Merricat's symbolic words, "safe" and "clean," pinpoint her singular focus: keeping the private world of the Blackwood estate free from intruders and perfectly in order (according to her own irrational logic). Her reliance on magical thinking makes her seem younger than she actually is; perhaps the reader is meant to think that, like the Betsy persona in *The Bird's Nest*, her development was arrested at a traumatic moment—in this case, the murder. While shopping in town, Merricat distracts herself by pretending that the sidewalk is a board game with squares for "Lose a turn" (if she has a difficult encounter) or "Advance three spaces" (if all goes smoothly). She stashes objects around the property to form "a powerful taut web which never loosened, but held fast to guard us": silver dollars by the creek, a doll buried in a field, a book nailed to a tree. "All our land was enriched with my treasures buried in it." She chooses magic words that will retain their protective force only as long as they are never spoken. After her magic fails and Charles gains access to the sanctum, she becomes obsessed with removing any traces of him. (This is why Jackson uses the word "neaten" to describe the sisters' regular housekeeping rather than the more usual "clean"; in *Castle*, the purpose of cleaning is to remove spiritual contamination.) The fire is the ultimate cleaning agent that will finally achieve Merricat's desired result: to erase Charles's presence from the house entirely.

Friends and neighbors who knew the Hymans in the early 1960s have suggested that Merricat was the image of Sarah, who was twelve years old—the same age as Merricat at the time of the crime—when Jackson began her major rewrite of *Castle*. Like Merricat, who was sent to her room without supper on the night of the poisoning, Sarah regularly managed to get herself ejected from the dinner table for making insolent remarks. (As Constance does for her sister in the novel, Jackson often brought food up to her later.) A slender girl with bright eyes and long, wild hair, Sarah also shared her mother's interest in magic and omens. She had become close to Jay Williams, who originally helped Jackson explore her own interest in magic; the two of them made up their own holidays, including the feast day of "Jay-Hey-Day" and a magic ceremony to be conducted on "Salli's Eve." In *Raising Demons*, Jackson humorously depicts Sarah's early attempts at domestic magic and the chagrin with which her father greeted them. Elizabeth Greene, a friend of Sarah's in those years, remembers her conducting a healing ritual on behalf of a friend: "She was always pushing at edges . . . living in this imaginary world." Other friends speak of her physical recklessness, including a former classmate who recounted an episode in which Sarah, exploring in the woods, accidentally tumbled over a cliff. Sarah was intensely interested in the novel: she read the chapters as her mother finished them and offered critiques. Hyman was reportedly annoyed when Jackson accepted some of Sarah's suggestions rather than his: "he says he is a professional critic and i take the advice of a thirteen-year-old girl over his."

Jackson told Joanne that Merricat and Constance were in some ways modeled after the two Hyman daughters—Merricat on Sarah, Constance on Joanne—but only loosely. Joanne had Constance's aura of common sense, but she did not share Constance's placid domesticity. "It was fluid. It wasn't firmly attached that I was Constance and Sarah was Merricat," Joanne says. "They were both of us . . . in fantasy versions."

Of course, the elements of Merricat that reflected Sarah were precisely the ways in which Sarah most resembled her mother. Jackson, too, was preoccupied with omens and signs, making note of her lucky and unlucky days even as an adolescent. She spoke openly—perhaps too openly—of her interest in witchcraft and magic. Like the alleged witches of Salem Village, Merricat and Constance are outsiders, living a nontraditional lifestyle, vulnerable to the ill will spread by gossip—which Jackson felt to be her own social status in North Bennington. (Merricat's witchiness is enhanced by her faithful black cat, Jonas, to whom she often speaks, just as Jackson conversed with her cats.) Witchcraft, in this context, is again best understood as a metaphor for female power and men's fear of it. It is a last resort for women who feel that they are powerless, the only way in which they can assert control over their surroundings. Even imaginary control is preferable to no control at all.

The domestic arts, which Constance practices to perfection and which were a source of both interest and anxiety for Jackson, are another way in which women have traditionally expressed control over their environment. It is no accident that the witch's symbols are, of all things, a broom and a pot. In *Castle*, the kitchen—Constance's center of command and the sisters' final refuge—is "the heart of our house," as Merricat says. (Recall that Jackson used nearly the same phrase in *Hill House* to describe the nucleus of the haunting, the cold spot in front of the nursery.) The significance of preparing and preserving food is gorgeously represented in the rainbow of preserves stockpiled in the cellar: "All the Blackwood women had taken the food that came from the ground and preserved it, and the deeply colored rows of jellies and pickles and bottled vegetables and fruit, maroon and amber and dark rich green stood side by side in our cellar and would stand there forever, a poem by the Blackwood women." (The only other "poem" that appears in the novel is the villagers' cruel ditty about Constance and Merricat.) Constance's contributions, we are told, are the product of her life's work, and "her rows and rows of jars were easily the handsomest, and shone among the others." Just as she painstakingly separates edible mushrooms from those that are poisonous, Constance will allow the family to eat only from her own preserves; the others, she says, will kill them.

Female power and creativity, bottled up too long, turn lethal. This is the closest the novel comes to offering an explanation for the murder. If Merricat and Constance are two halves of a whole, in some ways forming a single person, then it does not matter which of them put the arsenic in the sugar bowl—they are both responsible, and equally justified. The crime turns their house into a prison, but it is a prison of their own creation in which they shut themselves willingly, as they affirm: "We are going to be very happy." The happy ending to their fairy tale requires a new definition of happiness, severed from the traditional marriage plot. But it is not ironic. Within a few months of *Castle*'s publication, Jackson, too, would build herself a prison. The difference was that she would inhabit it alone.

"MY BOOK GOES along so well it scares me," Jackson wrote Carol Brandt in February 1962, shortly before submitting the manuscript. "I am most reluctant to give up my characters." Throughout the process, Pat Covici had expressed nothing but absolute faith in her ability to produce a novel of the highest quality. He especially admired her unusual skill at fine-tuning her own work. "What a relief it is to get a manuscript that is not only the product of a first-rate imagination but has also gone through the fires of criticism," he told her early on. "Don't you rush anything for anybody," he assured her in another letter. "Go about your business of sharpening your pencils and literally sniffing the air of murder and love and intrigue and cover the pages at your own pace and let no one dare disturb you or do aught that would detract from the quality of your work."

Now his confidence in her was rewarded. Aside from the most basic copy-edits—which, unfortunately, included mistakenly changing the common name of *Amanita phalloides* from "death cap" (as Jackson correctly had it in her manuscript) to "death cup"—"not a word" of *Castle* needed correction. Marshall Best, the head of Viking Press, cried when he read it. Hyman predicted that if the book could "bring tears to those mean old publishing eyes," it ought to make a million dollars. Jackson had her doubts. "i do not think this book will go far," she wrote to her parents. "it's short, for one thing, and stanley and the publisher and the agent all agree that it is the best writing i have ever done, which is of course the kiss of death on *any* book." Also, she warned, "the heroine of this one is *really* batty."

In terms of publicity, Viking pulled out all the stops. The book party took place on September 20, 1962, the eve of publication day, in the library of the luxurious St. Regis Hotel, an opulent wood-paneled room lined with leather-bound books in glass-front bookcases. The seventy guests included primarily reviewers—Orville Prescott of the *Times*, Brendan Gill of *The New Yorker*—with a few friends: the Ellisons, the Burkes, Louis Untermeyer. Viking publicist Julie Van Vliet set up a whirlwind schedule of interviews: two radio programs, *The Reader's Almanac with Warren Bower* on WNYC and *Arlene Francis at Sardi's* (a talk show hosted by the actress and TV personality famous for *What's My Line?*), plus print journalists for the *New York Times, New York Herald Tribune, New York Post*, and others. Jackson's days were so packed that Harry Hancock of the *Chicago Tribune* had to interview her at the party. John Barkham of the *Saturday Review* echoed earlier interviewers in finding her "a solid, substantial personality as far removed from her Alice-in-Wonderlandish characters as it is possible to be." With the press, she was open about her struggles over the novel, confessing that she had written the first chapter in many different forms—first person, third person, with narrators of different ages, and so on.

For the first time in Jackson's career, the critics were virtually unanimous: *Castle* was her masterpiece. Many quoted the opening paragraph in its entirety, with even the usually tough Prescott counting *Castle* among the best books of the year and declaring, "Only one woman alive could have written this paragraph . . . a literary sorceress of uncanny prowess." He and others marveled at how deeply she had infiltrated Merricat's character: "the most eerie yet oddly attractive child in recent fiction," as one put it. Critics compared her to Poe, Edward Gorey, Dostoevsky, Henry James, Isak Dinesen, even Faulkner—Merricat, with her stilted, strangely affectless diction, reminded at least one reviewer of Benjy in *The Sound and the Fury*. There was the usual confusion about what genre Jackson was writing in. Was *Castle* a whodunit, a horror novel, or a "shocker with a stunning denouement like 'The Lottery'?" asked Barkham, concluding that the book contained elements of all those genres, yet was "a better piece of writing than any of them." Jackson needed "no ghosts, werewolves or clanking chains to inculcate horror," wrote Beatrice Washburn in *The Miami Herald*. "She finds it where it really exists, in the secret passages of the human mind." Several reviewers found the book beyond criticism: "one to read, not to review, for the aura it generates cannot be confined or itemized," raved the *Boston Herald*.

Even reviewers who found the plot difficult to believe complimented Jackson's "elegant distinction of style": she wrote like "a demon-touched angel," as one of them said. "Shirley Jackson looks at the world as practically nobody else does and describes it in a way almost anybody would like to emulate," wrote Max Steele in the *New York Herald Tribune*. Kenneth Burke, writing for *The New Leader*, to which Hyman was now contributing regular reviews, called the novel "fanciful realism" and suggested that readers track Jackson's use of the words "black" and "wood": "In watching how they tie things up, you will discover for yourself the astounding kind of complexity implicit in the imaginary lines of this charming book's apparent simplicity." (This, incidentally, is an excellent demonstration of Burke's method of literary criticism.)

Not everyone was certain that the novel meant more than it appeared to on the surface, but many tied it convincingly to Jackson's other writings about man's inhumanity to man (or, more often, woman). *Castle* "manages the ironic miracle of convincing the reader that a house inhabited by a lunatic, a poisoner and a pyromaniac is a world more rich in sympathy, love and subtlety than the real world outside," wrote *Time*'s reviewer, who also called Jackson, in a line Hyman would later deplore, "a kind of Virginia Werewoolf among the séance-fiction writers." In *National Review*, Guy Davenport saw it as a product of its times, a fable of "camping on the brink" inspired by "the refrigerated horrors of the cold war and [the] icy emptiness of space." One of the most insightful pieces, in *The New York Times Book Review*, argued that Jackson offered "an alternative to the canonical view of 'seriousness' in literature" by exploring "a real world which is at once more sane and more mad than the world we see." The best line came from Dorothy Parker in *Esquire*: "This novel brings back all my faith in terror and death. I can say no higher of it."

Within a few weeks of publication, nearly 14,000 copies had been sold, and Viking doubled the size of its second printing, bringing the number of copies in print to 25,000. By late November 1962, close to 30,000 copies had been sold. In December, *Castle* became Jackson's only novel to hit the *New York Times* best-seller list, where it stayed for five weeks, alongside *Ship of Fools* by Katherine Anne Porter and *Fail-Safe* by Eugene Burdick and Harvey Wheeler, a thriller about nuclear war. A newspaper cartoon depicted a couple in bed, the man reading *Fail-Safe* and the woman reading *Castle*, gripping each other's hands in terror.

Jackson was thrilled by the reviews. But her elation did not last long. When she returned from her triumphant trip to New York, waiting for her at home was Geraldine's most recent summons. She had seen the review in *Time*. Her letter did not mention its content; instead, she focused on the new picture of Shirley by a *Time* photographer that accompanied it. "Why oh why do you allow the magazines to print such awful pictures of you," she lamented to her daughter (either not knowing or not caring that Jackson had no control over the choice of photograph). "If you don't care what you look like or care about your appearance why don't you do something about it for your children's sake—and your husband's. . . . I have been so sad all morning about what you have allowed yourself to look like. . . . You were and I guess still are a very wilful child and one who insisted on her own way in everything—good or bad."

This kind of criticism was nothing new—Jackson had been experi-

Jackson photographed by Alfred Statler for Time *magazine, 1962—the photo for which her mother gave her so much grief.*

encing it all her life. But this particularly blunt letter hit her in a very vulnerable place. For years Jackson had hated having her picture taken; the photograph that appeared on the jacket of *Castle* was the same one she had used for *The Lottery*, thirteen years earlier. Both Brandt and Covici respected her wishes on the matter—Brandt, who once reassured Jackson that "you and I seem to think quite differently about your face," constantly refused magazine editors permission to publish Jackson's picture alongside her stories. Jackson had been relieved that Alfred Statler, the photographer sent by *Time*, took more pictures of the cats than of her, but she hated the published picture nearly as much as her mother did. In truth, it was not that bad: wearing a sleeveless blouse and looking somewhat exhausted, Jackson slouches before her typewriter, an enigmatic expression on her face. The condescending caption was "Deranged but enchanting."

Even at this point in her career, with six published novels and two popular memoirs, Jackson still felt she had to prove her worth to her parents. She never missed an opportunity to emphasize how successful she had become, reporting back to them on just about every lecture, reading, and conference. She was embarrassed to shop at the bookstore Brentano's, she had disingenuously complained earlier that year, because her charge account was under the name Shirley Jackson and the staff always insisted that she sign autographs. For her part, Geraldine had never disguised her preference for Jackson's lighter work over the stories about "demented girls," which she confessed she didn't understand. And she still took every opportunity to criticize her daughter, even about minor things. When "Weep for Adonais," a lightly disguised story about Dylan Thomas's death, appeared in *Playboy*, she reprimanded Jackson for publishing in "that dreadful magazine." After hearing Jackson's recording of "The Lottery" and "The Daemon Lover," Geraldine complained that it didn't sound like her voice.

Normally Jackson ignored these criticisms. But for once, she indulged in a sharp reply to her mother's letter about *Time*. "i received your unpleasant letter last night when i got back from new york, and it upset me considerably, as you no doubt intended," she responded.

> i wish you would stop telling me that my husband and children are ashamed of me. if they are, they have concealed it very skilfully; perhaps they do not believe that personal appearance is the most important thing in the world. . . . as far as i am concerned [the picture] is a very minor thing. i am far more concerned with my book and the very good review which accompanied the picture. . . .
>
> will you try to realize that i am grown up and fully capable of handling my own affairs? i have a happy and productive life, i have many good friends, i have considerable stature in my profession, and if i decide to make any changes in my manner of living, it will not be because you have nagged me into it. you can say this is 'wilful' if you like, but surely at my age i have a right to live as i please, and i have just had enough of the unending comments on my appearance and my faults.

The letter remained unsent. Just as she had more than twenty years earlier, when Stanley confessed his infidelity with his upstairs neighbor while Shirley was away for the summer, she repressed her fury. Perhaps, like the murderous preserves lined up along the Blackwood pantry shelves, its bottled-up power frightened her. Instead, Jackson sent a cheerful note describing her trip to New York, emphasizing her lavish treatment at the hands of her publishers: a suite at the Royalton "with a refrigerator and bar, and big bowls of roses," the cocktail party at the St. Regis and a fancy dinner to follow. The reviews so far had been "simply fantastic." Geraldine seemed to get the hint. "I just remembered I hadn't told you how I liked your story—I enjoyed it very much," she wrote in her next letter. Even though she did still prefer the books about the children, she agreed with the critics: it was Shirley's best novel. In an unusually magnanimous gesture, she had even bought two copies— probably the first time she had ever spent money on one of her daughter's books rather than demanding free copies. For Geraldine—who never failed to mention the price of a large purchase, and who was so cheap that after Joanne's visit to California a few years earlier she sent Shirley an itemized bill requesting reimbursement for all the clothes and other items she had bought for her granddaughter—this was the closest she could come to apologizing.

But the damage was done. Within two months, Jackson had retreated into her house. After months of emotional and professional stress, her mother's letter was one of the final triggers. She would not emerge until the following year.

17.
WRITING IS THE WAY OUT

> Past the turn I might find a mark of Constance's foot,
> because she sometimes came that far to wait for me, but
> most of Constance's prints were in the garden and in the
> house. Today she had come to the end of the garden, and I
> saw her as soon as I came around the turn; she was stand-
> ing with the house behind her, in the sunlight, and I ran
> to meet her.
> "Merricat," she said, smiling at me, "look how far I
> came today."
>
> —*We Have Always Lived in the Castle*

THE FIRST SIGN OF TROUBLE CAME IN THE EARLY SUMMER OF
1962. With several of the children in tow, Shirley and Stanley made a trip
to New York: she bought some new clothes and met Pat Covici and Carol
Brandt for lunch, while he took the children to the Museum of Natural
History—an unusual reversal of their typical roles. The city was in the
midst of a heat wave, and Shirley, laden with shopping bags, suddenly felt
faint. A passerby took her arm and led her into the shade to wait while he
flagged down a taxi. The taxi got stuck in traffic, and in the heat and
smog, she struggled to breathe. At the sight of Barry, standing in the
doorway of their hotel, she nearly burst into tears. He took her shopping

"It's about somebody poisoning the table sugar, and they don't know who!"

*This cartoon, by Charles Saxon, ran in the March 23, 1963,
issue of* The New Yorker.

bags and brought her inside, where Stanley fixed her a large drink full of ice. She spent the next day holed up in the hotel while Stanley and the children went to the Metropolitan Museum of Art. Back in Bennington, Dr. Durand told her the main cause of her distress was probably just rushing around in the heat, "with a spot of anxiety thrown in."

The spot grew, cancerlike, all through the summer, which was unusually event-filled and stressful. In May, Laurence—then nearing the end of his sophomore year at Goddard College, a small, progressive coed school several hours from Bennington—had astonished his parents by announcing that he was about to get married. He had been dating Corinne Biggs, a local girl turned Bennington student whom Shirley had hired to babysit for Barry. Now she was pregnant. They had little choice but to marry: Corinne, a Catholic, probably did not consider abortion, which in any event was not easy to obtain in 1962. He was nineteen years old; she was twenty. Stanley referred to the situation as "Laurie faces life, the hard way."

In public and to her mother, as always, Shirley downplayed her dismay. Laurence and Corinne, she told Geraldine, were perfectly suited to each other and had been talking about marriage for some time; this was not "some unlucky accident." People were gossiping, but she and Stanley had been vocal in their support of the couple. The other children were extremely fond of Corinne, who was already like a member of the family. Corinne's parents were more of a problem: they were upset that Laurence would not participate in a Catholic ceremony. As it turned out, the local priest refused to perform a mixed marriage. The couple would be married in June by a justice of the peace, in a quiet garden on the Bennington campus, with only immediate family present and a small reception afterward, "provided corinne's mother can stop praying long enough to arrange for it." Geraldine initially and rather cluelessly wondered why they couldn't just be engaged instead of rushing to marry, but when the facts were spelled out she was supportive: marriage and a baby, she suggested, was just what Laurence needed to "make him grow up fast." She and Leslie did not attend the wedding— conveniently, they had already planned a vacation in Hawaii—but she insisted on sending the newlyweds a full set of silver, followed by a series of nagging letters to Shirley when her gift was not immediately acknowledged.

Laurence's godparents, Shirley and Stanley's college friends Frank Orenstein and June Mirken Mintz, did come up from New York for the wedding, as did Lulu Hyman, now a widow, and Stanley's brother, Arthur. Shirley wore a new dress of gray silk and even consented to put on a pair of high heels, which she had always hated; she felt vindicated when one of the heels broke during the reception. Corinne was accompanied by numerous family members, "all the women wearing flowered hats." Stanley was so nervous that he accidentally introduced Lulu to Corinne's mother as his grandmother, the judge got the bride's and groom's names wrong, and the best man handed them the wrong rings. But the ceremony was dispatched in ten minutes, just before it began to rain, and the guests trooped over to the Four Chimneys, a historic inn in Old Bennington, for the reception. There was champagne for everyone except Shirley, who loathed it; the headwaiter, recognizing her, brought her a glass of bourbon instead. The Republican governor of Vermont, also dining at the inn that night, came over to congratulate the young couple, to which Stanley promptly shot back that they were planning to raise a fine family of Democrats. Back at the house afterward, Laurence was in such high spirits—Shirley described him later as "wild with joy"—that he gave one of Corinne's aunts a trumpet lesson while Joanne taught Corinne's mother to do the twist. Then the newlyweds took off for Europe, where Laurence's band was once again touring for the summer, Corinne accompanying him for their honeymoon.

In public Shirley took an "all's well that ends well" attitude toward the situation, but there can be no doubt that she was disappointed. The problem wasn't Corinne, of whom she seems to have been genuinely fond. But a shotgun wedding at age nineteen hardly fit into the Exeter-to-Harvard track she had once dreamed of for her elder son. When Miles Hyman—named for Stanley's father—arrived in late September, making her a grandmother at age forty-five, Shirley treated the baby with nonchalance verging on aloofness. She enjoyed being around him for an hour or so, but she was "always very glad to give him back to his mother and father," she admitted to her parents. "She'd come over to our house and I'd make her a bourbon and she'd hold the baby. That was about it," Laurence remembers.

ALMOST AS SOON as Laurence's wedding was over, another upheaval took place in Shirley's personal life. Barbara Karmiller, the former student of Stanley's whose wedding Shirley had made a trip to New York to attend a few years earlier, and her husband, Murry, moved into the Hymans' back apartment. At Bennington, Barbara had struggled with emotional and psychological problems, including severe writer's block. As her counselor, Stanley took a close interest in her state of mind, suggesting alternate courses of study when she had trouble writing and worrying about how to encourage her without putting too much pressure on her. She also was one of the few students in whom Shirley, too, took a personal interest, perhaps sympathizing with her struggles. After her graduation in 1957, Barbara spent a few years working in New York, where she met Murry, a television writer. In the spring of 1958, when *The Sundial* appeared, she sent Shirley an effusive letter praising the book. That fall, when Barbara and Murry were married at City Hall in lower Manhattan, Shirley gave the newlyweds a marriage charm.

After Barbara came into an inheritance, she and Murry took off for Europe, where they lived for several years, sending the Hymans regular reports on their adventures in Antwerp, Rome, and elsewhere. By the summer of 1962, they were ready to return to America, and Shirley and Stanley invited them to stay at 66 Main Street until they decided where to live. Murry worked on his magazine writing and tutored Sarah in Latin. Barbara mainly helped around the house and enjoyed the country life. "Barbara chopped the vegetables, Murry chopped the wood," Sarah remembers. Twenty years younger than Shirley, she fit nicely into the smart-younger-sister role left newly vacant by Jeanne Beatty, whose letters had abruptly stopped without explanation. Shirley kept trying: she sent Jeanne a copy of *Castle* as soon as it appeared and wrote to her with the news of Miles's birth (although she pretended that Laurence had gotten married the year before). But Jeanne did not write again, even to acknowledge the gift. She never opened one of Shirley's last letters to her, though she kept it, along with all of Shirley's letters, until her death, at age eighty-four, in 2013. Perhaps she was angry that Shirley had neglected her during the intense year of work on *Castle*; perhaps she was too depressed to write and ashamed by her own neglect of their correspondence. Regardless, it was a sad ending to a friendship that had brought them both so much pleasure.

As if by magic, Barbara appeared to take her place. A talented pianist who had once thought of becoming a professional musician, she was a happy partner in the same piano duets that Shirley had played with Dorothy Ayling, her best friend in Burlingame, many years before. She baked a loaf of bread for Shirley and didn't care when one of the cats walked over it while it was rising and left footprints, delighting Shirley. And she and Murry, hoping to have a child soon, doted on the Hyman children. After they moved to a house of their own that fall, Barry took to dropping in to chat on his way home from school. When Miles was born, Barbara and Murry were named his godparents and often helped with the baby, who was nicknamed Big Moey: when Laurence and Corinne wanted to spend a weekend in New York, it was Barbara and Murry who took care of him. "grandma and grandpa not only did not offer . . . but were extremely deaf to all hints on the subject." At Christmas, Shirley bestowed upon them the sorts of gifts she lavished only on family and her closest friends: for Murry, a paperweight, desk supplies, a Zippo lighter, and records by Ella Fitzgerald and Billie Holiday; for Barbara, a black scarf, cigarette holders, harpsichord albums, and a ceramic serving platter.

Stanley, too, paid a good deal of attention to his former student. In December, he asked Barbara to collaborate with him on an anthology of Kenneth Burke's writings, which Burke had asked him to put together. It was a huge task, requiring someone to read all of Burke's dense literary theory and suggest ways to excerpt it. That Stanley trusted Barbara with the work shows how highly he valued her intelligence. It also gave them a reason to spend a significant amount of time together.

The year before Barbara came back into his life had been challenging for Stanley, both personally and professionally. After his Jackie Robinson profile failed to see the light of day, he had to accept that *The New Yorker* did not value his feature writing. *Poetry and Criticism*, a short book of lectures he published, failed to attract attention. Then a new opportunity arose. In January 1961, following the death of founder Sol Levitas, *The New Leader*, a small, biweekly opinion magazine, underwent a transition. Its focus had primarily been on foreign affairs, but Myron Kolatch, a longtime staffer and the newly minted managing editor, was interested in building up the magazine's arts criticism. (Kolatch became executive editor the following year.) Recognizing that Hyman's talents were being wasted at *The New Yorker* on capsule reviews, one of Kolatch's first acts as managing editor was to invite him to write a regular book review column, called "Writers and Writing," to lead the section. Hyman accepted. He remained on staff at *The New Yorker*—and continued to use its stationery for all his correspondence—but he was now the voice of *The New Leader*'s book criticism.

It was, from the start, a terrific pairing. From June 1961 until June 1965, when he decided to step down for health reasons, Hyman published a book review of around two thousand words every other week. The column was "an instant hit," Kolatch says. "People were just eager to read him." Hyman collected his favorites in *Standards* (1966), which included pieces on virtually all the important writers of the period: Hemingway, Ellison, Malamud, Mailer, Henry Miller, Marianne Moore, Djuna Barnes, Philip Roth, James Baldwin, Isaac Bashevis Singer, Truman Capote, Günter Grass, and John Barth, among many others. In his column, Hyman did not try to formulate an overarching theory of literary criticism. His goal, as he put it in his introduction to that book, was to confront "the literature of our time with a hard eye . . . insisting on standards of excellence at a time of general cultural debasement, trying to tell the truth when truth has become unfashionable in literary journalism." Though he acknowledged that his talents were "mainly of a destructive order, with a highly developed instinct for the jugular," he insisted that he had "sternly" restrained himself, allowing only nine "blasts" in his four years on the job. (The "blasts," inevitably, were the pieces that generated the most mail and were most widely read and discussed.) His column was "the core, the nucleus of the magazine," said John Simon, whom Kolatch hired as film critic around the same time as Hyman.

The reviews are witty, learned, and personal. In a piece about baseball books, Hyman mourned the departure of the Brooklyn Dodgers to Los Angeles in 1957: "I still feel drawn to them, but faintly, as by the moon's gravitation," he wrote. "Like the moon, they are so far away, and they shine while I sleep." Reviewing *Herzog* (1964), he aptly observed that "Bellow is a word-spinner, as a consequence of which the sources of his strength lie very close to the sources of his weakness." He judged John Updike, on the eve of his thirtieth birthday, as "the most gifted young writer in America." When he allowed "the old blood-lust" to sweep over him, the results were as wickedly withering as ever. He called Herman Wouk's novel *Youngblood Hawke* (1962) "the most fraudulent and worthless novel I have read in many years," its charac-ters "cereal-box cut-outs," written with "the most dazzling ineptitude." In the irresistibly titled "Norman Mailer's Yummy Rump," one of his final reviews, he wrote that "the awfulness" of Mailer's *An American Dream* (1965) was "really indescribable," its similes "deranged." But if the post of *New Leader* book critic was ideal for Hyman, it was also a tacit acknowledgment that his career at *The New Yorker*, to which he had devoted virtually all his working life, had not fulfilled his hopes.

A bigger disappointment, especially in contrast to the encomiums his wife had lately grown accustomed to receiving, was the reception that greeted *The Tangled Bank*, finally published in April 1962 after thir-teen years of research and writing. Hyman spent many of those years painstakingly working his way through the entire published works of Darwin, Marx, Frazer, and Freud, the book's four pillars. (It was dedi-cated to the children, "who are glad to see it done.") The book he wrote, amounting to nearly five hundred densely printed pages, represented a fusion of the interests that had preoccupied him all his life: his early fas-cination with natural science, his political sensibilities as a young man, myth and ritual criticism, and the reverberations of primitive beliefs in human psychology. "I believe their books to be art," he wrote of his four subjects, "but I believe art itself to have an ethical as well as an aesthetic dimension, in that it is the work of the moral imagination, imposing order and form on disorderly and anarchic experience. That this vision of order and form is primarily metaphoric makes it no less real, since lines of force radiate out from the work of art and order or reorder the world around."

Hyman followed essentially the same structure he had in *The Armed Vision*, beginning with a brief biographical note about each of his sub-jects and proceeding to an overview of their writings, punctuated with his commentary. In Darwin's account of natural selection, he found a version of the ritual stages of Greek tragedy as presented in the famous terms of classicist Gilbert Murray: *agon*, contest; *sparagmos*, tearing apart; *anagnorisis*, discovery; and *epiphany*, joyous culmination. (*Agon* and *sparagmos* constitute the struggle for existence; *anagnorisis* and *epiphany*, the survival of the fittest.) He confronted the blatant anti-Semitism—in this case, Jewish anti-Semitism—in Marx's correspondence with Engels. He saw Burke's theory of the scene-act ratio (the idea that a specific scene must require a specific act) at the heart of *The Golden Bough*. The book's conclusion gorgeously expresses Hyman's vision of the underlying tie among the four thinkers: the powerful beams of their works, he writes, illuminate "our wriggling ancestor, the bloodstain on our fancy clothes, the corpse from which our grain sprouts, our lustful and murderous wish"—in short, the fundamental underpinnings of modern life. It is a conclusion, not incidentally, that is wholly consonant with Jackson's fictional project of searching out the desires and fears hidden deep within the human psyche.

The book, alas, was not met with the literary huzzahs Hyman had hoped his long awaited magnum opus would generate. Critics reacted as if confronting a literary mausoleum: they were in awe of the amount of work that had gone into the book—"merely to read all the works of those four tireless researchers was no mean task," wrote one—but were underwhelmed by its argument. *The Tangled Bank* "notably accomplishes its chief purpose, that of making the minds of these innovators *present to us*," wrote Harold Rosenberg in *The New York Times*, but it was structured too much like a classroom reader, with "blocks of quotations shepherded by comments." Others were less kind. "Mr. Hyman undertakes a bold adventure, one which I am sure all will agree is highly commendable, the more so because it is hazardous and foredoomed to failure," sniffed the Harvard historian Perry Miller, an old acquaintance of Hyman's, arguing that his methods of analysis were inappropriate to his subject. Still others concurred with Rosenberg that the book smelled too strongly of the undergraduate lecture hall. *The Tangled Bank*, wrote James Gray in the *Saturday Review*, amounted to "an enormous instruction schedule for a do-it-yourself course in the humanities." Academic reviewers, too, were unimpressed. "Where his deductions are not

Hyman photographed by Philippe Halsman for the Saturday Evening Post, *1959.*

derivative they are extravagant," Ronald S. Berman wrote in *The Kenyon Review*. The reaction that gave Hyman the most pleasure was that of the U.S. government, which requested permission to print the section on Marx's *Capital* in a handbook on communism. Although his politics had changed since college, he appreciated the irony nonetheless.

Shirley, too, was dismissive. At "a quarter of a million words long not counting the introduction and the index," the book "ought to make a very handy doorstop," she wrote to her parents. Granted, Geraldine and Leslie were hardly Stanley's ideal readers; they could barely get through a dumbed-down essay about tragedy he had written for the *Saturday Evening Post*, their favorite publication. In public, Shirley mocked Stanley in an interview with the *New York Post* on the eve of *Castle*'s publication. Asked whether her husband had anything new in the works, she replied, laughing, "He published a book in the spring. That one took him thirteen years."

For all the rigor of his working habits, Stanley was a slow writer. Perhaps he had simply set out to do too much: one wonders if he truly needed to read every single word written by his subjects, other than to stake his authority. He watched from the sidelines while *Castle* shot onto the best-seller lists. It was a repetition of the same pattern of fourteen years earlier, when *The Armed Vision* was immediately eclipsed by "The Lottery." This time, it may have hurt even more.

Within a few months of *The Tangled Bank*'s publication, Barbara Karmiller—Stanley's lovely, intelligent former student, perhaps beginning to entertain doubts about her marriage—took up residence in his home. Many people who knew the Hymans at the time suspect that Stanley and Barbara fell in love. Stanley had already had other affairs, of course, but most were brief, and certainly none was as serious as the relationship with Barbara. Phoebe Pettingell, to whom Stanley confessed the infidelities of his prior marriage, says that aside from his wives, Barbara was the only woman Stanley ever loved, though Pettingell describes the affair as primarily emotional rather than sexual. Slim, with short red hair, Barbara was "very smart, very elegant," Barry says. "Very perceptive. I was ten years old and I thought she was enormously attractive." She and her husband may not have been well matched. Barbara was fiery and emotional, with an Irish background, while Murry, raised Jewish, was calm and laidback. "Very thin and pale. He didn't make any noise when he walked," Barry says. "But very kind. He never raised his voice."

Previously, Shirley had never revealed to the children her anguish about Stanley's infidelity. Joanne remembers often watching television in the front room of the house and overhearing her parents arguing in the study next door. "I could hear them talking, I couldn't hear the words, but I could hear her crying," Joanne says. "But she was careful not to reveal anything about her unhappiness." Now, betrayed not only by her husband but by a woman she regarded as a close friend, she allowed her façade to crack. Joanne and Barry both remember an evening when Shirley, drunk and hysterical, insisted on driving to the Karmiller house to confront Stanley. The children ran out into the snow after their mother, trying to persuade her not to do it; eventually they were able to calm her down and bring her inside. "I desperately did not want her to go there, and I didn't really know why," Joanne says. "But there was a lot of sexual tension." Later, after she heard gossip that her father and Barbara were having an affair, she realized what must have been going on. "We would go over to their house for dinner, and Murry and I would be in the living room at the piano singing show tunes, and Stanley and Barbara would disappear. It was very uncomfortable." Sarah, too, recalls Shirley's discovery of the affair as traumatic: "Barbara was her best friend."

THE "SPOT OF ANXIETY" Dr. Durand had observed in the summer continued to grow through the distressing fall of 1962. On October 22, Shirley and Stanley threw a big cocktail party in honor of Kenneth Burke, who had just finished giving a series of lectures at Bennington. The guests arrived fresh from hearing President Kennedy inform the nation that American spy planes had discovered Soviet missiles deployed in Cuba; it was all anyone could talk about. "After the President's broadcast last night my poor young Barry, who used to dream of being an astronaut, fled back to the Oz books for comfort. I feel the same way," Shirley wrote Carol Brandt the next day. To Joanne and Sarah, who were then attending boarding school outside Boston, she confided that she had been turning on the radio every hour to follow the news. The apocalypse she had satirized in *The Sundial* was turning out to be no joke; even the safety that Merricat and Constance finally found in turning their home into a kind of bomb shelter, with boards over the windows and a supply of canned goods in the cellar, might not be sufficient. The crisis would be resolved diplomatically within days, but its reverberations were felt for the remainder of the Cold War. Schoolchildren like Barry, taught to hide under their desks during air raid drills, were disturbed by the memories for years.

In the wake of *Castle*, Shirley didn't try to do much writing, but even the small amount she undertook was unusually difficult. Louis Untermeyer, whom she had gotten to know at Suffield, was editing a new children's series to be published by Collier Books and had asked her to contribute a picture book. She had an idea for a story to be called *Nine Magic Wishes*, a sweet and whimsical tale about a child who encounters a magician and wishes for various strange, enchanting things: an orange pony with a purple tail, "a squirrel holding a nut that opens and inside is a Christmas tree," a garden of flowers made of candy, a pocket-sized zoo, and finally a "little box and inside is another box and inside is another box and inside is another box and inside that is an elephant." But the publisher had supplied her with an "arrogant little list" of approved vocabulary, and many of the words she needed were not on it. It included "getting" and "spending," but not "wishing"; "cost" and "buy" and "nickel" and "dime," but not "magic." "I felt that the children for whom I was supposed to write were being robbed, persuaded to accept nickels and dimes instead of magic wishes," she wrote later. She got her way: the publisher eventually agreed that she could ignore the list.

At Halloween, Jeanne Beatty's daughter Shannon sent Sarah a birthday present, prompting Shirley to reach out again with a letter that started, "Jeanne?" There was no response. Shortly afterward, Shirley fell on the ice and twisted her ankle, which left her unable to drive her car. The only shoe that fit on her foot was a furry red bedroom slipper. She could not wear it into town, where she already felt self-conscious doing her errands. "so i just won't get the mail, and the store will send up my groceries, and i will spend a happy day with my foot on the hassock reading a mystery story," she wrote to her parents. She would not make it out of the house again until the following spring.

THE WINTER OF 1962–63 was unusually cold, with temperatures well below zero—"so terrible that even the vermonters are talking about it," Shirley wrote. In two days there were thirty inches of snow. Aside from her birthday and Christmas, which both passed quietly, the Hymans did almost no entertaining. Shirley stayed inside. Something new and unpleasant had begun to happen every time she tried to leave the house. She would begin to shake, her legs would give way, and everything would start spinning. If she did not go inside right away, she feared passing out. Her nightmares returned, stranger than ever; she paced the floor in the dark, crying. She suffered from delusions that even she recognized were irrational: she was afraid to go into the post office, for instance, because she believed the postmaster thought she was crazy. When Stanley tried to reassure her that it wasn't true, she lashed out at him. Eventually her anxiety was no longer associated only with leaving the house: anything could trigger a panic attack, even the phone ringing. Dr.

Durand prescribed tranquilizers, which she took around the clock, but "all they did was keep me kind of stupid but still frightened all the time." She was experiencing, she later realized, "a classic case of acute anxiety."

Shirley had never believed in psychoanalysis, which she felt was "a little bit like Christian Science." Years earlier, her "fancy doctor" in Westport had tried to sell her on it, but she had rejected him soundly. Now it took the combined ministrations of Stanley, the Karmillers, and Durand to persuade her to see Dr. James Toolan, a psychiatrist from New York who had recently set up shop in Bennington. Shirley initially doubted whether he was intelligent enough to help her, but she finally consented to try. Fortified with her "usual tranquilizers, a sedative injection from [Durand], two stiff drinks, and stanley and barbara"—Barbara drove, Stanley accompanied Shirley from the car into the office—she set out on a late-winter afternoon. "i think getting out of the car in front of the doctor's office was the most terrifying minute of my life," she wrote later. Together she and Stanley went down a long path and a flight of steps into a hallway and then a waiting room, where Toolan was waiting to usher her inside. The journey seemed "many million miles long." But she found Toolan a comfortable and reassuring presence. Of course he could help her, he said. Why had she waited so long? After the appointment, she had "a sudden very clear happy picture of what it might be like to be free again" and announced to Stanley proudly that she planned to have the "fastest analysis on record."

In the beginning, Shirley did progress quickly. The purpose of the therapy was simply to get her back into her established routine—groceries, getting the mail, driving Stanley to the college—rather than to delve into the underlying issues that had triggered her anxiety. "The whole idea was to get her back on track, not to examine how this woman wants to reshape her life," Corinne, her daughter-in-law, recalls. "You give her a bunch of pills and if she can go to Powers Market that means she's getting better." Two weeks after her first appointment, she was able to drive herself to Toolan's office, with Stanley along to help her get from the car to the waiting room. She managed the next visit entirely on her own. The next step was the post office. One morning she and Stanley got in the car and drove the few blocks. Then they went in together, "with stanley practically leading me." She managed to remember the mailbox combination—"thank heaven it opened the first time around"—and then raced back to the car while Stanley gathered the mail. Each new step was followed by "a terrible after-effect of terror and trembling and gasping for breath," but the aftershocks lessened with each repetition. Finally, she managed to complete the whole errand alone. "that one was a bad day afterwards but i was so triumphant that i didn't really care."

The same process had to be repeated for each new destination, such as going to the grocery store or into Bennington proper. The process, she wrote, "amazed and fascinated" her, "because it was so completely learning how to do things *alone*, like a baby learning to walk. . . . each step was a great triumph." By spring, "though at considerable cost in fear," she was able to function "almost normally." But there were many setbacks. As Toolan explained to her, she was not yet mentally strong enough to maintain the gains she made. One day in Powers Market, Larry Powers noticed that she seemed to be hanging onto her grocery cart for support; her knuckles were white. "How are things going?" he asked her. "The doctor says I'm all right," she replied. A few minutes later he saw that she had abandoned her cart, half filled, in the middle of the aisle. She called from home and asked him to finish filling her order and deliver it. "The doctor says I'm better," she told him, "but I'm not sure." A year later, she was still unable to enter the Grand Union supermarket in Bennington; it was simply too big.

Even though Shirley's ability to go through the motions of daily life improved, writing was impossible. All winter, Carol Brandt checked in regularly—did she have anything new on the horizon? At first, Shirley downplayed her illness: "I am anxious to get to work, and in that irritable state where I am furious with myself because nothing happens," she wrote in January. Brandt asked her to come into the city to meet with an editor at *Redbook* who was very interested in her writing, but the very thought of the trip sent her into "a quite serious paroxysm of terror." That was the most she let on until March, when she finally confessed what was going on. Brandt professed shock, but she must have suspected that something was seriously wrong. She sent Shirley a handwritten letter on her home stationery as a token of her friendship. "How grim for you—In our many telephone calls I never suspected it—That you are making progress is so good—That writing is your release is so natural and inevitable." Brandt passed on Shirley's letter about her difficulties to Pat Covici and asked him to destroy it. "It is your work that speaks for you in this curious city," she told Shirley.

Covici, too, was supportive. "I was moved and touched and saddened when I learned of your attack of anxiety," he wrote.

> That agonizing mental state is not unknown to me. Anxiety fights dirty and dies hard. But, oh, what a relief when it leaves you. The burden of mental depression is difficult to surmount. . . . But you have the capacity to throw it off. And when you do breathe freer and think clearer . . . your imagination will take hold and shape things to your liking.

He added a few words of reassurance that would have meant a great deal to Shirley at any time, but were especially meaningful now:

> With your last book, *We Have Always Lived in the Castle*, you have joined the few who can be called the masterful prose-painters of our time. With the very first paragraph in your book one is held and cannot help but go on reading, so vivid and rich and amusing is your prose, with so many felicities of wit and humor. You are exquisitely endowed with a fine sensibility, a rich vocabulary and a creative imagination. Never worry, you will soon be wrapped up in the writing of a new novel.

Geraldine and Leslie, so rarely able to provide emotional support, found the whole situation mystifying. Shirley tried to describe her condition in a letter that she was unable to finish; she did not write to them all spring, to Geraldine's dismay. Instead, she decided to explain it in a phone conversation that left the Jacksons bewildered. "what 'ails' me, pop, is what they used to call a nervous breakdown," she wrote bluntly afterward. The first signs had appeared perhaps eight years earlier, around the time of her breakdown after *The Bird's Nest*, when Durand had begun prescribing her tranquilizers "because i was so jumpy all the time." Geraldine, who had been considerably worried by her daughter's silence, was unsure of how to respond. "This thing that has been wrong with you—is it a very unusual thing?" she asked. Even more cluelessly, she wrote that Stanley sounded like "a good strong bulwark. . . . Poor man. It must have been tough for him."

Shirley did lean heavily on Stanley during these months. When he went to Michigan to lecture in May 1963, she came along as a visiting writer, managing the trip only by drinking steadily through it: they got on an evening train with a bottle of bourbon for her and a bottle of scotch for him and woke up in the morning in Detroit. ("Two bottles of liquor on an overnight trip sounds as though you will have to be poured off in the morning," Geraldine commented, unhelpfully.) For the rest of the year, their travel was minimal. In July, they went to New York to lecture at the Columbia Writers' Conference and attend a special screening of *The Haunting*. Shirley had been looking forward to seeing the film, but all her normal New York activities were now sources of anxiety. "My two big difficulties . . . are a reluctance to be packed in tightly anywhere (as in cocktail parties or traffic jams!) and a reluctance to go alone across open spaces (like walking down a street)," she confided to Brandt. Both were easier if she wasn't alone, but Stanley could not accompany her at every moment—he had responsibilities at Columbia. Julie Van Vliet, her publicist at Viking, was dispatched to help out if needed. The trip went well, including her lecture: "i was quite nervous ahead of time about getting frightened in the middle and having to stop, and stanley was ready to take over but actually once i started i forgot all about the panics and enjoyed myself," she wrote to her parents afterward. When she saw Toolan at his New York office the next day, he was "very proud."

For the most part, Stanley seems to have kept Shirley's problems private. Laura Nowak once caught him in a rare confessional moment: when she greeted him at a Bennington concert and asked why Shirley wasn't with him, he replied simply, "She doesn't want to go out anymore." But he was under significant pressure himself. In addition to his teaching, he had two new projects: a *Portable Darwin* reader and *The Promised End*, a collection of reviews and essays published between 1942 and 1962, from his early essay on John Steinbeck to more recent pieces on myth, ritual, and religion. And he and Barbara Karmiller were still working on the Burke anthology, which now looked like it would require two volumes. Joanne, who had graduated from boarding school in June and was planning to attend Bennington in the fall, spent the summer of 1963 at home, keeping Shirley company and helping her with her errands.

Sarah was sent home from school that fall after just a couple of months. Shirley was disappointed but resigned. Though Sarah was having problems of her own, it was useful to have her around: there was still "a long siege ahead." Throughout the winter and spring, the two of them both saw Toolan twice a week: one of them sat in the waiting room reading while the other had her session. In the spring of 1964, Sarah reapplied to school. Shirley felt too ill to accompany her to the interview—Stanley and Laurence took her—but wrote a letter describing how helpful she had been in running the house while her mother was unwell. In addition, she had written a short story that Shirley was sufficiently impressed with to send to Carol Brandt. While clearly less taken with the teenager's work, Brandt gamely offered to shop it around.

Shirley herself was not able to write. That was the worst part—worse than not being able to go to the post office or the supermarket, or to drive off alone in her car. "Today marks my official return to work," she wrote to Brandt happily, if prematurely, in April 1963, as she first began to see improvement. But she wasn't able to follow through on most of what she started. Buoyed by her enjoyment writing *Nine Magic Wishes*, she wrote another children's book, this one called *Famous Sally*, about a little girl who decides she wants everyone in the world to know her name. The heroine uses different methods to communicate with people in different places: for Tall City, where the buildings are "so high they wore clouds on their heads like hats," she writes her name on a thirty-one-mile-high kite; for Soft City, where "the people wore shoes made of cat fur so their feet would not make a sound on the streets," she asks the wind to whisper it; for Slow City ("Here the people moved like water dripping from a faucet. . . . When the people of Slow City ate their breakfasts they ate so slowly that when they were through it was time for lunch"), she paints her name on the back of a turtle. (The ideas for the cities were Sarah's—Shirley asked her permission before using them.) The book was charming, but editors were not as captivated by it as they had been by *Nine Magic Wishes*; it was rejected by several publishers as too odd before finding a home with Harlin Quist, the editor of *Nine Magic Wishes* at Collier, who had now moved to Crown. It would not be published until 1966, after Shirley's death.

With new material slow to come, she tried revising older stories, including "The Lie," in which a woman returns to her hometown to try to make right on a shameful incident in her past. The story had gone through various versions since she first submitted it in 1951 but had never sold. Money was not an issue—although Viking did not owe her anything more until she submitted a new novel, Brandt had sold the dramatic rights to *Castle*, which brought in an additional $10,000. "I don't seem to finish anything," Shirley told Brandt in July, "but I've got several lovely starts." Two months later, she admitted to her parents that she had "not been doing any writing at all, not even letters." The most she could manage were some book reviews for the *New York Herald Tribune*, including an ode to Dr. Seuss in honor of his latest ABC book (she praised him for bucking the current trends in children's reading, which tended more to "touching tributes to doctors and school-bus drivers" and directions for how to build a tree house than to imagination) and another piece on *The Pooh Perplex*, a parody of literary theory by the critic Frederick Crews, in which a fictional group of English professors apply Marxist, Freudian, and other trendy methods of analysis to the Winnie-the-Pooh books. ("Literary criticism may not survive her embrace," Stanley joked to Kenneth Burke.)

The problem, she told Brandt, was that she simply had no ideas: "I am in the disagreeable position of being most eager to get to work, with nothing at all to work on. If I do not find an idea soon I will have to steal one." Brandt tried to help, even suggesting that she visit Shirley in Vermont to "stir things up." In the end, Pat Covici offered the most useful advice. He told her to sit down at the typewriter every morning for an hour and write anything that came into her head. She promised she would do it—she was "ready to try anything."

WHAT SHIRLEY PRODUCED during those morning sessions at the type-writer, during the dark winter of 1963–64, would be her last diary. Now she was writing for only herself: not Stanley, not her parents, not the vanished Jeanne Beatty. She was skeptical at first about whether it would have the effect Covici had suggested of loosening her up, preparing her to write fiction again. "if this is going to be largely automatic writing and i always hated stream of consciousness then perhaps something to do will come out of it although after thinking about writing ever since i woke up when i was not feeling sorry for myself and hating stanley i have nothing but phrases in my head," she wrote on December 2, the first morning. "punctuate at least," she scolded herself at once.

"Why do you not write?" Howard Nemerov had asked her. He suffered from regular periods of depression, most recently after the death of his father, but the act of asking himself that question and answering it had led him to begin a new book of poems. For Shirley, the answer was not straightforward. "my mind is so full of troubles that there is no room for writing," she worried. "but the sound of the typewriter in the empty house is comforting." The pages were "a refuge, a pleasant hiding place from problems and troubles." Perhaps writing would help her not to think about Stanley. Perhaps the words she had been trying to use were all wrong; perhaps the "absolutely correct words," like Merricat's magic words, would help her "find a clear way through." After her first day's writing, she felt as if her mind had been "swept clean," purified. "there is a calm which begins to come. and my fingers are more limber." She told Dr. Toolan that the sheer act of writing again brought her happiness. "this is the most satisfying writing i have ever done." Here, among her familiar yellow pages, she was "at home," she wrote on December 3.

But her mind kept returning to Stanley. She could not write when he was at home because she could not tell him what she was doing, which he would regard as a "criminal" waste of time. She had internalized his criticism: "i feel i am cheating stanley because i should be writing stories for money." (Of course, if she had been able to write fiction, she wouldn't have had to write this diary.) When he was at the college, she felt an "enormous relief"; she waited to do her shopping in Bennington until the day he worked at home so that she could have some time away from him. It was an issue of control, she thought. How could she wrest control of her life, of her mind, back from Stanley? And if she could, would her writing change? "insecure, uncontrolled, i wrote of neuroses and fear and i think all my books laid end to end would be one long documentation of anxiety," she wrote.

> if i am cured and well and oh glorious alive then my books should be different. who wants to write about anxiety from a place of safety? although i suppose i would never be entirely safe since i cannot completely reconstruct my mind. but what conflict is there to write about then? i keep thinking vaguely of novels about husbands and wives, perhaps in suburbia, but i do not really think that this is my kind of thing. perhaps a funny book. a happy book. . . . plots will come flooding when i get the rubbish cleared away from my mind.

The diary pages are filled with references to an obsession that Shirley would not name.

> i cannot write about what i am going to call my obsession because i simply cannot bring myself to put down the words. i don't think that this is a refusal to face it because heaven knows i have thought recently about very little else, but i do think that being unable to write about it is a clear statement by my literary conscience . . . that i know the problem is not real, is imaginary . . . and i cannot in good faith write about it as though it were real. the emotion— let me see—is shame. . . . is it painful to write? i thought it was getting better and then it got worse, but it *can* get better, i know.

So consuming was her obsession that the assassination of John F. Kennedy, which had just taken place, is never mentioned in these pages. Even the most tumultuous events in the outside world could not break through her ruminations. She was entirely possessed with her own troubles.

What was she ashamed of? One possibility was her fears about Stanley and Barbara Karmiller—the idea of seeing Barbara now filled her with unease. As the diary continues, however, the issue takes on a new dimension. Shirley's obsession was not the affair itself; it was what the affair might finally drive her to do. She was consumed with the idea of leaving Stanley, of creating a new home for herself. She may have planned to take the children with her—Sarah and Barry, then fifteen and twelve, were still at home—but her fantasies are of leaving alone. In *Come Along with Me*, the novel she was about to begin, the narrator will do just that, taking a room in a boardinghouse where she hangs up her clothes, puts her sleeping pills on the nightstand, and places her reading glasses next to them. "I had no pets, no address books, no small effects to set around on tables or pin on walls, I had no lists of friends to keep in touch with and no souvenirs; all I had was myself," she tells the reader. It is a fantasy of total unencumbrance.

Shirley records a deeply suggestive dream in which Stanley tells her she is sick and sends her to a doctor. In the office, the doctor shows her a "most attractive picture": its title is something like *Exodus*. It depicts a woman "sliding out through a parting in the background." She does not dwell on what the dream might mean, but its significance seems obvious. It is a dream of leaving, of slipping away unnoticed through a crack in the wall. She no longer needed a daemon lover to sweep her away; she now imagined walking off on her own. But as long as she was unable to confront the fantasy in her conscious mind, she would continue to suffer from agoraphobia. How better could her psyche prevent her from acting on her desire? If she could not leave the house, she could not leave Stanley. "heaven knows i am learning enough about myself to develop a new style and i look forward every now and then to freedom and security (and i do mean security by myself) and that great golden world outside which i should be getting closer to every day," she wrote. "i wonder what i will be writing then." The "great golden world" cannot simply mean the world outside 66 Main Street, because by this point she was capable of doing errands like going to Bennington and to the post office (though she still dreaded the hour when the mail was due to arrive). It was the world in which she would live out her fantasy of total independence. "writing is the way out," she reminded herself.

"i think about the glorious world of the future. think about me think about me think about me. not to be uncontrolled, not to control. alone. safe," she wrote that December. As she contemplated it more and more seriously, she began to feel "a kind of sadness, almost a sense of loss; i am giving up something very precious, and withdrawing from something very important"—the family life that she and Stanley had spent so many years creating. "the new life is worth it, i do believe that. but i cannot always remember that what i am losing is cancerous." Still, she reminded herself that whatever the cost, it was worth it "to be separate, to be alone, to *stand* and *walk* alone, not to be different and weak and helpless and degraded . . . and shut out. not shut out, shutting out." Her vision mimics the transformation that Merricat and Constance experience in *Castle*. At the beginning of the novel, the two sisters are "shut out" from the world outside, intimidated by the villagers' hostility from pursuing the most minimal contact. By the end, they are "shutting out" intruders, barricaded in their kitchen, alone and in control and perfectly happy.

Shirley saw the process as "building a cover over the unbearable, now at first only a very thin crust, not enough to support my weight, not enough to walk on yet, but please constantly reinforced and made stronger. the focus is gradually turning on myself, which is where it should be." There would be a way through. She could almost see it. "on the other side somewhere there is a country, perhaps the glorious country of well-dom, perhaps a country of a story. perhaps both, for a happy book." The diary ends with a single repeated phrase:

laughter is possible laughter is possible laughter is possible

COVICI'S METHOD WORKED: plots did come flooding back. Between January and November 1964, Jackson wrote three new stories—a meager showing compared with her periods of greatest productivity, but a fine start after her fallow year and a half. All are variations on the theme of homes that have been corrupted. Places that seem secure become suddenly dangerous; the familiar turns menacing. In "The Little House," a young woman arrives to stake her claim to a house she has inherited from an elderly aunt, the first home that has ever belonged only to her. As she imagines the ways she will make it her own—"I can do anything I want here and no one can ever make me leave, because it's mine"— her peace is disturbed by the arrival of neighbors, a pair of creepy old ladies who needle her about the changes she intends to make and terrify her with the suggestion that her aunt may have been murdered by an intruder. After they leave, she is so frightened that she cannot go upstairs alone in the dark. "Don't leave me here alone," she repeats madly into the empty kitchen.

"Home," written later in the year, is a more typical ghost story, and a frightening one. Ethel Sloane and her husband, city people, have just moved to a house in the country, and when the story begins Mrs. Sloane is pleased with herself for going straight into the village and introducing herself to all the shopkeepers: "she liked knowing that people knew who she was." The locals are friendly if somewhat nonplussed by her self-assurance, particularly when she refuses to heed their warnings not to use the old road leading up the hill to her house when the weather is wet, as it is that day. On the way home she stops to pick up an old woman standing with a child on the side of the road, who surprises her by asking for a ride to her own house by its old name—"the old Sanderson place." The ride is slippery and dangerous, and the road requires all her attention; when she turns back to look at her passengers after reaching the top, they have vanished. When Mrs. Sloane tells the story to her husband, he confesses that he hasn't told her a local legend about their new house. Long ago, a boy who lived there was kidnapped by an old woman during a rainstorm; both were believed to have drowned in the creek. Mrs. Sloane is pleased that her house has its very own ghosts, but her pride evaporates when she gets in her car to head down to town the next morning and discover them once again in the backseat. After a wild ride in which she nearly skids off the road, she understands why the locals say not to use the road in the rain.

"The Bus" is the most complex of the three stories—a belated fourth part, perhaps, of the late-1940s trilogy of "Pillar of Salt," "The Daemon Lover," and "The Tooth." This time the protagonist is a disagreeable old woman traveling home alone at night. She falls asleep and is awakened by the bus driver, who abruptly puts her off at an empty crossroads she doesn't recognize. A truck driver picks her up and takes her to a roadhouse that was once a Victorian mansion, but is now a tacky saloon. She tries to tell the innkeeper that she grew up in a house like this— "One of those good old houses that were made to stand forever"—but is met with jeers. She finds a bedroom that looks like her own childhood room and drifts off to sleep, the noise from downstairs reminding her of her mother singing in the drawing room. A rattling disturbs her, and she opens the closet to find it full of her childhood toys, become alive and malevolent. "Go away, old lady," says her beautiful doll with golden curls, "go away." She awakens to find herself still on the bus, being shaken by the bus driver, who is about to put her off at the very same crossroads where the bus had stopped in her dream. The story is ambiguous, but its underlying message is reminiscent of "Louisa, Please Come Home": it is far easier to leave home than to find your way back again.

Jackson also managed to complete a well-paying piece for the *Saturday Evening Post*, a humorous riff on the same theme. Commissioned to write an essay for the magazine's "Speaking Out" section, in which writers were encouraged to take extreme, irreverent positions on topics of interest, she chose the subject "No, I Don't Want to Go to Europe." A few years earlier, Hyman was pleased to be selected as a host to lead a literary European tour for a company specializing in themed trips— "twenty or so lonely schoolteachers decide that their summer might best be spent touring europe with stanley (not me; i am too ignorant; i am just to smile) pointing out spots of literary interest, like westminster abbey. . . . we say hemingwayhemingway and lead them to a bullfight"—but her colitis made the trip impossible. Now, she declared, she had never wanted to go anyway. First of all, she hated to fly; travel by boat was "slow and dirty, and you have to sleep with the bananas." Even if it were possible to drive, she still wouldn't want to go. "I don't like leaving home in any case, but I dislike even more prying into someone else's country." Her traveler friends came back full of insufferable stories about dining on balconies with contessas. The food was supposed to be terrible—"head cheese tastes like gefüllte fish"—and border crossings were terrifying. In any event, her husband "cannot get through the day without *The New York Times*" and she herself is "mortally afraid of practically everything."

Although she found the piece difficult to write and the end result wasn't up to her best work—it came out sounding more misanthropic than humorous—Jackson was happy to be working. "I am beginning to be more myself again, and more optimistic and enthusiastic than for a long time," she wrote to Brandt. But she suffered a setback when the *Post* published her married name and address, unleashing a torrent of angry letters the likes of which she hadn't seen since "The Lottery." Not getting the joke, all the happy travelers she had caricatured wrote to castigate Jackson for her narrow-mindedness, one of them calling her piece a "nauseating little pack of distortions." The episode, not surprisingly, gave her a difficult month.

Brandt was thrilled to see Jackson back at work, and even happier to learn that she and Hyman were planning a visit to New York in March 1964. To celebrate, she suggested a shopping trip to Bergdorf Goodman, the most exclusive department store in Manhattan, and lunch at the Four Seasons, then only six years old and the ultimate statement in American culinary modernism. That visit had to be postponed— Jackson got the flu—but she and Hyman did travel together to Indiana University, where he lectured and they were given a tour of the Institute for Sex Research, founded by Alfred Kinsey, and its pornography library. Jackson was intrigued: "Some of the material would make an interesting book; you couldn't show it to your mother but my, wouldn't it sell." Dr. Toolan suggested that she book lecture dates into the following spring: the next one was scheduled for New York University in May. Sarah would accompany her—Jackson was still afraid to travel alone, though her goal was a solo trip to the Bread Loaf Writers' Conference that summer, where she had been invited to be on the faculty. "all of this i do with great trepidation, and batteries of pills, but i've been doing it. . . . each adventure takes a little less pushing from the doctor," she reported to her parents. At home, she kept her pills all around the house, in heart-shaped china boxes, so that she would always have them close at hand when she needed them.

Trepidation notwithstanding, the NYU lecture was a triumph. Brandt was out of town, so the Four Seasons lunch had to be postponed once again, but Jackson was in top form. She read an essay based on a set of rules for writing short stories she had drawn up the previous year, when Sarah had begun writing seriously; afterward, as if to demonstrate that the advice worked, she read a new story by her daughter. Titled "Notes for a Young Writer," the lecture repeated some of the instructions she had been giving for years at Suffield—the writer's main goal is to keep the reader's attention; avoid anything extraneous to the narrative—but she phrased them with uncommon elegance. A story must have "a surface tension, which can be considerably stretched but not shattered"; it must keep as much as possible to one time and place and lead the reader naturally from one setting to another. Instead of wasting a sentence on a simple action—"They got in the car and drove home"—she advised using it to advance the plot: "On their way home in the car they saw the boy and the girl were still standing talking earnestly on the corner." Characters don't need to waste time in needless conversation: "It is not enough to let your characters talk as people usually talk because the way people usually talk is extremely dull." Colorful words ought to be used sparingly for "seasoning," if at all: "Every time you use a fancy word your reader is going to turn his head to look at it going by and sometimes he may not turn his head back again." Simple language is usually best: "if your heroine's hair is golden, call it yellow." Textbooks insist that the beginning always must imply the ending, but "if you keep your story tight, with no swerving from the proper path, it will curl up quite naturally at the end." During the question-and-answer session, Jackson was inevitably asked about "The Lottery." "I hate it!" she answered. "I've lived with that thing fifteen years. Nobody will ever let me forget it."

After the lecture, an editor from Doubleday approached Jackson. Would she be interested in doing a children's chapter book for them—perhaps a fantasy in the style of the Oz books? Jackson was intrigued.

Brandt quickly shot down the idea—Jackson was already committed to Viking—but that was not enough to dissuade her. Within a month, she had embarked on a new children's novel on the off chance that Covici might want it. "Since I do not seem to be writing any other kind of book, I thought this might be a good running start," she told Brandt.

The Fair Land of Far begins with an ordinary, unpopular girl named Anne, "the kind of person who always seems a stranger." When she throws a party for herself, only two of her classmates show up. They are greeted with a surprise: because it is Anne's birthday, the three of them will be granted access to the Fair Land of Far, reached through a hidden doorway in the kitchen. There she is no longer ordinary Anne, but a princess doted on by her parents, the king and queen. But as they prepare to celebrate, a strange present is delivered: a gigantic creature in a cage. Somehow it gets out, and in a rush of wings it seizes Anne and flies away with her. Someone must go after them—perhaps the two classmates who reluctantly showed up at the party.

If Jackson got much further than that, her work has been lost. But the book served its purpose: to provide an imaginary country to which she could retreat at a difficult time. A rehearsal, perhaps, for the real escape she planned to make as soon as she was ready.

18.

LAST WORDS

COME ALONG WITH ME, 1964–1965

> "I've just buried my husband," I said.
> "I've just buried mine," she said.
> "Isn't it a relief?" I said.
> "What?" she said.
> "It was a very sad occasion," I said.
> "You're right," she said, "it's a relief."
>
> —*Come Along with Me*

O N APRIL 27, 1965, SHIRLEY JACKSON TOOK THE STAGE of Syracuse University's Gifford Auditorium. Wearing a bright red dress, with her hair loose down her back, she began to read the opening chapter of her new novel, speaking slowly and carefully:

I always believe in eating when I can. I had plenty of money and no name when I got off the train and even though I had had lunch in the dining car I liked the idea of stopping off for coffee and a doughnut while I decided exactly which way I intended to go, or which way I was intended to go. I do not believe in turning one way or another without consideration, but then neither do I

believe that anything is positively necessary at any given time. . . .
I needed a name and a place to go; enjoyment and excitement and
a fine high gleefulness I knew I could provide on my own.

Twenty-five years earlier, she had been interviewed on a college
radio program called "I Want a Job," in which people seeking employment could advertise themselves. Jackson said simply, "I want to write."
A month later, she left Syracuse with Hyman for New York, uncertain
of her future.

Now she was the author of eight published books for adults, two

Jackson photographed by her son Laurence, early 1960s.

of them best sellers, one a National Book Award finalist. After more than two years of struggling with agoraphobia, she was at the start of a lecture tour that would take her to five different cities. She had two novels under way, with a lucrative new contract from Viking. While at Syracuse, she learned that in June the university planned to award her its prestigious Arents Medal for distinguished alumni. Leonard Brown was no longer alive to appreciate it, but in her lecture she credited her college education with starting her writing career. After she spoke, students swarmed her with questions about her writing methods, her work, and her time at Syracuse. By any measure, she was in top form.

Less than three months later, she was dead.

IN AUGUST 1964, Howard Nemerov and Jackson drove together along the winding roads from North Bennington to Bread Loaf Mountain. It was her first time attending the famous writers' conference, founded in 1926 by her old friend John Farrar. In 1954, John Ciardi, a poet and regular columnist for the *Saturday Review*, had taken over as director. More formal and regulated than Suffield, it was the most prestigious summer program for writers. In addition to Robert Frost, who was a long-standing teacher there, many of the most important American writers came through the program as either fellows or faculty, including Eudora Welty, Carson McCullers, Anne Sexton, Ralph Ellison, and Joan Didion. "Being invited there meant something," says Jerome Charyn, who was a Bread Loaf fellow in 1964.

At meals, the faculty sat at a central table, separate from the students and fellows: they were "a little private group, eating together and gathering every day at twelve and five in our private little bar, where we had a bartender and an inexhaustible supply of bloody marys," Jackson wrote later. Pictures of her with the other faculty that summer show her relaxed and smiling, often with a cigarette in her hand. For her public lecture, she delivered "Biography of a Story," her account of the publication of and reaction to "The Lottery," and read the story yet again. Her voice was "dour yet direct," and projected a "quiet sense of doom," recalled Mark Mirsky, another Bread Loaf fellow that summer. Hearing her read,

Jackson at Bread Loaf, August 1964 (first row, second from right).
Howard Nemerov is in the back row, second from left.

he said, was "a hypnotizing experience." When she wasn't teaching, she
mainly rested.

It had been an exhausting summer. She and Stanley spent part of July
in New York, where they both lectured again at the Columbia Writers'
Conference and she and Brandt finally had their long planned lunch at the
Four Seasons. They had to leave the city in a rush when Stanley abruptly
fell ill. A New York doctor said he should go directly to the hospital for
treatment in an oxygen tent. Stanley, who always put off medical care until
it could wait no longer, refused and headed home instead. Back in North
Bennington, Dr. Durand warned that if he didn't change his lifestyle,
he risked an imminent coronary. Durand instructed him to cut down on
smoking and drinking, reduce the amount of salt in his diet, and lose 50
pounds: he currently weighed 230.

Shirley sprang into action, acquiring numerous low-calorie and low-
salt cookbooks and sweeping the pantry clean of canned and processed
foods, "all the lovely chili and rich soups we liked so well." She developed imitation versions of his favorite foods, including a low-calorie kugel
made from cauliflower instead of potatoes, which she admitted was terrible. They also both started using Metrecal, a new brand of liquid protein

drinks designed to provide 900 calories per day. She left Joanne and Sarah in charge of Stanley's diet while she went to Bread Loaf and came back to find them all 15 pounds thinner. Stanley was appropriately grumpy about the whole ordeal. "Currently teetering at 202 [pounds], hungry and mean," he reported to Kenneth Burke. "I can stand every part of the diet except the congratulations, the people who say 'Look at the way you bound up the stairs. Don't you feel *much* better? . . . I think that bounding up stairs is a ridiculous infantile substitute for a free adult life of eating and drinking one's self comatose."

When Stanley went back to school that fall, his students were shocked to see how loose his clothing was. "Mr. Hyman lost a lot of weight, but his suits stayed fat," one remarked. He wouldn't have them altered, because he was still dieting. Despite the weight loss, he still seemed unwell. "He looked not slender but wasted," Brendan Gill commented, his clothes hanging in "grotesque billows." Stanley made light of it, complaining that the wind caught in his clothing and slowed him down when he tried to chase girls. Gill wondered whether Stanley's prey was "only sometimes imaginary."

As Shirley cared for Stanley, the fall brought another sadness. After a brief illness, Pat Covici died suddenly on October 14, at age seventy-five. Brandt had sent word to him in the hospital that Jackson's work on

*Jackson at
Bread Loaf.*

her new book was going well. "I knew this would be the kind of message that would give him great cheer," she told Jackson. In the six years they worked together, he had proved an ideal editor for her: supportive, enthusiastic, and above all patient. When she found calendar deadlines too stressful, he came up with "Dogwood Day" as a gentle substitute. During her time of acute anxiety, he expressed unconditional sympathy and encouragement. Jackson, who still avoided travel when possible, did not go down to New York for his funeral at Riverside Memorial Chapel, which was attended by Bellow, Steinbeck, and Arthur Miller, among many others. "A great editor is father, mother, teacher, personal devil, and personal god," said Steinbeck, who often kick-started a day's work by pretending he was writing a letter to Covici. He called the editor "my collaborator and my conscience." Brandt, too, felt the loss acutely. "It seems to me I have known him forever and ever," she wrote to Jackson. "He was a wonderful man, a wonderful person and a wonderful editor."

Thankfully, Covici's death did not derail the progress Jackson was making. At the end of October, she submitted "The Bus" to Brandt with the news that she had put aside *The Fair Land of Far* for the moment. As her agent had suspected, the book had served its purpose of getting her limbered up for a "more grownup type of thing," as Jackson called her new project. "Working, working," she assured Brandt in November. They were both eager to match her with a new editor at Viking. After considering the options, Brandt proposed Corlies (Cork) Smith, a young editor whose literary taste ranged from highbrow to commercial and who had recently pulled Thomas Pynchon's debut novel from the slush pile. Jackson was enthusiastic, and she and Smith hit it off when they met for lunch in January 1965. Brandt promptly negotiated a new contract for $20,000 that would allow Jackson to continue to draw $1,000 each month, allowing her just over eighteen months to finish the novel. "It is Viking's wish and intention to give you peace of mind in which to work," she assured Jackson. Brandt also negotiated a higher royalty rate.

"I am full of awe for you," Jackson responded. By now she was "seriously at work at last" on the new book, which she thought she could easily finish within eighteen months, and "certainly with peace of mind under these terms." It was to be called *Come Along with Me*.

———

IN HER LAST DIARY, Jackson had imagined writing a different kind of book, "perhaps a funny book. a happy book . . . [in] a new style." *Come Along with Me* was her attempt at a novel in this new style, markedly different from anything she had previously written, a comic novel featuring an unnamed heroine who outwardly resembles Jackson in middle age more than any other character in her work. Her age and size are both forty-four, she announces on the first page, "in case it's vital to know," and she "dabble[s] in the supernatural." Her husband has recently died, and she is moving to a new city to begin a new life. There are shades of "Louisa, Please Come Home," especially as she tries on new names searching for one that fits, but this woman is an adult, in full control of her destiny. The name she settles on, as we know, is Angela Motorman.

This narrator's idiosyncratic, superstition-inflected voice contains something of Merricat, but a Merricat who somehow managed to grow up, leave the house, and get married. After her husband's death—the circumstances of which are never made clear—she put all his possessions in the barn, just in case he "might turn up someday asking, the way they sometimes do." In addition to his paintings and half-finished canvases—"my God, he was a lousy painter"—there were boxes and cartons of letters and other files. After selling all the furniture, she simply got on the train and left for the next city available: "I hadn't ever been there and it seemed a good size and I had enough in my pocket to pay for the fare." Again like Louisa, she has no trouble finding a room in a boardinghouse—"perfectly square, which was good"—and makes friends with the landlady, Mrs. Faun, who offers her tea and cookies. The house rules are simple: no smoking in bed, no pets, "and anything you raise by way of spirits you have to put back yourself."

There is a jocular inflection here that is altogether new. This "happy book" is no *Bird's Nest* or *Castle*: Jackson is thoroughly enjoying herself. "In case you are wondering about me having lunch on the train and coffee and a doughnut in the station, and now a cup of tea and cookies, let me just remark that I have plenty of room to put it all," the narrator jokes in an aside. This is a comfort in largeness that has never appeared before in Jackson's work, a sharp contrast to the woman who counts calories and drinks Metrecal. Even her supernatural powers are mainly of a cozy, domestic type: as a child, she knew who would be on the phone before it rang and could see creatures—"what the cat saw"—under the dining room table. "i'm a kind-hearted mama who studies evil all the time," she says in an early draft. When she decides to give a séance for the other rooming-house residents, Mrs. Faun is initially worried: "Are you sure . . . that you are not tampering with things better left alone?" The narrator assures her that "it's exactly like taking a long-distance call. Once you hang up, it's over."

The novel amounts to only about seventy-five typescript pages; it's not clear where Jackson intended to take it. There is no real plot, only a series of episodes featuring this singular narrator and her "fine high gleefulness." "I think you understand me," she tells the reader. "I have everything I want." How close Jackson was to getting it.

IN EARLY FEBRUARY 1965, Jackson fell ill, probably with pneumonia, and was hospitalized for a week. She recovered just in time to travel with Hyman to Georgia to see Flannery O'Connor's estate, including her famous peacocks. Hyman was planning a short book about O'Connor, who had died of lupus the previous year at age thirty-nine. The trip, Jackson reported to Brandt, was "splendid but tiring"; as of early March she was still not supposed to climb stairs, lift anything heavy, or "overdo in any fashion." Her confidence had been shaken by the illness: "My whole life has been turned upside down in some lunatic fashion, and I can't seem to come to terms with things yet." But she was happy to be writing again, if only "half back at work . . . the hardest part of all is taking it easy."

She could not afford to convalesce for long. At the urging of her psychiatrist, James Toolan, she had planned the five college lectures for the spring, with stops in Syracuse, Madison, Akron, South Bend, and Chicago. Since the Morris was wearing out, she treated herself to a new MG sedan for the trip: the lecture fees, she bragged to her parents, covered the cost of the car. The students, as always, adored her, even

when Hyman was the purported headliner: when he spoke at Naza-
reth College in Rochester, students hung around afterward until he
got the hint and offered to introduce them to his wife. But the trip was
difficult. The weather was unseaonably hot, consistently over ninety
degrees, and Jackson "dripped all over" the pages she read. At Syracuse, one of her hosts worried that she looked like "a sick lady." At the
University of Chicago, she participated in an arts festival that required
her to live in a student dorm for four days, taking her meals in the cafeteria, which she hated. "the schedule was so wearing that i thought i
wouldn't make it," she confessed afterward. Compared with Bennington students, "full of ideas and enthusiasm," she found the Chicago
undergrads "dull drab creatures" who "only wanted to get their papers
written and their homework done so they could get out of the place."
Even the mood of student rebellion, palpable at every other college she
visited, had not infected them: when she asked if there had been any
civil rights demonstrations at the university, "these kids just stared at
the idea, completely apathetic."

Exhausted, Shirley spent most of June and July at home, though she
and Stanley did take Barry, along with his cousin Scott, on a road trip
to Canada. Though she must have been weak, her mood, Barry recalls,
was "gleeful." She drove with the MG's top down; Stanley, in the passenger seat, would light two Pall Malls off the lighter and hand one to
her. They spent the nights in one of the roadside motels newly popping
up beside the interstates, with the exception of a splurge at the Château
Frontenac, a historic hotel in Quebec City. On Bastille Day, Shirley and
Stanley let the boys buy Roman candles, which they set off along the
waterfront. Even after the police showed up to stop them, Shirley—
uncharacteristically—didn't get angry. "My cousin and I were into
all kinds of mischief that went entirely and intentionally unpunished,"
Barry remembers. "It was a really happy time when Shirley and Stanley
seemed to be getting along fine . . . no dark clouds on the horizon at all."
Perhaps the dynamic between them had shifted back to symbiosis. Or
perhaps Shirley was preparing to take the decisive step.

Later, a couple of Shirley's friends would say that she had acted
unusually during that summer, as if she had a premonition that her death

was approaching. She visited June Mirken Mintz unexpectedly in New York, bringing a huge box of chocolates for June's son. In general, she seemed relaxed and happy. And, in the very last days of her life, she sent Carol Brandt a strange, vaguely worded letter. She was about to leave for a wonderful journey, she said, where she would meet many new people. Though she offered no details, Brandt had the sense she was not talking about an ordinary trip. And it was clear that she was going alone.

Brandt, too, wondered later whether Shirley had foreseen her death. But there is a simpler explanation. The journey she was about to make was the journey she had been planning for so many years. Like the wife in "A Day in the Jungle," or Eleanor in *Hill House*, or Angela Motorman, she would step through a crack and disappear.

THE AFTERNOON OF August 8, 1965, was warm and pleasant. Shirley went upstairs to take her customary nap after lunch. Several hours later, Stanley tried to rouse her and found that he could not. In fear, he called out for Sarah. "I can't wake your mother," he said in a tone she had never heard before. Madly, he held a mirror in front of Shirley's nose and mouth to see if it would fog. "Dad, I think she's dead," Sarah told him.

Since it was Sunday, they had a hard time reaching a doctor. Durand finally arrived several hours later. By then, they knew. The official cause was a coronary occlusion due to arteriosclerosis, with hypertensive cardiovascular disease as a contributing factor.

Stanley made phone calls: Geraldine and Leslie, Lulu, the Karmillers, the Ellisons. Word quickly spread in tiny North Bennington. Visitors began to arrive: friends from the college, Stanley's poker group. It felt as if "hundreds of people" came to the house that day, Sarah, who was then sixteen, recalled. As Shirley might have done, Stanley told her to go upstairs and put on a girdle and stockings. Thirteen-year-old Barry sat alone on the porch, strumming the same guitar riff over and over. Joanne, nineteen, was in Rochester for the summer, working in theater; she was away that day and did not make it back to North

Bennington until two days later, after Shirley had already been cremated, in accordance with her wishes. Laurence, age twenty-two, and Corinne were living in New York, where he was teaching music at a school in Spanish Harlem. That weekend he wandered into a voodoo shop and bought some "goofer dust," said to bring money. The next day, Stanley called to tell him his mother had died. "That was my get-rich-quick—five hundred dollars [inheritance] or something," he recalled. He always wondered if in some way he had been responsible.

In New Hampshire, the *New Yorker* writer Francis Steegmuller heard the news on the radio. Many others, on vacation, learned about Shirley's death from *The New York Times*, which ran an obituary on August 11, or from *Newsweek* or *Time*, both of which ran short appreciations. Irving Kristol picked up the *Times* at the airport in Lebanon, New Hampshire, and saw the obituary: "That airport will, for me, remain forever haunted," he wrote to Stanley. Leonard Brown's daughter heard about Shirley's death on CBS news and wrote to say how much Brown had always admired her writing. In Baltimore, Jeanne Beatty clipped the obituary from the *Times* and put it away in the file where she kept Shirley's letters. She did not write to Stanley, who probably never knew of her existence.

Condolence telegrams and letters—as many as the "Lottery" letters, if not more—poured in from colleagues, friends, strangers. Roger Straus, Shirley's first publisher, who would later recall her as "a rather haunted woman." Marshall Best from Viking, who wrote of "Shirley's rare talents and wonderfully warm spirit." Jay Williams, who had long ago terrified Shirley by seeming to conjure a demon in front of her. Tom and Kit Foster, neighbors for so many years. Stanley's *New Yorker* colleagues: William and Cecille Shawn, Philip and Edith Hamburger, E. B. and Katharine White, Brendan Gill, Andy Logan. Bruce Bliven, Stanley's onetime boss at *The New Republic*. Norman Podhoretz and Midge Decter. Fred Burkhardt, the Bennington College president who had brought Stanley back to the campus. Florence Shapiro, whose presence on *Spectre* and in Stanley's life had irked Shirley so in college and after. Louis Untermeyer, Shirley's friend from Suffield. Virginia and Bill Olsen, neighbors in Westport. Jesse Zel Lurie, Stanley's long ago

Communist comrade, now the editor of *Hadassah Magazine*. College friends: Ben Zimmerman, Frank Orenstein (June Mirken Mintz was traveling and could not be reached). Walter Lehrman, Stanley's fellow blues scholar. Myron Kolatch, his editor at *The New Leader*. Bernard and Ann Malamud. Kenneth and Libbie Burke. Stanley's students, current and past, including Sandra Hochman, who was traveling in Hong Kong and heard the news there. The folksinger Tom Glazer, who recalled attending Stanley and Shirley's wedding, nearly twenty-five years earlier to the day: "so different, I am sure, from any other wedding." The renowned cookbook author Julia Child and her husband, Paul, who had met Shirley the previous summer at Bread Loaf and remembered her "wonderful talent" and "warm and wonderful personality." Isaac Bashevis Singer, who had read a number of Shirley's books after meeting Stanley in New York and saw her as "a kindred spirit in many ways." "Shirley is the main reason I don't even try to write fiction," wrote a classmate from Syracuse. "It was too humiliating to go to school with her." Many readers did not bother to sign their names, but instead identified themselves only as "a devoted fan." "She was one of us, and greater and smarter and funnier than any of us," wrote a housewife on Long Island. "It was so good to know she was *there*."

One of the condolence letters came from Phoebe Pettingell, a shy, awkward Bennington student from Chicago who had taken Stanley's introductory English class her freshman year. In December of the following year, she and Stanley would be married. The marriage lasted until Stanley's sudden death, from a heart attack, on July 29, 1970.

STANLEY SPENT THE first month in shock. He had no idea how to manage his day-to-day routine without Shirley; he could not even make coffee. Joanne and Sarah stayed with him, alternating nights. They cooked him dinner or, more often, took a taxi to a restaurant somewhere. He made them answer the condolence letters, ten a day, at random. That fall he taught his usual schedule—Myth, Rit, and Lit—and he tried to finish the short book about Flannery O'Connor that he had begun earlier that summer. "More than usual, it isn't very good," he told Kenneth

Burke. Now that Shirley was gone, he was unable to continue using the yellow paper she had loved; after sharing it with her for nearly a quarter century, he went back to white. In October, Burke nominated him for the National Institute of Arts and Letters, but even that honor did nothing for him. "I do not give a damn whether or not I am admitted," he wrote to Burke. "If Shirley never made it, I do not need it."

What energized Stanley most, in those early months, were his efforts on behalf of Shirley's reputation. The day after Shirley died, Nemerov prepared a press release that included his own perceptive assessment of her talent. "In an age whose most-praised novels are given to descriptions of how it feels to sit on a real toilet seat, she told her fables of the real and abstract life . . . in sentences that read about as crisp and clean as those of Jane Austen," Nemerov wrote. "By her power of writing such sentences she achieved her wonderful strangeness, which has to do with the power of magic both black and white in our lives." Unfortunately, the journalists who wrote her obituaries ignored this aspect of her fiction, preferring to concentrate on the sensationalistic. The headline of her *Times* obituary identified her as "Author of Horror Classic," reducing her body of work, as would many other such assessments in the coming years, to "The Lottery" (a "horror" story only in the loosest sense). *Newsweek* judged her an "absolute original" but emphasized the supernatural aspect of both her personality and her fiction, calling her "the most benign, warm-hearted, humorous and generous of witches." The *New York Herald Tribune* repeated the old line about her writing with "a broomstick, not a pen"—in its headline, no less—and wondered yet again at her ability to write both family humor and ghost stories.

Stanley set out to "dissipate some of the 'Virginia Werewoolf of seance-fiction' fog." The *Saturday Evening Post* still had one last story of Jackson's: "The Possibility of Evil," originally written in 1958. It ran on December 18, 1965, with Stanley's introduction, for which he sought approval from the children, Nemerov, and Barbara Karmiller before publishing. The surprise of readers upon discovering that Shirley Jackson, author of "violent and terrifying" fiction, was also an "apparently happy" wife and mother, he wrote, was "the most elementary misunderstanding of what a writer is and how a writer works, on the order of expecting Herman Melville to be a big white whale." Whether or not she was, in fact, a happy wife and mother—a judgment Stanley finally was too honest to offer without a qualifier—his observation is undoubtedly correct. "Shirley Jackson wrote in a variety of forms and styles because she was, like everyone else, a complex human being, confronting the world in many different roles and moods," Stanley continued. She had eschewed publicity, he said, because "she believed that her books would speak for her clearly enough over the years."

The *Post*'s readers, presented with this introduction, might well have expected that a story in an entirely new style would follow—something like *Come Along with Me*. What they found, rather, was one that epitomized the method Jackson had been perfecting ever since "Janice," the story that first caught Stanley's attention: the deceptively simple but finally devastating exposure of hypocrisy, cruelty, or inhumanity in all its many forms. As usual, a woman is at its center.

Like "When Things Get Dark," Jackson's wartime story about the innocuous-seeming Mrs. Hope, who sends letters of support to whomever she meets, "The Possibility of Evil" tells of an elderly woman who takes pleasure in sending anonymous letters to unwitting recipients. In this case, however, the letters are intended not to lift people's morale, but to destroy it by confirming their worst fears. A young mother who has been worrying about her baby's development gets a note that reads, "Didn't you ever see an idiot child before?" A woman who is about to have an operation gets one that says, "You never know about doctors. . . . Suppose the knife slipped accidentally?" The writer of the letters, Adela Strangeworth, considers it her duty to sow these seeds of discontent. Otherwise, her neighbors "would have gone unsuspectingly ahead with their lives, never aware of possible evil lurking nearby." But one day she is discovered, and the townspeople take their revenge.

Shirley Jackson saw herself, it seems clear, as a version of Miss Strangeworth: she believed her role as a writer was to draw back the curtain on the darkness within the human psyche. The disturbance experienced by the recipients of Miss Strangeworth's letters must have been something like the sensation that overcame the thousands of unsuspecting readers who opened *The New Yorker* on June 26, 1948, and were confronted by a story unlike anything they had ever read before. They admired it, they raged at it, they were puzzled by it; but no matter their reaction, it illuminated their world. Jackson paid a high price for the evil she exposed: her hate mail, her ostracism from her neighbors, her crippling anxiety. Her insistence on telling unpleasant truths is surely part of the reason her work has been less appreciated than it deserves to be. Nonetheless, she kept it up until the end, sending her literary bombs unerringly to their targets, then standing back to watch them explode.

Select Bibliography

SHIRLEY JACKSON'S
PUBLISHED WORKS

The original editions of each of Shirley Jackson's books are listed below. As explained at the beginning of the Notes, I often consulted a different edition in writing this biography.

NOVELS AND STORY COLLECTIONS

The Road Through the Wall. New York: Farrar, Straus, 1948.
The Lottery: or, The Adventures of James Harris. New York: Farrar, Straus, 1949.
Hangsaman. New York: Farrar, Straus and Young, 1951.
The Bird's Nest. New York: Farrar, Straus and Young, 1954.
The Sundial. New York: Farrar, Straus and Cudahy, 1958.
The Haunting of Hill House. New York: Viking, 1959.
We Have Always Lived in the Castle: New York: Viking, 1962.

NONFICTION

Life Among the Savages: An Uneasy Chronicle. New York: Farrar, Straus and Young, 1953.
Raising Demons. New York: Farrar, Straus and Cudahy, 1957.
Special Delivery: A Useful Book for Brand-New Mothers. Boston: Little, Brown, 1960.

CHILDREN'S BOOKS

The Witchcraft of Salem Village. New York: Random House, 1956.
Nine Magic Wishes. New York: Crowell-Collier, 1963.
Famous Sally. New York: Harlin Quist, 1966.

POSTHUMOUS COLLECTIONS

Hyman, Stanley Edgar, ed. *Come Along with Me*. New York: Viking, 1966. Includes the unfinished novel *Come Along with Me*, fourteen previously uncollected stories, and three lectures.

Hyman, Stanley Edgar, ed. *The Magic of Shirley Jackson*. New York: Farrar, Straus and Giroux, 1966. Includes eleven stories from the *Lottery* collection, *The Bird's Nest*, *Life Among the Savages*, and *Raising Demons*.

Hyman, Laurence Jackson, and Sarah Hyman Stewart, eds. *Just an Ordinary Day*. New York: Bantam, 1997. Includes thirty-one previously unpublished stories and articles and twenty-three published but uncollected stories.

Oates, Joyce Carol, ed. *Shirley Jackson: Novels and Stories*. New York: Library of America, 2010. Includes the entire *Lottery* collection, *The Haunting of Hill House*, *We Have Always Lived in the Castle*, a selection of stories from *Come Along with Me* and *Just an Ordinary Day*, and the lecture "Biography of a Story."

Hyman, Laurence Jackson, and Sarah Hyman DeWitt, eds. *Let Me Tell You*. New York: Random House, 2015. Includes thirty unpublished or uncollected short stories; twenty-one unpublished or uncollected essays, reviews, or articles; and five lectures.

Notes

The following abbreviations are used in the notes.

PEOPLE

SJ	Shirley Jackson
SEH	Stanley Edgar Hyman
BB	Bernice Baumgarten
CB	Carol Brandt
KB	Kenneth Burke
RE	Ralph Ellison
GJ	Geraldine Jackson
LJ	Leslie Jackson
JW	Jay Williams

Jackson's children are referred to in notes by the names they now use: Laurence Jackson Hyman, Jai Holly (Joanne Hyman), Sarah Hyman DeWitt, and Barry Hyman.

ARCHIVES

SJ-LOC	Shirley Jackson Papers, Manuscript Division, Library of Congress, Washington, D.C. The vast majority of SJ's publicly available papers are here. (The University of Colorado at Boulder has drafts and notes for around twenty stories, some of which duplicates material in the LOC.) The archive exists in two parts: Part I was donated to the Library in 1967 by SEH. Part II consists mainly of material transferred from the SEH Papers (see below) in 1993, plus small additional later gifts from Sarah Hyman DeWitt and Virginia Olsen.
SEH-LOC	Stanley Edgar Hyman Papers, Manuscript Division, Library

of Congress, Washington, D.C. SEH's archive was donated by Phoebe Pettingell, his second wife, in 1979.

AK-HRC   Alfred A. Knopf, Inc., Records, Harry Ransom Center, University of Texas at Austin. The Knopf archives contain correspondence between SEH and his editors at Knopf during the period preceding the publication of his book *The Armed Vision* (1948).

FSG-NYPL   Farrar, Straus and Giroux Records, New York Public Library, New York, New York. SJ's first seven books for adults were published by Farrar, Straus. The archive includes correspondence between SJ and John Farrar, Roger Straus, and Robert Giroux.

JW-BU   Jay Williams Papers, Howard Gotlieb Archival Research Center, Boston University, Boston, Massachusetts. The actor and author Jay Williams was a friend of both SJ and SEH.

KB-PSU   Kenneth Burke Papers, Pennsylvania State University Libraries, State College, Pennsylvania. Burke, a major literary critic, and his wife, Libbie, were close friends of SJ and SEH and corresponded regularly with SEH. Correspondence from SJ to Libbie Burke is presumed lost.

LH-AJA   Louis Harap Papers, American Jewish Archives, Cincinnati, Ohio. Louis Harap, a magazine editor, corresponded frequently with SJ and SEH in the early 1940s.

NY-NYPL   *New Yorker* Records, New York Public Library, New York, New York. *The New Yorker*'s vast archive includes correspondence between SJ and Gustave Lobrano, one of the fiction editors, as well as between SEH and William Shawn, SEH's editor.

RE-LOC   Ralph Ellison Papers, Manuscript Division, Library of Congress, Washington, D.C. Ellison was a close friend of both SJ and SEH and corresponded regularly with SEH.

Several important collections of SJ's letters are held privately. These include her letters to her agents Bernice Baumgarten and Carol Brandt and to her friend Jeanne Beatty.

WORKS

CAWM   *Come Along with Me: Classic Short Stories and an Unfinished Novel*, ed. Stanley Edgar Hyman. New York: Penguin, 2013.

JOD	*Just an Ordinary Day*, ed. Laurence Jackson Hyman and Sarah Hyman Stewart. New York: Bantam, 1997.
LMTY	*Let Me Tell You*, ed. Laurence Jackson Hyman and Sarah Hyman DeWitt. New York: Random House, 2015.
LOA	*Shirley Jackson: Novels and Stories*, ed. Joyce Carol Oates. New York: Library of America, 2010.
RTW	*The Road Through the Wall*. New York: Penguin, 2013.
Savages	*Life Among the Savages*. New York: Penguin, 2015.

Editions of the other books by SJ referred to in these notes:

The Bird's Nest. New York: Penguin, 2014.

Famous Sally. New York: Harlin Quist, 1966.

Hangsaman. New York: Penguin, 2013.

Nine Magic Wishes. New York: Farrar, Straus and Giroux, 2001.

Raising Demons. New York: Penguin, 2015.

Special Delivery: A Useful Book for Brand-New Mothers. Boston: Little, Brown, 1960.

The Sundial. New York: Penguin, 2014.

The Witchcraft of Salem Village. New York: Scholastic, 2001.

INTRODUCTION: A SECRET HISTORY

1 **"I didn't want to fuss"**: "Biography of a Story," in *CAWM* and LOA. A slightly different version of SJ's inspiration for "The Lottery" appears in "How I Write" in *LMTY*.

2 **"I have read"**: "Lottery" scrapbook, SJ-LOC, Box 32.

2 **"perhaps the only contemporary writer"**: The author's note appears on the jacket of the first edition of *RTW*.

2 **"Miss Jackson writes"**: W. G. Rogers, "Literary Guidepost" (a review of *The Lottery: or, The Adventures of James Harris*), Associated Press, April 13, 1949.

2 **"a rather haunted woman"**: Oral history interview with Roger W. Straus Jr., 1979, Columbia University Center for Oral History, New York, N.Y.

3 **"strange stirring"**: Betty Friedan, *The Feminine Mystique* (1963; repr., New York: W. W. Norton, 1997), 1.

4 **"One would sooner expect"**: Nathaniel Benchley, "Never a Dull Moment by This Family's Not So Peaceful Hearth," *New York Herald Tribune*, June 28, 1953.

5 **"I'll just put down housewife"**: SJ, *Savages*, 65–66.

5   **"babies and bed and brilliant friends"**: Karen V. Kukil, ed., *The Unabridged Journals of Sylvia Plath* (New York: Anchor Books, 2000), 221.

5   **"Some women marry houses"**: Anne Sexton, *The Complete Poems* (Boston: Houghton Mifflin, 1981), 77.

6   **"the decade of Jackson"**: Linda Wagner-Martin, *The Mid-Century American Novel* (New York: Twayne, 1997), 107.

6   **"faintly disreputable"**: Bernice M. Murphy, " 'Do You Know Who I Am?' Reconsidering Shirley Jackson," in *Shirley Jackson: Essays on the Literary Legacy*, ed. Bernice M. Murphy (Jefferson, N.C.: McFarland & Company, 2005), 11.

7   **"I have always loved"**: SJ-LOC, Box 14. This line comes from a document that Judy Oppenheimer, SJ's first biographer, identifies (I believe incorrectly) as an unsent letter from SJ to Howard Nemerov; see chapter 16.

7   **"since I hope"**: SJ to GJ and LJ, n.d. [March 1960]. All of SJ's letters to her parents can be found in SJ-LOC, Box 3. These letters are usually undated; I have given dates in brackets when possible.

8   **"Her character"**: Libbie Burke to SEH, September 1965, SEH-LOC, Box 46, folder 7.

9   **"hard / As it is"**: Howard Nemerov, *The Collected Poems of Howard Nemerov* (Chicago: University of Chicago Press, 1981), 436.

9   **"For all her popularity"**: Stanley Edgar Hyman, "Shirley Jackson," *Saturday Evening Post*, December 18, 1965. Reprinted as the introduction to *The Magic of Shirley Jackson*.

1. FOUNDATIONS

11   **"the witchery of a tropic moon"**: The description of the ship comes from United States Lines Company, *The New S.S. California* (New York: International Mercantile Company, 1927), unpaged pamphlet.

13   **"which means a suburb"**: "Autobiographical Musing," *LMTY*, 192.

13   **"My grandfather was an architect"**: "The Ghosts of Loiret," *LMTY*, 241.

14   **Samuel Bugbee came**: The Bugbee family history is drawn from family trees and newspaper clippings courtesy of Laurence Jackson Hyman.

15   **"It would start to play"**: Interview with Laurence Jackson Hyman, February 17, 2013.

16   **"large and elegant mansion"**: "The Building Season," *San Francisco Chronicle*, May 5, 1870.

16   **Attorney David Douty Colton's**: Details on the Colton house and the other Bugbee-designed mansions in this paragraph come from Patricia J.

Lawrence, "Four Mansions on Nob Hill in the 1870s" (master's thesis, University of California, Davis, 1976).

16   **Charles Crocker's home:** Ibid., 30–38.

17   **"an entertainment":** *California Spirit of the Times,* October 21, 1879, quoted in ibid., 56.

17   **The menu included:** Lawrence, "Four Mansions," 67–68.

17   **"All the old New England houses":** SJ to GJ and LJ, January 14, 1958, SJ-LOC, Box 3.

17   **"possible architectural orgies":** GJ to SJ, n.d. [January 1958]. All of GJ's letters to SJ are in SJ-LOC, Box 2.

18   **"Glad [it] didn't survive":** GJ to SJ, January 2 [1959].

18   **"shadow of misfortune":** "Palatial Houses: The Shadow That Rests on San Francisco's Nob Hill," *Morning Call* (San Francisco), October 5, 1891.

19   **"an air of disease":** "Experience and Fiction," *CAWM,* 227-28.

19   **"big old california":** SJ to GJ and LJ, January 14, 1958.

19   **a prayer book:** SJ to GJ and LJ, n.d. [early 1963].

20   **"a cultivated, refined gentleman":** Undated clipping, courtesy Laurence Jackson Hyman.

20   **"You think things":** Interview with Sarah Hyman DeWitt, February 17, 2013.

20   **At its height:** The movement has since been in decline. As of 2000, there were fewer than 100,000 Christian Scientists in the United States.

21   **President Woodrow Wilson:** Anne Grosvenor-Ayres, "The Mystery of the Ouija Board," *San Francisco Chronicle,* November 24, 1918.

21   **"ouijamania":** "Residents of Contra Costa Found Crazed—Ouija Board Séance Drives 7 Insane," *San Francisco Chronicle,* March 4, 1920. The *Chronicle* reported on the phenomenon nearly every day for a month. See, for instance, "Town of 1200 Faces Ouija Board Inquiry," March 5, 1920; "Ouija Board Drives Two More Insane," March 6, 1920; "Ouija Board Not Insanity Case, Says Professor," April 18, 1920.

21   **"Sickness is a dream":** Mary B. Glover Eddy, *Science and Health,* vol. 1 (Cambridge: Cambridge University Press, 1881), 188.

21   **"You could make a story":** GJ to SJ, n.d. [November 1958].

21   **A wealthy English family:** Ibid. LJ's father, Edward Henchall, was reportedly a classmate of British prime minister Herbert Asquith. See Judy Oppenheimer, *Private Demons: The Life of Shirley Jackson* (New York: Putnam, 1988), 13.

22   **"one of the prettiest girls":** Undated newspaper clipping, courtesy Laurence Jackson Hyman.

22   **In an unpublished story:** SJ-LOC, Box 15.

23   **"The pregnancy":** Interview with Jai Holly, July 16, 2015.

23   **"Seeing her":** Louise Albert to SJ, October 18, 1945, SJ-LOC, Box 43, folder 1.

23   **"She was a lady":** Interview with Laurence Jackson Hyman, February 17, 2013.

24   **"I don't think":** Interview with Barry Hyman, July 22, 2013.

24   **"Geraldine wanted":** Interview with Jai Holly, July 16, 2015.

25   **The unofficial motto:** Joanne Garrison, *Living in Burlingame Is a Special Privilege: Burlingame Centennial, 1908–2008* (Burlingame: Burlingame Historical Society, 2007), vii.

25   **"far enough away":** "Dorothy and My Grandmother and the Sailors," LOA, 108–13.

26   **"like something out of England":** Garrison, *Living in Burlingame*, 6.

26   **"perhaps the most exclusive hometown":** Ibid., 17.

27   **"new, modern, spick and span":** Elbert Hubbard, *A Little Journey in San Mateo County* (East Aurora, N.Y.: Roycroft Shop, 1915), 19, quoted in ibid., 43.

27   **"You are a stranger":** Garrison, *Living in Burlingame*, 58.

27   **a town modeled on Burlingame:** SJ's brother noted the similarities when the book came out. "I understand that I'm not to be surprised if I find myself in it. . . . I certainly recognize the setting and I'm sure most of the characters will seem somewhat familiar." Barry Jackson to SJ, April 1, 1948, SJ-LOC, Box 2.

29   **In her notes:** SJ-LOC, Box 27.

29   **"The weather falls":** *RTW*, 1.

30   **the only Jewish child:** It is unlikely that there were any Jews in Burlingame at the time. The town's first synagogue was established in 1955.

30   **"the first book":** Oppenheimer, *Private Demons*, 125.

30   **"a wilful child":** GJ to SJ, n.d. [September 1962].

30   **"gawking at nothing":** *CAWM*, 19.

31   **her little brother:** Interview with Jai Holly, July 22, 2013.

31   **"died of Christian Science":** Ibid.

31   **"one of my grandmother's":** "Hex Me Daddy, Eight to the Bar," *LMTY*, 199.

32   **"Writing used to be":** "Autobiographical Musing," *LMTY*, 191.

33   **the lock on the desk broken:** Keys, which often give a false sense of security, are an important symbol in SJ's work. In the story "Like Mother Used to Make," having the key to another person's apartment creates a sense of false ownership. In "Trial by Combat," a woman whose privacy

is invaded in a rooming house learns that the same key can be used to open many doors; in *Hangsaman*, Natalie finds out the same thing about her dorm, to her horror. See also "Desk," SJ-LOC, Box 19, for a description of the scene of invaded privacy.

33   **"He was not"**: Interview with Jai Holly, July 22, 2013.

33   **Her excitement**: Lenemaja Friedman, *Shirley Jackson* (New York: Twayne, 1975), 18.

33   **"lonely wood"**: For "The Pine Tree" and other childhood poems, see SJ-LOC, Box 13.

34   **"two for a nickel"** . . . **"unladylike"**: Draft of "The Clothespin Dolls," SJ-LOC, Box 13.

34   **"so careful"** . . . **"sanity"**: SJ-LOC, Box 42.

35   **"worked overtime"**: SJ-LOC, Box 1.

35   **"My mother told us"**: "Dorothy and My Grandmother and the Sailors," LOA, 108–13.

35   **"My mother used to be"**: SJ-LOC, Box 13.

36   **"I do believe"**: *Raising Demons*, 125.

36   **Hawthorne is said**: Malcolm Cowley, introduction to *The Portable Hawthorne* (New York: Viking, 1948), 6–7.

36   **The earliest surviving diary**: Most of SJ's diaries can be found in SJ-LOC, Box 1.

37   **"write down just what"**: SJ-LOC, Box 1.

37   **"A lady doesn't"**: Interview with Sarah Hyman DeWitt, February 17, 2013.

37   **"You have too many"**: GJ to SJ, n.d. [October 1962].

38   **"Shirley—it would be very interesting"**: SJ-LOC, Box 1.

38   **a tablet-size notepad**: SJ-LOC, Box 42.

38   **"my girl-shy violinist"**: SJ-LOC, Box 42.

38   **she kept both diaries simultaneously**: It's possible that the datebook was intended as a decoy diary that SJ kept more accessible in case her mother went looking through her desk; finding the more innocent diary, GJ would have been less likely to probe further.

39   **"Today I shall write "** . . . **"you don't know it"**: SJ-LOC, Box 42.

39   **"To my friend"**: SJ-LOC, Box 42.

40   **she began a new diary**: SJ-LOC, Box 1.

40   **She also started a five-year diary**: SJ-LOC, Box 1.

40   **"horribly unhorrifying"**: SJ-LOC, Box 1.

40   **"Wrote all evening"**: SJ-LOC, Box 1.

40   **"I've been"** . . . **"yellow streak"**: SJ-LOC, Box 1.

41   **"Somehow I think"**: "The Intoxicated," LOA, 5–9.

41   "This is the last time": SJ-LOC, Box 1.

41   "Get thee behind me": SJ-LOC, Box 1.

41   undated story fragment: SJ-LOC, Box 42.

2. THE DEMON IN THE MIND

43   "an odd corner": *Hangsaman*, 3.

43   "the sweet sharp sensation": Ibid., 10.

44   "ultimate publication": Ibid., 30.

44   "her bruised face": *Hangsaman*, 44.

44   "sticky touch": Judy Oppenheimer, *Private Demons* (New York: Putnam, 1988), 26–27.

44   "I feel like a package": SJ-LOC, Box 1.

45   "the ruination of what" . . . "Absolved of sin": SJ-LOC, Box 1.

46   "Golly, how I hate this town": SJ-LOC, Box 1.

46   "people were on": Telephone interview with Marion Strobel, August 12, 2015.

46   Alta Williams: SJ-LOC, Box 14.

46   "the sick inadequate feeling": "Autobiographical Musing," *LMTY*, 192.

47   "She used to wear": Oppenheimer, *Private Demons*, 34.

47   "didn't give a darn": Interview with Strobel, August 12, 2015.

48   "We just don't know": Ibid.

48   "odd duck": Ibid.

48   "i hate that school": "Scapegoat," SJ-LOC, Box 18. The story's title suggests that SJ wrote it after reading *The Golden Bough* during her sophomore year at Rochester, and its action mimics the rituals of imitative magic Frazer describes.

48   "My father doesn't like": "Catharine," SJ-LOC, Box 15. The draft in SJ's archive is a revised version, hence the normal capitalization.

48   "fat, and badly dressed" . . . "proud of them": "The Lovely Night," SJ-LOC, Box 17.

49   "When have I ever": Letter inserted in 1933 diary, SJ-LOC, Box 1.

49   "I was just wondering": Dorothy Ayling to SJ, December 16, 1933, SJ-LOC, Box 4.

49   "Sometimes after I read": Dorothy Ayling to SJ, April 14, 1934, SJ-LOC, Box 4.

49   "I beg your pardon": SJ-LOC, Box 42.

49   "Hereafter see that": SJ-LOC, Box 1.

50   "Irish has gone" . . . "To be happy": SJ-LOC, Box 1.

50 an ornamental mask: SJ to GJ and LJ, June 16 [1958], SJ-LOC, Box 3.

50 "a study of the grotesque": Quoted in Pierre Louis DuChartre, *The Italian Comedy*, trans. Randolph T. Weaver (London: George G. Harrap and Co., 1929), 17. In college, SJ teased SEH that this was the only book she had ever read that he hadn't.

51 "of acrobatics and unseemly noises": Ibid., 134.

51 "I can't understand": SJ-LOC, Box 1.

51 "Knowing myself to desire": SJ-LOC, Box 1.

52 "Life is such a casual thing": SJ-LOC, Box 1.

52 "There's a little covered wagon": *RTW*, 111.

53 The 1934 University of Rochester admissions application: University of Rochester file on SJ, University of Rochester Archives, Rochester N.Y. Archivist Melissa Mead graciously provided me with this material.

54 Richard Morton: Interview with Strobel, August 12, 2015.

54 "more serious": Arthur J. May, *University of Rochester History*, chapter 27, accessed September 7, 2015, http://rbscp.lib.rochester.edu/2333.

54 essay questions: SJ-LOC, Box 1.

54 Her parents may have insisted: Oppenheimer, *Private Demons*, 37. In *Hangsaman*, Natalie's father selects her college for her.

55 "sick at the things": SJ-LOC, Box 1.

55 "the persecution of new students": *Hangsaman*, 60.

55 "senior queens": Ibid., 52.

55 in the middle of the night: Interview with Strobel, August 12, 2015.

55 "spooky" and "crazy": *Hangsaman*, 68–69.

57 "A true Parisian": SJ-LOC, Box 1.

57 "a bad caricature of Beethoven": SJ to SEH, June 21, 1938, SEH-LOC, Box 2.

57 "Slightly mad, we were": SJ-LOC, Box 1.

57 "I adore gangsters" . . . "cafeteria[s]": SJ-LOC, Box 1.

57 "in one hour": SJ-LOC, Box 1.

57 "revenge": Jeanne Marie Bedel to SJ, February 3, 1947, SJ-LOC, Box 6.

58 *Caucasian Sketches* . . . *Carmen*: SJ-LOC, Box 1.

58 "Don't fall too hard" . . . "poor husbands": Dorothy Ayling to SJ, January 22 and February 3, 1935, SJ-LOC, Box 4.

58 "Nobody recognized your picture": Dorothy Ayling to SJ, April 5, 1935, SJ-LOC, Box 4.

58 "I shall *never* be able": SJ-LOC, Box 1.

58 an invented language called Lildsune: SJ-LOC, Box 40.

59 Jackson published her first story: *Meliora* 12, no. 1 (Spring 1935). University of Rochester Archives, Rochester, N.Y.

59   "I must really go": SJ-LOC, Box 1.

59   "a month of evil omen": SJ-LOC, Box 1.

59   "I die a million deaths of tears": SJ-LOC, Box 40.

59   "Why does life" . . . "than the last": SJ-LOC, Box 1.

60   "spoiled" and "selfish": Jeanne Marie Bedel to SJ, June 16, 1936. SJ-LOC, Box 6.

60   "unbearable": Quoted in letter from Dorothy Ayling to SJ, June 15, 1935, SJ-LOC, Box 4.

60   "I thought you would understand": Note in SJ's 1935 diary, SJ-LOC, Box 1.

60   "Poor Jeanou": Ayling to SJ, June 15, 1935.

60   "Write to me": Bedel to SJ, n.d., SJ-LOC, Box 6. Sadly, SJ's letters to Bedel are lost. Bedel's relatives, in accordance with her wishes, burned her papers after her death, in 1966.

61   "has the stubborn persistency": Ezra Pound, *The Spirit of Romance* (London: J.M. Dent and Sons, 1930), 178; accessed September 7, 2015 via archive.org: https://archive.org/stream/spiritofromanceaoopounrich#page/178/mode/2up.

61   "I know all things—except myself": SJ-LOC, Box 1.

61   "She gave me": SJ-LOC, Box 1.

61   "i went to college" . . . "i was all alone": "Notes for a Story on the Grotesque," SJ-LOC, Box 14.

62   *Hangsaman* may be read: See Judie Newman, "Shirley Jackson and the Reproduction of Mothering," and John G. Parks, "Chambers of Yearning," in *Shirley Jackson: Essays on the Literary Legacy*, ed. Bernice M. Murphy (Jefferson, N.C.: McFarland & Company, 2005), 176, 242.

62   "She *wants* me": *Hangsaman*, 214.

62   "barely escapes a Lesbian seduction": SJ-LOC, Box 45.

63   must have deeply sympathized: This sympathy is also evident in "The Lovely Night," a story SJ rewrote in different forms, but which draws on an early draft of *Hangsaman* in which Natalie, in high school, accompanies her friends Doris and Ginny to a dance. The story indicates that Doris and Ginny, who dance together in defiance of others' stares and comments, are lesbians. In the published version, at the dance Natalie meets a popular girl who encourages her to shun Doris and Ginny; the story ends with a boy escorting her home. But in a draft, Natalie wants to come to her friends' defense: "they're only here to have fun. . . . they don't mean any real harm. . . . it's just that they're different, and they want a different kind of fun." SJ-LOC, Boxes 17 and 45.

63   **discover herself mentioned:** In fact, the book makes it clear that Tony is "the other half of [Natalie's] split personality. . . . The drama in *Hangsaman* is that of an abnormally sensitive girl's narrow escape from schizophrenia": Jeannette H. Foster, *Sex Variant Women in Literature* (Tallahassee, Fla.: Naiad Press, 1985), 332.

63   **"i happen to know":** SJ-LOC, Box 14.

64   **"there was a devil":** SJ-LOC, Box 45. Asmodeus is mentioned by Dr. Wright in *The Bird's Nest*; see chapter 12.

64   **"glorious" . . . "like some privacy":** SJ-LOC, Box 1.

65   **"Wrote an allegory":** SJ-LOC, Box 1.

65   **"The idea is":** SJ-LOC, Box 1.

65   *Story* **magazine:** SJ-LOC, Box 11.

65   **"Wrote a play tonight":** SJ-LOC, Box 1.

66   **"very nice" . . . "technically known as Hell":** SJ-LOC, Box 1.

66   **"For people who do not care":** SJ-LOC, Box 1.

66   **"because i refused":** "Notes for a Story on the Grotesque," SJ-LOC, Box 14.

67   **A psychiatrist who treated her:** Oppenheimer, *Private Demons*, 45.

67   **likely influenced by *Hangsaman*:** Bernice M. Murphy, "'Do You Know Who I Am?' Reconsidering Shirley Jackson," in *Shirley Jackson: Essays on the Literary Legacy*, 8.

67   **Plath . . . admired Jackson:** Linda Wagner-Martin, *Sylvia Plath: A Biography* (New York: Simon and Schuster, 1987), 97.

67   **"deadening" . . . "when it comes?":** SJ-LOC, Box 1.

67   **"old fears of people":** SJ-LOC, Box 1.

67   **"nerves and overwrought temperament":** SJ-LOC, Box 1.

67   **"the fearful cold waters below":** SJ-LOC, Box 1.

67   **"'you were just going to'":** "Fugue: A Short Story," SJ-LOC, Box 17.

68   **"You don't mind":** SJ-LOC, Box 44. The letter is filed, hilariously, under "Letters to unknown correspondents."

68   **a thousand words a day:** Oppenheimer, *Private Demons*, 45. This number has been repeated often by others, but I was unable to confirm it independently.

68   **"stay there and behave":** "Preface (to be read aloud to a group of sympathetic listeners)," SJ-LOC, Box 30.

69   **"I wish to further":** Syracuse University file on SJ, Syracuse University Archives, Syracuse, N.Y.

69   **"a hotbed of communism":** Michael Palmer to SJ, n.d., SJ-LOC, Box 10.

69   **"Since there were no books" . . . make her bed:** "All I Can Remember,"

JOD, xii–xiv. After SJ left home, she and her brother were barely in contact. "A fine brother and sister we are! We scarcely know where each other lives," Barry Jackson wrote to SJ in 1948, (SJ-LOC, Box 2).

3. INTENTIONS CHARGED WITH POWER

70   "I wanted to see": http://philippehalsman.com/?image=jumps.

72   "My ancestors were": SEH-LOC, Box 33.

72   "paid, even in Russia": SEH-LOC, Box 33. Elsewhere, SEH said his grandfather was a pawnbroker.

72   Stanley would later tell stories: Interview with Phoebe Pettingell, March 26, 2013.

72   "sensitive, idealistic, and deeply religious soul": SEH-LOC, Box 32.

73   "She was one of those women": Interview with Pettingell, April 6, 2015.

73   "It has not yet been declared": SEH-LOC, Box 33.

73   a case of pneumonia: In another version of this story, Lulu was told by the doctor who delivered Stanley that the baby was certain not to live. She left the hospital thinking her son was dead, only to be told two weeks later that he had survived after all. Interview with Pettingell, March 26, 2013.

73   "a willful, independent, unemotional man": SEH-LOC, Box 32.

74   "peremptory," with "a tough demeanor": Interview with Walter Bernstein, February 27, 2013.

74   "I was scared": Ibid.

74   "I invariably took her side": SEH-LOC, Box 32.

74   Stanley's IQ test: Interview with Sarah Hyman DeWitt, February 17, 2013.

74   "frightened of his intelligence": Interview with Pettingell, August 12, 2011.

75   "full of savage little children": John Wakeman, *World Authors, 1950–1970* (New York: H. H. Wilson, 1975), 699.

75   he delighted a student: Interview with Catherine Morrison, November 6, 2013.

75   he raised his hand: Judy Oppenheimer, *Private Demons* (New York: Putnam, 1988), 56.

75   "competed with great success": Wakeman, *World Authors*, 699.

75   structure a story: Unpublished story ("i would have said that i knew every grocery in this town"), SJ-LOC, Box 26.

76   "militant atheist": Wakeman, *World Authors*, 699.

76   "freed my mind": SEH-LOC, Box 32.

76   "Jesus is a myth": Wallace Fowlie, *Journal of Rehearsals* (Durham, N.C.: Duke University Press, 1977), 158.

77   "became stagnant physically": SEH-LOC, Box 32.

77   "For the first time" . . . "without being ashamed": Ibid.

77   "watch—with dazzling cruelty": Claude Fredericks, *The Journal of Claude Fredericks*, October 25, 1961. Marc Harrington of the Claude Fredericks Foundation generously provided me with excerpts from Fredericks's journal.

77   "One got used to seeing": Malcolm Cowley, *The Dream of the Golden Mountains: Remembering the 1930s* (New York: Viking, 1964), 22.

78    $2.39 per week: Ibid., 22–23.

78   "His idea of a good time": Interview with Laurence Jackson Hyman, February 17, 2013.

78   "Mom has periodical": SEH to Moe Hyman, May 19, 1932, SEH-LOC, Box 1.

79   an underage girl: Interview with Pettingell, April 6, 2015.

79   Lulu once discovered: Ibid.

79   "At least I do": SEH to Moe Hyman, May 29, 1932, SEH-LOC, Box 1.

79   "perhaps the greatest": SEH-LOC, Box 33.

79   "He knew where": Interview with Sarah Hyman DeWitt, February 17, 2013.

80   funny, if probably apocryphal, story: Bernard Malamud, "Stanley's Files," *Quadrille* 7, no. 2 (Winter/Spring 1973), 14.

80   campus on Flatbush Avenue: Janna Malamud Smith, *My Father Is a Book* (Boston: Houghton Mifflin, 2006), 40.

80   "either cut down" . . . "completely disregarded": SEH-LOC, Box 33.

81   "miserably lonely" . . . "like a harelip": SEH-LOC, Box 32.

81   "dreadfully serious" . . . "learns to walk": Ibid.

81   Walter even snuck out: Walter Bernstein, *Inside Out* (New York: Da Capo, 2000), 36.

82   "enter the fold": SEH-LOC, Box 18.

82   "He was born": Interview with Bernstein, February 27, 2013.

82   "I have read": SEH-LOC, Box 33.

82   "lyric and exquisite": SEH-LOC, Box 33.

83   "as picturesque and checkered": SEH-LOC, Box 32.

83   "an infrequent and shamefaced" . . . "my body since": Ibid.

83   "It was my father's theory" . . . "high school can be": Ibid.

84   "exotic" . . . "showing off": Interview with Bernstein, February 27, 2013.

84   A comic sketch: SEH-LOC, Box 33.

84   "ultimately their excitement": Malamud Smith, *My Father Is a Book*, 187.

84   "small, round, red-haired girl": SEH-LOC, Box 32.

86 **"take communism away"**: Cowley, *The Dream of the Golden Mountains*, 19–20.

86 **"tinged with pink"**: Ibid., 289.

86 **"to clarify the principles"**: Ibid., 136.

87 **"He wrote in English"**: Ibid., 271.

87 **"Hundreds of poets"**: Ann George and Jack Selzer, *Kenneth Burke in the 1930s* (Columbia: University of South Carolina Press, 2007), 13.

87 **the term "the people"**: Ibid., 17.

88 **"constant doubts"**: SEH-LOC, Box 32.

88 **"on the same wavelength"**: Interview with Florence Shapiro Siegel, March 5, 2014.

88 **"sociological position"**: Syllabus from Main Currents in Modern Literature, SEH-LOC, Box 34.

89 **"What I am attempting"**: Ibid.

89 **Stanley's last known Communist affiliation**: File 100-HQ-366428, National Archives at College Park, College Park, Md. I am grateful to Mark Murphy of the National Archives for expediting my request for SEH's FBI file.

4. S & S

90 **"I was in that first sweet"**: Judy Oppenheimer, *Private Demons* (New York: Putnam, 1988), 50.

92 **Herrington's course in folklore**: See chapter 8.

92 **"I am going to write"**: SJ-LOC, Box 38.

92 **"it seemed that everyone"**: "Preface (to be read aloud to a group of sympathetic listeners)," SJ-LOC, Box 30.

92 **A story Shirley wrote around this time**: SJ-LOC, Box 37.

93 **"I have . . . seldom" . . . "in my hand"**: SJ-LOC, Box 37.

93 **"People are beginning"**: Draft of letter in college notebook, SJ-LOC, Box 37.

93 **"epochal novel"**: Michael Palmer to SJ, January 4, 1938, SJ-LOC, Box 10.

93 **"He knew [his roommates]"**: SJ-LOC, Box 10.

94 *The Threshold*: Syracuse University Archives, Syracuse, N.Y.

94 **"Surprisingly enough"**: SJ-LOC, Box 37.

94 **"Darn near killed myself"**: LOA, 565.

94 **After Y showed**: SJ to SEH, summer 1938 ("hawney"), SEH-LOC, Box 2. Since it is not possible precisely to date many of the letters between SJ and SEH, I have used their first lines as identifiers. Some of the letters are dated in pencil by an unknown hand; some of those dates are demonstrably

inaccurate (e.g., the letter is dated "Wednesday" but the date given is for a Thursday). For the sake of simplicity, I have used those dates when available, with the knowledge that they may be off by a day or more.

95   **"specious scientific conditioning"**: *The Threshold*, Syracuse University Archives.

95   **"You were the only live thing"**: SEH to SJ, summer 1938 ("darling, I worked eleven hours today"), SJ-LOC, Box 42.

96   **"no idea what the things"**: Interview with Walter Bernstein, February 27, 2013.

96   **"wrote painfully, it was a tedious"**: Oppenheimer, *Private Demons*, 76.

96   **"He talked a lot"**: Ibid., 73.

97   **"looking enough of a bum"**: SEH to SJ, summer 1938 ("oh darling, i am such a damn fool"). SJ-LOC, Box 42.

97   **"Your intellect is"**: SJ-LOC, Box 13.

97   **"no one can really love"**: *Hangsaman*, 106.

98   **"He wants to know"**: SJ-LOC, Box 38.

98   **"single antagonist"**: *Hangsaman*, 203.

98   **"Stanley left me tonight"**: SJ-LOC, Box 38.

98   **"all along"** . . . **"the summer began"**: SEH to SJ, summer 1938 ("darling, i am sick unto death"). SJ-LOC, Box 42.

98   **"He is absolutely"**: SJ-LOC, Box 38.

98   **"I leaned my head back"**: SJ-LOC, Box 38.

98   **a note to herself**: SJ-LOC, Box 38.

98   **"he could break me"**: SJ-LOC, Box 38.

99   **"Did I remember"**: SJ-LOC, Box 37.

99   **"I must beg him"**: Draft of letter in college notebook, SJ-LOC, Box 38.

99   **the abbreviation "cf."**: SJ-LOC, Box 37.

99   **"Marx knows"**: SJ-LOC, Box 38.

100   **"less than does sanskrit"**: SJ to SEH, summer 1938 ("dear, monopoly established by mother"), SEH-LOC, Box 2.

100   **"I think any nation"**: SJ-LOC, Box 1.

100   **His response**: SEH to SJ, June 1938 ("beloved, since i wrote the first half"), SJ-LOC, Box 42.

101   **"My fashion has been acting up"**: SEH to SJ, summer 1938 ("cynara darling), SJ-LOC, Box 42.

101   **notorious for his affairs**: This dynamic—of a philandering man and a distraught woman—was common among the Greenwich Village radicals Stanley admired. Couples such as John Reed and Mabel Dodge and Ben Reitman and Emma Goldman had almost verbatim arguments. See Russ

Wetzsteon, *Republic of Dreams: Greenwich Village: The American Bohemia, 1910–1960* (New York: Simon & Schuster, 2002), 105, 212.

101   "I'll do anything": SJ-LOC, Box 38.

101   "He kept making remarks": Interview with Florence Shapiro Siegel, March 5, 2014.

101   "Stanley, crawling, is still powerful": SJ-LOC, Box 38.

102   "they will eat": SEH to SJ, June 1938 ("dearest boopsie"), SJ-LOC, Box 42.

102   "for god's sake": SJ to SEH, June 7, 1938, SEH-LOC, Box 2.

102   "i ought to stop": SEH to SJ, June 11, 1938. SJ-LOC, Box 42.

102   "every once in awhile": SEH to SJ, June 9, 1938, SJ-LOC, Box 42.

103   "genuine bohemia" . . . "save my life": SEH to SJ, June 1938 ("beloved, since i wrote the first half").

103   "i promised you": SEH to SJ, July 1938 ("darling, a thing as terrible"), SJ-LOC, Box 42.

103   "typical jewish" . . . "mother and daughter": SEH to SJ, summer 1938 ("drujok, this continuation"), SJ-LOC, Box 42.

104   "you have forever": SEH to SJ, summer 1938 ("darling, i just got home"), SJ-LOC, Box 42.

104   "all sick inside": SJ to SEH, July 1938 ("i read the stupid poem to pan") SEH-LOC, Box 2.

104   "if it turns you queasy": SEH to SJ, summer 1938 ("immortal beloved"), SJ-LOC, Box 42.

104   "it was a copulation": Ibid.

104   "o mightiest among men" . . . "*good* novel": SJ to SEH, August 1938 ("o mightiest among men"), SEH-LOC, Box 2.

105   "i think you are potentially": SEH to SJ, August 1938 ("cynara darling").

105   a to-do list: SJ to SEH, August 1938 ("this is the hardest letter"), SEH-LOC, Box 2.

105   "Pride is nice": Jeanne Marie Bedel to SJ, September 14, 1938, SJ-LOC, Box 43.

105   "Have you performed": "Meeting Jay Williams," SJ-LOC, Box 19.

107   "an intricate thing" . . . "too great for the devil": "Meeting Jay Williams."

107   "filled with books" . . . "in the world": Ibid.

108   skiing accident: See chapter 8.

108   "You mustn't be so timid": "Meeting Jay Williams."

109   "Everybody here": Bedel to SJ, September 14, 1938.

109   "the next world war": SEH to SJ, September 1938 ("drujok, i sit here"), SJ-LOC, Box 42.

109   **Earl Browder:** Ibid.

109   **"we stayed up":** Walter Bernstein to SEH, April 21, 1939, SEH-LOC, Box 4.

109   **"composed mainly of semi-illiterate":** SEH, "The Need for a New Poetic Form," *Spectre* 1, no. 1 (Fall 1939).

110   **"truly liberating":** SEH, *Standards: A Chronicle of Books for Our Time* (New York: Horizon, 1966), 118.

110   **"Love Sonnet After Munich":** SEH-LOC, Box 33.

110   **"i don't use":** SEH to JW, fall 1938, JW-BU, Box 30.

110   **"Letter to a Soldier":** SJ-LOC, Box 13.

111   **"knocked the class":** SEH to JW, fall 1938.

111   **"Y and I":** *Syracusan* 4, no. 2 (October 1930), Syracuse University Archives.

112   **"Y and I and the Ouija Board":** *Syracusan* 4, no. 3 (November 1938), ibid.

112   **"The Smoking Room":** *JOD*, 3–8.

113   **"All you need":** Pages torn from college notebook, SJ-LOC, Box 41.

113   **"What do you do":** Walter Bernstein to SEH, May 7, 1939, SEH-LOC, Box 4.

113   **"one-sided":** SJ-LOC, Box 38.

113   **"to know and understand":** "We the Editor," *Spectre* 1, no. 4 (Summer 1940), Syracuse University Archives.

114   **she even sent him a sketch:** SJ to SEH, June 27, 1939, SEH-LOC, Box 2.

114   **"People don't just part":** SJ-LOC, Box 37.

114   **"i decided i wanted":** SJ to SEH, June 27, 1939.

115   **"marvelous" . . . "great deal more":** SEH to SJ, June 28, 1939, SJ-LOC, Box 42.

115   **"read or fuck":** SEH to SJ, July 1939, SJ-LOC, Box 42.

115   **"look at someone's face":** SEH to SJ, July 10, 1939, SJ-LOC, Box 42.

115   **he had dropped out of Columbia:** Thomas P. Brockway, *Bennington College: In the Beginning* (Bennington, Vt.: Bennington College Press, 1981), 94.

115   **"there was not much talk":** Malcolm Cowley, "Notes on a Writers' Congress," *The New Republic*, June 21, 1939.

115   **"an intellectual thrill" . . . "believed them":** SEH to SJ, July 19, 1939, SJ-LOC, Box 42.

116   **"Aha, your subconscious":** SEH to SJ, July 23, 1939, SJ-LOC, Box 42.

116   **"i didn't realize":** SEH to SJ, August 6, 1939, SJ-LOC, Box 42.

116   **"Minnesota comes close":** SJ to SEH, July 25, 1939, SEH-LOC, Box 2.

116   **"a foot and a half":** SJ to SEH, July 26, 1939, SEH-LOC, Box 2.

116   **"acutely homesick" . . . "this vast quiet":** SJ to SEH, July 29, 1939, SEH-LOC, Box 2.

117 "the most delicate": SJ to SEH, August 3, 1939, SEH-LOC, Box 2.

117 "i'd forgotten" . . . "barry to sleep": SJ to SEH, August 2, 1939, SEH-LOC, Box 2.

117 "movie-travelogue" . . . "not from lack of trying": SEH to SJ, July 31, 1939, SJ-LOC, Box 42.

118 "a form of fish": SJ to SEH, July 20, 1939, SEH-LOC, Box 2.

118 "one of the finest modern novels": SEH to SJ, June 1939, SJ-LOC, Box 42.

119 "My daughter's" . . . "please help me": SJ to SEH, August 9, 1939, SEH-LOC, Box 2.

119 "a first-class bigot" . . . "tell me so regularly": SJ to SEH, August 12, 1939, SEH-LOC, Box 2.

119 "i've read your letter" . . . "fuck her": SJ to SEH, August 14, 1939, SEH-LOC, Box 2.

119 This one was solely about the book: SJ to SEH, August 16, 1939 (incorrectly dated August 13), SEH-LOC, Box 2.

120 "guess what started it" . . . "down the hall": SJ to SEH, August 26, 1939, SEH-LOC, Box 2.

120 "i was half certain": SEH to SJ, September 14, 1939, SJ-LOC, Box 42.

120 "have some music" . . . "more apart": SEH to JW, October 7, 1939, JW-BU, Box 30.

121 "the most beautiful" . . . "uncomplimentary tenor": Ibid.

121 "If it's all you say": Walter Bernstein to SEH, n.d., SEH-LOC, Box 4.

122 "We called the magazine": "We the Editor," *Spectre* 1, no. 1 (Fall 1939), Syracuse University Archives.

122 "We haven't any editorial policy": Ibid.

123 "If you want to have": "We the Editor," *Spectre* 1, no. 2 (Winter 1940), Syracuse University Archives.

123 "Censorship, or Repression": Ibid.

124 "sells out every time": "We the Editor," *Spectre* 1, no. 3 (Spring 1940), Syracuse University Archives.

124 "The overwhelming majority": "We the Editor," *Spectre* 1, no. 4 (Summer 1940), Syracuse University Archives.

124 "We wish them": Ibid., 3.

124 "race records": William Howland Kenney, *Recorded Music in American Life: The Phonograph and Popular Memory, 1890–1945* (New York: Oxford University Press, 1999).

125 "Bessie talks" . . . "a heavy surf": SEH, "Big Brown Woman," *Spectre* 1, no. 4 (Summer 1940).

125 Three of her poems: *Spectre* 1, no. 2 (Winter 1940).

126 "advocat[ing] retreat and weakness": "The Muse Hits Syracuse," *Spectre* 1, no. 4 (Summer 1940).

126 "The college was glad": SEH to Robert Phillips, April 4, 1961, Robert Phillips Papers, Syracuse University Archives, Syracuse, N.Y.

126 "most of which I wrote": SEH to SJ, August 27, 1939, SJ-LOC, Box 42.

126 "'If we had fifty dollars'": SJ, "Had We but World Enough," *Spectre* 1, no. 3 (Spring 1940).

127 A cartoon Shirley drew: SJ-LOC, Box 37.

5. THE MAD BOHEMIANS

128 "a brief three-minute thing" . . . "that sort of wedding": SEH-LOC, Box 47.

129 "that Mick": SEH to SJ, summer 1938 ("drujok, it was cool today"), SJ-LOC, Box 42.

130 first serious talk: SEH to SJ, March 24, 1940, SJ-LOC, Box 42.

130 his synagogue: Gershon Greenberg, "Kristallnacht: The American Ultra-Orthodox Theological Response," in *American Religious Responses to Kristallnacht*, ed. Maria Mazzenga (New York: Palgrave Macmillan, 2009), 180.

130 "he would be awfully sore": SEH to SJ, March 24, 1940.

130 "the real business": SEH to SJ, March 27, 1940, SJ-LOC, Box 42.

130 "they will do anything": SJ to SEH, May 26, 1940, SEH-LOC, Box 2.

130 "i have come to the conclusion": SJ to SEH, March 26. 1940, SEH-LOC, Box 2.

131 After visiting Shirley: Joan Schenkar, *The Talented Miss Highsmith* (New York: Picador, 2010), 242.

132 "being barred from certain circles": Anonymous, "I Married a Jew," *The Atlantic Monthly*, January 1939.

132 "The disease was growing": Irwin Shaw, "Select Clientele," *The New Yorker*, August 17, 1940.

132 "Whispering": Interview with Florence Shapiro Siegel, March 5, 2014.

133 "still messing around": College notebook, SJ-LOC, Box 37.

133 "I Cannot Sing the Old Songs": *LMTY*, 61–62.

133 Leslie and Geraldine did not know: Interview with Jai Holly, July 16, 2015.

133 "bounced it off Stan's skull": College notebook, SJ-LOC, Box 37.

133 *Anthony*: SJ-LOC, Box 30.

134 "i'm not made": Ibid.

134 "jealousy had no part": Ibid.

134 **"When you get out of college"**: SJ-LOC, Box 38. The speech comes from an unpublished story that appears to track closely to a real-life argument.

135 **A real estate market analysis:** *New York City Market Analysis*, compiled by *The News*, *The New York Times*, *Daily Mirror*, and *Journal-American*, 1943, accessed October 21, 2015, www.1940snewyork.com.

135 **homeless scribe Joe Gould:** Joseph Mitchell, *Up in the Old Hotel* (New York: Vintage, 2008), 52–70 and 623–716.

136 **"[t]he guests at those dinners"**: Mary McCarthy, *Intellectual Memoirs: New York, 1936–38* (New York: Harcourt Brace, 1993), 60–61.

136 **"1919 all over again"**: Ross Wetzsteon, *Republic of Dreams: Greenwich Village: The American Bohemia, 1910–1960* (New York: Simon & Schuster, 2002), 498.

136 **"The city had never looked"**: James Atlas, *Bellow: A Biography* (New York: Random House, 2000), 82.

136 **"The Villager"**: LOA, 41–46.

137 **"Every time a train"**: Ruth McKenney, *My Sister Eileen* (New York: Harcourt, Brace & World, 1938), 107.

137 **"pleasure-loving robber"**: Ibid., 108.

137 **"village urchins"** . . . **"symphony of noise"**: Ibid., 109.

137 **"he is highly intelligent"**: SEH-LOC, Box 12.

137 **"i choose you"**: SEH-LOC, Box 44.

138 **job in a sweatshop:** Phoebe Pettingell, e-mail to author, March 27, 2013.

138 **"we have to have oranges"**: Unpublished essay, SJ-LOC, Box 19.

138 **scripts for a radio station:** SJ-LOC, Box 20.

138 **"i am twenty-three"**: Unpublished essay, SJ-LOC, Box 19.

138 **"My Life with R. H. Macy"**: LOA, 47–49.

139 **a few short poems:** The poems appeared under two of SJ's pseudonyms, Agatha Nunnbush and Meade Lux, in February and May 1941.

139 **"Portrait of the Artist"**: SJ-LOC, Box 13.

139 **"Not for us, it seems"**: SJ-LOC, Box 13.

139 **"song for all editors"**: SJ-LOC, Box 13.

140 **"a thousand years"**: *The New Yorker*, April 8, 1933.

140 **"Americans' philosophy seems to be"**: *The New Yorker*, March 7, 1936.

140 **"In almost everything I wrote"**: Ben Yagoda, *About Town: The* New Yorker *and the World It Made* (New York: Scribner, 2000), 63.

140 **an anti-Nazi demonstration:** Irwin Shaw, "Sailor off the Bremen," *The New Yorker*, February 25, 1939.

140 **a newsboy continually shouts "Hitler!":** Irwin Shaw, "Weep in Years to Come," *The New Yorker*, July 1, 1939.

140   advice that Eleanor Roosevelt: *The New Yorker*, July 5, 1941.

141   "The terrain unquestionably favored": *The New Yorker*, August 16, 1941.

141   "tense and humid days": "Heat Stays with Us and May Get Worse," *The New York Times*, July 1, 1941.

141   a man in Coney Island: *The New Yorker*, August 16, 1941.

141   Five people died: *The New Yorker*, July 19, 1941.

141   "This is a week": SJ to SEH, July 7, 1941, SEH-LOC, Box 2.

141   "Like always I don't know how": Ibid.

142   "there is some incredible": SEH to SJ, July 8, 1941, SJ-LOC, Box 42.

142   "The house looks fresh": Gwynne Ross to SEH, July 21, 1941, SEH-LOC, Box 14.

142   "Have you ever lived": Gwynne Ross to SEH, August 12, 1941, SEH-LOC, Box 14.

142   "With reasonable care": Ibid.

142   "a real tin lizzie": Interview with Siegel, March 5, 2014.

142   "It has been wonderfully warm": SEH to Louis Harap, October 22, 1941, LH-AJA.

143   "The farm seems to agree": William Shawn to SEH, October 20, 1941, SEH-LOC, Box 15.

143   "He's either drowning or fishing": SJ-LOC, Box 36.

143   a "familiar": SJ-LOC, Box 37.

143   "there is still wood": SEH to Harap, October 22, 1941.

144   "Shirley Jackson, the wife of Stanley Hyman": *The New Republic*, December 22, 1941.

144   "mentor and friend": Walter Bernstein, e-mail to author, April 23, 2014.

145   "thin and frightened": "Catharine," SJ-LOC, Box 15. The published version, "I Know Who I love," is in LOA, 733–44.

145   "worse for Catharine" . . . "than Catharine did": Ibid.

146   "The Fable of Philip": SJ-LOC, Box 15.

146   "I cannot, as a friend": Louis Harap to SJ, January 27, 1942, SJ-LOC, Box 43.

146   "We should prosecute": *The New Republic*, September 1, 1941.

147   Stanley resolved to keep a journal: SEH's journal is in SEH-LOC, Box 1; SJ's can be found in SJ-LOC, Box 1.

148   Arthur, his brother, would later remark: Skype interview with Corinne Biggs, September 3, 2015.

149   "Shirley is still working": SEH to Louis Harap, February 4, 1942, LH-AJA.

149   "have to put it down": SJ-LOC, Box 38.

149   "thinking about it": Harvey Breit, "Talk with Miss Jackson," *The New York Times Book Review*, June 26, 1949.

149 **"accurate account of an incident"**: Notes for a lecture on writing, SJ-LOC, Box 14.

149 **"wow ending"**: SJ-LOC, Box 38.

149 **whose collected stories**: SEH, *Standards: A Chronicle of Books for Our Time* (New York: Horizon, 1966), 28.

150 **"we want fiction"**: Yagoda, *About Town*, 55.

150 **"the same anonymous person"** . . . **"the subordinate"**: Lionel Trilling, " 'New Yorker' Fiction," *The Nation*, April 11, 1942. In *Commentary*, nearly ten years later, Saul Bellow made a similar complaint: "The 'good' writing of *The New Yorker* is such that one experiences a furious anxiety, in reading it, about errors and lapses from taste; finally what emerges is a terrible hunger for conformism and uniformity. The smoothness of the surface and its high polish must not be marred" ("Dreiser and the Triumph of Art," *Commentary*, May 1951).

150 **"It is worth noting"**: SEH, "The Urban New Yorker," *The New Republic*, July 20, 1942.

151 **"just didn't click"**: SEH-LOC, Box 1.

151 **"a very good slick"**: Ibid.

151 **It described a young woman**: "Lunch with Aunt Cassandra," SJ-LOC, Box 17.

152 **"Simon Hyman"**: SJ-LOC, Box 1; SEH-LOC, Box 1.

152 **"probably but not certainly pregnant"**: SEH-LOC, Box 1.

152 **"too dull to record"**: SJ-LOC, Box 1.

153 **"he was more interested"**: Ibid.

153 **"mild as water"**: SEH-LOC, Box 1.

153 **"if I had to marry"**: SJ-LOC, Box 1.

153 **"coarse and vulgar"** . . . **"am too fat"**: Ibid.

154 **"it got quieter"** . . . **"being left alone"**: "Meadelux," SJ-LOC, Box 17.

155 **"why should i be"**: "Scapegoat," SJ-LOC, Box 18.

155 **"poor little boy"**: SJ-LOC, Box 1.

155 **"no more"**: Ibid.

156 **"If it's sex"**: Notebook marked 1942, SJ-LOC, Box 37.

156 **"my rape"**: SJ to SEH, June 7, 1938 ("portrait of the artist at work"), SEH-LOC, Box 2. Judy Oppenheimer provides a conflicting account of SJ's loss of virginity based on interviews with SJ and SEH's friends, in which their first attempt to consummate their relationship was ruined by friends who barged in on them; on their second attempt, Hyman was supposedly too nervous to perform (*Private Demons*, 68–69). These stories are impossible to verify. Oppenheimer does not mention the letter or the journal entry.

156   **teenaged Sarah Hyman**: Janna Malamud Smith, *My Father Is a Book* (Boston: Houghton Mifflin, 2006), 187.

156   **not to "get fucked"**: SJ to SEH, July 7, 1941, SEH-LOC, Box 2.

156   **"We should never"**: SJ-LOC, Box 37.

157   **"Maybe when I have my baby"**: Ibid.

6. GARLIC IN FICTION

158   **"My menagerie now includes"**: SEH to Louis Harap, May 19, 1942, LH-AJA.

158   **He gathered food**: Claude Fredericks, *The Journal of Claude Fredericks*, October 25, 1961. Fredericks recounts hearing SEH describe "how—in the year they lived, the first of their marriage, in the woods—he had six kinds of snakes and would set out in the morning to gather food. . . . Each needed a different kind, live warmblooded animals, live coldblooded animals, live insects. . . . He could steal, with a can of tunafish, a live mouse from a clever cat."

159   **"Sometimes we have such good luck"**: These details about RE's relationship with SEH come from a series of notes about SEH in RE-LOC, Box I:188. Although undated, they seem to represent RE's attempts to write a tribute after Hyman's sudden death in 1970.

160   **"discussions concerning the relationship" . . . "sharply honed minds"**: Ibid.

160   **But the initial response**: Ibid. Malcolm Cowley was among the critics who turned RE down. It could not have helped that RE had no money to offer: he asked all his contributors to write for free.

160   **he immediately sent Ellison**: The initial postcard has been lost, but RE writes of it in his reminiscence. The earliest existing letter between them is RE to SEH, dated June 22, 1942, thanking him for his note and suggesting two possible books for review.

160   **"Between the sophisticated *New Yorker*"**: Arnold Rampersad, *Ralph Ellison: A Biography* (New York: Alfred A. Knopf, 2007), 159.

160   **he followed T. S. Eliot's footnotes**: Bryan Crable, *Ralph Ellison and Kenneth Burke: At the Roots of the Racial Divide* (Charlottesville: University of Virginia Press, 2011), 34.

160   **an essay in *The New Masses***: RE, "Camp Lost Colony," *The New Masses*, February 6, 1940.

161   **"A Jew married to a gentile"**: Rampersad, *Ralph Ellison*, 160.

161   ***The Child's Garden of New Hampshire***: SJ-LOC, Box 20.

161   **she may have seriously considered**: Phoebe Pettingell, introduction to *The*

Critic's Credentials: Essays and Reviews by Stanley Edgar Hyman (New York: Atheneum, 1978), x.

162   **their only local friends:** SEH to Louis Harap, October 22, 1941, LH-AJA.

162   **"I can't understand":** SJ-LOC, Box 36.

162   **"mutual assistance":** Gwynne Ross to SEH, August 6, 1942, SEH-LOC, Box 14.

162   **Jackson would later say:** Interview with Jai Holly, July 22, 2013.

162   **"a worse madhouse than ever":** E. B. White to Stanley Hart White, March 2, 1944, in *Letters of E. B. White*, ed. Dorothy Lobrano Guth (New York: Harper & Row, 1976), 239.

163   **a source of guilt:** Thomas Kunkel, *Man in Profile: Joseph Mitchell of The New Yorker* (New York: Random House, 2015), 136.

163   **"living in New York":** William Shawn to SEH, July 27, 1942, SEH-LOC, Box 15.

163   **"magic briefcase":** Brendan Gill, *Here at the New Yorker* (1975; repr., New York: Da Capo, 1997), 247.

163   **"the borough of homes":** *The WPA Guide to New York City: The Federal Writers' Project Guide to 1930s New York* (New York: Random House, 1939), 555.

164   **Laurence Jackson Hyman (Laurie):** In her family writings, including letters, SJ always referred to the children by their nicknames. I have chosen to use their given names in the text, except in the context of SJ's writing about them.

164   **"Bring 'em to me":** Interview with Sarah Hyman DeWitt, February 17, 2013.

164   **"man who sits in chair reading":** SJ to Louis Harap, October 18, 1944, LH-AJA.

164   **"Insist on your cup of stars":** LOA, 256.

165   **Diana Trilling:** Interview with Midge Decter, March 13, 2013.

165   **"it was the men" . . . "bohemian life":** Ibid.

165   **"The first was young Miss Grattan":** LOA, 397.

165   **"She was afraid she would lose us":** Interview with Sarah Hyman DeWitt, February 17, 2013.

166   **Shirley went into the kitchen:** Telephone interview with Walter Lehrman, August 13, 2014.

166   **"All we could figure":** SJ to GJ and LJ, n.d. [end of November 1950], SJ-LOC, Box 3.

166   **"She could go":** Interview with Jai Holly, July 23, 2013.

166   **"listen to the house":** Interview with Jai Holly, July 16, 2015.

167 "reeling from one birthday cake": Unpublished article, SJ-LOC, Box 14.

167 "irregular income": SJ-LOC, Box 43.

167 "They would put sheets": Interview with Sarah Hyman DeWitt, February 17, 2013.

168 "dog candy": "No Christmas Cookies" (unpublished article), SJ-LOC, Box 14.

168 "Shut up and deal": Interview with Laurence Jackson Hyman, February 17, 2013.

169 "Every month, our family was exposed": Interview with Sarah Hyman DeWitt, February 17, 2013.

169 "The nicest thing" . . . "pleasure and delight": Unpublished article, SJ-LOC, Box 14.

170 "i do very little writing": SJ to Louis Harap, n.d., LH-AJA.

170 "looks just like every other baby": Postscript by SEH on ibid.

170 "6 o'clock feeding": SJ-LOC, Box 37.

170 "Dear, you know the doctor": SJ-LOC, Box 37.

171 "I did three paragraphs": SJ-LOC, Box 37.

171 "Oh, no, we haven't got company": SJ-LOC, Box 37.

171 "Honest to God, Stanley": SJ-LOC, Box 37.

171 she steals up: SJ-LOC, Box 37.

171 a pile of books: SJ-LOC, Box 37.

171 "I understand she's trying": SJ-LOC, Box 37.

171 But on Christmas Eve: Phyllis Meras, "Her Husband Turned Green," *Providence Sunday Journal*, August 14, 1960.

171 Gus Lobrano had finally taken: Even though the stories were sold at the same time, "After you, My Dear Alphonse" appeared in the issue of January 16, 1943, but "Afternoon in Linen" didn't run until the issue of September 4, 1943.

172 "We're going to be hitched!": Frances Pindyck to SJ, January 27, 1943, SJ-LOC, Box 43.

172 "now that we are making": SJ to Louis Harap, n.d. [early 1943], LH-AJA.

172 "nagging thoughts": SJ to GJ and LJ, April 1950.

172 "All the time that I am" . . . "always noticing": "Memory and Delusion," *LMTY*, 377.

173 drafts on yellow paper: SJ used several different shades of paper, depending on what was available. The shade she favored is technically called goldenrod. Since SJ refers to it several times in her writings as "yellow," I have followed her lead.

173 "A book is": "Private Showing," *LMTY*, 220.

173   "In the country of the story": "Notes for a Young Writer," *CAWM*, 263.

173   "their stories are, far too often": "Garlic in Fiction," *LMTY*, 396.

173   "unless the writer": Ibid., 397.

173   "garlic in fiction": Ibid.

174   "move as naturally": "Notes for a Young Writer," 264.

174   "It is not enough": Ibid., 266–67.

174   "a character who says": Ibid., 267.

174   "Alphonse": LOA, 69–72.

174   "I guess all of you": LOA, 71. There may be something of Geraldine in Mrs. Wilson. Some of her letters contain racist remarks. SJ seems to have taken special pains to mention black friends in her own letters to her mother, perhaps deliberately to discomfit her.

174   "Unlike most *New Yorker* stories": RE to SEH, June 16, 1945, SEH-LOC, Box 6.

175   "Afternoon in Linen": LOA, 78–82.

175   his family's lodge: Blake Bailey, *Cheever: A Life* (New York: Alfred A. Knopf, 2009), 116.

175   a male-bonding activity: Despite the presence of notable women on staff—Katharine White, Janet Flanner, and others—the writing published in *The New Yorker* thoroughly reinforced gender stereotypes. A typical example was James Thurber's "The Case Against Women" (October 24, 1936), a poisonous little satire.

175   "the patronizing sniffing": Irwin Shaw to Gus Lobrano, October 1, 1943, quoted in Ben Yagoda, *About Town: The New Yorker and the World It Made* (New York: Scribner, 2000), 22.

176   "Pretty formula[ic] and unconvincing": Gus Lobrano to Frances Pindyck, February 11, 1943, SJ-LOC, Box 43.

176   "A lady does not permit": SJ, "Little Old Lady in Great Need," *Mademoiselle*, September 1944.

176   "Come Dance with Me in Ireland": LOA, 171–76.

177   "On the House": *JOD*, 217–21.

177   "It Isn't the Money I Mind": *LMTY*, 51–55.

177   "Colloquy": LOA, 117–18.

177   "a nice big old place": SEH to KB, October 8, 1943, KB-PSU.

178   Laurence's crib piled: Judy Oppenheimer, *Private Demons* (New York: Putnam, 1988), 98.

178   "hideously green mashed potatoes": Interview with Jesse Zel Lurie, June 1, 2014.

178 **"rustling up dinner"**: Andy Logan Lyon to SEH, December 15, 1965, SEH-LOC, Box 46.

179 **"The baby's diaper was always full"**: Interview with Walter Bernstein, February 27, 2013.

179 **Bellow would joke**: Zachary Leader, *The Life of Saul Bellow: To Fame and Fortune, 1916–1964* (New York: Alfred A. Knopf, 2015), 255.

179 **"hatless and wearing"**: RE-LOC, Box I:188.

179 **"The thing to do"**: SEH, "No Roots at All," *Negro Quarterly*, Fall 1942.

179 **"Where Ralph tended"**: Rampersad, *Ralph Ellison*, 159.

179 **"Myth is neither"**: SEH, "Myth, Ritual, and Nonsense," *Kenyon Review* 11, no. 3 (Summer 1949).

180 **Hyman also introduced**: Despite SEH's attempts to keep it going, the relationship between RE and KB would later become strained over KB's failure to congratulate RE on *Invisible Man*. See Crable, *Ralph Ellison and Kenneth Burke*, chapter 3.

180 **"going a-blintzing"**: KB to SEH, September 26, 1943, SEH-LOC, Box 4.

181 **"I am writing a novel"**: Crable, *Ralph Ellison and Kenneth Burke*, 80. In one sense, RE was thanking KB for recommending him for the fellowship that had allowed him to spend time focusing on the novel, but in the context of the letter, the lines can also be read as a statement of his broader intellectual debt to KB.

181 **"reluctant" . . . "hard covers"**: RE-LOC, Box I:188.

181 **"This section of the novel"**: RE to SEH, August 21, 1945, SEH-LOC, Box 6.

181 **Ellison would regularly call upon Hyman**: Rampersad, *Ralph Ellison*, 211, 232; Crable, *Ralph Ellison and Kenneth Burke*, 87.

181 **Rampersad and others**: RE valued SEH's judgment enough to name him his literary executor, together with Albert Murray (Albert Murray and John F. Callahan, eds., *Trading Twelves: The Selected Letters of Ralph Ellison and Albert Murray* [New York: Modern Library, 2000], 82). RE outlived SEH; his wife, Fanny, became his executor. The Ellisons also promised to be guardians of the Hyman children in the event of disaster.

181 **Jeanou was struggling**: Jeanne Marie Bedel to SJ, December 18, 1944, SJ-LOC, Box 6.

182 **He would bring her**: Alexander Taylor to SJ, March 22, 1945, SJ-LOC, Box 16.

182 **"we live quietly"**: SJ to Louis Harap, February 20 [1944], LH-AJA.

182 **"muscles in his back"**: SJ to Louis Harap, July 16 [1944], LH-AJA.

182 **"young Samson"**: LJ to SJ, December 22, 1944, SJ-LOC, Box 3.

182   "A Fine Old Firm": LOA, 153–56.

183   "the most terrible day": SJ to Harap, July 16 [1944], LHP-AJA.

183   "they were chasing her": *Soldier Leaving*, SJ-LOC, Box 29.

184   a teacher mistakes: "Henrietta," SJ-LOC, Box 16.

184   a soldier home on leave: SJ, "The Gift," *Charm*, December 1944.

184   "Trial by Combat": LOA, 35–40.

184   "As High as the Sky": *LMTY*, 299–304.

184   "Homecoming": *LMTY*, 285–92.

184   "When Things Get Dark": *JOD*, 227–31.

185   "The Possibility of Evil": LOA, 714–24.

185   "after a while": SJ-LOC, Box 19.

185   "the acts of criticism": Jacket copy for SEH, *The Armed Vision* (New York: Alfred A. Knopf, 1948).

186   "The general outline": KB to SEH, September 26, 1943, SEH-LOC, Box 4.

186   Scott Mabon: Scott Mabon to SEH, September 26, 1941, SEH-LOC, Box 3.

186   Hyman was floored: Alfred A. Knopf to SEH, December 23, 1942, SEH-LOC, Box 3.

186   "a swell little piece": Alfred A. Knopf to SJ, January 18, 1943, SJ-LOC, Box 43.

186   "bold and piratical": Geoffrey T. Hellman, "A Very Dignified Pavane," *The New Yorker*, November 20, 1948.

186   "eating squab and drinking god-knows-what": SEH to Louis Harap, March 1, 1943, LH-AJA.

187   His ambitious plan: SEH to Alfred A. Knopf, February 11, 1944, AK-HRC.

187   "he seems to be writing": SJ to Louis Harap, October 18, 1944, LH-AJA.

187   "did stanley tell you": SJ to Louis Harap, May 11, 1944, LH-AJA.

187   "He promised her Money" . . . "all things": Joseph Glanvill, *Saducismus Triumphatus: Or, Full and Plain Evidence Concerning Witches and Apparitions*, 3rd ed. (London, 1700), 73, 81.

188   called simply "Elizabeth": LOA, 119–52.

188   Instead, Jackson decided: The table of contents for this proposed collection is in SJ-LOC, Box 16.

188   Harap was critical: Louis Harap to SJ, March 12, 1945, SJ-LOC, Box 8.

188   "if you think": SJ to Louis Harap, April 1, 1945, LH-AJA.

189   "can't you just see": SJ to Harap, July 16 [1944].

189   "illiterate in the arts": "Blue Jeans with a Difference," *Time*, February 3, 1947.

189   **140 hilltop acres:** Thomas P. Brockway, *Bennington College: In the Begin-ning* (Bennington, Vt.: Bennington College Press, 1981), 46. The campus now occupies 440 acres.

189   **"real cows":** SJ to Harap, October 18, 1944.

7. SIDESTREET, U.S.A.

191   **"the actual":** Thomas P. Brockway, *Bennington College: In the Beginn*ing (Bennington, Vt.: Bennington College Press, 1981), 49. For the story of Bennington's founding, see also Barbara Jones, *Bennington College: The Development of an Educational Idea* (New York: Harper & Brothers, 1946).

192   **"It was a wild and wonderful place":** Interview with Barbara Fisher, September 20, 2013.

192   **"as much a state of mind":** Susan Cheever, *E. E. Cummings: A Life* (New York: Pantheon, 2014), 116.

192   **"significant, vital, and representative in the field":** Brockway, *Bennington College*, 53.

192   **"Bennington regards education":** www.bennington.edu/About/traditional-commencement-statement; accessed September 19, 2015.

193   **"We are not educating":** Quoted in Betty Friedan, *The Feminine Mystique* (1963; repr., New York: W. W. Norton, 1997), 182.

193   **"social paternalism":** Mabel Barbee Lee, "Censoring the Conduct of College Women," *The Atlantic*, April 1930.

194   **"It was the kind of place":** Interview with Marilyn Seide, April 19, 2013.

194   **"We do count":** Kathleen Norris, *The Virgin of Bennington* (New York: Riverhead, 2001), 9.

194   **"very bright":** Bernard Malamud to Rosemarie Beck, quoted in Janna Malamud Smith, *My Father Is a Book* (Boston: Houghton Mifflin, 2006), 164.

194   **a full-length evening gown:** Interview with Betty Aberlin, September 21, 2014.

195   **"this wild man":** Interview with Suzanne Stern Shepherd Calkins, October 16, 2014.

195   **"The idea was":** Interview with Fisher, September 20, 2013.

195   **a golden age:** In terms of artistic star power, the only comparable institution was North Carolina's Black Mountain College, founded a year after Bennington and according to similar principles. It closed in 1957.

195   **hired in haste:** Dana Goodyear, "The Gardener," *The New Yorker*, September 1, 2003.

195   "kick around a few notions": Interview with Calkins, October 16, 2014.

196   "When we had parties": Interview with Victoria Kirby, January 22, 2015.

196   "It was a model for sexist behavior": Interview with Joan Schenkar, June 8, 2012.

196   "the little red whorehouse on the hill": Norris, *Virgin of Bennington*, 10.

196   "More than once": Ibid., 12.

196   "caricatures" . . . "faculty scalps": Interview with Phoebe Pettingell, April 6, 2015.

196   "He was as brilliant as Shakespeare": Interview with Sandra Hochman, June 4, 2014.

196   "learning something" . . . "the stuff": SEH to Bernard Smith, July 24, 1945, and January 6, 1946, AK-HRC.

197   "the mating combat of male elks": Sonya Rudikoff Gutman, untitled memorial tribute to SEH, *Quadrille* 7, no. 2 (Winter/Spring 1973), 51.

197   "has frequently read": *Raising Demons*, 147.

198   "Mimosa": Interview with Calkins, October 16, 2014.

198   excellent potato pancakes: Interview with Miriam Marx Allen, December 3, 2014.

198   "He would invite": Telephone interview with Joan Constantikes, August 13, 2014.

198   "She was kind of overshadowed": Interview with Allen, December 3, 2014.

198   "My mother used to enjoy": Interview with Sarah Hyman DeWitt, February 21, 2013.

198   "always seemed a little annoyed": Telephone interview with Marjorie Roemer, September 24, 2014.

198   "I sometimes think": *Hangsaman*, 123–24.

198   "What kind of woman": Friedan, *The Feminine Mystique*, 6.

198   "By the end": *Raising Demons*, 154.

199   "The Church of Christ Hyman": Judy Oppenheimer, *Private Demons* (New York: Putnam, 1988), 113.

199   nothing had been touched: Much of *Life Among the Savages* is fictionalized, but that particular story meshes with SJ's descriptions of the house elsewhere.

199   "little nest" . . . "we've ever seen": SJ to Louis Harap, April 1, 1945, LH-AJA.

199   "Our house" . . . "a well": *Savages*, 1.

199   Jeanou, for one: Jeanne Marie Bedel to SJ, January 28, 1946, SJ-LOC, Box 6. In response, SJ urged Jeanou to settle down.

200   "where they do": *Savages*, 2.

201   "not only knew": Ibid., 9.

201   "Vermonters generally": Malamud Smith, *My Father Is a Book*, 163.

201   "Those young ladies": Interview with Larry Powers, July 23, 2013.

202   "The students were seen": Interview with Anna Fels, August 3, 2013.

202   "Commies" or "pinkos": Interview with Barry Hyman, July 22, 2013.

202   "added color to the village": Interview with Powers, July 23, 2013.

202   "wasn't your ordinary housewife": Interview with Laura Nowak, July 24, 2013.

202   one of the canes: Phoebe Pettingell, introduction to *The Critic's Credentials: Essays and Reviews by Stanley Edgar Hyman* (New York: Atheneum, 1978), xiii.

202   "I would walk": Interview with Barry Hyman, July 22, 2013.

202   The garbageman gossiped: Larry Powers, *The Store and Other Stories of North Bennington* ([North Bennington, Vt.?]: printed by author, n.d.).

203   "Men with Their Big Shoes": LOA, 199–206.

204   "As a black man": Arnold Rampersad, *Ralph Ellison: A Biography* (New York: Alfred A. Knopf, 2007), 239. The lecture at Bennington was RE's first public lecture: "He believed that I had something to say, saw that I was provided a platform from which to say it, and I discovered that I did and could. I'm still paying the rent out of his generous good faith," RE wrote many years later: RE-LOC, I:188.

204   "the oldest family in town": "Flower Garden," LOA, 83.

205   "The nerve of her": Ibid., 106.

205   In an early draft: "The Flower Garden," SJ-LOC, Box 16.

205   "they're all beautiful": LOA, 93.

206   "a solid respectable": Ibid., 102.

206   "What he needs is a baby sister": SJ-LOC, Box 37.

206   "seems as arbitrary" . . . "the weather": SJ-LOC, Box 50.

206   Joanne nicknamed herself: I refer to her in the text as Joanne Hyman and in notes as Jai Holly, which is now her name.

207   "We don't have any Charles": "Charles," LOA, 77. The story appeared in *Mademoiselle* in July 1948, nearly simultaneous with "The Lottery."

207   "a thousand" . . . "Only these few": Catherine Osgood Foster, "The Hymans of Prospect Street," *Quadrille* 7, no. 2 (Winter/Spring 1973), 53.

207   "I'm good, aren't I?": *Savages*, 39.

207   "the second Mrs. Ellenoy": Ibid., 107.

207   "Jannie is our beauty": SJ-LOC, Box 14.

208   "He had a little jacket": Interview with Nowak, July 24, 2013.

208   "She was always working": Interview with Jai Holly, July 23, 2013.

208   playing Monopoly: Foster, "Hymans of Prospect Street," 53.

208   "tense and even impatient" . . . "not a story": Ibid.

209   "Half the people": Thomas Kunkel, *Man in Profile: Joseph Mitchell of The New Yorker* (New York: Random House, 2015), 103. Mitchell himself insisted on having a salary rather than a drawing account, which "terrified" him.

209   the magazine also rejected: Ben Yagoda, *About Town: The New Yorker and the World It Made* (New York: Scribner, 2000), 233.

209   earned $365: Blake Bailey, *Cheever: A Life* (New York: Alfred A. Knopf, 2009), 123.

209   Stafford's first story . . . Cheever's signing bonus: Yagoda, *About Town*, 219; Bailey, *Cheever*, 319.

210   "Be a darling": Frances Pindyck to SEH, September 5, 1945, SJ-LOC, Box 43.

210   "Our authors": Pindyck to SJ, October 17, 1945, SJ-LOC, Box 43.

210   "a well-earned rest": Jean Rogers to SJ, February 1, 1946, SJ-LOC, Box 43.

210   After Thompson died: "Woman, Widow Two Weeks, Ends Life with Pistol Shot," *New London* (Conn.) *Day*, July 20, 1953.

211   "In a crisis": Jim Bishop to SJ, October 4, 1946, SJ-LOC, Box 43.

211   "still very dear": Ibid.

211   "You can bait": SJ to Jim Bishop, August 16, 1946, SJ-LOC, Box 43.

211   *I Know Who I Love*: SJ-LOC, Box 29.

212   "Shirley has finished": SEH to JW, November 26, 1946, JW-BU.

212   "Seventy thousand words": SEH to Ben Zimmerman, January 5, 1947. Zimmerman's daughter Anne generously shared their correspondence with me.

212   "I have never known": Jim Bishop to SJ, February 13, 1947, SJ-LOC, Box 43.

212   The winning match: Roger Straus to Tom Foster, January 25, 1949, and April 23, 1954, FSG-NYPL, Box 173.

212   For the sake of comparison: Boris Kachka, *Hothouse: The Art of Survival and the Survival of Art at America's Most Celebrated Publishing House, Farrar, Straus and Giroux* (New York: Simon & Schuster, 2013), 94.

212   "My goodness, how you write": John Farrar to SJ, July 29, 1947, SJ-LOC, Box 43.

213   "We must expect": *RTW*, 148.

214   "something more than a housewife": Ibid., 125.

214   "In ten years" . . . "what I say": Ibid., 164.

214   Harriet agonizes: In an excruciating scene near the end of the novel, a senile old woman tells Harriet she's lucky she won't ever be pretty.

"Harriet knew already that this would keep her heartsick for months, per-haps the rest of her life, and she said thickly, 'I'm losing weight right now.' 'It isn't that you're so *fat*,' Miss Tyler said critically. 'You just don't have the *air* of a pretty woman. All your life, for instance, you'll walk like you're fat, whether you are or not'" (ibid., 170).

214 "Herewith the baby": SJ to John Farrar, June 3, 1947, FSG-NYPL, Box 174.

215 "a magnificent job": Roger Straus to SJ, August 5, 1947, FSG-NYPL, Box 174.

215 "Helen dressed": *RTW*, 60.

215 "a recent regrettable pink stucco": Ibid., 2.

215 swim "insanely": Ibid., 81.

215 "wry unpalatable fruit": Ibid., 45.

215 "grotesque effect" . . . "he giggled": "Notes for a Young Writer," *CAWM*, 269.

215 "No man owns": *RTW*, 1.

216 "He seemed to possess": Kachka, *Hothouse*, 56.

216 "everything of quality": Ibid., 47.

216 "A new imprint": Ibid., 46.

217 "an owlish aspect" . . . "vile temper": Ibid., 39–40.

217 "I hope": John Farrar to SJ, May 7, 1947, FSG-NYPL, Box 174.

217 "so beautiful": Margaret Farrar to SJ, August 19, 1947, SJ-LOC, Box 43.

217 "She plays the guitar": SJ-LOC, Box 40.

218 "a man of distinction": SJ to Margaret Farrar, November 20, 1947, FSG-NYPL, Box 174.

218 "perfectly delightful and fetching": Margaret Farrar to SJ, undated, SJ-LOC, Box 7.

219 "we hope": Barbara Ely to SJ, December 16, 1947, FSG-NYPL, Box 174.

219 "ritual week": SEH to Ben Zimmerman, February 10, 1948.

219 "mediocre market" . . . "an unknown quantity": Roger Straus to SJ and SEH, February 11, 1948, FSG-NYPL, Box 174.

219 "little secret nastinesses": Victor P. Hass, "Strange Folk Who Grew Up on Pepper St.," *Chicago Sunday Tribune*, March 21, 1948.

220 "direct, unsentimental way": Leonora Hornblow, "Pepper St. Has 11 houses but No Good People Live in Them," *Los Angeles Daily News*, April 3, 1948.

220 "If you sometimes": Cothburn O'Neal, "Village and Artist in Three Novels," *Dallas Times Herald*, February 22, 1948.

220 "supple and resourceful": Unsigned review, *The New Yorker*, February 21, 1948.

8. A CLASSIC IN SOME CATEGORY

221   **Jackson's neighbors:** Judy Oppenheimer, *Private Demons* (New York: Putnam, 1988), 130.

221   **"choosing a victim for a sacrifice":** "How I Write," *LMTY*, 390.

222   **"Biography of a Story":** LOA, 787–801.

223   **June 26, 1948:** SJ's lecture mistakenly gives the magazine's cover date as June 28.

223   **March 16, 1948:** "How I Write" corroborates that it was written in the spring. Drafts of "The Lottery" are in SJ-LOC, Box 17.

223   **"some reservations" . . . "take it":** SJ-LOC, Box 43. SJ would claim in "Biography of a Story" that her agent at the time did not like "The Lottery," but there is no evidence in her files to support this.

224   **"It was the pure thing":** Oppenheimer, *Private Demons*, 128.

224   **"It is not likely":** John Farrar to SJ, August 9, 1948, SJ-LOC, Box 43.

224   **"No one writes":** Joseph Henry Jackson to SJ, July 7, 1948, "Lottery" scrapbook, SJ-LOC, Box 32.

224   **"preservation of" . . . "human behavior":** I was unable to find this memo in SJ's archive. It is quoted in Oppenheimer, *Private Demons*, 125.

225   **"the smoothest and roundest" . . . "their husbands":** LOA, 227.

225   **"Wouldn't have me":** Ibid., 230.

225   **"time and energy":** Ibid., 228.

225   **"It wasn't fair!":** Ibid., 233. The critic Joseph Church speculates that Mr. Summers may be manipulating the outcome; see his "Getting Taken in 'The Lottery,'" *Notes on Contemporary Literature* 18, no. 4 (September 1988).

226   **"The children":** LOA, 235.

226   **Jackson would claim:** LOA, 788.

226   **"The most important" . . . "original ritual":** Gus Lobrano to SJ, April 9, 1948, NY-NYPL, Box 463.

227   **"'They do say'":** LOA, 232.

227   **"Nothing but trouble":** Ibid.

227   **that line is written:** SJ-LOC, Box 17.

227   **"so large":** Ibid., 235. The critic Gayle Whittier points out that no men are shown holding or throwing stones—the women are the ones who display "blood lust." See her "'The Lottery' as Misogynist Parable," *Women's Studies* 18 (1991). The lottery is run by men, but—as in *The Road Through the Wall*—women are responsible for enforcing social norms.

227   **"I could not" . . . "thought it meant":** SJ to James Thurber, n.d. [c. spring

1958; in response to his letter of April 22, 1958], SJ-LOC, Box 11. Thurber quotes the letter in *The Years with Ross* (Boston: Little, Brown, 1958), 263.

228   **"We've never been"**: "The Enormous Radio," *John Cheever: Collected Stories and Other Writings*, ed. Blake Bailey (New York: Library of America, 2009), 49.

228   **"He'd say"**: Ben Yagoda, *About Town: The New Yorker and the World It Made* (New York: Scribner, 2000), 155.

228   **"contrived" and "heavy-handed"**: Interview by Thomas Kunkel with William Maxwell, March 1, 1992. Kunkel, who touches on the editorial debate surrounding "The Lottery" briefly in *Genius in Disguise: Harold Ross of The New Yorker* (New York: Random House, 1995, 397–98), generously shared his transcript of the interview.

228   **"I think"**: Brendan Gill to SJ, n.d., "Lottery" scrapbook, SJ-LOC, Box 32. Gill would use almost the same terms in 1957 about Saul Bellow in a review of *Seize the Day* that Bellow biographer Zachary Leader characterizes as "condescending": Gill calls Bellow "one of the three or four most talented writers to come along in this decade." Leader, *The Life of Saul Bellow: To Fame and Fortune, 1916–1964* (New York: Alfred A. Knopf, 2015), 510.

229   **"Shirley Jackson's 'The Lottery'"**: Unless otherwise noted, all the "Lottery" letters quoted here are in the "Lottery" scrapbook, SJ-LOC, Box 32.

230   **Friend still remembered**: Telephone interview with Miriam Friend, June 9, 2013. "I don't know how anyone approved of that story," she said.

230   **"not counting"**: SEH to Ben Zimmerman, July 22, 1948.

230   **up to 150**: SEH to JW, August 3, 1948, JW-BU.

231   **"and they were mostly from friends"**: LOA, 789.

231   **"bewilderment, speculation"**: Ibid., 790.

231   **"could be considered"**: Ibid., 789.

232   **"because as a social anthropologist"**: Ursula Kroeber Le Guin, e-mail to author, June 20, 2013.

233   **Jackson wrote back**: Lenemaja Friedman, *Shirley Jackson* (New York: Twayne, 1975), 21.

233   **"one of the most"**: Herbert Weinstock to SJ, July 1, 1948, AK-HRC.

233   **"a very profound conceit"**: KB to SEH, July 31, 1948, "Lottery" scrapbook, SJ-LOC, Box 32.

233   **"presented the rite"** ... **"same vein"**: RE to SEH, August 13, 1948, SEH-LOC, Box 6. Arnold Rampersad hears a note of jealousy in Ellison's tone over the fact that "Jackson had dipped into the well of myth and ritual from which he had been hauling water": see Rampersad, *Ralph Ellsion: A*

Biography (New York: Alfred A. Knopf, 2007), 237. But the well was surely deep enough for both of them.

233   **"certainly a great success"**: Harold Ross to SEH, July 1948, "Lottery" scrapbook, SJ-LOC, Box 32.

234   **Her friend Helen Feeley:** Oppenheimer, *Private Demons*, 131.

234   **its theme is strikingly consonant:** "Normal men do not know that everything is possible," Rousset wrote. "The concentrationees do know." Quoted in *The New Yorker*, July 26, 1947.

234   **an early version:** "How I Write," *LMTY*, 390. Larry Powers, who insisted that he had never read the story, affirmed that some of the townspeople believed that they were models for the characters (interview, July 23, 2013). The writer Jonathan Lethem, who attended Bennington College in the mid-1980s, writes that "a handful of the townspeople portrayed in thin disguise . . . were still around": see his "Monstrous Acts and Little Murders," *Salon*, January 6, 1997.

234   **"Shirley's beautiful piercing eyes"**: Wallace Fowlie, *Journal of Rehearsals* (Durham, N.C.: Duke University Press, 1977), 156–57. But in 1953 SJ told a newspaper reporter, "If you'll notice, the village is not even in New England. It doesn't have any location": *"Life Among the Savages* Wins Acclaim for Area Author," *Albany Sunday Times-Union*, November 29, 1953.

234   **the brief period she and Hyman spent:** Interview with Jai Holly, July 22, 2013.

234   **"If you can't"**: Telephone interview with Jennifer Feeley, February 23, 2015.

234   **"rural harshness"**: Janna Malamud Smith, *My Father Is a Book* (Boston: Houghton Mifflin, 2006), 162.

234   **"The Renegade"**: LOA, 57–68.

235   **"I suppose I hoped"**: Joseph Henry Jackson, "How a Story Puzzled Readers, Critics (and the Author)," *San Francisco Chronicle*, July 22, 1948.

235   **"It seems to us"**: SJ-LOC, Box 48.

235   *The Crucible*: Carolyn Wolf to SJ, July 6, 1953, SJ-LOC, Box 8.

236   **in many ways resembles Jackson:** Compare Tessie's embarrassed explanation of her lateness—"Wouldn't have me leave m'dishes in the sink, now, would you?"—to SJ's comments in the posthumously published essay "Here I Am, Washing Dishes Again": "If I were any sort of a proper housewife at all I'd start my dishwashing at a specific hour in the morning, duly aproned, trim and competent, instead of heaping the dishpan high while my neighbors and no doubt the rest of the world are off on some blissful pursuit" (*LMTY*, 317).

236 **Female sacrifice:** Gayle Whittier points out, in " 'The Lottery' as Misogynist Parable," that the story depicts Tessie as a "bad mother" who is willing to sacrifice her children before herself: "She may be sacrificed . . . because she is not sacrificial enough."

236 **"One of the most terrifying":** LOA, 789. A similar anxiety about mail can be found in "Mrs. Spencer and the Oberons": "Mrs. Spencer detested letters on principle, because they always seemed to want to entangle her in so many small, disagreeable obligations . . ." (*LMTY*, 29).

237 **"Exalted Rollers":** This letter, not included in the "Lottery" scrapbook, can be found in Box 14 among the pages of a draft of one of SJ's lectures.

237 **"I am out":** LOA, 801.

237 **"The razor's edge":** *Biographia Literaria*, chapter 7.

238 **"villains to heroes":** Reader's report by William York Tindall, AK-HRC.

238 **"the ideal critic":** SEH, *The Armed Vision* (New York: Alfred A. Knopf, 1948), 395.

239 **"Stanley himself felt":** Phoebe Pettingell, e-mail to author, March 27, 2013.

239 **weekly "allowance":** SEH to JW, October 7, 1948, JW-BU. This allowance was not a salary, but a "drawing account," as described in the previous chapter. Being constantly in debt to the magazine created stress for many of *The New Yorker*'s writers. "I do not draw enough to live on (and buy books on) from The New Yorker," SEH wrote to JW. "It has to be supplemented regularly by checks for Shirley's stories or my miscellaneous activities [lecturing or writing reviews]. When those do not come, we run into debt. When a big check comes, it pulls us out of debt, but leaves nothing in the bank. That happened in July and left us almost on our feet, but since then no check for more than $25 has come in, and three such months put us right back in. Only the next big check can pull us out (an advance on my new book, a slick sale for Shirley) but I doubt that we will ever be ahead, with money in the bank like other people."

239 **"The Daemon Lover":** Because the story appears under a different title ("The Phantom Lover"), with certain details changed, some critics have assumed that it constitutes an earlier version. In fact, SJ revised the story as her editors at *Woman's Home Companion* insisted, but restored the original version and title in *The Lottery*. See Elliott Schryver to SJ, November 6, 1947, SJ-LOC, Box 44.

240 **"on the theory that":** SEH, outline for *Four Poets*, AK-HRC.

240 **"what is loosely":** Herbert Weinstock to SEH, May 8, 1947, SEH-LOC, Box 3.

240 "The basic point": Alfred A. Knopf to SEH, July 7, 1947, AK-HRC.

240 A profile of Knopf: Geoffrey T. Hellman, "A Very Dignified Pavane," *The New Yorker*, November 20, 1948.

241 Knopf's *New York Times* obituary: Herbert Mitgang, "Alfred A. Knopf, 91, Is Dead," *The New York Times*, August 12, 1984.

241 "We will rest": Alfred A. Knopf to SEH, July 14, 1947, AK-HRC.

241 In the scrapbook: The *Armed Vision* scrapbook is held privately.

241 "one of the prestige": Jim Bishop to SEH, September 10, 1947, SEH-LOC, Box 12.

241 "criminal and farcical": SEH to Herbert Weinstock, November 23, 1947, AK-HRC.

241 "You see our difference in scale": SEH to RE, November 20, 1947, RE-LOC.

241 "If Alfred A. Knopf": SEH to Weinstock, November 23, 1947.

242 "everything for me": SEH, *Armed Vision*, xiv.

242 an interviewer asked her: W. G. Rogers, "Shirley Jackson Is 'Sure 'Nuff' Witch," Associated Press, May 21, 1949.

242 "I am delighted": SEH to Herbert Weinstock, October 24, 1947, AK-HRC.

243 "makes the author": SEH to Herbert Weinstock, March 15, 1948, *Armed Vision* scrapbook.

243 "The literary future": SEH to Herbert Weinstock, March 2, 1948, *Armed Vision* scrapbook.

243 "exciting" . . . "the pool": Herbert Weinstock to SEH, May 21, 1948, *Armed Vision* scrapbook.

243 "I feel certain": *Armed Vision* scrapbook.

243 When Saul Bellow: James Atlas, *Bellow: A Biography* (New York: Random House, 2000), 60.

243 "brilliant display": W. G. Rogers, "Literary Guidepost," Associated Press, May 29, 1948.

243 "distinguished" and "explosive": "Critics Under Critic's Knife," *Omaha World Herald*, June 13, 1948.

244 "One lays down": Joseph Wood Krutch, "About Writing About Writing," *New York Herald Tribune*, June 20, 1948.

244 "questionable" and its evaluations "arbitrary": John Farrelly, "Goals of Criticism," *The New Republic*, June 21, 1948.

244 "uncomplicated and often witty": *The New Yorker*, May 29, 1948.

244 "nasty petulance": SEH to RE, June 21, 1948, RE-LOC.

244 "Aside from being": SEH to JW, September 25, 1948, JW-BU.

245 **Vladimir Nabokov**: Nabokov's copy of the book is in the Berg Collection of the New York Public Library.

245 **"We may be"**: SJ to Pyke Johnson, July 15, 1949, FSG-NYPL, Box 174.

245 **"An ugly story"**: Harriet van Horner, untitled clipping, *Washington Times*, March 16, 1951.

245 **"anti-prejudice message"**: Untitled newspaper clipping (interview with Rod Serling), 1960, SJ-LOC, Box 49.

245 **"she felt that *they*"**: SEH, preface to *The Magic of Shirley Jackson* (New York: Farrar, Straus & Giroux, 1966), viii.

245 **One scholar analyzed the method**: Richard R. Williams, "A Critique of the Sampling Plan Used in Shirley Jackson's 'The Lottery,'" *Journal of Modern Literature* 7, no. 3 (September 1979), 543–44. See also, among others, Peter Kosenko, "A Marxist/Feminist Reading of Shirley Jackson's 'The Lottery,'" *The New Orleans Review* 12, no. 1 (Spring 1985).

246 **"let the poor old chestnut"**: SJ to CB, July 16, 1963. SJ's letters to CB are held privately.

9. NOTES ON A MODERN BOOK OF WITCHCRAFT

249 **As she would tell it**: *Savages*, 65–66.

250 **"fat and happy"**: SJ to GJ and LJ, November 18 [1948], SJ-LOC, Box 3.

250 **"Three children are enough"**: GJ to SJ, n.d. [c. late 1948], SJ-LOC, Box 2.

251 **"Her general appearance"**: "Sunday, Eleven A.M." (an early draft of a portion of *Savages*), SJ-LOC, Box 14.

251 **"any notion"**: *Savages*, 138.

251 **"mischievous"**: Interview with Laura Nowak, July 24, 2013.

251 **"She always presented herself"**: Interview with Barry Hyman, July 22, 2013.

251 **"I tried to be"**: Interview with Sarah Hyman DeWitt, February 21, 2013.

251 **a question about sex**: Interview with Jai Holly, July 16, 2015.

251 **"sally has always"**: Unpublished essay, SJ-LOC, Box 14.

252 **"She had a lot of light"**: Telephone interview with Elizabeth Greene, October 16, 2013.

252 **she attempted suicide**: Interview with Sarah Hyman DeWitt, February 21, 2013.

252 **"There is a rightness"**: John Farrar to SJ, July 7, 1948, SJ-LOC, Box 43.

252 **now to be titled**: In addition to *The Intoxicated* for a somewhat different collection, another previous title was *Merry Meet and Merry Part* (also spelled *Marie Meet and Marie Part*), a ritual greeting among witches. See

memo from Margaret Farrar to Roger Straus and John Farrar, June 3, 1948, FSG-NYPL, Box 174.

252 **"I never heard anything"**: SJ to Pyke Johnson, November 22, 1948, FSG-NYPL, Box 174.

252 **"so excruciating"**: SJ to GJ and LJ, December 18 [1948].

252 **the postmaster overruled**: Albert Goldman to Farrar, Straus, December 3, 1948, FSG-NYPL, Box 174.

253 **"Like Mother Used to Make"**: LOA, 26–34.

253 **inspired by an anecdote**: Telephone interview with Anne Zimmerman, June 12, 2014. See also Judy Oppenheimer, *Private Demons* (New York: Putnam, 1988), 102.

253 **In an early draft**: SJ-LOC, Box 17.

253 **feminine gifts for homemaking**: SJ may be dropping a veiled hint that Ben Zimmerman, who did not come out to his family until much later, was gay. "Paranoia," another story with a male subject written around the same time, was left out of the volume, possibly because SJ could not make it fit with the James Harris theme.

254 **The case dominated**: SJ's file on Paula Welden shows that the *Bennington Banner* published updates on the case every day from December 3, 1946, until December 21, 1946, when the search for Welden was apparently abandoned. SJ-LOC, Box 45.

254 **"run away"**: *Bennington Banner*, December 7, 1946.

254 **Jackson wrote one story explicitly**: Oppenheimer and others have claimed that *Hangsaman* was inspired by the Paula Welden case. As far as I can tell, there is no evidence for this.

254 **"Got a Letter from Jimmy"**: LOA, 225–26.

254 **based closely**: Oppenheimer, *Private Demons*, 104.

255 **Hyman jokingly compared**: SEH to Ben Zimmerman, November 3, 1947.

255 **"Pillar of Salt"**: LOA, 184–98.

255 **"The Daemon Lover"**: LOA, 10–25.

255 **"The Tooth"**: LOA, 207–24. According to SEH's letters to Zimmerman, SJ wrote "Pillar of Salt" (originally titled "Vertigo"—see SJ-LOC, Box 18) in May 1947, "The Daemon Lover" in June 1947, and "The Tooth" (originally titled "Persephone"—SJ-LOC, Box 19) in September 1947. SJ's manuscript of "The Tooth" shows that she submitted it to her agent on October 15, 1947.

255 **"The Beautiful Stranger"**: *CAWM*, 63–71.

256 **"Sometimes a woman"**: Betty Friedan, *The Feminine Mystique* (1963; repr., New York: W. W. Norton, 1997), 8.

256 "Document of Loneliness": SJ-LOC, Box 15.

257 "you once wrote me": SEH-LOC, Box 2.

257 "He promised her": SEH, obviously under SJ's influence, quoted this passage facetiously in a March 22, 1948, letter to Herbert Weinstock during his contract dispute with Knopf: "She saith, That when the Devil doth any thing for her, she calls for him by the name of Herbert, upon which he appears, and when in the Shape of Man, she can hear him speak, but his voice is very low. He promised her when she made her Contract with him, that she should want nothing, but ever since she hath wanted all things"(*Armed Vision* scrapbook).

257 "Once in a long while": FSG-NYPL, Box 174.

257 "very pleased": GJ to SJ, n.d. [c. 1949], SJ-LOC, Box 2.

257 "the most terrifying": SJ to GJ and LJ, n.d. [late December 1948].

258 "Boy, that story": SJ to GJ and LJ, April 11 [1949].

258 "With attractive features": W. G. Rogers, "Shirley Jackson is 'Sure 'Nuff' Witch," Associated Press, May 21, 1949.

258 "fortunately he had": SJ to GJ and LJ, April 11, 1949.

258 "writers i admire" . . . "night before": Ibid.

258 "I can't persuade myself": Harvey Breit, "Talk with Miss Jackson," *The New York Times Book Review*, June 26, 1949.

259 "i don't like housework": Biographical notes, SJ-LOC, Box 40.

259 "I am tired": "The Real Me," *LMTY*, 357. The title was given by the book's editors, Laurence Jackson Hyman and Sarah Hyman DeWitt.

260 "i'm a kind-hearted mama": Draft of *Come Along with Me*, SJ-LOC, Box 15.

260 One of her favorite "tricks": Oppenheimer, *Private Demons*, 189.

260 "I suggest": John Buck to John Farrar, n.d. [c. October 1949], SJ-LOC, Box 43.

261 "with a string of rattles": "Shirley Jackson, Novelist, Dies at Vermont Home." *New York World Telegram and Sun*, August 9, 1965.

261 "i like writing fiction" . . . "magic equals fiction": SJ-LOC, Box 14.

262 "She loved me": *Savages*, 71.

262 "full of ultra-violet rays": SJ to RE, November 16, 1948, RE-LOC.

262 "one of the first": Telephone interview with Virginia Bush, August 25, 2015.

262 "now that i am not": SJ to GJ and LJ, June 13 [1949].

263 "very brave" . . . "little girl": GJ to SJ, n.d. [1949], SJ-LOC, Box 2.

263 expulsion of Miriam Marx: Frederick Burkhardt, Bennington's president at the time, later said that he had to uphold the judgment of the college's Judicial Committee, to test "whether student democracy and student input

should be real or not." Frederick Burkhardt, interview by Stephen Sandy, August 15, 2005, Bennington College Archives.

263   "What do you say first?": Wallace Fowlie, *Journal of Rehearsals* (Durham, N.C.: Duke University Press, 1977), 156.

263   "the girls and i": SJ to GJ and LJ, June 13, 1949.

263   One of the students: Gail Newman, letter to the editor, *The New Yorker*, September 22, 2003.

263   "interminably": SEH to Ben Zimmerman, August 1949.

264   Hyman was invited: Margaret Farrar to SEH, April 20, 1949, SEH-LOC, Box 7.

264   "modesty" and the "supreme skill": Margaret Farrar to SJ, August 24, [1949], SJ-LOC, Box 8 (misfiled).

264   "had a fine time": SJ to GJ and LJ, August 23 [1949].

264   "no one but me ever remembers": SJ to GJ and LJ, November 18 [1948].

264   "perfect wives and mothers" . . . "the home": Friedan, *The Feminine Mystique*, 5, 28.

265   "Here I Am, Washing Dishes Again": *LMTY*, 317–22.

265   "any kind of problem": "Put It in a Box," Shirley Jackson Papers (MS 336), University of Colorado at Boulder.

265   "before going out" . . . "every wrinkle": "Pillar of Salt," LOA, 195.

265   "anything natural" . . . "deserve it, too": "Something Less than a Good Cigar," SJ-LOC, Box 50.

266   "even the bookends": SJ to SEH, summer 1938 ("snookums"), SEH-LOC, Box 2.

266   "The crack in the kitchen linoleum": *LMTY*, 291.

266   In a piece called "Fame": *JOD*, 429–31.

266   "William Barber": SJ-LOC, Box 33.

267   "Mrs. Spencer and the Oberons": *LMTY*, 29–49.

268   "literary reputation" . . . "great thing": SJ to Lucy Grey Black, March 9, 1948, FSG-NYPL, Box 174.

268   "The general consensus": Interview with Barry Hyman, July 24, 2013.

268   "you can imagine": SJ to GJ and LJ, June 13 [1949].

268   "no more teaching": SJ to GJ and LJ, n.d. [summer 1949].

268   "The Summer People": LOA, 594–607.

268   "the biggest dog in town": SJ to GJ and LJ, June 13 [1949].

269   One of Hyman's: SEH to JW, October 18, 1949, JW-BU.

269   "in a position": SEH to JW, November 26, 1948, JW-BU.

269   He and Williams: SEH to JW, September 14, 1949, JW-BU.

269   This time Hyman: SEH-LOC, Box 8.

269   **Charles Jackson received:** Blake Bailey, *Farther and Wilder: The Lost Weekends and Literary Dreams of Charles Jackson* (New York: Alfred A. Knopf, 2013), 265.

269   **"The Wishing Dime":** *JOD*, 248–57. Contrast this saccharine treatment of the theme with a passage in *Hangsaman*, written the following year: " 'I found a wishing stone,' little Natalie was telling her mother. 'I knew it was a wishing stone because when I dug it up it *looked* like a wishing stone, so I held it tight in my hand and closed my eyes and wished for a bicycle, and then nothing happened. . . .' Natalie could still, this many years later, see her mother's stricken eyes. She remembered that her father had laughed, and that her mother had begged for the bicycle for Natalie. . . . Too, Natalie saw now that if she had kept the wishing stone until the right time came, she could have used it to wish for a bicycle on that Christmas Eve when a bicycle was so obviously awaiting her under the Christmas tree. Then, magic would have been sustained, and cause and effect not violated for that first, irrecoverable time. . . . Mustn't violate the sacred rules of magic. . . . Never wish for anything until it's ready for you."

270   **"at a thousand bucks":** SJ to GJ and LJ, n.d. [October 1949].

10. THE LOVELY HOUSE

271   **"Smart New Yorkers":** Nina Leen (photo essay), "Fairfield County: Smart New Yorkers Are Flocking to It," *Life*, August 8, 1949.

272   **restricted to WASPs:** Lisa Prevost, *Snob Zones: Fear, Prejudice, and Real Estate* (Boston: Beacon Press, 2013), 94.

273   **an entire moving truck:** Interview with Larry Powers, July 23, 2013.

273   **seven or eight thousand volumes:** SJ to GJ and LJ, n.d. [c. January 1950], SJ-LOC, Box 3.

273   **"plump, disarmingly affable":** All quotations in this and the next paragraph are from SEH, "Book Scout," *The New Yorker*, November 8, 1952.

274   **every year he accompanied Scher:** SEH to Ben Zimmerman, July 13, 1950, and SJ to GJ and LJ, n.d. [c. April 1950].

274   **"vicious French game":** "Book Scout."

274   **her godfather:** Interview with Sarah Hyman DeWitt, February 17, 2013.

274   **"Life at Castle Jackson":** SEH to Zimmerman, July 13, 1950.

274   **"a vast improvement":** SJ to GJ and LJ, n.d. [c. January 1950].

275   **"before the World Series":** SJ-LOC, Box 45.

275   **Shirley made the entire basement:** SJ to GJ and LJ, n.d. [c. January 1950].

275   **"sheltered and private":** SJ to GJ and LJ, n.d. [c. April 1950].

275   "**big enough**": SEH to Ben Zimmerman, July 13, 1950.

275   "**about the same**" . . . "**just like everyone else**": SJ to GJ and LJ, n.d. [c. July–August 1950].

275   "**one of the things**": SJ to GJ and LJ, n.d. [August 1950].

275   "**There is no reason**": GJ to SJ, n.d. [August 1950], SJ-LOC, Box 2.

276   "**She always had one red arm**": Interview with Sarah Hyman DeWitt, February 17, 2013.

276   **Salinger**: Interview with Laurence Jackson Hyman, February 17, 2013. Salinger, like the Hymans, would eventually leave Westport after his privacy was exposed: see Kenneth Slawenski, *J. D. Salinger: A Life* (New York: Random House, 2010), 184, 190, 205.

276   **a neighbor stopped by**: Telephone interview with Walter Lehrman, August 13, 2014.

276   "**finished most**" . . . "**I was on**": Albert Murray and John F. Callahan, eds., *Trading Twelves: The Selected Letters of Ralph Ellison and Albert Murray* (New York: Modern Library, 2000), 19.

277   **Pen and Brush**: SJ to GJ and LJ, n.d. [January 1950].

277   **a piece by Cowley**: Malcolm Cowley, "New Tendencies in the Novel," *The New Republic*, November 28, 1949.

277   "**a rich writer**" . . . "**work it right**": SJ to GJ and LJ, n.d. [April 1950].

277   "**Don't you like**": GJ to SJ, n.d. [April 1950].

277   "**if i don't**": SJ to GJ and LJ, n.d. [April 1950].

278   "**as long as he is amused**": SJ to GJ and LJ, n.d. [May 1950].

278   "**we'll take four**": SJ to GJ and LJ, n.d. [June 1950].

278   "**intriguing**" and "**wonderful as hell**": Rae Everitt, telegram to SJ, June 17, 1950, SJ-LOC, Box 43.

278   "**a brilliant job**": Roger Straus to SJ, June 28, 1950, SJ-LOC, Box 8.

278   "**a subsidiary theme**": Gus Lobrano to SJ, August 1, 1948, SJ-LOC, Box 43. SEH rated it more highly: the story "not only seems scarier than Lottery but is probably better" (SEH to JW, August 3, 1948, JW-BU).

278   "**With six thousand**": SEH to Zimmerman, July 13, 1950.

278   **Jackson bought a spinet**: SJ to GJ and LJ, n.d. [June 1950].

278   **fur coat**: SEH-LOC, Box 33, folder 2 (note on yellow paper misfiled with "early writings: poetry").

279   "**should take ten years**": SEH to Zimmerman, July 13, 1950.

279   "**the greatest blessing**": SJ to GJ and LJ, n.d. [April 1950].

279   "**You'd better**": GJ to SJ, n.d. [April 1950].

279   **Dylan Thomas, on his first**: John Malcolm Brinnin, *Dylan Thomas in*

America (Boston: Little Brown, 1955), 3–25; Paul Ferris, *Dylan Thomas* (New York: Dial Press, 1977), 237–38.

280   **"As usual, we stayed too late"**: Brinnin, *Dylan Thomas in America*, 35–36.

280   **"Now you know exactly"**: Ferris, Dylan Thomas, 239.

280   **"Shirley Jackson Hyman"**: Brendan Gill, *Here at the New Yorker* (1975; repr., New York: Da Capo, 1997), 247.

280   **"a tubby little man"** . . . **"jogging past him"**: Ibid., 248.

280   **"fooling about"**: Ferris, *Dylan Thomas*, 240.

280   **In an untitled fragment**: SJ-LOC, Box 19. SJ later told her friend Helen Feeley that "she was one of those women Dylan Thomas screwed on the back porch." Feeley did not entirely believe her. See Judy Oppenheimer, *Private Demons* (New York: Putnam, 1988), 151.

283   **"[e]ven farther"**: LOA, 211.

283   **"A visit"**: *CAWM*, 101–25.

283   **a great-aunt**: The stone tower, with the old lady inside, foreshadows the library tower in *Hill House*, the room Eleanor fears to enter because of the decay only she can smell.

284   **"Come downstairs"** . . . **Emma was gone**: "Emma," Shirley Jackson Papers (MS 336), University of Colorado at Boulder.

284   **"which heaven knows"** . . . **"not very serious"**: SJ to GJ and LJ, n.d. [June 1950].

284   **"You sound"**: GJ to SJ, n.d. [June 1950].

285   **"that was [the week of]"**: SJ to GJ and LJ, n.d. [summer 1950].

285   **"a nice girl from the South"**: SJ to GJ and LJ, n.d. [summer 1950].

285   **"real fancy doctor"** . . . **"magic pills"**: SJ to GJ and LJ, n.d. [summer 1950].

285   **waist size by now was up to 40**: SEH to Zimmerman, July 13, 1950.

285   **other prescriptions**: Interview with Sarah Hyman DeWitt, February 21, 2013.

286   **And Shirley was initially successful**: SJ to GJ and LJ, n.d. [end of August 1950].

286   **Dexamyl**: A friend of Shirley's described the experience of taking Dexamyl: "we have both discovered dexamil [sic] and are fair delirious with it. especially in a capsule form containing little pellets which melt at different rates and you take one and just when life is getting drab and foolish another one melts and you tingle down to your tippy-toes" (SJ-LOC, Box 10).

286   **"Think how much"** . . . **"love them too"**: "The Fresh Air Fund," *The New York Times*, July 6, 1949.

286   **"Perhaps these days"**: "Fresh Air Diary" (unpublished manuscript), SJ-LOC,

Box 48. Unless otherwise identified, all the quotes in this section are from this document.

288   "overtax": GJ to SJ, n.d. [August 1950]. The strain on SJ's writing—the unpublished "Fresh Air Diary" was the only thing she wrote that summer—was also evident.

288   **Laurence rode his bicycle:** Different accounts of the accident are in SJ-LOC, Box 23 and Box 50. See also SJ to GJ and LJ, n.d. [October 1950], and SEH-LOC, Box 1 ("Hyman v. Weidlich, 1950–53"). SJ's account in Box 23 begins with the detail about the weather; as in "The Lottery," terrible things tend to take place on beautiful days.

289   **"Except for a splitting headache":** SJ to GJ and LJ, n.d. [October 1950].

289   **she found painful to recount:** *Savages*, 156–63.

289   **"there is nothing":** SJ to GJ and LJ, n.d. [October 1950].

290   **"a highly neurotic"** . . . **"and today":** Ibid.

290   **"sweet-faced old lady"** . . . **"very likely win":** SJ-LOC, Box 23.

290   **"half our town":** SJ to GJ and LJ, n.d. [end of November 1950].

291   **"we are thinking":** SJ to GJ and LJ, n.d. [December 1950].

291   **to recover any money:** SEH-LOC, Box 1.

291   **"Gallows Pole":** The song was popularized by Leadbelly and has also been recorded by Almeda Riddle; Peter, Paul and Mary; and others. SJ would have likely known the Leadbelly and Almeda Riddle versions.

291   **When Jackson read tarot:** Jai Holly showed me some of SJ's tarot cards. Elizabeth Greene recalls that when SJ did a tarot reading for her, she used the Waite-Smith deck.

292   **"suggests deep entrancement"** . . . **"Resurrection":** Arthur E. Waite, *The Pictorial Key to the Tarot* (New York: University Books, 1959), 116–19.

292   **the Hanged Man:** T. S. Eliot, *The Waste Land*, lines 43–55.

292   **a god of vegetation named Attis:** James Frazer, *The Golden Bough* (New York: Macmillan, 1949), 347–52.

293   **"a novel with contemporary setting":** Andre Bernard of the Guggenheim Foundation kindly provided me with a copy of SJ's application.

293   **"He seems perpetually":** *Hangsaman*, 11.

293   **"You overlook one":** Ibid., 13.

293   **some of his friends commented:** See, for instance, JW to SJ, April 25 [1951], in her *Hangsaman* scrapbook, SJ-LOC, Box 31. SEH acknowledged that he was the source for Mr. Waite in a letter to KB, May 15, 1951, KB-PSU; the letter also indicates that Natalie was modeled on SJ as an undergraduate at Rochester.

293   **"fuzzy tweed jacket":** *Hangsaman*, 26–27.

294   "I always used": Ibid., 19.

294   **In an early draft**: SJ-LOC, Box 45. Another draft of *Hangsaman* is misfiled in SEH-LOC, Box 32, as "Untitled novella."

294   "Male, I should say": *Hangsaman*, 22.

294   **as Jackson acknowledged**: SJ-LOC, Box 45. See also SEH to KB, May 15, 1951.

294   "It was decided": *Hangsaman*, 48-49.

295   "confiscated from the common bathrooms": Ibid., 119.

295   "Natalie, I want to die": Ibid., 133. Elizabeth echoes the famous line of the Cumaean Sibyl quoted by T. S. Eliot as an epigraph to *The Waste Land*: "I saw with my own eyes the Sibyl at Cumae hanging in a cage, and when the boys said to her, 'Sibyl, what do you want?' she answered: 'I want to die.'" According to the legend, Apollo had granted her immortality but not eternal youth.

295   "if she had lost": *Hangsaman*, 99.

295   "the girl Tony": Ibid., 143.

296   "old and large": Ibid., 177

296   "side by side, like two big cats": Ibid., 180.

296   "Still she haunts me phantomwise": Ibid., 190. The yearbook chronicling SJ's sophomore year at Rochester had an *Alice in Wonderland* theme.

296   "strange, one-armed man": SJ-LOC, Box 1.

296   "As she had never been before": *Hangsaman*, 218.

296   "an elaboration": SEH, "Myth, Ritual, and Nonsense," *Kenyon Review* 11, no. 3 (Summer 1949).

297   **Jackson saved the clipping**: SJ-LOC, Box 51.

297   "Still Life with Teapot and Students": *LMTY*, 15–20. In the published version, the girls' names are changed to Joan and Debbi.

298   "with his latest tomato": Interview with Jai Holly, July 16, 2015.

298   "You know what": Telephone interview with Walter Lehrman, August 13, 2014.

298   "Stanley didn't do that": Interview with Suzanne Stern Shepherd Calkins, October 16, 2014.

298   "There was nothing inherently": Interview with Marjorie Roemer, September 24, 2014.

298   "hundred-mile rule": Telephone interview with Lyn Sprogell, March 4, 2014.

298   "This was the world": Interview with Phoebe Pettingell, April 6, 2015.

299   "just ordinary drunken curiosity": Interview with Lehrman, August 13, 2014.

299   "i used to think": SEH-LOC, Box 2.

299   "A Day in the Jungle": *CAWM*, 146–60.

300   "Shirley finished the novel": SEH to Ben Zimmerman, November 29, 1950.

300   "in peonage": SEH to John Fischer (his editor at Harper and Brothers), December 7, 1950, Harpers Papers, Harry Ransom Humanities Research Center, University of Texas at Austin.

300   Brooklyn Bridge: He finished that piece in February 1951; it ran in May 1952.

300   "my novel is coming out": SJ to GJ and LJ, n.d. [December 1950].

300   Nemerov . . . Jay Williams: Both letters are in SJ's *Hangsaman* scrapbook, SJ-LOC, Box 31.

300   "It's a story": Elliot Schryver to Rae Everitt, December 20, 1950, SJ-LOC, Box 31.

300   "wrung dry": Margaret Cousins to Rae Everitt, December 29, 1950, SJ-LOC, Box 31.

301   "one of the most successful": "The Year in Books," *Time*, December 17, 1951.

301   "a considerable advance": "Mrs. Foster Reviews 'Hangsaman,'" *Bennington Weekly*, undated clipping, SJ-LOC, Box 31.

301   "a beautifully written": Orville Prescott, "Books of the Times," *The New York Times*, April 24, 1951.

301   "One cannot doubt": Alice S. Morris, "Adventure into Reality," *The New York Times Book Review*, April 22, 1951.

301   "the structure of the novel": W. T. Scott, "Dreaming Girl," *Saturday Review*, May 5, 1951.

301   "part magic": W. G. Rogers, "Author of the Week," Associated Press, April 23, 1951.

301   "so complex" . . . "all of us": Diana Trilling, "Speaking of Books," *The New York Times Book Review*, June 15, 1952.

302   "fashionable poses" . . . "cultural situation": John Aldridge, "Speaking of Books," *The New York Times Book Review*, June 22, 1952.

303   "What language is it": Saul Bellow, "Man Underground," *Commentary*, June 1952.

303   "suffered a schizophrenic split": Friedan, *The Feminine Mystique*, 39.

11. CABBAGES AND SAVAGES

305   "this compound of creatures": SJ-LOC, Box 1.

305   "a thunderstorm from a zephyr": Margaret Parton, *New York Herald Tribune*, June 23, 1953.

305   **An early draft went further:** This appeared as "The House" in *Woman's Day*, May 1952, and in *LMTY* as "Good Old House."

306   **"No matter how much":** *Savages*, 17–18.

306   **"always believed in ghosts":** Ibid., 166.

306   **"the reason i always think":** SJ to GJ and LJ, n.d. [c. October 1955], SJ-LOC, Box 3.

306   **"It is just like a visit":** GJ to SJ, n.d. [September 1957], SJ-LOC, Box 2.

306   **"helter skelter way of living":** GJ to SJ, n.d. [September 1953].

307   **"Was there a lot of blood?":** *Savages*, 158.

307   **"an accurate account":** This particular line comes from notes SJ made for a lecture about writing given in the late 1950s or early 1960s (Box 14), but versions of it appear in many other places.

307   **"the awesome vagaries"** . . . **"everywhere":** Arthur Finch, *Book of the Month Club News*, undated, SJ-LOC, Box 23.

307   **"She not only":** Interview with Midge Decter, March 13, 2013.

307   **"This is a remark":** SJ-LOC, Box 48.

308   **"Why, I asked":** Mrs. David Brooks Westwater to SJ, July 13, 1953, SJ-LOC, Box 46.

308   **Jackson occasionally wrote back:** For an extensive analysis of SJ's fan letters, see Jessamyn Neuhaus, "'Is It Ridiculous for Me to Say I Want to Write?': Domestic Humor and Redefining the 1950s Housewife Writer in Fan Mail to Shirley Jackson," *Journal of Women's History* 21, no. 2 (Summer 2009).

308   **"Despite interference":** SJ to BB, April 1, 1952. The correspondence from SJ to her Brandt & Brandt agents is privately held.

308   **"there was nothing":** SJ-LOC, Box 23.

308   **"This was a falsehood":** *Savages*, 50.

308   **"Not for me":** *Savages*, 90–91.

309   **"pang of honest envy":** Ibid., 139.

309   **"sweetly and falsely":** Ibid., 125.

309   **"open-mouthed"** . . . **"their own paths":** Ibid., 164.

309   **"with complete abandon"** . . . **"editorial comment":** Ibid., 167–68.

309   **"I'm a sweetie":** Ibid., 172.

309   **"When I ask you":** Ibid., 186.

309   **"I don't believe it":** Ibid., 174.

310   **"Who was Aristedes":** Ibid., 174.

310   **"contemptuously":** Ibid., 37.

310   **150 coins:** Compare the account in SJ to GJ and LJ, n.d. [November 1950]: "stanley had a tragedy and is still in a nervous fever. he ordered two shipments of coins from germany, one of a hundred and fifty selected coins of

the world, and the other of a hundred selected counterfeit coins of the world and the two shipments got mixed, so stanley got a package of two hundred and fifty coins of which a hundred were counterfeit."

310   **"She has her career"**: C. R. Roseberry, " 'Life Among Savages' Wins Acclaim for Area Author," *Albany Times-Union*, November 27, 1953.

310   **"good red, white, and blue publicity"**: Katherine M. Scardino, "Diabolical Humor in Family Routine," *Savannah* (Ga.) *News*, January 13, 1957.

310   **As movers were unloading**: File 100-HQ-366428, National Archives at College Park, College Park, Md. All quotations and information in this and the next two paragraphs about the FBI investigation are from SEH's FBI file.

312   **"a growing tension"**: SJ-LOC, Box 23.

313   **"the famed short story"** . . . **"right now"**: " 'Shirley Jackson' Is Westport Mother-to-Be," *Bridgeport Sunday Herald*, July 1, 1951.

313   **"The Lie"**: SJ first submitted "The Lie" in August 1951, rewrote it in October, and revisited it several more times over the years. It finally appeared in *LMTY*.

314   **"it was a novel"**: SJ to Jeanne Beatty, September 29, 1960. (See chapter 16.) SJ's letters to Beatty are privately held.

314   **"a flowery character"**: SJ to GJ and LJ, n.d. [May 1951].

314   **he rejected almost everything**: Margaret Cousins to SJ, February 27, 1950, August 15, 1950, August 28, 1950, et al., SJ-LOC, Box 43.

314   **"a quite definite idea"**: Herbert Mayes to BB, July 19, 1951, SJ-LOC, Box 43.

315   **Mayes demanded that she repay**: BB to SJ, March 7, 1951, SJ-LOC, Box 43.

315   **"the toughest agent in the business"**: SJ to GJ and LJ, n.d. [May 1951].

315   **"small, quiet, and neat"**: Interview with Stanley Kauffmann, August 27, 2012.

315   **"there is nothing"**: SJ to GJ and LJ, n.d. [May 1951].

315   **Porcellian Club**: Matthew Bruccoli, *James Gould Cozzens: A Life Apart* (New York: Harcourt Brace Jovanovich, 1983), 88.

315   **"Personally I think"**: BB to SJ, September 11, 1951, SJ-LOC, Box 43.

315   **She told her client**: Bruccoli, *James Gould Cozzens*, 289–90.

316   **"When we come"**: Ibid., 290.

316   **Mayes wanted her to promise**: BB to Margaret Cousins, July 30, 1952, and BB to SJ, May 20, 1953, SJ-LOC, Box 4.

316   **"The damn baby wouldn't show up"**: Judy Oppenheimer, *Private Demons* (New York: Putnam, 1988), 157.

317   **"This one's for you"**: Interview with Jai Holly, July 15, 2015.

317 "quiet determination": SJ to GJ and LJ, January 14, 1958.

317 "Barry was always good": Interview with Sarah Hyman DeWitt, February 21, 2013.

317 "Mr. Beekman" . . . "thoughtful": SJ to GJ and LJ, October 31, 1952.

317 "a rational conversation": Interview with Sarah Hyman DeWitt, February 21, 2013.

317 "barry is unbearable": SJ to GJ and LJ, n.d. [November 1960].

318 "the least accurate nickname possible": Interview with Laurence Jackson Hyman, February 17, 2013.

318 "quiet and unobtrusive": Telephone interview with Lyn Sprogell, March 4, 2014.

318 "loved Barry" . . . "listen and nod": Interview with Sarah Hyman DeWitt, February 21, 2013.

318 "I guess it will be nice": *Savages*, 226.

319 "the sordid Westport experiment": SEH to John Fischer, November 26, 1952, Harpers Papers, Harry Ransom Humanities Research Center, University of Texas at Austin. Describing the move in *Raising Demons*, SJ considerably simplified the family's living situation: they moved from one house in their town to another, with Westport omitted.

319 "Shirley, no friend": SEH to KB, April 4, 1952, KB-PSU.

319 "I feel ten years younger": SJ to BB, April 25, 1952.

319 "You had to wash": Interview with Jai Holly, July 16, 2015.

319 "beethoven sits there": SJ to GJ and LJ, n.d. [May 1952].

320 the Durands: Oliver Durand took care of all the Hymans. Laurence remembers his lax approach to house calls: "He'd come and have a big glass of bourbon, and then he'd go see the sick child" (interview, February 17, 2013).

320 "there is a constant pack": SJ to GJ and LJ, n.d. [May 1952].

320 "Been away": SJ to BB, May 8, 1952.

320 a comic account: "An International Incident," *The New Yorker*, September 12, 1953. In SJ's story, the Japanese students show up at the Hymans' house unannounced, and she and the children spend an afternoon trying to entertain them in true American style. A letter to her parents about the incident makes it clear that the reality was less involved: "we met one japanese character, named takehashi, who persisted in calling stanley 'mr stanley', and we finally realized that of course that's the way they run names, the formal one first. he said to me, 'madam i am happy to be meeting of you, how are you feeling?' and that did it, as far as i am concerned; i leave the foreigners to laurie and stanley. he kept clicking his

heels and bowing every time sally or jan came into the room, and since it is the first time a gentleman has ever stood up for jannie she was impressed. sally just thought it was screwy." Another day she offered a ride to a group of foreign students lost in North Bennington: "sally stood up peering over the seat to the back where they were sitting, and finally one of them, trying to be polite, said, 'the curls, is it hair?' which polished off sally."

320 **Bread Loaf School for English**: This program is separate from the Bread Loaf Writers' Conference, where SJ was on the faculty in 1964.

320 **the Hymans still had not found**: The reality contrasts sharply with SJ's description of the situation in *Raising Demons*, in which she presents the move to the house on Main Street as driven by "an extraordinary feeling of inevitability" (9).

320 **"picturesque, ancient, expensive"**: SJ to Virginia Olsen, September 16, 1952, SJ-LOC, Box 52.

321 **"inexplicably" double**: SEH to Herbert Weinstock, September 29, 1952, AK-HRC.

321 **"*disintegrated* personality" . . . "memories"**: Morton Prince, *The Dissociation of a Personality* (London: Longmans, Green, and Co., 1906), 3.

322 **the voice inside Natalie's head**: In a draft of *The Bird's Nest*, Dr. Wright refers to Elizabeth's demon as Asmodeus, the same demon that possessed Natalie in an early draft of *Hangsaman*.

322 **"dismal little house"**: SJ to GJ and LJ, December 30, 1953.

322 **"completely delightful"**: Memo from Margaret Farrar to John Farrar and Roger Straus, May 15 [1952], FSG-NYPL, Box 173.

322 **"Every time I think of"**: Margaret Farrar to SJ, August 8, 1952, SJ-LOC, Box 8.

322 **"warm and affectionate"**: Memo from Stuart Young to John Farrar and Roger Straus, July 18, 1952, FSG-NYPL, Box 173.

322 **"With the proper enthusiasm"**: FSG-NYPL, Box 173.

322 **"It seems too bad"**: FSG-NYPL, Box 173.

323 **"so they can admire" . . . "Cabbages"**: SJ to John Peck, n.d. [early March 1952], FSG-NYPL, Box 173.

323 **"the funniest, the most engaging"**: Orville Prescott, "Books of the Times," *The New York Times*, June 22, 1953.

323 **Jackson was so delighted**: SJ to BB, June 23, 1953.

323 **"Staggered"**: SJ to BB, July 14, 1953.

323 **"when i am making"**: SJ to GJ and LJ, n.d. [July 1953].

323 **"Funny how people"**: GJ to SJ, n.d. [fall 1953].

323 "If you don't": SJ-LOC, Box 11.

324 "very cute": M.M., "Cute Kids, but Mommy's Better When She's Sinister," *New York Post*, June 21, 1953.

324 "There is no reason": "Sterling North Reviews the Books," *New York World Telegram*, June 22, 1953.

324 "Never, in this reviewer's opinion": Jane Cobb, "Chaos Can Be Beautiful," *The New York Times Book Review*, June 21, 1953.

325 "it is the very familiarity": Margaret Parton, *New York Herald Tribune*, June 23, 1953.

325 "chilling objectivity": Joseph Henry Jackson, "Bookman's Notebook," *San Francisco Chronicle*, June 23, 1953.

325 "Shirley Jackson has built" . . . "like home": Edmund Fuller, "Life Among the Savages," *Chicago Sunday Tribune Magazine of Books*, July 5, 1953.

325 "female Thurber": "A Female Thurber: Mother of Four Also Produces Wit," *Miami Herald*, January 27, 1957.

325 "i thought she might": SJ to GJ and LJ, n.d. [July 1953].

326 "You're such a nice woman": Mary Margaret McBride to SJ, July 1, 1953, SJ-LOC, Box 9.

326 "the most uncooperative": SJ to Lynn Caine, February 26, 1958, FSG-NYPL, Box 174.

326 "You *must* learn": GJ to SJ, n.d. [June 1953].

326 "big, in that fine old": SJ to Virginia Olsen, September 2, 1953, SJ-LOC, Box 52.

326 "an extremely reasonable price": SJ to GJ and LJ, n.d. [May 1953].

326 "It seemed to go on": Telephone interview with Anne Zimmerman, June 12, 2014.

327 "totems . . . and masks": Claude Fredericks, *The Journal of Claude Fredericks*, October 13, 1961.

327 On the wall: Phoebe Pettingell, "s.e.h.—a biography," *Quadrille* 7, no. 2 (Winter/Spring 1973).

327 the Virgin Mary: Interview with Jai Holly, July 22, 2013.

328 Friends recalled: Interview with Midge Decter, March 13, 2013.

328 "Whatever you do": Interview with Naomi Decter, August 11, 2011.

328 "It was full of life": Interview with Midge Decter, March 13, 2013.

328 Some guests would complain: Oppenheimer, *Private Demons*, 120.

328 "It was writing clutter": Interview with Midge Decter, March 13, 2013.

328 "The doors were always open": Interview with Marilyn Seide, April 19, 2013.

329 exotic delicacies: For Altman's, see SJ to GJ and LJ, n.d. [c. January 1955]; Sahadi's order is in SJ-LOC, Box 41.

329 "**Everything was somehow provided**": Interview with Catherine Morrison, November 6, 2013.

329 "**There was this great spread**": Interview with Midge Decter, March 13, 2013.

329 "**rarely letting anybody**": Sarah Hyman DeWitt, "Shirley Jackson's Daughter Remembers," ReaderCon pamphlet, 2013.

329 "**took up literally**": Oppenheimer, *Private Demons*, 220.

329 "**Stanley and Shirley**": Interview with Morrison, November 6, 2013.

329 "**Don't stop!**": Interview with Suzanne Stern Shepherd Calkins, October 16, 2014.

330 "**She began to speak**": Fredericks, *The Journal of Claude Fredericks*, October 13, 1961.

330 "**We'd all be sitting**" . . . "**lose them**": Interview with Morrison, November 6, 2013.

330 "**sitting on the edge**": Robert Zimmerman to SEH, August 10, 1965, SEH-LOC, Box 46.

330 "**it may be bad luck**": SJ to GJ and LJ, July 1953.

12. DR. WRITE

331 **Bell Telephone ad**: Reprinted in Marta Caminero-Santangelo, *The Madwoman Can't Speak: Or Why Insanity Is Not Subversive* (Ithaca, N.Y.: Cornell University Press, 1998), 99.

331 "**business manager**": Dorothy Thompson in *Ladies' Home Journal*, March 1949, quoted by Betty Friedan, *The Feminine Mystique* (1963; repr., New York: W. W. Norton, 1997), 34.

332 "**the tension**" . . . "**wives work**": Quoted in Glenna Matthews, *Just a Housewife: The Rise and Fall of Domesticity in America* (New York: Oxford University Press, 1989), 208.

332 "**Split personality**": Unsigned review, *Time*, June 21, 1954.

333 "**innermost skeleton**": *The Bird's Nest*, 3.

333 "**It is not proven**": Ibid., 2. In an early draft, SJ disavowed the relationship between the building and Elizabeth: "it is not probable that elizabeth's personal equilibrium was set off balance by the interesting slant of her office floor." In another early version, Elizabeth is a college student and the main lecture building of the university is falling down; the hole is in the wall of the office of a professor on whom she has a crush. Both in SJ-LOC, Box 20. The connection between Elizabeth's psyche and the

building prefigures a crucial element of *Hill House*: the dangerous symbiosis between Eleanor and the house.

334   **"blank and unrecognizing"**: *The Bird's Nest*, 4.

334   **"no friends"**: Ibid., 3–4.

334   **"ha ha ha"**: Ibid., 17.

334   **sneaking off . . . aches**: SJ borrowed many of these details from Morton Prince's description of Miss Beauchamp's condition in *The Dissociation of a Personality* (London: Longmans, Green and Co., 1906).

334   **"I'm frightened"**: *The Bird's Nest*, 35.

334   **"A man's vanity"**: In an early draft, SJ left a blank space where she would later fill in the quotation, suggesting that she began the book while living in Erich Fromm's house, without her own library at hand. SJ-LOC, Box 20.

334   **mental blockage**: Caminero-Santangelo draws attention to the overt sexuality of this metaphor: "Miss Richmond's problem, then, must be 'relieved' through a manful creeping down her pipe; all she really needs is a good screw" (*Madwoman Can't Speak*, 105).

334   **"the dreadful grinning face"**: *The Bird's Nest*, 50.

334   **"the smile upon"**: Ibid., 49.

334   **"Dr. Wrong"**: Ibid., 55 and elsewhere.

334   **"Someday I am going"**: Ibid., 56.

335   **"Hence, Asmodeus"**: Ibid., 54.

335   **"one who has raised"**: Ibid., 50.

335   **"normal whole self"**: Prince, *Dissociation of a Personality*, 3.

335   **He initially hopes**: As Caminero-Santangelo points out, Dr. Wright initially plans to cure Elizabeth "not by integrating her multiple personalities but by choosing the one that seems to him the most perfectly feminine— that is, the one most perfectly compliant with his own opinions" (*Madwoman Can't Speak*, 11).

335   **nursery rhyme**: The original version is:

> Elizabeth, Elspeth, Betsy and Bess,
> All went together to seek a bird's nest.
> They found a bird's nest with five eggs in,
> They all took one, and left four in.

335   **"much like a Frankenstein"**: *The Bird's Nest*, 143.

335   **"one for each of you"**: Ibid., 190.

336   **"a vessel emptied"**: Ibid., 248.

336   **DR WRITE**: SJ-LOC, Box 20.

336   "I daresay a good writer": *The Bird's Nest*, 32.

336   "You have written": Roger Straus to SJ, April 7, 1954, SJ-LOC, Box 8.

336   "it's really more": SJ to GJ and LJ, December 30 [1953], SJ-LOC, Box 3.

337   "a chameleon personality": *The Bird's Nest*, 199.

337   "deny reality": Friedan, *Feminine Mystique*, 65.

337   "hungry to go back to teaching": SEH to KB, March 19, 1952, KB-PSU.

337   "I assume that all this": SEH to KB, May 13, 1953, KB-PSU.

338   Form in the Novel: SEH-LOC, Box 41.

338   "changed my life" . . . "in a woman": SEH, *Standards: A Chronicle of Books for Our Time* (New York: Horizon, 1966), 103.

338   "spoken correlative" . . . "and not vice versa": SEH, "Myth, Ritual, and Nonsense," *Kenyon Review* 11, no. 3 (Summer 1949).

338   "the projection": Jane Ellen Harrison, *Themis: A Study of the Social Origins of Greek Religion* (Cambridge: Cambridge University Press, 1927), 49.

339   "found Greece marble": SEH, *Standards*, 107.

340   "a hand was laid upon their ark": Harrison, *Themis*, viii.

340   "That's what Stanley found": Interview with Phoebe Pettingell, April 6, 2015.

340   "a kind of Pauline": Richard Tristman, "Myth, Ritual, Stanley," *Quadrille* 7, no. 2 (Winter/Spring 1973), 41.

340   "Its formal beauty": Jean McMahon Humez, "Myth, Ritual and Literature: A Student's Eye View," *Quadrille* 7, no. 2 (Winter/Spring 1973), 42.

340   Mondays: SEH's syllabi can be found in SEH-LOC, Box 41.

340   Students were required to complete: Interview with Joan Schenkar, June 8, 2012.

341   "The life of that course": Humez, "Myth, Ritual, and Literature."

341   "before each class": Nicholas Delbanco, untitled reminiscence, *Quadrille* 7, no. 2 (Winter/Spring 1973), 50.

341   Birkenstock sandals: A *New Yorker*–style cartoon by Janna Pratt, a Bennington alumna, shows one student saying to another, "I *know* it's Mr. Hyman. I can tell by the sox." SEH-LOC, Box 46.

341   Toulouse-Lautrec: Interview with Barbara Fisher, September 20, 2013.

341   "He was a very large": Interview with Anna Fels, August 3, 2013.

341   "an almost legendary figure": Wallace Fowlie, *Journal of Rehearsals* (Durham, N.C.: Duke University Press, 1977), 155–56.

341   "big black-bearded": Claude Fredericks, *The Journal of Claude Fredericks*, November 30, 1961.

341   "A man who": Harold Kaplan, "Stanley Hyman's Bennington," *Quadrille* 7, no. 2 (Winter/Spring 1973), 19.

341   "one of the most": Francis Golffing, untitled reminiscence, *Quadrille* 7, no. 2 (Winter/Spring 1973), 48.

341   "he dominated": Fowlie, *Journal of Rehearsals*, 158.

342   "infinitely giving": Greta Einstein Eisner, untitled reminiscence, *Quadrille* 7, no. 2 (Winter/Spring 1973), 48.

342   "when we saw": Kaplan, "Stanley Hyman's Bennington," 19.

342   "your three hundred" . . . "the world you love": SEH-LOC, Box 2.

343   "Shirley and two friends": This dream note and the two that follow are my paraphrase of a document titled (in SJ's handwriting) "Three Dreams and a Terror," SJ-LOC, Box 20.

344   "a sudden and unusual": The description of SJ's physical and mental symptoms comes from another document found among the *Bird's Nest* drafts. Three and a half single-spaced pages, it may be notes she wrote to a therapist. SJ-LOC, Box 20. All quotations not otherwise identified in this section are from this document.

345   To meet the deadline: SJ to GJ and LJ, n.d. [November 1953].

345   "steaming away": BB to Roger Straus, November 4, 1953, FSG-NYPL, Box 173.

345   "I've always wanted": Outline/memo for *The Bird's Nest*, SJ-LOC, Box 21.

345   "it scared them to death": SJ to GJ and LJ, December 30 [1953].

346   "I am myself": SJ to BB, December 1, 1953.

347   "she must on no account": *The Bird's Nest*, 82.

347   "My mother loves me best": Ibid., 89.

347   "Why did Robin": Ibid., 115. Robin also happens to be the name one of Glanvill's witches uses for the devil. See chapter 6.

347   "I *hate* that child": Ibid., 100.

347   "My mother loves me best": Ibid., 89–90.

348   "as though promising": Ibid., 84.

348   "going crazy": SJ to GJ and LJ, November 9 [1953].

349   "i am tangling" . . . "existing emotions": SJ-LOC, Box 20.

350   mothers who are not good enough: D. W. Winnicott introduced the concept of the "good-enough mother" in his article "Transitional Objects and Transitional Phenomena," published in 1953.

350   "How about you": GJ to SJ, n.d. [spring 1949], SJ-LOC, Box 2.

350   "We're so proud": GJ to SJ, n.d. [March 1950].

350   "Dear, you are getting": GJ to SJ, n.d. [September 1953].

351   loans during their dry spells: SJ to GJ and LJ, n.d. [May 1953].

351   "all my ailments": SJ-LOC, Box 40.

351 **"The Rock"**: *CAWM*, 126–45. The published story is dated "c. 1951," for unknown reasons. I could find no rough draft in SJ's archives.

351 **"There once were two cats"**: *The Bird's Nest*, 238.

352 **"I can think of"**: John Barkham, "Author Exploits 'Four in One,'" *Roanoke Times*, June 27, 1954.

352 **"anybody who gives away"**: George A. Minot, "Will Keep You on Edge," *Boston Herald*, June 27, 1954.

352 **"Shirley Jackson the housewife"**: Dan Wickenden, "Shirley Jackson Once More Weaves Her Dramatic and Satiric Spell," *New York Herald Tribune*, June 20, 1954.

352 **"more gripping"**: John Metcalf, "New Novels," *The Spectator*, February 11, 1955.

352 **"Most men"** ... **"plural monogamy"**: "Sterling North Reviews the Books," *New York World Telegram*, June 22, 1954.

352 **"the most horrifying"**: Florence Zetlin, "Four Beings in One Girl's Body," *Norfolk* (Va.) *Pilot*, June 20, 1954.

352 **"too bizarre"**: Orville Prescott, "Books of the Times," *The New York Times*, June 22, 1954.

353 **"an old souse"**: Joe Hymans, "This Is Hollywood," unidentified clipping, SJ-LOC, Box 44.

353 **"arty and pretentious"**: SJ to BB, March 4, 1955.

353 **"Abbott and Costello meet a multiple personality"**: SJ to GJ and LJ, June 12 [1955].

353 **"Major mental muddle melodramatized"**: "Psychiatry Steps In," *Newsweek*, March 11, 1957.

354 **"the all-purpose female malady"**: Lavinia Reedy, "From Peaceful N. Bennington ... A Tale of Warring Personalities," *The Knickerbocker News* (Albany, N.Y.), September 1, 1954.

354 **"they made"**: SJ to GJ and LJ, n.d. [c. March 1957].

13. DOMESTIC DISTURBANCES

355 **"fiendish book"** ... **"sleep for a year"**: SJ to BB, December 1, 1953.

355 **Cerf proposed**: BB to SJ, March 27, 1953.

355 **"enough of a library"**: SJ to BB, March 30, 1953.

356 **"by a kind of dogged"**: SJ to GJ and LJ, December 21 [1954], SJ-LOC, Box 3.

357 **"The main trouble"**: SJ to BB, October 6, 1953.

357 **"disturbed and uneasy"**: *The Witchcraft of Salem Village*, 6.

357 "They could not" . . . "half crazy": Ibid., 27.

358 "spent a large part": Ibid., 28.

358 "Their mothers had surely talked": Ibid., 29.

358 "uncontrollable hysteria" . . . "had an audience": Ibid., 31.

358 "a wonderful way of attracting attention": Ibid., 33.

358 "as concretely dangerous": Ibid., 61.

359 "As in all such epidemics": Ibid., 89.

359 "People simply stopped": Ibid., 123.

359 The term "witch hunt": "Senate Inquiry Set on Acheson Staff," *The New York Times*, February 26, 1950.

360 "intelligent and thoughtful people": *The Witchcraft of Salem Village*, 12.

360 "If the bewitched" . . . "over the world": SJ-LOC, Box 12.

361 "i've been feeling" . . . "little as possible": SJ to GJ and LJ, October 15 [1954].

361 one went to *McCall's*: SJ to GJ and LJ, December 21 [1954].

361 "eating and sleeping": Ibid.

362 "stanley says": Ibid.

362 "You were trying": GJ to SJ, December 31 [1954], SJ-LOC, Box 2.

362 "When do you start": GJ to SJ, n.d. [September 1955].

362 "obviously . . . must be": SJ to BB, January 29, 1955.

362 "our small clown": SJ-LOC, Box 14.

363 "i actually like": SJ to GJ and LJ, January 11 [1957].

363 "since we have been in despair": SJ to GJ and LJ, n.d. [summer 1955].

363 "Our whole family life": SJ to BB, June 26, 1955.

364 "some real jazz" . . . "one more number": SJ to GJ and LJ, May 21 [1956].

364 "a little chip": M.M., "Miss Jackson—Life Among the Demons," *New York Post*, January 5, 1957.

365 almost verbatim from a letter: SJ to Virginia Olsen, September 16, 1953, SJ-LOC, Box 23 (misfiled).

365 "Barry Sunday": *Raising Demons*, 75–76.

365 A note she actually once left: SJ-LOC, Box 51.

365 "gone to Fornicalia to live": *Raising Demons*, 43.

365 "had not come home": Ibid., 45.

365 "almost illiterate": Ibid., 95.

366 "by a series": Ibid., 102.

366 "since we were": Ibid., 99.

366 1939 New York World's Fair: SEH and St. Clair McKelway, "The Time Capsule," *The New Yorker*, December 5, 1953.

366 William Shawn accepted: Phoebe Pettingell argues that the culture of secrecy Shawn encouraged at *The New Yorker* undermined the

self-confidence of many writers. "You never knew why Shawn suddenly went off. It was not only controlled but also the most repressed and repressive environment. . . . People who stayed at *The New Yorker* kept feeling that if they were really good Shawn would be running their stuff." (Interview, August 12, 2011.)

367   "if i can sell": SJ to GJ and LJ, January 30 [1956].

367   "Nothing is ever wasted": *CAWM*, 219.

367   "potential writing time": SJ to GJ and LJ, December 30 [1953].

367   "stanley cannot say": SJ to GJ and LJ, n.d. [summer 1953].

368   "'Daddy is going to see'": *Raising Demons*, 179.

368   "the classically dogmatic": Derland Frost, "Shirley Jackson's Family," *Houston Post*, January 6, 1957.

368   "the author's husband": Esther Greenberg, "Raising Demons Is a Frolic, or So It Would Seem," *Washington Post and Times Herald*, January 6, 1957.

368   The admissions director: SJ to GJ and LJ, October 4 [1956].

368   "typewriters": *Raising Demons*, 20.

369   "how strange it was going": Ibid., 142.

369   "I drove home": Ibid., 145.

369   "a new breed" . . . "lives are a joke?": Betty Friedan, *The Feminine Mystique* (1963; repr., New York: W. W. Norton, 1997), 52–53.

369   "somehow one expects more": Jean Campbell Jones, "The Writer as Mother," *Saturday Review*, January 19, 1957.

369   "if Miss Jackson's": Silence Buck Bellows, "Children and Parents," *Christian Science Monitor*, January 3, 1957.

370   "the humor" . . . "tangy flavor": Edmund Fuller, "Shirley Jackson's Tangy Vein: Frustrated Humor," *Chicago Sunday Tribune Magazine of Books*, January 6, 1957.

370   "writer with two heads": "A Female Thurber: Mother of 4 Also Produces Wit," *Miami Herald*, January 27, 1957.

370   "310 pages from life": Paul Molloy, "Mother Sees Funny Side of Household," *Chicago Sun-Times*, January 6, 1957.

370   "charm in writing": FAP, "American Family Life at Its Best," *Rochester Democrat and Chronicle*, January 27, 1957.

370   "an unusual but not really": Untitled review, *Burlington Free Press*, March 18, 1957.

370   "as normal": "A Female Thurber."

370   "someone trapped" . . . "spinsterhood": Mary McGrory, "Unsparing Album of Family Snapshots Sans Retouching," *Washington Star*, January 6, 1957.

371   "The savages are older": Lewis Gannett, "Laurie, Jannie, Sally, and
        Barry—Demons at Home and Charmers Abroad," *New York Herald Tri-
        bune,* January 6, 1957.

371   "the two best lines": Roger Straus to SJ, April 12, 1956, SJ-LOC, Box 8.

371   "Last Christmas": *Raising Demons,* 306.

371   "it's not a real": Unpublished story, SJ-LOC, Box 26.

371   "It was the standard": Interview with Barry Hyman, July 22, 2013.

372   "She liked being": Interview with Laurence Jackson Hyman, February 17,
        2013.

372   "a classic fat girl": Brendan Gill, *Here at the New Yorker* (1975; repr., New
        York: Da Capo, 1997), 247.

372   "Each of them ordered": Ibid., 246.

372   Kenneth Burke recalled: Judy Oppenheimer, *Private Demons* (New York:
        Putnam, 1988), 219.

373   "for reasons" . . . "like a goose": Ibid.

373   "our doctor": SJ to Jeanne Beatty, September 29 [1960].

373   "i have suddenly realized" . . . "creams and sweets": Unpublished essay,
        SJ-LOC, Box 50.

374   "Mrs. Melville Makes a Purchase": *JOD,* 269–83.

374   Gardner Botsford: Interview with Janet Malcolm (Botsford's widow),
        February 1, 2012.

374   "the claptrap": Unpublished essay, SJ-LOC, Box 50.

374   Dr. Durand warned her: SJ to GJ and LJ, n.d. [October 1956].

374   a strict weight-loss plan: SJ-LOC, Box 35.

374   "SINFUL": SJ-LOC, Box 35.

374   "i figure" . . . "eating potatoes": SJ to GJ and LJ, October 1956.

375   Miltown: See Tony Dokoupil, "America's Long Love Affair with Anti-
        Anxiety Drugs," Newsweek.com, January 21, 2009, and Andrea Tone,
        The Age of Anxiety: A History of America's Turbulent Affair with Tranquilizers
        (New York: Basic Books, 2008). By 1957, Americans had filled more than
        36 million prescriptions for Miltown. Sarah Hyman DeWitt confirms that
        Miltown was among her mother's prescriptions.

375   "I know excess weight": GJ to SJ, n.d. [December 1956].

375   Shirley's plan for apportioning: BB to SJ, November 26, 1956.

375   "stanley and i": SJ to Beatty, September 29 [1960].

376   "If you wanted to spend time": Interview with Barry Hyman, July 22, 2013.

377   "who wants" . . . "christmas": SJ to GJ and LJ, January 11 [1957].

377   "brilliantly intelligent": SJ recorded this incident in two separate

documents—one a rough draft, the other more polished. All quotes in this section, unless otherwise identified, are from these documents. Both are in SJ-LOC, Box 14.

378   "She was a bitter": Interview with Sarah Hyman DeWitt, February 17, 2013.

378   "the most mischievous": Interview with Laura Nowak, July 24, 2013.

378   "very intense . . . very intellectual": Interview with Alison Nowak, October 14, 2014.

379   "When a teacher": Interview with Jai Holly, July 22, 2013.

379   "letters of appreciation" . . . "understanding": "Board Hears Defenders of Miss Holden," *Bennington Banner*, April 25, 1957.

380   "without terror": SJ to Jeanne Beatty, January 14 [1960].

380   "the old sadist": SJ to GJ and LJ, n.d. [May 1957].

380   "in an institution": SJ to Beatty, January 14 [1960].

380   "a tremendous story": BB to SJ, May 3, 1957.

380   "The people of the village": LOA, 424.

382   "thirty-two times": "Films of H-Bomb Now Being Shown," *The New York Times*, April 2, 1954.

382   *Operation Ivy*: For a description, see Betsy Hartmann, Bau Subramaniam, and Charles Zemer, *Making Threats: Biofears and Environmental Anxieties* (Lanham, MD.: Rowman & Littlefield, 2005), 57. The film is available online: www.youtube.com/watch?v=LQp8_fhY9YA.

383   "The sun's rising in the west!": David Halberstam, *The Fifties* (New York: Ballantine, 1993), 346.

384   "when it became clear": Susan Sontag, "The Imagination of Disaster," in *Against Interpretation* (New York: Farrar, Straus & Giroux, 1966), 224.

384   "Bulletin": *LMTY*, 115–18.

385   "Prominent in every book" . . . "everything outside": "Shirley Jackson Reverses Pattern," *Syracuse Summer Orange*, July 30, 1957. The lecture appears in *LMTY* as "About the End of the World," 373–74.

385   Halloran estate: The protagonist in "Paranoia," an earlier story, shares the name Halloran.

385   "so that all": *The Sundial*, 7. SJ's notes for *The Sundial* reveal that the Halloran estate, like the estate in *The Road Through the Wall*, was based on La Dolphine, the Newhall mansion near her childhood home in Burlingame.

385   "could think of": Ibid., 8.

385   "summer house": Ibid., 9.

385   "that the human eye": Ibid., 11.

387   "Humanity, as an experiment": Ibid., 37.

387   "Splendid. I was": Ibid., 40.

387   "one night" . . . "their inheritance": Ibid., 35–36.

387   The date of the apocalypse: "Shirley Jackson Reverses Pattern."

387   "a pervasive sense": R. W. B. Lewis, *Trials of the Word* (New Haven: Yale University Press, 1965), 184–85.

387   "chosen people": *The Sundial*, 38.

387   "No one needs": Ibid., 5.

387   "Well, that, and the house": Ibid., 11.

388   "Nothing I have ever written": *LMTY*, 374.

388   "an immediate need": *The Sundial*, 81.

388   "You Can Survive": Eugenia Kaledin, *Mothers and More: American Women in the 1950s* (Boston: Twayne Publishers, 1984), 6.

389   "contain everything": *The Sundial*, 8.

389   "this furniture had been built": Ibid., 158.

389   "a tiny island": Ibid., 209.

389   "the waffle iron" . . . "hurt you": "Memory and Delusion," *LMTY*, 375.

390   "always a little behind": Tom Foster to Roger Straus, June 12, 1954, FSG-NYPL, Box 173.

390   "millions of petty irritations": SJ to BB, February 21, 1956.

390   "fond little notes" . . . "the head": Ibid.

390   fulfilled the option clause: BB to SJ, July 26, 1955, SJ-LOC, Box 4.

391   "probably the best editor": BB to SJ, February 23, 1956, SJ-LOC, Box 4.

391   In his office: Kachka, *Hothouse: The Art of Survival and the Survival of Art at America's Most Celebrated Publishing House, Farrar, Straus & Giroux* (New York: Simon & Schuster, 2013), 105.

391   "completely delightful": BB to SJ, April 19, 1956, SJ-LOC, Box 5.

391   Jackson's account: SJ to BB, March 23, 1956.

391   "What is the biggest": SJ to BB, April 2, 1956.

392   "How you managed": Robert Giroux to SJ, March 11, 1957, SJ-LOC, Box 8.

392   "the chosen Ark" . . . "part of the book": Robert Giroux to SJ, July 25, 1957, SJ-LOC, Box 8.

392   "decided on the spot" . . . "whiskey in it": SJ to GJ and LJ, July 7 [1957].

393   "when a set of soldiers": SJ to Robert Giroux, August 22 [1957], FSG-NYPL, Box 174.

393   "I would not like": *LMTY*, 373.

393 "an impenetrable, almost intangible": *The Sundial*, 132.

393 "millions of idiotic": SJ to GJ and LJ, n.d. [August 1957].

393 "stanley was so annoyed": SJ to GJ and LJ, July 12 [1957].

393 "world of loveliness and peace": *LMTY*, 374.

394 "I am most anxious": SJ to Giroux, August 22 [1957].

394 "violently" . . . "too hard": SJ to Robert Giroux, November 1 [1957], FSG-NYPL, Box 174.

394 congratulatory telegram: Notes for the telegram are in SJ's handwriting on the back of a letter from BB dated May 22, 1956.

394 "development of great importance": Robert Giroux to someone identified only as "Frank," "Thanksgiving Eve" 1957, FSG-NYPL, Box 506.

395 "spent more time" . . . "doing business with her": SJ to GJ and LJ, n.d. [May 1951].

395 Baumgarten generally: Matthew Bruccoli, *James Gould Cozzens: A Life Apart* (New York: Harcourt Brace Jovanovich, 1983), 291.

395 "tremendous, never-failing": Ibid., 290.

396 National Institute of Arts and Letters: BB to SJ, October 18, 1956, SJ-LOC, Box 5.

396 "I know that": BB to SJ, December 24, 1957, SJ-LOC, Box 5.

396 "i keep getting": SJ to GJ and LJ, January 14 [1958].

396 he continued to receive: Thomas H. Foster and Catherine Osgood Foster Papers, Yale University, Box 9.

396 "an old old man": SJ to GJ and LJ, January 14 [1958].

397 "one of those men": Saul Bellow, *To Jerusalem and Back* (New York: Penguin Classics, 1998), 72.

397 "What it does": BB to SJ, December 24, 1957.

397 "like she killed my daddy": *The Sundial*, 1.

397 "the deadly mannered charm": Derland Frost, "Symbolism and Reality Combined in New Novel," *Houston Post*, February 23, 1958.

397 "i always start": SJ to Jeanne Beatty, March 1960.

397 "As a satire": Edmund Fuller, "Absorbing, Puzzling Novel," *Chicago Sunday Tribune*, February 23, 1958.

398 "an assemblage of weirdies": Stella Suberman, "But Shirley Is Terribly Game," *Raleigh* (N.C.) *Observer*, August 24, 1958.

398 "A bizarre tale": John Barkham, "The End of the World," *Saturday Review Syndicate*, n.d.

398 "all the big brains puzzled": Beatrice Washburn, "Black Magic—and Mathematics," *Miami Herald*, February 23, 1958.

398   "hell bombs": Charles Poore, "Books of the Times," *The New York Times*, February 18, 1958.

398   "As H-Hour": William Peden, "The 'Chosen Few,'" *Saturday Review*, March 8, 1958. In his book *The American Short Story*, Peden would later dismiss SJ as a writer of "sick stories."

398   "the hub": Robert E. Krieger, "Symbolism Is Varied," *Worcester* (Mass.) *Telegram*, February 23, 1958.

398   "Mother Church": Jean Holzhauer, "Interpretation," *Commonweal*, April 4, 1958.

398   "A novel such as this": Robert Kirsch, "The Book Report," *Los Angeles Times*, February 24, 1958.

398   "Some kind of dissociation": Unsigned review, *Washington Post and Times-Herald*, February 16, 1958.

398   "ahead of all" . . . "throwing bricks": William Bittner, "Promise Still Unfulfilled," *New York Post*, February 16, 1958.

399   "a very bright lady": Marsh Maslin, "The Browser," *S.F. Gate Bulletin*, March 13, 1958.

399   "a nasty little novel": SJ to BB, April 2 [1956].

399   "One is tempted": Daniel L. Stevenson, "The Lost Audience," *The Nation*, August 2, 1958.

399   "Miss Jackson is": Eleanor M. Bloom, "An Exciting Writer Spins Original Tale," *Minneapolis Tribune*, March 23, 1958.

399   "Louisa, Please Come Home": LOA, 673–90.

399   The first version: SJ-LOC, Box 17.

400   "I hope your daughter": LOA, 689.

400   "powerful and brilliant horror story": CB to SJ, May 28, 1958, SJ-LOC, Box 5.

400   *The Haunted House*: "Shirley Jackson Finishes New Novel, 'The Sundial,'" *Bennington Banner*, March 4, 1958.

401   "the most hideous" . . . "only a dream": "The Ghosts of Loiret," *LMTY*, 244–45. A version of this story also appears in "Experience and Fiction."

401   "When we got": "Experience and Fiction," *CAWM*, 226.

401   229 West 140th Street: "Tenement Blaze in Harlem Kills 3," *The New York Times*, April 19, 1957. The previous year, the only fatal fire was at 125 West 115th Street, also not visible from the train: "Fire in Harlem Flat Kills Two Children," *The New York Times*, March 9, 1956.

402   "I have always": "Experience and Fiction," 227.

402   "the kind of novel": SJ-LOC, Box 22.

402 "type which wouldn't be haunted": SJ to GJ and LJ, January 14, 1958.

403 A picture of the mansion: SJ-LOC, Box 51.

403 "pictures and information": SJ to GJ and LJ, January 14, 1958.

404 the novel mentions: LOA, 315.

404 "No human eye" . . . "concession to humanity": LOA, 265.

404 "We live over in the town": Ibid., 268.

404 "It had an unbelievably": Ibid., 269.

404 "A masterpiece": Ibid., 316. By contrast, Natalie in *Hangsaman* is pleased to find her dorm room "exactly right-angled at the corners," the number 27 on the door "a good number, owning a seven for luck and a two for work and adding, triumphantly, to nine" (*Hangsaman*, 51–52).

405 In her notes for the novel: SJ-LOC, Box 22.

405 "a symbol": Milton Bracker, "Mystery in L.I. House Deepens; Family, Experts, Police Stumped," *The New York Times*, March 4, 1958.

405 The episodes continued: "Bouncing Bottle Plague Still Puzzles L.I. Family," *New York Herald Tribune*, February 12, 1958; "L.I. Bottles Again Blow Tops, So Family Departs," *New York Herald Tribune*, February 21, 1958; "Professor Seeks L.I. Mystery Key," *The New York Times*, February 26, 1958—all clippings in SJ-LOC, Box 51.

406 "It is a legitimate inference": *Haunted People* (New York: E. P. Dutton, 1951), 108.

406 Even had she not acknowledged: Nandor Fodor to SJ, October 8, 1963: "I had my suspicion on reading your book that my writings may have had some bearing on your treatment. I am glad to have your confirmation." SJ-LOC, Box 8.

15. THE HEART OF THE HOUSE

407 "there are going to be" . . . "told me": SJ to SEH, September [1958], SEH-LOC, Box 2.

409 "Carrie wanted": SJ-LOC, Box 22.

409 her cultural moment: The critic Tricia Lootens writes that what Hill House ultimately reveals is "a brutal, inexorable vision of the 'absolute reality' of nuclear families that kill where they are supposed to nurture. In this perception, Jackson touches on the terror of her entire culture." Lootens, " 'Whose Hand Was I Holding?' Familial and Sexual Politics in Shirley Jackson's *The Haunting of Hill House*," in *Haunting the House of Fiction: Feminist Perspectives on Ghost Stories by American Women*, ed. Lynette

Carpenter and Wendy K. Kolmar (Knoxville: University Press of Tennessee, 1991), 167.

410   **"No live organism"**: LOA, 243.

410   **"there are few"** . . . **"parts"**: Stephen King, *Danse Macabre* (1981; repr., New York: Gallery Books, 2010), 282.

410   **"An atmosphere"**: LOA, 330.

410   **"lifting a cross"**: Ibid., 246.

410   **"Her years"**: Ibid., 245.

411   **"someday something would happen"**: Ibid., 246.

412   **"round and rosy"**: Ibid., 282.

412   **"during which time"**: Ibid., 245.

412   **"oppressive to be"**: Ibid., 283–84.

412   **In an early draft**: Lootens, " 'Whose Hand Was I Holding?' " 174.

413   **"Gossip says"**: LOA, 298. "A Visit" is an obvious precursor.

413   **"the heart of the house"**: Ibid., 326.

413   **"Help Eleanor Come Home"**: Ibid., 345.

413   **"What do you want?"**: Ibid., 378.

413   **"It is too much"**: Ibid., 387.

413   **"I think we are"** . . . **"being alone"**: Ibid., 355.

414   **"God God"**: Ibid., 358.

414   **"key line"**: SJ-LOC, Box 22.

414   **holding her own hand**: Darryl Hattenhauer, *Shirley Jackson's American Gothic* (Albany, N.Y.: State University of New York Press, 2003), 162.

414   **Another scholar**: Lootens, " 'Whose Hand Was I Holding?' " 178–79.

414   **"Fear and guilt are sisters"**: LOA, 365.

414   **"housemother"**: Ibid., 392.

414   **"padded"** . . . **"unwelcoming"**: Ibid., 390.

415   **"FAMILY FAMILY"**: SJ-LOC, Box 22. In a version of the lecture that appears in *LMTY* as "Memory and Delusion," SJ tells a very similar story regarding a friend's husband's rifle number.

415   **"The house *is* the haunting"** . . . **"Eleanor"**: SJ-LOC, Box 22.

415   **"Somewhere upstairs"**: LOA, 400.

415   **"I am home, I am home"**: Ibid., 407.

416   **"outrageous"** . . . **"the way it is"**: SJ to Jeanne Beatty, February 12 [1960].

417   **"one [new] lecture"**: SJ to GJ and LJ, July 21 [1958], SJ-LOC, Box 3.

417   **"always noticing"** . . . **"potential paragraphs"**: *LMTY*, 377–78.

417   **a lecture called "Garlic in Fiction"**: *LMTY*, 395–406.

418   **question-and-answer sessions**: For a transcript of one of these sessions,

see Thelma Finefrock, "Shirley Jackson on the Short Story," *Writer's Digest*, May 1966.

418 "it is now one of": SJ to SEH, September 9 [1958], SEH-LOC, Box 2.

418 "frightened enough" . . . "radio city": SJ to GJ and LJ, July 21 [1958].

418 "the pride and joy of my life": SJ to GJ and LJ, n.d. [July 1958].

418 "the sports car type": SJ to CB, September 5, 1962.

419 "sailing along in my little car": SJ to GJ and LJ, September 17 [1958].

419 long spontaneous drives: SJ to Jeanne Beatty, February 4, 1960.

419 Massachusetts and Maine: SJ to GJ and LJ, n.d. [September 1960].

419 "Hill House is really swinging": SJ to CB, August 19, 1958.

419 every week she threw out: SJ to GJ and LJ, September 17 [1958].

420 "yell and swear": SJ to Jeanne Beatty, February 4, 1960.

420 "when the dogwood": Pat Covici to SJ, May 2, 1958, SJ-LOC, Box 11.

420 "The Very Strange House Next Door": *JOD*, 365–77.

420 a housekeeper named Mallie: See also "Dinner for a Gentleman" (*JOD*, 52–63) and "Family Magician" (*JOD*, 236–47).

421 "as it usually": *Special Delivery*, 119.

421 "No one has ever solved": Ibid., 116.

421 "No baby ever developed": Ibid., 37.

421 "in ninety-nine cases": Ibid., 92.

421 "only appear": SJ to GJ and LJ, n.d. [September 1960].

422 "burying the hatchet": CB to SJ, November 26, 1958, SJ-LOC, Box 5.

422 "[she] thinks she is": SJ to Jeanne Beatty, February 4, 1960.

422 "eight feet tall" . . . "gray suit": Ibid.

423 she reprimanded her daughter: GJ to SJ, n.d. [November 1958], SJ-LOC, Box 2.

423 "Shirley, from my experience": CB to Betty Pope, January 18, 1960, SJ-LOC, Box 5.

423 "Don't press" . . . "gently": CB to SJ, March 31, 1959, SJ-LOC, Box 5.

423 "You are the most reasonable": Marshall Best to SJ, June 18, 1959, SJ-LOC, Box 11.

424 "the most spine-chilling" . . . "folk tale": Orville Prescott, "Books of the Times," *The New York Times*, October 21, 1959.

424 "When busy Housewife": "Mom Did It," *Time*, October 19, 1959.

424 "never read more than": SJ to GJ and LJ, November 2 [1959].

424 "a strong and scary parable": Harvena Richter, "The Ghosts of Illusion," *Providence Journal*, October 18, 1959.

424 "when i left": SJ to GJ and LJ, November 2 [1959].

425 "you come after": SJ to GJ and LJ, n.d. [December 1959].

425   "i just deposited": SJ to GJ and LJ, n.d. [c. February 1961].

425   the idea of colored sheets: Judy Oppenheimer, *Private Demons* (New York: Putnam, 1988), 149.

425   Wise decided: Press release for *The Haunting*, SJ-LOC, Box 45.

425   "Shirley Jackson writes" . . . "draperies": Will Jones, "After Last Night: A Return to Old Haunts," *Minneapolis Star-Journal*, August 15, 1963.

425   For the soundtrack: Edith Lindeman, " 'Haunting' May Mark Return of the Good Spooky Movie," *Richmond Times-Dispatch*, August 18, 1963.

426   Gidding told her . . . "good idea": Richard C. Keenan, *The Films of Robert Wise* (Lanham, Md.: Scarecrow Press, 2007), 125.

426   ads ran in the New York papers: SJ-LOC, Box 45.

426   "a top-notch ghost story": Judith Crist, "Haunting—Of Ghosts and Ghouls," *New York Herald Tribune*, September 19, 1963.

426   "Most of the devices": Brendan Gill, "The Current Cinema: Love and Ghosts," *The New Yorker*, September 28, 1963.

426   "When I saw it": Michael Pilley, "Film Terrifies Book's Author," unidentified clipping, SJ-LOC, Box 45.

427   "I have written myself": Oppenheimer, *Private Demons*, 237.

16. STEADY AGAINST THE WORLD

428   "how Violet" . . . "I suspect": SJ, "The Lost Kingdom of Oz," *The Reporter*, December 10, 1959.

429   "better than *Treasure Island*": Jeanne Beatty to SJ, December 12, 1959, SJ-LOC, Box 4. After discovering Beatty's letters in SJ's archive, I tracked down her daughter Shannon Beatty, who initially thought SJ's letters to Beatty had been lost. They turned up in May 2015 in a barn at the Beattys' former home in Pennsylvania. Excerpts are published here for the first time, courtesy of Shannon Beatty.

429   "I have looked forward" . . . "never can": SJ to Jeanne Beatty, December 29, 1959. SJ's first letter to Beatty uses standard capitalization; the rest are lowercase.

429   "lovely" . . . "to remember": Pat Covici to CB, January 22, 1960, SJ-LOC, Box 5.

430   "i cannot really remember": SJ to Jeanne Beatty, February 12, 1960.

430   "Dear Master Parent": Jeanne Beatty to SJ, May 23, 1960, SJ-LOC, Box 4.

430   "do you know": SJ to Jeanne Beatty, February 4, 1960.

431   "he taught me to say": SJ to Jeanne Beatty, February 26, 1960.

431   She joked about her moods: SJ to Beatty, February 12, 1960.

431   "with no trains": SJ to Jeanne Beatty, March 1960.

431   "my husband": SJ to Jeanne Beatty, January 14, 1960.

432   "every minute" . . . "forty dollars a page": SJ to Beatty, February 12, 1960. Ironically, in *The Tangled Bank* SEH quoted Marx on marriage: "The bourgeois sees in his wife a mere instrument of production" (101).

432   "he sits down": SJ to Beatty, February 26, 1960.

432   "Of course I will" . . . "baby away": Jeanne Beatty to SJ, February 18, 1960.

433   "he solidifies": Beatty to SJ, May 23, 1960.

433   "purest saturated envy": Beatty to SJ, February 18, 1960.

433   "make me a poem": Jeanne Beatty to SJ, January 20, 1960, SJ-LOC, Box 4.

434   "it is a wonderful": SJ to Beatty, January 14, 1960.

434   "my book is": SJ to Beatty, February 12, 1960.

434   "my turn my turn": SJ to Beatty, March 1960.

434   "I resent" . . . "daily days": Beatty to SJ, February 18, 1960.

435   "damned book" . . . "old sponge": SJ to Beatty, February 26, 1960.

435   "a big old brown house" . . . "mushroom from another": SJ to Beatty, March 1960.

436   made careful notes: SJ's notes on the mushrooms are included in a draft of the novel shown to me by Laurence Jackson Hyman.

436   "cooking now": SJ to Beatty, March 1960.

436   "do not impose" . . . "dogwood day": SJ to Jeanne Beatty, September 3, 1960.

436   "i would have sent": Ibid. Beatty's silence was likely caused by depression. "It is because I'd rather write to you than do anything else that I can't," she wrote to SJ that fall. "I become absorbed, and the pretense of good-wife-and-mother becomes so quickly submerged, the whole scaffolding shakes, and it may be hard enough on the kids later when I chase them up a tree like a mother bear and walk off, without the emphasis of a day-to-day desertion." Jeanne Beatty to SJ, October 24, 1960, SJ-LOC, Box 4.

437   "a lovely evening": SJ to GJ and LJ, n.d. [September 1960], SJ-LOC, Box 3.

437   "i am really seared": SJ to Jeanne Beatty, September 29, 1960.

437   "pact-with-the-devil series": SJ to Jeanne Beatty, November 14, 1960.

437   "maybe i will write": SJ to Beatty, September 29, 1960.

437   "Good food helps": Pat Covici to SJ, October 31, 1960, SJ-LOC, Box 11.

437   "these times come": SJ to GJ and LJ, n.d. [November 1960].

438   "She lived on Alka-Seltzer": Interview with Sarah Hyman DeWitt, February 21, 2013.

438   "sulfa pills" . . . "lots of garlic": SJ to GJ and LJ, n.d. [May 1961].

438   "every time" . . . "thank heaven": Ibid.

439 "a lot of silk shirts": SJ to GJ and LJ, n.d. [September 1961].

439 "didn't want to take": Interview with Laura Nowak, July 24, 2013.

439 "terror of such things" . . . "didn't belong": SJ to GJ and LJ, n.d. [September 1961].

439 "there's nothing like": SJ to GJ and LJ, n.d. [November 1961].

439 "No one has the desire": CB to SJ, September 21, 1961, SJ-LOC, Box 6.

439 "half-seriously" . . . "novel about lesbians": SJ-LOC, Box 14.

440 an unsent letter to Howard Nemerov: Judy Oppenheimer, *Private Demons* (New York: Putnam, 1988), 232.

440 the summer of 1960: The letter must date prior to September 3, 1960, because in her letter to Jeanne Beatty of that date, SJ refers to the book's heroine as Merricat. She was named Jenny in a previous version.

440 "now, can you help me?": Owing to what appears to be a slip of SJ's typewriter, it is possible to misread "now" as "how." This could be the reason that Oppenheimer identified the addressee as Nemerov. But looking at the page closely, it's clear that SJ intended to type "now"; the first word on the second line ("every," unambiguously) has the same typographical irregularity.

440 "completely disintegrated *castle*": Unless not otherwise specified, all the quotes in this section come from the letter.

442 "four people have read": SJ to Jeanne Beatty, January 3, 1962.

442 In draft after draft: Laurence Jackson Hyman generously shared with me some of SJ's drafts and notes for the novel.

443 longtime family mansion: In an early version, the house was named Blackwood Farm.

443 "She was the most": LOA, 438.

444 "Merricat, said Connie": Ibid., 435.

444 "neatening the house" . . . "against the world": Ibid., 421.

445 "with a musical cry": Ibid., 520.

445 "We are going to be": Ibid., 549.

445 Jackson's friends would later say: Oppenheimer, *Private Demons*, 234.

445 "We knew" . . . "self-conscious": Interview with Jai Holly, July 16, 2015.

445 reenact the scene: Oppenheimer gives this as SJ's strategy for *Hill House*, but Sarah Hyman DeWitt confirms that the book in question was actually *Castle* (Interview, February 21, 2013).

446 "those people deserved": LOA, 455.

446 "give anything": Ibid., 441.

446 "Yiddish Hawthorne": SEH, "Isaac Singer's Marvels," *The New Leader*, December 21, 1964.

446   "**European in spirit**": Isaac Bashevis Singer to SJ, January 26, 1963 [misdated 1962], SJ-LOC, Box 11.

446   "**there were newspapers**": Draft of *Castle* courtesy of Laurence Jackson Hyman.

447   "**My name is**": LOA, 421.

448   "**All our land**": Ibid., 459.

448   **Sarah regularly managed**: Interview with Sarah Hyman DeWitt, February 17, 2013.

448   "**Jay-Hey-Day**" . . . "**Salli's Eve**": SJ to Jeanne Beatty, December 29, 1959.

448   "**She was always**": Telephone interview with Elizabeth Greene, October 16, 2013. Greene also kindly shared an unpublished story she wrote about a visit to the Hyman house.

449   "**he says he is a professional critic**": SJ to GJ and LJ, February 1962.

449   "**It was fluid**": Interview with Jai Holly, July 16, 2015.

449   "**the heart of our house**": LOA, 472.

449   "**All the Blackwood women**" . . . "**among the others**": Ibid., 460.

450   "**My book goes along**": SJ to CB, February 21, 1962.

450   "**What a relief**": Pat Covici to SJ, June 24, 1960, SJ-LOC, Box 11.

450   "**Don't you rush**": Pat Covici to SJ, February 2, 1960, SJ-LOC, Box 11.

451   "**death cap**": Pat Covici to SJ, June 11, 1962, SJ-LOC, Box 11.

451   "**not a word**" . . . "**this one is *really* batty**": SJ to GJ and LJ, n.d. [late April/early May 1962].

451   "**a solid, substantial personality**": John Barkham, "A Tale of Two Sisters," *Saturday Review*, October 13, 1962.

452   "**Only one woman alive**": Orville Prescott, "Books of the Times," *The New York Times*, October 5, 1962.

452   "**the most eerie**": Paul Carroll, "Rare Magic in a Novel," syndicated review, November 14, 1962.

452   *The Sound and the Fury*: Leslie J. Stanford, untitled review, *Jamestown (N.Y.) Post-Journal*, March 30, 1963.

452   "**shocker**" . . . "**any of them**": Barkham, "A Tale of Two Sisters."

452   "**no ghosts**" . . . "**human mind**": Beatrice Washburn, "Shirley Jackson Creates Another 'Spine Chiller,'" *Miami Herald*, undated clipping.

452   "**one to read**": "Hermitage," *Boston Herald*, September 23, 1962.

452   "**elegant distinction of style**": Gilbert Highet, "We Have Always Lived in the Castle," Book of the Month Club News, December 1962.

452   "**a demon-touched angel**": John Hutchens, "Shirley Jackson Leads Us Again to Haunted House," *Philadelphia Inquirer*, November 11, 1962.

452 "Shirley Jackson looks": Max Steele, " 'I Like the Death Cup Mushroom,' " *New York Herald Tribune*, September 23, 1962.

452 "fanciful realism" . . . "apparent simplicity": KB, "Imaginary Lines," *The New Leader*, December 10, 1962.

452 "manages the ironic miracle": "Nightshade Must Fall," *Time*, September 21, 1962.

453 "camping on the brink" . . . "space": Guy Davenport, "The Dust Witch, the Red October Moon," *National Review*, December 31, 1962.

453 "an alternative": Chab Hassan, "Three Hermits on a Hill," *The New York Times Book Review*, September 23, 1962.

453 "This novel brings back": Dorothy Parker, "We Have Always Lived in the Castle," *Esquire*, December 1962.

453 close to 30,000 copies: Pat Covici to SJ, November 26, 1962, SJ-LOC, Box 11.

453 "Why oh why": GJ to SJ, September 1962, SJ-LOC, Box 2.

454 "you and I seem to think": CB to SJ, January 13, 1960, SJ-LOC, Box 5.

455 "that dreadful magazine": GJ to SJ, June 1960.

455 "i received": SJ to GJ, unsent letter, n.d. [c. September 1962], SJ-LOC, Box 3.

456 "with a refrigerator" . . . "simply fantastic": SJ to GJ and LJ, September 1962.

456 "I just remembered": GJ to SJ, October 1962.

17. WRITING IS THE WAY OUT

458 "with a spot of anxiety thrown in": SJ to GJ and LJ, n.d. [July 1962], SJ-LOC, Box 3.

459 "Laurie faces life" . . . "arrange for it": SJ to GJ and LJ, n.d. [May 1962].

459 "make him grow up fast": GJ to SJ, n.d. [June 1962], SJ-LOC, Box 2.

460 "all the women wearing flowered hats": SJ to GJ and LJ, n.d. [July 1962].

460 "wild with joy": SJ to Libbie Burke, September 5, 1962, KB-PSU.

460 "always very glad": SJ to GJ and LJ, n.d. [November 1962].

460 "She'd come over to our house": Interview with Laurence Jackson Hyman, February 16, 2013.

461 As her counselor, Stanley took: SEH-LOC, Box 10.

461 marriage charm: SJ-LOC, Box 9.

461 "Barbara chopped the vegetables": Interview with Sarah Hyman DeWitt, January 21, 2015.

462 "grandma and grandpa": SJ to GJ and LJ, n.d. [November 1962].

462   **the sorts of gifts**: SJ-LOC, Box 51.

463   **one of Kolatch's first acts**: Interview with Myron Kolatch, April 9, 2013.

463   **"an instant hit"**: Ibid.

463   **"the literature of our time"** . . . **"blasts"**: SEH, *Standards: A Chronicle of Books for Our Time* (New York: Horizon, 1966), 279.

463   **"the core, the nucleus"**: John Simon to SEH, June 21, 1965, SEH-LOC, Box 16.

463   **"I still feel drawn"**: SEH, "The National Pastime," *The New Leader*, August 6, 1962.

463   **"Bellow is a word-spinner"**: SEH, "Saul Bellow's Glittering Eye," *The New Leader*, November 28, 1964.

464   **"the most gifted"**: SEH, "The Artist as a Young Man," *The New Leader*, March 19, 1962.

464   **"the most fraudulent"** . . . **"dazzling ineptitude"**: SEH, *Standards*, 69–70.

464   **"the awfulness"** . . . **"deranged"**: Ibid., 275–78.

464   **"I believe their books"**: SEH, *The Tangled Bank* (New York: Atheneum, 1962), x.

465   **"our wriggling ancestor"** Ibid., 447.

465   **"merely to read"** . . . **"by comments"**: Harold Rosenberg, "Four Men Who Helped to Shape the Way We Think Today," *The New York Times*, April 22, 1962.

465   **"Mr. Hyman undertakes"**: Perry Miller, "Dubious," *New York Herald Tribune*, April 22, 1962.

465   **"an enormous instruction schedule"**: James Gray, "They Changed Our Minds," *Saturday Review*, April 1962.

465   **"Where his deductions"**: Ronald S. Berman, "Taken in by Metaphor," *The Kenyon Review* 25, no. 1 (Winter 1963).

466   **Marx's *Capital***: SJ to GJ and LJ, n.d. [February 1962].

466   **"a quarter of a million words"**: SJ to GJ and LJ, n.d. [January 1962].

466   **"He published a book"**: Martha MacGregor, "A Talk with Shirley Jackson," *New York Post*, September 30, 1962.

467   **"very smart"** . . . **"raised his voice"**: Interview with Barry Hyman, July 16, 2015.

467   **"I could hear"** . . . **"It was very uncomfortable"**: Interview with Jai Holly, July 16, 2015.

468   **"Barbara was her best friend"**: Interview with Sarah Hyman DeWitt, January 21, 2015.

468   **"After the President's broadcast"**: SJ to CB, October 23, 1962.

468   **"a squirrel"** . . . **"an elephant"**: *Nine Magic Wishes*.

469 "arrogant little list": Harlin Quist to CB, December 12, 1962, SJ-LOC, Box 5.

469 "getting" . . . "magic wishes": SJ, "A Vroom for Dr. Seuss," *LMTY*, 212–13.

469 "Jeanne?": SJ to Jeanne Beatty, November 13, 1962. This is the letter Beatty did not open.

469 "so i just won't get the mail": SJ to GJ and LJ, n.d. [November 1962].

469 "so terrible that even the vermonters": SJ to GJ and LJ, n.d. [early 1963].

470 "all they did" . . . "analysis on record": SJ to GJ and LJ, unsent letter, n.d. [spring 1963].

470 "The whole idea": Skype interview with Corinne Biggs, September 3, 2015.

471 "with stanley" . . . "a great triumph": SJ to GJ and LJ, unsent letter, n.d. [spring 1963].

471 "How are things" . . . "not sure": Powers, *The Store and Other Stories of North Bennington* ([North Bennington, Vt.?]: printed by author, n.d.).

471 "I am anxious" . . . "paroxysm of terror": SJ to CB, January 27, 1963.

472 "How grim" . . . "curious city": CB to SJ, March 18, 1963, SJ-LOC, Box 4.

472 "I was moved" . . . "a new novel": Pat Covici to SJ, March 25, 1963, SJ-LOC, Box 11.

472 "what 'ails' me" . . . "all the time": SJ to GJ and LJ, n.d. [spring 1963].

473 "This thing" . . . "tough for him": GJ to SJ, n.d. [May 1963].

473 "Two bottles": GJ to SJ, n.d. [May 1963].

473 "My two big difficulties": SJ to CB, July 2, 1963.

473 "i was quite nervous" . . . "very proud": SJ to GJ and LJ, September 4, 1963.

473 "She doesn't want": Interview with Laura Nowak, July 24, 2013.

474 "a long siege ahead": SJ to GJ and LJ, September 4, 1963.

474 a letter describing how helpful: SJ to Mr. Cheek, undated, SJ-LOC, Box 7.

474 "Today marks": SJ to CB, April 11, 1963.

474 "so high" . . . "time for lunch": *Famous Sally.*

475 "I don't seem": SJ to CB, July 23, 1963.

475 "had not been doing": SJ to GJ and LJ, September 4, 1963.

475 "touching tributes": "A Vroom for Dr. Seuss," 212.

475 "Literary criticism": SEH to KB, October 29, 1963, KB-PSU.

475 "I am in the disagreeable position": SJ to CB, November 7, 1963.

475 "stir things up": CB to SJ, November 20, 1963, SJ-LOC, Box 6.

475 "ready to try anything": SJ to CB, December 2, 1963.

476 the dark winter of 1963–64: The diary pages are dated by month and day, but not with a year. The only internal evidence to date them is a reference to the recent death of Howard Nemerov's father, which took place in June

1963. The letter to CB in which SJ reports that she has resolved to try Covici's system is dated December 2, 1963. For these reasons, I conclude that the diary began that December day and ended on February 7, 1964.

476   **"if this is going to be"**: SJ-LOC, Box 1. Unless otherwise specified, all quotes in this section are from this diary.

476   **"Why do you not write?"**: In *Whose Woods These Are*, his history of the Bread Loaf Writers' Conference (New York: Ecco, 1993), David Haward Bain dates this conversation to Nemerov and Jackson's trip to Bread Loaf together in 1964. This cannot be accurate if the diary was written in the winter of 1963–64. Bain gives no source.

478   **"I had no pets"**: CAWM, 16.

480   **"The Little House"**: LOA, 691–99.

480   **"Home," written later in the year:** *JOD*, 397–405.

480   **"The Bus" is the most complex**: LOA, 700–713.

481   **"twenty or so lonely schoolteachers"**: SJ to Jeanne Beatty, February 4, 1960.

481   **"slow and dirty"** . . . **"afraid of practically everything"**: SJ, "No, I Don't Want to Go to Europe," *Saturday Evening Post*, June 6, 1964.

482   **"I am beginning to be"**: SJ to CB, March 20, 1964.

482   **"nauseating pack of distortions"**: William M. Farley to SJ, June 3, 1964, SJ-LOC, Box 8.

482   **"Some of the material"**: SJ to CB, February 21, 1964.

482   **"all of this i do"**: SJ to GJ and LJ, April 1964.

483   **heart-shaped china-boxes**: Interview with Sarah Hyman DeWitt, February 21, 2013.

483   **"Notes for a Young Writer"**: *CAWM*, 263–73.

483   **"I hate it"**: Martha MacGregor, "The Week in Books," *New York Post*, May 10, 1964.

484   **"Since I do not seem to be writing"**: SJ to CB, June 2, 1964.

484   **"*The Fair Land of Far* begins with"**: SJ-LOC, Box 50.

18. LAST WORDS

485   **"I always believe in eating"**: *CAWM*, 3.

486   **"I want to write"**: Alfred J. Farnett to *Daily Orange*, May 6, 1940, SJ-LOC, Box 8.

486   **"Being invited there"**: Telephone interview with Jerome Charyn, July 3, 2015.

487   **"a little private group"**: SJ to GJ and LJ, n.d. [September 1964], SJ-LOC Box 3.

487   "dour yet direct" . . . "hypnotizing experience": Mark Mirsky, e-mails to author, August 31 and September 1, 2015.

488   "all the lovely chili": SJ to GJ and LJ, n.d. [September 1964].

489   "Currently teetering": SEH to KB, August 25, 1964, KB-PSU.

489   "Mr. Hyman lost": Interview with Patty Burrows, September 5, 2014.

489   "He looked" . . . "sometimes imaginary": Brendan Gill, *Here at the New Yorker* (1975; repr. New York: Da Capo, 1997), 246.

490   "I knew this would be": CB to SJ, October 15, 1964, SJ-LOC, Box 6.

490   "A great editor" . . . "my conscience": John Steinbeck, *Working Days: The Journals of The Grapes of Wrath, 1938–1941* (New York: Viking, 1989), 143; accessed via Google Books.

490   "It seems to me": CB to SJ, October 15, 1964.

490   "more grownup type of thing": SJ to CB, October 30, 1964.

490   "Working, working": SJ to CB, November 6, 1964.

490   "It is Viking's wish": CB to SJ, January 18, 1965, SJ-LOC, Box 6.

490   "I am full" . . . "under these terms": SJ to CB, January 20, 1965.

491   Her age and size: SJ began writing the book just before her forty-eighth birthday, so the two women are the same age, once her customary deduction of three years is factored in.

491   "in case it's vital": *CAWM*, 4.

491   "dabble[s] in the supernatural": Ibid., 12.

491   "might turn up": Ibid., 4.

491   "my God, he was a lousy painter": Ibid., 3.

491   "I hadn't ever been there": Ibid., 5.

491   "perfectly square, which was good": Ibid., 16.

491   "and anything you raise": Ibid., 14.

491   "In case you are wondering": Ibid., 11.

492   "what the cat saw": Ibid., 19.

492   "i'm a kind-hearted mama": SJ-LOC, Box 15.

492   "Are you sure" . . . "hang up, it's over": *CAWM*, 24.

492   "fine high gleefulness" . . . "everything I want": Ibid., 3.

492   "splendid but tiring" . . . "taking it easy": SJ to CB, March 8, 1965.

493   "dripped all over": SJ to GJ and LJ, May 12, 1965.

493   "a sick lady": Frank P. Piskor to SJ, May 25, 1965, SJ-LOC, Box 11.

493   "the schedule" . . . "completely apathetic": SJ to GJ and LJ, May 12, 1965.

493   "gleeful" . . . "horizon at all": Telephone interview with Barry Hyman, July 16, 2015.

494   She visited June Mirken Mintz: Judy Oppenheimer, *Private Demons* (New York: Putnam, 1988), 266.

494   **a strange, vaguely worded letter**: Ibid., 271. The description of this letter was confirmed with Sarah Hyman DeWitt, with whom Brandt shared the letter.

494   **"I can't wake"** . . . **"she's dead"**: Interview with Sarah Hyman DeWitt, February 21, 2013.

494   **"hundreds of people"**: Facebook post by Sarah Hyman DeWitt, August 12, 2015.

495   **"goofer dust"** . . . **"or something"**: Interview with Laurence Jackson Hyman, February 17, 2013.

495   **"That airport"**: Kristol to SEH, August 16, 1965. All condolence letters quoted in this section are in SEH-LOC, Box 46.

495   **"Shirley's rare talents"**: Marshall Best to SEH, undated telegram.

496   **"so different"**: Tom Glazer to SEH, n.d. [c. August 1965].

496   **"wonderful talent"** and **"warm and wonderful personality"**: Paul and Julia Child to SEH, August 10, 1965.

496   **"a kindred spirit"**: Isaac Bashevis Singer to SJ, January 26, 1963 [misdated 1962], SJ-LOC, Box 11.

496   **"Shirley is the main reason"**: Dede Annin to SEH, August 11, 1965.

496   **"She was one of us"**: Shelley Ellman to SEH, September 30, 1965.

496   **"More than usual"**: SEH to KB, August 27, 1965, KB-PSU.

497   **"I do not give a damn"**: SEH to KB, October 22, 1965, KB-PSU.

497   **Nemerov prepared a press release**: SEH-LOC, Box 46.

497   **The headline**: "Shirley Jackson, Author of Horror Classic, Dies," *The New York Times*, August 10, 1965.

497   **"absolute original"** . . . **"of witches"**: "School of One," *Newsweek*, August 23, 1965.

497   **the old line**: Albin Krebs, "She Wrote With 'Broomstick, Not Pen,'" *New York Herald Tribune*, August 10, 1965.

497   **"dissipate some of the"**: SEH to KB, August 27, 1965.

497   **"violent and terrifying"** . . . **"over the years"**: Reprinted in SEH, ed., *The Magic of Shirley Jackson* (New York: Farrar, Straus and Giroux, 1966), vii.

498   **"The Possibility of Evil"**: LOA, 714–24.

Acknowledgments

"Her character was so tremendous it was always hard to believe she was just one person," one of Shirley Jackson's friends once remarked about her. For their help in corraling this character within the pages of a book, I have a small army of people to thank.

For their cooperation, including permission to quote from Jackson's archives without restriction or contingency, I am deeply grateful to her children: Laurence Jackson Hyman, Jai Holly, Sarah Hyman DeWitt, and Barry Hyman. They retained the right to read the manuscript before publication and to comment on it, but they ceded approval of its final version. In addition, each of them sat for numerous interviews and made themselves available for queries by telephone and email. I appreciate the faith in me they showed from the beginning of this project.

Phoebe Pettingell, Stanley Edgar Hyman's widow, also granted unrestricted access to her late husband's archive, including personal letters and photographs, and sat for lengthy interviews. I am equally grateful for her generosity and trust.

I conducted the majority of the research for this book at the Library of Congress, which holds both Jackson's and Hyman's archives. For their assistance and their patience, I'm grateful to the entire staff of the Manuscript Reading Room, especially Alice Birney, the archivist in charge of Jackson's papers. Melissa Mead, an exceptional archivist at the University of Rochester, found treasures in the archives there, including Jackson's first known publication. Sandra Steltz at Pennsylvania State University helped me navigate Kenneth Burke's unwieldy archive, Danielle Rougeau offered direction in the Bread Loaf archives at Middlebury College, and Sarah Pratt assisted at Boston University's Howard Gotlieb

Archival Research Center. Staff at the New York Public Library, Chicago's Newberry Library, the Lilly Library at Indiana University, the University of Colorado at Boulder, the Harry Ransom Humanities Research Center at the University of Texas, and the Getty Center in Los Angeles were also generous with their time and knowledge.

William Brennan was the most enthusiastic and devoted research assistant a biographer could hope for, returning to the Library of Congress time and again to retrieve anything I asked for. Prashansa Taneja did research and fact-checking at Bennington College, and Ummekulsoom Ghadai helped with Kenneth Burke's archive. Allison Bulger analyzed all the letters Jackson received in response to "The Lottery" and also helped with transcription, as did Victoria Beale.

Marc Harrington of the Yoshitsune Foundation kindly searched Claude Fredericks's journal—itself a remarkable document—for mentions of Jackson and Hyman. Anne Zimmerman shared many pages of Stanley Hyman's letters to her father, Ben Zimmerman, which were invaluable in dating some of Jackson's stories. Shannon Beatty spent a long and dusty day tearing apart a barn with me in search of Jackson's letters to her mother. Mattie Rogers Kroiz, the truest of friends, not only showed up to help but figured out the right place to look.

Many people who knew Jackson and Hyman generously shared their memories and insights in interviews, including Betty Aberlin, Miriam Marx Allen, Walter Bernstein, Corinne Biggs, Patty Burrows, Virginia Bush, Suzanne Stern Shepherd Calkins, Jerome Charyn, Joan Constantikes, Midge Decter, Naomi Decter, Anna Fels, Elizabeth Greene, Sandra Hochman, Victoria Kirby, Myron Kolatch, Jesse Kornbluth, Walter Lehrman, Jesse Zel Lurie, Catherine Morrison, Alison Nowak, Laura Nowak, Larry Powers, Harriet Fels Price, Marjorie Roemer, Joan Schenkar, Marilyn Seide, Florence Shapiro Siegel, Barbara Herrnstein Smith, Ruth Smith, Lyn Sprogell, Marion Strobel, and Anne Zimmerman.

I was privileged to receive financial support for this book from the Cullman Center for Scholars and Writers, the Guggenheim Foundation, and the Leon Levy Center for Biography. Gary Giddins at the Levy Center was an invaluable source of advice and support, as were my colleagues at the Women Writing Women's Lives seminar. The New York Institute for the Humanities, where I presented an early version of the book, has been my intellectual community for years. A fellowship at the MacDowell Colony during the summer of 2014 allowed me three weeks of blissfully uninterrupted writing.

The members of the Narrative Writing Group—Patricia Auspos, Betty Boyd Caroli, Barbara Fisher, Dorothy O. Helly, and Melissa Nathanson—read and commented on every page of the manuscript. I think they came to care about Shirley nearly as much as I do. Trish Harnetiaux was present at the creation and never tired of hearing about my discoveries.

I owe so much to Sarah Burnes, my dedicated and tireless agent, who believed in this book from the moment I mentioned the idea to her. She found it the perfect home with Robert Weil at Liveright/W. W. Norton, the editor of every writer's dreams. At Liveright, I'm grateful also for the work of Will Menaker, Bill Rusin, Don Rifkin, Peter Miller, and Cordelia Calvert. Trent Duffy copyedited the manuscript impeccably.

Sam and Phoebe more than earned their promised dedication. They took far more of an interest in Shirley Jackson than I ever imagined they would, and it was tremendous fun to see her works—from *Life Among the Savages* to "The Lottery"—through their eyes. Ariel showed me that the third baby actually can be the easiest. And from literally the day we met, my husband, Joseph Braude, was devoted to this book. From Delray Beach, Florida, to Sonoma County, California, and countless places in between, he was my companion on this journey.

Permissions

ILLUSTRATIONS

Photographs on pages 4, 219, and 356 used by permission of Erich Hartmann/Magnum Photos.

Photographs on pages 71 and 466 used by permission of Philippe Halsman/Magnum Photos.

Photographs on pages 12, 24, 28, 32, 47, 56, 65, 169, 222, 249, 383, 408, and 486 courtesy of Laurence Jackson Hyman.

Photographs on pages 75, 78, 85, 95, 99, 180, and 238 courtesy of Phoebe Pettingell.

Photographs on pages 191 and 193 courtesy of Bennington College.

Photograph on page 223 courtesy of Trinity College Library, Cambridge University.

Photograph on page 246 courtesy of *The State News* (Michigan State University).

Photograph on page 250 courtesy of The Ralph and Fanny Ellison Charitable Trust.

Photograph on page 281 used by permission of Hulton Archive/Getty Images.

Photographs on page 311 and 314 courtesy of the *Knickerbocker News*.

Photographs on page 324 and 363 courtesy of Lloyd Studio.

Photograph on page 333 courtesy of AT&T Archives and History Center.

Photograph on page 339 reproduced with permission of the Principal and Fellows of Newnham College, Cambridge.

Photograph on page 395 used by permission of Princeton University Library.

Photograph on page 403 used by permission of Bennington Museum, Bennington, Vermont.

Photograph on page 454 used by permission of Grapefruit Moon Gallery.

Cartoon on page 458 used by permission of Charles Saxon/The New Yorker Collection/The Cartoon Bank.

Photographs on page 488 and 489 courtesy of Middlebury College Special Collections and Archives.

TEXT

Selections from unpublished letters written by Bernice Baumgarten and Carol Brandt used by arrangement with Brandt & Hochman Literary Agents, Inc.

Selections from unpublished letters written by Jeanne Marie (Jeanou) Bedel used courtesy of J. P. Trystram.

Selections from unpublished letters written by Kenneth and Libbie Burke used by arrangement with The Kenneth Burke Literary Trust.

Selections from unpublished letters written by Ralph Ellison used by arrangement with The Ralph and Fanny Ellison Charitable Trust.

Selections from unpublished letters written by John and Margaret Farrar, Roger Straus, and Robert Giroux to Shirley Jackson. Copyright © 2016 by Farrar, Straus and Giroux, LLC. Printed by permission of Farrar, Straus and Giroux, LLC.

Selections from unpublished letters written by Herbert Mayes used by arrangement with Alexandra Mayes Birnbaum and Victoria Mayes.

Selections from "Myth and Ritual" by Howard Nemerov used by permission of the University of Chicago Press.

Selections from unpublished letters from Howard Nemerov used by arrangement with the Estate of Howard Nemerov.

Selections from *Come Along with Me* by Shirley Jackson, edited by Stanley Edgar Hyman, copyright 1948, 1962, © 1960 by Shirley Jackson; copyright 1944, 1950, © 1962, 1965, 1968 by Stanley Edgar Hyman. Used by permission of Viking Books, an imprint of Penguin Publishing Group, a division of Penguin Random House LLC.

Index

Page numbers in *italics* refer to illustrations.
Page numbers beginning with 505 refer to endnotes.

ABOUT THE AUTHOR

Ruth Franklin is a book critic and former senior editor at *The New Republic*. She has written for many publications, including *The New Yorker*, *Harper's*, *The New York Times Book Review*, and *The New York Review of Books*. She is the recipient of a Guggenheim Fellowship in biography, a Dorothy and Lewis B. Cullman Fellowship, a fellowship at the Leon Levy Center for Biography, and the Roger Shattuck Prize for Criticism. Her first book, *A Thousand Darknesses: Lies and Truth in Holocaust Fiction* (Oxford University Press, 2011), was a finalist for the Sami Rohr Prize for Jewish Literature. She lives in Brooklyn, New York.